OTHER BESTSELLERS
From Josh McDowell

A Ready Defense: The Best of Josh McDowell (compiled by Bill Wilson)

He Walked Among Us: Evidence for the Historical Jesus (with Bill Wilson)

Why Wait? What You Need to Know About the Teen Sexuality Crisis (with Dick Day)

Teens Speak Out: "What I Wish My Parents Knew About My Sexuality"

The Dad Difference: Creating an Environment for Your Child's Sexual Wholeness (with Norm Wakefield)

The Love, Sex and Dating Gift Set (Series Editor)

Evidence That Demands a Verdict, Vol. 1

Answers to Tough Questions (with Don Stewart)

Handbook of Today's Religions (with Don Stewart)

His Image . . . My Image

The Resurrection Factor

The Secret of Loving

Understanding the Cults (with Don Stewart)

Understanding Non-Christian Religions (with Don Stewart)

Understanding the Occult (with Don Stewart)

Understanding Secular Religions (with Don Stewart)

Jesus: A Biblical Defense of His Deity (with Bart Larson)

JOSH McDOWELL

EVIDENCE

THAT DEMANDS A VERDICT

VOLUME II

HISTORICAL EVIDENCES FOR THE CHRISTIAN FAITH

Publishers Since 1798

THOMAS NELSON PUBLISHERS
Nashville

Published in Nashville, Tennessee, by Thomas Nelson, Inc., Publishers, and distributed in Canada by Word Communications, Ltd., Richmond, British Columbia, and in the Untied Kingdom by Word (UK), Ltd., Milton Keynes, England.

Library of Congress Cataloging-in-Publication Data

McDowell, Josh.
Evidence that demands a verdict : historical evidences for the Christian faith / Josh McDowell.
  p cm
  Vol. 1 previously publishing: Rev. ed. San Bernardino, Calif.: Here's Life Publishers, c1979.
  Vol. 2 previously published: More evidence that demands a verdict.
  Includes bibliographical references and index.
  ISBN 0-8407-4379-3 (v. 2 : pbk.)
  1. Documentary hypothesis (Pentateuchal criticism)—Controversial literature. 2. Bible. O.T. Pentateuch—Criticism. Interpretation. etc. 3. Bible. N.T. Gospels—Criticism, Form—Controversial literature. 4. Bible—Evidences, authority, etc. I. McDowell, Josh. More evidence that demands a verdict. II. Title.
BS1225.2.M33 1993
220.6'01—dc20   93-24923
                                  CIP

Printed in the Untied States of America

FOREWORD

Webster's Collegiate Dictionary, fifth edition, defines an apologist as, "One who apologizes or who argues in defense of a cause, institution, or the like; specifically one who argues in defense of Christianity." Even a casual glance at church history reveals that through the years the Holy Spirit has given to certain theologians the gift of apologetics. Names like Athanasius, Augustine and Calvin come to the fore to document the authenticity of this claim.

In our day one of the truly gifted men in this intellectual and spiritual discipline is Josh McDowell. Back in 1972 he published *Evidence That Demands a Verdict.* In it he presents with great convicting power hundreds of historical evidences which validate the teachings of the Christian faith. I make bold to say that no intelligent person can read this with an open mind without coming to the conclusion that Jesus Christ is the unique Son of God and man's only sufficient Savior. I consider this volume one of the most valuable I have in my library.

And now Mr. McDowell has completed his second major work, *More Evidence That Demands a Verdict.* From perusing it in its unedited form I have discovered that it has the same characteristics as the first, i.e., sound scholarship, penetrating exegesis and convincing proofs which are simply stated. Thousands of hours of competent research based on an extensive bibliography made up of books and periodicals representing every point of view have gone into its production. It is a valuable tool for the serious-minded Christian worker as he seeks to come to grips with the pagan philosophical, psychological and economic concepts of our day. I am grateful to Campus Crusade for Christ for their backing and their encouragement in making it possible for this gifted author to bring this volume into being. I intend to make full use of it in my ministry.

Harold L. Fickett, Jr., ThD, Pastor
Faith Evangelical Church
Chatsworth, California

PREFACE

WHY *MORE EVIDENCE THAT DEMANDS A VERDICT?*

There are various reasons for adding this volume to my first book, *Evidence That Demands a Verdict:*

(1) All the material could not be put into one volume.

(2) I have received many requests from students, professors and pastors for material dealing with the Documentary Hypothesis and Form Criticism. University students are taking courses from professors steeped in one view, and the student, because of a lack of background, finds himself being brainwashed, not educated. He has no basis from which to answer and usually no sources to develop a positive response to what he is taught. Instead of responding with positive evidence, the student is intimidated.

(3) There seems to be a need to counteract the "absoluteness" of so many university textbooks on these two subjects.

DO WHAT WITH IT?

It is my desire that this book give Christian believers the confidence and knowledge to speak up. Christian students will be able to use this material to write papers, give speeches and interject their convictions about Jesus Christ and the Scriptures in the classroom.

After reading the manuscript of *More Evidence That Demands a Verdict*, the following comments were made:

A university student: "If I would have had this material last year, I could have intelligently answered almost every negative assertion of the professor in my Old Testament class."

A professor: "Your book provided much of the material I had been looking for to give in my class. Thanks a lot."

A pastor: "The knowledge I gained from reading your book has answered the nagging doubts I had left over from seminary."

A layman: "Your research has helped me to evaluate the Sunday school material I have been asked to teach."

THE TERM "RADICAL CRITIC"

The terms "radical critic" and "radical criticism" have been chosen as convenient ones to indicate those who not only adhere to the Documentary Hypothesis and Form Criticism but basically advocate a naturalistic world view (see page 3). The label is not used in an invidious sense.

A "COCKSURE COMPLACENCY" OR
A "CAREFUL CONSIDERATION"?

Bernard W. Anderson says that "in these days we speak less dogmatically of the 'assured gains' of Biblical Criticism, for someone is just apt to pull the rug out from under our feet." 2/81

About the present need of examining the evidence further, Anderson speaks of "the serious undergraduate himself who may be quite skeptical but is no longer able to dismiss the Bible with cocksure complacency." 1/81

THE CRITICS AND CRITICISM

It seems that every time the term "critic" is used, it denotes a negative discipline or study. That should not be the case. The word critic or criticism is a positive term. A basic definition of criticism is the examination of a problem, a text or issue, etc., to determine its authenticity, reliability or meaning.

For example, Higher Criticism, rightly understood, "is simply the careful scrutiny, on the principles which it is customary to apply to all literature, of the actual phenomena of the Bible, with a view to deduce from these such conclusions as may be warranted regarding the age, authorship, mode of composition, sources, etc., of the different books; and everyone who engages in such inquiries, with whatever aim, is a 'Higher Critic,' and cannot help himself." 1/9 Therefore, anyone who studies the authenticity of a book is a "Higher Critic," whether he is a liberal or a conservative.

The problem that usually leads to a misunderstanding of its use is that High Criticism, as well as other types, has almost exclusively been associated with a "method yielding a certain class of results."

The critical method, so often attached to liberal theology, has been falsely assumed to be strictly a liberal discipline. The various names used for God in Genesis, the similarity of passages in the Synoptic Gospels, etc. are facts to be recognized. This is the job of criticism. The "collation and sifting of evidence, with a view to the obtaining of a satisfactory explanation . . . is a critical process." 1/9

I in no way want to discredit the function of criticism. However, and it shall be apparent in the following pages, I do disagree with the humanistic view that often determines the results of the radical critics. It is the subjective analysis of the critical results with which I take issue. Too many of the objective results are made to coincide with a subjective, rationalistic, anti-supernatural, humanistic outlook.

A DIFFICULT TASK

I realize that when I state a view of radical criticism, it does not necessarily mean that all the radical critics adhere to that particular assumption or view.

It would be impossible, as well as boring, to give all the various views and differences of opinion of the critics on any one problem or assertion. The radical critics, between themselves, differ as much in their assumptions as the conservative scholars often do in their answers.

Each person receiving the early drafts of the manuscript suggested another author or book that should be represented. Finally the line had to be drawn or the work would have gone on *ad infinitum.*

THE PURPOSE

I did not have in mind, nor have I in practice expected, to replace or supersede the use of many excellent works in these fields by very competent biblical and literary scholars.

But much of the research and many of the writings in this book are not available at most secular universities. Therefore students and faculty are often limited in their examination of the subjects dealt with in the classroom and in this book. Some of the best works are unavailable to the student, especially in the area of answers to the radical assumptions.

I will probably be accused of being unfair or lopsided in the presentation of the material in this volume. It will more than likely be said that more space was given to the answers to radical criticism than to its assumptions and their support.

I am of the opinion that the university textbooks are abounding with explanations of the assumptions of radical criticism. However, there seem to be few answers in textbooks (if any in the majority of them) to these views, especially by capable conservative critics. Perhaps *More Evidence That Demands a Verdict* will help to offset this imbalance. Thus it will contribute to the process of education.

ATTITUDE

The purpose of this book is not to "kill a critic" or to "destroy a hypothesis," but rather to provide material that can be used to better understand the issues involved and to answer many of the conclusions of the naturalistic critics and their methods. Often I hear various believers incorrectly pass off the radical critics as "infidels" or "blind skeptics."

I am at odds with many of the radical critics over various issues and methods of approach to biblical criticism, but I respect them as individuals and often admire their dedication and research.

The proper motivation behind the use of these lecture notes is to glorify and magnify Christ—not to win an argument. Apologetics is not for proving the Word of God but simply for providing a basis for faith.

One should have a gentle and reverent spirit when using these notes: "But sanctify Christ as Lord in your hearts, always being ready to make a defense to every one who asks you to give an account for the hope that is in you, yet with gentleness and reverence" (I Peter 3:15).

These notes, used with a proper attitude, will help to motivate a person to honestly consider Jesus Christ and will head him toward the central and primary issue—the gospel (such as is contained in the Four Spiritual Laws at the end of this book).

When I share Christ with someone who has some honest doubts, I give him enough apologetics to answer his questions or satisfy his curiosity and then turn the conversation back to his relationship with Christ. The presentation of evidence (apologetics) should never be a substitute for using the Word of God.

A FOIBLE OF SCHOLARSHIP

For years the hackneyed phrases "Documentary Hypothesis," "JEDP," "Moses didn't write the Pentateuch," "Form Criticism," etc., have been heard again and again in the classrooms of our universities.

Today, it often seems that a theory is accepted because of its place in a textbook and its continued repetition and recognition.

Often repetition is a foible of scholarship. One scholar notes: "Another common and natural phenomenon is the repetition of hypotheses once proposed. As in other fields, so in Bible study, what begins as a very tentative guess becomes by repetition an assumed fact and represents 'the consensus of scholarly opinion.'"

The above should be a warning, not only to the radical critic, but to the conservative critic as well.

SOME CRITICISMS

(1) One criticism of my first book, *Evidence That Demands a Verdict,* (and it will certainly be made of this book too) has been that the quotes are too long. I have included long quotes so that individuals using the material can better understand the context and, therefore, not misuse a reference. It is easy for quotations to be misleading. I have tried to avoid a misrepresentation of any writer.

(2) Another criticism is that many quotes are very similar and therefore unnecessary. Again my purpose here is to give the person using the material ample sources so that he can choose what he thinks is relevant. Most books have limited documentation and, therefore, if several people use them, they begin to sound like parrots. *More Evidence That Demands a Verdict* has sufficient sources to allow its use by various people without their sounding like a broken record. Also, it permits those using the material to be creative.

(3) Still another criticism is that some references are used several times. Yes, a few quotes are used two times. The reason for this is that they are appropriate in each situation and aid the reader in understanding the issue.

(4) Others will criticize that I didn't deal with Source Criticism, Historical Criticism, the New Quest, the Post-Bultmannian influence, Existentialism, Demythologization, the Q document or the Synoptic Problem, epistomology, etc. The purpose of this book is to clarify the issues and give some practical answers to the questions that students have asked me over the last three years. It is not to give the pros and cons of the multitudes of problems, questions and schools of criticism.

RESEARCH TEAM MEMBERS

Working with me in compiling this research was a team of 14 students from 14 universities. It all started after my first book, *Evidence That Demands a Verdict*, was published. Several students approached me about working on the project so they could receive credit at their universities.

Ron Lutjens	Bowling Green University RESEARCH: Historic Reliability of the Old Testament
James Davis	Louisiana Polytechnic Institute RESEARCH: Archaeology
Frank Dickerson	Ohio State University RESEARCH: Presupposition of Anti-Supernaturalism
Jay Gary	Georgia Tech RESEARCH: Synoptic Problem
Roy Moran	Baylor University RESEARCH: Documentary Hypothesis
John Austin	University of Virginia (Campus Crusade for Christ Director) RESEARCH: Documentary Hypothesis
Richard Beckham	Louisiana State University RESEARCH: Dating of Daniel
Dave Wilson	Trinity Seminary RESEARCH: Documentary Hypothesis
Terry Shope	University of Arkansas RESEARCH: Form Criticism
John Sloan	West Texas State University RESEARCH: Form Criticism
Faith Osteen	Arizona State University Research Assistant
Stephanie Ross	North Texas State University Research Assistant
Beth Veazie	University of Arizona Research Assistant
Nancy Thompson	Chaffey College Research Assistant

After eight years of traveling and lecturing in universities, I see a great need for Christian students to invest their lives in research.

Robert Mounce, dean of the Potter College of Arts and Humanities at Western Kentucky University speaks of the commitment and vision necessary for such an endeavor:

"The task of scholarship is in fact a lowly role which demands tremendous dedication. My own personal feeling is that young men with a gift of conceptualization and perception need to be encouraged to really believe that God can be served in the solitude of one's study surrounded by the fruits of scholarly labor."

WHY COPYRIGHTED?

The reason that these notes have been copyrighted is not to limit their use, but to protect them from misuse and to safeguard the rights of the authors and publishers of the multitude of quotations I have used and documented.

OUTLINE FORM

Because the notes are in outline form and the transitions between various concepts are not extensively written out, the effective use of this material will result as a person spends time thinking through individual sections and developing his own convictions. Thus, it becomes his message and not the parroting of someone else's.

GODISNOWHERE

means

GOD IS NO WHERE? or GOD IS NOW HERE?

The outline structure of the notes can sometimes cause a person to misunderstand an illustration or concept. Be cautious in drawing conclusions one way or another when you do not clearly understand something. Study it further and investigate other sources.

A LIFETIME INVESTMENT

The following are books that I recommend a person buy for his library. Also, these would be good books to buy and donate to your university library. (Often university libraries will buy books if you fill out a request slip.)

1. Archer, Gleason, Jr. *A Survey of Old Testament Introduction.* Moody Press.
2. Cassuto, U. *The Documentary Hypothesis.* Magnes Press, The Hebrew University.
3. Free, Joseph P. *Archaeology and Bible History.* Scripture Press.
4. Guthrie, Donald. *New Testament Introduction.* Inter-Varsity Press.
5. Harrison, R.K. *Introduction to the Old Testament.* Wm. B. Eerdmans Publishing Company.
6. Kistemaker, Simon. *The Gospels in Current Study.* Baker Book House.
7. Kitchen, K.A. *Ancient Orient and Old Testament.* Inter-Varsity Press.
8. Ladd, G.E. *The New Testament and Criticism.* Wm. B. Eerdmans Publishing Co.

   (The following are three excellent books for understanding New Testament Criticism.)

9. Marshall, Howard I. *Luke: Historian and Theologian.* Zondervan Publishing House
10. McNight, Edgar V. *What is Form Criticism?* Fortress Press (any in this series).
11. Perrin, Norman. *What is Redaction Criticism?* Fortress Press.

    (The following is an excellent workbook to understand "forms" according to Form Criticism.)

12. Montgomery, Robert M. and Richard W. Stegner. *Auxiliary Studies in the Bible: Forms in the Gospels, 1. The Pronouncement Story.* Abingdon Press.

BIBLIOGRAPHY

1. Allis, Oswald T. *The Old Testament, Its Claims and Its Critics.* The Presbyterian and Reformed Publishing Company.
2. Anderson, Bernard W. "Changing Emphasis in Biblical Criticism," *Journal of Bible and Religion.* April, 1955. Vol. 23, pp. 81-88.

EXPLANATION OF GENERAL FORMAT

FOOTNOTES: After each quote there will be two sets of numbers divided by a diagonal (example: 47/21-23). The number to the left of the diagonal is the reference to the source in the bibliography at the end of each section. The number on the right refers to the page or pages where the quote is located in the reference source.

BIBLIOGRAPHY: The entire bibliography is not placed at the back of the lecture notes. There are five individual bibliographies placed at the ends of the various divisions of the notes.

This enables a person to remove a section of the notes and have its bibliography with it to facilitate the locating of reference sources.

OUTLINE: I have chosen not to use the traditional method of outlining. Instead I am employing a method that is easy to use in locating specific references in printed notes while lecturing.

Traditional	Method Used Here
I.	1A.
A.	1B.
1.	1C.
a.	1D.
(1)	1E.
(a)	1F.

INDEXES: Located at the back of the notes are two separate indexes to help you in using these notes: 1. Author Index; 2. Subject Index.

BIOGRAPHICAL SKETCHES: At the back of the book is a limited biography of various authors. This will give the reader a background on some of the authors quoted.

TABLE OF CONTENTS

section I

introduction

This section deals with anti-supernaturalism and archaeology. These topics relate to both the Documentary Hypothesis and Form Criticism.

SECTION OUTLINE

the
presupposition
of
anti-supernaturalism

Before entering the study of the Documentary Hypothesis (see page 29) and Form Criticism (see page 183) there is a very crucial and often misunderstood area that needs to be dealt with—anti-supernaturalism.

If there is any subject where ignorance abounds it is here. So many sincere students and laymen are led astray because of conclusions that are allegedly based upon objective historical or literary investigation and method. However, in reality, the conclusions are the result of a subjective world view.

1A. PRESUPPOSITION

1B. Definition

A presupposition is something that is assumed or supposed in advance. A good definition would be "to require or involve necessarily as an antecedent condition." One could say that to "presuppose" is to conclude something before the investigation is commenced.

2B. Synonyms

Prejudge, assume as true, prejudice, forejudgement, preconceived opinion, fixed conclusion, preconceived notion, jump to a conclusion.

3B. Unavoidable

Presuppositions are to a degree inevitable. Thomas Whitelaw of Great Britain cites the German theologian, Biedermann (*Christliche Dogmatik),* who put it this way:

It is "not true but sand in the eyes, if one asserts that genuinely scientific and historic criticism can and should proceed without dogmatic presuppositions. In the last instance the consideration of the so-called purely historic grounds always reaches the point where it can and will decide concerning this, whether it can or cannot hold some particular thing in and of itself to be possible.... Some sort of boundary definitions, be they ever so elastically held, of what is historically possible, every student brings with him to historical investigations; and these are for that student dogmatic presuppositions." 36/172

"It is perfectly true," continues James Orr, "that it is impossible in any inquiry to dispense with guiding principles of investigation, and with presuppositions of some kind, and there is no criticism on earth that does so.... Only these should not be allowed to warp or distort the facts, or be applied to support a preconceived conclusion. The scientist also finds it incumbent on him to 'anticipate nature' with his interrogations and tentative hypotheses, which, however, have to be brought to the test...of experimental verification." 16/14

Commenting on the need for presuppositions, John Warwick Montgomery makes the following observation: "First, though Kant was quite right that all arguments begin with *a prioris*, it does not follow that one presupposition is as good as another" 1/388

Thomas Whitelaw says both the radical and conservative critics presuppose too much:

"So long as Higher Critics believe in a God, they have no right to postulate His noninterference with the ordinary line of causation or to assume beforehand that 'miracles do not happen,' or that 'prediction' in the sense of foretelling future events 'is impossible.' Admitting that it would be a violation of sound reasoning to make the contrary suppositions, viz. that in God's providential government of the world and revelation of Himself miracles and predictions must occur, one has ground to contend that the argumentation is equally unfair—is a virtual begging of the question—which starts from the premise, No supernatural except within the lines and limits of the natural. Impartial inquirers will severely restrict themselves to investigating the reality or non-reality of so-called facts, *i.e.* to examining and proving phenomena with a view to ascertaining their true character, whether they are natural or not." 36/178

In all fairness to the radical critic, it needs to be realized that "sometimes professedly conservative writers take great liberties with the simple facts of Scripture and put forward conclusions which are quite as baseless as the conclusions of radical criticism." 37/339

Oswald Allis observes the prejudices on both sides:

"The 'scientific scholar' is, generally speaking, quite as dogmatic in rejecting the authority of the Old Testament, as the conservative is in accepting and defending it. He is just as insistent on fitting the Old Testament into a world view, which rejects the redemptive supernaturalism of the Bible and the uniqueness of its history, religion and cultus, as the Bible defender is in insisting on the uniqueness of Old Testament history and the supernaturalism which pervades it.... To charge an opponent with bias and dogmatism, is an easy way of avoiding the issue." 37/338

4B   Do We Have a Right?

One needs to constantly and consciously be aware of his presuppositions. I had to ask myself, "Do I have a right to my presuppositions?" A key issue is, "Do one's presuppositions coincide with reality with what really is? Is there sufficient evidence to support them?"

2A. ANTI-SUPERNATURALISM

Since this concept of anti-supernaturalism is prevalent among the radical critics of both the Documentary Hypothesis and Form Criticism schools, I decided to deal with it here rather than in these respective sections.

1B. Definition

For our purposes we will define anti-supernaturalism as disbelief either in God's existence or His intervention in the natural order of the universe. In the Pentateuch it is explicitly stated no less than 235 times that either God "spoke" to Moses, or God "commanded" Moses to do something (according to an examination of *Strong's Exhaustive Concordance of the Bible*). A critic with an anti-supernaturalism bias (presupposition) would immediately reject these accounts as being unhistorical prior to his investigation.

A.J. Carlson, in *Science and the Supernatural*, defines the supernatural as "information, theories, beliefs and practices claiming origins other than verifiable experience and thinking, or events contrary to known processes in nature." 1/5-8

2B. Explanation

1C. STATEMENT OF POSITION

Since we purportedly live in a *closed* system or universe, there can be no interference or intrusion from the outside by an alleged God. This closed system or continuum means that every event has its cause within the system. To put it plainly, every event or happening has its natural explanation. Therefore, any reference to a divine act or event is futile, since it is presumed there has to be a natural explanation for all phenomena.

2C. BASIC TENETS

It is difficult to summarize the tenets of those holding to an anti-supernatural viewpoint because they vary among themselves. The following are held by many:

1D. We live in a closed system (every cause has its natural effect).

2D. There is no God. (For many critics it would be more appropriate to state it thus: "For all practical purposes, there is no God.")

3D. There is no supernatural.

4D. Miracles are not possible.

3B. Some Illustrations

1C. A group of students gave my first book to a professor, who was also head of the history department of a large, well-known university. They asked him to read *Evidence That Demands A Verdict* and give them his opinion.

Several months later one of the students returned to his office to inquire about his progress. The professor replied that he had finished the book. He continued that "it contained some of the most persuasive arguments that he had read and didn't know how anyone could refute them." At this point he added, "However, I do not accept Mr. McDowell's conclusions." The student, slightly baffled, asked, "Why?" The head of the history department answered, "Because of my world view!" His final rejection was not because of the evidence but in spite of the evidence. The motivating factor for refusing to acknowledge the evidence was his presupposition about the supernatural and not an investigation of the historical.

2C. At another university I was lecturing in a philosophy class. Upon my conclusion the professor immediately began to badger me with questions about the validity of the resurrection. After several minutes the discussion almost became obnoxious.

Finally a student asked the professor what he believed took place that first Easter morning. After a brief pause, the professor honestly replied: "To tell you the truth, I really don't know." Then he immediately added rather forcefully, "But it wasn't the resurrection!"

After a short period of interrogation he reluctantly admitted this was because of his world outlook and bias against God acting within the realm of history.

3C. During another class lecture in which I was speaking on Christianity and philosophy, the professor interrupted me and said, "This is all ridiculous. We all know that there has to be some other explanation for the empty tomb."

4C. The above is one of many reasons why I often make the statement in history classes that "following the modern historical approach I would never come to believe in the resurrection of Jesus as Savior and Lord." Most Christians at this point look askance at me because they know I teach that Christianity is a historical faith. Then I have to point out that I said "following the modern historical approach." I could not justify my examination of history adhering to the "modern approach." The reason is that it presupposes certain conclusions before an investigation is commenced. The average "modern" historian rules out any reference to the supernatural as being unhistorical, or to use a hackneyed expression as "myth."

They approach history with a preconceived notion and then adjust the evidence accordingly. In other words, before they even begin their historical examination they have determined the content of their results.

Many historians approach history with certain presuppositions and these presuppositions are not historical biases but rather philosophical prejudices. Their historical perspective is rooted within a philosophical framework, and the metaphysical conviction usually determines the "historical" content and results. The "modern" researcher, when presented with the historical evidence for the resurrection, will usually reject it, but not because of historical examination.

The response will often be: "Because we know there is no God"; or "The supernatural is not possible"; or, "We live in a closed system"; or "Miracles are not possible"; etc., etc., *ad infinitum*. I usually reply, "Did you come to this conclusion by studying the historical evidence or did you think it up philosophically?" All too often it is the offshoot of *philosophical speculation* and not historical homework.

The above men rejected my contentions, not because of any weakness in the material, but rather because they were confirmed naturalists.

Clark Pinnock clearly describes the problem: "Until he (the naturalist) will admit the possibility of a theistic world, no amount of evidence will convince modern man that the Resurrection is not absurd." 39/6,7

Bernard Ramm clarifies the naturalistic approach and its effect upon the results of one's study:

"If the issue is over the existence of the supernatural, very obviously such an approach has made the conclusion its major premise. In short, before the criticism actually begins, the supernatural is ruled out. All of it must go. The conclusion is not therefore purely a result of openminded study of the supernatural, but a conclusion dictated dogmatically by an antisupernatural metaphysics. On what other basis could critics *completely* rule out the supernatural in a document that admittedly has historical value?" 13/204

5C. A VIVID EXAMPLE OF A COMMITMENT TO A PRESUPPOSED CONCLUSION

For many years I have been telling a joke that illustrates a presuppositional viewpoint. J. Warwick Montgomery tells this humorous anecdote:

"Once upon a time there was a man who thought he was dead. His concerned wife and friends sent him to the friendly neighborhood psychiatrist. The psychiatrist determined to cure him by convincing him of one fact that contradicted his belief that he was dead. The psychiatrist decided to use the simple truth that dead men do not bleed. He put his patient to work reading medical texts, observing autopsies, etc. After weeks of effort, the patient finally said, 'All right, all right! You've convinced me. Dead men do not bleed.' Whereupon the psychiatrist stuck him in the arm with a needle, and the blood flowed. The man looked down with a contorted, ashen face and cried: 'Good Lord! Dead men bleed after all!'"

Montgomery comments:

"This parable illustrates that if you hold unsound presuppositions with sufficient tenacity, facts will make no difference at all, and you will be able to create a world of your own, totally unrelated to reality and totally incapable of being touched by reality. Such a condition (which the philosophers call solipsistic, psychiatrists call autistically psychotic, and lawyers call insane) is tantamount to death because connection with the living world is severed. The man in the parable not only thought he was dead, but in a very real sense, he *was* dead because facts no longer meant anything to him." 33/21, 22

4B. Examples of Proponents

This section will basically deal with those who advocate either the Documentary Hypothesis or Form Criticism.

1C. THE DOCUMENTARY HYPOTHESIS

Here is an exact summary of their presupposition as given by the German scholar Frank *(Geshichte und Kritik der Neuren Theologie,* p. 289): "The representation of a course of history is *a priori* to be regarded as untrue and unhistorical if supernatural factors interpose in it. Everything must be naturalised and likened to the course of natural history."

In one of his works *(De Profeten en de Profetie onder Israel,* Vol. I, pp. 5, 585) A. Kuenen states his anti-supernaturalist position:

"So long as we attribute a part of Israel's religious life directly to God and allow supernatural or immediate revelation to intervene even in one instance, just so long does our view of the whole remain inexact, and we see ourselves obliged to do violence here or there to the well-assured content of the historical accounts. It is only the assumption of a natural development that takes account of all the phenomena."

In *De Godsdienst van Israel* (Vol. I, p 111) Kuenen confesses that "the familiar intercourse of the divinity with the patriarchs constitutes for me one of the determining considerations against the historical character of the narratives."

The idea that there was no supernatural intervention on the part of God in the affairs of the Israelites has not been abandoned.

Langdon B. Gilkey, formerly of Vanderbilt University, now with the University of Chicago, describes the biblical account of the entire Exodus-Sinai experience as "the acts Hebrews believed God might have done and the words he might have said had he done and said them — but of course we recognize he did not." 40/148

Julius Wellhausen, in his *Israelitische und Juedische Geschichte* (p. 12), ridicules the account of the miracles that occurred at Sinai when God gave Moses the law with the scornful exclamation, "Who can seriously believe all that?"

Referring to the Hebrews' crossing of the Red Sea, Gilkey says: "We deny the miraculous character of the event and say its cause was merely an East wind, and then we point to the unusual response of Hebrew faith." 40/150

In contrast to these anti-supernaturalist views, W.H. Green concludes that "we cannot intelligently nor safely overlook the palpable bias against the supernatural which has infected the critical theories....All the acknowledged leaders of the movement have, without exception, scouted the reality of miracles and prophecy and immediate divine revelation in their genuine and evangelical sense. Their theories are all inwrought with naturalistic presuppositions, which cannot be disentangled from them without their falling to pieces."41/157

J. Orr, in speaking of the 19th century documentation scholarship (very much applicable to the 20th century), states that "for now the fact becomes apparent, there is, indeed, not the least attempt to disguise it, — that, to a large and influential school of critical inquirers—those, moreover, who have had the most to do with the shaping of the current critical theories— this question of a supernatural origin for the religion of Israel is already foreclosed; is ruled out at the start as a 'a priori' inadmissible." 42/12

2C. FORM CRITICISM

Rudolph Bultmann, one of the foremost proponents of Form Criticism lays the initial groundwork for his discipline:

"The historical method includes the presupposition that history is a unity in the sense of a closed continuum of effects in which individual events are connected by the succession of cause and effect. This does not mean that the process of history is determined by the causal law and that there are no free decisions of men whose actions determine the course of historical happenings. But even a free decision does not happen without cause, without a motive; and the task of the historian is to come to know the motives of actions. All decisions and all deeds have their causes and consequences; and the historical method presupposes that it is possible in principle to exhibit these and their connection and thus to understand the whole historical process as a closed unity.

"This closedness means that the continuum of historical happenings cannot be rent by the interference of supernatural, transcendent powers and that therefore there is no 'miracle' in this sense of the word. Such a miracle would be an event whose cause did not lie within history....It is in accordance with such a method as this that the science of history goes to work on all historical documents. And there cannot be any exceptions in the case of biblical texts if the latter are at all to be understood historically." 44/291, 292

Bultmann presupposes that 20th century men take it for granted that the events of nature and of history are nowhere interrupted by the intervention of supernatural powers.

Also, according to Bultmann, "an historical fact which involves a resurrection from the dead is utterly inconceivable." 44/39

Norman Perrin, in *The Promise of Bultmann*, says that "perhaps most important of all for Bultmann is the fact that not only are there no unique events in history, but also that history which historians investigate is a closed chain of cause and effect. The idea of God as a force intervening in history as an effective cause is one which a historian cannot contemplate." 45/38

"It follows," adds Perrin, "from what we have said that God cannot be the effective cause of an event with history; only a man or a people's faith in God can be that. Moreover, since the process of history is uniform and not random—if it were random any kind of historical existence would become impossible—then it follows that there never has been and there never will be an event within history (that is, world history) of which God has been or will be the effective cause." 45/90, 91

Bultmann rejects "miracles." Writing in *Jesus Christ and Mythology*, he says that "therefore, modern man acknowledges as reality only such phenomena or events as are comprehensible within the framework of the rational order of the universe. He does not acknowledge miracles because they do not fit into this lawful order." 46/37, 38

Bultmann continues his argument in Kerygma and Myth:

"It is not at all relevant for critics to point out that the world-picture of natural science today is no longer that of the nineteenth century, and it is naive to seek to use the relativization of the causal law to refurbish the belief in miracle, as if by this relativization the door had been opened for the intrusion of transcendent powers. Does science today renounce experiment? So long as it does not, it stands in the tradition of thought that began in Greece with the question of the cause, and the demand that a reason be given for things." 44/120, 121

Writing on anti-supernaturalism and Bultmann, Herman Ridderbos said:

"It is inconceivable to a modern thinker that it is possible for one who is dead to be brought again into physical existence; for modern man has learned to understand the organization of the human body. Modern man can conceive of God's action only as an event which intervenes and transforms the reality of his own 'essential' life; that is to say, an event in the reality of his existence as spirit. He cannot conceive of the acts of redemption insofar as they are concerned with man as a natural reality and with the natural reality of the whole cosmos. It is at the same time implied that the conception of Christ, as a pre-existent heavenly being, and of the removal of man into a heavenly world of light, and the clothing of man in a heavenly body, is not only rationally unthinkable but also is meaningless: it says nothing." 47/18

Pierre Benoit, after analyzing the method of Form Criticism concludes:

"Behind all these relatively new methods, new at least in their technical application, we discover one fundamental thesis which is not itself new at all. This is the denial of the supernatural which we are so accustomed to meeting in works of modern rationalist criticism. It is a thesis which, once it is stripped of its various masks, literary, historical or sociological analysis, reveals its true identity—it is a philosophical one." 43/39

3C. OTHER PROPONENTS

W.J. Sparrow-Simpson points out that David Strauss "long ago fully admitted that 'the origin of that faith in the disciples is fully accounted for if we look upon the Resurrection of Jesus, as the Evangelists describe it, as an external miraculous occurrence' (New Life, i, 399). Nothing can be more genuine that Strauss' acknowledgment that he was controlled by *a priori* considerations, to which the fact of a resurrection was inadmissible· cf. p. 397:—

"'Here, then, we stand on that decisive point where, in the presence of the accounts of the miraculous Resurrection of Jesus, we either acknowledge the inadmissibility of the natural and historical view of the life of Jesus, and must consequently retract all that precedes and give up our whole undertaking, or pledge ourselves to make out the possibility of the results of these accounts, *i.e.* the origin of the belief in the Resurrection of Jesus without any correspondingly miraculous fact.'

"This is his conscious, deliberate undertaking—to give an explanation of the evidence on the presupposition of a certain view of the universe. It invariably amounts to this. At the grave in Joseph's garden two antagonistic world-theories confront each other (cf. Ihmels, *Auferstehung*, p. 27; Luthardt, *Glaubenslehre*).

"The ultimate reasons for rejecting the Resurrection evidence are not historical. As Sabatier truly says, 'Even if the differences were perfectly reconciled, or even did not exist at all, men who will not admit the miraculous would none the less decisively reject the witness. As Zeller frankly acknowledges, their rejection is based on a philosophic theory, and not on historic considerations' *(L'Apôtre* Paul, p.42)." 48/511

Schubert Ogden, a form critic, cites Glauben and Verstehn ("The Problem of Miracles," *Religion in Life,* I, Winter, 1957-58, p.63): "The idea of miracle has become impossible for us today because we understand nature as a lawful occurrence and must therefore understand miracle as an event that breaks this lawful continuum. Such an idea.   is no longer acceptable to us." 49/33

F.C. Burkitt in *Jesus Christ* acknowledges the following: "I confess that I see no way to treat the Feeding of the Five Thousand except by a process of frank rationalization . . . . The solution which alone appeals to me is that Jesus told the disciples to distribute their scanty store, and that their example made those who were well provided share with those who had little." 50/32

Ernst Käsemann vividly expresses the opinion of the anti-supernaturalist. He writes about the words and deeds of Jesus in the Gospels as "an unbroken series of divine revelations and mighty acts, which have no common basis of comparison with any other human life and thus can no longer be comprehended within the category of the historical." 51/30

3A. SCIENCE AND MIRACLES

1B. The Limitations of Science in the Realm of Miracles and the Supernatural

J.W.N. Sullivan, in his book *The Limitations of Science,* shows that since the publication of Einstein's *Special Theory of Relativity* (1905) and Planck's endeavors on "black-body radiation," the scientists are faced with "the vicissitudes of so-called natural law in an uncharted and unobstructed universe." 3/79

Sullivan writes:

"What is called the modern 'revolution in science' consists in the fact that the Newtonian outlook which dominated the scientific world for nearly two hundred years, has been found insufficient. It is in process of being replaced by a different outlook, and, although the reconstruction is by no means complete, it is already apparent that the philosophical implications of the new outlook are very different from those of the old one." 3/138

James R. Moore, in *Christianity for the Tough Minded* (edited by John Warwick Montgomery), adds that "today scientists will admit that no one knows enough about 'natural law' to say that any event is necessarily a violation of it. They agree that an individual's non-statistical sample of time and space is hardly sufficient ground on which to base immutable generalizations concerning the nature of the entire universe. Today what we commonly term 'natural law' is in fact only our *inductive and statistical descriptions of natural phenomena.*" 58/79

John Montgomery denotes that the anti-supernatural position is both "philosophically and scientifically irresponsible." First of all, philosophically "because no one below the status of a god could know the universe so well as to eliminate miracles *a priori.*" Secondly, scientifically "because in the gage of Einsteinian physics (so different from the world of Newtonian absolutes in which Hume formulated his classic anti-miraculous argument) the universe has opened up to all possibilities, 'any attempt to state a "universal law of causation" must prove futile' (Max Black, *Models and Metaphors*), and only a careful consideration of the empirical testimony for a miraculous event can determine whether in fact it has or has not occurred." 2/32

An explanation of the above continues in *History and Christianity:*

"But can the modern man accept a 'miracle' such as the resurrection? The answer is a surprising one: The resurrection has to be accepted by us just because we are modern men, men living in the Einstein relativistic age. For us, unlike people of the Newtonian epoch, the universe is no longer a tight, safe, predictable playing-field in which we know all the rules. Since Einstein no modern has had the right to rule out the possibility of events because of prior knowledge of 'natural law.'

"The only way we can know whether an event can occur is to see whether in fact it has occurred. The problem of 'miracles,' then, must be solved in the realm of historical investigation, not in the realm of philosophical speculation." 4/75, 76

"And note," continues Montgomery, "that a historian, in facing an alleged 'miracle,' is really facing nothing new. All historical events are unique, and the test of their factual character can be only the accepted documentary approach that we have followed here. No historian has a right to a closed system of natural causation, for, as the Cornell logician Max Black has shown in a recent essay, the very concept of cause is 'a peculiar, unsystematic, and erratic notion' *(Models and Metaphors*, p. 169)." 4/75, 76

Vincent Taylor, a prominent form critic, warns against too great a dogmatism with regard to the miraculous:

"It is far too late to-day to dismiss the question by saying that 'miracles are impossible'; that stage of the discussion is definitely past. Science takes a much humbler and truer view of natural law than was characteristic of former times; we now know that the 'laws of Nature' are convenient summaries of existing knowledge. Nature is not a 'closed system,' and miracles are not 'intrusions' into an 'established order.' In the last fifty years we have been staggered too often by discoveries which at one time were pronounced impossible. We have lived to hear of the breaking up of the atom, and to find scientists themselves speaking of the universe as 'more like a great thought than like a great machine.' This change of view does not, of course, accredit the miraculous; but it does mean that, given the right conditions, miracles are not impossible; no scientific or philosophic dogma stands in the way." 52/135

2B. Hume's Philosophical Argument

1C. HUME'S POSITION

"A miracle is a violation of the laws of nature; and as a firm and unalterable experience has established these laws, the proof against a miracle, from the very nature of the fact, is as entire as any argument from experience can possibly be imagined....Nothing is esteemed a miracle if it ever happens in the common course of nature. It is no miracle that a man, seemingly in good health, should die on a sudden; ..But it is a miracle that a dead man should come to life; because that has never been observed in any age or country. There must, therefore, be a uniform experience against every miraculous event, otherwise the event would not merit that appellation." 5/126, 127

2C. C.S. Lewis cogently answers Hume's assertion that "nothing is esteemed a miracle if it ever happens in the common course of nature."

Lewis writes:

"Now of course we must agree with Hume that if there is absolutely 'uniform experience' against miracles, if in other words they have never happened, why then they never have. Unfortunately, we know the experience against them to be uniform only if we know that all the reports of them are false. And we can know all the reports of them to be false only if we know already that miracles have never occurred. In fact, we are arguing in a circle." 6/105

Merald Westphal, in his review of "The Historian and the Believer," writes:

"If God exists, miracles are not merely logically possible, but really and genuinely possible at every moment. The only condition hindering the actualisation of this possibility lies in the divine will. (For the theologian to say that scientific knowledge has rendered belief in miracles intellectually irresponsible is to affirm that scientific knowledge provides us with knowledge of limits within which the divine will always operates.) Since the question of morality has been introduced, one may perhaps be permitted to inquire about the intellectual integrity of such an affirmation. Is peace with one's age to be purchased at any cost?" 57/280

4A. A PROPER APPROACH TO HISTORY

1B. A Critical Method

1C. The Erlangen historian Ethelbert Stauffer gives us some suggestions on how to approach history:

"What do we [as historians] when we experience surprises which run counter to all our expectations, perhaps all our convictions and even our period's whole understanding of truth? We say as one great historian used to say in such instances: 'It is surely possible.' And why not? For the critical historian nothing is impossible." 7/17

2C. The historian Philip Schaff adds to the above:

"The purpose of the historian is not to construct a history from preconceived notions and to adjust it to his own liking, but to reproduce it from the best evidence and to let it speak for itself." 54/175

3C. Ronald Sider, professor of history at the Messiah College campus at Temple University, details how a historian should deal with presuppositions:

"What does the critical historian do when his evidence points very strongly to the reality of an event which contradicts his expectations and goes against the naturalistic view of reality? I submit that he must follow his critically analyzed sources. It is unscientific to begin with the philosophical presupposition that miracles cannot occur. Unless we avoid such one-sided presuppositions, historical interpretation becomes mere propaganda.

"We have a right to demand good evidence for an alleged event which we have not experienced, but we dare not judge reality by our limited experience." 12/31

4C. Montgomery concludes that "we have no right to begin with the presupposition that Jesus can be no more than a man. For then, obviously, our conclusions may simply reflect our preconceptions instead of representing the actual content of the documents. We must, in other words, objectively try to discover the picture Jesus and his contemporaries had of him, whether we agree with it or not. The question for us is not whether Jesus is pictured as a man. Virtually no one today would question this, for the records tell us that he was hungry and tired, that he wept, that he suffered and died, in short, that he was human.

"The question we face today is whether he was depicted as no more than a man." 4/48, 49

2B. An Appropriate Investigation

A critical historian should "decide the historicity of alleged miracles on the basis of the evidence that can be adduced for each individual case." 8/313

The application of the above historical inquiry is greatly enhanced with the scientific knowledge we have today. "The scientific description," comments Professor Sider, "of the observed regularity of nature was a very significant factor in the development of a more critical attitude toward reports of unusual events of all kinds. The fact that an alleged event is not what one would expect on the basis of observed regularity in a given scientific field 'activates a warning light' [Harvey, "The Historian and the Believer," p. 225]." 8/314

At this point one realizes that he must proceed with caution and carefully examine the data about the alleged event.

For example—the resurrection of Jesus: A critical historian would want to check out the witnesses; confirm the death by crucifixion; go over the burial procedures; confirm the reports of Jesus being alive on the third day and the tomb being empty. Then it would be sensible to consider every possible explanation of the above data. At this stage one would want to peruse other corroborative evidence and then draw an appropriate conclusion.

The historian cannot prove that the resurrection and subsequent empty tomb was a direct intervention by God. Ronald Sider clearly states that "the historian *qua* historian of course could never prove that an unusual event was inexplicable in terms of natural causes, much less that it was due to direct divine activity. (At best the historian could say that the evidence for the event was strong enough to warrant his affirming its historicity even though the event was inexplicable in terms of present scientific knowledge.) But he could never rule out the possibility that future scientific knowledge would be able to explain the event as one instance of a regularly recurring pattern. [See Patrick Nowell-Smith, 'Miracles,' in *New Essays in Philosophical Theology*, ed. A. Flew and A. MacIntyre (Macmillan, New York, 1964), pp.243-53, and especially p. 245.] But the historian's inability to prove that the unusual event is a 'miracle' does not preclude his ruling on its facticity. In the case of the alleged resurrection of Jesus of Nazareth, the historian *qua* historian could never demonstrate that *God* raised Jesus, but he might, if he found the evidence adequate, conclude that Jesus was probably alive on the third day." 8/317, 318

The affirmation or step of commitment to one's conclusion could only come after sufficient evidence indicates that "Jesus probably was alive on the third day."

Orr warns us that "whatever our personal convictions—and of these, of course, we cannot divest ourselves—we must, in conducting our argument place ourselves in as absolutely neutral an attitude of mind as we can. We must try to see the facts exactly as they are. If differences emerge, let them be noted. If the facts are such as to compel us to assume a special origin for this religion, let that come to light in the course of the inquiry." 42/14

"The ultimate test," continues Orr, "in either case is fitness to meet the facts." 42/14

George E. Ladd, speaking of the inability to speak of the resurrection in natural terms, writes that the Christian faith affirms that "in the resurrection of Christ an event occurred in history, in time and in space, among men which is without historical explanation or causality, but is a direct unmediated act of God. Indeed, *when the historian can explain the resurrection of Jesus in purely human terms*, those who hold anything like an evangelical faith will be faced with a problem of shattering dimensions. Faith does not, however, mean a leap in the dark, an irrational credulity, a believing against evidences and against reason. It means believing in the light of historical facts, consistent with evidences, on the basis of witnesses. It would be impossible to believe in the resurrection of Jesus apart from the historical facts of His death, His burial, and the witness of the disciples." 9/187

"If historical criticism," concludes Ladd, "could establish that the great events of redemptive history did not occur, any evangelical faith would be impossible. If the historical critic could prove that Jesus never rose from the tomb, Christian faith would be shattered. Scripture itself affirms as much (I Corinthians 15:12-19)." 9/86

The very story of Christianity is that God has intervened in history, and these acts or interventions are beyond natural explanation when it comes to analyzing their cause. The author firmly believes that a living God who acts within history would obviously be beyond "natural human explanation."

What men have done today is to rule God out by a narrow naturalistic definition of history. "If historical study," advises Wolfhart Pannenberg, "keeps itself free from the dogmatic postulate that all events are of the same kind, and at the same time remains critical toward its own procedure, there does not have to be any impossibility *in principle* in asserting the historicity of the resurrection of Jesus." 10/264, 265

Robert M. Horn (*The Book That Speaks for Itself,* used by permission of Inter-Varsity Press, Downers Grove, Ill.) is very helpful in understanding people's biases in approaching history:

"To put it at its most obvious, a person who denies God's existence will not subscribe to belief in the Bible."

"A Muslim, convinced that God cannot beget, will not accept as the Word of God, a book that teaches that Christ is the only begotten Son of God.

"Some believe that God is not personal, but rather the Ultimate, the Ground of Being. Such will be predisposed to reject the Bible as God's personal self-revelation. On their premise, the Bible cannot be the personal word of 'I AM WHO I AM' (Ex. 3:14).

"Others rule out the supernatural. They will not be likely to give credence to the book which teaches that Christ rose from the dead.

"Still others hold that God cannot communicate His truth undistorted through sinful men; hence they regard the Bible as, at least in parts, no more than human." 53/10

Gerhardus Vos is very explicit in his analysis of anti-supernaturalism's approach:

Historical study has become a powerful instrument in the service of the anti-supernaturalistic spirit of the modern age. Professing to be strictly neutral and to seek nothing but the truth it has in point of fact directed its assault along the whole line against the outstanding miraculous events of Sacred History. It has rewritten this history so as to make the supernatural elements disappear from its record. It has called into question the historicity of one after the other of the great redemptive acts of God. We need not say here that the apologetic answer to these attacks has been able and fully satisfactory to every intelligent believer. But the Christian public at large is not always able to distinguish between well-authenticated facts as such and historical constructions in which the facts have been manipulated and their interpretation shaped by *a priori* philosophical principles. People are accustomed to look upon history as the realm of facts *par excellence,* second only to pure science in the absolute certainty of its concrete results. They do not as easily detect in historical argumentation as they would in philosophic reasoning the naturalistic premises which predetermine the conclusions. It is not difficult, therefore, to give the popular mind the impression that it is confronted with an irrefutable array of evidence discrediting the Bible facts, whereas in reality it is asked to accept a certain philosophy of the facts made to discredit the Bible. Hence there has arisen in many quarters a feeling of uneasiness and concern with regard to the historical basis of facts on which Christianity has hitherto been supposed to rest." 11/293

Bultmann, one of the more radical form critics, speaks about the need for objectivity and the need for a freedom from presuppositions:

"And just for this reason the demand for freedom from presuppositions, for an unprejudiced approach, which is valid for all science, is also valid for historical research. The historian is certainly not allowed to presuppose the results of his research, and he is obliged to keep back, to reduce to silence, his personal desires with regard to these results." 14/122

Bultmann continues this thought in *Existence and Faith*: "The question whether exegesis without presuppositions is possible must be answered affirmatively if 'without presuppositions' means 'without presupposing the results of the exegesis.' In this sense, exegesis without presuppositions is not only possible but demanded."

Bultmann qualifies this by saying that in another sense there is no such thing as presuppositionless research. He asserts: "However the one presupposition that cannot be dismissed is the historical method of interrogating the text." 15/289, 290

With regard to presuppositionless scholarship Swedish scholar Seth Erlandsson states:

"But at the same time that this is maintained it is often said that we must presuppose that the Bible is of the same nature as any other human literature. By this assertion it is not merely meant that the Bible was written in human language and contains the literary finesses or expressions found in human literature. It is presupposed that the Bible 'like all other products of human activity contains mistakes and inaccuracies' and that all that is related in it including its ideological content, is altogether conditioned by human forces and has a complete explanation in this—worldly factors. If an other-worldly factor has intervened, then it cannot be analyzed historically, and for this reason we must presuppose that such an other-worldly factor, if it exists, has only made use of this-worldly causes, (so that what hapened can be fully explained in terms of these latter, that is, this-worldly, causes)." 3/8, 9

Erlandsson's point being that even those who advocate no presuppositions still approach the Scriptures with them.

I contend that by using the historical method, as Bultmann defines it, as a closed continuum of effects, closed to transcendental intervention, the presuppositions will inevitably presuppose the results.

Orr correctly concludes that "to assume beforehand, in an inquiry which turns on this very point that the religion of Israel presents no features but such as are explicable out of natural causes,—that no higher factors are needed to account for it,—is to prejudge the whole question." 16/13

To the radical critic, the presence of the miraculous is sufficient evidence for rejecting its historicity or at least sufficient reason to reject the "credibility of its witnesses."

One would wonder, as A.H. Sayce has speculated, that "if there was no record of miracles in the Old and New Testaments, it may be questioned whether so much zeal would have been displayed in endeavouring to throw doubt on the authenticity of their contents." 17/126

The Christian should not permit the "modern historians" or "radical critics" to determine the "limits of its discipline." 9/190 "On the contrary," writes Ladd, "Christian theology must recognize that the critical-historical method is a child of rationalism and as such is based on a naturalistic world view." 9/190

The radical critics are not lacking when it comes to ability and scholarship, etc.

The problem area is not their lack of knowledge of the evidence but rather their hermeneutics or approach to biblical criticism based upon their world view.

Birger Gerhardsson has appropriately said, "But the validity of its results depends on the validity of its first principles." 55/6

5A. IN SUMMARY

1B. The anti-supernaturalist bases his thinking on the *presupposition* that God has not intervened in history. Therefore he rejects evidence indicating the supernatural no matter how convincing.

2B. Both conservative and radical critics must beware of prejudices.

3B. Modern science no longer views nature as a "closed system" and therefore cannot insist that miracles do not exist.

4B. The historian should draw his conclusions from the facts at his disposal, not force the facts to conform to his presuppositions.

chapter 2

archaeology
and
criticism

The discipline of archaeology is basically a recent study. It has made a significant contribution in the area of biblical criticism.

1A. DEFINITION

The word archaeology is composed of two Greek words: (1) *Archaios* means "old" or "ancient" and (2) *Logos* signifying "word, treatise or study." A literal definition is "the study of antiquity." It is basically "a science devoted to the recovery of ancient civilizations with a view to reconstructing the story... progress and fall."

2A. BASIC REASONS FOR THE RAPIDLY INCREASING INTEREST IN ARCHAEOLOGY

William F. Albright gives four factors for the steady advance in the area of archaeology:

1B. "A rapid increase in the number of serious archaeological expeditions from many different countries, including Japan. Museum space and volume of publication have kept pace with the field work.

2B. "An improvement of archaeological method that has been little short of phenomenal. This applies both to the analysis of superimposed layers of occupation (stratigraphy) and to classification and relative dating of objects found (typology).

3B. "Use of innumerable new techniques derived from the natural sciences, among them radiocarbon (carbon isotope 14) for dating.

4B. "Decipherment and interpretation of the flood of new inscriptions and texts in many scripts and languages, many quite unknown until recent decades. The application of sound linguistic and philological method to well-preserved cuneiform tablets and Egyptian hieratic papyri makes it possible to publish them with speed and accuracy. A new script is deciphered quickly, if there are a few good clues or sufficient material to permit decoding. The number of cuneiform tablets from three millennia preserved under debris of occupation in Western Asia and Egypt seems to be practically unlimited, and new methods of baking and reproduction have reduced losses to a surprisingly low proportion.

With the aid of statigraphy, scientific analysis, and museum research, the archaeologist can now reconstruct the daily life of ancient peoples with remarkable completeness." 19/3

3A. BASIC CONTRIBUTIONS TO BIBLICAL CRITICISM

1B. Archaeology Enhances the "Scientific Study" of the Text

Archaeological insight helps in the areas of manuscript accuracy, understanding of technical words and the development of more dependable lexicons.

2B. Archaeology Acts as a Check in the Area of Critical Studies (Both Radical and Conservative)

H.M. Orlinsky in *Ancient Israel* discusses how a new attitude has developed in regard to the negative results of previous radical criticism;

"More and more the older view that the biblical data were suspect and even likely to be false, unless corroborated by extra-biblical facts, is giving way to one which holds that, by and large, the biblical accounts are more likely to be true than false, unless clear cut evidence from sources outside the Bible demonstrate the reverse." 20/6

Reformed Jewish scholar, Nelson Glueck, has affirmed:

"It is worth emphasizing that in all this work no archaeological discovery has ever controverted a single, properly understood Biblical statement." 2/6

L.H. Grollenberg adds that it greatly illumines the biblical background of many passages:

"The views (of the older documentary critics) proceeded from a rather hasty application of the evolutionary pattern and were based too exclusively upon textual criticism. Thanks to the work of the archaeologist, the modern scholar is in closer contact with the actual world in which Israel had its roots ... Today... many scholars feel a renewed confidence in the skilful narrators of chapters 12-50 of Genesis,.... the stories of the patriarchs must be based on historical memories." 21/35

The University of Chicago professor, Raymond A. Bowman, denotes that archaeology helps provide a balance between the Bible and critical hypothesis: "The confirmation of the biblical narrative at most points has led to a new respect for biblical tradition and a more conservative conception of biblical history." 22/30

Albright, in "Archaeology Confronts Biblical Criticism," says that "archaeological and inscriptional data have established the historicity of innumerable passages and statements of the Old Testament." 23/181

Archaeology does not prove the Bible to be the Word of God. All it can do is confirm the basic historicity or authenticity of a narrative. It can show that a certain incident fits into the time it purports to be from. "We shall probably never," writes G.E. Wright, "be able to prove that Abram really existed... but what we can prove is that his life and times, as reflected in the stories about him, fit perfectly within the early second millennium, but imperfectly within any later period." 27/40

Millar Burrows of Yale recognized the value of archaeology in confirming the authenticity of the Scriptures:

"The Bible is supported by archaeological evidence again and again. On the whole, there can be no question that the results of excavation have increased the respect of scholars for the Bible as a collection of historical documents. The confirmation is both general and specific. The fact that the record can be so often explained or illustrated by archaeological data shows that it fits into the framework of history as only a genuine product of ancient life could do. In addition to this general authentication, however, we find the record verified repeatedly at specific points. Names of places and persons turn up at the right places and in the right periods." 24/6

Joseph Free comments that he once "thumbed through the book of Genesis and mentally noted that each of the fifty chapters are either illuminated or confirmed by some archaeological discovery—the same would be true for most of the remaining chapters of the Bible, both Old and New Testaments." 25/340

A.T. Olmstead in "History, Ancient World, and the Bible," speaks about the unfolding of the Documentary Hypothesis: "While Old Testament Higher Critics spun out their increasingly minute dissections, and more and more took an agnostic attitude toward the recorded facts, this attitude was sharply challenged by exciting discoveries in the Near East." 26/13

3B. Archaeology Helps to Illustrate and Explain Various Biblical Passages

It enhances our knowledge of the economic, cultural, social and political background of biblical passages. Also, archaeology contributes to the understanding of other religions that bordered Israel.

S.H. Horn, an archaeologist, gives an excellent example of how archaeological evidence helps in biblical study:

"Archaeological explorations have shed some interesting light on the capture of Jerusalem by David. The biblical accounts of that capture (II Sam. 5:6-8 and I Chron. 11:6) are rather obscure without the help obtained from archaeological evidence. Take for example Second Samuel 5:8, which in the King James Version reads: 'And David said on that day, Whosoever getteth up to the gutter, and smiteth the Jebusites, and the lame and the blind, that are hated of David's soul, he shall be chief and captain.' Add to this statement First Chronicles 11:6—'So Joab the son of Zeruiah went first up and was chief.'

"Some years ago I saw a painting of the conquest of Jerusalem in which the artist showed a man climbing up a metal downspout, running on the outside face of the city wall. This picture was absurd, because ancient city walls had neither gutters nor downspouts, although they had weeping holes in the walls to drain water off. The Revised Standard Version, produced after the situation had become clear through archaeological discoveries made on the spot, translates the pertinent passages: 'And David said on that day, 'Whoever would smite the Jebusites, let him get up the water shaft to attack the lame and the blind, who are hated by David's soul.'' 'And Joab the son of Zeruiah went up first, so he became chief.' What was this water shaft that Joab climbed?

"Jerusalem in those days was a small city lying on a single spur of the hills on which the large city eventually stood. Its position was one of great natural strength, because it was surrounded on three sides by deep valleys. This was why the Jebusites boastfully declared that even blind and lame could hold their city against a powerful attacking army. But the water supply of the city was poor; the population was entirely dependent on a spring that lay outside the city on the eastern slope of the hill.

"So that they could obtain water without having to go down to where the spring was located, the Jebusites had constructed an elaborate system of tunnels through the rock. First they had dug a horizontal tunnel, beginning at the spring and proceeding toward the center of the city. After digging for ninety feet they hit a natural cave. From the cave they dug a vertical shaft forty-five feet high, and from the end of the shaft a sloping tunnel 135 feet long and a staircase that ended at the surface of their city, 110 feet above the water level of the spring. The spring was then concealed from the outside so that no enemy could detect it. To get water the Jebusite woman went down through the upper tunnel and let their water skins down the shaft to draw water from the cave, to which it was brought by natural flow through the horizontal tunnel that connected the cave with the spring.

"However, one question remained unanswered. The excavations of R.A.S. Macalister and J.G. Duncan some forty years ago had uncovered a wall and a tower that were thought to be of Jebusite and Davidic origin respectively. This tract of wall ran along the rim of the hill of Ophel, west of the tunnel entrance. Thus the entrance was left outside the protective city wall, exposed to the attacks and interference of enemies. Why hadn't the tunnel been built to end inside the city? This puzzle has now been solved by the recent excavations of Kathleen Kenyon on Ophel. She found that Macalister and Duncan had given the wall and tower they discovered wrong dates; these things actually originated in the Hellenistic period. She uncovered the real Jebusite wall a little farther down the slope of the hill, east of the tunnel entrance, which now puts the entrance safely in the old city area.

"David, a native of Bethlehem, four miles south of Jerusalem, may have found out about the spring and its tunnel system in the days when as a youth he roamed through the countryside. Later, as king he based his surprise attack on this knowledge, and made the promise that the first man who entered the city through the water shaft would become his commander-in-chief. Joab, who was already general of the army, did not want to lose that position and therefore led the attack himself. The Israelites apparently went through the tunnel, climbed up the shaft, and were in the city before any of the besieged citizens had any idea that so bold a plan had been conceived.

"This water system, constructed more than three thousand years ago, is still in existence and can be examined by any tourist. Some good climbers have even climbed the shaft in modern times, though it is not easy to do so because the rock walls are smooth and slick and give little hold for hand or foot. The shaft is also a little too wide for a comfortable climb, as I learned in my unsuccessful attempt to climb it." 34/15, 16

4B. Archaeology Helps to Supplement Areas Not Dealt with in the Bible

A good example here is the intertestamental period, kings, military campaigns, and empires not mentioned in the Scriptures.

4A. A WORD OF PRECAUTION

All too often we hear the phrase, "Archaeology proves the Bible." There needs to be a word of caution. Archaeology cannot "prove" the Bible, if by that you mean "prove it to be inspired and revealed by God." If by prove, one means "showing some biblical event or passage to be historical," then it would be a correct usage.

I believe archaeology contributes to biblical criticism, not in the area of inspiration or revelation, but in historical accuracy and trustworthiness about the events that are recorded. Let's say the rocks on which the Ten Commandments were written are found. Archaeology could confirm that they were rocks, the Ten Commandments were written on them and that they came from the period of Moses; it could not prove that God had written them.

Millar Burrows writes that archaeology "can tell us a great deal about the topography of a military campaign. It can tell us nothing about the nature of God." 30/290

One limitation of archaeology is the paucity of evidence. "Historians of antiquity," writes Edwin Yamauchi, "in using the archaeological evidence have very often failed to realize how slight is the evidence at our disposal. It would not be exaggerating to point out that what we have is but one fraction of a second fraction of a third fraction of a fourth fraction of a fifth fraction of the possible evidence." 28/9

Joseph Free in *Archaeology and Bible History* answers the question of archaeology and its relationship to the Bible: "We pointed out that numerous passages of the Bible which long puzzled the commentators have readily yielded up their meaning when new light from archaeological discoveries has been focused on them. In other words, archaeology illuminates the text of the Scriptures and so makes valuable contributions to the fields of Biblical interpretation and exegesis. In addition to illuminating the Bible, archaeology has confirmed countless passages which have been rejected by critics as unhistorical or contradictory to known facts." 29/1

One also needs to realize that archaeology has not refuted the "radical critics." Burrows is quite clear on this point: "It is quite untrue to say that all the theories of the critics have been overthrown by archaeological discoveries. It is even more untrue to say that the fundamental attitudes and methods of modern scientific criticism have been refuted." 30/292

However, as you will see in this book, archaeology has shown that many tenets of radical criticism are invalid and has called into question what has often been taught as "assured results of higher criticism."

Albright comments about the evidence for the extensive reign of Solomon which had been questioned by the radical critics. He writes: "Once more we find that the radical criticism of the past half-century must be corrected drastically." 31/22

Some people will make the unfounded assertion that supernaturalists and the nonsupernaturalist can never agree on the results of archaeology because they exist in two totally different planes. Therefore, some conclude that you interpret archaeological findings according to your own viewpoint.

Joseph Free in "Archaeology and Higher Criticism," answers this assertion in a very convincing way. "According to this view," contends Free, "a given archaeological discovery means one thing to a supernaturalist, and something different to a non-supernaturalist, and therefore archaeology has only an incidental bearing on the whole matter of apologetics.

"Actually, this is not the whole picture. To illustrate: in the nineteenth century, the Biblical critic could hold with good reason that there never was a Sargon, that the Hittites either did not exist or were insignificant, that the patriarchal accounts had a late background, that the sevenfold lampstand of the tabernacle was a late concept, that the Davidic Empire was not as extensive as the Bible implied, that Belshazzar never existed, and that a host of other supposed errors and impossibilities existed in the Biblical record.

"Archaeological discoveries showed, on the contrary, that Sargon existed and lived in a palatial dwelling some twelve miles north of Nineveh, that the Hittites not only existed but were a significant people, that the background of the patriarchs fits the time indicated in the Bible, that the concept of a sevenfold lamp existed in the Early Iron Age, that a significant city given in the record of David's Empire lies far to the north, that Belshazzar existed and ruled over Babylon, and that a host of other supposed errors and contradictions are not errors at all.

"It is of course true that in certain peripheral areas, one's theology will have a bearing on his interpretation of a given fact or a particular archaeological discovery. But in the broad outline as well as in a host of small details, facts are facts whether discovered by a supernaturalist or nonsupernaturalist. The writer knows of no nonsupernaturalist who still argues that Sargon never existed, that there never were any Hittites, or that Belshazzar is still a legend. There are many points on which all candid scholars can agree, regardless of their theology. There are certain areas, however, where the liberal has not taken the evidence, archaeological or otherwise, sufficiently into account. This is true, we believe, in the realm of the documentary theory and in the question of authorship, date, and integrity of the books of the Bible." 32/30,31

Note: For some examples of archaeology affecting criticism, see the appendix "The Stones Cry Out—Archaeology and Criticism."

5A. IN SUMMARY

1B. Archaeology does not *prove* the Bible; it confirms its historicity and explains various passages.

2B. Archaeology has not refuted the radical critics, but has caused a questioning of many of their presuppositions.

BIBLIOGRAPHY

1. Carlson, A.J. *Science and the Supernatural* (Pamphlet). Yellow Springs, Ohio: American Humanist Association, n.d.

2. Montgomery, Jonn W. (ed.). *Christianity For the Tough Minded.* Minneapolis: Bethany Fellowship, Inc., 1973.

3. Sullivan, J.W.N. *The Limitations of Science.* New York: Mentor Books, 1963.

4. Montgomery, John W. *History and Christianity.* Downers Grove, Ill: Inter-Varsity Press, 1964.

5. Hume, David. *An Enquiry Concerning Human Understanding.* Chicago: Open Court, 1958.

6. Lewis, C.S. *Miracles.* New York: Macmillan, 1947.

7. Stauffer, Ethelbert. *Jesus and His Story.* Translated by Dorothea M. Barton. New York: Knopf, 1960.

8. Sider, Ronald. "The Historian, The Miraculous and Post-Newtonian Man," *Scottish Journal of Theology.* August, 1972. Vol. 25, No. 3, pp. 309-319.

9. Ladd, George E. *The New Testament and Criticism.* Grand Rapids: Wm. B. Eerdmans Publishing Co., 1967.

10. Pannenberg, Wolfhart. *Revelation As History.* Translated by David Granskou. New York: Macmillan, 1968.

11. Vos, Gerhardus. *Biblical Theology: Old and New Testament.* Grand Rapids: Wm. B. Eerdmans Publishing Co., 1948.

12. Sider, Ronald. *"A Case for Easter," His Magazine.* April, 1972. pp. 27-31.

13. Ramm, Bernard. *Protestant Christian Evidence.* Chicago: Moody Press, 1953.

14. Bultmann, Rudolf. *History and Eschatology.* Edinburgh: The Edinburgh University Press, 1957.

15. Bultmann, Rudolf. *Existence and Faith.* Shorter writings of R. Bultmann selected, translated and introduced by Schubert M. Ogden. Cleveland and New York: Meridian Books—The World Publishing Co., 1960.

16. Orr, James. *The Problem of the Old Testament.* New York: Charles Scribner's Sons, 1917.

17. Sayce, A.H. *Monuments, Facts and Higher Critical Fancies.* London: The Religious Tract Society, 1904.

18. Allis, Oswald T. *The Old Testament, Its Claims and Its Critics.* Nutley, New Jersey: The Presbyterian and Reformed Publishing Company, 1972.

19. Albright, Wm. R. "Archaeological Discovery of the Scriptures," *Christianity Today*. June 21. 1968. Vol. 12, No. 19, pp. 915-917.

20. Orlinsky, Harry. *Ancient Israel*. Ithaca: Cornell University Press, 1954.

21. Grollenberg, Luc H. *Atlas of the Bible*. Translated and edited by Joyce M.H. Reid and H.H. Rowley. London: Nelson, 1956.

22. Bowman, Raymond. "Old Testament Research between the Great Wars," *The Study of the Bible Today and Tomorrow*. Ed. by Harold H. Willoughby. Chicago: University of Chicago Press, 1947.

23. Albright, W.F. *Archaeology Confronts Biblical Criticism*," *The American Scholar*. Spring, 1938. Vol. 7, pp. 176-188.

24. Burrows, Millar. "How Archaeology Helps the Student of the Bible," *Workers with Youth*. April, 1948. pp. 6-10

25. Free, Joseph P. "Archaeology and the Bible," *His Magazine*. May, 1949. Vol. 9, pp. 17-20.

26. Olmstead, A.T. "History, Ancient World, and the Bible," *Journal of Near Eastern Studies*. January, 1943. pp. 1-34.

27. Wright, G.E. *Biblical Archaeology*. Philadelphia: Westminster Press, 1957.

28. Yamauchi, Edwin M. "Stones, Scripts, Scholars," *Christianity Today*. February 14, 1969. Vol. 13, pp. 8ff.

29. Free, Joseph P. *Archaeology and Bible History*. Wheaton, Ill.: Scripture Press, 1969.

30. Burrows, Millar. *What Mean These Stones?* New York: Meridian Books, 1956.

31. Albright, Wm. F. "New Light on the Early History of Phoenician Colonization," *Bulletin of the American Schools of Oriental Research*. October, 1941. Vol. 83, pp. 14-22.

32. Free, Joseph P. "Archaeology and Higher Criticism," *Bibliotheca Sacra*. January, 1957. Vol. 114, pp. 23-29.

33. Montgomery, John W. *The Altizer-Montgomery Dialogue*. Chicago: Inter-Varsity, 1967.

34. Horn, S.H. "Recent Illumination of the Old Testament," *Christianity Today*. June 21, 1968. Vol. 12, pp. 925-929.

35. Livingston, Herbert G. *The Pentateuch in Its Cultural Environment*. Grand Rapids: Baker Book House, 1974.

36. Whitelaw, Thomas. *Old Testament Critics*. London: Kegan, Paul, Trench, Trubner & Co., Ltd., 1903.

37. Allis, Oswald T. *The Five Books of Moses*. Philadelphia: The Presbyterian and Reformed Publishing Co., copyright 1943, revised 1969.

38. *Strong's Exhaustive Concordance of the Bible*. New York, London: Hodder and Stoughton, 1903.

39. Pinnock, Clark. *Set Forth Your Case*. Nutley, New Jersey: Craig Press, 1967.

40. Gilkey, Langdon B. "Cosmology, Ontology, and the Travail of Biblical Language," *Concordia Theological Monthly*. March, 1962. Vol. 33, pp. 143-154.

41. Green, William H. *The Higher Criticism of the Pentateuch*. New York: Charles Scribner's Sons, 1895.

42. Orr, James. *The Problem of the Old Testament*. New York: Charles Scribner's Sons, 1917.

43. Benoit, Pierre. *Jesus and the Gospels*. Vol. I. Translated by Benet Weatherhead. Herder and Herder, 1973.

44. Bultmann, Rudolf. *Kerygma and Myth*. Ed. by H.W. Bartsch. Translated by Reginald M. Fuller. New York: Harper and Row, 1961.

45. Perrin, Norman. *The Promise of Bultmann*. In the series, The Promise of Theology, edited by Martin E. Marty. New York: J.P. Lippincott Co., 1969.

46. Bultmann, Rudolf. *Jesus Christ and Mythology*. New York: Charles Scribner's Sons, 1958.

47. Ridderbos, Herman N. *Bultmann*. Translated by Dr. David H. Freeman. Grand Rapids: Baker Book House, 1960.

48. Sparrow-Simpson, W.J. "Resurrection and Christ," *A Dictionary of Christ and the Gospels*. Vol. 2. Edited by James Hastings. Edinburgh: T. & T. Clark, 1908.

49. Ogden, Schubert M. *Christ Without Myth*. New York: Harper and Row Publishers, 1961.

50. Burkitt, F.C. *Jesus Christ*. London and Glasgow: Blackie and Sons, Ltd., 1932.

51. Käsemann, Ernst. *Essays on New Testament Themes*. Naperville, Ill.: Alec R. Allenson, Inc., SCM Press Ltd., 1964.

52. Taylor, Vincent. *The Formation of the Gospel Tradition*. London: Macmillan and Co. Limited, Second edition, 1935.

53. Horn, Robert M. *The Book That Speaks for Itself*. Downers Grove, Ill.: Inter-Varsity Press, 1970.

54. Schaff, Philip. *History of the Christian Church*. Vol. I. New York: Charles Scribner's Sons, 1882.

55. Gerhardsson, Birger. *Tradition and Transmission in Early Christianity*. Translated by Eric J. Sharpe. Copenhagen: Ejnar Munksgaard, 1964.

56. Driver, S.R. *An Introduction to the Literature of the Old Testament*. New York: Charles Scribner's Sons, 1891.

57. Westphal, Merald. "The Historian and the Believer," *Religious Studies*. 1967. Vol. 2, No. 2, pp. 277-282.

58. Moore, James R. "Science and Christianity: Towards Peaceful Coexistence," *Christianity for the Tough Minded*. Edited by John W. Montgomery. Minneapolis: Bethany Fellowship, Inc., 1973.

section II

documentary
hypothesis

The discipline of literary criticism applied to the Pentateuch is examined along with evidence for Mosaic authorship.

SECTION OUTLINE

chapter 3

introduction to the
documentary hypothesis

Julius Wellhausen in 1895 added the finishing touches to a hypothesis which is prevalent in modern biblical circles. The hypothesis is known as the Documentary Hypothesis (JEDP hypothesis). Using literary criticism as its basis for argument, this hypothesis sets forth the idea that the Pentateuch (Genesis to Deuteronomy) was not written by Moses, as the Bible claims, but was completed years after Moses died.

Those adhering to the Documentary Hypothesis teach that the first five books of the Bible were written close to one thousand years after Moses' death and were the result of a process of writing, rewriting, editing and compiling by various anonymous editors or redactors.

Citing literary variations within the text (divine names, doublets, repetition of accounts), style and diction, the documentarians assert that there are four different documents, J, E, D and P, which make up the Pentateuch. The J stands for the divine name YHWH which is the name for God characteristically used by the anonymous J writer. This writer had a flowing style and a peculiar vocabulary. E denotes the Elohist document which is known for its use of Elohim as the name for God. J and E are often difficult to separate within the text so they are often referred to as one source, JE. The letter D describes the Deuteronomic code which was found in 621 B.C. Finally P represents the Priestly writer. This writer was the last compiler to work with the Old Testament. He put the finishing touches on it. P is characterized by its use of the name Elohim for God and its acrid style. "Its language is that of a jurist, rather than a historian." 18/12 P is not to be confused with the Elohist document which has a fresh flowing style.

Chronologically these came in the same order as the letters, J, E, D, P. The following is an excellent description of the background and purpose of each writer:

"J, or the Yahwist, was the first writer to bring together the legends, myths, poems even well-known stories from other peoples, such as the Babylonians, into one great history of God's people. Some of the sources J used were oral traditions; some were already in written form. This anonymous writer lived about the time of David or Solomon. He was concerned to save the old traditions when Israel was becoming a nation and, as a world power, was coming into contact with other nations and ideas. In planning his work, J seems to have used the old confessions of faith or creeds about what God had done for his people. As an example see *Deut. 26:5-10.* Around this basic outline of creeds, he grouped the narratives. This writer is called the Yahwist because he used Yahweh as the name for God. German scholars, who first discovered this writer, spell Yahweh with a 'J'.

"E, or the Elohist, was the second writer to gather all the traditions into one history. He wrote about 700 B.C., perhaps when the Northern Kingdom, Israel, was threatened by enemies. E used traditions that had been passed down among northern tribes. Some of these were the same as those used by J; others were different. E used the name Elohim for God in stories before the time of Moses. He believed that the name Yahweh was revealed to Moses. E gave special emphasis to Moses. See his description in *Deut. 34:10-12.* E was a good writer of stories, for example, the story of Joseph.

"JE. The works of these two writers were put together into one history by an unknown editor after Jerusalem was destroyed. Sometimes the editor kept both J's and E's telling of a story, even when they differed in details. Other times he would use one as the basic material and add details from the other. In *Ex., ch. 14,* the basic material is from J; very little from E is used. Occasionally the editor added sentences of his own.

"P may have been a priest or a group of priests who lived during the exile in Babylon. They worked out a code of holiness for the people, that is, the ways of worship and the laws that ought to be observed. This Priestly Code was at first a separate book. Sometime in the fourth century B.C. it was worked into parts of the JE book. It was 'as if someone were to take a stirring account of American history and insert into it at key points the American Constitution or legislation of Congress.' Usually the P material is not so lively as the JE parts. The P writers were interested in details of worship and sacrifice, in laws, in genealogies, in specific locations and dates, in exact descriptions and measurements, and the like. When they added to the stories of J and E, they were likely to emphasize and even overemphasize the intervention of God and to make some actions almost magical." 82/11-14

The D or Deuteronomy document has as its purpose reform in religious practices. J, E and P were not yet united into a single work when D was composed.

"It was a great manifesto," writes Driver, "against the dominant tendencies of the time. It laid down the lines of a great religious reform. Whether written in the dark days of Manasseh, or during the brighter years which followed the accession of Josiah, it was a nobly-conceived endeavour to provide in anticipation a spiritual rallying-point, round which, when circumstances favoured, the disorganized forces of the national religion might range themselves again. It was an emphatic reaffirmation of the fundamental principles which Moses had long ago insisted on, loyalty to Jehovah and repudiation of all false gods: it was an endeavour to realize in practice the ideals of the prophets, especially of Hosea and Isaiah, to transform the Judah demoralized by Manasseh into the 'holy nation' pictured in Isaiah's vision, and to awaken in it that devotion to God, and love for man, which Hosea had declared to be the first of human duties." 18/89

"Throughout the discourses the author's aim is to provide motives, by which to secure loyalty to Him. . . . Deuteronomy may be described as the *prophetic re-formulation, and adaptation to new needs, of an older legislation.* It is highly probable that. . . the bulk of the laws contained in Dt. is undoubtedly far more ancient than the time of the author himself: and in dealing with them as he has done, in combining them into a manual for the guidance of the people, and providing them with hortatory introductions and comments." 18/91

Herbert Livingston gives an excellent summary of the dates of the four documents of Wellhausen's theory:

"How then did the Wellhausen theory date the four documents? Since the D document was declared to be written in the seventh century and made public in Josiah's reform of 621 B.C., that document became the keystone for the procedure. It was decided that D knew about the contents of J and E, but not of the contents of P; hence, J and E were written before 621 B.C., and P, at a later date.

"Dialectically, the J document, with its naive concepts, could be dated before E, and the early phases of the divided kingdom seemed to provide a good historical setting. It could be argued that J was the kingdom of Judah's reaction against the establishment of the kingdom of north Israel. The purpose of J, then, was to provide Judah with a 'historical' document that would justify Judah's and Jerusalem's claim to be the governmental center of all Israel. Likewise, E would be the antithetical production of the kingdom of north Israel, led by the tribe of Ephraim, to show that there were historical antecedents in the Patriarchs and in Joshua for the governmental center to be located in the north.

"The theory continued to conclude that after the destruction of the northern kingdom of Israel, in 721 B.C., broadminded men during the reign of Manasseh (first half of seventh century B.C.) felt that the E document was too valuable to lose, so they blended it with the J document. This new JE document became a new thesis and the D document its antithesis. The thinking of the D document is said to have triumphed, substantially, during the Exile in Babylon and colored the composition of the historical books Joshua through II Kings. However, the 'Holiness Code,' tied with Ezekiel, arose as another antithesis to D; and slowly, for perhaps a century, the priests in exile and then in Jerusalem put together the P document and made it the framework of a grand synthesis, the Pentateuch.

"In summary, the J document is dated a bit later than 900 B.C., and the E document somewhat later in the ninth century B.C. The two were put together about 650 B.C., and were written about that same time and made public in 621 B.C. The P document appeared in the fifth century and the Pentateuch composed in approximately its present form about 400 B.C." 120/228, 229

As a result of the above assertions, those adhering to the Documentary Hypothesis reject the Mosaic authorship of the Pentateuch.

Moses, who may be dated around 1,400 B.C., purports to have written the Pentateuch. The documentarians reject this date and say it was not completed until sometime between the eighth and fifth centuries B.C.

The Documentary Hypothesis calls into question the credibility of the entire Old Testament. One would have to conclude, if their assertions are correct, that the Old Testament is a gigantic literary fraud. Either God did speak to and through Moses or we have to acknowledge that we possess a *belles-lettres* hoax.

The primary issue is not the "unit of the pentateuch" but "how did this unity come about?" In other words, the literary section of Genesis through Deuteronomy is one continuous narrative. The question posed here is, "How did this continuous narrative come into existence?" Was it, as traditional Christianity asserts and the Bible teaches, written by Moses, or was it compiled years later? The whole issue calls into question the trustworthiness of Jesus, the accuracy of both the Old and New Testament writers and the integrity of Moses himself.

Livingston makes an acute observation:

"Almost every book that promotes the theory has a listing of chapters and verses originally belonging to the independent documents. All isolated fragments that are left over are attributed, much too easily, to redactors or compilers. It should be understood, however, that there are no literary references, no extant manuscripts of any kind, which mention the J, E, D, or P documents, either singly or as a group. They have been created by separating them, with the aid of the above mentioned criteria, from the extant text of the Pentateuch." 120/227

Livingston gives consequences of adherence to the theory of the Documentary Hypothesis:

"(a) Mosaic authorship is rejected, with only bits of the Pentateuch attributed to the Mosaic period; (b) for many of the scholars who accept the Wellhausen view, the men and women of the Pentateuch were not actual human beings—at best they were idealized heroes; (c) the Pentateuch does not give us a true history of ancient times, but it reflects instead the history of the divided kingdom through the early part of the postexilic period; (d) none of the people in the Pentateuch were monotheistic, and it was the postexilic priests who made them look like believers in one God; (e) God never spoke to any individuals in ancient times, but again, it was the work of the priests that gives that impression; (f) very few of the laws in the Pentateuch were prekingdom in origin; (g) very few of the cultic practices recorded in the Pentateuch were prekingdom, and many were postexilic; (h) the early Israelites never had a tabernacle such as described in Exodus; (i) all claims in the Pentateuch that God acted redemptively and miraculously in behalf of Israel are erroneous; (j) any concept that the present structural unity of the five books was original with Moses is erroneous, and, finally; (k) the skepticism inherent in the theory creates a credibility gap with the ordinary layman to the extent that the Pentateuch becomes practically useless to him." 120/229

The following section is written (1) to present the evidence for Mosaic authorship; (2) to clarify the assertions of those who advocate and propagate the Documentary Hypothesis; (3) to give some basic answers to the documentarian assumptions.

Documentary Hypothesis

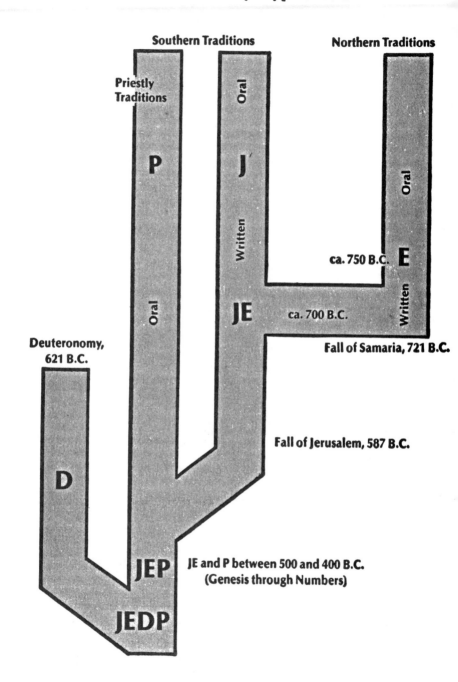

chapter 4

introduction to biblical criticism

1A. DEFINITIONS

"The word *criticism* denotes, primarily, a judgment, or an act of judging; its derivation from a Greek verb (. . . [*krino*]) meaning *to discern*, or *to try*, or *to pass judgment upon*, or *to determine*, gives it this signification. As applied to literary matters, it conveys the idea, not of fault-finding, but of fairly and justly estimating both merits and defects. In other words, it is simply an impartial judgment, or as nearly such as the given critic can render, on whatever question is under consideration." 59/70, 71

This kind of study can be applied to the Bible and is therefore called biblical criticism. It is defined by the *Christian Cyclopedia* as:

"the science by which we arrive at a satisfactory acquaintance with the origin, history, and present state of the original text of Scripture." 25/206

Biblical criticism has been divided into two kinds:

(1)   Lower criticism "which is more of a verbal and historical nature, and is confined to the words, or the collocation of the words, as they stand in the manuscript or printed texts, the ancient versions, and other legitimate sources of appeal." 25/206 Lower criticism is also known as textual criticism.

(2)   Higher criticism "consists in the exercise of the judgment in reference to the text, on grounds taken from the nature, form, method, subject, or arguments of the different books; the nature and connection of the context; the relation of passages to each other; the known circumstances of the writers, and those of the persons for whose immediate use they wrote." 25/206

1B. Higher Criticism

The questions of the higher criticism are questions of integrity, authenticity, credibility and literary forms of the various writings that make up the Bible.

The term "higher criticism" is not, in and of itself, a negative term. James Orr, former Professor of Apologetics and Systematic Theology in the United Free Church College, Glasgow, Scotland, stated it this way:

"The truth is, and the fact has to be faced, that no one who studies the Old Testament in the light of modern knowledge can help being, to some extent, a 'Higher Critic,' nor is it desirable he should. The name has unfortunately come to be associated all but exclusively with a method yielding a certain class of results; but it has no necessary connection with these results. 'Higher Criticism,' rightly understood, is simply the careful scrutiny, on the principles which it is customary to apply to all literature, of the actual phenomena of the Bible, with a view to deduce from these such conclusions as may be warranted regarding the age, authorship, mode of composition, sources, etc., of the different books; and everyone who engages in such inquiries, with whatever aim, is a 'Higher Critic,; and cannot help himself." 50/9

Green adds that higher criticism in its modern implication has a negative connotation, but in fact it properly means an inquiry into the origin and character of the writings to which it is applied. By using all available materials the higher critic seeks to ascertain the author of a work, period in which it was written, the circumstances surrounding the writing, and the design with which the writing was produced. Investigations conducted in such a manner will prove most important in understanding and appreciating the writing. 26/6

Higher criticism should remain as objective as possible. Orr said:

"The age, authorship, and simple or composite character of a book are matters for investigation, to be determined solely by evidence, and it is justly claimed that criticism, in its investigation of such subjects, must be untrammelled: That faith cannot be bound up with results of purely literary judgments." 50/16

This includes faith in theories and presuppositions as well as "religious" faith.

2B. History of Higher Criticism

Although higher criticism as an exacting science had been applied to some classical literature before the 19th century, J.G. Eichhorn, a German rationalist of the late 1700's was the first to apply the term to the study of the Bible. He introduced the second edition of his *Einleitung in das Alte Testament* (O.T. Introduction) in 1787 with these words:

"I have been obliged to bestow the greatest amount of labor on a hitherto entirely unworked field, the investigation of the inner constitution of the particular writings of the Old Testament, by the Higher Criticism (a new name to no humanist)." 16/19

Eichhorn has been called the "Father of Old Testament Criticism."

Although the term "higher criticism" did not become associated with biblical studies until Eichhorn, it was Jean Astruc's publication of his treatise on Genesis in 1753 that actually marked the beginning of higher critical methodology as applied to the Old Testament. While Astruc defended Moses as the author of Genesis, he concluded that there were independent sources woven together throughout the book. Subsequently the entire Pentateuch (Genesis-Deuteronomy) was subjected to extensive source analysis. Higher criticism therefore may be said to have been spawned and developed in Pentateuchal analysis. It was the highly complex conclusions regarding the authorship and dating of the Pentateuch (the Documentary Hypothesis) by European (especially German) higher critics promulgated primarily during the 1800's that formed the foundation for most subsequent critical inquiry into the Old Testament. Therefore, an investigation of modern Old Testament higher criticism in general will have to consider, first of all, past

Pentateuchal analysis. It is the key to a proper evaluation of all higher criticism of the Old Testament since Astruc.

Unfortunately, the higher critical school which grew up out of German scholarship in the last century employed some faulty methodology and tenaciously held to some questionable presuppositions. This seriously undermined the validity of many of their conclusions. Entire books were rent into numerous "sources"; most of the books in the Old Testament were dated later—by almost a 1000 years in some cases—than the actual witness of the documents themselves would allow. The biblical account of the early Hebrews' history was replaced by a complicated and well-thought-out theory in contradiction to Israel's own account of her history in almost every major point.

Because of its wholesale reconstruction of Israelite literature, and its radical remaking of Hebrew history, this school, which has dominated Old Testament studies since its inception, together with the methodology that achieved these drastic results, came to be known in some circles as "destructive higher criticism."

2A. THREE SCHOOLS OF RADICAL PENTATEUCHAL CRITICISM

1B. Documentary Hypothesis—Statement of Theory

The Pentateuch, although traditionally ascribed to Moses, was actually a compilation of four basic documents written by independent authors over a period of approximately 400 years beginning ca. 850 B.C. and gradually combined by unknown redactors who put it in its basic form by about 400 B.C. The main criterion for this theory was a close analysis of the text itself through which it was thought the actual documents could be isolated. The classic expression of this theory came from a German scholar, Julius Wellhausen, in 1878. 32/19-27

2B. Form Criticism (Formgeschichte)

The form critical school likewise held that the Pentateuch was the product of a compilation process and not the work of Moses. But it differed from the Documentary Hypothesis in that it held the individual documents were themselves compilations developing from early oral tradition and being placed in writing only during or after the exilic period (586 B.C.). Very little could be known about the literary development of these documents and it was clear to this school that the neat isolation of documents achieved by the documentary school was impossible. The only practical approach was to go behind the sources in their written form and examine the types of categories to which the original material belonged in its oral state and then follow the probable course of development of each one of these oral units until it finally reached its written form. Great emphasis was placed upon the *Sitz im Leben* (life situation) of these different categories in determining through what kind of process they evolved into their written form. Herman Gunkel and Hugo Gressmann, two German scholars, have been credited with founding this school at the beginning of the 20th century. (Gunkel's *Die Sagen der Genesis*, 1901; *Die Schriften des Alten Testaments*, 1911; Gressmann's *Die Alteste Geschichtsschreibung und Prophetie Israels*, 1910.) 32/35-38

3B. Oral Traditionists ("Uppsala School")

Similar to the form critical school, the oral traditionists held that the Pentateuch is not Mosaic in origin but is rather a collection of material compiled over centuries and committed to writing not before the Exile. Totally rejecting the Documentary Hypothesis as an occidental solution to a literary problem of the vastly different ancient Near East, this Scandinavian school placed even more emphasis on oral tradition than Gunkel and the form critics. Some even claimed that oral tradition was more important in the transmission of material than was writing in the ancient Orient. It is not written documents which must be dealt with but rather units of oral tradition, circles of tradition, and various "schools" within these traditionist circles.

They seek to classify the material into literary categories such as narratives, legal, prose, poetry and especially subdivided types called *Gattungen*. These subdivided types *(Gattungen)* are given "laws" as to how they develop in "life situations" *(Sitz im Leben)*.

There are two basic sources of tradition in the Pentateuch: one extends from Genesis through Numbers and points to a P (priestly) type school of tradition. The other is a D (Deuteronomy through II Kings) work which exhibits a different style than P, and points to a D circle of traditionists. Largely responsible for this most recent trend in Pentateuchal analysis were Johannes Pedersen *(Die Auffassung vom Alten Testament,* 1931) and Ivan Engnell *(Gamla Testamentet en Traditionshistorisk Inledning,* 1945). 32/66-69

chapter 5

introduction
to the
pentateuch

As was noted earlier, the first five books of the Old Testament, Genesis through Deuteronomy (also called the Five Books of Moses), are known as the Pentateuch, deriving from the Greek word *pentateuchos* meaning "five-volumed [sc. book]." 49/957

The collection of these five books was first called the Pentateuch by Origen in the third century A.D. in his commentary on the Gospel of John. 32/495 Jewish tradition has called these five books the Torah (deriving from the Hebrew word tôrâ, meaning "instruction"), the Book of the Law, the Law of Moses or simply the Law.

Harrison breaks down the contents of the Pentateuch as follows:

1. Primeval History with a Mesopotamian Background, Gen. 1–11
2. History of the Patriarchs, Gen. 12–50
3. The Oppression of Israel and Preparations for the Exodus, Exod. 1–9
4. The Exodus, Passover, and the Arrival at Sinai, Exod. 10–19
5. The Decalogue and the Covenant at Sinai, Exod. 20–24
6. Legislation Relating to the Tabernacle and Aaronic Priesthood, Exod. 25–31
7. The Idolatrous Violation of the Covenant, Exod. 32–34
8. The Implementation of Regulations Concerning the Tabernacle, Exod. 35–40
9. The Law of Offerings, Lev. 1–7
10. The Consecration of the Priests and Initial Offerings, Lev. 8–10
11. The Laws of Cleanliness, Lev. 11–15
12. The Day of Atonement, Lev. 16
13. Laws Concerning Morality and Cleanliness, Lev. 17–26
14. Vows and Tithes, Lev. 27
15. Numberings and Laws, Num. 1–9
16. The Journey from Sinai to Kadesh, Num. 10–20
17. Wanderings to Moab, Num. 21–36
18. Historical Retrospect to the Wilderness Period, Deut. 1–4
19. Second Speech, with an Hortatory Introduction. Deut. 5–11

32/496

1A. PURPOSE AND IMPORTANCE OF THE PENTATEUCH

The Bible is history, but of a very special kind. It is the history of God's redemption of mankind, and the Pentateuch is chapter one of that history. 61/187, 188

Unger elaborates:

"The author of the Pentateuch had a definite plan. He did not apply himself to recording the story of human history. His task was rather to give an account of God's gracious provisions for man's salvation. The Pentateuch, accordingly, is history with a motive behind it, a deep, religious motive, which imbues the whole. The religious principle underlying it, on the other hand, does not render the events recounted any less historical. It merely gives them a permanent importance far transcending the times in which and about which they were written and far out-reaching in importance their application to any one nation or people, investing them with an inestimable and abiding value for all mankind...

"Failure to comprehend the precise character and purpose of the Pentateuch has led many critics to deny its historicity altogether or to adopt low views of its reliability. If, for instance, the account of the Egyptian sojourn, the miraculous deliverance and the wilderness wanderings were fictitious, its vital connection not only with Hebrew history but with the whole Biblical plan of salvation raises the insoluable [sic] problem of how this extraordinary record could ever have been fabricated." 61/188, 189

D.A. Hubbard speaks of the prime importance of the Pentateuch in understanding Israel's relationship with God:

"A record of revelation and response, the Pentateuch testifies to the saving acts of God who is sovereign Lord of history and nature. The central act of God in the Pentateuch (and indeed the Old Testament) is the Exodus from Egypt. Here God broke in upon the consciousness of the Israelites and revealed Himself as the redeeming God. Insights gained from this revelation enabled them under Moses' leadership to reevaluate the traditions of their ancestors and see in them the budding of God's dealings which had bloomed so brilliantly in the liberation from Egypt." 49/963

Even Langdon B. Gilkey, hardly a conservative scholar, calls the Exodus-Sinai experience "the pivotal point of biblical religion." 26/147

Therefore, the Pentateuch occupies an important place in the Christian view of the universe since it records God's initial revealing of Himself to mankind.

As Gilkey puts it:

"The Exodus event has a confessional as well as a historical interest for us. The question of what God did at Sinai is, in other words, not only a question for the scholar of Semitic religion and theology, it is even more a question for the contemporary believer who wishes to make his witness today to the acts of God in history." 26/147

2A. ORIGIN AND HISTORY OF NON-MOSAIC AUTHORSHIP THEORY

According to John of Damascus, the Nazarites, a sect of Christians of Jewish birth living during the second century, denied that Moses wrote the Pentateuch. 71/113 The Clementine Homilies, a collection of ancient writings somewhat later than the second century, stated that the Pentateuch was written by 70 wise men after Moses' death. (For a study of the unreliability of these writings and the invalid methodology of historical and biblical interpretation which they employed, see E.J. Young's *An Introduction to the Old Testament*, pp. 118, 119.) 71/112

Although there were several groups and individuals from the first two centuries A.D. who denied the essential Mosaic authorship of the Pentateuch, the following passage from Young should be noted:

"During the first two centuries of the Christian era there is no recorded instance of criticism that is hostile to the Bible among the Church fathers or in the orthodox Church itself. The Apostolic Fathers and the subsequent Ante-Nicene Fathers, in so far as they expressed themselves on the subject, believed Moses to be the author of the Pentateuch, and the Old Testament to be a divine book...

"Such instances of hostile criticism as are extant from this period come either from groups that were considered to be heretical or from the external pagan world. Furthermore, this criticism reflected certain philosophical presuppositions and is of a decidedly biased and unscientific character." 71/113,114

The allegation that Moses was not the author of the Pentateuch thus had its beginning during the first two centuries A.D. The primary basis upon which this charge rested was the presence of passages supposedly written after Moses' time.

There was some minor activity in the question of Mosaic authorship during the following centuries but it was not until the 18th century when the argument moved to a new foundation, that of literary criticism, that the theory of non-Mosaic authorship was extensively developed. (For a survey of the developments from the third century to the 1700's see E.J. Young, *An Introduction to the Old Testament*.) 71/116-120

chapter 6

the development of the documentary hypothesis

1A. IMPORTANCE OF THE DOCUMENTARY HYPOTHESIS IN RADICAL HIGHER CRITICISM

We have already referred to the important role that the Documentary Hypothesis has played in the establishment of a whole school of higher critical scholarship that has undeniably undermined the literary and historical integrity of the Old Testament. The radical conclusions reached by this school therefore necessitate a careful and searching investigation of its position by all serious students of the Old Testament. Any such investigation must start with the analysis of the Pentateuch as set forth in the Documentary Hypothesis. Whether this radical higher criticial position is indeed a valid one or whether it ought to be discarded in favor of one which is better suited to the facts at hand will be determined largely by an objective assessment of the classic Documentary Hypothesis and its subsequent revisions.

2A. HISTORY OF ITS DEVELOPMENT

1B. First Documentary Theory

As far as is known, a Protestant priest, H.B. Witter, in the early part of the 18th century, was the first to assert that there were two parallel accounts of creation and that they were distinguishable by the use of the different divine names. He was also the first to suggest the divine names as criteria for distinguishing the different documents. (See his *Jura Israelitarum in Palestina,* 1711.) 15/9; 71/118

The first significant treatment of the documentary theory was set forth in 1753 by the French physician Jean Astruc in his book *Conjectures Concerning the Original Memoranda which it Appears Moses Used to Compose the Book of Genesis.*

Astruc held that there were distinct documents in Genesis, discernible primarily by the unique usage of the divine names Elohim and Jehovah in the opening chapters. Astruc realized that the divine name phenomenon could not be used as a criterion for testing any portions of the Pentateuch beyond Genesis. Alleged repetition of events (i.e., the creation and flood stories) and chronological inaccuracies were also cited by Astruc as evidence for underlying sources. Although he developed a documentary theory, Astruc defended Moses as being the compiler of the documents. 71/118-121

The first to introduce Astruc's theory to Germany was J.G. Eichhorn. In his three-volume introduction to the Old Testament, *Einleitung in das Alte Testament* (1780-1783), Eichhorn suggested that criteria for source analysis in the Pentateuch should include literary considerations (i.e., diversity in style, words peculiar to previously isolated documents, etc.), in addition to Astruc's divine name criterion. 32/14

2B. Fragmentary Hypothesis

1C. THE THEORY

In 1800 a Scottish Roman Catholic priest, A. Geddes, called Astruc's two-document theory a "work of fancy." He held there was a mass of fragments, large and small, (not actual documents) that were pieced together by a redactor about 500 years after Moses' death. From 1802-1805 the German, Johann Vater, developed Geddes' theory. He tried to demonstrate the gradual growth of the Pentateuch from individual fragments. He held that there were at least 38 different fragment sources. Although some of the particular fragments were from Moses' time, the Pentateuch as we now have it was compiled about the time of the Jewish Exile (586 B.C.). This theory was developed more fully in 1831 by the German scholar A.T Hartmann. 71/123-127

2C. ESSENTIAL DIFFERENCE FROM ASTRUC'S DOCUMENTARY THEORY

Those who hold this theory believe there are no continuous documents, but rather a mass of fragments of documents impossible to isolate.

3B. Supplementary Theory

1C. THE THEORY

In 1823, Heinrich Ewald dealt the "death blow" to the fragmentary hypothesis in his book *Die Komposition der Genesis Kritisch Untersucht,* in which he defended the unity of Genesis. By 1830 he had developed a new theory which held that the basis of the first six books of the Bible lay in an Elohistic writing, but that later a parallel document which used the divine name "Jehovah" arose. Still later, an editor took excerpts from this J document and inserted them into the initial E document. Numerous versions of this basic hypothesis subsequently developed, with some like De Wette (1840) and Lengerke (1844) holding not to one supplementation but three. 71/127-129

2C. ESSENTIAL DIFFERENCE FROM FRAGMENTARY HYPOTHESIS

There is not a hodge-podge of sources but rather a unity with one basic document (E) running throughout Genesis with supplements (J) being added later.

4B. Crystallization Theory

1C. THE THEORY

By 1845 Ewald had rejected his own supplementary theory. In its place he offered that instead of one supplementer there were five narrators who wrote various parts of the Pentateuch at different times over a period of 700 years. The fifth narrator, supposedly a Judean of the time of King Uzziah, constantly used the name Jehovah and was the final editor. He completed the Pentateuch about 790-740 B.C. Ewald also held that

Deuteronomy was an independent work added around 500 B.C. Others who held to a simpler form of this theory were August Knobel (1861) and E. Schraeder (1869). 71/129, 130

2C. ESSENTIAL DIFFERENCE FROM SUPPLEMENTARY THEORY

There is not one supplementer but rather five different narrators who wrote different parts of the Pentateuch at various times.

5B. Modified Documentary Theory

1C. THE THEORY

In 1853, Herman Hupfeld sought to show:

a) that J sections in Genesis were not supplements but rather they formed a continuous document.

b) that the basic E document (supplementary theory) was not one continuous document but rather a composite of two separate documents (which he called P and E).

c) that these three documents were put into present form by a redactor.

d) that Deuteronomy was an entirely separate document, added last (designated by D).

Therefore, Hupfeld held that there were actually four distinct documents woven into the fabric of the Pentateuchal narrative: P (early Elohist), E, J. D. 71/130, 131

2C. ESSENTIAL DIFFERENCE FROM CRYSTALLIZATION THEORY

Not five narrators but one redactor combined the documents: J document, early Elohist P document, late Elohist E document.

6B. Development Hypothesis (Revised Documentary Theory)

1C. THE THEORY (today most commonly called "Documentary Hypothesis")

Whereas Hupfeld had established the chronological order of the documents as being P E J D, during the 1860's Karl H. Graf completely reversed the order to J E D P, holding that the basic document (first Elohist or P) was not the earliest portion of the Pentateuch but the last. Graf's theory was strengthened by Abraham Kuenen's book *De Godsdienst Van Israel* (1869-70).

Julius Wellhausen *(Die Komposition des Hexateuchs*, 1876 and *Prolegomena zur Geschichte Israels,* 1878) skillfully and eloquently formulated Graf's and Kuenen's revised documentary theory and gave it the classic expression that brought it to prominence in most European (and later American) scholarly circles. Wellhausen restated the Documentary Hypothesis (later to be called the Graf-Wellhausen Hypothesis) in terms of the evolutionary view of history which was prevalent in philosophical circles at that time.

He held:

1) The earliest part of the Pentateuch came from two originally independent documents, the Jehovist (850 B.C.) and Elohist (750 B.C.).

2) From these the Jehovist compiled a narrative work (650 B.C.).

3) Deuteronomy came in Josiah's time and its author incorporated this into the Jehovist's work.

4) The priestly legislation in the Elohist document was largely the work of Ezra and is referred to as the Priestly Document. A later editor(s) revised and edited the conglomeration of documents by about 200 B.C. to form the extant Pentateuch we have today.

In England, W. Robertson Smith *(The Old Testament in the Jewish Church*, 1881) interpreted and propounded the writings of Wellhausen.

But it was Samuel R. Driver who, in his *Introduction to the Literature of the Old Testament*, (1891), gave Wellhausenism its classic presentation to the English-speaking world. The most notable early advocate of the Wellhausen school in America was Charles A. Briggs, *(The Higher Criticism of the Hexateuch*, 1893). 11/79; 71/136-138

2C. ESSENTIAL DIFFERENCE FROM MODIFIED DOCUMENTARY THEORY

P is not the earliest document but the latest JEDP sequence as worked out on a systematic evolutionary pattern.

7B. **The Development and Modern Revisions of the Documentary Hypothesis Since Wellhausen.**

1C. Rudolph Smend *(Die Erzählung des Hexateuchs auf Ihre Quellen Untersucht*, 1912)—Not one J document but two: J^1 and J^2. 11/91

2C. Otto Eissfeldt *(Hexateuchsynopse*, 1922)—L document within J document, written in 860 B.C. 11/91

3C. R.H. Kennett in *Deuteronomy and the Decalogue* (1920); Gustav Hölscher in *Komposition und Ursprung des Deuteronomiums* (The Composition and Origin of Deuteronomy) (1922). Both held:

Deuteronomy was later than the Josiah period. Thus, the "book of the law" found in the temple in 621 B.C. was not Deuteronomy. 11/100, 101

4C. Martin Kegel in *Die Kultusreformation des Josias* (Josiah's Reformation of the Cultus) (1919), Adam C. Welch in *The Code of Deuteronomy (1924)*, Edward Robertson in *Bulletin of John Rylands Library* (1936, 1941, 1942, 1944), all concluded that Deuteronomy was written much earlier than Josiah's time (621 B.C.). 11/101, 102

5C. Max Löhr, in his *Der Priestercodex in der Genesis* (The Priestly Code in Genesis) (1924), asserted:

1. An independent P source never existed.

2. The Pentateuch was composed by Ezra who drew upon preexilic written materials.

3. These written materials could not be identified with any specific documents (e.g. J, E, etc.). 11/97

6C. Julius Morgenstern *(The Oldest Document of the Hexateuch*, 1927)—K document (somewhat similar to Eissfeldt's L) present in J. 11/91

7C. Paul Volz and Wilhelm Rudolph, in their *Der Elohist als Erzähler: Ein Irrweg der Pentateuchkritik?* (The Elohist as a Narrator: a Mistake in Pentateuchal Criticism?) (1933), concluded:

1. There were no grounds for the existence of a separate E document.

2. Only one writer in the whole book of Genesis, with a few additions made by a later editor. 11/100

8C. Robert Pfeiffer *(Introduction to the Old Testament*, 1941)—S Document found in J and E sections of Genesis 1-11 and 14-38, dated 950 B.C. 11/91

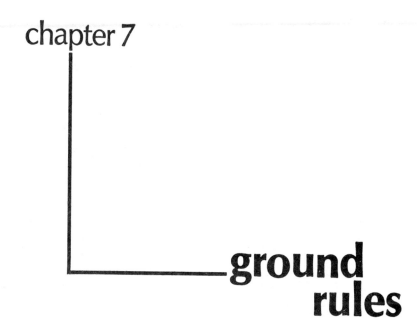

chapter 7

ground rules

The ancient oriental environment of the Old Testament provides many very close literary parallels. And while many ignore it, no one can well deny the truth that principles found to be valid in studying ancient oriental history and literature should be applied to the Old Testament history and literature. Likewise principles that are decidedly false when applied to ancient Near Eastern literature and history should not be applied to Old Testament literature and history. 42/28

Three elementary principles should permeate this investigation:

1A. APPROACH THE HEBREW SCRIPTURES AS OTHER ANCIENT LITERATURE—HARMONISTICALLY

Literary genius and critic Coleridge established this basic rule for literature long ago:

"When we meet an apparent error in a good author, we are to presume ourselves *ignorant of his understanding,* until we are certain that we *understand his ignorance.*" cited by 10/125

Historian John Warwick Montgomery states that in the determination of the essential historicity of an ancient document "historical and literary scholarship continues to follow Aristotle's dictum [*De Arte Poetica,* 14606-14616] that the benefit of the doubt is to be given to the document itself, not arrogated [unjustly assumed] by the critic to himself." 48/29

Kitchen has more recently emphasized the necessity of this principle in Old Testament studies as well as Egyptology:

"It is normal practice to assume the general reliability of statements in our sources, unless there is good, explicit evidence to the contrary.... The basic harmony that ultimately underlies extant records should be sought out, even despite apparent discrepancy. Throughout ancient history, our existing sources are incomplete and elliptical." 42/28-33

Allis labels this approach the "harmonistic method," and elaborates on its application to the Hebrew writings:

"It has two obvious advantages. The one is that it does justice to the intelligence and common sense of the writers of the Bible. To claim that the writers, compilers, editors of the biblical records would introduce or combine conflicting accounts of the same event into a narrative is to challenge their intelligence, or their honesty, or their competence to deal with the data which they record. The second is that it is the biblical method of interpretation. The many times and various ways in which the biblical writers quote or refer to one another implies their confidence in the sources quoted. Their method is a harmonistic method. Most important of all, this method of interpretation is the only one which is consistent with the high claims of the Bible to be the Word of God." 90/35

2A. EXERCISE AN OPEN MIND

Bewer, a firm defendant of the documentary position, has provided an outstanding exposition of this principle:

"A truly scientific criticism never stops. No question is ever closed for it. When new facts appear or a new way of understanding old facts is shown, the critic is ready to reexamine, to modify or to overthrow his theory, if it does not account for all the facts in the most satisfactory way. For he is interested in the truth of his theory, and indifferent to the label, old or new; orthodox or heterodox; conservative, liberal or radical, that others may place upon it." 94/305

Another radical critic, W.R. Harper, heartily agrees:

"It should be remembered that, after all, it is not a question of opinion, but of fact. It matters not what any particular critic may think or say. It is the duty of every man who studies this question to take up one by one the points suggested, and to decide for himself whether or not they are true." 108/73

R.K. Harrison is likewise insistent upon such an attitude:

"As the result of the impact of what T.H. Huxley once called 'one ugly little fact,' the truly scientific investigator will make whatever changes are demanded by the situation, even if he is compelled to begin his research *de novo* to all intents and purposes." 32/508

The direction in which the facts lead may not be palatable, but it must be followed. Kitchen reasons that even if "some of the results reached here approximate to a traditional view or seem to agree with theological orthodoxy, then this is simply because the tradition in question or that orthodoxy are that much closer to the real facts than is commonly realized. While one must indeed never prefer mere orthodoxy to truth, it is also perverse to deny that orthodox views can be true." 42/173

The highly respected Jewish scholar Cyrus Gordon, formerly of Brandeis University and New York University, concludes that "a commitment to any hypothetical source structure like JEDP is out of keeping with what I consider the only tenable position for a critical scholar: *to go wherever the evidence leads him.*" 27/3

3A. SUBMIT TO EXTERNAL, OBJECTIVE CONTROLS

These all-important facts to which our minds must necessarily remain open are discovered by an archaeological examination of the ancient Orient. Cassuto exhorts us "to conduct our investigation without prejudgment or anticipatory fear, but to rely on the objective examination of the texts themselves and the help afforded by our knowledge of the ancient East, in the cultural environment of which the children of Israel lived when the Torah was written. Let us not approach the Scriptural passages with the literary and aesthetic criteria of our time, but let us apply to them the standards obtaining in the ancient East generally and among the people of Israel particularly." 15/12

Kitchen establishes this as an axiom:

"Priority must always be given to tangible, objective data, and to external evidence, over subjective theory or speculative opinions. Facts must control theory, not vice versa." 42/28-33

Certainly Cassuto is to be commended for attributing much respect to the documentarians because of their labor. There should be no attempt to belittle them, but we do have the right to examine rigidly the hypothesis they put forth and their method of obtaining their evidence for this hypothesis. Since there is a tremendous amount of archaeological evidence existing today that these documentarians were lacking when they constructed their theories, we may discover something they missed or solve a problem which left them perplexed. 15/13

"In view of the grave shortcomings," writes Harrison, "of the Graf-Wellhausen approach to the problems of the Pentateuch, and to the Old Testament in general, any new study will need to be based firmly upon an accredited methodology that will utilize the vast quantities of control material now available to scholars throughout the world, and will argue inductively from the known to the unknown instead of making pronouncements from a purely theoretical standpoint that bears only a slight relation to some of the known facts." 32/533

Elsewhere, Harrison affirms that "it is only when criticism is properly established upon an assured basis of ancient Near Eastern life rather than upon occidental philosophical or methodological speculations that Old Testament scholarship can expect to reflect something of the vitality, dignity, and spiritual richness of the law, prophecy, and the sacred writings." 32/82

Kyle very effectively epitomizes this principle:

"Theory must always give way to fact. In the settlement of disputes, facts are final. Even so staunch a defender of the rights and function of criticism as Dr. Driver, (*Authority and Archaeology,* p. 143.) recognized this principle, *at least in theory.* For he says: 'Where the testimony of archaeology is direct, it is of the highest possible value, and, as a rule, determines the question decisively: even where it is indirect, if it is sufficiently circumstantial and precise, it makes a settlement highly probable.'" 117/32

4A. CONCLUSION

These principles are implicit in ancient Near Eastern studies. One point that should be stressed is that a positive approach does not exclude critical study of material but it avoids the distortions that hypercriticism brings. If positive studies had been pursued, the modern critical school would have a different position and many of the supposed problems would be in correct proportion. 42/34

The present condition in Old Testament criticism is summed up by Kitchen:

"Through the impact of the Ancient Orient upon the Old Testament and upon Old Testament studies a new tension is being set up while an older one is being reduced. For the comparative material from the Ancient Near East is tending to agree with the extant structure of Old Testament documents as actually transmitted to us, rather than with the reconstructions of nineteenth-century Old Testament scholarship—or with its twentieth-century prolongation and developments to the present day.

"Some examples may illustrate this point. The valid and close parallels to the social customs of the Patriarchs come from documents of the nineteenth to fifteenth centuries B.C. (agreeing with an early-second-millennium origin for this material in Genesis), and not from Assyro-Babylonian data of the tenth to sixth centuries B.C. (possible period of the supposed 'J,' 'E' sources). Likewise for

Genesis 23, the closest parallel comes from the Hittite Laws which passed into oblivion with the fall of the Hittite Empire about 1200 B.C. The covenant-forms which appear in Exodus, Deuteronomy and Joshua follow the model of those current in the thirteenth century B.C.—the period of Moses and Joshua—and *not* those of the first millennium B.C." 42/25

Instead of starting biblical studies with the presupposition that the Old Testament has error throughout, many contradictions, historical inaccuracies, and gross textual errors, the proper study should include a meticulous examination of the Hebrew text in light of modern archaeology and the knowledge existing of cultures of the ancient Near East in the third millennium B.C. 32/532

Orlinsky remarks that the modern flow of thinking is going in this direction:

"More and more the older view that the Biblical data were suspect and even likely to be false, unless corroborated by extra-biblical facts, is giving way to one which holds that, by and large, the Biblical accounts are more likely to be true than false, unless clear-cut evidence from sources outside the Bible demonstrates the reverse." 213/81

chapter 8

documentary
presuppositions

1A. INTRODUCTION

Underlying much of the radical higher critical methodology are some very important presuppositions. This is not necessarily objectionable, and is to a degree, inevitable. Orr cites the German theologian, Biedermann *(Christliche Dogmatik)*, who put it this way:

It is "not true but sand in the eyes, if one asserts that genuinely scientific and historic criticism can and should proceed without dogmatic presuppositions. In the last instance the consideration of the so-called purely historic grounds always reaches the point where it can and will decide concerning this, whether it can or cannot hold some particular thing in and of itself to be possible.... Some sort of boundary definitions, be they ever so elastically held, of what is historically possible, every student brings with him to historical investigations; and these are for that student dogmatic presuppositions." 50/172

The radical critics are not lacking when it comes to ability and scholarship, etc. The problem area is not their lack of knowledge of the evidence but rather their hermeneutics or approach to biblical criticism based upon their world view.

Gerhardsson has appropriately said, "But the validity of its results depends on the validity of its first principles." 223/6

So often discussion in the area of biblical criticism is carried out on the level of conclusions or answers, rather than at the level of presuppositions or our basis of thinking.

Talking at the level of presuppositions reveals whether people have the right to come to a logical conclusion. If a person has reasonable presuppositions in light of known evidence, his logical conclusions may well be correct.

But if his presuppositions are faulty, his logical conclusions will only magnify original errors as an argument is extended.

In the study of the Bible there have always been various philosophical presuppositions. Evaluating these is beyond the scope of this work. But archaeology has given us much to consider today in the objective realm. Any presuppositions regarding the Bible must consider this as well.

One of the first needs in this study is the harmonizing of presuppositions with the objective data available, before serious discussion on other points begins.

The question as it relates to the documentarians is, "What were their presuppositions and were they admissible?

The most basic presupposition of the majority of radical critics is anti-supernaturalism. This presupposition is treated in chapter one.

2A. PRIORITY OF SOURCE ANALYSIS OVER ARCHAEOLOGY

One of the major weaknesses of the radical higher critical school was that in much of their analysis and isolation of alleged documents conclusions were based almost exclusively upon their own subjective theories regarding the history of Israel and the probable development and compilation process of the supposed sources, with little reference to the more objective and verifiable information that was being provided by archaeology.

The methodological parallels which continue between Pentateuchal and Homeric studies are due to reciprocal influence and also to mutual profit from the progress made in general techniques of research.

"Undoubtedly," writes Cassuto, "it is affected also by the opinions and concepts, the trends and demands, the character and idiosyncrasies of each age. This being so, it may well be that we have not before us an objective discovery of what is actually to be found in the ancient books, but the result of the subjective impression that these writings have on the people of a given environment. If among peoples so different from one another ... scholars find literary phenomena so complex and yet so similar, and precisely one trend in one epoch and another trend in another, and yet a third period, the suspicion naturally arises that the investigators' conceptions are not based on purely objective facts but that they were appreciably motivated by the subjective characteristics of the researchers themselves." 15/12

Harrison points this out:

"Whatever else may be adduced in criticism of Wellhausen and his school, it is quite evident that his theory of Pentateuchal origins would have been vastly different (if, indeed, it had been formulated at all) had Wellhausen chosen to take account of the archaeological material available for study in his day, and had he subordinated his philosophical and theoretical considerations to a sober and rational assessment of the factual evidence as a whole. While he and his followers drew to some extent upon the philological discoveries of the day and manifested a degree of interest in the origins of late Arabic culture in relation to Semitic presursors, they depended almost exclusively upon their own view of the culture and religious history of the Hebrews for purposes of Biblical interpretation." 32/509

Harrison continues:

"Wellhausen took almost no note whatever of the progress in the field of oriental scholarship, and once having arrived at his conclusions, he never troubled to revise his opinion in the light of subsequent research in the general field." 32/509

Even as late as 1931 some critics were still claiming that analyzing alleged sources was the most accurate method for determining the historical background of the Pentateuch. J. Pedersen, a Swedish scholar and one of the pioneers of the oral tradition school made the following statement ("Die Auffassung vom Alten Testament" in *Zeitschrift fur die Alttestamentliche Wissenschaft*, 1931, Vol. 49, p. 179) here cited by C. R. North:

"All the sources of the Pentateuch are both pre-exilic and post-exilic. When we work with them and the other sources, we have no other means than that of intrinsic appraisement *(innere Schatzung)*; in every single case the character of the material must be examined and the supposed background be inferred from that." 77/62

Such dependence upon so subjective a methodology as source analysis has been criticized by many scholars.

Mendenhall says:

"The value of literary analysis for history and its success in convincing the scholarly world today depends upon the isolation of more adequate criteria for judgment than has evidently so far been produced by its adherents. The results, consequently, must be judged to fall in the category of hypotheses, not of historical fact. For the reconstruction of history itself, something more than literary analysis is needed, valuable and necessary as hypotheses are." 68/34

"Literary criticism," cautions Wright, "is an indispensable tool for the introductory study of written documents, but it is not in itself the key to *historical* reconstruction. As Mendenhall has expressed it, 'The isolation of a source in the Pentateuch or elsewhere could give no more historical information other than the fact that it was reduced to written form, at some more or less fixed chronological period, by a person with a particular view of Israel's past. It could not produce criteria for the evaluation of the sources it isolated, beyond a possible demonstration that a later source used an earlier' ("Biblical History in Transition"). Consequently, external criteria are needed, and these are precisely what the archaeologist has provided in abundance." 199/46

A.H. Sayce adds that:

"Time after time the most positive assertions of a skeptical criticism have been disproved by archaeological discovery, events and personages that were confidently pronounced to be mythical have been shown to be historical, and the older writers have turned out to have been better acquainted with what they were describing than the modern critic who has flouted them." 137/23

G.E. Wright warns that "we must attempt to reconstruct the history of Israel, as historians do that of other early peoples, by the use of every tool available, and that by no means permits the neglect of archaeology." 199/51

Similarly Albright calls for verifiable methods:

"The ultimate historicity of a given datum is never conclusively established nor disproved by the literary framework in which it is imbedded: there must always be external evidence." 3/12

The following statement by Mendenhall is well worth noting:

"It is significant that most of the important new results in historical studies have little to do with literary analysis." 68/50

Finally, Gunkel, a radical critic whose own method is quite arbitrary, says that he "at this point cannot conceal his conviction that the reigning school of literary criticism is all too zealous to explain as not genuine the passages which do not exactly fit in with its construction of the history, or which are hard to be understood by the modern investigator, and that a powerful reaction must follow on the period of this criticism." 214/113

Wright, speaking of external data to check hypercriticism (which leads to hyper skepticism), says that:

"When the basic attitudes of higher criticism were being formed in the last century, there was an insufficient amount of extra-biblical data to serve as a check to hyperskepticism. Consequently, passage after passage was challenged as being a literary forgery, and the possibility of 'pious fraud' in the compilation of written documents was exaggerated beyond the limits even of common sense.

When such a critical attitude is established, constructive work becomes increasingly difficult, since emotional as well as rational actors are involved in the general negativism." 200/80

Albright comments with regard to the historicity of the Old Testament:

"Archaeological and inscriptional data have established the historicity of innumerable passages and statements of the Old Testament; the number of such cases is many times greater than those where the reverse has been proved or has been made probable." 4/181

Albright further states:

"Wellhausen still ranks in our eyes as the greatest Biblical scholar of the nineteenth century. But his standpoint is antiquated and his picture of the evolution of Israel is sadly distorted." 4/185

3A. NATURAL VIEW OF ISRAEL'S RELIGION AND HISTORY (EVOLUTIONARY)

Concomitant with Hegel's evolutionary concept applied to history is its application to religion, especially to the Old Testament. Rationalistic critics hypothesized that religious development went through an evolutionary process which commenced with "a belief in spirits in the days of primitive man, and then went through various stages, which included manism or ancestor worship; fetishism or belief in objects indwelt by spirits; totemism or the belief in a tribal god and a tribal animal related to the members of the tribe; mana, or the idea of an indwelling power; magic, the control of the supernatural. Finally man conceived of clear-cut deities (polytheism) and later elevated one deity above the others, a stage called henotheism." 166/332

G.E. Wright explains the view of Wellhausen and many other radical critics:

"The Graf-Wellhausen reconstruction of the history of Israel's religion was, in effect, an assertion that within the pages of the Old Testament we have a perfect example of the evolution of religion from animism in patriarchal times through henotheism to monotheism. The last was first achieved in pure form during the sixth and fifth centuries. The patriarchs worshipped the spirits in trees, stones, springs, mountains, etc. The God of pre-prophetic Israel was a tribal deity, limited in his power to the land of Palestine. Under the influence of Baalism, he even became a fertility god and sufficiently tolerant to allow the early religion of Israel to be distinguished from that of Canaan. It was the prophets who were the true innovators and who produced most, if not all, of that which was truly distinctive in Israel, the grand culmination coming with the universalism of II Isaiah. Thus we have animism, or polydemonism, a limited tribal deity, implicit ethical monotheism, and finally, explicit and universal monotheism." 200/89, 90

Orr says that "if, on impartial consideration, it can be shown that the religion of Israel admits of explanation on purely natural principles, then the historian will be justified in his verdict that it stands, in this respect, on the same footing as other religions. If, on the other hand, fair investigation brings out a different result,—if it demonstrates that this religion has features which place it in a different category from all others, and compel us to postulate for it a different and higher origin,—then that fact must be frankly recognised as part of the scientific result, and the nature and extent of this higher element must be made the subject of inquiry. It will not do to override the facts—if facts they are— by a *priori* dogmatic assumptions on the one side any more than on the other. Thus far we agree with Kuenen, that we must *begin* by treating the religion of Israel exactly as we would treat any other religion." 50/14

Orr continues:

"First, and perhaps deepest, of the reasons for this rejection is the *a priori* one, that such a conception of God as the Old Testament attributes to the patriarchs and to Moses was *impossible* for them at that stage of history. It is too elevated and spiritual for their minds to have entertained. The idea of the unity of God has for its correlates the ideas of the world and of humanity, and neither of these ideas, it is asserted, was possessed by ancient Israel." 50/127, 128

Wellhausen, speaking on the creation of the world, says that "in a youthful people such a theological abstraction is unheard of, and so with the Hebrew we find both the word and the notion only coming into use after the Babylonian exile." 63/305

Wellhausen adds that "the religious notion of *humanity* underlying Gen. ix. 6 is not ancient with the Hebrews any more than with other nations." 63/312

The Dutch scholar, Kuenen, stated this position in the chapter entitled, "Our Standpoint," in his book, *The Religion of Israel.* He lays down the principle that no distinction can be made between the religion of Israel and other religions. Kuenen says, "For us the Israelitish religion is one of those religions; nothing less, but also nothing more." 116/N.P.

Orr's evaluation of this position is well taken:

"To assume beforehand, in an inquiry which turns on this very point, that the religion of Israel presents no features but such as are explicable out of natural causes, — that no higher factors are needed to account for it, — is to prejudge the whole question." 50/13

Here we note what the critics' interpretation of Israel's history actually was. Gleason Archer, a graduate of Harvard University, Suffolk Law School, Princeton Theological Seminary, and currently chairman of the Department of Old Testament at Trinity Evangelical Divinity School, provides us with an introduction to this point.

An evolutionary understanding of history and an anthropocentric view of religion dominated the 19th century. The prevailing thinkers viewed religion as devoid of any divine intervention, explaining it as a natural development produced by man's subjective needs. Their verdict was that the Hebrew religion, as its neighbor religions, certainly must have begun with animism and then evolved through the stages of polydemonism, polytheism, menolatry, and finally monotheism. 11/132, 133

That the then-current evolutionary philosophy of Hegel had a definite effect on Old Testament studies is clearly attested to by Herbert Hahn:

"The conception of historical development was the chief contribution of the liberal critics to the exegesis of the Old Testament. It is true, of course, that this conception did not grow merely from an objective reading of the sources. In a larger sense, it was a reflection of the intellectual temper of the times. The genetic conception of Old Testament history fitted in with the evolutionary principle of interpretation prevailing in contemporary science and philosophy. In the natural sciences, the influence of Darwin had made the theory of evolution the predominant hypothesis affecting research. In the historical sciences and in the areas of religious and philosophical thought, the evolutionary concept had begun to exercise a powerful influence after Hegel had substituted the notion of 'becoming' for the idea of 'being.' He had arrived at the notion by *a priori* reasoning without testing it by scientific application to observable fact, but Hegel was none the less the intellectual progenitor of the modern point of view. In every department of historical investigation the conception of development was being used to explain the history of man's thought, his institutions, and even his religious faiths. It was not strange that the same principle should be applied to the explanation of Old Testament history. In every age exegesis has concormed to the thought forms of the time, and in the latter half of the nineteenth century thought was dominated by the scientific methos and an evolutionary view of history." 31/9, 10

Paul Feinberg writes of Hegel's historical approach:

"Hegel believed that the problem of philosophy was to find the meaning of history. From this fundamental presupposition he attempted to explain the whole of human history. The history of Israel, covering nearly two millennia, was a likely starting place. In his *Philosophy of Religion*, Hegel assigns the Hebrew religion a defined and necessary place in the evolutionary development of Christianity, the absolute religion. Hegel's view of Hebrew religion and his general schematization of history offered an irresistible framework in which Hegelians would attempt to interpret the Old Testament." 22/3

The *Encyclopedia Britannica* summarizes Hegel's philosophy:

"Hegel presupposes that the whole of human history is a process through which mankind has been making spiritual and moral progress; it is what human mind has done in the course of its advance to self-knowledge. . . . The first step was to make the transition from a natural life of savagery to a state of order and law." 75/202, 203

Hegel's influence on 19th century Old Testament scholars can be seen in this statement by Kuenen *(Religion of Israel,* p. 225) cited here by Orr:

"To what we might call the universal, or at least the common rule, that religion begins with fetishism, then develops into polytheism, and then, but not before, ascends to monotheism—that is to say, if this highest stage be reached—to this rule the Israelites are no exception." 50/47

Such a position either ignores or discredits Israel's own account of her history as we have it in the Old Testament.

The Wellhausen school approached the Hebrew religion with the preconceived notion that it was a mere product of evolution, untouched by the supernatural. This approach completely ignored the fact that *only* the Hebrew religion and its branches have produced a genuine monotheism, and that the singular message throughout the entirety of the Hebrew Scriptures is monotheism. Thus, the accounts of the Israelite fathers such as Abraham, Isaac, Jacob, and Moses have been re-examined with intent to show that their early polytheism was camouflaged by the later Deuteronomic and Priestly writers. 11/98

That this whole presupposition—the evolutionary view of Israel's history and religion—was crucial to the entire Documentary Hypothesis is stated in this summary of the foundations of the theory found in *The Interpreter's Dictionary of the Bible:*

"In its standard form the documentary hypothesis rested upon arguments of two kinds: those based upon literary and linguistic evidence, which resulted in the division of the Pentateuchal material into various written sources; and those based upon historical evidence for the evolution of religious institutions and ideas in Israel, which produced an analytical description of the interrelationships among the documents, and a chronological arrangement to account for them." 37/713

W.F. Albright, W.W. Spence Professor of Semitic Languages from 1929-1958 at John Hopkins University and a sometime director of the American Schools of Oriental Research in Jerusalem, was, until his death in 1971, considered by many to be the foremost biblical archaeologist in the world. His work has forced many critics to completely reassess their conclusions regarding the history of Israel. About Wellhausen's application of Hegel's philosophical theories to the history of Israel, Albright said:

"He tried, by means of Hegelian analogy with pre-Islamic and Islamic Arabia, to build a system for the development of Israel's history, religion, and literature which would fit his critical analysis. Wellhausen's structure was so brilliant and afforded such a simple, apparently uniform interpretation that it was adopted almost universally by liberal Protestant scholars, and even largely by Catholic and Jewish scholars. There were, of course, some exceptions, but in nearly all places where men were thoroughly schooled by learning Hebrew and Greek and absorbing the critical method, they also learned Wellhausenian principles. Unfortunately all of this was developed in the infancy of archaeology, and was of very little value in interpreting history." 6/15

Critics have often restricted advanced theological concepts to Israel's later history, concluding that early concepts must have been primitive.

Kitchen has conclusively demonstrated that many such "advanced concepts" were common property of the ancient Orient as early as the third millennium B.C. Their widespread presence in so many written documents makes the familiarity of these ideas to the Hebrews likely at any point of their history. For example, many have attributed the personification of wisdom in Proverbs eight and nine to influence of the third and fourth century B.C. Greeks. But exactly the same type of personification of truth, justice, understanding, etc. is found as early as the third millennium B.C. in Egypt and Mesopotamia, as well as in the second millennium B.C. in Hittite, Hurrian, and Canaanite literature. The concept of a universal God was demonstrated as early as 1940 to be widespread during the third millennium B.C., yet some radical critics are still insistent upon attributing this biblical idea (as seen in Psalm 67) to "relatively late times." 42/126, 127

John Mackay, former president of Princeton Seminary, reflects this language of the evolutionary school when he says, concerning the Old Testament: "The narrative, taken as a whole, aims at conveying the idea that, first under the lowly form of a *tribal deity*, the one universal God, the 'god of the whole earth,' manifested himself in the life of Israel" (*Heritage and Destiny*, p. 17). Cited by 167/131

William F. Albright sums up this view when he states:

"The entire school of Wellhausen has agreed on a refusal to admit Mosaic monotheism, and a conviction that Israelite monotheism was the result of a gradual process, which did not culminate until the eighth century B.C." 209/163

The radical critics are here expressing the obvious results or conclusions of their anti-supernatural presuppositions appled to the religion of Israel in the Old Testament. Since a direct revelation from God is ruled out, their monotheism must have developed through regular evolutionary channels like other religions.

Therefore, the radical critics conclude that a piece of literature can be dated by its stage of religious teaching. One is supposed to deduce that the earlier the literary source, the more primitive the religious concepts.

When monotheism appears in a book purporting to be dated at the time of Moses (ca. 1400 B.C.) it is immediately rejected by many radical critics because the "roots of monotheism" writes Pfeiffer, "were not planted until the time of Amos." 85/580

The following are a few of the assumptions of those who advocate the evolutionary presupposition."

1B. Monotheism

1C. DOCUMENTARY ASSUMPTION

It was not until the time of Amos that monotheism found a beginning in Israel's religion and definitely not during the Mosaic age (ca. 1400 B.C.). As Harrison says, "Wellhausen rejected the idea that the Torah as a whole was the starting point for the history of Israel as a community of the Faith." 32/352

Concerning monotheism, Wellhausen says:

"It is extremely doubtful whether the actual monotheism, which is un-doubtedly presupposed in the universal moral precepts of the Decalogue, could have formed the foundation of a national religion at the downfall of the nation, and thereupon kept its hold upon the people in an artificial manner by means of the idea of a covenant formed by the God of the universe with, in the first instance, Israel alone." 146/20, 21

Monotheism was not considered to be present in the Mosaic age but rather a result of the purifying effects of the Babylonian exile and not characteristic of Israel until after the sixth century B.C.

"The Hebrews," Kuenen agrees, "were undoubtedly polytheists. This is shown, not only by the sequel of their history, but also by positive evidence of later date, it is true, but still admissible, because it is not contradicted by a single account of former times." 116/270

Kuenen continues:

"At first the religion of Israel was polytheism. During the eighth century B.C. the great majority of the people still acknowledged the existence of many gods, and, what is more, they worshipped them. And we can add that during the seventh century, and down to the beginning of the Babylonish exile (586 B.C.), this state of things remained unaltered." 116/223, 224

Kuenen explains his reasons for evolution of religion, "To what one might call the universal, or at least the common rule, that religion begins with fetishism, then develops into polytheism, and then, but not before, ascends to monotheism—that is to say, if this highest stage be reached—to this rule the Semites are no exception." 116/225

Kuenen summarizes his theory:

"The lowest conception of religion will no doubt have had most adherents. This we know as fetishism, which continues to exist even where less childish ideas have already arisen and, for instance, the adoration of the heavenly bodies, of the sun, moon, and planets, has been introduced. Therefore we certainly shall not err if we assume that the worship of trees and especially of stones, which for some reason or other were held to be abodes of the deity, was very common among the Hebrews. The Old Testament still contains many reminiscences of that stone-worship, which was by no means limited to the land of Goshen, but was continued in Canaan also. When Jahveh was afterwards acknowledged by many as the only god, these holy stones were brought into connection with him in various ways. It is here worthy of note, that most of them are said to have been set up by the patriarchs during their wanderings through Canaan, either as altars in honor of Jahveh or as memorials of his presence: this is easily accounted for, if the worship of stones had really been common in former times." 116/270, 271

Pfeiffer concludes:

"Amos, without discrimination of race or nation, planted the roots of a universal religion, from which were to grow the great monotheistic religions of salvation, Judaism, Christianity, and Islam." 132/580

2C.   BASIC ANSWER

William F. Albright says that "it is precisely between 1500 and 1200 B.C., i.e., in the Mosaic age, that we find the closest approach to monotheism in the ancient Gentile world before the Persian period." 7/178

Joseph Free continues that an "examination of the archeological inscriptional material shows that a monotheistic type of worship of the god Aton came into Egypt in the period between 1400 and 1350 B.C. Monotheistic tendencies in Babylonia are evidenced in the period 1500-1200 B.C. in a famous Babylonian text which identifies all important Babylonian deities with some aspect of the great god Marduk; Zababa is Marduk of battle, Sin is Marduk as illuminer of night, Adad is Marduk of rain. There is one great god, with various functions. Monotheistic tendencies also appear in Syria and Canaan in this same period of the fourteenth century B.C. Certain names were given to gods worshiped in many different places, all of whom were considered as variant forms of one great deity: there was a Teshup of Nirik, a Teshup of Khalab (Aleppo), a Teshup of Shamukha; it seems that finally Teshup was thought of as the great and sole god, who manifested himself in many places." 166/334, 335

Albright writes that he had "gathered archaeological data from many quarters for the purpose of filling in the historical background of religious syncretism and conflict against which the prophets fulfilled their mission. Thanks to archaeology we can see, more clearly that the prophets of Israel were neither pagan ecstatics or religious innovators." 7/178

Albright not only concludes that Amos "was no religious innovator, much less the earliest monotheistic teacher of Israel," but that "orthodox Yahwism remained the same from Moses to Ezra." 9/313

E.G. Wright observes that "we can assert with confidence that by the time of the patriarchs the religion of all parts of the Near East was a long distance removed from the animistic stage, if the latter in any approved textbook form ever existed at all." 200/0)

"It is an incontestable fact of history," concludes Archer, "that no other nation (apart from those influenced by the Hebrew faith) ever did develop a true monotheistic religion which commanded the general allegiance of its people. Isolated figures may be pointed out like *Akhnaton* and Xenophanes (both of whom also spoke of 'gods' in the plural number), but it remains *incontrovertible* that neither the Egyptians nor the Babylonians nor the Greeks ever embraces a monotheistic faith on a national basis." 11/134

James Orr observes that the monotheism of the Israelites is one of the first characteristics to be noted when studying the Old Testament. This is quite a feat in itself, in view of the fact that polytheism and idolatry were the modern trend. The religions of the Babylonians, the Assyrians, the Egyptians, and even Israel's Palestinian neighbors were incorrigibly corrupt and polytheistic. Only in Judah was God known. 50/40, 41

Thus Wellhausen's theory of unilinear evolutionary development on a simple, one-dimensional time line from the "simple" to the "complex" has come to be regarded by most archaeologists as erroneous.

Kitchen concludes:

"Unilinear evolution is a fallacy. It is valid only within a small field of reference for a limited segment of time and not for whole cultures over long periods of time. One thinks of Egypt's thrice repeated rise and fall in and after the Old, Middle and New Kingdoms respectively, or of the successive flowerings of Sumerian civilization, Old Babylonian culture and the Assyro-Babylonian kingdoms in Mesopotamia. This oscillation and mutation applies to all aspects of civilization: artistic standards, literary output and abilities, political institutions, the state of society, economics, and not least religious belief and practice. Intertwined with the multicoloured fabric of change are lines of continuity in usage that show remarkable consistency from early epochs." 42/113, 114

Ronald Youngblood adds that "it cannot be shown that there is a universal tendency on the part of polytheistic religions to gradually reduce the number of deities until finally arriving at one deity. In some instances, in fact, such a religion may even add *more* deities as its adherents become aware of more and more natural phenomena to deify! At any rate, the Old Testament teaches that monotheism, far from having evolved through the centuries of Israel's history, is one of the inspired insights revealed to the covenant people by the one true God Himself." 225/9

Here would be that appropriate place to ask, "Was Moses a monotheist?"

"If by 'monotheist,'" writes Albright, "is meant a thinker with views specifically like those of Philo Judaeus or Rabbi Aquiba, of St. Paul or St. Augustine, of Mohammed or Maimonides, of St. Thomas or Calvin, of Mordecai Kaplan of H.N. Wieman, Moses was not one. If, on the other hand, the term 'monotheist' means one who teaches the existence of only one God, the creator of everything, the source of justice, who is equally powerful in Egypt, in the desert, and in Palestine, who has no sexuality and no mythology, who is human in form but cannot be seen by human eye and cannot be represented in any form—then the founder of Yahwism was certainly a monotheist." 9/271, 272

The degree to which Moses can be considered as a true monotheist has been a topic of much discussion by scholars. However, R.K. Harrison believes that there is little "justification for not attributing monotheism to Moses, although care should be taken not to understand that concept in a speculative Hellenic sense. A more accurate designation of the situation might well be framed in terms of an empirical ethical monotheism." 32/403

Waltke adds:

"Many scholars argue for a devolution in religion from monotheism to polytheism. Study of Ras Shama shows that

"The existence of a particular god named El is not only important for the origins of the religion of Israel, but it raises the problem of a primitive Semitic monotheism formerly defended by Renon. The thesis of an original monotheism has been upheld more recently and with more convincing arguments by scholars of such varied outlook as Andrew Lang, N. Soederblom, R. Pettazzoni, Father W. Schmidt and Geo Widengren, Upsala and finally, and on the particular grounds of the religion of Israel, I. Enguell believes that El, the supreme god of the Caupanites, was a 'high god' who was worshipped in the whole of the west Semitic world under the names of El Shadday, El Elyon, Shaelem, and Hadad." (E. Jacobs, *Theology of the Old Testament*, 1958, pp. 44f.) 5/2

2B. Environmental Conditioning

1C. DOCUMENTARY ASSUMPTION

The natural evolutionary process through conditioning by environmental and geographical conditions produced the Israelite religion. Basically, the religious tenets were borrowed by Israel from the pagan religions surrounding Israel.

2C. BASIC ANSWERS

"The faith of Israel," writes G.E. Wright, "even in its earliest and basic forms is so utterly different from that of the contemporary polytheisms that one simply cannot explain it fully by evolutionary or environmental categories. Such a contention runs somewhat counter to the habits of thought and the methodological assumptions of many leading scholars of the last two generations. Yet it is difficult to see how any other conclusion is justified by the facts as we now know them from the vast accumulation of knowledge about the Biblical world." 148/7

W.F. Albright points out that it is impossible that the Israelite religion could be accounted for by saying it was borrowed from the adjacent religions:

"Every new publication of North-Canaanite inscriptions or literary documents will thus add to our knowledge of the literary background of the Old Testament. On the other hand, every fresh publication of Canaanite mythological texts makes the gulf between the religions of Canaan and of Israel increasingly clear. A common geographical environment, a common material culture, and a common language were not enough to quench the glowing spark of Israelite faith in the God of Moses or to assimilate the cult of Yahweh to that of Baal." 154/24

The Israelites were able to resist the pressure of syncretism with the pagan religions that surrounded them.

Alexander Heidel describes the differences between the contemporary Babylonian polytheism and Israelite monotheism:

"The Babylonian creation stories are permeated with a crude polytheism. They speak not only of successive generations of gods and goddesses proceeding from Apsû and Tiâmat, with all of them in need of physical nourishment, since all consist of matter as well as of spirit, but they speak also of different creators.

"Against all of this, the opening chapters of Genesis as well as the Old Testament in general refer to only one Creator and Maintainer of all things, one God who created and transcends all cosmic matter. In the entire Old Testament, there is not a trace of a theogony [battle of the gods], such as we find, for example in Enûma elish and in Hesiod. To this faith the Babylonians never attained." 176/96, 97

The danger of environmental corruption is indicated by Merrill Unger:

"The patriarchs, sojourning in the midst of polytheism with its divination and other forms of occultism, were constantly in danger of corruption. The teraphim of Rachel (Gen. 31:19), 'the strange gods' which Jacob ordered put away from his household (Gen. 35:2) and hid under an oak in Shechem (v. 4), are indicative of contamination. However, the patriarchs were remarkably free from the divinatory methods of surrounding pagan peoples." 193/127

One of the many major differences is the duality of pagan religion in terms of sex.

"For some reason," writes G.E. Wright, "perhaps in part because of the historical nature of God's revelation, the Israelite did not combine the complementary forces of nature by means of a duality expressed in terms of sex. While the category of personality is, of course, applied to Yahweh and while the pronouns used are in their masculine gender, there is no complementary feminine. The duality of male and female is to be found only in the created world; it is not a part of the Godhead, which is essentially sexless. Biblical Hebrew has no word for goddess. Equally phenomenal is the preservation of God's mystery and holiness by the prohibition of images, either of God himself or of any other spiritual being in heaven or on earth, a prohibition preserved in the oldest law which the Old Testament contains." 148/23

Albright concludes:

"This is not the place to describe the total breakdown of Wellhausenism under the impact of our new knowledge of antiquity; suffice it to say that no arguments have been brought against early Israelite monotheism that would not apply equally well (with appropriate changes in specific evidence) to postexilic Judaism. Nothing can alter the now certain fact that the gulf between the religions of Israel and of Canaan was as great as the resemblance between their material cultures and their poetic literatures." 150/545

To the above Wright adds that "it is increasingly realized today that the attempt to make of the Old Testament a source book for the evolution of religion from very primitive to highly advanced concepts has been made possible only by means of a radical misinterpretation of the literature." 148/12

3B. The Second Commandment

1C. DOCUMENTARY ASSUMPTION

The second commandment, although attributed to Moses, could not have been a part of the early Israelite religions because of its probhibition of images. The radical critics reject Mosaic authorship and early dating of the decalogue because it is believed that they in fact did worship images. Julius Wellhausen states that "the prohibition of images was during the older period quite unknown." 63/439 Wellhausen says this is one of the main reasons for rejecting the authenticity of Mosaic authorship.

R.W. Smith writes:

"Even the principle of the second commandment, that Jehovah is not to be worshipped by images. . . cannot, in the light of history, be regarded as having so fundamental a place in the religion of early Israel." 208/63

2C. BASIC ANSWER

It is rather obvious that, if the prohibition of image worship was a late addition to the Pentateuch and the Israelites worshipped images, then one should find images of Jehovah.

However this has not been the case. G.E. Wright records that the excavation of Megiddo by the University of Chicago failed to turn up images of Jehovah. He says "tremendous amounts of debris was moved from the first five town levels (all Israelite), and not a single example has been found as far as this writer is aware." 201/413

Wright continues: "There is no image of deity ever mentioned in Patriarchal worship, nor in connection with the instution of the Tabernacle which served as the central shrine of the tribal amphictyony, nor in the Temple of Solomon. On the other hand, we know from archaeology that Israelites possessed small plaques or figures of the Canaanite fertility and mother goddesses in great number. This indicates the widespread syncretism which went on in early Israel, precisely as the literature frankly testifies. When the Aramaeans and Philistines settled in Canaanite territory, they adopted Canaanite customs. When the Amorites settled in Mesopotamia, they took over Sumerian religion, adjusting their own religious pantheon to it. Similarly, the people of Israel were tempted to adopt the customs of their environment. Yet in the vast mass of debris dug out of Israelite towns there is yet to be found an image of a male deity." 148/24

Many of the misunderstandings are the result of not discerning between the "official doctrines" of Israel's religion and the "actual practices" of some of the common people.

Wright concludes that "the evidence is vividly clear that the prohibition against images of Yahweh was so deeply fixed in early Israel, that even the unenlightened and the tolerant understood that Yahweh was simply not to be honored in this way." 148/24, 25

To the above he adds:

"The basic character and antiquity of the second commandment thus receives as strong a support as archeology will probably ever be able to produce for it." 200/93

4B. Moral Level

1C. DOCUMENTARY ASSUMPTION

The laws, moral tone, and social level ascribed to Moses are too lofty to be found so early in Israel's development.

2C. BASIC ANSWER

Various archaeological discoveries have discouraged the continuation of this assumption. Millar Burrows writes:

"The standards represented by the ancient law codes of the Babylonians, Assyrians, and Hittites, as well as the high ideals found in the Egyptian Book of the Dead and the early Wisdom Literature of the Egyptians, have effectively refuted this assumption." 156/46

Speaking of the Israelites, of the conquest of Canaan, and the pagan worship encountered by Israel, Albright says that their gross mythology and worship "were replaced by Israel, with its nomadic [although they were not nomads] simplicity and purity of life, its lofty monotheism, and its severe code of ethics." 9/214

5B. The Priestly Code

1C. DOCUMENTARY ASSUMPTION

"The Priestly Code," writes Pfeiffer, "like all legislation, notwithstanding its deliberate timelessness and fictitious Mosaic background, bears the earmarks of its age, the first half of the Persian period (538-331 B.C.)." 132/257

Joseph P. Free in "Archaeology and Higher Criticism" explains further the situation when he explains that "another body of supposedly very late material in the Pentateuch is the record of the Levitical sacrificial laws, assigned to the P document.... If the bulk of much of the Pentateuch, assigned to the P document, is to be dated 500 B.C., the Mosaicity of the Pentateuch is definitely set aside.

"Archaeological evidence, on the contrary, shows that there is no valid reason for dating the Levitical sacrificial laws late, for they appear in the Ugaritic material from the fourteenth century B.C." 164/33

2C. BASIC ANSWER

1D. Tenure in Egypt

Apparently the skeptics of the early dating believe that the Israelites were simply too primitive in Moses' day to write such a law. Archer disagrees:

"It can hardly be objected that the Israelites were too primitive to be governed by laws such as these back in Moses' time, since according to their own explicit record they had been living in the midst of one of the most advanced civilizations of ancient times for over four hundred years, and would naturally have entertained more advanced concepts of jurisprudence than tribes indigenous to the desert." 11/162

2D. Code of Hammurabi

Also, it seems the other half of the skepticism comes from the belief that no primitive civilization could have written such a work as the code we have today. J.P. Free in *Archaeology and Bible History* takes issue with this:

"Archaeological discoveries, however, have shown that the advanced laws of Deuteronomy and the rest of the Pentateuch do not have to be dated late in accordance with the supposition of the critical school. The Code of Hammurabi (written within the period 2000-1700 B.C.) was found by a French archaeological expedition under the direction of M. Jacques de Morgan in 1901-1902 at the site of ancient Susa, to the east of the region of Mesopotamia. The code was written on a piece of black diorite, nearly eight feet high, and contained two hundred eighty-two sections or paragraphs.

"The Code of Hammurabi was written several hundred years before the time of Moses (c. 1500-1400 B.C.), and yet it contains some laws which are similar to those recorded by Moses. In the light of this, the liberal has no right to say that the laws of Moses are too advanced for his time, and could not have been written by him." 162/121

Meredith G. Kline in the "Is the History of the Old Testament Accurate?" chapter of *Can I Trust the Bible]* (edited by Howard Vos) adds:

"Archaeology speaks decisively against Wellhausen's notion that Pentateuchal legislation is too complex and its cultic provisions too elaborate for so early a time as that of Moses, to whom the authorship of the Pentateuch is attributed in both Old and New Testaments. As evidence of the antiquity of codified law, there are Assyrian and Hittite law codes from approximately the time of Moses, the Code of Hammurabi some three centuries before Moses, and the more recently discovered fragments of other Babylonian and Sumerian predecessors of Hammurabi's Code, dating back to Abraham's day." 62/146

A.H. Sayce *(Monument Fact and Higher Critical Fancies)* answers Pfeiffer soundly:

"In other words, the Mosaic code must belong to the age to which tradition assigns it, and presupposes the historical conditions which the Biblical narrative describes. Not only has the code of Khammu-rabi [i.e. Hammurabi] proved that the legislation of Moses was possible, it has also shown that the social and political circumstances under which it claims to have arisen are the only ones under which it could have been compiled." 137/82

If the equal caliber of the codes is not enough to convince one of the possibility of the early date, then Archer gives even added evidence in that the "Babylonian Code of Hammurabi... shows numerous similarities to the provisions in Exodus, Leviticus and Numbers relative to the punishment of crimes and the imposition of damages for torts and breaches of contract." 11/161

Not only is the quality comparable, but even some of the laws are similar. Free sums it up:

"The Code of Hammurabi was found in 1901-2 by a French expedition at the site of ancient Susa, east of Mesopotamia. On the surface of this monument some 282 laws were recorded, comprising the legislation of the Babylonian king Hammurabi, who lived within the period of 2000-1700 B.C.... Some critics held that the laws of Moses (1500-1400 B.C.) were too advanced for his day and assigned them to a much later period (800-400 B.C.). The discovery of Hammurabi's code, which precedes Moses by several centuries, effectively answered this objection." 163/20

3C. COUNTER ASSUMPTION

Unfortunately this has created an obvious accusation by the documentarians.

"Then it was suggested," Free continues, "that Moses borrowed his laws from the Code of Hammurabi. A comparison of the two over a period of years, however, has convinced most critics that there are essential differences and that the laws of the Old Testament are in no essential way dependent upon the Babylonian." 163/20

Sayce explains the issue at hand:

"Certain German Assyriologists have been at great pains to discover similarities between the codes of Khammu-rabi and Moses, and to infer from this a connection between them. And there are cases in which the similarity is striking." 137/71

Merrill Unger says:

"Again, higher critical views which have placed the origin of many of the laws ascribed to Moses in the ninth, eighth, or seventh century B.C., or even later, have had to be drastically revised or entirely rejected. On the other hand, the discovery of the early extra-Biblical legal material has led many to adopt an equally faulty view that Hebrew legislation is merely a selection and adaptation of Babylonian law." 193/154, 155

4C. FURTHER ANSWERS

1D. Contrast of the Codes

Archer explains that "it should be understood, of course, that the differences between the Torah and the Code of Hammurabi are far more striking than the resemblances. But the differences proceed largely from the entirely different ideology to which each of the two cultures adhered." 11/162

And again:

"The Babylonian code is alleged to have been received by Hammurabi from the sun god, Shamash. Moses received his laws directly from God. Hammurabi, despite his purported reception from Shamash, takes credit for them in both the prologue and epilogue of the Code. He, not Shamash, established order and equity throughout the land. Moses, in contrast, is only an instrument. The legislation is, 'Thus saith Yahweh.'" 193/156

Further, "in the Hebrew laws a greater value is set upon human life, a stricter regard for the honor of womanhood is discernible, and a more humane treatment of slaves is enjoined. Moreover, the Babylonian Code has nothing in it corresponding to that twofold golden thread running through the Mosaic legislation—love to God and love to one's neighbor (Matt. 22:37-40)." 193/157

He goes on to say that "Hammurabi's laws are adapted to the irrigation-culture and the highly commercialized urban society of Mesopotamia. The Mosaic injunctions, on the other hand, suit a simple agricultural, pastoral people of a dry land like Palestine, much less advanced in social and commercial development, but keenly conscious in all phases of their living of their divine calling." 193/156

And finally, "the Hebrew Code contains many purely religious injunctions and ritual regulations. The Code of Hammurabi is civil. However, the priestly laws of Leviticus contain many points of contact with corresponding priestly ritual and practice in Western Asia, whether in Canaan and Phoenicia or in Mesopotamia." 193/156

Free speaks of "no real connection between the Mosaic laws and the Code of Hammurabi. Such an acknowledgment was made by G.A. Barton, liberal professor at the University of Pennsylvania, who said, 'A comparison of the Code of Hammurabi as a whole with the Pentateuchal laws as a whole, while it reveals certain similarities, convinces the student that the laws of the Old Testament are in no essential way dependent upon the Babylonian laws....' The Code contains many laws peculiar to itself, including those relating to soldiers, tax-collectors, and wine-merchants." 162/121

Sayce, an Assyriologist, makes the conclusion that "the difference between the two codes in this last particular is characteristic of a difference which runs through the whole of them, and makes the contrast between them far greater and more striking than any agreement that can be pointed out." 137/72

2D. Ugarit (Ras Shamra) Discoveries

It seems that this section thus far indicates the only evidence available is the Hammurabi Code. This is not true, and we will now see how the Priestly Code compares with another archaeological find. To begin with, Joseph P. Free says that "the fact that the Ras Shamra Tablets [Ras Shamra is a Canaanite city located on the Syro-Palestinian coast just opposite the tip of Cyprus.], dating back to about 1400 B.C. record several laws similar to those of Leviticus, shows that the liberal has no right to deny the possibility of such a code of sacrificial laws as early as the time of Moses." 162/112

Millar Burrows in *What Mean These Stones?* goes further to explain that "texts from Ras Shamrah name many kinds of sacrificial animals, including some that were used also in the Hebrew religion and some which were excluded by the laws of the Old Testament. Several of the terms employed in the Hebrew Old Testament for the various types of offering also have appeared in the Ras Shamrah tablets, for example the burnt offering, the whole burnt offering, the guilt offering, and the peace offering." 156/234

Would not mutual sacrifices mean Moses used Ras Shamra as a source? Free concludes by answering thus:

"We believe that there are at least two possible answers. In the first place, they may have been diffused from Israel at the time they were revealed to Moses (about 1450 B.C.) and have come into the practices of the Canaanites and people of Syria, being reflected in the Ras Shamra tablets (1400-1350 B.C.). The second possibility is that the laws and statutes revealed by the Lord at a much earlier time (and later given to Moses) were handed down among various peoples and appear in a modified and often corrupted form among such people as those of Ras Shamra." 162/112

3D. Lipit-Ishtar Law Code

Briefly, the Lipit-Ishtar Code is another discovery, as Francis Steele in "Lipit-Ishtar Law Code" *(American Journal of Archeology)* explains:

"The importance of the Lipit-Ishtar law code can scarcely be overemphasized. Its discovery extends the history of codified law by nearly two centuries and thereby paves the way for a comparative study of law almost four thousand years old." 191/164

Waltke quoting S.N. Kramer concerning the Lipit-Ishtar Law Code writes:

"All seven pieces date from the Early Post-Sumerian period, that is, they were actually inscribed sometime in the first half of the *second* millennium B.C. As for the first compilation of the code, it must have taken place sometime during the eleven-year reign of Lipit-Ishtar, who ruled probably during the first half of the nineteenth century B.C., it thus antedates the Hammurabi Code by more than a century and a half." (S.N. Kramer, *ANET*, 1953, p. 159) 5/1

4D. The Laws of Eshnunna

The same can be said of the Eshnunna law code of the old Babylon period (1830-1550 B.C.). Hammurabi apparently incorporated some of this code into his own system. Two tablets found in 1945 and 1947 near Baghdad contain these ancient laws.

Reunen Yaron points out that archaeology confirms that these tablets could not be dated after the reign of King Dadusha. The last year of Dadusha's reign is set in the seventh year of Hammurabi. However, archaeology cannot set the date of its composition. The usual date given to the Eshnunna Law Codes is about 200 years before Hammurabi. 224/1, 2

The kingdom of Eshnunna "fell... victim to the expansionist policies pursued with success by Hammurabi of Babylon, during the fourth decade of his reign." 224/1

The discovery of the above two tablets adds additional evidence that the Hammurabi Codes were not the only source of an early codified law.

The Laws of Eshnunna: "The code, written during the twentieth century B.C. in the Akkadian language, contains sixty paragraphs of law dealing with such subjects as the price of commodities, the hire of wagons and boats, the wages of laborers, marriage, divorce and adultery, assault and battery, and the placing of responsibility for the ox that gores a man and the mad dog that bites a man." *(Biblical World,* 1966, p. 232) 5/1

6B. Additional Comments

Albright says that Wellhausen's "standpoint is antiquated and its picture of the early evolution of Israel is sadly distorted." 2/185

Wright speaking of Albright says that he "has amassed archeological fact upon fact in his review of the Bible's setting in the world in order to show that Wellhausen's developmental scheme, ultimately drawn from the idealistic philosophy of Hegel, no longer fits the facts as they are now known." 199/45

Ira Maurice Price in *The Monuments and the Old Testament* writes that "the critical views of the origin of many of the laws ascribed to Moses locating them in the ninth, eighth, and seventh centuries, and even later B.C., must not only be modified, but in some cases, entirely rejected." 188/219

M.J. Lagrange ("L' Authenticité Mosaique de la Genése et la Théorie des Documents"), a man who was involved in biblical and archaeological endeavors in Jerusalem for nearly 40 years, concludes:

"It is a fact that the historical work of Wellhausen is more than compromised. The evolution which starts from fetishism to rise to monolatry and then to monotheism, or from a very rudimentary rustic worship to complicated social and sacerdotal institutions, cannot be maintained in face of the evidence of the facts revealed by the recent discoveries." Cited by 190/312, 313

Where did this archaeological evidence come from?

George Mendenhall, of the University of Michigan, speaking of the actual excavations that have led archaeologists to the preceding conclusion, says:

"The starting point was the introduction of new evidence from Ras Shamra and Mari, which excluded from the realm of probability certain theories about the Patriarchal narratives previously held, and which, together with many details from other sources, called for a new theory to account for the new evidence. . . . if those who made up the twelve tribes of Israel included some at least who had first been in contact with Mesopotamian civilization, then for a period of centuries lived in a land surrounded by a cosmopolitan complex of many cultures in process of amalgamation, then it follows that they can hardly have been childlike, cultureless, traditionless barbarians. It follows that the earliest stages of the religion of Israel need not have been as primitive as earlier scholars had thought—not on the grounds of evidence, but on the basis of an *a priori* theory of how religion *must* evolve." 68/40

So Albright had taught:

"History is not a meaningless record of chance happenings, or even a mere chain of related occurrences; it is a complex web of interacting patterns, each of which has its own structure, however difficult it may be to dissect the structure and to identify its characteristic elements. Moreover, the web is itself constantly changing, and by comparing successive states which it exhibits to the trained eye of the historian we can detect the direction in which it is changing—in other words, its evolution. We also emphasized the fact that the evolution of historical patterns is highly complex and variable; it may move in any direction and it cannot be detected by *a priori* hypotheses nor can it be explained by any deterministic theory. We also pointed out that this organismic nature of history makes unilinear 'historicism' unsuitable as a clue to the complexities of the history of religion. For this reason Wellhausen's Hegelian method was utterly unsuited to become the master-key with which scholars might enter the sanctuary of Israelite religion and acquire a satisfying understanding of it." 7/3

Albright's conclusion seems final:

"In the light of the ancient orient nothing seems more artificial and contrary to analogy than the postulated evolution of Hebrew religion within the limits of time and circumstance allowed by the school of Wellhausen." 2/182

7B. Implications

These conclusions seriously undermine the entire Documentary Hypothesis both in its classical form and in its present state of flux, since current Pentateuchal analysis is, for the most part, still solidly based on the classical Documentary Theory.

Kitchen's conclusion is justified:

"As extended unilinear development is, therefore, an invalid assumption, there is no reason whatever to date supposed literary fragments or sources by the imaginary level of their concepts on a scale from 'primitive' to 'advanced.'" 42/114

4A. NO WRITING IN ISRAEL AT MOSES' TIME (ca. 1500-1400 B.C.)

1B. Documentary Assumption

Writing was virtually unknown in Israel during Moses' time and consequently Moses could not have written the Pentateuch.

Wellhausen himself said:

"Ancient Israel was certainly not without God-given bases for the ordering of human life; only they were not fixed in writing." 63/393

Schultz, in 1893, states in his book *Old Testament Theology:*

"Of the legendary character of the pre-Mosaic narrators, the time of which they treat is a sufficient proof. It was a time prior to all knowledge of writing, a time separated by an interval of more than four hundred years, of which there is absolutely no history, from the nearest period of which Israel had some dim historical recollection, a time when in civilised countries writing was only beginning to be used for the most important matters of State. Now wandering herdsmen have invariably an instinctive dislike to writing. In fact, at the present day, it is considered a disgrace among many Bedouin tribes in the peninsula of Sinai to be able to write. It is therefore impossible that such men could hand down their family histories, in themselves quite unimportant, in any other way than orally, to wit, in legends. And even when writing had come into use, in the time, that is, between Moses and David, it would be but sparingly used, and much that happened to the people must still have been handed down simply as legend." 138/25, 26

There is every reason to believe that in the time of Moses language was highly usable as a vehicle of literary expression, and most likely had been so for centuries. Concerning this point, Driver believes "it is not denied that the patriarchs possessed the art of writing" but the use of documents from the patriarchal age is "a mere hypothesis, for the truth of which no positive grounds can be alleged." 17/xlii

And speaking of hypothesis, Orr reminds us that the critical view itself is surely "built on hypothesis. The value of a hypothesis is the degree in which it explains facts, and, in the silence of the Book of Genesis, we can only reason from general probabilities. But the probabilities, derived from the state of culture at the time, from the fixed and circumstantial character of the tradition, and from the archaeological notices embedded in the book, are, we think, strong, that the Hebrews, even in the patriarchal age, were to some extent acquainted with books and writing. If so, we may believe that at an early period, in Egypt under Joseph, if not before, attempts would be made to set down things in writing." 50/375

When it was believed that Israel's beginnings dated to the early dawn of civilization, the position was more tenable that the Hebrews were unacquainted with writing. It was likewise respectable to doubt their capacity to conceive such lofty ideas as expressed in Moses' laws or David's psalms.

2B. Basic Answer

1C. EVALUATION AND CULTURAL CLIMATE

The British Assyriologist A.H. Sayce evaluates this late date of writing theory. He claims that "this supposed late use of writing for literary purposes was merely an assumption, with nothing more solid to rest upon than the critic's own theories and presuppositions. And as soon as it could be tested by solid fact it crumbled into dust. First Egyptology, then Assyriology, showed that the art of writing in the ancient East, so far from being of modern growth, was of vast antiquity, and that the two great powers which divided the civilized world between them were each emphatically a nation of scribes and readers. Centuries before Abraham was born Egypt and Babylonia were alike full of schools and libraries, of teachers and pupils, of poets and prose-writers, and of the literary works which they had composed." 137/28, 29 He cites Crete as another example.

A.J. Evans found evidence of pre-Mosaic writing on Crete. Not only were Egypt and Babylon writing in hieroglyphic and cuneiform respectively, but Crete had three, perhaps four systems, i.e. pictographs, linear symbols, etc. 137/41

Albright, speaking of the various writing systems that existed in the ancient Orient even during pre-Mosaic patriarchal times, says:

"In this connection it may be said that writing was well known in Palestine and Syria throughout the Patriarchal Age (Middle Bronze, 2100-1500 B.C.). No fewer than five scripts are known to have been in use: Egyptian hieroglyphs, used for personal and place names by the Canaanites; Accadian cueniform; the hieroglyphiform syllabary of Phoenicia, used from the 23rd century or earlier (as known since 1935); the linear alphabet of Sinai, three inscriptions in which are now known from Palestine (this script seems to be the direct progenitor of our own); the cuneiform alphabet of Ugarit (used also a little later in Palestine), which was discovered in 1929. This means that Hebrew historical traditions need not have been handed down through oral transmission alone." 2/186

Cyrus Gordon, formerly professor of Near Eastern Studies and chairman of the Department of Mediterranean Studies at Brandeis University and an authority on the tablets discovered at Ugarit, concludes similarly:

"The excavations at Ugarit have revealed a high material and literary culture in Canaan prior to the emergence of the Hebrews. Prose and poetry were already fully developed. The educational system was so advanced that dictionaries in four languages were compiled for the use of scribes, and the individual words were listed in their Ugaritic, Babylonian, Sumerian, and Hurrian equivalents. The beginnings of Israel are rooted in a highly cultural Canaan where the contributions of several talented peoples (including the Mesopotamians, Egyptians, and branches of the Indo-Europeans) had converged and blended. The notion that early Israelite religion and society were primitive is completely false. Canaan in the days of the Patriarchs was the hub of a great international culture. The Bible, hailing from such a time and place, cannot be devoid of sources. But let us study them by taking the Bible on its own terms and against its own authentic background." 27/133, 134

The archaeological evidence serves not only to refute the older critics' antequated theory but also serves as positive evidence to support the probability that Moses kept written records.

Sayce makes a shuddering conclusion:

"The Babylonia of the age of Abraham was a more highly educated country than the England of George III." 137/35

Why can archaeologists make such statements? Several archaeological finds bring them to the above conclusion. We will study four.

2C. UGARIT (RAS SHAMRA)

William F. Albright explained the Ugarit discoveries. The cuneiform writing of Ugarit is a system completely native to Syria-Palestine and was recovered in 1929 by C.F.A. Schaeffer on the Syrian north coast. The most prominent deposits of tablets with this writing are at Ugarit and Ras Shamra. Artifacts with this script are dated as early as 1400 B.C., though the alphabet itself is probably older. 5/187; 11/157

Albright says:

"It is difficult to exaggerate the importance of the Canaanite alphabetic tablets from Ugarit, north of Canaan proper. Thanks to them, we have a vast body of texts from the age of Moses (fourteenth and thirteenth centuries B.C.). They are partly in local prose dialect of Ugarit at that time, but mostly in a generalized poetic dialect that corresponds closely to such early Hebrew poetic language as the Song of Miriam (thirteenth century B.C.) and the Son of Deborah (twelfth century), as well as to many of the early Psalms. They have enormously widened our knowledge of biblical Hebrew vocabulary and grammar." 149/3, 4

3C.   EGYPTIAN LETTERS

Sayce noted that Egypt was a very literate nation. During the reign of Ikhnaton (or Amenhotep IV), about 1375-1358 B.C., who tried to change the entire religious system of Egypt, great amounts of correspondence, called the Amarna tablets, were exchanged between Egypt, Syria, Palestine and Babylon. Many of these have been discovered at Amarna since 1887. Not only do these show writing to have been in use, but further, they are not in hieroglyphics but Babylonian cuneiform. This indicates a close contact between the two, so much so that a standard diplomatic language of the day was used. The art of writing was well entrenched by this time. 137/38, 39

4C.   MT. SINAI INSCRIPTIONS

S.H. Horn explains yet another find:

"In 1917 Alan Gardiner, noted British Egyptologist, made the first decipherment of the Proto-Semitic inscriptions found at Mt. Sinai by Flinders Petrie more than ten years earlier. These inscriptions, written in a pictorial script by Canaanites before the middle of the second millennium B.C., prove that alphabetic writing existed before the time of Moses." 177/14

5C.   GEZER CALENDAR

The Gezer Calendar, written in 925 B.C. (found by Macalister in the 1900's) is obviously an exercise performed by a child. It proves that writing was well established in society at that time even to the point of being taught to children. 11/157

Compare Judges 8:14 where a youth picked at random from the town of Succoth was able to "write down" the names of the 77 elders for Gideon.

Albright shows the importance of this definitely Semitic writing:

"The oldest important Israelite inscription is the Gezer Calendar, a schoolboy's exercise tablet of soft limestone, on which he had awkwardly scratched the text of a ditty giving the order of the chief agricultural operations through the year. It dates from the late tenth century, if we may judge from the agreement of the evidence for forms of letters from contemporary Byblus with the stratigraphic context in which it was discovered." 5/132

6C.   CONCLUSION: CRITICS CRITICIZED

This issue constitutes a major upset for skeptics of Bible history. Sayce said it well when he asserted:

"As late as 1862, Sir George Cornewall Lewis denied it [writing in Moses' day], and as late as 1871 the eminent Semitic scholar Professor Noldeke declared that the results of Assyriology in both linguistic and historical matters had 'a highly suspicious air.' It was subjective theory against objective fact, and in accordance with the usual 'critical' method fact had to give way to theory." 137/35, 36

He then concludes, "Moses not only could have written the Pentateuch, but it would have been little short of a miracle had he not been a scribe." 137/42, 43

James Orr in *The Problem of the Old Testament* explained the trans formation of modern thought in the following manner:

"Formerly Israel was looked upon as a people belonging to the dim dawn of history at a period when, except in Egypt, civilization had hardly begun. It was possible then to argue that the art of writing did not exist among the Hebrews, and that they had not the capacity for the exalted religious ideas which the narratives of their early history implies. Moses could not have given the laws, nor David have written the psalms, which the history ascribes to them. This contention is now rendered impossible by the discovery of the extraordinary light of civilization which shone in the Tigro-Euphrates valley, and in the valley of the Nile, millenniums before Abraham left Ur of the Chaldees, or Moses led his people out of Egypt. The transformation of opinion is revolutionary." 50/396, 397

5A. THE LEGENDARY VIEW OF PATRIARCHAL NARRATIVES

1B. Documentary Assumption

The question of historicity of the Abraham accounts has been a favorite battleground between believer and skeptic. It is difficult to remain neutral on this issue and consider the Bible important for man today. Merrill Unger in his *Archaeology and the Old Testament* shows that the historicity of Abraham is no mean issue, but vital to New Testament faith:

"The figure of Abraham emerges from the ancient Mesopotamian world of his time with such remarkable vividness and assumes a role of such importance in the history of redemption that he is not overshadowed by even Moses, the great emancipator and lawgiver of Israel. Throughout the Old Testament and especially the New Testament the name of Abraham stands for the representative man of faith (cf. Rom. 4:1-25)." 193/105

Therefore we can turn to Gleason Archer in *A Survey of Old Testament Introduction* for a phrasing of the allegation. He explains that the documentarians believe "the Genesis accounts of the career of Abraham and his descendants are untrustworthy and often unhistorical. Noldeke even went so far as to deny the historical existence of Abraham altogether." 11/158

From the pen of noted critics we have explanatory material. Julius Wellhausen writes:

"From the patriarchal narratives it is impossible to obtain any historical information with regard to the patriarchs; we can only learn something about the time in which the stories about them were first told by the Israelite people. This later period, with all its essential and superficial characteristics, was unintentionally projected back into hoary antiquity and is reflected there like a transfigured mirage." 63/331

Wellhausen viewed Abraham as "a free creation of unconscious art." 63/320

Hermann Schultz says:

"The result may be given in outline as follows:—Genesis is the book of sacred legend, with a mythical introduction. The first three chapters of it, in particular, present us with revelation-myths of the most important kind, and the following eight with mythical elements that have been recast more in the form of legend. From Abraham to Moses we have national legend pure and simple, mixed with a variety of mythical elements which have become almost unrecognisable. From Moses to David we have history still mixed with a great deal of the legendary, and even partly with mythical elements that are no longer distinguishable. From David onwards we have history, with no more legendary elements in it than are everywhere present in history as written by the ancients." 138/31

And finally, from Robert H. Pfeiffer:

"Our sharp distinction between story and history, fancy and fact, seems meaningless when applied to the body of Old Testament narratives which present all the gradations between pure fiction (as in the stories about Adam, Noah, Samson) and genuine history (as in the ancient biography of David and in the Memoirs of Nehemiah). Only in the recital of events on the part of an eyewitness (unless he be lying as in I Sam. 22:10a and II Sam. 1:7-10) may exact historicity be expected in the Old Testament narratives. Their credibility decreases in the ratio of their distance in time from the narrator." 132/27

2B. Basic Answer

In the next few pages we will examine what we know about the patriarchal period and show that archaeology has played a big part in increasing this knowledge. G. Ernest Wright points out:

"There are numerous illustrations of the service which archaeology has rendered along this line. Perhaps the most noteworthy is the partial 'recovery' of the patriarchal period of biblical history." 200/80

1C. INSCRIPTIONAL MATERIAL

In this section we will investigate certain finds; in the next we will see how the finds have contributed to filling out our understanding of patriarchal culture. Unger has struck the balance between the two.

"As a result of archaeological research, particularly that of the last three decades, a large quantity of inscriptional material is now available to scholars, which has an important bearing on the patriarchal age. This material is of the greatest importance." 193/120, 121

He goes on to add that, though much has so far been unprinted, it has been crippling to skeptical theories, and analysis of the material has raised the standing of the Old Testament history. It does not establish such accounts as inviolate, but "it does mean that it has furnished a great deal of indirect evidence showing that the stories fit into the background of the age, as that age can now be recovered from the new sources of knowledge available, and that customs which appear in the stories prevailed in the world in which the patriarchs are set." 193/120, 121

Professor David Noel Freedman of the University of Michigan, and director of the William F. Albright School for Archaeological Research in Jerusalem, states specifically regarding the historicity of the patriarchs:

"In the same mood, that is the search for truth, I now bring you word, not about Moses and his generation, the historicity of which continues to be questioned by many leading scholars, but about an earlier generation still, that of the patriarchs, and to be more specific, the father of them and of us all, that is by faith if not in fact—Abraham or Abram. Even to talk about the possible historicity of the stories of Genesis and the figures who play leading roles in them is to jeopardize one's standing in the profession and to lay oneself open to the charges of pseudo-scholarship.

"Nevertheless, there have been outstanding scholars in the past who held these peculiar notions, and I do not hesitate to identify myself with this viewpoint and as an adherent of that school of thought, I recall an interesting and remarkable ultimate ancestor, for the members of the three great monotheistic faiths—Judaism, Christianity and Islam—all trace their descent from Abraham himself, which makes the subject of his historicity of something more than academic interest, Professor W.F. Albright, whom we all acknowledge as an Abrahamic figure in the scholarship of our day, and the father-professor of a legion of us, his followers and disciples, was quite circumspect about a historical reconstruction of the Genesis narratives and about precise circumstances and activities of the patriarchs, as well as their beliefs. At the same time, the illustrious cuneiformist at the University of Pennsylvania, E. Speiser, who unlike Albright did not profess a personal religion, had hardly any reservations at all; he did not merely assert the historicity of Abraham and his extensive family, but insisted on his monotheistic faith. Together these eminent scholars were an island fortress of conservative, almost traditional views, in an age of skepticism, but, of the two, Speiser was the more outspoken and direct, while Albright was more reticent and nuanced. Now that vindication is on its way, it is clear that Speiser was closer to historical reality, but even the presently known facts go far beyond what either of these great thinkers could have imagined.

"I am here to inform you that recent archaeological discoveries have proved to be directly pertinent to the question of the historicity of the patriarchal traditions, as they are preserved in the Genesis narratives. Generally they confirm or at least support the basic positions maintained by giants like Albright and Speiser, while effectively undercutting the prevailing skepticism and sophistry of the larger contingent representative of continental and American scholarship." 19/144

1D. The Mari Tablets

William F. Albright in his *From the Stone Age to Christianity* comments,

"The latest discoveries at Mari on the Middle Euphrates... have strikingly confirmed the Israelite traditions according to which their Hebrew forefathers came to Palestine from the region of Harran in northwestern Mesopotamia." 9/197

In his article "The Bible After Twenty Years of Archaeology," he goes further:

"The excavation of Mari began in 1933, under the direction of Andre Parrot. Situated on the Middle Euphrates, Mari was one of the most important centers of the Northwest Semitic life of Patriarchal times. In 1936, M. Parrot unearthed many thousands of cuneiform tablets dating mostly from about 1700 B.C., which are now in course of being studied and published. These tablets throw direct light on the background of the Patriarchal traditions of Genesis." 150/538

He goes on further to explain the impact of the Mari Tablets:

"Now we can speak even more emphatically, and with a wealth of additional detail. For example, the 'city of Nahor' which plays a role next to Harran in the Patriarchal stories (Gen. 24:10) turns up frequently along with Harran in the Mari documents about 1700 B.C. The name of a prince of Mari, Arriyuk, is evidently the same as the Arioch of Genesis 14. 'Benjamin' often appears as a tribal name at Mari." 150/541, 542

In the 1950 edition of *The Archaeology of Palestine*, one gets the feel of the impact of these tablets by noting the following:

Dossin and Jean are editing the thousands of tablets from Mari; every new publication of theirs helps us better to understand the life and times of the Hebrew Patriarchs. Abraham, Isaac, and Jacob no longer seem isolated figures, much less reflections of later Israelite history; they now appear as true children of their age, bearing the same names, moving about over the same territory, visiting the same towns (especially Harran and Nahor), practising the same customs as their contemporaries. In other words, the patriarchal narratives have a historical nucleus throughout, though it is likely that long oral transmission of the original poems and later prose sagas which underlie the present text of Genesis has considerably refracted the original events." 5/236

2D. The Law Codes

We have come to understand many of the actions of the patriarchs through the law codes of the Hittites, who exerted a strong influence on culture at that time. Archer notes the findings of one archaeologist:

"As Manfred Lehmann brings out [*Bulletin of the American Schools of Oriental Research*, No. 129, Feb. 1953, p. 18], the account in Genesis 23 exhibits such an intimate knowledge of Hittite procedure as to make it certain that the episode antedated the destruction of the Hittite power in the thirteenth century B.C." 11/161

Henry T. Frank in *Bible, Archaeology, and Faith* elucidates an Abrahamic episode:

"Similarly, a number of once puzzling incidents associated with the patriarchs are also shown by archaeological discoveries to have been commonplace in the early second millennium. We have already seen that Abraham's haggling with Ephron concerning the purchase of the Cave of Machpelah was in accordance with common ancient practice. Apparently Abraham wished to purchase only the cave itself in which to bury his wife, Sarah. Yet governed by Hittite practice he had to buy not only the cave but the land and the arbors associated with it. This assumption of feudal obligation described in Genesis 23:1-20 is exactly in accord with the recovered Hittite documents from Boghazköy in which such details are stressed." 161/74

3D. The Egyptian Execration Texts

Unger explains what these denunciatory artifacts are:

"The so-called 'Execration Texts' add their evidence to attest the authentic background of the patriarchs as presented in Genesis. These curious documents are statuettes and vases inscribed in Egyptian hieratic script with the names of potential enemies of the Pharaoh. If threatened by rebellion the Egyptian king had only to break the fragile objects on which were written the names and accompanying formulae, to the accompaniment of a magical ceremony, and forthwith the rebels would somehow come to grief. The group of vases from Berlin, published by Kurt Sethe (1926), probably date from the end of the twentieth century B.C., while the collection of statuettes from Brussels, published by G. Posener (1940), date from the late nineteenth century." 193/127

4D. The Nuzi Tablets

S.H. Horn in his *Christianity Today* article, "Recent Illumination of the Old Testament," introduces the Nuzi Tablets:

"The discovery of a whole archive of legal and social texts at Nuzi, a small place in northeastern Iraq, has revealed that the social and legal background of the patriarchal age is reflected accurately and in great detail in the Old Testament patriarchal narratives." 177/14

G.E. Wright in his "Present State of Biblical Archaeology" (1947) in *The Study of the Bible Today and Tomorrow* and Cyrus Gordon in "Biblical Customs and the Nuzu Tablets" *(The Biblical Archaeologist)* provide good background material. Wright includes certain key points:

Nuzi (or Nuzu) is located southeast of Nineveh. Some of the patriarchal episodes seem unusual, even to the later Israelites but this find at Nuzu clears the picture. The Nuzians were Hurrians (biblical Horites), formerly thought of as 'cave dwellers," and are now understood as Armenoid, non-Indo-Europeans of North Mesopotamia, who flourished in the 1500 and 1400's B.C. 200/43

Gordon follows up by explaining that though the patriarchs were not Nuzians, the cultures of the two were alike due to similar time and place. Therefore the Nuzi Tablets help us to understand Abraham, Isaac and Jacob. 172/2

Wright points out that the "Nuzi tablets elucidate many a custom typical of the patriarchal age in the second millennium, but not of Israelite life in the first." 200/87

Cyrus Gordon contends:

"Thanks to the Nuzu texts we may feel confident that the social institutions have come down to us authentically " 172/9

What are some specific instances in which the Nuzi Tablets help us to understand Genesis? Horn answers:

"First, in the patriarchal stories we find several strange accounts of a barren wife who asked her husband to produce a child for her by her maid servant. Sarah did this, and later also Jacob's two wives, Rachel and Leah. Today we know that this practice was not unusual during the patriarchal age. The laws of that period as well as ancient marriage contracts mention it. For example, in a marriage contract from Nuzi, the bride Kelim-ninu promises in written form to procure for her husband Shennima a slave girl as a second wife, if she fails to bear him children. She also promises that she will not drive out the offspring of such a union. In no other period besides the patriarchal age do we find this strange custom." 177/14

Gordon in another article refers to the Documentary Hypothesis:

"The cuneiform contracts from Nuzu have demonstrated that the social institutions of the patriarchs are genuine and pre-Mosaic. They cannot have been invented by any post-Mosaic. They cannot have been invented by any post-Mosaic J, E, D or P." 173/241

In Gordon's "Biblical Customs and the Nuzu Tablets," we find yet another custom explained.

"It was a custom at Nuzu for childless people to adopt a son to serve them as long as they lived and to bury and mourn for them when they died. In exchange for these services the adopted son was designated as heir. If, however, the adoptor should beget a son after the adoption, the adopted must yield to the real son the right of being the chief heir.... Once we know of this proviso, we have the legal meaning of God's reply in Genesis 15:4: 'This (slave) shall not inherit thee, but he that shall come out of thine inwards shall inherit thee.'" 172/2, 3

Albright concludes the worth of the Nuzi Tablets:

"When we add the fact that our present knowledge of social institutions and customs in another part of northern Mesopotamia in the fifteenth century (Nuzi) has brilliantly illuminated many details in the patriarchal stories which do not fit into the post-Mosaic tradition at all, our case for the substantial historicity of the tradition of the Patriarchs is clinched." 8/4, 5

5D. The Ebla Tablets

The tremendous archaeological discovery of Tell Mardikh of the ancient city of Ebla is revealing a wealth of new light on the patriarchal narratives. Although very little has come to publication as yet, the evidence points to exciting new gains and significant inroads for Near Eastern studies of the third millennium B.C., especially as related to the Old Testament accounts.

Referring to the patriarchal narratives, with general reference at first to Ebla and then specifically to a tablet that has been uncovered, David Noel Freedman states:

"Nevertheless, in spite of the bad examples from the past and the ample warnings by those associated with the Ebla finds, I believe firmly that there is a link between the Ebla tablets and the Bible, not only of the general linguistic and literary type already mentioned, which is almost inevitable, or even in terms of a common pool of names of persons and places, but much more direct in terms of history, chronology and fact." 19/148

Some of the specifics that Dr. Freedman mentions with regard to history, chronology and fact all center on a tablet for which its exact translation is now a clouded issue. Some of the information first released to Dr. Freedman has been revised (as he himself mentions in his article 19/143-164.) Hopefully with its publication the evidence will support the original reading of the tablet. But while that is pending, Dr. Freedman also pointed out that there is still a link between Ebla and the Bible, and time should surface to what extent.

2C. THE LIVING CONDITIONS

All these finds and more are combined to give us a picture of the culture of Middle Bronze Age Palestine (2000-1500 B.C.). For convenience, the following part is broken into the social-cultural setting and the geographical setting.

1D. The Social-Cultural Setting

Millar Burrows introduces the area:

"Specific archaeological evidence that this or that event in the stories of the patriarchs actually occurred may not be forthcoming, but the social customs reflected by the stories fit the patriarchal period; they also fit the region from which the patriarchs are said to have come." 156/278, 279

Albright is even stronger:

"The picture of movements in the hill country of Palestine, of seasonal migration between the Negreb and central Palestine, and of easy travel to Mesopotamia and Egypt is, accordingly, so perfectly in accord with conditions in the Middle Bronze Age that historical skepticism is quite unwarranted." 8/4

For some specific instances, Fred H. Wight mentions the question of travel.

"Men who have doubted the historic character of the patriarchs have questioned the migration of Abraham from Ur of the Chaldees to the land of Canaan, and also the military expedition from Babylonia to Palestine as indicated in Genesis 14, because they have insisted that extensive travel was not known in that day. But Babylonian excavators [at Mari] have uncovered a tablet that shows there was much travel between these two lands in those days. This tablet is dated in the era of

Abraham, and it was a wagon contract. The owner of the wagon leased it to a man for a year on condition that it not be driven to Kittim (i.e., the coast land of the Mediterranean Sea). Evidently, it was quite customary for men to drive their wagons over this route from Babylonia to Canaan or vicinity, and this owner stipulated that this should not be done with his wagon. This is clear evidence of wide travel between these two sections of the ancient world." 198/61, 62

Joseph P. Free even mentions the custom of heavy doors during Lot's time. He mentions Genesis 19:9 where the evil men of Sodom could not get through Lot's doorway. Keil and Albright studied Tell Beit Mirsim which is Kirjath-Sepher of the Bible and found walls and doors of 2200-1600 B.C. to be heavy and strong. At the 900-600 B.C. level homes most likely had used archways or curtains, but no doors were found. In Lot's day, the police force was not so strong and forbidding doors were needed. But with stronger law and order, doors were no longer needed for protection. 162/62

Free then took the offensive:

"Lot's heavy door fits precisely in this period. The critics, however, date the writing of the accounts of Abraham in the ninth and eighth centuries B.C. How did the writer know the conditions a thousand years or more before his time? 162/63

Concerning the name of Abraham, John Elder explains:

"It is not to be expected that the histories which kings of those times have left will contain mention of such a man as Abraham. But a tablet found in Babylonia bears the name Abarama and records that he paid his rent. At the least it shows that Abraham was one of the names used in that period."

To summarize, Albright sets forth a broad analysis:

"Numerous recent excavations in sites of this period in Palestine, supplemented by finds made in Egypt and Syria, give us a remarkably precise idea of patriarchal Palestine, fitting well into the picture handed down in Genesis." 8/3

2D. The Geographical-Topographical Setting

Unger speaks of the topographical accuracy of Genesis and shows that "it is significant, too, in this connection that the topographical allusions in the patriarchal stories fit the archaeological indications of the Middle Bronze Age (200-1500 B.C.) extremely well." 193/114

And further,
"The five cities of the plain (circle) of the Jordan, Sodom, Gomorrah, Admah, Zeboiim and Zoar, also belong to the early patriarchal age. The Biblical notices that the district of the Jordan, where these cities were located, was exceedingly fertile and well-peopled around 2065 B.C. but that not long afterwards was abandoned, are in full accord with the archaeological facts." 193/114

Earlier scholars maintained that the Jordan Valley was hardly populated in Abraham's day. Archer, however, shows that "Nelson Glueck has in recent decades uncovered more than seventy sites in the Jordan Valley, some of them as ancient as 3000 B.C." 11/159

Archer continues that "as for Abraham's career in Palestine, the excavations at Shechem and Bethel show that they were inhabited in Abraham's time." 11/159

Joseph Free speaks of Shechem, Ai, and Bethel:

"When Abraham came into Canaan, he dwelt for a time near Shechem

(Shichem, Gen. 12:6), about thirty miles north of Jerusalem, in a plain within the central mountain ridge of Palestine. Later he moved a few miles to the south and pitched his tent between Bethel and Ai (Gen. 12:8), some twelve miles north of Jerusalem (ISBE, article on 'Bethel'). Here he built an altar to the Lord and worshipped." 162/53

He goes on to say that "practically all of the towns mentioned in connection with Abraham (such as Shechem, Ai, Bethel) have been excavated, and the findings show that these go back to Abraham's time." 162/53

Concerning the "Table of Nations" in Genesis 10, and the listings in chapter 11, Burrows comments that the lists of Genesis 10 and 11 have been enlightened by archaeology, since many names remained lost to outside sources until recent material was discovered. 156/258

Free in his article "Archaeology and the Historical Accuracy of Scripture," works from Albright here:

"Archaeological monuments, however, have yielded the names of peoples and countries mentioned in this record [Gen. 10]. Many of them were unknown until discovered in ancient archaeological records. W.F. Albright, in his 1955 revision of the article, 'Recent Discoveries in Bible Lands,' pointed out what he had said earlier, that this chapter stands absolutely alone in ancient literature *(Young's Analytical Concordance to the Bible*, p. 30). We find that the monuments attest:

> Tubal in the form Tabal
> Meshech as Mushke
> Ashkenaz as Ashkunz
> Togarmah as Tegarama
> Elishah as Alashi (Alashiyah)
> Tarshish as Tarsisi (Assyrian Tarshish)
> Cush as Kusi (pronounced Kush in Assyrian)
> Phut as Putu
> Dedan as Ddn
> Accad as Akkadu
> Shinar as Shanghar

Many other parallels appear in the monuments, and this evidence leads Dr. Albright to conclude that The Table of Nations remains an astonishingly accurate document." 165/215

Summing up in his *Archaeology and Bible History,* Free closes:

"The fact, however, that the cities mentioned in connection with Abraham are shown by archaeological discoveries to have existed in his time constitutes a definite argument for the accuracy of the background of the Abrahamic accounts in the Scriptures." 162/53

3C. THE COUNTER-ISSUE: ABRAHAM IN EGYPT

Before moving to a conclusion, one final point must be dealt with. Some critics will maintain that Abraham could not have visited Egypt due to a closed-door policy. This is brought out by Edgar Banks:

"Frequently it has been asserted that neither Abraham nor any other of his people and age was ever down in Egypt, and that it would have been impossible for him or for any other stranger to enter the country from which all strangers were excluded." 222/58

This question has been brought to my attention by Joseph Free in his *Archaeology and Bible History.* He explains the situation:

"Popular books on archaeology frequently allude to the critical view that strangers could not have come into Egypt in earlier times, and often refer the basis of such an idea back to the first century historians, Strabo or Diodorus, but ordinarily no further documentation is given." 162/54

Free also cited Millar Neatby:

"Neatby says that the critic could quote Strabo, the Greek geographer and historian, who stated shortly before the time of Christ that 'Not till the time of Psammetichus (654 B.C.) did Egypt open its ports to strangers or grant security to foreign traders.' T. Millar Neatby, *Confirming the Scriptures*, (London: Marshall, Morgan and Scott, n.d.), Vol. II, pp. 114, 115." 162/54

"A detailed examination of the writings of Strabo and Diodorus has shown, however, that such an implication is given by Strabo, and a point blank statement is made by Diodorus." 162/54

Strabo:

"Now the earlier kings of the Egyptians, being content with what they had and not wanting foreign imports at all, and being prejudiced against all who sailed the seas, and particularly against the Greeks (for owing to scarcity of land of their own the Greeks were ravagers and coveters of that of others), set a guard over this region and ordered it to keep away any who should approach." 78/27

Diodorus:

"Psammetichus... regularly treated with kindness any foreigners who sojourned in Egypt of their own free will... and, speaking generally, he was the first Egyptian king to open to other nations the trading-places through the rest of Egypt and to offer a large measure of security to strangers from across the seas. For his predecessors in power had consistently closed Egypt to strangers, either killing or enslaving any who touched its shores." 79/235

There is only one problem. Archaeology has shown the Old Testament to be the accurate work and not the first century historians:

"Archaeological discoveries, however, show that people from the region of Palestine and Syria were coming to Egypt in the period of Abraham. This is clearly indicated by a tomb painting at Beni Hassan, dating a little after 2000 B.C. It shows Asiatic Semites who have come to Egypt.... Furthermore, the archaeological and historical indications of the coming of the Hyksos into Egypt c. 1900 B.C. provides another piece of evidence showing that strangers could come into that land. Their entrance was almost contemporary with that of Abraham. The Bible is correct in this indication and Diodorus was wrong." 162/54, 55

4C. CONCLUSION

G.E. Wright gives the story behind an extra-biblical reference to Abraham, which is most rare:

"The first great disaster since the reign of Saul descended upon the two kingdoms about 918 B.C. Our books of Kings give us scant information about it:

'And it came to pass in the fifth year of King Rehoboam that Shishak, king of Egypt came up against Jerusalem. And he took away the treasures of the house (Temple) of the Lord, and the treasures of the king's house.... And he took away all the shields of gold which Solomon had made (I Kings 14:25-6).'

"This king of Egypt thought more highly of his campaign, however, and on the walls of the great temple of Karnak in Upper Egypt he had his artists carve a picture of himself smiting the Asiatics in the presence of the god

Amon, who with a goddess is depicted as presenting to him ten lines of captives. Each captive symbolized a town or locality, the name of which was inscribed below. From these names we can gather the extent of his campaign. The biblical account implies that only Judah was affected, but all of Palestine apparently suffered, for the list includes cities in the Esdraelon, Transjordan, the hill country of both Israel and Judah, and even Edom. There is an interesting reference to the Field of Abram, presumably the Hebron area, and this is the first time that a source outside the Bible confirms that Patriarch's connection with a locality in Palestine." 200/148

W.F. Albright writes that "so many corroborations of details have been discovered in recent years that most competent scholars have given up the old critical theory according to which the stories of the Patriarchs are mostly retrojections from the time of the Dual Monarchy (ninth- eighth centuries B.C.)." 9/183

Albright concludes that "as a whole the picture in Genesis is historical, and there is no reason to doubt the general accuracy of the biographical details and the sketches of personality which make the Patriarchs come alive with a vividness unknown to a single extrabiblical character in the whole vast literature of the ancient Near East." 8/5

Millar Burrows says:

"No longer can we think of Abraham as a lonely figure moving across uninhabited wastes to an almost unoccupied land, and taking possession of it as an arctic explorer claims the wastes of the north for his nation." 156/92

J.P. Free, citing Gordon, writes that "in regard to the background of the patriarchal narratives Cyrus Gordon, writing on the Nuzi tablets, points out that they show us that the picture of patriarchal society has come down to us authentically *(Biblical Archaeologist,* 3:1:9, January, 1940)." 164/34

Jack Finegan says that "certainly the Patriarchal stories fit with thorough congruity and often with surprising relevance of detail into the historical setting of life in Mesopotamia during the early second millennium B.C."

Even W.A. Irwin of Southern Methodist University, not a conservative in his views, in his article "The Modern Approach to the Old Testament," writes:

"An extreme skepticism in regard to the patriarchal stories has given place to recognition that they preserve valid reminiscences of historic movements and social conditions." 178/14

W.F. Albright concludes:

"Turning to Israel, I defend the substantial historicity of patriarchal tradition, without any appreciable change in my point of view, and insist, just as in 1940-46, on the primacy of oral tradition over written literature. I have not surrendered a single position with regard to early Israelite monotheism but, on the contrary, consider the Mosaic tradition as even more reliable than I did then. Without altering my general view of the growth of the social and political institutions of Israel, I now recognize that Israelite law and religious institutions tend to be old and more continuous than I had supposed—in other words, I have grown more conservative in my attitude to Moasic tradition." 9/2

J. Bright states:

"We can assert with full confidence that Abraham, Isaac, and Jacob were actual historical individuals." 14/82

Any discussion of the historicity of the patriarchs will have to consider

Bright's recommendation:

"The only safe and proper course lies in a balanced examination of the traditions against the background of the world of the day and, in the light of that, making such positive statements as the evidence allows. Hypothetical reconstructions, plausible though these may be, are to be eschewed. Much must remain obscure. But enough can be said to make it certain that the patriarchal traditions are firmly anchored in history." 14/69

3B. Genesis 14 - An Additional Example

One area which was continuously criticized in regard to its historicity is the abstruse chapter 14 of Genesis. This chapter narrates Abraham's victory over Chedorlaomer and the Mesopotamian kings.

The first person to apply the "German rationalistic criticism" to Genesis 14 was Theodore Noldeke (1826-1930). He wrote a pamphlet titled "The Unhistorical Character of Genesis 14," in which he labels it a forgery and describes the expedition as being "ficititous."

Julius Wellhausen writes of its "historical unreliability":

"That 'at the time of Abraham' four Kings from the Persian Gulf made a razzia (or raid) as far as the peninsula of Sinai; that they, on that occasion, surprised and captured five city-princes who reigned in the Dead Sea; that finally Abraham, at the head of 318 servants, fell upon the departing victors, and recaptured what they had robbed, — these are simply impossibilities." 207/312

Wellhausen continues:

"From the patriarchal narratives it is impossible to obtain any historical information with regard to the Patriarchs. We can only learn something about the time in which the stories about them were first told by the Israelite people. This later period, with all its essential and superficial characteristics, was unintentionally projected backward into hoary antiquity, and is reflected there like a transfigured mirage." 207/331

William F. Albright in 1918 wrote an article entitled "Historical and Mythical Elements in the Story of Joseph." He concluded that chapter 14 "must be regarded, with Asmussen... and Haupt... as a political pamphlet, designed (so Haupt) to strengthen the hands of the patriotic Jews who were supporting the rebellion of Zerubbabel against the Persian monarch." 203/136

Albright concludes that "the Hebrew material was either borrowed from extant legends like the saga of the cities of the plain and the legend of Melchizedek, or invented by use of haggadic processes." 203/136

However, as a result of his own archaeological discoveries in 1929, he had his skeptical views radically changed and concluded that "this account represents the invading host as marching down from Hauran through eastern Gilead and Moab to the southeastern part of Palestine. Formerly the writer considered this extraordinary line of march as being the best proof of the essentially legendary character of the narrative. In 1929 however, he discovered a line of Early and Middle Bronze Age mounds, some of great size, running down along the eastern edge of Gilead, between the desert and the forest of Gilead. Moreover, the cities of Hauran (Bashan) with which the account of the campaign opens, Ashtaroth and Karnaim, were both occupied in this period, as shown by archaeological examination of their sites. The same is true of eastern Moab, where the writer discovered an Early Middle-Bronze city at Ader in 1924. This route called "The Way of the King," in later Israelite tradition, does not appear to have ever been employed by invading armies in the Iron Age." 209/142, 143

The following is indicative of his change in view when he writes that Genesis 14 "can no longer be considered as unhistorical, in view of the many confirmations of details which we owe to recent finds." 204/140

Joseph Free lists several specific accusations made by the radical critics against the historicity of Genesis 14. They shall be dealt with briefly.

1C. THE MESOPOTAMIAN KINGS

1D. Documentary Assumption

The Mesopotamian kings' names were said to be fictitious or unhistorical.

2D. Basic Answer

The Mari tablets (18th century B.C.) discovered in 1933 contain the name Arriyuk (or Arriwuk) identified with the name Arioch of Genesis 14. 150/542

K.A. Kitchen points out:

"Tid'al is a Tidkhalia, a Hittite name known from the nineteenth century B.C. onwards, and borne by four or five Hittite kings in the eighteenth to the thirteenth centuries B.C. Chedorla'-omer is typically Elamite... of the Old Babylonian period (2000-1700 B.C.) and later.... The individuals themselves have not yet been identified in extra-biblical documents, but this is not surprising when one considers the gaps in our knowledge of the period." 42/44

Howard Vos concludes:

"For a long time the names of the four kings of the East were thought to be unhistorical, but most scholars now find some means of identifying them with known persons or at least identifying them as historical name forms." 197/68, 69

Nahum Sarna recognizes that events in Genesis 14 are based upon documents of great antiquity. He writes that "the prose style has preserved indications of an archaic substratum in verse form. For instance, the names of the Canaanite Kings are arranged in two alliterative pairs, Bera-Birsha and Shinab-Shemeber. The language contains some unique or very rare words and phrases. One such, *hanikh* (v. 14), meaning 'an armed-retainer,' appears but this once in the bible, but it is found in the Egyptian execration texts of the nineteenth-eighteenth centuries B.C.E. and in a fifteenth-century B.C.E. cuneiform inspription from Taanach, Israel.

"It will be noticed that only four of the local monarchs are mentioned by name, the fifth being called simply, 'the king of Bela' (v. 2). Had the whole episode no historical foundation, the writer would surely not have been at a loss for a name." 210/111

2C. THE EXTENSIVE TRAVEL

1D. Documentary Assumption

There could not have been "extensive travel" such as the military campaign in Genesis 14.

2D. Basic Answer

Vos states that "the assertion made formerly that travel was not so extensive in the patriarchal period as indicated in this chapter and that military control of Palestine by Mesopotamian kings did not exist at that time must now be discarded. The expedition of kings of Elam and Babylonia appears in different light when we learn, for instance, that as early as 2300 B.C. Sargon of Akkad (near Babylon) made raids on the Amorites of Syria and Palestine." 197/70, 71

Another example of extensive travel as implied in Genesis 14 is given by G.A. Barton. The paragraph is entitled: "Travel between Babylonia and Palestine." Barton translates a document from a Babylonian clay tablet containing a wagon contract. He writes:

"The date of the above interesting document has not been identified with certainty. It is thought by some to belong to the reign of Shamsuiluna, the successor of Hammurabi. The writing clearly shows that at any rate it comes from the period of this dynasty... *Kittim* in the contract is the word used in the Hebrew of Jeremiah 2:10 and Ezekiel 27:6 for the coast lands of the Mediterranean. It undoubtedly has that meaning here. This contract was written in Sippar, the Agade of earlier times, a town on the Euphrates a little to the north of Babylon. It reveals the fact that at the time the document was written there was so much travel between Babylonia and the Mediterranean coast that a man could not lease a wagon for a year without danger that it might be driven over the long route to Syria or Palestine. . . ." 205/347

Joseph Free relates that "other implication of long-distance travel is found in one of the Mari Tablets, which indicated that the King of ancient Ugarit on the Mediterranean coast planned to visit the King of Mari on the Euphrates. Such discoveries do not support the idea of limited travel, but rather the implication of the extensive travel involved in the campaign of the four kings of the east." 165/217, 218

3C. THE ROUTE OF MARCH

1D. Documentary Assumption

It was not reasonable that the route of the march would follow the geographical lines as indicated.

2D. Basic Answer

Fred Wight states that "archaeological discoveries have compelled an increasing recognition of the value of this Scripture from the historical viewpoint." 198/105

William F. Albright confesses that "the underlying account of the campaign waged by the Eastern kings appears to be historical. This account represents the invading host as marching down from Hauran through eastern Gilead and Moab to the southeastern part of Palestine." 109/142

However, Albright did not always attest to the historicity of the campaign. For a long time he "considered this extraordinary line of march as being the best proof of the essentially legendary character of the narrative." 209/142

He retracted his above legendary view when he wrote (also a quote previously used):

"In 1929, however, he [Dr. Albright referring to himself] discovered a line of Early and middle Bronze Age mounds, some of great size, running down along the eastern edge of Gilead, between the desert and the forests of Gilead. Moreover, the cities of Hauran (Bashan) with which the account of the campaign opens, Ashtaroth and Karnaim, were both occupied in this period, as shown by archaeological examination of their sites. The same is true of eastern Moab, where the writer discovered an Early-Middle Bronze city at Ader in 1924." 209/142

If the account of the invasion is historical, there would be various areas of developed regions of permanent sedentary occupation existing very early along the route followed.

Nahum Sarna writes that "extensive archaeological surveys of Transjordan and the Negeb have indeed shown this to have been the case during what is known as the Middle Bronze I period, i.e. between the twenty-first and nineteenth centuries B.C.E. A civilization of a high order of achievement flourished throughout this period, and a truly amazing number of settlements has been discovered. Strangely enough, there occurs a complete and sudden interruption in settled life in Transjordan and the Negeb just at the end of the period, apparently as a result of some historic catastrophic invasion that systematically wiped out everything in its path. For the next six hundred years, Transjordan remained desolate until the founding of the Kingdoms of Edom and Moab in the thirteenth century B.C.E. In the Negeb, the break in civilization lasted nearly a thousand years.

"In the light of all this, it is not unreasonable to assume that the story of the battle of the Kings in the Book of Genesis preserves an authentic echo of a great military expedition which put an end to the Middle Bronze I settlements. The annals recording the catastrophic events may well have furnished the basis for the biblical account." 210/113, 115

The evidence has caused Albright to conclude that "Genesis 14 can no longer be considered as unhistorical, in view of the many confirmations of details which we owe to recent finds." 204/140

4C. AUTHORITY OVER CANAAN

1D. Documentary Assumption

The Mesopotamian kings had no sovereignty over Canaan.

2D. Basic Answer

Joseph Free writes concerning their control over Canaan:

"Archaeological evidence of their control or attempt at control over the region of Canaan was found in an inscription in which the King of Elam (Persia) called himself 'the prince of the Land of Amurru' (M.G. Kyle, *Deciding Voice of the Monuments,* p. 133). Amurru, the land of the Amorites, included Syria and Canaan." 165/218, 219

5C. SOME ADDITIONAL COMMENTS:

Kenneth Kitchen contends that "the system of power-alliances (four kings against five) is typical in Mesopotamian politics within the period c. 2000-1750 B.C., but not before or after this general period when different political patterns prevailed." 42/44

Millar Burrows:

"According to the fourteenth chapter of Genesis, eastern Palestine was invaded by a coalition of kings in the time of Abraham. The route taken by the invading armies led from the region of Damascus southward along the eastern edge of Gilead and Moab. The explorations of Albright and Glueck have shown that there was a line of important cities along this route before 2000 B.C. and for a century or two thereafter, but not in later periods." 156/71

Howard Vos:

"As we continue to investigate the historicity of Genesis 14, we might well ask if any of the towns mentioned in verses 5 through 7 have yet been identified. At least three have been." 197/72

S.L. Caiger states that "there seems no reason to question a factual basis of Genesis 14." 157/34

William Albright:

"A generation ago most critical scholars regarded this chapter as very late and as quite unhistorical. Now we cannot accept such an easy way out of the difficulties which the chapter presents, since some of its allusions are exceedingly early, carrying us directly back into the Middle Bronze Age." 209/237

6A. CONCLUSION REGARDING PRESUPPOSITIONS OF DOCUMENTARY HYPOTHESIS

1B. Presuppositions as the Basis

The importance of presuppositions in the formulation of the Documentary Hypothesis is brought out by George Mendenhall when he says:

"Wellhausen's theory of the history of Israelite religion was very largely based on a Hegelian philosophy of hisotry, not upon his literary analysis. It was an *a priori* evolutionary scheme which guided him in the utilization of his sources." 68/36

This suspicion that the founders of the Documentary Theory were not as scientifically objective in their handling of the material as modern critics would have us believe (31/17) seems to be supported by these two statements of Wellhausen in which we see employment of careless and subjective methodology and the priority that *a priori* theories took over the textual evidence itself:

"At last, in the course of a casual visit in Gottingen in the summer of 1867, I learned through Ritschl that Karl Heinrich Graf placed the Law later than the Prophets, and, almost without knowing his reasons for the hypothesis, I was prepared to accept it; I readily acknowledged to myself the possibility of understanding Hebrew antiquity without the book of the Torah." 63/3, 4

"Almost more important to me than the phenomena themselves, are the presuppositions which lie behind them." 63/368

Thus, Whitelae's criticism is certainly justified:

"It is not questioned that hypothesis as a tentative method of proof is perfectly legitimate. Frequently no other means of arriving at the solution of hard problems in science and philosophy is possible than by testing the applicability of first one supposition and then another.... In this way Grotefend, Rawlinson, and other Assyriologists deciphered the cuneiform inscriptions which have so wondrously enriched our knowledge of antiquity. Hence no real objection can be taken to the adoption by Biblical scholars of the same plan when confronted by knotty questions which cannot otherwise be answered. What is complained of is the making of *a priori* assumptions which rather raise difficulties than remove them, and holding these assumptions as demonstrated truths without having previously established them by convincing argument." 64/188, 189

Finally, all six of the documentarians' presuppositions that we have examined must be regarded as invalid. Anti-supernaturalism (see page 3) must be rejected on the grounds that it claims to have absolute truth regarding the existence of God or the extent and nature of His intervention in the natural order of the universe, i.e., either His existence or His divine intervention is ruled out as an *impossibility* on an *a priori* basis.

Another of these presuppositions (an *a priori* distrust of the Old Testament record) must be rejected since it flies in the face of an accepted cannon of criticism that has stood the test of time, having guided literary and historical scholars since the time of Aristotle.

The remaining four presuppositions (evolutionary view of Israel's history; priority of source analysis over verifiable methodology; legendary view of patriarchal narratives; and the assumption that there was no writing in Israel during the Mosaic age) have all been soundly refuted by archaeology. (For additional development between archaeology and criticism, see appendix page 327.)

2B. Presuppositions and Contemporary Biblical Criticism

Some students of the Bible are under the assumption that in the field of biblical study the age of "the *a priori* assumption" has been rendered obsolete, having been replaced by "the conclusion that is reached only after the application of the totally objective scientific method in an analysis of the data." If preconceived positions are held, it is the conservative "Fundamentalists" who hold them and not the unbiased adherents of higher liberal criticism whose interest in the Bible is not hampered by "dogmatic religious beliefs." Indeed, the term "liberal" connotes in many minds one who is less biased than the "conservative."

But such conclusions are, at best, wishful thinking. Although of a decidedly different nature, modern liberal critics, like conservatives, maintain certain preconceived positions. This important fact cannot be overstressed and failure to recognize it invites the serious charge of intellectual dishonesty.

Gilkey, himself a documentarian, concludes his article, "Cosmology, Ontology, and the Travail of Biblical Language," with this reminder to the entire school of liberal biblical criticism to which he belongs:

"And for all of us, a contemporary understanding of ancient Scriptures depends as much on a careful analysis of our present presuppositions as it does on being learned in the religion and faith of the past." 26/154

chapter 9

consequences of radical higher criticism

Acceptance of the conclusions of radical higher criticism necessitates embracing the following consequences:

1A. THE OLD TESTAMENT IS ESSENTIALLY UNHISTORICAL

For most adherents of the radical higher critical schools, the Old Testament does not contain an accurate history of Israel. It has, to be sure, isolated events which in themselves may be considered historical, but when viewed as a whole it gives a false picture of Israelite chronological history. Working from this premise, the critics have constructed their own account of early Hebrew history which, as can be seen from the chart below, quite contradicts the Old Testament record in many major points.

Walther Eichrodt's comment regarding the critics' treatment of the book of Ezekiel points out the difficulties of constructing theories that contradict the actual text:

"This unsatisfactory fluctuation in the theories is no mere matter of chance; it is the necessary result of all the difficulties encountered by any attempt to work out such a fundamental theory on the basis of a text which states the exact opposite. Whenever they do not fit in with the theory, the established pieces of information about dates and geographical locations must now be accepted, and again dismissed as doubtful, without any reliable methodological basis for the conclusions. There is also a readiness to take those elements of the tradition that are difficult to accommodate to this interpretation, and either make them mean something else or else try to eliminate them by critical methods." 19/8, 9

The following chart compares the Hebrew's account of their own history (some of the major events) with that of the modern higher critics. This chart represents only the general trend in radical higher criticism and therefore cannot be said to represent the view of every critic. However, it is the general outline prominent in most destructive higher critical circles today. In passing, it should also be noted

89

that Wellhausen's reconstruction of early Hebrew history was even more radical than the view represented here.

OLD TESTAMENT RECORD		DOCUMENTARIAN VIEW	
1445-1405 B.C.	Moses gives "the Law" and writes Genesis, Exodus, Leviticus, Numbers, Deuteronomy	1400 B.C.	Covenant Code (Material in Exodus 20-23)
1000	David's reign	1000	David's reign
960	Solomon's temple	960	Solomon's temple
850(?)	Obadiah—first writing prophet	950	J document
850-550	Golden Age of the Prophets	930	Kingdom divides
		850	E document
722	End of northern kingdom (Israel)	750	Amos—first writing prophet
586	Jerusalem falls; Exile	750-550	Golden Age of the Prophets
539	Restoration of Israel	722	End of northern kingdom (Israel)
450	Ezra reforms second Jewish Commonwealth on basis of the Law (Torah)	622	Deuteronomic Code
		586	Jerusalem falls; Exile
		575	H (Holiness) Code (Leviticus 17-20)
		550	Deuteronomic circle edits Deuteronomy— II Kings
		539	Restoration of Israel
		450	P document written for the purpose of instituting Second Jewish Commonwealt
		450-400	P circle compiles Tetrateuch (Genesis—Numbers); Deuteronomy added later to form Pentateuch

We see that the biblical sequence of the Law being given early and *followed* by the prophets has been exactly reversed; for, according to the critics, the Law, comprised of the Deuteronomic Code, Holiness Code, and the Priestly Code (the bulk of the legislative material in the Pentateuch) did not come into existence until long after the prophets. And yet it is clear from the text that many of the prophets appealed to a body of law which was already in existence in their time and which was authoritatively binding upon the people. Amos even refers to this law as "the *Torah* ['Law'] of Yahweh" (Amos 2:4).

Thus, the critics have created a crucial and irreconcilable contradiction regarding both the chronology and the theological development of Israel's history.

This contradiction leaves us with an insurpassable gulf between an authoritative Word of God on the one hand and "a tattered miscellany of half-mythical and historically unreliable literary fragments" on the other. And even more fundamentally, we are left with extreme tension between the scriptural portrayal of Israelite history and the reconstruction of the radical critics.

"It does not put the matter too strongly to say that, to the more radical school of critics, the Old Testament is in the main *unhistorical*. Not necessarily, of course, that there is not in parts—some would acknowledge in considerable parts—a historical substratum. Everyone may not go so far, at one end of the history, as Stade, who doubts whether Israel as a people was ever in Egypt at all; or, at the other end, as Kosters, who denies the return from the exile at Babylon under Zerubbabel. But the books as they stand are, for all that, held not to be, at least till the days of the kings, and even then only very partially, genuine history." 50/56

This implies that the clear picture we see in the Old Testament of the development of a coherent and unified divine plan (teleological element) in Israel's history beginning in Genesis with Adam, and to be culminated in the promised Messiah as witnessed to by the prophets, was contrived.

Kautzsch, of Halle, in a lecture on *"The Abiding Value of the Old Testament,"* cited by Orr, writes:

"The abiding value of the Old Testament lies above all in this, that it guarantees to us with absolute certainty the fact and the process of a divine plan and way of salvation, which found its conclusion and fulfillment in the new covenant, in the Person and work of Jesus Christ." 50/61

Orr says that the reply which "comes from the side of the criticism that seeks to get rid of the teleological element in the history is, that the Biblical representation is an unreal and artificial one: not a development in accordance with the actual history, but an *imaginary* development, the result of a reading back into the primitive legends of the ideas of the prophetic age. The appearance of development is superimposed on the historical tradition by the manner in which its materials are manipulated. Grant, it is said, the critical scheme—its analysis and partition of documents—and the illusion of teleology in the Old Testament story disappears; so far at least as any extraordinary cause is required to account for it. In the words of Professor Robertson: 'What they maintain is, that the scheme of the Biblical writers is an afterthought, which by a process of manipulation of older documents, and by a systematic representation of earlier events in the light of much later times, has been made to appear as if it were the original and genuine development.'" 50/61, 62

2A. ISRAEL'S RELIGION IS TOTALLY NATURAL, NOT SUPERNATURAL IN ORIGIN AND DEVELOPMENT (In other words, God did not *really* act in Israel's history; the Hebrews only *thought* He did.)

How is this derived from the literary analysis of the Pentateuch? Orr explains:

"Nothing, it may be plausibly argued, depends, for the decision of the supernatural origin of the religion, on whether the Pentateuch, as we have it, is from the pen of Moses, or is made up of three or four documents, put together at a late date; or at what period the Levitical law as finally codified; or whether the Book of Isaiah is the work of one, or two, or of ten authors; or whether the Psalms are pre-exilic, or post-exilic, in origin. Yet, as will be seen more fully later, the dependence of the literary criticism on the religious theory is really very close. For, if it be true, as every fair mind must admit, that there are many scholars who succeed, to their own satisfaction, in combining the acceptance of the main results of the critical hypothesis of the Old Testament, even in its advanced form, with firm belief in the reality of supernatural revelation in Israel it is equally true that, in the case of others, and these pre-eminently, in Dr. Cheyne's phrase, 'The Founders of Criticism,' the decisions arrived at on purely literary questions, — the date of a psalm, e.g., the genuineness of a passage, or the integrity of a book, — are largely controlled by the view taken of the origin and course of development of the religion; and, with a different theory on these subjects, the judgments passed on the age, relations and historical value, of particular writings, would be different also. This dependence of many of the conclusions of criticism—by no means, of course, all—on the religious and historical standpoint is practically admitted by Wellhausen, (63/12) when he declares that 'it is only within the region of religious antiquities and dominant religious ideas—the region which Vatke in his *Biblische Theologie* had occupied in its full breadth, and where the real battle first kindled—that the controversy can be brought to a definite issue.'" 50/4, 5

Gilkey, an honest spokesman for this view, states it quite unequivocally:

"Now this assumption of a causal order among phenomenal events, and therefore of the authority of the scientific interpretation of observable events, makes a great difference to the validity one assigns to biblical narratives and so to the way one understands their meaning. Suddenly a vast panoply of divine deeds and events recorded in Scripture are no longer regarded as having actually happened. Not only, for example, do the six days of creation, the historical fall in Eden, and the flood seem to us historically untrue, but even more the majority of divine deeds in the biblical history of the Hebrew people become what we choose to call symbols rather than plain old historical facts. To mention only a few: Abraham's unexpected child; the many divine visitations; the words and directions to the patriarchs; the plagues visited on the Egyptians; the pillar of fire; the parting of the seas; the verbal deliverance of covenantal law on Sinai; the strategic and logistic help in the conquest; the audible voice heard by the prophets; and so on—all these "acts" vanish from the plane of historical reality and enter the never-never land of "religious interpretation" by the Hebrew people. Therefore when we read what the Old Testament seems to say God did, or what precritical commentators said God did (see Calvin), and then look at a modern interpretation of what God did in biblical times, we find a tremendous difference: the wonder events and the verbal divine commentaries, commands, and promises are gone. Whatever the Hebrews believed, *we* believe that the biblical people lived in the same causal continuum of space and time in which we live, and so one in which no divine wonders transpire and no divine voices were heard." 26/144, 145

He brings this view to its logical conclusion:

"The vast panoply of wonder and voice events that preceded the Exodus-covenant event, in effect the patriarchal narratives, are now taken to be Hebrew interpretations of their own historical past based on the faith gained at the Exodus. For us then, these narratives represent not so much *histories* of what God actually did and said as *parables* expressive of the faith the post-Exodus Jews had, namely, belief in a God who was active, did deeds, spoke promises and commands, and so on. Third, the biblical accounts of the post-Exodus life—for example, the proclamation and codification of the law, the conquest, and the prophetic movement—are understood as the covenant people's interpretation through their Exodus faith of their continuing life and history. For modern biblical theology the Bible is no longer so much a book containing a description of God's actual acts and words as it is a book containing Hebrew interpretations, 'creative interpretations' as we call them, which, like the parable of Jonah, tell stories of God's deeds and man's responses to express the theological beliefs of Hebrew religion. Thus the Bible is a book descriptive not of the acts of God but of Hebrew religion." 26/146

The radical nature of this position is realized by Gilkey when he admits:

"The difference between this view of the Bible as a parable illustrative of Hebrew religious faith and the view of the Bible as a direct narrative of God's actual deeds and words is so vast that it scarcely needs comment." 26/146

3A. THE HISTORY AND RELIGION OF ISRAEL ARE BASICALLY FRAUDULENT

It is clear upon reading the Hebrews' account of their own history and religion as laid out before us in the Old Testament that they *intended* the account to be accepted by readers as truly historical. The sequence of Moses giving the Law and then later the prophets judging the people by harking back to the Mosaic Law was meant to be an account of what really happened—and in what precise order it happened.

Unger makes a similar point:

"Again, Deuteronomy if not published till 621 B.C., yet professing to be from Moses' mouth and pen, cannot be cleared of the suspicion of pious forgery. The same may be said of the Priestly Code, not completed till about 500 B.C., but repeatedly professing to be directly and divinely commanded to Moses. Under these circumstances the honesty and integrity of the redactors can scarcely be unchallenged." 61/231

Whoever wrote the Old Testament books and canonized them wanted us to think that the history depicted in them was indeed the real history of Israel. If the documentarians are right, the historians of the Old Testament are wrong, and there does not seem to be any reasonable way of getting around the implications of a "contrived" history.

chapter 10

evidence
for
mosaic
authorship

1A. INTERNAL EVIDENCE

1B. Witness of Pentateuch

The Pentateuch itself clearly states that these portions of its contents were written by Moses:

1C. BOOK OF THE COVENANT, extending from Exodus 20:22-23:33

"And Moses wrote down all the words of the Lord. Then he arose early in the morning, and built an altar at the foot of the mountain with twelve pillars for the twelve tribes of Israel.... Then he took the Book of the Covenant and read it in the hearing of the people; and they said, 'All that the Lord has spoken we will do, and we will be obedient!'" Exodus 24:4, 7

2C. RENEWAL OF THE COVENANT, referring to Exodus 34:10-26

"Then the Lord said to Moses, 'Write down these words, for in accordance with these words I have made a covenant with you and with Israel.'" Exodus 34:27

3C. DEUTERONOMIC CODE, which comprises the bulk of Deuteronomy 5-30

"So Moses wrote this law and gave it to the priests, the sons of Levi who carried the ark of the covenant of the Lord, and to all the elders of Israel." Deuteronomy 31:9

"And it came about, when Moses finished writing the words of this law in a book until they were complete, that Moses commanded the Levites who carried the ark of the covenant of the Lord, saying, 'Take this book of the law and place it beside the ark of the covenant of the Lord....'" Deuteronomy 31:24-26

Such a passage cannot be used to prove that Moses wrote the Pentateuch; but it does presuppose a considerable book which at least refers to

Deuteronomy 5-26, and indicates a large amount of literary activity by Moses. 53/86

4C. GOD'S JUDGMENT OF AMALEK

"Then the Lord said to Moses, 'Write this in a book as a memorial, and recite it to Joshua, that I will utterly blot out the memory of Amalek from under heaven.'" Exodus 17:14

5C. ITINERARY OF ISRAELITES FROM RAMSES TO MOAB

"And Moses recorded their starting places according to their journeys by the command of the Lord, and these are their journeys according to their starting places." Numbers 33:2

6C. THE SONG OF MOSES IN DEUTERONOMY 32

"Now therefore write this song for yourselves, and teach it to the sons of Israel; put it on their lips, in order that this song may be a witness for Me against the sons of Israel.

"For when I bring them into the land flowing with milk and honey, which I swore to their fathers, and they have eaten and are satisfied and become prosperous, then they will turn to other gods and serve them, and spurn Me and break My covenant.

"Then it shall come about when many evils and troubles have come upon them, that this song will testify before them as a witness (for it shall not be forgotten from the lips of their descendants); for I know their intent which they are developing today, before I have brought them into the land which I swore.

7C. When we speak of Moses as having "written" the Pentateuch or being its "author," it should be noted, as has previously been pointed out, that quite in accord with ancient Mesopotamian practice, this does not necessarily mean he himself wrote the words with his own hand, although such may have been the case. It is quite possible that the bulk of the Pentateuch was, like Hammurabi's Law Code, dictated to scribes. This in no way undermines the essential Mosaic authorship of the contents of the Pentateuch.

8C. THE LEGAL DOCUMENTS IN THESE PASSAGES ATTRIBUTE THEIR AUTHORSHIP TO MOSES in either the superscription or subscription:

Exodus - 12:1-28; 20-24, 25-31, 34

Leviticus - 1-7, 8, 13, 16, 17-26, 27

Numbers - 1, 2, 4, 6:1-21, 8:1-4, 8:5-22, 15, 19, 27:6-23, 28, 29, 30, 35

Deuteronomy - 1-33

9C. MOSES CERTAINLY WAS IN A POSITION TO WRITE THE PENTATEUCH. He grew up in Pharoah's house and was, as Stephen said, "learned in all the wisdom of the Egyptians" (Acts 7:22). All now agree that this learning would have included the knowledge of writing.

Moses had the information necessary for the project. It is likely that records of pre-Mosaic history existed; and had they been in the possession of the Hebrews, they would have certainly become accessible to Moses, the champion of his people. Had they been kept in the Egyptian archives from Joseph's time, they would have likewise been available to Moses during his early adulthood.

Moses also had the time to record this history. He spent 40 years in Egypt and 40 years in Midian, and there was plenty of time in both of these periods to author Genesis. 53/93, 94

That Moses was pre-eminently prepared to author a work such as the Pentateuch is witnessed by the following qualifications:

(a) *Education* - he was trained in the royal Egyptian court in their highly developed academic disciplines. This without a doubt included a knowledge of writing, for even the women's toilet articles of the time were inscribed.

(b) *Tradition* - he undoubtedly received the Hebrew traditions of their early history and encounters with God.

(c) *Geographical familiarity* - Moses possessed an intimate knowledge of the climate and geography of Egypt and Sinai as displayed in the Pentateuch.

(d) *Motivation* - as the founder of the Commonwealth of Israel, he had more than adequate incentive to provide the nation with concrete moral and religious foundations.

(e) *Time* - 40 long years of wandering in the Sinai wilderness easily allowed ample opportunity to write this work.

At a time when even uneducated slaves working at the Egyptian turquoise mines were inscribing their records on the tunnel walls, it is inconceivable that a man of Moses' background would fail to record the details of one of history's most significant epochs.

Kurt Sethe, one of the greatest authorities of this century on ancient Egypt, in attempting to find the father of one of the greatest contributions to the literary progress of civilization, the North Semitic script, mentions Moses as a possibility [*Vom Bilde Zum Buchstaben*, (1939), p. 56]. 46/23

2B. Witness of the Other Old Testament Books

These Old Testament verses record that the Torah or "the Law," was from Moses:

Joshua 8:32 speaks of "the Law of Moses, which he had written."

(Those of the following verses which are marked by an asterisk refer to an actual *written* "Law of Moses," not simply an oral tradition):

Joshua 1:7, 8*; 8:31*, 34*; 23:6*
I Kings 2:3*
II Kings 14:6*; 23:25
I Chronicles 22:13
II Chronicles 5:10; 23:18*; 25:4*; 30:16; 33:8; 34:14; 35:12*
Ezra 3:2; 6:18*; 7:6
Nehemiah 1:7, 8; 8:1*, 14*; 9:14; 10:29; 13:1*
Daniel 9:11, 13*
Malachi 4:4

3B. Witness of the New Testament

The New Testament writers also held that the Torah or "the Law" came from Moses.

The apostles believed that "Moses wrote for us a law." (Mark 12:19)

John was confident that "the Law was given through Moses." (John 1:17)

Paul, speaking of a Pentateuchal passage, asserts "Moses writes." (Rom. 10:5)

Other passages which insist on this include:

Luke 2:22; 20:28
John 1:45; 8:5; 9:29
Acts 3:22; 6:14; 13:39; 15:1, 21; 26:22; 28:23
I Corinthians 9:9
II Corinthians 3:15
Hebrews 9:19
Revelation 15:3

They also record that Jesus believed the Torah to be from Moses:

Mark 7:10; 10:3-5; 12:26
Luke 5:14; 16:29-31; 24:27, 44
John 7:19, 23

Especially in John 5:45-47 Jesus states unequivocally his belief that Moses wrote the Torah:

"Do not think that I will accuse you before the Father; the one who accuses you is Moses, in whom you have set your hope.

"For if you believed Moses, you would believe Me; for he wrote of Me.

"But if you do not believe his writings, how will you believe My words?"

Eissfeldt states:

"The name used in the New Testament clearly with reference to the whole Pentateuch—the Book of Moses—is certainly to be understood as meaning that Moses was the compiler of the Pentateuch." 20/158

2A. EXTERNAL EVIDENCE

1B. Jewish Tradition

R.H. Pfeiffer says:

"There is no reason to doubt that the Pentateuch was considered the divine revelation to Moses when it was canonized about 400 B.C." 85/133

1C. ECCLESIASTICUS, one of the books of the Apocrypha which was written about 180 B.C., gives this witness:

"All this is the covenant-book of God Most High, the law which Moses enacted to be the heritage of the assemblies of Jacob" Ecclesiasticus 24:23 (New English Bible).

2C. THE TALMUD, *(Baba Bathra,* 146), a Jewish commentary on the Law *(Torah),* dating from about 200 B.C., and the MISHNAH, *(Pirqe Aboth,* I, 1), a rabbinic interpretation and legislation dating from about 100 B.C., both attribute the *Torah* to Moses.

3C. Likewise, PHILO, the Jewish philosopher-theologian born approximately 20 A.D. held Mosaic authorship:

"But I will... tell the story of Moses as I have learned it, both from the sacred books, the wonderful monuments of his wisdom which he has left behind him, and from some of the elders of the nation." 51/279

4C. The first century A.D. Jewish historian FLAVIUS JOSEPHUS says in his *Josephus Against Apion* (11:8):

"For we have not an innumerable multitude of books among us, disagreeing from and contradicting one another (as the Greeks have) but only 22 books [our present 39], which are justly believed to be divine; and of them, five belong to Moses, which contain his laws, and the traditions of the origin of mankind till his death." 39/609

2B. Early Christian Tradition

1C. JUNILIUS, an imperial official in the court of Justinian I, Byzantine emperor from 527-565 A.D., held to the Mosaic authorship of the Pentateuch as can be seen from this dialogue between himself and one of his disciples, recorded in *De Partibus Divinae Legis:*

"CONCERNING THE WRITERS OF THE DIVINE BOOKS

Disciple: How do you know who are the writers of the divine books?

Master: In three ways. Either from the titles and prefaces...or from the titles alone...or from the tradition of the ancients, as Moses is believed to have written the first 5 books of the History; although the title does not say so, nor does he himself write, 'the Lord spake unto me,' but as of another, 'the Lord spake unto Moses.'" 28/44, 45

2C. **LEONTIUS OF BYZANTIUM** (sixth century A.D.) said in his treatise *Contra Mestorianos:*

"As for these five books, all bear witness that they are (the work) of Moses." 28/45

3C. **OTHER CHURCH FATHERS** attributing the Pentateuch to Moses in their lists of the Old Testament canon:

1. Melito, Bishop of Sardis	175 A.D.
2. Cyril of Jerusalem	348-386 A.D.
3. Hilary	366 A.D.
4. Rufinus	410 A.D.
5. Augustine	430 A.D.

4C. The Pentateuch is ascribed to Moses also in the following canonical lists of the early church.

1D. Dialogue of Timothy and Aquila

2D. The Synopsis (revised by Lagarde)

3D. List of the Apostolic Canons

4D. Innocent I - 417 A.D.

3B. Covenant-form Analysis

1C. INTRODUCTION

In 1954 George Mendenhall published an epochal article in which he described the ancient suzerainty treaties which were established between victorious Near Eastern kings and their vanquished subjects. He pointed out striking similarities between these treaties and certain treaty forms in the Hebrew Scriptures. Meredith Kline took his work further by demonstrating the correlation of these treaties to the Book of Deuteronomy as a whole.

The renowned archaeologist, G. Ernest Wright, introduces us to Mendenhall's study:

"Another major discovery within the realm of law which I venture to predict will stand the test of time is George E. Mendenhall's pioneer work on the formal background of the Mosaic covenant. This background, he has shown, is not to be found in the covenants of Bedouin society, as Johannes Pedersen had supposed. Instead it is to be found in the realm of international law, specifically in the suzerainty treaties of the Late Bronze Age found among the Hittite archives. This discovery has meant a number of things, of which I can mention only one. For the first time, we can gain a clearer perception of the way Deity was conceived in Israel and of the reason why certain types of language were permissible when used of him and others were not. The God of Israel was not the head of a pantheon which represented the primary powers of the natural world. He was first and foremost a suzerain, not a king among kings but the Emperor, the 'King of kings and Lord of lords' who had no equal. Consequently, the Hebrew term, *melek*, rarely used of God before the time of David, was not strictly applicable to him because it had received its primary political definition from the rival Bronze Age dynasts of Syro-Palestinian city-states. The suzerainty of Israel's God concerned the whole world, and the focus of attention was not on the life of nature but on the administration of a vast empire. The language was thus closely geared to history and historical perspectives." 86/150

2C. DEUTERONOMY AND THE SECOND MILLENNIUM B.C. TREATY HITTITE SUZERAINTY TREATY OF THE SECOND MILLENNIUM B.C.

"1) *Preamble or title*, identifying the author of the covenant.

2) *Historical prologue* or retrospect, mentioning previous relations between the two parties involved; past benefactions by the suzerain are a basis for the vassal's gratitude and future obedience.

3) *Stipulations* basic and detailed; the obligations laid upon the vassal by the sovereign.

4) (a). *Deposition* of a copy of the covenant in the vassal's sanctuary and (b). *Periodic public reading* of the covenant terms to the people.

5) *Witnesses*, a long list of gods invoked to witness the covenant.

6) (a). *Curses*, invoked upon the vassal if he breaks the covenant and, (b). *Blessings*, invoked upon the vassal if he keeps the covenant.

Nearly all the known treaties of the fourteenth/thirteenth centuries B.C. follow this pattern closely. Sometimes some elements are omitted, but the order of them is almost invariable, whenever the original texts are sufficiently well preserved to be analyzed. This is, therefore, a stable form in the period concerned. Earlier than this, the pattern was apparently somewhat different." 42/92, 93

DEUTERONOMIC COVENANT

Sinai Covenant in Deuteronomy

1) *Preamble* - 1:1-5

2) *Historical prologue* - 1:6-3:29

3) *Stipulations* - 4-11 (basic); 12-26 (detailed)

4) a. *Deposition of text* - 31:9, 24-26

b. *Public reading* - 31:10-12

5) *Witnesses* - since pagan gods are excluded here, ancient oriental godlists are absent. Moses' song could have been the witness (31:16-30; 32:1-47), as Kitchen suggests.

6) *Curses and Blessings* - 28:1-14 (blessings); 28:15-68 (curses); the sequence here is blessings—curses—witness as opposed to the witness—curses—blessings sequence of ancient oriental treaties, possibly due to the different nature of the witness here in Deuteronomy. 42/96, 97

The close correspondence between the two has led Kitchen to observe that "there can be no serious doubt (on present evidence) that the greater bulk of Deuteronomy coincides very closely indeed with the fourteenth- and thirteenth-century treaties, even more strikingly than do Exodus and Joshua. The essential difference in literary nature is that the Near Eastern documents are formal legal documents of the covenants concerned, whereas Deuteronomy is cast as the report of an actual ceremony of renewing a covenant in acts and speech." 217/3

Kline displays equal confidence:

"In the light of the evidence now surveyed, it would seem indisputable that the Book of Deuteronomy, not in the form of some imaginary original core but precisely in the integrity of its present form, the only one for which there is any objective evidence, exhibits the structure of the ancient suzerainty treaties in the unity and completeness of their classic pattern." 44/41

But Kline and Kitchen are not alone in their observations. D.J. McCarthy has produced the most thorough examination of the ancient treaties in his scholarly *Treaty and Covenant*. Although he identifies more readily with the radical critics, the comparison has been unavoidable for him:

"Is there, therefore, a text in the Old Testament which exemplifies with sufficient fullness the treaty form? For an affirmative answer we need only look at the basic elements of the Book of Deuteronomy." 220/110

He goes on to assert that Deuteronomy's basic components "present an organic structure which is that of the treaty." 220/110

Elsewhere McCarthy emphatically states that "there can be no doubt that Deuteronomy does show some kind of relationship to the literary forms of these treaties." 219/230

Even G. von Rad, the form critic who dates Deuteronomy sometime after 701 B.C. admits:

"Comparison of the ancient Near Eastern treaties, especially those made by the Hittites in the fourteenth and thirteenth centuries B.C., with passages in the Old Testament has revealed so many things in common between the two, particularly in the matter of the form, that there must be some connection between these suzerainty treaties and the exposition of the details of Jahweh's covenant with Israel given in certain passages in the Old Testament." 52/132

The most recent extensive study of this issue has been undertaken by Weinfeld. While he goes to great length to maintain a late date for Deuteronomy, he is forced to acknowledge:

"The major sections of the Hittite state treaties. . . are all found in the book of Deuteronomy." 221/61

3C. DEUTERONOMY AND THE FIRST MILLENNIUM B.C. TREATIES

If we find no appreciable differences between the treaty forms of the first and second millennia B.C., then there is no reason on the basis of this particular investigation to assign to Deuteronomy the traditional early date as opposed to the sixth-seventh century B.C. date given by the radical critics. But this is not the case.

As early as 1954, Mendenhall recognized that the covenant type which is found in the second millennium B.C. in Deuteronomy "cannot be proven to have survived the downfall of the great empires of the late second millennium B.C. When empires again arose, notably Assyria, the structure of the covenant by which they bound their vassals is entirely different. Even in Israel, the writer submits that the older form of covenant was no longer widely known after the united monarchy." 47/30

The quite conspicuous differences which Mendenhall speaks of can be detailed thus:
1) Order
   (a) The earlier form almost invariably places divine witnesses between stipulations and curses; this is *never* found in later treaties. 42/95
   (b) The highly consistent order of the earlier treaties is replaced by more randomness. 42/96
2) Content
   (a) The customary historical prologue of the second millennium

B.C. is totally absent in the later treaties. 42/95, 44/43, 47/56, 216/84

(b) The first millennium B.C. treaties are also lacking in the earlier usage of blessings in conjunction with the cursings. 42/96, 44/42

What are the immediate implications of this?

Kline says:

"The implications of the new evidence for the questions of the antiquity and authenticity of Deuteronomy must not be suppressed. Though the tradition of the suzerainty form is attested down into the first millennium B.C., the full classic pattern is documented only in the Syro-Anatolian treaties of the fourteenth-thirteenth centuries B.C. Accordingly, the customary higher critical view of Deuteronomy's origins can be maintained only by scholars able to persuade themselves that a process of accretion in the first millennium B.C., with more or less of a conscious editorial assist, managed to reproduce exactly a complex legal pattern belonging to the second millennium B.C. To preserve any semblance of plausibility the hypothesis of these scholars must be so drastically modified in the direction of a greater antiquity for so much more of Deuteronomy as to leave practically meaningless any persistent insistence on a final seventh century B.C. edition of the book." 44/15

The Old Testament covenant form demonstrates an amazing correspondence to the pattern of the late-second millennium treaties as opposed to the pattern of the first millennium treaties. The Sinai covenant and its renewals *must* be classified with the former, for with the latter it shares only the essential common core (title, stipulation, witnesses, and curses). Recent evidence has only buttressed Mendenhall's original view that the Sinai covenant closely parallels the late-second millennium treaties and not those of the first millennium. 42/98

4C. CONCLUSION

Even if we may conclude with confidence that Deuteronomy uniquely reflects the covenant form of the second millennium B.C., does this give us reason to conclude that it was necessarily authored then? Kitchen answers with a resounding *yes*, reasoning that if Deuteronomy and the other passages displaying this form "first took fixed literary forms only in the ninth to sixth centuries B.C. and onward, why and how should their writers (or redactors) so easily be able to reproduce covenant-forms that had fallen out of customary use 300 to 600 years earlier (*i.e.*, after about 1200 B.C.), and entirely fail to reflect the first-millennium covenant-forms that were commonly used in their own day?" 42/100

In a recent article, Kitchen presents a forceful summary of the body of evidence we have considered:

"The present writer cannot see any legitimate way of escape from the crystal-clear evidence of the correspondence of Deuteronomy with the remarkably stable treaty or covenant form of the fourteenth-thirteenth centuries B.C. Two points follow here. First, the basic structure of Deuteronomy and much of the content that gives specific character to that structure *must* constitute a recognizable literary entity; second, this is a literary entity *not* of the eighth or seventh century B.C. but rather from ca. 1200 B.C. *at latest*. Those who so choose may wish to claim that this or that individual 'law' or concept appears to be of later date than the late thirteenth century B.C.; but it is no longer methodologically permissible gaily to remove essential features of the covenant-form on a mere preconception (especially if of nineteenth-century [A.D.] vintage) of what is merely thought—not proven—to be late." 217/4

And Kline concludes:

"Accordingly, while it is necessary to recognize a substantial continuity in pattern between the earlier and later treaties, it is proper to distinguish the Hittite treaties of the second millennium B.C. as the 'classic' form. And without any doubt the Book of Deuteronomy belongs to the classic stage in this documentary evolution. Here then is significant confirmation of the prima facie case for the Mosaic origin of the Deuteronomic treaty of the great King." 44/43

Many scholars will allow that archaeology has demonstrated the "essential reliability" of many historical facts within the biblical record, but they still contend that these facts, along with legend and myth were passed "orally" for a millennium or more. But Deuteronomy's form demonstrates that it had to be written in the middle of the second millennium B.C. Otherwise no account can be given for its literary format.

3A. THE ANTIQUITY OF THE ALLEGED D SOURCE

1B. Introduction

The crucial role which Deuteronomy plays in the entire documentary scheme is recognized by all. Radical critic George Dahl acknowledges this truth:

"By unanimous consent this book is accorded a central and pivotal position in the study of Old Testament history, literature and religion. The epochal reconstruction of the course of Hebrew history, which it has been the supreme service and merit of critical Biblical scholarship to mediate, depends for its validity first of all upon the essential correctness of our dating of Deuteronomy. In particular, the identification of the so-called Fifth Book of Moses with the book of the law mentioned in 2 Kings 22f. is generally regarded as the very keystone of the arch of Old Testament research." 94/360

"The Code of Deuteronomy," Rowley concurs, "is...of vital importance in Pentateuchal criticism, since it is primarily by relation to it that the other documents are dated." 54/29

There is also little disagreement among scholars of all positions that the book which was discovered in the temple in 621 B.C., sparking the reforms of King Josiah (II Kings 22 and 23), was essentially the book which we now call Deuteronomy. But there is much disagreement over the date of its original authorship: the radical critics assign it to a time not long before the 621 discovery, while others insist that it must be dated from the time of Moses.

2B. Statements

1C. STATEMENTS FREQUENTLY RECURRING

Von Rad, speaking of Deuteronomy, tells us that the most frequent phrases show the most important thoughts.

Research into the most common phrases reveals the following groupings:

(a) memories of the past in Egypt.

(b) Yahweh's covenant for protection from Canaanite influence in the land.

(c) entry into the land.

(d) national unity (with no mention of the split kingdom of the seventh century B.C.).

(e) sin and cleansing (all of an exceedingly different nature from the eighth century B.C. denunciations for moral evils).

(f) blessings when the land will be entered. 123/28-36

Pederson describes the purpose of the entire book thus: "The main object of the book, in its present shape, is to protect the Israelite community against Canaanite influence." 82/27

These theme ideas sharply contrast with any period in the first millennium B.C., but harmonize perfectly with the period the book claims for itself—immediately preceding the entrance into Canaan in the second millennium B.C.

2C. GEOGRAPHICAL STATEMENTS

Manley's words quite aptly summarize the geographical attestations for the antiquity of this book:

"When we review the geographical data as a whole," Manley observes, "the details appear to be much too accurate to be due either to chance or to oral tradition. The account of the journeyings in chapters i-iii is altogether realistic and quite unlike an introduction prefixed to a collection of old laws; it bears every sign of originality. The views described and the features of the Moabite country reproduced must have been seen by human eyes; the antiquarian notes also belong to the period and are not the result of archaeological research.

"The omissions also are significant: there is no hint of Jerusalem, nor of Ramah, dear to Samuel's heart, not even of Shiloh, where the tabernacle came to rest. Everything points to its historical character and early date." 123/64

3B. Style

Radical critic Norman Habel succinctly phrases this accusation that the D writing is different from the rest of the Pentateuch:

"The style and jargon of Deuteronomy are very obvious. They stand in sharp contrast to the literary characteristics of the rest of the Pentateuch. When compared with Genesis through Numbers, Deuteronomy presents a new world of terms, thought patterns, groups of expressions, and stereotype idioms." 107/12

Dahl mentions another distinctive aspect of this book's style:

"The developed oratorical style of Deuteronomy, smooth, flowing and sustained, presupposes a long literary history behind it." 94/372

But the alleged differences in style and the contradictions between Deuteronomy and the rest of the Pentateuch are mainly caused by their respective standpoints. Leviticus, for example is a codified law book which the priests are to use, while Deuteronomy is made up of popular addresses. Therefore, we are not surprised to find that in Deuteronomy Moses uses an oratorical style, edits details, emphasizes practical issues and often includes directions regarding the entrance of the Israelites into Canaan. 53/113

And to say with Dahl (as do many scholars) that the oratorical style indicates a long period of development is so irresponsible as to barely merit a response. It would seem probable that a book recording the speeches of a great orator would display a "developed oratorical style" without needing a long period of evolution. Besides that, examples abound of literature with a smooth and developed style which has no longer period of development.

A final stylistic point is emphasized by Manley:

"The same style can to some extent be perceived in some of the earlier speeches of Moses recorded in the Pentateuch." 123/27

4B. Antiquity of Legislation

The radical argument for a late date based on legislative consideration is competently related by Dahl:

"In general,....it would appear that the relationship of Deuteronomy lies in the general direction of expansion and development of the earlier laws. Its code reflects a distinctly more advanced and complicated community life than that underlying Ex. 21-23 (34)." 94/367

G.T. Manley, a respected British Old Testament scholar, conducted a detailed and thorough study of each of the Pentateuchal laws to discover if this bold claim were indeed true. His startling conclusions are quoted:

"It has to be admitted that the Wellhausen scheme breaks down upon a close examination of the laws.

"1. The absolute dating has no foundation. There is nothing specific to connect the laws of JE with the early monarchy, those of Deuteronomy with 621 B.C., nor those of P with the exile.

"On the contrary, laws of great antiquity are found in all these, and some are peculiar to each—rather they bear the appearance of contemporary layers of material.

"2. The statement that Deuteronomy xii-xxvi is an 'expansion' of the JE code is misleading. A few of the old laws and precepts are repeated, more of the same type are omitted; where a law is modified there is no sign that it has been adapted to the needs of the seventh century. The material peculiar to Deuteronomy includes much that is demonstrably old, and nothing manifestly of a late origin.

"The two groups of laws appear to be complementary and roughly contemporary.

"3. The argument for the chronological sequence JE, D, P, fares no better; it cannot rightly be said that Deuteronomy shows dependence on JE and ignorance of P; it has some elements in common with both, rather more with the latter.

"The laws of Lv. xi concerning food reappear in Dt. xiv in a different form, but one which shows no difference of period. Deuteronomy asserts the existence of a priestly law concerning leprosy, and assumes the existence of laws of sacrifice, such as are found in P.

"4. The laws of Dt. xii-xxvi follow naturally upon the preceding discourse in chapters v-xi and appear quite suitable to the place and occasion stated in iv. 44-49. The parenetic additions also, where they occur, belong to the period when the deliverance from the bondage of Egypt was a living memory, and are quite different from the exhortations which Isaiah addressed to a disillusioned and sophisticated people." 123/94, 95

Later in the same monograph (*The Book of the Law*), Manley adds these observations:

"If the author be a reformer addressing the people of Judah groaning under the evils of Manasseh's rule, he is wonderfully successful in concealing the fact. He encumbers his programme of reform with a number of obsolete, impracticable and irrelevant laws; he betrays no hint of the divided kingdom, or of the promises to David; and whilst the possibility of a king is envisaged, the civil law entirely ignores his existence.

"The author of Deuteronomy issues laws which he expects to be obeyed; this is not the attitude of the reforming prophets, who call upon Israel to repent over laws that have been broken. This contrast with the prophetic utterances goes down to the very heart of the book, and colours the legislation throughout.

"From this aspect also the only time which provides a suitable background for the legislation is the pre-prophetic period." 123/121

5B. Statements Alleged to Oppose Mosaic Authorship and Antiquity of D

(a) The phrase "beyond the Jordan" to refer to the region east of the Jordan. It is contended that, since Deuteronomy claims to have been written in that region, "beyond the Jordan" could only refer to Canaan proper, on the western side. However, it has been adequately demonstrated that this phrase was simply a technical term for that region, even as it was known as Paraea ("The Other-side Land") during the New Testament times and has more recently been known as Transjordania (even to its inhabitants). 11/244, 123/49

(b) The phrase "until this day." Here it is urged that this indicates a great lapse of time since the event mentioned. Yet in each instance of its usage, it is highly appropriate that Moses use this phrase in light of only the previous forty year period, to indicate that a situation has persisted until these final days of his life. 11/243

(c) The account of Moses' death in Deuteronomy 34. But it is quite reasonable to assume that Joshua included this account, just as often an obituary is added to the final work of a man of great letters. 11/244 And it is worthy of note here that the other events of the book cover all of Moses' life, and never transgress that limit. 123/172

6B. Centralized Worship
1C. DOCUMENTARY ASSUMPTION

The adherents to the Documentary Hypothesis assume that at the time of Moses there was a plurality of sanctuaries that were permitted or legitimate. Then at the time of Josiah (621 B.C.) there was a religious revival and the major reform was the establishing of a central sanctuary in Jerusalem.

The main function of the Code of Deuteronomy, which was found in the temple at the time of Josiah, was to put an end to the various places of worship.

It is held that Exodus 20:24 is an "old law" which commanded the building of altars in various parts of the land. 80/136-138. These locations of worship were appropriate and the Israelites were to worship Yahweh at these sanctuaries. Then, at the publication of Deuteronomy, the worshipping was to be permitted only at the central sanctuary in Jerusalem and worship at the multiplicity of sanctuaries was forbidden.

2C. BASIC ANSWER

1D. "You shall make an altar of earth for Me, and you shall sacrifice on it your burnt offerings and your peace offerings, your sheep and your oxen; in every place where I cause My name to be remembered, I will come to you and bless you" (Exodus 20:24).

Nowhere does this verse speak of sanctuaries. It mentions only altars. Since this is the first legal directive about worship in the Pentateuch (except for the second commandment), it is to be connected with the patriarchal and Mosaic period. Thus "in every place where I cause My name to be remembered" refers to such places as the plain of Moreh (Genesis 12:16), Mount Moriah (Genesis 22:2), Beersheba (Genesis 26:23), Bethel (Genesis 35:1) and Rephidim (Exodus 17:8, 15).

To this G.T. Manley adds that "the statement that when Deuteronomy was composed the old law 'was revoked, and worship centralized in Jerusalem' is also contrary to the facts and inconsistent with the theory itself. Would any author engaged on an 'expansion' of the JE code revoke an important element in it without a word of explanation?" 87/131

"If the legislator," writes G.C. Aalders, "was thinking of sanctuaries, of which no mention whatever had been made previously, he undoubtedly would have indicated it more clearly. So the text certainly does not mean a plurality of sanctuaries; at most it refers to a multiplicity of altars." 1/72

2D. To the above, one could say that a plurality of altars speaks of a multiplicity of sanctuaries.

The phrase "in every place where I cause My name to be remembered" does not necessarily mean that this is done simultaneously.

Aalders points out that "as a rule the Hebrew noun *kol*, when combined with another noun provided with the definite article, as is the case here, indicates rather a number of persons or things *in succession*, especially when the noun added is singular. We point to the well-known *kol hayom* of which 'always' is the ordinary sense, that is to say: 'all successive days'; to Ex. i. 22 where 'every son' and 'every daughter' naturally refers to all children born successively; to Gn. xx. 13 where 'every place whither we shall come' cannot but indicate a number of places reached by Abraham and Sarah in succession; and to Dt. xi. 24; I Sa. iii. 17, etc. It is therefore incorrect to state that the expression 'in all places where I record my name' *must* be understood of a number of places of worship existing at the same time." 1/73

3D. It is interesting that the exhortation chapters (5-11) of Deuteronomy do not once mention the place of worship. Deuteronomy 12 demands, not the unification of worship, but its purification. It needed to be protected from pagan and idolatrous influence and cleansed from the idols and abominations that had defiled it.

4D. Deuteronomy 12:13, 14 contains a warning about the central sanctuary:

"Be careful that you do not offer your burnt offerings in every cultic place you see, but in the place which the Lord chooses in one of your tribes, there you shall offer your burnt offerings, and there you shall do all that I command you."

The documentary assumption is that "in every cultic place you see" refers to the previous multiple sanctuaries that are now being forbidden. However, 12:15 must give it another connotation:

"However, you may slaughter and eat meat within any of your gates, whatever you desire, according to the blessing of the Lord your God which He has given you; the unclean and the clean may eat of it, as of the gazelle and the deer."

Verses 13 and 14 are limited by the word "however" in 15. Verse 13 is speaking of "burnt offerings" which are to be presented in a sanctuary whose existence is presupposed. But, the phrase "in every place" in verse 13 does not refer to a condemnation of previous altars but to be taken synonymously with "within any of your gates" in verse 15. Therefore, the meaning of verses 13-15 is that cattle can be slaughtered anywhere but burnt offerings are not to be presented everywhere.

Contrary to the documentary assumption verse 13 does not "require that there should be a concentration of worship in contrast to a previous time when various cult-places were legitimate, but it simply cautions the Israelite not to offer burnt offerings wherever he might wish, and limits these offerings to the one sanctuary whose existence is presupposed." 1/75

5D. There are many situations that presuppose a central sanctuary prior to Josiah's reformation in 621 B.C.: "the house of God" Judges 18:31; "the temple of the Lord" I Samuel 1:9, 3:3.

The following references refer to a simple sanctuary: I Samuel 1:3;

Exodus 23:17, 19; 34:23, 26 (cf. Deuteronomy 16:16). These are directly connected with the sanctuary: I Samuel 21:4; Exodus 25:30; Leviticus 24:5; I Samuel 21:9 (cf. Exodus 28:6).

6D. I Kings 8:4 records that the elders and priests brought the ark and all the holy vessels to the tabernacle. Aalders writes that "to understand how any one can imagine that even at that time a multiplicity of sanctuaries existed and was deemed legitimate. The beautiful temple with its glorious wealth and grandeur must naturally have occupied such a prominent place in the religious life of the people that it is utterly inconceivable how it could have had a number of rival sanctuaries. This is confirmed by the proceedings of Jeroboam, the first ruler of the Northern Kingdom, who feared lest the heart of the people might turn again unto Rehoboam, the king of Judah, if they went up to sacrifice in the house of the Lord at Jerusalem (I Ki. xii. 27). He therefore instituted two places of worship, one in Beth-el and the other in Dan (verses 28 f.). This proves that in his days the people were accustomed to bring their offerings to the temple, and that the temple was the central sanctuary for the whole people of Israel. It could not therefore have been necessary in the days of King Josiah to concentrate the cult at the temple, since the temple had been the uncontested centre of worship from its foundation." 1/79, 80

7D. The text of II Kings 22:8-13 beseeches us to conclude that the "book of the law" which was found was an old book. The phrase "our fathers have not listened to the words of this book" (II Kings 22:13) and this being the cause of the wrath of God indicate its antiquity.

G.T. Manley says: "It was at once recognized as the 'book of the law,' which suggests that such a book was known to have existed, but had been lost or forgotten. These things could not have been if the book were known by some to be the work of men still living." 87/125

8D. There is no apparent close connection between Deuteronomy and the events surrounding Josiah. They agree in their denouncing of the sins of wizardry and idolatry but these same sins are also denounced in other parts of the Pentateuch. "But certain evils of the time," writes Manley, "such as the $k^e m\bar{a}r\hat{i}m$ ('idolatrous priests'), though known to Hosea (x. 5) and Zephaniah (i. 4, 5), and put down by Josiah (II Ki. xxiii. 5), are ignored in Deuteronomy. The same is true of the burning of incense to Baal (Ho. ii. 13, xii. 2; II Ki. xxiii. 5), and of the 'sun-images' (Is. xvii. 8, xxvii. 9; II Ch. xxxiv. 4)." 87/125

"On the other hand," continues Manley, "there are many commands in Deuteronomy, such as the destruction of the Amalekites and the assigning of the cities of refuge, which are not mentioned as part of Josiah's reform, and would have been anachronisms at that time." 87/125

9D. Deuteronomy 27:1-8. One of the most formidable barriers to the documentary assumption of centralization is the command in Deuteronomy 27:1-8 in which Moses is told to build an altar on Mount Ebal. This passage uses the same words as Exodus 20:24 about an altar that Deuteronomy was supposed to forbid or revoke.

The construction of this altar, commanded by Yahweh (Deuteronomy 27) is accomplished in Joshua 8:30, 31. It is no wonder that S.R. Driver recognizes that this passage produces "considerable critical difficulties" and that "it stands in a most unsuitable place." 80/294

10D. Sacrifices at "altars" and "high places"

The writer is indebted to the publisher and author of *The Book of the Law* for allowing the generous quoting of the following treatment of the Hebrew *bamah*—"high places."

LOCAL SANCTUARIES

"The term 'local sanctuaries' is somewhat vague, and if used loosely is apt to mix together things which differ, and which need separate treatment. The information at our disposal concerning local altars is scanty, and the shortage of facts encourages speculation. It is tempting to group together every place of sacred memories or where a sacrifice is recorded, and to reckon them all as permanent sanctuaries, each with a complement of sacrificing priests who followed a particular ritual and built up its own body of traditions. The wiser course, however, is to adhere as closely as possible to the record and to observe certain obvious distinctions, such as between acts on the one hand which claimed divine sanction and, on the other, cases where the people 'did evil in the sight of the Lord.'

"We shall begin with a brief survey of what is recorded of sacrifices, (1) at altars and (2) at high places, in the books of Joshua to 2 Samuel, that is, before the temple was built.

"In these books there are seven instances of an 'altar' being erected, two in connection with theophanies (Jdg. vi. 26-28, xiii. 20), and five on other occasions (Jos. viii. 30; Jdg. xxi. 2-4; I Sa. vii. 17, xiv. 35; 2 Sa. xxiv. 25). Moreover there is the statement in Jos. ix. 27 concerning the Gibeonites serving the 'altar of the Lord,' presumably at the tabernacle, and the story of the 'altar of witness' in Jos. xxii.

"It is a curious fact, and may be only a coincidence, that both in these books and in the legislation of Deuteronomy, the plural 'altars' occurs only once, and then in each case in reference to those of the Canaanites (Jdg. ii. 2; Dt. xii. 2).

"We read also of sacrifices at Bethlehem (I Sa. xvi. 5, xx. 29) and Gilgal (I Sa. xiii. 8) and by the men of Beth-shemesh in the presence of the ark (I Sa. vi. 15).

"Gideon's altar was still standing when the story was written, and that at Shechem at the time of Joshua's death (Jos. xxiv. 26); the site of David's altar was used for the temple. The others fade into oblivion.

"The 'high place' *(bāmāh)* is not the same as the 'altar.' The two words differ in origin and meaning and call for separate treatment.

"The word *bāmāh* is absent from Joshua and Judges, but in I Samuel two are mentioned.

"There was one at Ramah to which Samuel 'went up' (I Sa. ix. 13), and one nearby the 'hill of God,' from which a band of musical prophets came 'down' (I Sa. x. 5). On the former was a 'guest chamber' where Samuel entertained thirty persons at a sacrificial feast. The language employed shows that these *bāmôth* were, or were situated upon, eminences.

"This ends our information about sacrifices offered to Yahweh, which are authorized and approved. When under the judges the people 'forsook the Lord and served Baal and Ashtaroth' (Jdg. ii. 13), this was something quite different, and was condemned.

"A new phase is introduced with the building of the temple; the tone changes, and the word *bāmāh* begins to acquire a new and evil connotation. A transition can be seen in I Ki. iii. 1-4, where the writer tells us that 'the people still sacrificed in high places because there was no house built to the name of the Lord until those days'; this practice on the part of 'the people' is deprecated rather than condemned.

"We next read that Solomon walked 'in the statutes of David his father; only he sacrificed and burned incense in high places,' which also involves a tone of disapproval. The writer adds: 'The king went to Gibeon to sacrifice there; for that was the great high place' (I Ki. iii. 4).

"Here the LXX translates ὑψηλοτάτη καὶ μεγάλη (highest and great), as if its lofty elevation was in mind (Gibeon being the highest point in the region); but possibly the reference is to the presence of the tabernacle there (cf. II Ch. i. 1-3). Up to this point the notion of height lingers about the word bāmāh; it now disappears, and it comes to represent some kind of structure which can be 'built' (I Ki. xiv. 23), and destroyed and rebuilt II Ki. xxi. 3), in a city or in a gateway (II Ki. xxiii. 8).

"The continued existence of the bāmôth is considered a blot on the record of otherwise good kings; the building of them by the people is condemned outright (I Ki. xiv. 22-24), a condemnation passed equally upon the bēth-bāmôth, whatever their exact nature may have been (I Ki. xii. 31; II Ki. xvii. 29, xxiii. 19).

"This disapproval cannot be attributed merely to the Deuteronomic bias of the author, for it is expressed with great vigour by the prophets also (Ho. viii. 11, x. 1; Am. iii. 14, iv. 4-6, v. 4-6; Mi. i. 7; Is. ii. 8).

"The ground of objection has no relevance to a centralizing law, but is to the idolatry and corruption introduced by syncretism with the Canaanite religion, against which stern warnings had been given not only in Dt. xii. 29-32, but earlier in Ex. xxxiv. 12-16 (J).

"In the northern kingdom the pure religion of Yahweh was threatened with extinction by the royal patronage of the Phoenician Ba'al worship under Ahab and Jezebel. This was fiercely contested by Elijah; the altars of Yahweh to which he referred (I Ki. xix. 10) may have been erected by pious Israelites who were prevented from going up to Jerusalem to worship, or were possibly some of more ancient origin.

"Archaeology has little to add to this picture. Canaanite shrines which have been discovered at Gezer and elsewhere belong to the pre-Israelite period, and 'it still requires explanation why no Hebrew high place or other shrine for worship, whether of Yahweh or of some "strange god," is known from the period of Hebrew domination and the area of Hebrew occupation in Palestine.'

"This is the historical background, cleared of conjecture, against which Wellhausen's interpretations must be judged." 87/128-131

11D. Aalders concludes: "The advocates of the documentary theory criticize it as 'subjective history'; but such a verdict is not scientific. On the contrary, we must apply the accusation to the theory itself, which having forced an interpretation upon the Pentateuchal code which has absolutely no foundation in the wording of the law, rewrites history in order to bring the facts in harmony with this interpretation; and finally assigns all historical evidence discordant with its supposition to a 'deuteronomic' redactor! Against such a method the most energetic protest must be raised." 1/81

7B. See the following section for information on the antiquity of P and the tabernacle.

8B. Conclusion

On the basis of the internal evidence, we are left with a number of extremely difficult problems if we tenaciously retain the late-date position for D. Besides the problems mentioned above, we must ask other questions of those holding to a seventh century B.C. date. Since the author was clearly a preacher of distinction and of power (even founding a 'Deuteronomic' school of writers, according to the documentarians), why are we left with no trace of his name or person in the mid-first millennium B.C.? If he is such an effective reformer, why does he only denounce the sins of his ancestors? If his code of rules is intended to revoke an old Mosaic law, why does he ascribe them to Moses himself? If his purpose is to centralize worship in Jerusalem, why does he never show a knowledge of its existence? And why would he hide his book in the temple? 123/142

Moreover, given that it is of a late date and thus a forgery, Raven has discussed the "many persons in Judah who had powerful motives for exposing this forgery if it was one. The wicked people whom the book condemned would have seized the opportunity of condemning it as a forgery." 53/112

4A. THE ANTIQUITY OF THE ALLEGED P SOURCE

1B. Documentary Assumption

Driver has asserted:

"The pre-Exilic period shows no indications of P being in operation." 18/136

And Wellhausen has confidently affirmed:

"To any one who knows anything about history it is not necessary to prove that the so-called Mosaic theocracy, which nowhere suits the circumstances of the earlier periods, and of which the prophets, even in their most ideal delineations of the Israelite state as it ought to be have not the faintest shadow of an idea, is, so to speak, a perfect fit for post-exilian Judaism, and had its actuality only there." 63/151

2B. Basic Answer

1C. We may discover if the Priestly writing is indeed a "perfect fit" for the post-exilic period by testing P in light of the writings of Ezra, Nehemiah, Esther, Haggai, Zechariah, and Malachi. If its ideas may be shown to be harmonious with these writers and contradictory to the earlier ones, the radical claim will be strengthened.

1D. Features present in P, but absent from the post-exilic period:

tabernacle
ark, ten commandments, Urim and Thummim
day of atonement
cities of refuge
test of adultery by ordeal
wave offerings
Korban

2D. Features present in P and in the pre-exilic period, but absent from the post-exilic period:

circumcision, which is heavily emphasized in pre-exilic Joshua and I and II Samuel
significance of blood
leprosy
Nazarites
various offerings

3D. Features present in P and in both periods:
sabbath
passover

feast of unleavened bread
feast of tabernacles

4D. Features absent from P, yet prominent in post-exilic period:

divine name "Yahweh of hosts"—86 times in post-exilic authors
singing and music as central in worship
scribes
use of sackcloth
designation of central sanctuary as the "temple"
mention of legislation concerning the post-exilic industrial revolution
    112/39
city of Jerusalem 10/196-199

The radical critics have failed to adequately deal with any of these astonishing discrepancies when assigning to P a date in the sixth century B.C. O.T. Allis is forced to conclude:

"The claim that the Priest Code fits the post-exilic period like a glove is as little justified as the claim that it does not fit the pre-exilic period." 10/201

2C. INTERNAL EVIDENCE AND P'S RELATION TO THE OTHER SOURCES

If P is the last source to be recorded, it follows that no other sources would show a knowledge of P. Many such statements have been issued, such as the declaration by Driver, "nor is the legislation of P presupposed in Deuteronomy." 18/137

However, the following facts make it difficult to honestly affirm that P was unknown until the sixth century B.C.

1D. Material dealing with Aaron is usually assigned to document P. According to Brightman, "Aaron is missing from J and only incidental in E." This is accomplished by deleting all 13 occurrences in J. 96/459

3D. *Deuteronomy 14:3-20* - a passage almost identical to one in Leviticus, forcing Driver to acknowledge:

"That it is borrowed by D from P—or at least from a priestly collection of *toroth*—rather than conversely, appears from certain features of style which connect it with P and not with Deuteronomy.... If so, however, one part of P was in existence when Deuteronomy was written." 18/137, 138

3D. The following list definitely substantiates the antiquity of the law and shows that P was known in the pre-exilic times.

Deuteronomy 15:1 - the year of release (as in Leviticus 25:2)
Deuteronomy 23:9, 10 - ceremonial impurity (as in Leviticus 15)
Deuteronomy 24:8 - a law of leprosy given to the priests (Leviticus 13 and 14)
Amos 2:11, 12 - Nazarites forbidden wine (Numbers 6:1-21 [P])
Amos 4:5 - proscription of leaven in sacrifices (Leviticus 2:11)
Amos 5:22 - burnt, meat, and peace offerings (Leviticus 7 and 8)
Amos 4:5 - free will offering (Leviticus 7, etc.)
Amos 5:21 - solemn assembly (Leviticus 23, etc.)
Hosea 12:9 - dwelling in booths (Leviticus 23:42) 42/150, 151

The list could be extended but the point has been established. We must decide with Archer that "already in 755 B.C. there was a written body of law, including both P and D, and labeled by the prophet himself as the Torah of Yahweh (Amos 2:4), and accepted by his public as an authentic and authoritative body of legislation binding upon them." 11/151

And Allis effectively expresses this conclusion:

"When the critics reject those statements in the record which indicate that the law was ancient, they are not only guilty of tampering with the evidence, but they also make the denunciations uttered by Israel's historians and prophets of her failure to keep the law both farcical and cruel. For these teachers of Israel insisted that all of Israel's sufferings were due to the failure of the people to keep a law which, if the critics are correct, was unknown to them." 10/202

3C. GENESIS 17

Samuel R. Külling in "The Dating of the So-Called 'P-sections' in Genesis," an abstract of his book published under the title *Zur Datierung Der "Genesis-P-Stucke" Namentlich Des Kapitels Genesis XVII*, writing about Genesis 17 and circumcision says that the "form, style and content of Genesis 17 belong to the 2nd millenium [sic] B.C. and have nothing to do with post-exilic writers. As Mendenhall (Law and Covenant, 1955), Baltzer (Das Bundesformular, 1960), M.G. Kline (Treaty of the Great King, 1963), have done, and previous to this Wiener (Studies in Biblical Law, 1904), among others, I draw a parallel to the Vassal Treaties and show how Genesis 17, as to construction and style, is similar to these treaties of the middle of the 2nd millenium [sic] B.C., which no longer exist in this form after the year 1200 B.C. There is, moreover, no motive for reproducing the chapter in this form later in view of the fact that the structure of the treaties of later periods is different." 196/68

4C. GENESIS 9

This section attributed to the P source is said to be late and is a reference to the Persian period. The critic often says that the eating and spilling of blood are a rejection of the holy war.

Külling concludes that the same reasons for "rejecting a priestly tendency writing for the exilic-postexilic period, also applies to a Persian period: 'Just why an exilic-postexilic priest should select from the food laws one that allows the eating of meat without blood is quite unexplainable, especially because no particular reason is given by the writer. For the exilic-postexilic period it appears superfluous to grant a general permission to eat meat (Genesis 9:3). In this period a law differentiating between prohibited and non-prohibited meats would be more understandable. It is just verse 3 which indicates that there is no exilic-postexilic priestly interest involved and that the levitical legislation is not yet in existence.

"'A priestly tendency cannot be recognized. If there had been any special danger of an undue consumption of blood in the exilic-postexilic period it would then not have been necessary to first permit meat to be eaten and after this to forbid the eating of blood. However, the so-called exilic-postexilic sources indicate no such danger and I Samuel 14:32-34 presumes such a prohibition.'" 196/75

5C. THE TABERNACLE

1D. Documentarian Assumption

Usually the documentarian passes off the tabernacle in Exodus as a "pure fantasy." The entire Exodus account is attributed to the P document and is considered late and unreliable.

The structure is thought to be too elaborate for the time of Moses. It is alleged to be the pure creation of the post-exilic imagination.

It has been proposed that the Hebrews of Moses' age did not have the skills necessary to construct such an *elaborate* tabernacle or tent.

Wellhausen writes:

"The temple, the focus to which the worship was concentrated, and which was not built until Solomon's time, is by this document regarded as so indispensable even for the troubled days of the wanderings before the settlement, that it is made portable, and in the form of a tabernacle set up in the very beginning of things. For the truth is, that the tabernacle is the copy, not the prototype, of the temple at Jerusalem." 63/36, 37

Wellhausen continues that "the tabernacle rests on an historical fiction. . . . at the outset its very possibility is doubtful." 63/39

A. Bentzen says the tabernacle is "quite unrealistic." 13/34

"The Tabernacle, *as described by P*, represents, not a historical structure, which once actually existed, but an ideal, — an ideal, based indeed upon a historical reality, but far transcending it, and designed as the embodiment of certain spiritual ideas." 81/426

2D. Basic Answer

Kenneth Kitchen, in "Some Egyptian Background to the Old Testament," enumerates the various archaeological discoveries that give a general background of portable structures very close in most essentials to the Mosaic tabernacle.

The first one is dated about 2600 B.C. and is the prefabricated, portable bed canopy of Queen Hetepheres I, who was the mother of Kheops who constructed the great pyramid.

"This remarkable structure," writes Kitchen, "is a framework of long beams along top and bottom separated by vertical rods and corner-posts on three sides of a rectangle, with a lintel beam and other horizontal 'roof-beams' across the top. The entire structure was of wood, was throughout overlaid with gold, had hooks for curtains all round, and consisted entirely of beams and rods fitting together with tenons in sockets for rapid and customary erection and dismantling, just like the Hebrew Tabernacle thirteen centuries later." 72/9

There are various prefabricated structures from the Archaic and Old Kingdom periods (ca. 2850-2200). G.A. Reisner and W.S. Smith describe further structures that were depicted on the walls of tombs of the fourth to sixth dynasties (ca. 2600-2200 B.C.). 76/14, 15

Another form of prefabricated structures going back to the third millennium B.C. is described by Kitchen. He writes about "the Tent of Purification (*ibw*) to which the corpses of royal and exalted personages were borne for the rituals of purification both before and after embalmment. From pictures in Old Kingdom tombs, it is clear that these portable 'tents' were sizeable structures having hangings of cloth (like curtaining) upon a framework of vertical poles or pillars linked along the top by horizontal bars and beams—again, directly reminiscent of the Tabernacle. (B. Grdseloff, *Das Aegyptische Reinigungszelt*, 1941, plus E. Drioton, *Annales du Service des Antiquités de l'Éypte*, 40, (1940), 1008. Good pictures of "Tent of Purification" showing construction in Blackman, *Rock Tombs of Meir*, V, 1952, Pls. 42, 43)." 252/9, 10

The relics of several of these "tents" have been discovered. See Kitchen (72/10) and Reisner and Smith (76/13-17) for further descriptions of these.

Kitchen indicates that "clearer evidence of the practicality and actual use at a remote age of the very constructional techniques exemplified by the Tabernacle could hardly be wished for." 72/9

R.K. Harrison concludes:

"In view of this evidence there seems to be no adequate reason for denying the existence of a structure such as the Tabernacle to the Hebrews of the Mosaic period." 32/405

Kitchen adds:

"Hitherto-neglected Egyptian evidence for prefabricated structures for religious and other uses definitively refutes the charge of late fantasy with very early examples of the constructional techniques so airily dismissed." 72/9

To this Kitchen says that "it is now entirely unnecessary to dismiss either the concept or construction of the Tabernacle of Ex. xxvi, xxxvi as fantasy or free idealisation. The Egyptian data here adduced cannot of course directly prove the early existence of that Tabernacle, but it does create a very strong presumption in favour of the reasonableness and veracity of the straightforward Biblical account." 72/11

Against the objection that the Hebrews at the time of Moses did not possess the necessary ability to construct such an elaborate structure, R.K. Harrison writes that "it need only be remarked that the Egyptians placed a high value upon Semitic craftsmanship in precious metals when it came to exacting tribute from subjugated areas of Syria and Palestine, as illustrated by a number of tomb-scenes." 32/405. See also 251/34

Kitchen concludes that "it is sometimes objected that as a subject-race before the Exodus, the Hebrews would have no skills such as the work of the Tabernacle required, and could hardly have obtained the necessary materials even from spoiling the Egyptians. However, this is far from being necessarily the case. . . . amply sufficient skills to furnish a Bezalel and an Oholiab, and from the Egyptians in the E. Delta at that particular epoch spoils (Ex. xii, 35-36) amply sufficient for the work of the Tabernacle." 72/12, 13

G.T. Manley writes:

"It is true that the unity of the nation and the one-ness of Yahweh called for one sanctuary round which the people could gather. But this was no discovery of later times, it went back to the covenant in Horeb (Ex. xxxiv. 23; Dt. v. 2, 6, vi. 2). The simple fact is that from Joshua onwards there always existed a national centre for worship, first the tabernacle, then the temple." 87/127

For further information on the tabernacle, see three excellent chapters on its antiquity in *The Unity of the Pentateuch* by A.H. Finn.

Concerning the belief that there were two different representations of the "Tent of Meeting," one in the early JE passages and another in the late P passages, see A.H. Finn above and also James Orr in *The Problem of the Old Testament*.

6C. See the preceding section for information on the antiquity of D and centralized worship.

7C. EXTERNAL EVIDENCE

Archaeology has recently provided us with two powerful supports for the early dating of the Priestly writings.

Kitchen describes the first find:

"Certain difficult expressions and passages in Leviticus could be solved only with cuneiform data of the eighteenth to fifteenth centuries B.C. . . .

these were archaic and obscure by the post-exilic period." 42/129

The Ras Shamra tablets (1400 B.C.), which contain a large amount of Ugaritic literature, render the Wellhausen post-exilic concept void. Many of the technical sacrificial terms of Leviticus were discovered in far removed Canaanite-speaking Ugarit (1400 B.C.). Such P terms as:

1) *ishsheh* - "offering made by fire"
2) *kālîl* - "whole burnt offering"
3) *shelāmîn* - "peace offering"
4) *āshām* (?) - "guilt offering"

Archer is correct in concluding that "these terms were already current in Palestine at the time of Moses and the conquest, and that the whole line of reasoning which made out the terminology of the Levitical cultus to be late is devoid of foundation." 11/149, 150

3B. External Evidence

See page 99, regarding covenant-form analysis.

5A. ARCHAEOLOGY

1B. Antiquity of the Pentateuch - Internal Evidence

Optimum objectivity in dating any written document may be achieved through examining internal evidence. Clues may be discovered in allusions to current events, geographical or climatic conditions, prevalent flora and fauna and eye-witness involvement. And from these clues can be established a reasonably accurate estimate of the place and date of the origin of the document. 11/101

There is a substantial amount of internal evidence that the Pentateuch, both in its form and content, is very much older than the ninth-fifth century B.C. dating scheme assigned to it by the critics.

The following are a few examples of the internal details which indicate the antiquity of the Pentateuch:

1C. THE DESERT SETTING OF EXODUS-NUMBERS

Exodus, Leviticus, and Numbers are quite obviously aimed at a people wandering in the desert, not a nation of farmers settled for centuries in their promised land. Otherwise, the frequent and detailed descriptions of the portable tabernacle are absurd. The meticulous instructions for encampment (Numbers 2:1-31) and for marching (Numbers 10:14-20) would be irrelevant for a settled nation, but eminently practical for the desert experience. Desert references are abundant, including sanitary instructions for desert life (Deuteronomy 23:12, 13) and the sending of the scapegoat into the desert (Leviticus 16:10). 11/106-108

2C. EGYPTIAN INFLUENCE IN PORTIONS OF THE PENTATEUCH

Much of the material in Genesis and Exodus has an obvious Egyptian background. We would expect this if it was written by Moses (reared in an Egyptian court) shortly after the Israelites' Exodus from Egypt. But it would hardly be explainable had it been written, as the documentarians claim, more than 400 years after the Hebrews left Egypt. [An ambitious work which discusses the Egyptian background of the stories of Moses and Joseph in Egypt is Abraham Yahuda's *The Language of the Pentateuch in Its Relationship to Egyptian* (1933).]

This Egyptian influence is manifest in at least these different areas:

1D. Geography

The geography of Egypt and Sinai is familiar to the author of these narratives (i.e., Genesis 37 – Numbers 10). Many authentic locales which have been confirmed by modern archaeology are referred to by the author. Conversely, this author knows little of the *Palestinian* geography except by patriarchal tradition. For example, in Genesis 13 when the author wants to convey a picture of the land of Canaan, he compares it with Egypt, (v. 10). Similarly, in a P passage the author refers to Hebron by its pre-exilic name Kirjath-arba (Genesis 23:2). And its founding is explained by the author in Numbers 13:22, in which the author refers to the building of Zoan in Egypt. The reference to Shalem, "a city of Shechem, which is in the land of Canaan," is improbable for a writer whose people had dwelt in Canaan for centuries. The writer of the Pentateuch generally regards Palestine as a new country which the Israelites will enter in the future. 11/106

This intimacy with Egyptian geography is especially noticeable in the case of the second book.

The writer of Exodus had a thorough knowledge of Egyptian territory. He knew the Egyptian papyrus (Exodus 2:3), the character of the Nile bank and was well acquainted with the sandy desert (Exodus 2:12). He knew of such places as Ramses, Succoth (Exodus 12:37), Etham (Exodus 13:20) and Pi-Hahiroth (Exodus 14:2). The mention in Exodus 14:3 that "the wilderness had shut them in" shows an intimate knowledge of the geography of Egypt. In fact, chapter 14 cannot be understood without knowledge of Egyptian geography. 53/109

2D. Diction

"He [author of Genesis and Exodus] uses a greater percentage of Egyptian words," writes Archer, "than elsewhere in the Old Testament. For example: (a) the expression *abrek* (Gen. 41:43—translated 'bow the knee') is apparently the Egyptian *'b rk* ('O heart, bow down!'), although many other explanations have been offered for this; (b) weights and measures, such as *zeret* ('a span') from *drt*—*'hand'*; *'ēphah* ('tenth of a homer') from *'pt;hīn* (about five quarts volume) from *hnw;* (c) *gōme'* ('papyrus') from *kmyt;* (d) *qemah* ('flour') from *kmhw* (a type of bread); (e) *ses* ('fine linen') from *ss* ('linen'); (f) *yᵉōr* ('Nile, river') from *'trw* - 'river' (which becomes *eioor* in Coptic)." 11/102, 103

This author also makes use of numerous names which are distinctively Egyptian. These include:

(a) *Potipherah* (Genesis 41:45; 46:20) and its shorter form *Potiphar* (Genesis 37:36; 39:1) meaning "whom Ra (the Sun-God) gave."

(b) *Zaphnath-paaneah* (Genesis 41:45), which Pharaoh named Joseph. The LXX interprets this to mean "saviour of the world"—a fitting title for the one who delivered Egypt from famine.

(c) *Asenath* (Genesis 41:45, 50), Joseph's wife.

(d) *On* (Genesis 41:45, 50; 46:20), the ancient Egyptian name for Heliopolis.

(e) *Rameses* (Genesis 47:11; Exodus 1:11; 12:37; Numbers 33:3, 5).

(f) *Pithom* (Exodus 1:11), likely the Egyptian Pi-Tum which is first mentioned in the 19th dynasty monuments, just as Exodus here records it. 53/107, 108

3D. Names of Egyptian Kings

A few Egyptologists committed to the position of radical criticism have argued that an early author would have certainly mentioned the names of the contemporary Egyptian kings. But in truth the absence of such names on Hebrew literature until the time of Solomon actually supports early authorship. The custom of the New Kingdom Egyptian official language was to refer to the king simply as "Pharaoh," without connecting his name with the title. While the Israelites were in Egypt, they conformed to this practice. 11/105

It is here also worthy of note that the antiquity of the Old Testament is supported in the mention of royalty wearing a signet ring and a chain of gold as a token of authority (Genesis 41:42; Esther 3:10, 12; 8:2, 8, 10; Daniel 5:29). This was unknown to Israel but existed in ancient Egypt, Persia and Babylon.

3C. ARCHAISMS IN LANGUAGE

Certain words and phrases that are used in the Pentateuch are known to have become obsolete after the Mosaic age.

Albright says this about chapter 15 of Genesis:

"The account of the covenant between Yahweh and Abraham... is replete with archaisms; its antiquity has been established by E.A. Speiser. Here we have an example of the central place held in early Hebrew religion by the special god of a man with whom he made a solemn compact, according to the terms of which the god would protect him and his family in return for an oath of allegiance. This is a primitive form of the suzerainty treaty.... In the Late Bronze Age the word *beritu*, Hebrew *berit*, 'compact,' appears in Syria and Egypt (where it was a Semitic loanword) in connection with contract labor and contractual hiring of persons listed in a given document." 8/8

Archer gives other examples of archaisms:

"...the word for the pronoun 'she' is frequently spelled *HW'* instead of the regular *HY'*. We also meet with *N'R* instead of the feminine form *N'RH* for 'young girl.' Occasionally (i.e., twice in Genesis) *HLZH (hallazeh)* appears for demonstrative 'that' instead of *hallaz*, the form in use in Judges, Samuel and thereafter. The verb 'laugh' is spelled *ṢHQ* (in Genesis and Exodus) instead of *ŚHQ*; 'lamb' is *KŚB* instead of the later *KBŚ (kebeś)*." 11/107

This body of evidence should also include the fact that there are places in the Old Testament where trivial details are mentioned that a later author would be unlikely to include. For example, when Joseph and the Egyptians were separated from Joseph's brothers at the table, included is the explanatory note, "the Egyptians could not eat bread with the Hebrews, for that is loathsome to the Egyptians" (Genesis 43:32). Would a later author include this? 53/109

On the basis of the above evidence, Archer makes this final evaluation:

"Judging therefore by the internal evidences of the Pentateuchal text we are driven to the conclusion that the author must have been originally a resident of Egypt (not of Palestine), a contemporary eyewitness of the Exodus and wilderness wandering, and possessed of a very high degree of education, learning and literary skill." 11/101

2B. Other Archaeological Evidence for Mosaic Authorship

1C. EARLY HEBREW LITERATURE

The traditional destructive higher critical view that Hebrew literature was, for the most part, comparatively late, still prevails today as can be seen from this statement by J. L. McKenzie:

"It is generally accepted that no Israelite literature was written extensively before the reign of David." 38/1073

But, because of the recent knowledge of the literacy of the ancient Near East, it is possible to assign an earlier date to the Pentateuch than has previously been suggested. It is a fact that the scribes of antiquity recorded events at the time of their occurrence or shortly after, thus shortening the time of oral transmission of the material before it was written down. It is now known that oral transmission was used to disseminate the material to the people and not primarily to preserve the material, since they had written records in existence.

That the majority of the Old Testament is of great antiquity is without question. 33/18, 19

2C. EARLY PARALLELS IN PENTATEUCHAL LAWS

Many of the laws and legal procedures recorded in the Pentateuch are now known to be much older than was formerly assumed as a result of the numerous discoveries of parallel laws of other Mesopotamian cultures.

We cite three specific examples:

1D. The Covenant Code

Mendenhall says:

"It is hard to conceive of a law code which could be more at variance from what we know of Canaanite culture than the Covenant Code (Exod. 21–23–JE).... The Canaanite cities were predominantly commercial, rigidly stratified in social structure.... The Covenant Code shows no social stratification, for the slaves mentioned are not members of the community, with the single exception of the daughter who is sold as an *amah* or slave-wife (who is herself strongly protected by law).... The laws of the Covenant Code reflect the customs, morality and religious obligations of the Israelite community (or perhaps some specific Israelite community of the North) before the monarchy... since it exhibits just that mixture of case law and apodictic law (technique and policy respectively) which we find in covenants from the Hittite sources and in Mesopotamian codes as well; any study which assumes that it is a later, artificial composite from originally independent literary sources may be assigned rather to rational ingenuity than to historical fact." 47/13, 14

Albright also establishes the antiquity of the Covenant Code:

"Moreover, the Eshnunna Code, which is nearly two centuries older than the Code of Hammurabi, contains the first exact parallel to an early biblical law (Ex. xxi. 35, dealing with the division of oxen after a fatal combat between the animals). Since the Code of Eshnunna is on any rational theory at least five centuries earlier than the Book of the Covenant, this parallel becomes particularly interesting. Of course, it is now becoming a truism that the cultural background of the Book of the Covenant lies in the Bronze Age, not in the Iron; i.e., it must go back substantially to the Mosaic Age." 55/39

    2D.   Land Transaction Recorded in Genesis 23

Archer discusses the antiquity of this particular procedure. **Genesis 23** describes Abraham's reluctance in purchasing an entire tract of land from Ephron the Hittite, rather desiring only the cave of Machpelah itself and the immediate grounds. The discovery of the Hittite Legal Code (dating from 1300 B.C.) provides amazing parallels, and explains that the owner of an entire parcel must carry out the duties of feudal service, including pagan religious observances. Thus, Abraham plainly refused to purchase any more than a portion of the tract so as to avoid any involvement with gods other than Yahweh. This narrative reflects such a grasp of Hittite procedure as to make it highly probable that it preceded the fall of the Hittites in the 13th century B.C. 11/161

    3D.   Three customs referred to in Genesis

Archer points out that the antiquity of three customs referred to in Genesis (chapters 16, 27, and 31 respectively) has been established by archaeology. Many of the ancient customs of Genesis have been proven to be common in the second millennium B.C., but not in the first millennium B.C. Nuzi yielded numerous 15th century B.C. legal documents which spoke of siring legitimate children by handmaidens (such as Abraham by Hagar); an oral deathbed will as binding (such as Isaac to Jacob); and need for having the family teraphim (such as Rachel took from Laban) to claim inheritance rights. 11/107

3C.   **CONCLUSION**

It should be clear at this point that archaeology has done much, not only to undermine the Documentary Hypothesis, but also to, in fact, add support to Mosaic authorship of the Pentateuch.

About the Pentateuch Albright says:

"New discoveries continue to confirm the historical accuracy or the literary antiquity of detail after detail in it." 5/225

Bright makes this statement about the patriarchal narratives:

"No evidence has come to light contradicting any item in the tradition." 14/67

Albright warns:

"It is. . .sheer hypercriticism to deny the substantial Mosaic character of the Pentateuchal tradition." 5/224

Meredith Kline gives an appropriate conclusion:

"The story of twentieth century Biblical archaeology is the story of the silencing of the clamorous voice of the modern western Wellhausen by the voiceless witnesses emerging from ancient eastern mounds. The plot of the story would be clearer were it not for the reluctance of critical scholars to part with their traditional teachings. But all are now obliged to admit that far from the Biblical narratives of patriarchal and Mosaic days being alien to the second millennium B.C. where the Biblical chronology locates them, they would be completely out of place in the first millennium B.D. The Biblical sequence of Law and Prophets has been vindicated." 83/139

chapter 11

the phenomenon of divine names

Otto Eissfeldt gives four major foundations of the Documentary Hypothesis:

1) Change in divine names

2) Linguistic usage—(a) persons, places, objects being designated by different names, (b) words, expressions, and stylistic peculiarities are said to be characteristic of different documents

3) Diversity of ideas—religious, moral, legal, political; also, the difference in the contemporary conditions and events which they presuppose

4) Literary phenomena—double accounts, interruption of a continuous narrative by extraneous material, etc. 20/182-188

1A. INTRODUCTION

ELOHIM occurs 33 times in the first 34 verses of Genesis. It is followed by JEHOVAH (YHWH) ELOHIM 20 times in the next 45 verses, and finally by JEHOVAH (YHWH) 10 times in the following 25 verses. It would seem that such selective usage of divine names was more than coincidenta. 10/23

2A. DOCUMENTARY ASSUMPTION

Critics have held that the isolated use of various divine names [i.e., Jehovah (English pronunciation) or Yahweh (Hebrew pronunciation) and Elohim] indicated more than one author. This is what initially led Astruc to the conclusion that various sources lay intertwined and combined in the Pentateuch. Notice this statement in his *Conjectures,* cited by *The Encyclopedia of Religion and Ethics:*

"In the Hebrew text of Genesis, God is designated by two different names. The first is Elohim, for, while this name has other meanings in Hebrew, it is especially applied to the Supreme Being. The other is Jehovah, יְהוָה , the great name of God, expressing his essence. Now one might suppose that the two names were used indiscriminately as synonymous terms, merely to lend variety to the style. This, however, would be an error. The names are never intermixed; there are whole chapters, or large parts of chapters, in which God is always called Elohim, and others, at least as numerous, in which he is always named Jehovah. If Moses were the author of Genesis, we should have to ascribe this strange and harsh variation to himself. But can we conceive such negligence in the composition of so short a book as Genesis? Shall we impute to Moses a fault such as no other writer has committed? It is not more natural to explain this variation by supposing that Genesis was composed of two or three memoirs, the authors of which gave different names to God, one using that of Elohim, another that of Jehovah or Jehovah Elohim?" 21/315

While it is often claimed that this criterion is no longer employed by the critics, the following statement by A. Bentzen shows how important it still remains to modern critics:

"If we are to distinguish between the traditions we must look for 'constants' along this line. The first 'constant' which was noticed was the peculiar changes in the use of the Divine names. The change in the use of the Divine names is however more than a simply linguistic 'constant.' It is a *material 'constant.'* We know that its use, at least in Gen. and in the beginning of Exodus follows a definite plan." Later, "Accordingly, in the parts of the Pentateuch from Gen. 1 to Exodus 6 we must be entitled to use the criterion of the Divine names to distinguish between different traditions." 13/vol. II 27, 28

3A. BASIC ANSWER

1B. Specific Uses of Various Divine Names

Each divine name had a special significance and they were not necessarily synonymous. The author used Jehovah, Elohim, or Jehovah-Elohim according to the context of the passage. Therefore there is a real purpose behind the isolated usage of divine names and not random choosing.

In the 12th century R. Jehuda Halevi wrote a book called *Cosri* in which he explained the etymology of each of the divine names. His conclusions are paraphrased here by E.W. Hengstenberg, professor of theology at the University of Berlin during the middle of the 19th century:

"[Elohim] is the most general name of the Deity; it distinguishes him only in his fullness of power without reference to his personality or moral qualities—to any special relation in which he stands to men—either as to the benefits he bestows, or to the requirements he makes. On this account, where God has witnessed of himself and is truly known, another name is added to *Elohim*—this is the name *Jehovah,* peculiar to the people who received his revelation and his covenant.... The name Jehovah is unintelligible to all who are not acquainted with that development of the Divine essence which is represented by it; while Elohim distinguishing him as God in those respects which are known to all men, is universally intelligible.... The name *Jehovah* is the *nomen proprium* [proper name] of God, and being one that expresses the inmost nucleus of his essence, is only intelligible where God has come forth, laid open the recesses of his heart, and has permitted his creatures to behold them, so that, instead of an obscure undefined being, of whom thus much only is known and affirmed, that he is powerful, that he is immense—he here exhibits himself the most personal of all persons, the most characteristic of all characters." 35/216, 217

Umberto Cassuto, the Jewish scholar and late professor at the Hebrew University, continues:

"First consider the characters of the two Names. They are not of the same type. The designation *'Elōhīm* was originally a common noun, an appellative, that was applied both to the One God of Israel and to the heathen gods (so, too, was the name *'El*). On the other hand the name YHWH is a proper noun, the specific name of Israel's God, the God whom the Israelites acknowledged as the Sovereign of the universe and as the Divinity who chose them as His people. Let me cite a parallel by way of illustration. A certain city may be called *Jerusalem* or simply *city*. The appellation *city* is common to her and to all other cities; the name *Jerusalem* belongs to her alone. When the ancestors of the Jewish people realized that there is but One God, and that only 'YHWH, He is *'Elōhīm*' (I Kings xviii 39), then the common substantive *'Elōhīm* also acquired for them the signification of a proper noun, and became synonymous with the name YHWH. If Jerusalem had been the sole city in the world of those who spoke Hebrew, then of course the word *city* would have become a proper name, synonymous with *Jerusalem*." 15/18

Cassuto sets forth these rules as an explanation for the use of divine names.

YHWH

1) "It selected the name YHWH when the text reflects the Israelite conception of God, which is embodied in the portrayal of YHWH and finds expression in the attributes traditionally ascribed to Him by Israel, particularly in His ethical character."

2) YHWH "is used, when expression is given to the direct intuitive notion of God, which characterizes the simple faith of the multitude or the ardour of the prophetic spirit.

3) "The name YHWH occurs when the context depicts the Divine attributes in relatively lucid and, as it were, palpable terms, a clear picture being conveyed."

4) YHWH "is found when the Torah seeks to arouse in the soul of the reader or the listener the feeling of the sublimity of the Divine Presence in all its majesty and glory.

5) "The name YHWH is employed when God is presented to us in His personal character and in direct relationship to people or nature."

6) YHWH "appears when the reference is to the God of Israel relative to His people or to their ancestors.

7) "YHWH is mentioned when the theme concerns Israel's tradition."

ELOHIM

1) "It preferred the name ELOHIM when the passage implies the abstract idea of the Deity prevalent in the international circles of 'wise men'—God conceived as the Creator of the physical universe, as the Ruler of nature, as the Source of life.

2) "The name Elohim when the concept of thinkers who mediate on the lofty problems connected with the existence of the world and humanity is to be conveyed.

3) "Elohim, when the portrayal is more general, superficial and hazy, leaving an impression of obscurity.

4) "Elohim, when it wishes to mention God in an ordinary manner or when the expression or thought may not, out of reverence, be associated directly with the Holiest name.

5) "Elohim, when the Deity is alluded to as a Transcendental Being who exists completely outside and above the physical universe.

6) "Elohim, when He is spoken of in relation to one who is not a member of the Chosen people.

7) "Elohim, when the subject-matter appertains to the universal tradition."

Sometimes, of course, it happens that two opposite rules apply together and come in conflict with each other; then, as logic demands, the rule that is more material to the primary purport of the relevant passage prevails. 15/30-41

These rules apply to certain types of literature in different ways:

PROPHETIC. The prophets of the Old Testament consistently used the divine name YHWH instead of Elohim. Jonah is an exception, employing the title Elohim for the God of Israel a number of times. But this exception only proves the rule, for Jonah actually belongs to the narrative literature because of its viewpoint. Isaiah is another exception; he replaces Yahweh, not with Elohim, but with El, a name for God which was originally a common noun. 15/20

LEGAL. Yahweh is the only personal name of God employed throughout the legal literature of the Pentateuch and Ezekiel. 15/20

POETIC. The literature classified as poetic normally uses YHWH. Some poems that belong to the wisdom literature or that have been influenced by it are an exception. In the second and third books, known as the Elohistic books, the use of 'El or 'Elohim are of the majority. 15/20

WISDOM. Wisdom literature is unique in that it is a universal literary style and similar writing may be discovered throughout the ancient Orient. An investigation of the similar literature among Israel's neighbors should prove quite beneficial.

But as one begins to study these books "we are struck by an amazing phenomenon. The wisdom books of the ancient East, irrespective of the people from which they emanated or the language in which they were written, usually refer to the Godhead by an appellative rather than by the proper names of the various divinities." 15/21

NARRATIVE. Narrative literature, as is found throughout the Pentateuch, the Earlier Prophets, Job, Jonah, etc., frequently uses both Yahweh and Elohim in close proximity. 15/21

CHARACTERISTICALLY JEWISH PASSAGES. Umberto Cassuto, the late professor at the Hebrew University, in explaining the use of Yahweh states that in "those categories that have a purely Israelite character, only the Tetragrammaton [Yahweh] occurs, this being the national name of God, expressing the personal conception of the Deity exclusive to Israel."

ANCIENT HEBREW. Ancient Hebrew letters found at Lachish illustrate the usage of Yahweh in daily life. It is employed not only in greetings and in oaths, but throughout the entire letter. Elohim never appears. A parallel is seen in the consistent use of Yahweh on scriptural greetings (Judges 6:12; Psalms 129:8; Ruth 2:4) and in the actual rabbinical dictum that required use of Yahweh in greeting another. 15/24

MODERN HEBREW. Even in modern Hebrew, Cassuto says, "We are exact in our choice of words, we employ the Tetragrammaton [Yahweh] when we have in mind the traditional Jewish idea of the Deity, and the name Elohim when we wish to express the philosophic or universal concept of the Godhead." 15/30

The following is a brief application of these rules to Genesis: In Genesis one, God appears as Creator of the physical universe and as Lord of the world who has dominion over everything. Everything that exists does so because of His fiat alone, without direct contact between Him and nature. Thus the rules apply here that Elohim should be used. 15/32

In the story of the Garden of Eden we find God as a moral ruler because He imposes certain rules on man. Also, a personal side of God is shown as He relates directly to man. Yahweh fits easily here as would be expected. The only place Elohim is used is when the serpent speaks and when the woman is talking to the serpent. Yahweh is avoided out of reverence to the national God of Israel. 15/33

In the same passage we find Yahweh linked with Elohim, because the Scriptures now wish to identify Elohim with Yahweh:

"In other words that the God of the ethical world is none other than the God of the physical world, that the God of Israel is the God of the entire universe, that the names YHWH and Elohim point only to two different aspects of His activity, or to two different ways in which He reveals Himself to the children of men." 15/33 This explains the double usage and in subsequent chapters the names are used individually according to context.

Cassuto explains:

"In the story of the Generation of Division (xi 1-9) YHWH appears. The reason is clear: in this narrative only the place of the occurrence is outside the Land of Israel; the story itself is wholly Israelite in character, and it contains not an iota of foreign material. Unlike the accounts of the Creation and the Flood, it has no cosmopolitan tradition as its background to serve as the basis of the Torah's portrayal; on the contrary, here we find the Israelite spirit in complete opposition to the attitude and aspirations of the proud heathen peoples, who dominate the world. Thus the Israelite conception of the relationship between man and God is conveyed by the Israelite name of the Deity." 15/37

In chapter 12 of Genesis, the story of Abraham starts. It seems fitting that the Israelite name for the Godhead should be used.

Archer applied this to the early chapters of Genesis. A careful study of the use of Yahweh and Elohim in the book of Genesis will reveal the purpose that the writer had in mind. Elohim (which is perhaps derived from a root meaning "powerful," "strong," or "foremost") refers to God as being the almighty Creator and Lord of the universe. Thus Elohim is appropriate for Genesis one because God is in the role of the almighty Creator, whereas Yahweh is the name of God when He is in the covenant engagement. Thus in Genesis two Yahweh is almost exclusively used because God is dealing with Adam and Eve in a covenant relationship. In Genesis three, when Satan appears, the name for God changes back to Elohim because God is in no way related to Satan in a covenant relationship. Thus, both the serpent and Eve refer to Him as Elohim. The name changes back to Jehovah as He calls out to Adam (3:9) and reproves Eve (3:13) and it is the covenant God that puts the curse on the serpent (3:14). 11/112

John H. Raven argues similarly:

"This argument ignores the etymology of the names of God and conceives of them as used interchangeably merely as a matter of habit. It is not claimed by the critics that J was ignorant of the name Elohim or P and E of the name Jehovah, but that each preferred one of these names. But if so, the question remains, why did J prefer the name Jehovah and E and P the name Elohim. To this important question the divisive hypothesis gives no satisfactory answer. If the Pentateuch however be the work of one author, the use of these names is sufficiently clear. It is precisely that which the so-called characteristics of P, J and E, require. P is said to be cold, formal, systematic, logical; but it is precisely in such passages that one would expect Elohim, the general name for God, the name which has no special relation to Israel but is used many times in reference to the deities of the Gentiles. J on the other hand is said to be naïve, anthropomorphic in his conception of God; but these evidences of religious fervor would lead us to expect the proper national name of God, the name which emphasized his covenant relations with Israel." 53/118, 119

Even Kuenen, one of the founders of the classic Documentary Hypothesis, admitted the uncertainty of this criterion:

"The original distinction between Jahweh [another spelling] and Elohim very often accounts for the use of one of these appellations in preference to the other." 45/56

"The history of critical investigation," continues Kuenen, "has shown that far too much weight has often been laid on agreement in the use of the divine names.... It is well, therefore, to utter a warning against laying an exaggerated stress on this one phenomenon." 45/61

More recently, the oral traditionalist, Engnell, charges that source division on the basis of differing usages is totally unwarranted (in *Swedish Bible Dictionary: Svenskt Bibliskt Uppslagsverk*, ii) and is here cited by North as saying:

"In so far as a certain 'constant' change of divine names is really to be found, a closer examination shows that this does not rest upon change of documents but upon a conscious stylistic practice of the traditionist, something which is bound up with the fact that the different divine names have different ideological associations and therewith different import. Thus, Yahweh is readily used when it is a question of Israel's national God, indicated as such over against foreign gods, and where the history of the fathers is concerned, &c., while on the other hand Elohim, 'God,' gives more expression to a 'theological' and abstract-cosmic picture of God, and is therefore used in larger and more moving contexts.... So, then, it is the traditionist, the *same* traditionist, who varies in the choice of divine names, not the 'documents.'" 77/66, 67

Cassuto boldly proclaims that there "is no reason, therefore, to feel surprise that the use of these Names varies in the Torah. On the contrary, we should be surprised if they were not changed about. The position is of necessity what it is. It is not a case of disparity between different documents, or of mechanical amalgamation of separate texts; every Hebrew author was compelled to write thus and to use the two Names in this manner, because their primary signification, the general literary tradition of the ancient East, and the rules governing the use in the Divine Names throughout the entire range of Hebrew literature, demanded this." 15/41

Archaeology provides an answer for the use of the compound name Yahweh-Elohim.

One of the major assumptions of the JEDP hypothesis is that the use of Jehovah is typical of a J document and Elohim of an E document. The combination of these two documents is the ground used by the radical critics to account for the compound name Yahweh-Elohim. Cyrus Gordon cites his personal experience on this subject, "All this is admirably logical and for years I never questioned it. But my Ugaritic studies destroyed this kind of logic with relevant facts." 27/132 At Ugarit, deities were found with compound names. For example: Qadish-Amrar is the name of one and Ibb-Nikkal another. Most of the time "and" was put between the two parts, but the conjunction can be omitted.

Thus it was common to use compound names for a god. Amon-Re, the most famous god with a compound name, was a deity that resulted from the Egyptian conquest under the 18th dynasty. Amon was the god of the city of Thebes where the political power existed, while Re was the universal sun god. These two gods were combined because of the political leadership in Thebes and the universalism of Re. But Amon-Re is one god. This sheds light on the combination of Yahweh-Elohim. Yahweh refers to the specifics of the deity, while Elohim is more of a general or universal designation of the deity. This consolidation of Yahweh-Elohim may be demonstrating that Yahweh equals Elohim, which can be restated "Yahweh is God." Yet the documentarians tell us that Yahweh-Elohim is the result of combining the two documents J and E. This is as unfounded as using an A document and R document to explain the compound deity Amon-Re. 27/132, 133

Kitchen adds: "For multiple terms for deity, compare the use of three names, a fixed epithet, and common noun 'god' for the god Osiris on the Berlin stela of Ikhernofret: Osiris, Wennofer, Khent-amentiu, 'Lord of Abydos' (Neb-'Abdju), and nuter, 'god' (cf. 'Elohim in Hebrew). But no Egyptologist bothers to invent 'Osirist,' 'Wennofrist,' 'Khentamentist,' Neb-'Abdjuist and Nuterist sources to match the Yahwist and Elohist of Old Testament studies. Ikhernofret shows what could be taken as 'prolixity' of expression, but it is certain that this commemorative inscription was composed (as one unit), carved and set up within weeks, or possibly even days, of the events to which it chiefly relates, and has no literary 'pre-history' of several centuries of 'hands,' redactors and conflation. This applies to other texts, a few cited here and many more not. Alongside Egypt, multiple divine names occur in Mesopotamia. We might cite Enlil also called Nunamnir in the prologue to the Lipit-Ishtar laws, and in the prologue to Hammurapi's laws we have Inanna/Ishtar/Telitum, and Nintu/Mama." 42/121

Raven, in material used previously, introduces a difficulty in using divine names as evidence for multiple authors:

"It is not claimed by the critics that J was ignorant of the name Elohim or P and E of the name Jehovah, but that each preferred one of these names. But if so, the question remains, why did J prefer the name Jehovah and E and P the name Elohim? To this important question the divisive hypothesis gives no satisfactory answer. If the Pentateuch however be the work of one author, the use of these names is sufficiently clear." 53/118

"The great innovation on the part of the Israelites," Cassuto observes, "consists in the fact that, while the writings of the pagans give expression, on the one hand, to the abstract and general notion of Divinity, and, on the other, make mention of some particular god, in Hebrew literature the concept of the specific God of Israel is completely identified with that of the God of the whole earth. YHWH, whom the children of Israel recognize and before whom they prostrate themselves, is none other than 'Elōhīm, of whose dominion over them all men are more or less clearly conscious, and whom they are destined to acknowledge fully in time to come. This is the sublime thought to which the Biblical poets give expression through the variation of the Names." 15/25

2B. Exegesis of Exodus 6:3

1C. DOCUMENTARY ASSUMPTION

This verse is taken by the critics to mean that the name Jehovah (Yahweh, YHWH) was not known in Israel until God revealed it to Moses at Sinai. Therefore, all the passages in Genesis and in Exodus before this one where "Jehovah" is used must have been written by a hand other than the one who wrote this Exodus passage; otherwise (if there is only one author) he would be guilty of an obvious contradiction: having the patriarchs use "Jehovah" throughout Genesis but then stating that the name was unknown until it was revealed to Moses.

This view is stated by the British scholar, H.H. Rowley: "Exodus 6:2f. says: 'I am Jehovah, and I appeared unto Abraham, unto Isaac, and unto Jacob as El Shaddai, but by my name Jehovah I was not known to them.' Yet there are several passages in the book of Genesis which declare that God was known to the patriarchs by the name Jehovah. The name is known to

Abram (Genesis 15:2, 8), to Sarai (16:2), to Laban (24:31); it is used by angelic visitors in conversation with Abraham (18:14) and with Lot (19:13); and God is represented as saying 'I am Jehovah' to Abram (14:7) and to Jacob (28:13)." 54/20, 21 (See also 23/115)

2C. BASIC ANSWER

[22]Correct exegesis of Exodus 6:3: This verse does not mean that the name "Jehovah" was literally unknown to the Israelites before Moses' time (i.e., that it did not *exist*), but rather that they didn't have the relationship with God that the name "Jehovah" implied. In other words, they knew God by His *name* "Jehovah" but not by his *character* "Jehovah."

W.J. Martin, in his book *Stylistic Criteria and the Analysis of the Pentateuch*, said:

"It might have been possible, of course, to have denied the implications by drawing attention to the full sense of the Hebrew word for 'name.' The field of meaning of this word covers not only that of 'name,' that is, a verbal deputy, a label for a thing, but also denotes the attributes of the thing named. It may stand for reputation, character, honour, name and fame. Hence the reference would not be so much to nomenclature as to the nature of the reality for which the name stood." 46/17, 18

J.H. Hertz, former chief rabbi in London, England, in his commentary on the Pentateuch and Haftorahs says:

"Exodus 6:3 is the focal point of critical scholarship. According to them, God here first reveals his name as YHWH to Moses. Thus all chapters in Genesis and Exodus where the name Yahweh appears are from another source. This is used as decisive proof of the multiple document hypothesis of the Pentateuch, and is proclaimed by all radical critics as the clue to the JEDP hypothesis.

"The current Critical explanation of this verse, however, rests on a total misunderstanding of Hebrew idiom. When Scripture states that Israel, or the nations, or Pharaoh, 'shall know that God is Adonay'—this does *not* mean that they shall be informed that His Name is Y H W H (Adonay), as the Critics would have it; but that they shall come to witness His power and comprehend those attributes of the Divine nature which that Name denotes. Thus, Jer. xvi, 21, 'I will cause them to know my hand and my might, and they shall know that my name is Adonay.' [Orthodox Jews do not pronounce YHWH's name lest they break the third commandment and thus substitute Adonay which means "Lord."] In Ezekiel the phrase, 'They shall know that I am Adonay,' occurs more than sixty times. Nowhere does it mean, They will know Him by the four letters of His Name. Every time it means, they will know Him by His acts and the fulfillment of His promise." 36/104

"The word to know in the Old Testament" states Raven, "generally includes the idea of apprehension and the expression 'to know the name of Jehovah' is used many times in this fuller sense of apprehending the divine attributes (I Kings 8:43; Psalms 9:11, 91:14; Isaiah 52:6, 64:1; Jeremiah 16:21; Ezekiel 39:6, 7). All this shows the meaning to be that Abraham, Isaac and Jacob knew God as a God of power but not as the God of the covenant." 53/121

Archer argues similarly that the radical critics reject the method of founding Christian doctrine on proof-text but yet they found one of their primary doctrines upon this very method. This method seeks a literal interpretation of two verses without considering context or the analogy of other scriptural teaching. This instance is found in Exodus 6:2, 3. ("I am YHWH and I appeared to Abraham, to Isaac and Jacob, as El Shaddai, but by My name, YHWH, I did not make Myself known to them.") The documentarians hold that this is the first time the name Yahweh was revealed to Moses in the E document. However, J did not know about this and assumed Yahweh was a suitable name for the pre-Mosaic ers. Yet, with a proper understanding both of the verb "to know" *yādra)* and of the implications in Hebrew of knowing someone's name, it becomes clear that the meaning is not literal. All ten plagues were surely not for the mere purpose that the Egyptians might know that the God of the Israelites was named Yahweh (Exodus 14:4, ". . . and the Egyptians will know that I am Yahweh.") Rather, the intent of the plagues is that the Egyptians might witness the covenant faithfulness of God to His people and thus know Him by experience as Yahweh, the covenant God. (See also Exodus 6:7, "You shall know that I am Yahweh your God, who brought you out from under the burdens of the Egyptians.") "Hebrew usage therefore indicates clearly enough that Exodus 6:3 teaches that God, who in earlier generations had revealed Himself as El Shaddai (God Almighty) by deeds of power and mercy, would not in Moses' generation reveal Himself as the covenant-keeping Jehovah by His marvelous deliverance of the whole nation of Israel." 11/113, 114

"The context of the passage," continues Raven, "and the *usus loquendi* of the expression, 'to know the name' show clearly that the meaning is to have an experimental knowledge of the attributes emphasized by the name." 53/121

G.T. Manley makes this observation on the Hebrew verbs involved:

"Where a name is made known for the first time the verb commonly used is *nāghadh* (hiph), as in Genesis 32:29. Here [Exodus 6:3] it is *yādra*, the same as is found in I Sam. 2:12 and 3:7, where the persons concerned were familiar with the name Yahweh but not with all that the name implied." 87/47

The critics use this verse as the basis for their division of the J document which uses the name Jehovah, from the E document which uses Elohim. But this verse distinguishes not Elohim from Jehovah, but El-Sahddai from Jehovah, as Merrill Unger points out:

"That this supposition regarding the meaning of Exodus 6:2, 3 is totally unwarranted and has no foundation outside the exigencies of the critical hypothesis is apparent *first, because of the clear distinction indicated in the passage itself:* 'God spake unto Moses, and said unto him, I am the Lord: and I appeared unto Abraham, unto Isaac, and unto Jacob, by the name of God Almighty (El Shaddai); but by my name Jehovah was I not known to them.' Significantly, the reference does not distinguish Jehovah from Elohim (occurring over 200 times in Genesis) but from El Shaddai (occurring five times in Genesis), the name denoting the particular character in which God revealed Himself to be the patriarchs (Genesis 17:1; 28:3; 35:11; 43:14; 48:3)." 61/251

Another important issue often overlooked in regard to Exodus 6:2, 3 is what is referred to in Hebrew as the *Beth Essential.*

The revised version renders this passage as follows: "I appeared. . . *as* El Shaddai, but *by* my name Yahweh. . . ."

This translation does not indicate that although there is a preposition (prefix *Beth*) in the original for "as," which governs "El Shaddai," there is no corresponding preposition for the word "by" which here governs "my name Yahweh." Grammatically there needs to be a preposition "by" or "as" in English.

Gesenius gives an excellent basis for the use of the preposition "as" in relationship to "my name Yahweh."

This would carry the meaning of "character or inner condition, as distinct from outer circumstances or designation." 128/14

Gesenius writes that "in poetic parallelism the governing power of a preposition is sometimes extended to the corresponding substantive of the second member [Gesenius - Kautzsch, *Hebrew* Grammar, Para. 119 hh, 1910]." 128/14

Isaiah is an excellent example of this "poetic parallelism": "For my name's sake I defer my anger, for the sake of my praise I restrain it for you" (Revised Standard Version). Although English demands two uses of "for the sake of" Hebrew allows only one (here used before the first noun).

In this case, as in others, "the preposition extends to the second word exactly the same [meaning] which it exercises over the first." 128/14

There is no reason why Exodus 6:2, 3 should not be governed by the same principle. "My name Yahweh" should be governed the same way as the *Beth Essential* governs "El Shaddai."

Motyer in *The Revelation of the Divine Name* gives an excellent treatment of the meaning of the *Beth Essential.*

"In this verse [Exodus 6:3]," writes Motyer, "the *Beth Essentiae* is appropriately translated 'as,' that is to say, it is used with a view to concentrating attention on character or inner condition, as distinct from outer circumstances or designation. When God revealed Himself 'as' El Shaddai, it was not with a view to providing the patriarchs with a title by which they could address Him, but to give them an insight into His character such as that title aptly conveyed. Likewise, in Exodus iii. 2, 'the angel of Yahweh appeared... *as* a flame of fire....' The outward circumstances may have served in the first instance to attract Moses' attention—though this is not necessary, for his attention was, in point of fact, caught by the continued existence of the bush in spite of the flame. The flame was the appropriate characterization of God Himself, designed to provide a suitable revelation of the divine Nature to Moses at that particular juncture of his career. When we carry this force over to the nouns 'my name Yahweh' we reach a conclusion in accordance with the translation we are seeking to justify: 'I showed myself... in the character of El Shaddai, but in the character expressed by my name Yahweh I did not make myself known." 128/14

Motyer continues:

"The accuracy of the proposed translation is further established by its suitability to its context. (The place of the verse in the scheme of revelation, as we see it, is this: not that now for the first time the name as a sound is declared, but that now for the first time the essential significance of the name is to be made known). The patriarchs called God Yahweh, but knew Him as El Shaddai; their descendants will both call Him and know Him by His name Yahweh. This is certainly the burden of Exodus vi. 6ff. where Moses receives the message he is to impart ot Israel. The message opens and closes with the seal of the divine authority, 'I am Yahweh,' and on the basis of this authority it declares the saving acts which, it is specifically stated, will be a revelation of Yahweh's nature, for, as a result of what He will do, Israel will 'know that I am Yahweh,' but, in point of fact, their knowledge will be, not the name merely, but also the character of Israel's God. This meaning of the phrase is consistent throughout the Bible." 128/14

Given the documentarians' interpretation of this passage, we are left with a most difficult question: Why did not one · f the many redactors involved in the compilation of the Pentateuch reconcile the obvious contradiction between the use of the name Jehovah by the patriarchs in Genesis and the statement in Exodus 6:3 that the name was first revealed to Moses at Sinai?

Unger says that, besides the problems both of the context and of the true meaning of the words, the radical critics' position on Exodus 6:2, 3 is further weakened by the common sense implication of their own hypothesis. The redactor to whom they attribute these accounts clearly did not understand the passage as they do, for he saw here no contradiction with the frequent usage of "Yahweh" throughout Genesis. Had he seen a contradiction, he surely would have either altered the verse or deleted the earlier occurrences of the name "Yahweh." 61/252

"The redactor of the Pentateuch, if such there were," Raven notes, "could not have considered the statement of Exodus 6:3 inconsistent with the frequent use of the name Jehovah by the patriarchs. Otherwise he would either have changed the statement in Exodus or the name Jehovah in Genesis. The many generations of Jews and Christians who were ignorant of the composite authorship of Genesis also saw nothing difficult in Exodus 6·3." 53/121

It is also possible that the passage has been incorrectly translated into English. Martin explains:

"There is, however, another possible translation which would eliminate all conflict with the remote context. The phrase, 'but by my name the LORD I did not make myself known to them' could be taken in Hebrew as an elliptical interrogative. The translation of the whole verse would then run: 'I suffered myself to appear *(Niph'al)* to Abraham, to Isaac, and to Jacob, as El-Shaddai, for did I not let myself be known to them by my name YHWH?' Hebrew possesses an interrogative particle but on a number of occasions it is as here omitted: a good example is in Genesis xviii. 12. It is possible that in the spoken language the intonation was usually sufficient to indicate a question, as is still the case in living Semitic languages. Intonation has been described as the subjective stratum in languages in contrast to words, the objective stratum. Writing can never be a full, but only to a greater or less degree a partial representation of the spoken word. No ancient script attempted to indicate intonation, and even at the present day with all our typographical aids no completely satisfactory system has been devised. It should not be a cause for surprise that, in the transference of speech to writing, such meagre aids as there were should on occasion, possibly because unexpressed in speech, be omitted altogether. Commentators have not always reckoned with the possibility. For instance, in Job xxiii. 17, 'For have I not been cut off on account of the darkness?' which is a parallel case to the one under discussion, Bick quite unashamedly deletes the negative.

"No objection could be taken to this translation of Exodus vi. 3, in the light of Semitic usage, even if it had only the context to commend it. There is, however, strong support forthcoming from the grammatical structure of the following sentence. This is introduced by the words 'and also.' Now in Hebrew common syntactical practice demands that where 'and also' is preceded by a negative it also introduces a negative clause and vice-versa, otherwise we would be faced with a *non sequitur.* In this instance the clause after 'and also' is positive, hence one would expect to find the preceding clause a positive one. The translation of the clause as an interrogative would thus remove any illogicality. A perfectly good reason can be given for the use of an interrogative form here: it is a well-known method of giving a phrase an asseverative character. A translation of 'and also' in this context by 'but' would be highly unsatisfactory if not altogether inadmissible on the ground that the next clause again is introduced by 'and also.' This makes it extremely hard to avoid drawing the conclusion that we are here dealing with a series of positive statements, the first couched for the sake of emphasis in an interrogative form, and the two subsequent ones introduced by 'and also' to bring them into logical co-ordination." 46/18, 19

Finally, it should be noted that the divine name criterion cannot be applied to any material after Exodus 6:3 since from that point on, according to the critics, E and P, like J are free to use Jehovah. Even Eissfeldt admits this:

"Admittedly the difference of divine names may only be used in the analysis of Genesis and the beginning of Exodus. For the two sources which we now call E and P avoid the name Yahweh at first and only use it from the moment when God makes this known as his name to Moses—E from Exodus 3:15 and P from Exodus 6:6 on." 20/183

Yet many critics have attempted to show composite authorship for the remaining portions of the Pentateuch on the basis of divine names. It should be obvious that all such attempts have no logical foundation and are therefore invalid.

3B. Similar Use of Divine Names in the Koran

The Koran provides a helpful parallel to the irregular distribution of the divine names on the Pentateuch. No one questions the single authorship of these Arabic scriptures. Yet they display the same phenomenon as their Hebrew relative. The name Allahu parallels with Elohim, and Rabbu ('lord') corresponds to Adonay ('lord') which the Jews used later to refer to Yahweh. In some suras (chapters) the names are intermingled, but in others only the one or the other appears. For example, the name never occurs in the following suras: 4, 9, 24, 33, 48, 49, 57, 59, 61, 62, 63, 64, 86, 88, 95, 101, 102, 103, 104, 107, 109, 111, 112. While the name Allahu is never used in these suras: 15, 32, 54, 55, 56, 68, 75, 78, 83, 87, 89, 92, 93, 94, 99, 100, 105, 106, 108, 113, 114.

This is conclusive evidence that ancient Semitic literature was capable of using two names for God, yet with one author. 11/111

4B. Difficulties with the Documentarians' Manipulation of Divine Names

1C. INCONSISTENCY

According to documentarians, the divine name Yahweh indicates J source, Elohim indicates E source, P source used Elohim up to Exodus 6:3 but thereafter used Jehovah also.

The following sample passages contain divine names that do not correspond with the right source from which the passage is supposed to come:

  a. Elohim occurs in these J source passages:
    1) Genesis 31:50
    2) Genesis 33:5, 11
  b. Yahweh occurs in these P source passages before Exodus 6:3:
    1) Genesis 17:1
    2) Genesis 21:1
  c. Yahweh occurs in these E source passages:
    1) Genesis 21:33
    2) Genesis 22:4, 11
    3) Genesis 28:21
    4) Exodus 18:1, 8, 9, 10, 11

2C. **APPEAL TO REDACTORS.** The critics' answer to these obvious contradictions is that the redactors (whose who compiled and edited the documents) either made a mistake by copying in the wrong name or took the liberty to arbitrarily interchange the names here and there. The second explanation is of course appealed to more than the first.

H.H. Rowley is an example:

"We need not, therefore, be surprised that the compiler of the Pentateuch should have extracted material from older sources, or should have worked material from more than one source into a continuous narrative, or should have felt himself free to make slight alterations in what he took over, or have composed the joins in his narratives. These alterations and joins are usually attributed to the Redactor, and it should occasion no surprise that the compiler or redactor has left some traces of his own work." 54/25 (See also R.H. Pfeiffer, *Introduction to the Old Testament,* (1941), pp. 282-289.)

Oswald T. Allis comments on such an assumption:

"Finally, it is to be noted that what cannot but be regarded as a major defect of the critical analysis appears already quite plainly in connection with the use of the divine names: it cannot be carried through without appeal to a redactor or redactors. This means that where simple, even if hairsplitting, partitioning of the text will not give the source analysis desired by the critics, it is alleged that a redactor has altered or edited the sources. If JEHOVAH is regarded as the name of Deity characteristicc of J, the addition of ELOHIM in the title Jehovah Elohim in Genesis 2:4b-3:24 has to be attributed to a redactor." 10/38, 39

Raven points out the fallacious circular reasoning of the critics' appeal to redactors:

"Sometimes they sweep aside difficulties by asserting that R altered the name, at others that the text is evidently corrupt. Neither of these suppositions however has any basis outside of the exigencies of the hypothesis. The hypothesis is said to be derived from the phenomena of the text, as we have it; but if those phenomena do not suit the hypothesis, they are rejected as worthless. May we not reasonably ask: If the text is corrupt how can we trust the hypothesis which is derived from it? The very existence of R and several R's is a baseless assumption made necessary by the difficulties of the divisive hypothesis." 53/120

The implication of all this is well-stated by Allis when he concludes:

"It is to be noted, therefore, that every appeal to the redactor is a tacit admission on the part of the critics that their theory breaks down at that point." 10/39

3C. **EXTENT OF SOURCE DIVISION**

Even single verses are chopped up into "sources." For example, Genesis 21:1, 2:

1) "Then the Lord [Yahweh] took note of Sarah as He had said, and the Lord [Yahweh] did for Sarah as He had promised.

2) So Sarah conceived and bore a son to Abraham in his old age, at the appointed time of which God [Elohim] had spoken to him."

Now, according to the critics, "Then the Lord [Yahweh] took note of Sarah as He had said;; is assigned to J; "and the Lord [Yahweh] did for Sarah as He had promised" is assigned to P (in spite of the documentarians' insistence that P didn't use "Yahweh" before Exodus 6:3); "So Sarah conceived and bore a son to Abraham in his old age" is assigned to J; and "at the appointed time of which God [Elohim] had spoken to him" is assigned to P.

Throughout this discussion we refer to the lists found in *The Interpreter's One-Volume Commentary on the Bible* (88/2, 34, 85) in which all the passages in Genesis, Exodus, and Numbers are assigned to their respective sources. These lists are found on pages: 2 (Genesis), 34 (Exodus), and 85 (Numbers).

Nearly 100 verses in Genesis, Exodus, and Numbers are likewise divided up into at least two sources by the documentarians:

Genesis:

2:4	21:1, 2, 6	41:46
7:16, 17	25:11, 26	42:28
8:2, 3, 13	31:18	45:1, 5
10:1	32:13	46:1
12:4	33:18	47:5, 6, 27
13:11, 12	35:22	48:9, 10
16:1	37:25, 28	49:1, 28
19:30		

Exodus:

1:20	12:27	25:18
2:23	13:3	31:18
3:4	14:9, 19, 20, 21, 27	32:8, 34, 35
4:20	15:21, 22, 25	33:5, 19
7:15, 17, 20, 21	16:13, 15	34:1, 11, 14
8:15	17:1, 2, 7	
9:23, 24, 35	19:2, 3, 9, 11, 13	
10:1, 13, 15	24:12, 15, 18	

Numbers

13:17, 26	16:1, 2, 26, 27
14:1	20:22

Professor F. Dornseiff of Germany, a student of Greek philology, drew parallels between Greek and Old Testament literature during the 1930's. His comments on the implausibility of the above conclusions (*Zeitschrift für die Alttestamentliche Wissenschaft*, 1934, pp. 57-75) are cited by Aalders:

"Who can picture the genesis of a first-rate literary work like the Greek Homer or the Pentateuch by 'redactors' cutting 'sources' into small pieces, and compacting these separate sentences into a new unit, and that in following out such a method they met with a great literary success?" 1/28

5B. Divine Name Variation in the LXX (Septuagint)

There is much more variation in the use of divine names in the LXX than there is in the Masoretic Text (MT). Documentarians have traditionally used the MT as the basis for their source division holding that it is by far the more reliable of the two, and have consequently almost totally ignored divine name usage in the LXX.

Archer points out that the usage of divine names as a means of separating documents was first rejected by A. Klostermann (*Der Pentateuch*, 1893), who insisted that the Hebrew text has not been accurately transmitted through the centuries. Johannes Dahse [212/n.p.] was the first to come up with a scholarly investigation of the relationship of the MT to the LXX, when he showed that the LXX had no less than 180 instances of non-corresponding names (e.g., *theos* for Yahweh or *kyrios* for Elohim). This gives pause to the assumption that the MT is sufficiently well known in all of its variants so that we may autonomically prefer the MT reading in every case over the LXX. Many of these decisions were made before the Dead Sea Scrolls were found and need to be re-evaluated.

J. Skinner, in 1914, replied to Dahse in a book called *The Divine Names in Genesis*, in which he showed that the agreement of divine names in the Masoretic Text and the Samaritan texts (earlier than the LXX) extends to over 300 cases, while there were only 8 or 9 differences. Critics have assumed that Skinner's "crushing reply" (55/79) to Dahse was final on the issue of divine names and the LXX. But as a result of the findings of the Dead Sea Scrolls scholars are now quite confident that there were at least three separate families of manuscripts existing before the Masoretic period. Therefore, the close agreement of the Masoretic Text with the Samaritan texts probably means nothing more than that they came from the same manuscript tradition. It does not prove that the MT is closer to the original text than the LXX.

In 1908, in his *Die Komposition der Genesis*, B.D. Eerdmans, Kuenen's successor at the University of Leiden, also admitted that this argument based on Septuagintal data was a powerful one and asserted that it was impossible to use the divine names as evidence for separate documents. 11/84, 85

Wellhausen himself admitted (in a private letter to J. Dahse, published in 1912) that the argument against using the divine names as a criterion in light of the variations in usage in the LXX had "touched the weak point of his theory." 1/21

Harrison speaks of how the Dead Sea Scrolls have strengthened the opinion that there was possibly more variation of divine names in the original text than the MT allows:

"That there were at least three distinct families of Hebrew manuscripts in existence in the pre-Massoretic period has been demonstrated convincingly as a result of the manuscript discoveries at Qumran, and in particular from the fragments recovered from 4Q, thereby confirming the opinion that there was considerably more variety in the text of early Pentateuchal manuscripts than was the case with the MT itself. Since the latter has traditionally been used as the basis of documentary analysis in view of the fact that it was regarded as the 'fixed' text, it is interesting to speculate as to what might have happened to the entire Graf-Wellhausen theory had one or more pre-Massoretic texts been available for the use of nineteenth-century literary critics. The answer has in fact been supplied to a large extent by Albright, who, as mentioned above, has stated that the fragmentary manuscripts recovered from 4Q have already seriously undermined the foundations of detailed literary criticism." 32/518

Harrison speaks about some of the textual evidence at Qumran "which shows that it was eminently possible for the translators of the LXX version to have had several manuscript families of the Pentateuch at their disposal, whose nature and contents were by no means identical in all respects with those of the Massoretic tradition." 32/518

chapter 12

the repetition of **accounts** and alleged **contradictions**

1A. REPETITION OF ACCOUNTS

1B. Introduction

Certain stories in the Pentateuch **are** said to be repeated twice. Other stories are said to have contradictory details (i.e., Creation—Genesis 1-2:4a-P; 2:4b ff-J; Flood—Genesis 6:1-8; 7:1-5, 7-10, 12, 16b, 17b, 22-23; 8:2b-3a, 6-12, 13b, 20-22-J; Genesis 6:9-22; 7:6, 11, 13-16a, 17a [except "forty days"], 18-21, 24; 8:1-2a, 3b-5, 13a, 14-19-P). 14/159

2B. Documentary Assumption

Since no author would have reason to repeat the same story twice, the repetition of certain narratives (parallel accounts) indicates more than one author at work. Also, since one author could hardly be charged with giving us obviously contradictory details, those stories in which such discrepancies occur are the work of a redactor or editor who wove together two different accounts of the same story (interwoven accounts).

Rollin Walker speaks for this view (*A Study of Genesis and Exodus,* p. 24) when he says the following, as cited by O.T. Allis:

"Toward the question of the precise historical accuracy of the stories of the books of Genesis and Exodus we ought to take somewhat the same attitude that the editor of the books took when he gave us parallel and conflicting accounts of the same event, and thereby confessed that he was not sure which of the two was exactly right." 10/123

Otto Eissfeldt lists no less than 19 allegedly repetitious or contradictory accounts. 20/189, 190

3B. Basic Answer

Supposed double and triple accounts of the same story are actually different stories with similar details.

Concerning the dual accounts of certain stories in the Pentateuch, Raven notes that "these accounts are not really parallel. Some of them are merely similar events, as the two instances in which Abraham lied concerning his wife and the same action by Isaac. The redactor must have considered these quite distinct. In other cases there is a repetition from a different standpoint, as the account of the creation in Genesis 2 is from the standpoint of the God of revelation and providence. Sometimes the repetition is a characteristic of Hebrew style, which often makes a general statement by way of introduction and then enlarges upon it." 53/124, 125

The supposed contradictory details in certain stories are in fact supplementary details and are seen as being contradictory only when the stories are misinterpreted.

1C. THE CREATION STORY

H.H. Rowley says: "For instance, between the two accounts of the Creation there is a disagreement as to the sequence of creation, a difference in the usage of the divine names, a difference in the conception of God, and a difference of style." 54/24 (See also 17/35, 36)

Attacking this position, Kitchen points out that two lines of argument have been drawn in favor of a double narrative of the creation accounts: theological and stylistic differences between Genesis one and two and a seemingly different order of creation. The style differences have no weight as an argument and simply reflect changes in subject matter; and the understanding of a transcendent God in Genesis one as opposed to an anthropomorphic God in Genesis two is "vastly overdrawn and frankly, illusory." 42/118

E.J. Young illustrates this: "The anthropomorphic God of Genesis 2 'fashions,' 'breathes,' 'plants,' 'places,' 'takes,' 'sets,' 'brings,' 'closes up,' 'builds,' 'walks.' But the critics have quite a superficial argument. Man in his finite mind cannot express ideas about God in anything but anthropomorphisms. Chapter 1 of Genesis expresses God in such equally anthropomorphic terms as, 'called,' 'saw,' 'blessed,' 'deliberated' (verse 26 'let us make'), God 'worked' for six days then He 'rested.'" 71/51

Kitchen continues: "The same may be said of the order of events. In Genesis 2:19, there is no explicit warrant in the text for assuming that the creation of animals here happened immediately before their naming (*i.e.*, after man's creation); this is eisegesis, not exegesis. The proper equivalent in English for the first verb in Genesis 2:19 is the pluperfect ('...had formed...'). Thus the artificial difficulty over the order of events disappears." 42/118

There is an essential difference in the two accounts which must be appreciated: Genesis one describes the creation of the world, while Genesis two details and further describes the specific creation of Adam and of his immediate environment in the Garden of Eden. This is accented by the introductory phrase in Genesis 2:4, "These are the generations of the heavens and of the earth when they were created, in the day that Yahweh Elohim made the earth and the heavens." Throughout Genesis the phrase "these are the generations" occurs nine other times, each time introducing an account of the offspring descended from a specific ancestor. This would then indicate that in the verses following Genesis 2:4, we will find an account of the offspring of the heavens and earth after the initial creation has taken place. And that is just what we find here in the case of Adam and

Eve (v. 7—"Yahweh Elohim formed man of *dust from the ground*"). 11/118 It must be emphasized that we do not have here an example of incompatible repetition. We have an example of a skeletal outline of creation as a whole, followed by a detailed focus on the final point of the outline—man. Lack of recognition of this common Hebrew literary device, in the words of Kitchen, "borders on obscurantism." 42/116, 117

Kitchen then shows how archaeology has brought this type of literary pattern to light. For just such a literary pattern is commonplace in other texts of the ancient Near East. On the Karnak Poetical Stela from Egypt, the address of Amun to King Tuthmosis III breaks down thus:

Paragraph one—expressing his general supremacy (Would the diversified style indicate a J source?)

Paragraph two—more precise poetical expression of supremacy (Would the rigidity indicate a P source?)

The Gebel Barker Stela is similar:

Paragraph one—general royal supremacy (J source?)

Paragraph two—specific triumphs in Syria-Palestine (P source?)

Several of the royal inscriptions of Urartu are likewise enlightening:

Paragraph one—victory over specified lands ascribed to the chariot of the god Haldi (Would an "H" source be indicated by the brief, rigid style?)

Paragraph two—detailed repetition of description of these victories, this time as achieved by the king (Is a "K" source indicated by this detailed, varied style?)

Just as an assignment of the various portions of these Egyptian texts to different documents is unheard of in scholarly circles, so is it absurd to practice a dissection of sources in their contemporary literature found in Genesis one and two. 42/117

Orr explains it this way:

". . . to the *beginnings of things*, how constantly is it alleged that 'we have two contradictory accounts of the *creation*.' It is certain that the narratives in Gen. i.-ii. 4 and chap. ii. 4 ff. are quite different in character and style, and view the work of creation from different standpoints. But they are not 'contradictory'; they are, in fact, bound together in the closest manner as complementary. The second narrative, taken by itself, begins abruptly, with manifest reference to the first: 'In the day that Jehovah Elohim made earth and heaven' (ver. 4). It is, in truth, a misnomer to speak of chap. ii. as an account of the 'creation' at all, in the same sense as chap. i. It contains no account of the creation of either earth or heaven, or of the general world of vegetation; its interest centers in the making of man and woman, and everything in the narrative is regarded from that point of view." 50/346, 347

2C. THE NAMING OF ISAAC

It is theorized that the accounts of three different documents regarding the naming of Isaac have been included in Genesis (Genesis 17:17 from P, 18:12 from J and 21:6 from E). But is it unreasonable to assume that both Abraham and Sarah laughed with disbelief when they were individually told that Isaac would be born, and that they later laughed with joy at his birth?

3C. ABRAHAM'S DECEIT

The critics allege that the two occurrences of Abraham passing Sarah off as his sister are merely variations of the same event. It is naive to assume that men never make the same mistake twice nor yield to the same temptation more than once. In this case, the weakness of the assumption is magnified by the consideration that Abraham profited financially on both occasions. 11/120

4C. ISAAC'S DECEIT

When Isaac allowed his wife to be regarded as his sister while Abimelech was king of the Philistines in Gerar (Genesis 26:6-11), he provided striking similarities to the E account of Abraham and Sarah in Genesis 20. If these are to be understood as differing versions of the same event which have been incorporated into Genesis by the redactor, several very difficult assumptions must be made: 1.) that sons never follow the bad example of the parents, 2.) that the sexual habits of the people of Gerar had changed for the better by the time of Isaac, 3.) that the Philistine dynasties never handed down the same name from ruler to ruler, (i.e., Abimelech I, Abimelech II, etc.), even though in Egypt the 12th dynasty practiced the exact same thing (Amenemhat I, II and III, and also Senwosret I, II and III). The same practice occurred in Phoenicia. A series of Hirams or Ahirams ruled in Tyre and Byblos. It is noteworthy that the account of Abraham's first deception concerning his relationship to Sarah (Genesis 12) is assigned to J along with the similar Genesis 26 account of Isaac and Rebekah. Another instance of "repetitive" accounts being allowed by the critics to stand as genuinely separate events is seen in the assigning to E of both of Jacob's visits to Bethel (Genesis 35:1-8 and Genesis 28:18-22). 11/120, 121

5C. THE NAMING OF THE WELL AT BEERSHEBA

In Genesis we discover two stories of the naming of the well at Beersheba — first by Abraham in Genesis 21:31 (assigned to E) and then by Isaac in Genesis 26:33 (attributed to P). But there is no evidence that these are actually two (J and P) versions of the same original episode. In light of the nomadic habits of Abraham and Isaac, it is more likely that the well was stopped up by Abraham's enemies upon his departure, only to be reopened by Isaac when he returned to his father's old rangeland. And it is reasonable to see Isaac reviving the old name and reconfirming the treaty which gave him the right to the well. 11/121

6C. JACOB'S FLOCKS PROSPER

Driver divides Genesis 30:25 - 31:18 into two sections: Genesis 30:25-31 which comes mainly from the J source and Genesis 31:2-18 taken mainly from the E source. He confirms:

"The two sources give a different account of the arrangement between Jacob and Laban, and of the manner in which, nevertheless, Jacob prospered. The success which in 30, 35 ff. is attributed to Jacob's stratagem, with the effect of the striped rods upon the ewes in the flock, is in 31:7-12 attributed to the frustration by Providence of Laban's attempt, by repeatedly altering his terms, to overreach Jacob, and to the fact that only the striped he-goats leaped upon the ewes." 18/15

When these two chapters are heard for what they are saying and are evaluated in light of the rest of Scripture as well as the ancient Near East, they neither contain any discrepancy nor require divergent sources. Chapter 30 contains the author's objective description of the selective breeding which Jacob practiced in this situation. In chapter 31, the author relates the event from Jacob's perspective (by dialogue) as Jacob, speaking to his wives, ascribes to the all-provident God the credit for both his knowledge and success in the venture. Jacob had to acknowledge in the end that it was not any prenatal influence stratagem at work (does it at all work?) but only God! So Genesis 30 *reports* what Jacob did and hoped for, but Genesis 31 *teaches* what was actually so and even Jacob had to agree. In the process, Jacob relates complementary but not contradictory details.

Numerous examples of an event being described from both the human and the divine perspective may be found in Scripture (Judges 7:7, 21-23; Exodus 14:21; Genesis 4:1).

This may also be found in other ancient Near Eastern cultures. Kitchen cites the royal inscriptions at Urartu, in which one paragraph attributes victory over specified nations to the chariot of the god Haldi and the next paragraph repeats the same victories in more detail as accomplished by the king. No scholar would think of dividing this account into various sources upon such grounds. 42/117

7C. THE CONTINUITY OF ISOLATED DOCUMENTS

Eissfeldt states that one of the characteristic features of the Pentateuchal narratives is "the interweaving of compiled parallels, which are therefore incomplete." 20/189 (See also 18/8 and 16/76, 77)

One of the destructive higher critics' reasons for holding that there are various sources interwoven in certain narratives is the argument that when these sources are isolated and all the J passages put together and all the P passages put together, there are formed two separate continuous and coherent stories.

In his book, *The Higher Criticism of the Pentateuch*, the late William H. Green gave a brilliant illustration of the arbitrary nature of this argument. He took the New Testament parable of the prodigal son and subjected it to the same treatment to which the documentarians were subjecting some of the Pentateuchal narratives. Here are his results: (Phrases in parentheses Green attributes to a "redactor.")

THE PRODIGAL SON, Luke xv. 11-32.

A

11. A certain man had two sons: 12. and the younger of them said to his father, Father, give me the portion of thy substance that falleth to me. ... 13. And not many days after the younger son gathered all together,... and there he wasted his substance with riotous living....

14b. and he began to be in want.

16b. And no man gave unto him.

20. And he arose, and came to his father; ...and he ran, and fell on his neck, and kissed him. 21. And the son said unto him, Father, I have sinned against heaven, and in thy sight: I am no more worthy to be called thy son. 22. But the father said to his servants,

B

(A certain man had two sons:)

12b. and he divided unto them his living.

13b. And (one of them) took his journey into a far country.... 14. And when he had spent all, there arose a mighty famine in that country.... 15. And he went and joined himself to one of the citizens of that country; and he sent him into his fields to feed swine. 16. And he would fain have been filled with the husks that the swine did eat. ... 17. But when he came to himself he said, How many hired servants of my father's have bread enough and to spare, and I perish here with hunger! 18. I will arise and go to my father, and will say unto him, Father, I have sinned against heaven, and in thy sight: 19. I am no more worthy to be called thy son:

Bring forth quickly the best robe, and put it on him; and put a ring on his hand, and shoes on his feet:...24. for this my son was dead, and is alive again.... And they began to be merry. 25. Now his elder son was in the field: and as he came and drew nigh to the house,... 28. he was angry, and would not go in: and his father came out, and entreated him. 29. But he answered and said to his father, Lo, these many years do I serve thee, and I never transgressed a commandment of thine: and yet thou never gavest me a kid, that I might make merry with my friends: 30. but when this thy son came, which hath devoured thy living with harlots, thou killedst for him the fatted calf. 31. And he said unto him, Son, thou art ever with me, and all that is mine is thine. 32. But it was meet to make merry and be glad: for this thy brother was dead, and is alive again.

make me as one of thy hired servants. ... 20b. But while he was yet afar off, his father saw him, and was moved with compassion:...23. and (said) Bring the fatted calf, and kill it, and let us eat, and make merry. ... 24b. he was lost, and is found....25b. (And the other son) heard music and dancing. 26. And he called to him one of the servants, and inquired what these things might be. 27. And he said unto him, Thy brother is come; and thy father hath killed the fatted calf, because he hath received him safe and sound... 32b. and he was lost and is found. 29/119, 120

Although these two stories were arbitrarily manufactured by Green out of the one story, each has unique characteristics which, by someone unfamiliar with Green's clever scheme, might be induced as evidence for composite authorship:

"A and B agree that there were two sons, one of whom received a portion of his father's property, and by his own fault was reduced to great destitution, in consequence of which he returned penitently to his father, and addressed him in language which is nearly identical in both accounts. The father received him with great tenderness and demonstrations of joy, which attracted the attention of the other son.

"The differences are quite as striking as the points of agreement. A distinguishes the sons as elder and younger; B makes no mention of their relative ages. In A the younger obtained his portion by solicitation, and the father retained the remainder in his own possession; in B the father divided his property between both of his sons of his own motion. In A the prodigal remained in his father's neighborhood, and reduced himself to penury by riotous living; in B he went to a distant country and spent all his property, but there is no intimation that he indulged in unseemly excesses. It would rather appear that he was injudicious; and to crown his misfortunes there occurred a severe famine. His fault seems to have consisted in having gone so far away from his father and from the holy land, and in engaging in the unclean occupation of tending swine. In A the destitution seems to have been chiefly want of clothing; in B want of food. Hence in A the father directed the best robe and ring and shoes to be brought for him; in B the fatted calf was killed. In B the son came from a distant land, and the father saw him afar off, in A he came from the neighborhood, and the father ran at once and fell on his neck and kissed him. In B he had been engaged in a menial occupation, and so bethought himself of his father's hired servants, and asked to be made a servant himself; in A he had been living luxuriously, and while confessing his unworthiness makes no request to be put on the footing of a servant. In A the father speaks of his son having been dead because of his profligate life; in B of his having been lost because of his absence in a distant land. In A, but not in B, the other son was displeased at the reception given to the prodigal. And here it would appear that R has slightly altered the text. The elder son must have said to his father in A, 'When this thy son came, which hath devoured thy substance with harlots, thou didst put on him the best robe.' The redactor has here substituted the B word 'living' for 'substance,' which is used by A; and with the view of making a better contrast with 'kid' he has introduced the B phrase, 'thou killedst for him the fatted calf.'" 29/121, 122

Green points out another similar experiment, a work entitled "Romans Dissected" by E.D. McRealsham, the pseudonym of Professor C.M. Mead, formerly of Hartford Theological Seminary. Green Comments:

"The result of his ingenious and scholarly discussion is to demonstrate that as plausible an argument can be made from diction, style, and doctrinal contents for the fourfold division of the Epistle to the Romans as for the composite character of the Pentateuch." 29/125

1D. The Flood Story

Rowley says:

"Again in the story of the Flood we find that according to Gen. vi. 19f. Noah is commanded to take a single pair of every species into the Ark, whereas according to Gen. vii. 2 he is bidden to take seven pairs of clean beasts and a single pair of unclean. Gen. vii. 8f. emphasizes this contradiction with its specific statement that of clean and unclean a single pair went into the Ark, though it is possible that the emphasis on the contradiction is not original. Similarly there is disagreement in the duration of the Flood. According to Gen. vii. 12 the rains lasted forty days, after which, according to vii. 6ff., Noah waited for certain periods of seven days before the waters were abated, whereas according to Gen. vii. 24 the waters prevailed for a hundred and fifty days, and were not finally abated until a year and ten days after the beginning of the Flood (vii. 14; cf. vii.)." 54/18

Kitchen argues:

"It has often been claimed, for example, that Genesis 7 to 8 gives two different estimates for the duration of the Flood, but in fact these are purely the invention of the theory. The biblical text as it stands is wholly consistent in giving a year and ten days (eleven, if first and last are both counted) as the total duration of the Flood episode, as clearly pointed out by Aalders, Heidel and others long ago. Likewise, the supposed clash between Genesis 6:19, 20 (cf. Gn. 7:8, 9) and Genesis 7:2, 3 over 'two by two' or 'seven pairs' is imaginary. In Genesis 6:20 *shenayim*, 'pair,' is probably being used as a collective por 'pairs,' seeing that one cannot form a plural of a dual word in Hebrew (no *shenayimiml*); Genesis 6:19, 20 and 7:8, 9 are general statements while Genesis 7:2, 3 (clearly twos and sevens) is specific." 42/120

Alexander Heidel provides us with a thorough investigation of the question on the biblical account of the duration of the Flood:

"Modern biblical criticism, as is well known, sees in the Genesis account of the deluge a blending of two main, in several respects irreconcilably contradictory, sources put together by a redactor. According to the one source, called P (or the Priestly Code), the flood began on the seventeenth day of the second month (7:11) and ended on the twenty-seventh day of the second month of the following year (8:13-14), the whole occurrence thus extending over a period of one year and eleven days. But according to the other source, called J (or the Yahwistic Narrative), it rained for forty days and forty nights (7:12), at the end of which Noah opened the window of the ark and sent forth four birds at intervals of three successive periods of seven days (8:6-12), whereupon he removed the covering of the ark and found that the face of the ground was dry (vs. 13b); accordingly, the duration of the flood was only sixty-one days.

"With this view I cannot agree. However, this is not the place to enter upon a detailed discussion of the problems involved; a few words will have to suffice. I do by no means deny that a number of different documents may have been utilized in the composition of the biblical flood story, for the Scriptures themselves indicate unmistakably that the sacred penmen employed written records and the like in the preparation of their books. But, in spite of the claims that have been made, I am not at all convinced that the biblical material can be resolved into its constituent elements with any degree of certainty. Moreover, I am not in sympathy with the common practice of treating the alleged remnants of each supposed document as if it constituted the whole, with the result that the Genesis account of the deluge, with which alone we are at present concerned, fairly teems with discrepancies. It must be apparent to every unprejudiced reader that the Genesis version of the flood, as divided by modern biblical criticism, shows several important gaps in the portions assigned to J and P. Therefore, if we had access to the complete text of the supposed documents denominated J and P (assuming, for the sake of argument, that such documents ever existed), we might see at once that there were no discrepancies at all between the two. But even without such access, it has been demonstrated repeatedly that the alleged contradictions in the Genesis narrative are capable of a simple and reasonable solution if the story is left as we find it in the Hebrew text.

"A good illustration of this we have in the point under examination— the duration of the flood. If we leave the biblical text as it stands and treat the story as one whole, the numerical data on the duration of the deluge are in perfect harmony, as shown by the following.

"According to 7:11, the flood began in the six hundredth year of Noah's life, on the seventeenth day of the second month, coming seven days after Noah had received the command to enter the ark (7:1-4, 10). For forty days and forty nights it rained upon the earth (vs. 12). It is not said anywhere that after this period the downpour stopped altogether. On the contrary, the rain and the gushing-forth of the subterranean springs continued; for it is clearly stated that the fountains of the deep and the windows of heaven were not closed and that the rain from heaven was not stopped... until the end of the one hundred and fiftieth day after the outbreak of the flood, for which reason the waters kept rising or maintained their maximum height during all this time (7:24-8:2). But while the flow of the subterranean waters may have continued with great force even after the first forty days, the uninterrupted and unrestrained torrential downpour from heaven must have ceased and the rain must have continued much more moderately, for we read in 7:12: 'The rain came upon the earth forty days and forty nights,' and in verse 17: 'The flood (mabbûl) came upon the earth forty days.' As pointed out before, the term mabbûl in verse 17 undoubtedly describes the unprecedented stream of rain from above, which made the waters mount on the surface of the earth. From this it seems quite obvious that it was the unchecked torrential rain or the sheets of water from the sky which ceased after the first forty days.

"At the end of the 150 days the waters began to decrease (8:3), and on the seventeenth day of the seventh month the ark rested on one of the

mountains of Ararat (vs. 4). This was exactly five months and 1 day from the beginning of the flood (cf. 7:11). The obvious conclusion appears to be that the 150 days constituted 5 months and that each month, consequently, consisted of 30 days. On the day that the waters began to abate, i.e., on the one hundred and fifty-first day from the commencement of the flood, the ark grounded. The waters continued to decrease until, on the first day of the tenth month, the tops of the mountains became visible (8:5). If a month is reckoned at 30 days, this gives us 74 additional days, yielding a total of 225 days. At the end of 40 days from this date, i.e., the first of the tenth month, Noah opened the window of the ark and sent forth four birds at intervals of three successive periods of 7 days (vss. 6-12). Since the first bird was released on the forty-first day, these figures add up to 62 more days and bring the total up to 287 days. The last bird was sent forth on the two hundred and eighty-seventh day from the beginning of the deluge, or (adding the 46 days of the year which elapsed before the outbreak of the flood) on the three hundred and thirty-third day of the year. We have, accordingly, arrived at the third day of the twelfth month. Twenty-eight days later, on the first day of the following year, in the six hundred and first year of Noah's life, the waters were dried up from off the earth (but the surface of the ground was not yet fully dry) and Noah removed the covering of the ark (vs. 13). A month and 26 days after that, on the twenty-seventh of the second month, the earth was again dry and firm, and Noah left the ark (vss. 14 ff.). These two periods amount to 84 days. Adding these days to the 287, we gain a grand total of 371 days, or 1 year and 11 days, beginning with the outbreak of the flood. There is here no discrepancy whatever."
34/245-247

Not only are the alleged discrepancies nonexistent, but the two accounts are organically dependent upon one another and thus already form a unit. Raven demonstrates this:

"The critics have been unable to extract two records of the flood even tolerably complete. The beginning of chapter seven is assigned to J. If so, we are told by J that God commanded Noah to come with all his house into the ark, without telling a word about the building of the ark or the members of Noah's family. Chapter seven needs precisely the statement of Chap. 6:9-22 to make it complete or comprehensible. Gen. 8:13 says: 'And Noah removed the covering of the ark and looked and behold the face of the ground was dry—' This is assigned to J but not another word of J is recorded till verse 20 where we read: 'And Noah builded an altar unto the Lord.' This serious gap is bridged by the intervening statements which the critics assigned to P. Furthermore Gen. 9:1-17 (P) is not a useless repetition of Gen. 8:12-22 (J) but an enlargement of God's covenant with Noah after he had built the altar to Jehovah and recommenced his life upon earth." 53/125

2D. Abraham's Journey

The critics also have "discovered" two interwoven stories in chapters 11-13 of Genesis which Orr describes and answers thus:

"After many variations of opinion, the critics have settled down to give Gen. xi. 28-30 to J, and ver. 27, 31, and 32 to P; beyond this only chaps. xii. 4b, 5, and xiii. 6, 11b, 12 are assigned to P in chaps. xii., xiii. But this yields some remarkable results. In chap. xi. 28, the J story begins quite abruptly, without telling us who Terah, Haran, Abram, and Nahor are; i.e., it needs ver. 27 for its explanation. The residence of the family is placed by J in Ur of the Chaldees (elsewhere given as a P mark), and nothing is related of the migration to Haran (cf. P, vers. 31, 32). Yet this migration is apparently assumed in the call to Abraham in Gen. xii. 1. In ver. 6, Abraham is said to have 'passed through the land into the place of Sichem,' but we are not told *what* land. It is P alone who tells of his departure from Haran, and coming to the land of Canaan (ver. 4*b*, 5). But this very fragment in P assumes the departure from Haran as a thing known (ver. 4*b*), and so needs the first part of the verse, given to J. In other words, the story, as it stands, is a unity; divided, its connection is destroyed." 50/351

3D.   Isaac's Blessing

Genesis 27 has likewise failed to escape the scalpel of the critics. The chapter opens with the account of Isaac's preparations to bestow his blessing upon Esau. The first four verses provide an excellent example of arbitrary methods by the critics in dissecting passages.

Verse one reads "Now it came about, when Isaac was old, and his eyes were too dim to see, that he called his older son Esau and said to him, 'My son.' And he said to him, 'Here I am.'" Because this passage is given to J, the final phrase "and said to him, 'My son.' And he said to him, 'Here I am.'" is deleted as a feature unique to E. But certainly such a basic formula cannot be reasonably assigned to one author and excluded from all others. This is not even supported by the text, for Genesis 22:11 records the words, "But the Angel of Yahweh called to him from heaven, and said, 'Abraham, Abraham!' And he said, 'Here I am.'" Not only do the critics here replace Yahweh with Elohim, but they go on to assign to E every passage containing the formula but no divine name. This is a blatant example of arguing in a circle. And further, if in Genesis 27:1 the formula were removed, we would expect verse two to read, "And Isaac said *to him*." But this word is missing from the Hebrew text and confirms that this sentence is not the conversation opener.

Verses 2-4 continue, "And Isaac said, 'Behold now, I am old and I do not know the day of my death. Now then, please take your gear, your quiver, and your bow, and go out to the field and hunt game for me; and prepare a savory dish for me such as I love, and bring it to me that I may eat, so that my soul may bless you before I die.'" Claiming that the words "and prepare a savory dish for me... that I may eat," represent a variant motif of the same story, the phrase is deleted and assigned to E. The other variant of this motif, majoring on "game" as opposed to the "savory dish," goes to J. Thus J reads, "Now then, please take your quiver... and hunt game for me, so that my soul may bless you before I die." Yet this totally eliminates the crucial point that Esau return with the game and serve it to his father. On the other hand, J reads, "And prepare a savory dish for me such as I love... so that my soul may bless you before I die." Here our story is further twisted so that Esau, the valiant hunter, is relegated to a housewife's role.

Taken as we have it, this passage is clearly a sensible, lucid unit; dissected, it is meaningless. 15/87-97

4D.   The Story of Joseph

Rowley speaks of contradictions in this story also:

"In Gen. xxxvi. 27 Judah proposes that Joseph should be sold to some Ishmaelites, and the following verse states that this was done, while Gen. xxxix. 1 says the Ishmaelites sold him to an Egyptian. But Gen. xxxvii 28a introduces Midianites who passed by and kidnapped Joseph from the pit, without the knowledge of his brethren (29f.), and who later sold Joseph to Potiphar (xxxvii. 36)." 54/18, 19

Kitchen again answers the charge:

"It is also often asserted that Genesis 37 contains parts of two irreconcilable accounts of how Joseph was sold into Egypt: (a) by his brothers to the Ishmaelites and so into Egypt (Gn. 37:25, 28b; cf. 45:4, 5), and (b) by the Midianites who took him from the pit (Gn. 37:28a, 36; cf. 40:14, 15). The truth is much simpler.

"First, the terms 'Ishmaelites/Midianites' overlap, and refer to the same group in whole or in part (*cf.* Jdg. 8:24).

"Secondly, the pronoun 'they' in Genesis 37:28 refers back to Joseph's brothers, not to the Midianites. In Hebrew, the antecedent of a pronoun is not always the last preceding noun. If this were not so the phrase 'he has brought an evil name . . .' in Deuteronomy 22:19 would refer to the innocent father; likewise the pronouns 'his' and 'he' in Deuteronomy 22:29 go back to an erring other man; and so elsewhere in Hebrew. In Egypt, after talking to Tuthmosis II, Ineni mentions the accession of 'his (Tuthmosis II's) son,' Tuthmosis II, and then the real rule of 'his sister, . . . Hatshepsut.' But 'his' here refers back to Tuthmosis II, not to his son.

"Thirdly, in private conversation Joseph could be blunt with his own brothers (Gn. 45:4, 5, 'you sold. . . .'), but in seeking a favour from the royal butler, an alien, he could not very well reveal the humiliating fact that his own blood brothers wanted to be rid of him (Gn. 40:14, 15)—however unjustly, what kind of impression would that admission have made on the butler?" 42/119-120

(It should be noted that this reference to being "kidnapped" in Genesis 40:14, 15 is totally accurate since Joseph was literally kidnapped from his father by his brothers and it was ultimately because of them that he was taken out of "the land of the Hebrews.")

Lamenting a critical attack upon a passage much like the instances described above, Cassuto appropriately remarks that the passage "affords a classic example of outstandingly beautiful narrative art, and by dismembering it we only destroy a wonderful literary work, the like of which it is hard to find." 15/96

8C. OTHER EVIDENCE EXPLAINING REPETITIOUS ACCOUNTS

Hebrew style is marked by three distinctive traits which illuminate the problem of repetitious accounts:

1D. *Paratactic sentence structure* is the practice, says Archer, "by which subordinate or interdependent ideas are linked together by the simple connective "and" (Heb. W^e)." 11/122 This word thus may be used to convey the meaning of "in order that," "when," "while," "then," "even," or "that is to say"—a versatility which all Hebrew grammarians acknowledge.

Allis agrees and elaborates further:

"The Hebrew not infrequently uses dependent clauses as the English does. But very often coordinates clauses by "and" where we would subordinate one to the other. . . . It is to be noted, therefore, that this tendency to join complete sentences together loosely by "and" may make it appear that the writer is repeating himself; and these loosely connected sentences which all refer to the same event or topic may seem more or less repetitious and to be lacking in strictly logical or chronological sequence. And the very simplicity of the syntax makes it a relatively easy matter to cut apart such sentences, to assert that they describe the same event from different and even conflicting viewpoints and must be assigned to different sources. Were the Biblical narratives written in complicated periodic sentences in the style of an Addison, such analysis would be far more difficult if not impossible." 10/96, 97

A misunderstanding of this basic principle allows many to assume that a late editor clumsily glued his sourcces together with the word "and." But a similar dissection would be impossible in languages which are more precise in this respect, such as classical Greek and Latin. 11/122

2D. *Repetition for emphasis* is seen in the "tendency to repeat in slightly varied form those elements of the narrative which are of special importance," states Archer. 11/122

Allis develops this idea, explaining that "the Bible is a very emphatic book. Its aim is to impress upon the hearer or reader the great importance of the themes of which it treats. The most natural way of securing emphasis in a narrative is by amplification or reiteration. Consequently the Biblical style is often decidedly diffuse and characterized by elaborateness of detail and by repetition." 10/97

The account of the 10 plagues (Exodus 7-11) provides an excellent example of this. Some of the plagues are described in as many as five steps: threat, command, enaction, prayer for removal and termination. By misunderstanding the emphatic nature of this repetition, the radical critics have given seven plagues to J, five plagues to E, and only four to P (not including a fifth which is threatened but not executed). This leaves us with three incomplete accounts, each needing the material in the others to form a sensible entity. 11/122, 123

3D. *Poetic parallelism*, in Archer's words, is the "balanced structure of paired clauses which is employed so extensively in Hebrew verse." 11/123

Again, Allis provides a clear statement of the issue:

"In dealing with the question of repetitions, it is important to note that repetition or parallelism in phraseology and content (*parallelismus membrorum*) is a characteristic feature of Hebrew poetry. This is so obvious that proof is unnecessary. A familiar illustration of practically synonymous parallelism is the following:

> 'The law of Jehovah is perfect, restoring the soul,
> The testimony of Jehovah is sure, making wise the simple'
> (Ps.xix. 7)." 10/108

And in demonstrating the role of such parallelism beyond the boundaries of poetry, Allis expresses that "it has been clearly shown that the dividing line between prose and poetry is not fixed and sharply defined but that elevated or impassioned prose may approximate very closely to poetry, balanced repetition or parallelism." 10/108, 109

When the divine names are alternated in such a parallel fashion, it should clearly be attributed to the poetic style, not to divergent sources. Genesis 30:23, 24 illustrates this:

"*Elohim* has taken away ("*asaf*") my reproach.... May *Yahweh* add ("*yosef*") to me another son."

To divide this passage into E and J due to the divine names (as the critics do) is to fail to recognize the poetic purpose of the alternation of the names and to violate the clear poetic parallelism of "asaf" and "yosef." 11/122, 123

4D. Gordon correlates the Hebrew style with other ancient oriental styles:

"One of the commonest grounds for positing differences of authorship are the repetitions, with variants, in the Bible. But such repetitions are typical of ancient Near East literature: Babylonian, Ugaritic, and even Greek. Moreover, the tastes of the Bible world called for duplication. Joseph and later Pharaoh, each had prophetic dreams in duplicate. In Johan 4, the Prophet's chagrin is described at two stages, each accompanied by God's asking 'Are you good and angry?' (vv. 4, 9). Would anyone insist that such duplicates stem from different pens?" 27/132

5D. The critics' inconsistency

Allis points out also the inconsistency of the documentarians in not claiming as repetitious references to Moses' and Aaron's deaths:

"Three statements are made in Numbers regarding the death of Moses and Aaron. (1) Chap. xx. 24 declares that Aaron is to die because Moses and Aaron sinned, but says nothing of Moses' death; (2) chap. xxvi. 13 says that Moses shall die as Aaron did and for the same reason; (3) chap.xxxi. 2 declares that Moses shall die, but gives no reason of any kind. It would be easy to assert that the first passage belongs to a source which knew only of Aaron's death as a punishment for their joint act of disobedience, that the third knew of Moses' death but of no reason for it unless it be that his work was finished. But all are given to P. This is especially noteworthy because the critics cite as proof that Num. xiii.-xiv. is composite the fact that xiii. 30 and xiv. 24 do not mention Joshua along with Caleb, while xiv. 6, 39, do mention him. So they assign these passages to JE and P respectively." 10/94

2A. ALLEGED CONTRADICTIONS

1B. Introduction

Upon a casual reading of the text, certain contradictions regarding nomenclature, geography, legislation, customs, ethics, etc. seem to appear.

2B. Documentary Assumption

The contradictions are. in fact, real. This is further evidence that there are different authors from different backgrounds, writing at different times. Rather than try to correct the contradictions by deciding which one was right and rejecting the other, the redactors incorporated both accounts into the work.

3B. Basic Answer

Upon careful analysis of the text, the Hebrew language and the ancient oriental cultural background in which the Israelites lived, one finds that these alleged contradictions can be justly harmonized and do in fact, in many cases, disappear.

This truth is tacitly acknowledged by the critics, as Raven perceptively notes:

"The admission of a final redactor is fatal to the assertion of irreconcilable contradictions in the Pentateuch. A man of such marvelous ability as he must have possessed would have seen the contradictions if they were as patent as they are said to be, and would have removed them." 53/127

1C. NOMENCLATURE

The critics hold that different names given to the same person or place is an indication that there is more than one author. (See 17/13; 13/47; 20/182-188)

Examples:

(1). *Amorite* is used in Genesis 10:16 and Deuteronomy 2:24 but *Canaanite* in Genesis 10:18 and Deuteronomy 1:7.

(2). *Horeb* is used in Exodus 33:6 and 17:6 but *Sinai* in Exodus 34:2 and 16:1.

(3). *Jethro* is used in Exodus 3:1 and 4:18 but *Reuel* in Genesis 36:17 and Exodus 2:18.

R.K. Harrison offers a much more plausible and verifiable alternative, making it clear that such a criterion involves utter disregard for its only possible source of objective verification—the evidence from the ancient Near East. The hundreds of examples from Egypt include such personal name variations as Sebekkhu, a military commander, being likewise referred to as Djaa. 32/521

K.A. Kitchen has provided us with many other helpful instances:

"In Egypt, many peope had double names like the Israel/Jacob or Jethro/Reuel of the Old Testament, *e.g.*, Sebek-khu called Djaa whose stela in Manchester University Museum exemplifies the use of three names for one Palestinian populace: Mentiu-Setet ('Asiatic Beduin'), Retenu ('Syrians') and 'Amu' ('Asiatics')—just like the Ishmaelites/Midianites or Canaanites/Amorites of the Old Testament. For personal and group names elsewhere, *cf.* in Mesopotamia the sage Ahiqar (or Ahuqar) who is Aba'-enlil-dari (not to mention Tiglath-pileser III = Pul, and Shalmaneser V = Ululai). In the Hittite Empire, a series of kings had double names, while 'Mitanni' and 'Hanigalbat' and 'Mitanni' and 'Hurrians' occur as double designations of the state and people of Mitanni.

"For place-names like Sinai/Horeb, compare in the text of Merenptah's 'Israel Stela' two names for Egypt (Kemit, Tameri) and five names and variants for Memphis (Mennefer; Ineb-hedj, Inbu, Ineb-heqa; Hatkup-tah). Similarly, examples can be found elsewhere." 42/123, 124

The two alleged accounts of Aaron's death at Mount Hor (Numbers 20:22; 21:4; 33:33; Deuteronomy 32:50) and at Moserah (Deuteronomy 10:6) provide good evidence for the multiple document theory, or so a documentarian would say. But a careful scrutiny of the passages will show that in fact there is no contradiction and thus no ground for a multiple source conclusion. The word Moserah in Deuteronomy 10:6 means "chastisement" and designates the *event* of Aaron's death, not the *place*. This makes it clear that his death on Mount Hor was a reproof, a chastisement for his sin at Meribah (Numbers 20:24; Deuteronomy 32:51). He received the same recompense for his rebellion that Moses received: never to enter the Promised Land. The two accounts are thus in harmony and preserve the fact that Aaron did die at Mount Hor while the people were camped below. Moses marked the sad occasion by naming the camp site Moseroth (Numbers 33:31; Deuteronomy 10:6). 32/510, 511

2C. LEGISLATION

Critics have consistently held that certain laws contained in the Pentateuch are contradictory and that others are identically repeated. This can be seen in this statement by Hahn:

"The theory that separate groups of cultic regulations originated at the local shrines raises the possibility that the duplications and inconsistencies in the Pentateuchal law may have been due to independent, parallel developments rather than successive stages in the history of the law." 31/32

These differences in and repetitions of some of the legislative material are held to be evidence of composite authorship since one writer could hardly be guilty of such obvious inconsistency. Harrison supplies a feasible solution:

"Thus it is quite possible that in the post-Mosaic period some of the enactments were altered somewhat to suit changing circumstances, a process that is perfectly legitimate in any culture, and which does not in any sense vitiate the provenance of the original legislation. No doubt some of the duplications and inconsistencies in Pentateuchal law of which Hahn speaks were due, not to the rise of separate though parallel cultic regulations, as he and many other liberal writers suppose, but to the deliberate attempt on the part of the responsible authorities, whether priestly or other, to adapt the traditional legislation to the point where new conditions of life would be properly accommodated. This doubtless underlies the situation whereby the provisions of Numbers 26:52-56 relating to inheritance were modified by the circumstances detailed in Numbers 27:1-11 and Numbers 36:1-9, or where the regulations for an offering to cover sins of ignorance or inadvertence (Lev. 4:2-21) were changed by the provisions of Numbers 15:22-29. Again, it is of importance to note the witness of the text to the fact that some later additions were made to the Book of the Covenant in the time of Joshua (Josh. 24:26)." 32/539, 540

3C. CUSTOMS

In examining the customs of naming the children, the negative critics cite a proof for multiple documents. They say that in the P document the father names the children, while the mother has this privilege in J and E documents. Thus, each of these documents originated in separate environments.

When one looks at the cases in J and E, it is found that there are 19 or 20 examples that conform to the rule; but there are also 14 exceptions. The number of exceptions is enough to arouse suspicion, especially when it is noted that every instance connected with Jacob is counted as one instance. This weakens the credibility of the case, especially in the light of the fact that two of these instances are classified as P simply because the father names the son. A third instance is unclear as to whether the father named the son or not, which leaves only one instance; and this is nothing on which to base an hypothesis.

The Torah informs us of the reason why there is a difference in the naming of children. Usually the reason for naming a child is etymological and concerns the circumstances at birth. When the circumstance concerns the father he names it, and the same with the mother. This rule is simple and logical, and is valid in every case. When the circumstances apply to the son only or in the rare event that etymological explanation is given, the rule does not apply; in these instances it is once the father, once the mother, and otherwise indefinite. 15/66

4C. ETHICS

J and E are said to have a defect in their moral sensitivity, while P is alert and sensitive. One evidence for this is cited from the story in which Jacob tricks Isaac into giving him Esau's blessing. The moral character of the story must be judged by what attitude the text takes toward the transgressors. In narratives of this nature, it is fundamental that the text does not express its judgment explicitly and subjectively, but it relates the story objectively and allows the reader to learn the moral from the way the events unfold.

It is a fact that Jacob and Rebekah sinned in tricking Isaac, but what did they receive? Jacob was exploited by Laban in the same manner that he exploited his father, and Scripture makes it clear that Jacob received the wrong wife, Leah, as a punishment.

Rebekah too received her heartache when she had to send away the son she loved so much. She once asked him to obey her in the deceitful plot, and again she had to ask him to obey her in leaving. Thus, the moral ethic of the Torah is preserved and source division is again shown to be without grounds.

P is void of a single passage which requires close examination in order to learn its moral. P's complete silence concerning the transgressions of the patriarchs, however, does not necessitate a divergency of sources. For it is significant to note that only *two* narratives concerning the patriarchs are assigned to P (the Cave of Machpelah and the Circumcision). On the other hand, P abounds with dry reports, chronologies and genealogies. Certainly the point on ethics is meaningless when applied to material with *no* didactic content and with no relevant narratives. 15/63-65

3A. ANACHRONISMS—LATE WORDS

1B. Introduction

Certain words are used in the Pentateuch that seem to have come from a later time period. Also, there are words that occur only a few times in the Old Testament and then reappear only much later in other Jewish writings.

2B. Documentary Assumption

The occurrence of such anachronistic words shows that the Pentateuch was written at a time much later than Moses'.

3B. Basic Answer

Some of these words can be attributed to later scribal glosses. Others are, in fact, early and not late words, and with still others it is difficult to tell whether they are early or late.

1C. SCRIBAL GLOSSES

Three examples of words that obviously came (that is, to radical critics) from a period of history later than the Mosaic age:

(1). "Philistines" in Exodus 13:17

(2). "Dan" in Genesis 14:14, Deuteronomy 34:1

(3). Canaan called "land of the Hebrews" in Genesis 40:15
(See 17/15; 54/17)

Harrison suggests that such supposed anachronisms may be explained to be successive scribal revisions that brought the text up to date in some areas.

Other examples are the description of Moses as a prophet of Israel (Deuteronomy 34:10), as well as the various scribal glosses that give later forms of earlier names (Genesis 14:8, 15, 17; 17:14; 23:2; 35:6). Weiser alleges that the reference to a king in Deuteronomy 17:14 is anachronistic; but this shows lack of perception because the passage is foretelling events to take place, and is not recording the present situation. 32/524

Harrison continues:

"Along with revisions of spelling and the inclusion of glosses on the text, the scribes of antiquity frequently replaced an earlier proper name by its later form. This latter phenomenon may well account for such apparent anachronisms as the mention in the Pentateuch of the 'way of the land of the Philistines' (Exod. 13:17), at a time when the Philistines had yet to occupy the Palestinian coastal region in any strength." 32/523

2C. RARE WORDS

Archer paraphrases the critics' argument regarding rare words:

"If a word occurring less than three or four times in the Old Testament recurs only in later Hebrew literature (the Talmud and Midrash), then the word is of late origin, and the Old Testament passage must be of late composition." 11/125

This is invariably the interpretation offered by Old Testament scholars; but there are in fact *three* viable explanations:

(a) as stated above, that the "early" occurrence is actually within a body of writing which had a later origin;

(b) that the "early" occurrence provides evidence that the word was actually in common usage at the earlier date;

(c) that a truly "late" word may only demonstrate that the word itself was originated in the text (having been substituted for an obsolete, offensive or obscure word), and shows nothing as to the date of the body of writing.

While most scholars ignore the last two principles, the validity of the principles may be proven by an examination of literary remains of the ancient Orient which are objectively dated.

An example of (b) presents itself in the well-known phenomenon of the sporadic occurrence of words in, for instance, the Pyramid Texts of 2400 B.C. The word may then totally disappear, only to be found 21 centuries later (about 300-30 B.C.) in the writings of the Greco-Roman period. To compact more than two millennia of Egyptian history into a two and a half century period is, of course, absurd. Yet a wholesale application of this criterion leads scholars to just such absurdities with Hebrew literature. 42/141, 142

Likewise, Ecclesiasticus 50:3, dated in the second century B.C., provided the earliest occurrence of *swh* ("reservoir"), leading to the conclusion that it was a late word. But the more recent surprise discovery of the same word on the Moabite Stone added a sudden seven centuries to its age. 11/126, 127

One of many examples of (c) is seen in the Ashmolean text of the story of Sinuhe, which is definitely dated in the 20th century B.C. due to internal statements. However, the occurrence of *yam* for "sea" and the Late-Egyptian *bw* for "no" point to a date of 1500 B.C., according to principle (a). Manuscripts from about 1800 B.C. provide us with the answer—that the two words were actually substituted for early forms. The future discovery of very ancient Old Testament manuscripts may show the same truth in the Hebrew Scriptures. 42/141-143

Further, the Old Testament provides only a bare representation of the entire Hebrew literary output. Three thousand Old Testament words appear less than six times; 1500 occur but once. Certainly a greater knowledge of Hebrew literature and conversation would establish many of these as everyday Hebrew terms. Similarly, no one would argue that words like "invasion" (I Samuel 30:14), "jumping" (Nahum 3:2) and "lance" (Jeremiah 50:42) are rare in English, yet they are found only once in the English Bible. 11/126, 127

Robert Dick Wilson has done an excellent study of the words used five or less times in the Old Testament. He has shown that "a large part of the words that are produced as evidence [by the critics] of the late date of documents containing them cannot themselves be proved to be late. For, first, no one can maintain that because a word occurs only in a late document the word itself is therefore late; for in this case, if a late document was the only survival of a once numerous body of literature, every word in it would be late; which is absurd. Nor, secondly, can one maintain that a document is late merely because it contains words which do not occur in earlier ones, which are known to us. Every new find of Egyptian Aramaic papyri gives us words not known before, except, if at all, in documents written hundreds of years later. Nor, thirdly, is a word to be considered as evidence of the lateness of a document in which it occurs simply because it occurs again in documents known to be late, such as the Hebrew parts of the Talmud. And yet, this is frequently affirmed by the critics.... it is obvious that a kind of proof that will prove almost everything to be late, and especially the parts considered late to be early, is absurd and inadmissible as evidence in a case designed to prove that some documents are later than others because they contain words of this kind. For it is certain that if all are late, then none are early—a conclusion which would overthrow the position of all critics, radical as well as conservative; and since this conclusion is desired and maintained by none, it must be dismissed as *absurd*.

"In proof, however, that such words are found in every book, and in almost every part of every book, of the Old Testament we subjoin the following tables. These tables are based on special concordances of every book and of every part of every book of the Old Testament, prepared by and now in the possession of the writer of this article. In accordance with the laws of evidence, that 'witnesses must give evidence of facts,' and 'an expert may state general facts which are the result of scientific knowledge, and that an expert may give an account of experiments [hence, also of investigations] performed by him for the purpose of forming his opinion,' it may add force and clearness to the evidence about to be presented, if an account is first given of the way in which the facts upon which the tables are based were collected. One whole summer was spent in gathering from a Hebrew concordance all the words in the Old Testament that occur there five times or less, giving also the places where the words occur. A second summer sufficed for making from this general concordance a special concordance for each book. In the third summer, special concordances were made for J, E. D, H, and P, for each of the five books of the Psalter and for each of the psalms; for each of the parts of Proverbs, and of the alleged parts of Isaiah, Micah, Zechariah, Chronicles, Ezra, Nehemiah; and for such parts as Gen. xiv and the poems contained in Gen. xlix, Ex. xv, Deut. xxxii, xxxiii and Judges v. Then, each of the words of this kind was sought for in the Aramaic and in the Hebrew of the post-biblical Jewish writers. The evidence of the facts collected is manifest, and we think conclusive.

"A study of these percentages should convince everyone that the presence of such words in a document is no proof of its relative lateness.*

	Number of words occurring in O.T. five times or less	Percentage of these words in Talmud
Psalms lxxix	3	00.0
Prov. xxxi. 1-9	0	00.0
Isaiah xxiv-xxvii	0	00.0
Obadiah	7	14.3

Isaiah xxxvi-ix	7	14.3
Judges-Ruth	107	15.8
Nahum	36	16.7
Ezra i-vi	6	16.7
Micah ii	11	18.2
Isaiah xxxiv-v	5	20.0
Isaiah xiii-xiv	10	20.0
Isaiah (1st pt.)	121	22.3
Malachi	13	23.1
Ezekiel	335	24.9
Lamentation	56	25.0
Haggai	4	25.0
Ezra vii-x	8	25.0
Zechariah ii	16	25.0
Isaiah xl-lxvi	62	25.8
Proverbs i-ix	69	27.5
Daniel	47	29.8
Zecharia [sic] i	22	30.8

*In explanation of these tables it may be said that they are prepared with special reference to the critical analysis of the O.T. Thus the Pentateuch is arranged according to the documents, J, E, D, H and P; and the Proverbs are divided into seven portions (following LOT). The first column of the tables gives for each book or part of a book the number of words occurring five times or less in the Old Testament that are found in it; and the second column the percentage of these words that are to be found in the same sense in the Hebrew of the Talmud.

	Number of words occurring in O.T. five times or less	Percentage of these words in Talmud
Zecharia [sic] iii	12	30.8
Micah i	22	31.8
Job	374	31.0
Jeremiah	278	32.1
Psalms	514	33.1
Book I	123	35.8
Book II	135	31.1
Book III	76	30.3
Book IV	61	31.1
Book V	118	34.7
Micah iii	15	33.3
Prov. x-xxii. 16	80	33.8
Proverbs xxii. 17-xxiv	30	36.7
Sam.-Kings	356	37.2
Habakkuk	34	38.2
Joel	28	39.3
Jonah	15	40.0
Hosea	65	41.5
Jehovist (J)	162	44.4
Zephaniah	31	45.2
Amos	50	46.0
Elohist (E)	119	48.7
Prov. xxxi. 10-31	6	50.0
Holiness Code (H)	48	50.0
Chronicles	144	51.5

Prov. xxv-xxix	52	51.9
Esther	57	52.6
Priest Code (P)	192	53.1
Deuteronomist (D)	154	53.2
Proverbs xxx	15	53.5
Song of Songs	99	54.6
Nehemiah	48	56.3
Ecclesiastes	77	57.1
Memoirs of Nehemiah	27	59.3

"A careful reading of this table will justify the statement made above that a 'kind of proof that will prove almost everything to be late, and especially the parts considered late to be early, is absurd and inadmissible as evidence in a case designed to prove that some documents are later than others because they contain words of this kind.' This kind of evidence would simply prove almost all the documents of the Old Testament to be late. If admitted as valid, it would militate as much against the views of the radicals as it would against those of the conservatives.

"Take, for example, the number of these words occurring in the alleged documents of the Pentateuch. J and E together have 281 words in about 2,170 verses (one in less than every 7⁷⁄₁₀ verses) and about 46 per cent of these words are found in the Talmud; D has 154 words in about 1,000 verses (or one in every 6⁶⁄₁₀ verses) and about 53 per cent of them in the Talmud, and PH 201 words in 2,340 verses (or one in every 8⁸⁄₁₀ verses) and about 52 per cent of the words in the Talmud. Surely, no unbiased judge of literature would attempt to settle the dates of documents on such slight variations as these from one word in 6⁶⁄₁₀ to one in 8⁸⁄₁₀ and from 46 to 53 per cent in the Talmud! Besides, in regard to the relative proportion in verses the order is PH, JE, D and in percentages in the Talmud JE, PH, D; but according to the Wellhausians, it should in both cases be JE, D, PH. The slight variations in both cases point to unity of authorship and likeness of date." 65/131-136

3C. ARAMAISMS

The Babylonian Capitivity (607-538 B.C.) marked the beginning of the Jews' abandonment of their ancestral Hebrew language in favor of the more widely spoken Aramaic language. Therefore, the critics held that the presence of an Aramaic word in the biblical text was evidence that the passage had a post-exilic origin. They asserted that many such "Aramaisms" do in fact appear in the Pentateuch. This supports their theory of a late origin for their written sources (J, E, D, P, etc.).

But Archer offers this philological evidence:

"A great number of Hebrew words which they [documentarians] have classified as Aramaisms turn out, on closer examination, to have a very good claim to the status of authentic Hebrew words, or else to be derivable from Phoenician, Babylonian or Arabic dialects, rather than from Aramaic. For example, many critics have carelessly assumed that Hebrew nouns ending in -ōn are necessarily Aramaic because the -ān ending is so common in Aramaic. Yet the fact of the matter is that this ending is also found with fair frequency in Babylonian and Arabic, and further proof is necessary to demonstrate that it could not have been native in Hebrew from Canaanite times." 11/129

The Jewish scholar M.H. Segal concludes similarly:

"It has been the fashion among writers on the subject to brand as an

Aramaism any infrequent Hebrew word which happens to be found more or less frequently in Aramaic dialects. Most of the Aramaisms are as native in Hebrew as they are in Aramaic. Many of them are also found in other Semitic languages." 57/8

Kautzsch (*Die Aramaismen im Alten Testamente*) has listed about 350 words as being possibly of Aramaic origin. On this basis, over 1500 Old Testament verses in which the words occur are assigned a late date. Yet the thorough scholarship of R.D. Wilson has revealed the following information:

(a) 150 of these 350 words are *never* found in an Aramaic dialect.

(b) 235 of these 350 words are *never* found in Aramaic literature before the second century A.D.

(c) Only 40 of those found earlier than the second century A.D. are unique to Aramaic among the Near Eastern languages.

(d) Only 50 of the list of 350 words are found in the Pentateuch.

(e) More than two-thirds of these 50 "Aramaic" words in the Pentateuch had to be replaced by an genuinely Aramaic word to make them intelligible in the Aramaic translations.

(f) Most of the words which were *not* replaced in the Aramaic translations are still not unique to Aramaic among the Near Eastern Languages.

Even using the dating of the radical critics, we find that a full 120 of these alleged 350 "Aramaic words" are used by Old Testament writers as much as 700 years before they are found in any Aramaic documents. While it is easy to understand these as Hebrew words which were incorporated into Aramaic as more and more Jews made the transition, it is difficult to believe that the biblical writers borrowed so many Aramaic words which are apparently not used until seven centuries later. 65/155-163

chapter 13

incongruities___

1A. INTRODUCTION

The Pentateuch was supposed to have been written by Moses, yet many passages regarding Moses are written in the third person, rather than the first. Also, if the Pentateuch was written by Moses, how could it contain the account of his death?

2A. DOCUMENTARY ASSUMPTION

Such incongruities are an indication that in reality Moses did not write the Pentateuch.

3A. BASIC ANSWER

There are two very plausible alternatives to the critics' third person argument. And the account of Moses' death need not necessarily be attributed to Moses.

1B. Third Person Phenomen

1C. POSSIBLY DICTATED

Moses may have dictated his work to scribes.
Harrison suggests this:

"Equally uncertain is the actual extent to which Moses recorded personally the written material credited to him. It may well be that the presence of third person pronouns in various sections of the Mosaic enactments indicate that these sections were dictated. Quite possibly many of the small or isolated sections in the Hebrew text were committed initially to the priests for safekeeping, and only at a later period were the manuscript pieces assembled into some sort of mosaic and joined together into a roll." 32/538

This would be quite consistent with ancient oriental practice as R.D. Wilson argues:

"Is one to allege, then, that Hammurabi cannot be called the author of the code named after him, unless, forsooth, he inscribed it with his own hand? And yet the monument expressly ascribes itself to Hammurabi in the words of the epilogue (Col. Li. 59-67): 'In the days that are yet to come, for all future times, may the king who is in the land observe the words of righteousness which I have written upon my monument....' Are we to suppose that Moses cannot have recorded his thought and words and deeds just in the same way that his predecessors, contemporaries, and successors, did?" 65/24, 25

2C.   POSSIBLY WRITTEN BY MOSES IN THIRD PERSON

Moses may have actually written in the third person. This does not seem too unreasonable in light of the fact that the following authors of antiquity wrote about themselves, either in part or in full, in the third person:

Josephus, *The Wars of the Jews* (first century A.D.)
Xenophon, *Anabasis* (fifth century B.C.)
Julius Caesar, *Gallic War* (first century B.C.) 41/23, 24; 61/265

2B. Moses' Death

The account of Moses' death was a later addition.

The Talmud [*Baba Bathra* 146] attributes this section relating to Moses' death to Joshua. 32/661

Archer says this about Deuteronomy:

"Chapter 34 is demonstrably post-Mosaic, since it contains a short account of Moses' decease. But this does not endanger in the slightest the Mosaic authenticity of the other thirty-three chapters, for the closing chapter furnishes only that type of obituary which is often appended to the final work of great men of letters." 11/224

G. Aalders in his book, *A Short Introduction to the Pentateuch,* treats the various views on the death of Moses recorded in chapter 34 of Deuteronomy. 1/105-110

chapter 14

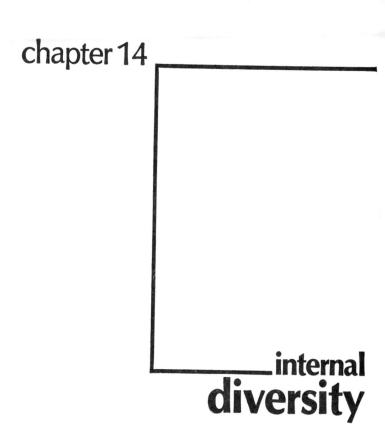

internal
diversity

1A. INTRODUCTION

There is considerable diversity in the Pentateuch as to subject matter, style, and diction.

2A. DOCUMENTARY ASSUMPTION

This internal diversity highly suggests that the Pentateuch was written by different men at different times each of whom had his own individual point of view and technique. This is much more plausible than believing that only one man is responsible for a work characterized by such diversity as the Pentateuch.

3A. BASIC ANSWER

Diversity of subject matter, style, and diction can be legitimately accounted for without resorting to composite authorship.

1B. Subject Matter

Regarding the ancient orientals' ability to write different subject matter, Harrison says:

"The concentration in one man of the ability to write historical narrative, to compose poetry, and to collate legal material is by no means as unique as earlier critical writers were wont to assume. As Kitchen has pointed out, an illustration of this kind of ability from ancient Egypt at a period some seven centuries prior to the time of Moses has been furnished in all probability by

Khety (or Akhtoy), son of Duauf, a writer who lived in the time of the pharaoh Amenemhat I (*ca.* 1991-1962 B.C.). This versatile individual apparently combined the functions of educator, poet, and political propagandist, and wrote the *Satire of the Trades* as a text for use by students in the scribal schools. He was probably commissioned to give literary form to the *Teaching of Amenemhat I*, which was a political pamphlet popular in the Eighteenth to Twentieth Dynasties as an exercise to be copied by schoolboys. In addition, he may have been the author of a popular *Hymn to the Nile,* which with the foregoing works was also frequently copied out by scribes. Quite clearly, then, it is by no means inherently impossible for a talented individual to have engaged during the Amarna period in the kind of literary activity traditionally ascribed to Moses." 32/538

2B. Style

Driver states, "If the parts assigned to P be read attentively, even in a translation, and compared with the rest of the narrative, the peculiarities of style will be apparent." 18/20 (See the quote by Driver below in the Diction section.)

Raven deals well with this phenomenon as it occurs in passages relating specifically to God:

"P is said to be cold, formal, systematic, logical but it is precisely in such passages that one would expect Elohim, the general name for God, the name which has no special relation to Israel but is used many times in reference to the deities of the Gentiles. J on the other hand is said to be naive, anthropomorphic in his conception of God; but these evidences of religious fervor would lead us to expect the proper national name of God, the name which emphasized his covenant relations with Israel. There are passages in which we cannot explain why one name of the deity is used rather than another; but in the great majority of cases, any other name would be inappropriate." 53/119

Dante's *Divine Comedy* provides a helpful example of a work which has only one author but has divergent styles in presenting God's nature. Many passages colorfully depict the intervention of God into human affairs (as J and E), while immediately beside them are passages rich in systematic doctrine (as P). Yet here we have one author and one document—no more. 15/59

Indeed, it cannot be contested that in the P document one finds a cold, dry atmosphere that has an affinity for details and a fondness of stereotyped phrases. In contrast to P, J and E are marked by their vividness, color and life. But let us not be deceived by appearances. The reason P is dull and dry is because the material attributed to it is that way by nature. How is it possible to give vitality and charm to a genealogical record? But the few narratives given to P contain vividness and grace of diction, just as the genealogies assigned to J are frigid, insipid and schematic. Thus one finds, affirms Cassuto, that "change of style depends on change of subject matter, not on different sources." 15/53, 54

Raven further develops this central issue:

"The claim of a distinct vocabulary for P and JE can be maintained only by mutilating the record. If an expression usually found in P occurs in a JE section, the chapter and sometimes even the verse is divided. If narratives were left entire except in case of an expression which might be a later gloss, the argument would be much weakened. By this method any literary work could be divided into several sources, more or less complete." 53/124

Kitchen very aptly drives home this weakness in the critics' methodology, stating that "the supposed consistency of criteria over a large body of writing is contrived and deceptive (especially on vocabulary, for example), and will hold for 'style' only if one in the first place picks out everything of a particular kind, then proclaims it as all belonging to one document separate from the rest, and finally appeals to its remarkable consistency—a consistency obtained by deliberate selection in the first place, and hence attained by circular reasoning. 'P' owes its existence mainly to this kind of procedure, and was not even recognized to have existed for the one hundred years from Astruc in 1753 until Hupfeld in 1853." 42/115-116

Many radical critics are confident that a difference in style within the same subject matter would tend to indicate different authors. But any one author will use different styles for different subject matter. A lawyer, for example, will use a different style in a letter to his mother than in a brief he has prepared. Here again a clergyman uses a different style talking to his children in the morning than he does in his benediction. A physician will only use a prescription style of writing when writing a prescription. In the same vein, the technical description of the ark in Genesis is no more evidence of different authorship from the surrounding narrative than a naval architect's style of describing a vessel makes him a different author than the same architect writing a love letter to his fiancée. 27/132

Finally, archaeological data indicate that the existence of stylistic differences in a literary work was characteristic of much of the ancient Orient. Kitchen has described the inscription of Uni, an Egyptian official (2400 B.C.), which contains a flowing narrative (J, E?), summary statements (P?), a victory hymn (H) and two different refrains (R_1, R_2?) which are repeated often. Yet the fact remains that there is no question of different documents in the monumental inscription which was engraved in stone at the request of the one it commemorates. 42/125, 126

Another helpful parallel is discovered in the royal inscriptions of the kings of Urartu. There is a set formula for going forth of the god Haldi (P?), a triple formula for the going forth of the king (K_1, K_2, K_3,?), a compact statement of success (S?) or first personal narrative (N?) and every so often there are statistics of the Urartian army or of the spoils they have taken (P again?). This is unquestioned as a document because it has no prehistory or rival proto-author and its style has lasted a century. 42/125, 126

3B. Diction

Certain words are considered to be unique to the J document, others to the P document, and so on. Driver gives an extensive list of those words and phrases that are said to be an indication of composite authorship. (see 18/131-135

About Genesis, Driver says:

"In short, the Book of Genesis presents two groups of sections, distinguished from each other by differences of phraseology and style." 17/IV

Even allowing that there was no other plausible explanation for this phenomenon, W.J. Martin points out that inducing composite authorship from a variation in vocabulary is groundless:

"The invalidity of such criteria has long been recognized by classical scholars, and no one would now think of attaching any significance to, say, the fact that beans are mentioned in the Iliad but not in the Odyssey; that the Iliad is rich in words for wounds and wounding, whereas such words are rare in, or absent from, the Odyssey; that the words for grasshopper, crane, eel, maggots, snow, sparrow, and donkey occur only in the Iliad, palm-tree only in the Odyssey. In fact the Iliad uses 1,500 words none of which occurs in the Odyssey. Or again, no deductions of any kind could be made from the fact that in the works of Shakespeare the word 'pious' is found only in Hamlet and subsequent plays. Even inconsistencies may occur in one and the same author; Virgil in a single book makes the wooden horse of fir in one passage, of maplewood in another, and of oak in yet another." 46/13

Cassuto establishes the following ground rules for the proper handling of linguistic diversity:

"(a) we must not rely upon the differences in language in order to determine the origin of the sections, which we shall subsequently use to decide the linguistic characteristics of the sources, for in that case we shall indeed fall into the snare of reasoning in a circle; (b) nor emend the texts in order to make them conform to our theory; (c) nor consider words and forms mechanically, as though they were divorced from their context and the latter could have no bearing on their use. As we shall soon see, the exponents of the documentary hypothesis were not always careful to avoid all these pitfalls." 15/44

While it is readily admitted that there is considerable variation of vocabulary in the Pentateuch (i.e., that different words denote the same thing, that certain phrases and words appear in some sections but not in others, etc.), the evidence for the existence of unique diction in each "source" is the result of the critics' circular reasoning. They compile a list of all the passages that contain certain words, labelling these passages as being from a particular "source," and then announce that since these words do not appear elsewhere in the text outside that "source" they are, in fact, characteristic of that "source" only. Thus, the phenomenon is created by the hypothesis itself. (See above, Kitchen's first quote on variation in style.)

Here is one example:

There are two words in Hebrew for "female slave," one being *amah* and the other *shiphah*. Critics have assigned *amah* to the Elohist as being the word he used for "female slave" and *shiphah* to the Yahwist as being his term for the same thing. 11/111

Some critics assert that when speaking of a female slave the Yahwist *invariably* uses the Hebrew word *shiphah* and the Elohist *always* uses *amah*. Driver quite prudently concedes that E's use of *amah* is not invariable, but only preferable. Yet even this is strong. E uses *amah* six times in Genesis (20:17; 21:10, 12, 13; 30:3; 31:33), yet *shiphah* occurs almost as often in E or in solidly unified contexts (assigned to E: Genesis 20:14; 29:24, 29; assigned to P: 30:4, 7, 18.)

Orr reacts harshly to the methodology practiced here, retorting:

"It is pure arbitrariness and circular reasoning to change this single word in chap. xx. 14 and xxx. 18, on the ground that 'the regular word for women slaves in E is *Amah*,' and that 'J on the other hand always employs *Shiphah*' — the very point in dispute. In chap. xxix. 24, 29, the verses are cut out and given to P; chap. xxx. 4, 7 are similarly cut out and given to J." 50/231

Genesis 20 furnishes the first substantial E portion in Genesis; yet *shiphah* (the J word) appears in verse 14, then followed by *amah* (the E word) in v. 17. Holzingar, asserting that "E does not use the word," deletes *shiphah*, as he also does in Genesis 30:18. To presuppose that E uses this word and to then attribute every exception to J's insertion or to the redactor's blunder is to simply build one's conclusion into his premise. Such a method is logically fallacious, unscientific and would allow one to prove anything he likes. 11/111

Cassuto provides us with another very beneficial example. He believes that a lack of scholarship is shown when the proponents of the theory deal with the Hebrew words *beterem* and *terem*. Each place *beterem* appears is ascribed to

E and where *terem* is found, it is ascribed to J. Unfortunately for the documentarians, these words are not synonyms. They are two totally different words; *beterem* means "before" and *terem* means "not only." It is apparent since these words mean two different things that their usage would be different. There is no question here of different sources. 15/51

Diversity of diction is also the issue when the documentarians argue that the use of the words "to bring up from Egypt" (which are employed by the E document) and "to bring forth from Egypt" (which are employed by the J document) are proof of multiple documents.

But in understanding the meaning of each phrase we reach a different conclusion. When the phrase "to bring up from Egypt" is used, it means they came from Egypt and entered into the Promised Land, while "to bring forth from Egypt" simply means to leave Egypt. In Genesis 46:4, God tells Jacob "I will also surely bring you up." This means H will bring him back to the Promised Land. On the other hand, in Genesis 15:14, it says, "and afterwards they will come out with many possessions" which when read with the context clearly shows that the Exodus is being talked about. When the inner meaning of the words is sought and the passage is not looked at mechanically, the underlying principles become clear. 15/48

We find a further example in the fact that the Pentateuch records numbers in two different ways: ascending order, such as the number "twenty and a hundred," and descending order, "a hundred and twenty." The critics postulate that J, E and D employ the descending order, while ascending order is characteristic of P.

A more logical explanation can be found in the fact that the ascending order is consistently associated with technical or statistical dates. On the other hand, solitary numbers are almost always in descending order, except in a few cases where special circumstances operate. Examples of this rule are seen when Moses was addressing the children of Israel, saying, "I am an hundred and twenty" (Deuteronomy 31:2), and in the passage concerning the offering of princes, where it states, "all the gold of the dishes being twenty and a hundred shekels" (Numbers 7:86, RSV).

In the light of this explanation one may ask how it is possible to explain the fact that the ascending order is to be found only in the P sections. The answer is very simple: P is formulated on the basis of its assumed constituency of all chronological and genealogical tables, all statistical records, all technical descriptions of services and the like. Thus, it is obvious that the ascending order will occur more often in the supposed P document. 15/51 ff

A final example is supplied by the word *yalad*. This Hebrew word for "beget" is alternately used in its causative form and in its regular form (but with causative meaning). Critics explain this by assigning the former to P and the latter to J. Their reasons? Apparently so that in passages of doubtful source, a precedent may now be established for assigning to J those which use the regular form with a causative meaning and to P those which use the strictly causative form. 15/43

1C. SUBJECT MATTER

In answer to the argument that words peculiar to the supposed documents are evidence for the documentary theory, Raven points out that the real reason for word variation is a difference in subject matter:

"Of course the argument has no weight unless the words or expression is one which both writers had occasion to use. Many of the words in Driver's list are confined to P because neither J, E, nor D had occasion to use them." 53/122

This should be obvious. We would expect the vocabulary used in a systematic genealogy (e.g. Genesis 10) to be somewhat different from the vocabulary used in a flowing narrative (e.g. Genesis 8-9). Upon investigation we find that it is not because it was written by two different people but because one is a genealogy and one is a narrative.

2C. VARIETY

It is essential to remember that a single author will utilize variety to attain vividness or emphasis. A helpful example is seen in the Exodus account of pharaoh's refusal to release the Israelites from Egypt. His obstinacy in the face of the plagues is referred to by three verbs meaning "to make strong or bold" (assigned to P and E), "to make hard" (assigned to P), and "to make heavy and insensible" (given to J). But an examination of the sequence of their usage yields the recognition of a natural psychological order—from boldness, to hardness, to insensibility. This is clearly due to the design of the author, not the mingling of documents. 11/116

3C. OUR POSSESSION OF ONLY A FRACTION OF THE ARCHAEOLOGICAL EVIDENCE THAT COULD SHED MUCH LIGHT ON ANCIENT HEBREW USAGE OF CERTAIN WORDS

The radical critics have traditionally held that the longer form of the pronoun "I" *(anoki)* is earlier in usage than the shorter form *(ani)*. This distinction is employed as a criterion for source division, even though an investigation of the text shows that the alternation of the two forms is frequently due to cliche. "I *(ani)* am Yahweh" is obviously a conventional phrase which is regularly found in contexts which freely·use the longer form *anoki*. And the entire argument has recently been proven a fabrication by the discovery of fifteenth century B.C. inscriptions at Ras Shamra in which *both* forms of the pronoun are seen side by side.

Another example:

Two Hebrew words for "window" are used in the Flood story. *Arubbah* is used in Genesis 7:11 and 8:2a. But in 8:6 the word for "window" is *challon* (10/78, 79). The documentarians hold that *arubbah* is the word that the P author used for window, and consequently Genesis 7:11 and the first part of 8:2 are part of the P document. *Challon* is the word that the J author used for "window" and so Genesis 8:6 is part of the J·document.

Is there another way to account for the use of both of these words that seem to denote the very same thing in so short a narrative as the Flood story?

The answer is yes. Although we do not yet know why both these terms were used in such close proximity to each other, archaeological excavations at Ras Shamra uncovered a tablet on which *both* of these words appear, thus rendering it highly untenable that the same usage in Genesis must mean two authors. 251/88, 98

Such archaeological discoveries have seriously undermined the arguments of the Documentary Hypothesis and there is every reason to believe that further excavations will continue to provide us with verifiable data regarding the *real* literary techniques of the ancient Hebrews.

While it has already done much to defend the integrity of Israelite literature, it should be realized that archaeology has barely even scratched the surface, as Edwin Yamauchi, formerly of Rutgers University and now of Miami University (Ohio), points out:

"If one could by an overly optimistic estimate reckon that ¼ of our materials and inscriptions survived, that ¼ of the available sites have been excavated, that ¼ of the excavated sites have been examined, and that ¼ of the materials and inscriptions excavated have been published, one would still have less than 1/1000 of the possible evidence ($\frac{1}{4} \times \frac{1}{4} \times \frac{1}{4} \times \frac{1}{4}$). Realistically speaking the percentage is no doubt even smaller." 70/12

4B. The Unity of the Pentateuch

The entire Pentateuch is founded upon a unity of arrangement and is linked together into an organic whole, with only rare overlapping and restatement due to the progressive nature of God's revelation to Moses. Even the critics acknowledge this unity by their introduction of the hypothetical redactor to account for the Pentateuch's present order and harmony. 11/108

An example of such a concession is provided by Edward Riehm (*Einleitung in das Alte Testament*, 1889, I, p. 202), here cited by Archer:

"Most of the laws of the middle books of the Pentateuch form essentially a homogeneous whole. They do not indeed all come from one hand, and have not been written at one and the same time.... However, they are all ruled by the same principles and ideas, have the same setting, the like form of representation, and the same mode of expression. A multitude of definite terms appear again and again. In manifold ways also the laws refer to one another. Apart from isolated subordinate differences, they agree with one another, and so supplement each other as to give the impression of a single whole, worked out with a marvelous consistency in its details." 11/108

W.J. Martin states:

"Genesis possesses all the characteristics of a homogeneous work: articulation, the unwitting use of forms and syntactical patterns which indicate the linguistic and geographical milieu of the writer, the function of particles, and in particular the definite article passing through the stages from demonstrative to definitive, as well as here the fluid state of grammatical gender. The writer of Genesis was a man of such pre-eminent literary gifts, as almost to suggest a facility and preoccupation with models in another literary medium. He has all the characteristics of genius: variety and diversity, multiplicity of alternatives, wide range of colours, a full gamut of notes exploited with masterly skill. No man now would dream of deducing from diversity of style diversity of authorship; diversity is part of the very texture of genius. It is not in the uniformity of diction or style but in the uniformity of quality that unity is discerned. It is easier to believe in a single genius than to believe that there existed a group of men possessing such pre-eminent gifts, so self-effacing, who could have produced such a work." 46/22

chapter 15

conclusion
to the
documentary
hypothesis

1A. SUGGESTED STRENGTHS

1B. Collective Force of the Hypothesis

Critics readily admit that each criterion by which the Pentateuch is divided into sources is not, by itself, a convincing argument. However, when taken collectively, these criteria do in fact present a powerful case for composite authorship.

Along these lines the British documentarian, A.T. Chapman, says:

"The strength of the critical position is mainly due to the fact that the same conclusions are reached by independent lines of argument." 16/39 Hence they appeal to the cumulative effect of these "independent lines of argument" (criteria).

But as Kitchen points out: "It is a waste of time to talk about the 'cumulative force' of arguments that are each invalid; $0+0+0+0=0$ on any reckoning. The supposed concordance of assorted criteria whose independence is more apparent than real has had to be rejected ...on evidence far too bulky to include in this book." 42/125

2B. The Reason for the Widespread Acceptance of the Theory

Why, it may be asked, if the Documentary Hypothesis is as invalid as this investigation has attempted to show, was it so eagerly received and defended in most scholarly circles throughout continental Europe, Great Britain, and the United States?

W.H. Green answers this way:

"A large number of eminent scholars accept the critical partition of the Pentateuch in general, if not in all its details. It has its fascinations, which sufficiently account for its popularity. The learning, ability, and patient toil which have been expended upon its elaboration, the specious arguments arrayed in its support, and the skill with which it has been adapted to the phenomena of the Pentateuch and of the Old Testament generally, have given to it the appearance of great plausibility. The novel lines of inquiry which it opens make it attractive to those of a speculative turn of mind, who see in it the opportunity for original and fruitful research in the reproduction of ancient documents, long buried unsuspected in the existing text, which they antedate by centuries. The boldness and seeming success with which it undertakes to revolutionize traditional opinion and give a new respect to the origin and history of the religion of the Old Testament, and its alliance with the doctrine of development, which has found such wide application in other fields of investigation, have largely contributed to its popularity." 29/131, 132

Green continues:

"Its failure is not from the lack of ingenuity or learning, or persevering effort on the part of its advocates, not from the want of using the utmost latitude of conjecture, but simply from the impossibility of accomplishing the end proposed." 29/132

2A. FATAL METHODOLOGICAL WEAKNESSES

Gleason Archer, a graduate of Suffolk Law School, sums up the fallacious methodology in this way:

"It is very doubtful whether the Wellhausen hypothesis is entitled to the status of scientific respectability. There is so much of special pleading, circular reasoning, questionable deductions from unsubstantiated premises that it is absolutely certain that its methodology would never stand up in a court of law. Scarcely any of the laws of evidence respected in legal proceedings are honored by the architects of this Documentary Theory. Any attorney who attempted to interpret a will or statute or deed of conveyance in the bizarre and irresponsible fashion of the source-critics of the Pentateuch would find his case thrown out of the court without delay." 11/99

Some specific examples of these weaknesses are outlined below.

1B. The Imposition of a Modern Occidental View on Ancient Oriental Literature

The radical critics' approach is highly questionable when it is assumed that (a) the date of composition of each document can be confidently fixed, even with *no* other contemporary Hebrew literature available for comparison, and that, (b) unexpected or rare words in the Masoretic Text can be readily replaced by a more suitable word.

These practices are especially doubtful in light of Archer's observation:

"As foreigners living in an entirely different age and culture, they have felt themselves competent to discard or reshuffle phrases or even entire verses whenever their Occidental concepts of consistency or style have been offended.

"They have also assumed that scholars living more than 3,400 years after the event can (largely on the basis of philosophical theories) more reliably reconstruct the way things really happened than could the ancient authors themselves (who were removed from the events in question by no more than

600 or 1000 years even by the critic's own dating)." 11/99

2B. The Lack of Objective Evidence

Even the most dogmatic documentarian must admit that there is no objective evidence for the existence or the history of the J, E or any of the documents that are alleged to make up the Torah. There is no manuscript of any portion of the Old Testament dating from earlier than the third century B.C. 42/23

W.H. Green's comment on this point (in Chambers, *Moses and His Recent Critics*, pp. 104, 105) cited by Torrey, is well taken:

"All tradition and all historical testimony as to the origin of the Pentateuch are against them. The burden of proof is wholly upon the critics. And this proof should be clear and convincing in proportion to the gravity and the revolutionary character of the consequences which it is proposed to base upon it." 60/74

Bruce K. Waltke, Ph.D., Harvard University and Fellow of the Hebrew University in Jerusalem states firmly:

"Though one who has read only the popular literature advancing the conclusions of the literary analytical approach might not realize it, even the most ardent advocate of the theory must admit that we have as yet not a single scrap of tangible, external evidence for either the existence or the history of the sources J, E, D, P." 5/2

3B. Substitution of Disintegrative Approach for Harmonistic Approach

The harmonistic approach is the standard methodology in the study both of literature and of ancient documents. Anytime it is abandoned for an attempt to find contradictions, literature will yield such "contradictions" by virtue of its inherent diversity. The same is true of biblical studies.

Allis has aptly noted:

"Disintegration must result inevitably from the application of the disintegrative method of interpretation, whether the variations or differences appealed to are found in the form or in the content of the document to which it is applied." 10/126

Kyle maintains a similar line of thinking:

"Criticism is not faultfinding, but it very easily becomes so. And when it sets out on a course of reconstruction which questions the integrity and trustworthiness of the documents to which it is applied, the disposition to find fault, to look for discord, is irresistible; indeed, it is essential to the process. But it is a fallacious method which is very apt to nullify processes of thought." 117/178

One of the most painful features of this weakness is its tendency to fabricate problems which are normally not there.

"Some of the alleged difficulties," avers Kitchen, "are merely the illegitimate product of the literary theory itself. Theories which artificially *create* difficulties that were previously non-existent are obviously wrong and should therefore be discarded." 42/114

The fallacy of this approach is lucidly epitomized by O.T. Allis' illustration:

"It is to be noted, therefore, that the quest for such differences is a relatively simple and easy one. It would be a simple matter to break a crystal ball into a number of fragments and then to fill a volume with an elaborate description and discussion of the marked differences between the fragments thus obtained, and to argue that these fragments must have all come from different globes. The only conclusive refutation would be the proof that when fitted together they form once more a single globe. After all is said it is the unity and harmony of the Biblical narratives as they appear in the Scriptures which is the best refutation of the theory that these self-consistent narratives have resulted from the combining of several more or less diverse and contradictory sources." 10/121

4B. The Number of "Original Documents" Is Unlimited

Due to the disintegrative nature of the methodology and the absence of any objective controls, any consistent analysis of the text becomes ridiculous.

North has described some early instances of such effects.

"Baentsch, it may be remembered, in his Leviticus Commentary (1900), worked with no less than seven P-sigla: P, Ps, Pss, Ph (xvii-xxvi), Po (i-vii), Pr (xi-xv), and Rp. Any one of the secondary sources might have a second (Ph^s, Pr^s) or third (Pr^{ss}) hand, together with redactors (Rpo, Rph) and even secondary redactors (Rp^s). We even meet with refinements like Po^1,Po^2, Po^s, Po^{2s}. This is surely the *reductio ad absurdum* of the analytical method." 77/56

Recent analysis has fared no better; new sources such as J^1, J^2, L, K, and S have abounded. This has led North, a prominent spokesman for the radical critics, to a telling conclusion:

"It seems likely that with sufficient analytical ingenuity it would be possible to sort out more such documents." Cited by 55/55

Green clearly perceives the reasoning behind such boundless fragmentation.

"It is," he notes, "the inevitable nemesis of the hypothesis reacting upon itself. The very principles and methods which are employed in dividing the Pentateuch into different documents, can be applied with like success and quite as much cogency in the division and subdivision of each of the documents to any assignable extent." 108/164

Equally perceptive is Allis, who points out that "if consistently applied the principles and methods of the higher criticism would lead to the complete disintegration of the Pentateuch and that it is only the failure on the part of the critics to apply them in thoroughgoing fashion which prevents this fiasco from occurring." 10/89

Alan Cole rings the death knell:

"The old and tidy 'documentary hypothesis' has largely failed by its own success, with ever smaller and smaller units, or unconnected fragments postulated by scholars, instead of major and continuous written sources." 100/13

5B. Irresponsible Logic

The logical fallacy committed by the radical critics is variously referred to as *petitio principii,* begging the question or arguing in a circle. Putting it simply, this is the practice of building one's desired conclusions into his premises so as to assure that said conclusions will result. At least two blatant occurrences of this may be found.

1C.   THE FORMULATION OF DOCUMENTS J, E, D AND P

In the construction of the four primary documents, the characteristics of each document were predetermined. Then each passage containing the appropriate characteristics was assigned to the corresponding document.

S.R. Driver writes that "Elohim is not here accompanied by the other criteria of P's style, [that] forbids our assigning the sections thus characterized to that source." 18/13

The result is four documents, each containing material with distinctive traits. But to then triumphantly assert that this demonstrates the original existence of these four documents is logically untenable, for the resulting "sources" are only the product of a predetermined purpose, totally devoid of any objective evidence or any parallel occurence in the world of literature. And so the argument spins in its unverifiable and meaningless circle.

2C. THE UTTER DEPENDENCE UPON REDACTORS

With the introduction of the redactor, the radical critics add another example of a solution which originates in their construction and not in fact. The redactor stretches their logic even thinner, for his presence insures the fact that no evidence can arise which cannot, at least hypothetically, be falsified by evidence is removed from the arenas of logic and evidence, and thus is unsupportable.

Allis solemnly contends that "in assigning to the redactor the role of editor and making him responsible for all the cases where the analysis does not work out as they think it should, the critics resort to a device which is destructive of their whole position. For the critics to blame the failure of the analysis to work out satisfactorily on an unknown redactor who has changed the text of his sources is equivalent to changing the actual text which the critics have before them in the interest of their theory as to what the text originally was. To put it bluntly, it is what is called 'doctoring the evidence.' By such means any theory can be proved or disproved." 10/60

And he elsewhere reminds us that "every appeal to the redactor is a tacit admission on the part of the critics that their theory breaks down at that point." 10/39

The renowned Jewish novelist, Herman Wouk, undertook a searching investigation of the Documentary Hypothesis and his reaction to the presence of the redactor deserves close attention. "With the discovery of the interpolater, writes Wouk, "Wellhausen's difficulties were at an end. As a tool of controversial logic this figure is wonderful.... When all else fails Wellhausen—grammar, continuity, divine names or outright falsifying of the plain sense of the Hebrew—he works an interpolater." He declares that Engnell "dealt the death blow to the *Prolegomena* by analysing Wellhausen's villainous ghost, the interpolater, and driving it from the field with a polite scholarly horse laugh." 67/315-317

3A. ULTIMATE FAILURE OF THE HYPOTHESIS

In his book, *The Documentary Hypothesis*, the late Umberto Cassuto devotes six entire chapters to the investigation of the five most significant criteria the documentarians offer as evidence that Moses did not write the Pentateuch. He compares the five basic objections to pillars which hold up a house. (Naturally, these objections to Mosaic authorship are also supports for the Documentary Hypothesis.) About these supports or "pillars" of the Documentary Hypothesis, Cassuto says in his concluding chapter:

"I did not prove that the pillars were weak or that each one failed to give decisive support, but I established that they were not pillars at all, that they did not exist, that they were purely imaginary. In view of this, my final conclusion that the documentary hypothesis is null and void is justified." 15/100, 101

Another Jewish scholar, M.H. Segal, after an investigation of the Pentateuchal problem in his book, *The Pentateuch—Its Composition and Its Authorship*, concludes:

"The preceding pages have made it clear why we must reject the Documentary Theory as an explanation of the composition of the Pentateuch. The Theory is complicated, artificial and anomalous. It is based on unproved assumptions. It uses unreliable criteria for the separation of the text into component documents.

"To these defects may be added other serious faults. It carries its work of analysis to absurd lengths, and neglects the synthetic study of the Pentateuch as a literary whole. By an abnormal use of the analytical method, the Theory has reduced the Pentateuch to a mass of incoherent fragments, historical and legalistic, to a collection of late legends and of traditions of doubtful origin, all strung together by late compilers on an artificial chronological thread. This is a fundamentally false evaluation of the Pentateuch. Even a cursory reading of the Pentateuch is sufficient to show that the events recorded therein are set out in logical sequence, that there is some plan combining its various parts and some purpose unifying all its contents, and that this plan and purpose find their realization in the conclusion of the Pentateuch which is also the end of the Mosaic age." 58/22

Thus, Wellhausen's Documentary Hypothesis must, in the final analysis, be regarded as unsuccessful in attempting to substantiate its denial of Mosaic authorship in favor of the JEDP source theory.

4A. SOME CLOSING COMMENTS

1B. The Jewish scholar, Yehezkel Kaufmann, relates the present state of affairs:

"Wellhausen's arguments complemented each other nicely, and offered what seemed to be a solid foundation upon which to build the house of biblical criticism. Since then, however, both the evidence and the arguments supporting this structure have been called into question and, to some extent, even rejected. Yet biblical scholarship, while admitting that the grounds have crumbled away, nevertheless continues to adhere to the conclusions." 40/1

2B. Mendenhall speaks of the continued acceptance of the documentarian evolutionary religious development:

"It is at least a justified suspicion that a scholarly piety toward the past, rather than historical evidence, is the main foundation for their position." 68/36

3B. Bright adds that even today the "documentary hypothesis still commands general acceptance, and must be the starting point of any discussion." 14/62

4B. The renowned Jewish scholar, Cyrus Gordon, relates the almost blind adherence of many critics to the documentary theory:

"When I speak of a 'commitment' to JEDP, I mean it in the deepest sense of the word. I have heard professors of Old Testament refer to the integrity of JEDP as their 'conviction.' They are willing to countenance modifications in detail. They permit you to subdivide (D_1, D_2, D_3, and so forth) or combine (JE) or add a new document designated by another capital letter but they will not tolerate any questioning of the basic JEDP structure." 27/131

Gordon concludes:

"I am at a loss to explain this kind of 'conviction' on any grounds other than intellectual laziness or inability to reappraise." 27/131

5B. The British scholar, H.H. Rowley, will not reject the theory simply because he sees nothing better to replace it with:

That it [the Graf-Wellhausen theory] is widely rejected in whole or in part is doubtless true, but there is no view to put in in its place that would not be more widely and emphatically rejected.... The Graf-Wellhausen view is only a working hypothesis, which can be abandoned with alacrity when a more satisfying view is found, but which cannot with profit be abandoned until then." 54/46

According to this view it is better to hold to an invalid theory than to have to admit to not holding one at all.

6B. **Cyrus Gordon,** in the end of an article in which he uncompromisingly criticized the entire Wellhausen theory, gave a striking example of this unquestioned allegiance to the Documentary Hypothesis:

"A professor of Bible in a leading university once asked me to give him the facts on JEDP. I told him essentially what I have written above. He replied: 'I am convinced by what you say but I shall go on teaching the old system.' When I asked him why, he answered: 'Because what you have told me means I should have to unlearn as well as study afresh and rethink. It is easier to go on with the accepted system of higher criticism for which we have standard textbooks.'" 27/134

7B. Such a statement would seem to justify Mendenhall's suspicion of many modern biblical critics:

"It is much easier to follow the accepted pattern of the 19th century, especially since it has received some academic respectability, mostly through default, and to be content with pointing out a few inadequacies here and there which will show that one is keeping up to date." 68/38

8B. **Herman Wouk,** the Jewish author and playwright, while not a professional biblical scholar as such, nevertheless provides some honest suggestions as to why there remains a general basic acceptance of the theories propounded by Wellhausen and his followers. In his book, *This Is My God,* Wouk, in the chapter on the Pentateuch, offers this poignant evaluation:

"It is a hard thing for men who have given their lives to a theory, and taught it to younger men, to see it fall apart." 67/318

To this Wouk adds:

"What the scholars had found out at long last, of course, was that literary analysis is not a scientific method. Literary style is a fluid, shifting thing, at best, a palimpsest or a potpourri. The hand of Shakespeare is in the pages of Dickens: Scott wrote chapters of Mark Twain; Spinoza is full of Hobbes and Descartes. Shakespeare was the greatest echoer of all, and the greatest stylist of all. Literary analysis has been used for generations by obsessive men to prove that everybody but Shakespeare wrote Shakespeare. I believe literary analysis could be used to prove that I wrote both *David Copperfield* and *A Farewell to Arms.* I wish it were sound." 67/317

BIBLIOGRAPHY

1. Aalders, G.A. *A Short Introduction to the Pentateuch.* Chicago: Inter-Varsity Christian Fellowship, n.d. (originally published in 1949).

2. Albright, W.F. "Archaeology Confronts Biblical Criticism," *The American Scholar.* April, 1938. Vol. 7, pp. 176-188.

3. Albright, W.F. "The Israelite Conquest of Canaan in the Light of Archaeology,"*Bulletin of the American Schools of Oriental Research.* 1939. Vol. 74, pp. 11-23.

4. Albright, W.F. *Recent Discoveries in Bible Lands.* New York: Funk and Wagnalls, 1955.

5. Albright, W.F. *The Archaeology of Palestine.* Baltimore: Penguin Books, revised 1960.

6. Albright, W.F. *Archaeology, Historical Analogy, and Early Biblical Tradition.* Baton Rouge: Louisiana State University Press, 1966.

7. Albright, W.F. *Archaeology and the Religion of Israel.* Baltimore: John Hopkins Press, 1942

8. Albright, W.F. *The Biblical Period From Abraham to Ezra.* New York: Harper & Row, 1963.

9. Albright, W.F. *From the Stone Age to Christianity.* Baltimore: John Hopkins Press, 1940.

10. Allis, Oswald T. *The Five Books of Moses.* Philadelphia: The Presbyterian and Reformed Publishing Co., revised 1969.

11. Archer, Gleason, Jr. *A Survey of Old Testament Introduction.* Chicago: Moody Press, ©1964, 1974. Moody Press. Moody Bible Institute of Chicago. Used by permission.

12. Beattie, F.R. *Radical Criticism.* New York: Fleming H. Revell Co., 1894.

13. Bentzen, A. *Introduction to the Old Testament.* 2 Vols. Copenhagen: G.E.C. Gad, 1948.

14. Bright, John. *A History of Israel.* Philadelphia: The Westminister Press, 1959.

15. Cassuto, U. *The Documentary Hypothesis.* Jerusalem; Magnes Press, the Hebrew University, 1941. First English edition, 1961.

16. Chapman, A.T. *An Introduction to the Pentateuch.* Cambridge: The University Press, 1911.

17. Driver, S.R. *The Book of Genesis.* London: Methuen & Co., 1904.

18. Driver, S.R. *Introduction to the Literature of the Old Testament.* New York: Charles Scribner's Sons, 1913.

19. Eichrodt, Walther. *Ezekiel.* Translated by Coslett Quin. Philadelphia: The Westminster Press, 1970.

20. Eissfeldt, Otto. *The Old Testament—An Introduction.* New York: Harper and Row Publilshers, 1965.

21. *Encyclopedia of Religion and Ethics.* Edited by James Hastings. Edinburgh: T. & T. Clark, 1935.

22. Feinberg, Paul D. *The Doctrine of God in the Pentateuch.* Doctoral Dissertation. Dallas Theological Seminary, 1968.

23. Fohrer, Georg. *Introduction to the Old Testament.* Initiated by Ernst Sellin. Translated by David Green. Nashville: Abingdon Press, 1965.

24. Freedom, D.N. and J.C. Greenfield, eds. *New Directions in Biblical Archaeology.* Garden City: Doubleday, 1969.

25. Gardner, James. *The Christian Cyclopedia.* Glasgow: Blackie and Son, 1858.

26. Gilkey, Langdon B. "Cosmology, Ontology, and the Travail of Biblical Language," *Concordia Theological Monthly.* March, 1962. Vol. 33, pp. 142-154.

27. Gordon, Cyrus H. "Higher Critics and Forbidden Fruit," *Christianity Today.* November 23, 1959. Vol. 4, pp. 131-133.

28. Gray, Edward M. *Old Testament Criticism.* New York and London: Harper & Brothers, 1923.

29. Green, William H. *The Higher Criticism of the Pentateuch.* New York: Chas. Scribner's Sons, 1895.

30. Gunkel, Hermann. *What Remains of the Old Testament?* London: George Allan and Unwin LTD., 1928.

31. Hahn, Herbert F. *The Old Testament in Modern Research.* Philadelphia: Fortress Press, 1966.

32. Harrison, R.K. *Introduction to the Old Testament.* Grand Rapids: William B. Eerdmans Publishing Company, 1970.

33. Harrison, R.K. *Old Testament Times.* Grand Rapids: William B. Eerdmans Publishing Company, 1970.

34. Heidel, Alexander.*The Gilgamesh Epic and the Old Testament Parallels.* Chicago: University of Chicago Press, 1949.

35. Hengstenberg, E.W. *Dissertations on the Genuineness of the Pentateuch.* Vol. 2. Edinburgh: James Nisbet & Co., 1847.

36. Hertz, J.H. *The Pentateuch and Haftorahs.* Vol. 2. London: Oxford University Press, 1930, 1951.

37. *The Interpreter's Dictionary of the Bible.* Vol. 2. Edited by George A. Buttrick. New York: Abingdon Press, 1962.

38. *The Interpreter's One-Volume Commentary on the Bible.* Edited by Charles Laymon. New York: Abingdon Press, 1971.

39. Josephus, Flavius. *The Works of Flavius Josephus.* Translated by William Whiston. Grand Rapids: Associated Publishers and Authors, Inc., 1860.

40. Kaufmann, Yehezkel. *The Religion of Israel.* Chicago: University of Chicago Press, 1960.

41. Kim, Chi Syun. *The Mosaic Authorship of the Pentateuch.* Doctoral Dissertation. Dallas Theological Seminary, 1935.

42. Kitchen, K.A. *Ancient Orient and the Old Testament.* Chicago: Inter-Varsity Press, 1966.

43. Kline, Meredith G. *Treaty of the Great King.* Grand Rapids: William B. Eerdmans Publishing Co., 1963.

44. Kline, Meredith G. "Dynastic Covenant," *Westminster Theological Journal.* November, 1961. Vol. 23, pp. 1-15.

45. Kuenen, Abraham. *An Historico-Critical Inquiry into the Origin and Composition of the Hexateuch.* Translated by P.H. Wicksteed. London: MacMillan & Co., 1886.

46. Martin, W.J. *Stylistic Criteria and the Analysis of the Pentateuch.* London: Tyndale Press, 1955.

47. Mendenhall, George E. *Law and Covenant In Israel and the Ancient Near East.* Pittsburgh: Biblical Colloquium, 1955.

48. Montgomery, John Warwick. *History and Christianity.* Downers Grove: Inter-Varsity Press, 1964.

49. *The New Bible Dictionary.* Edited by J.D. Douglas. Grand Rapids: Wm. B. Eerdmans Publishing Co., 1962.

50. Orr, James. *The Problem of the Old Testament.* New York: Charles Scribner's Sons, written 1905, printed 1917.

51. Philo, Judaeus. *The Works of Philo.* Vol. 4. Translated by F.H. Colson. Cambridge: Harvard University Press, 1935.

52. Von Rad, G. *Old Testament Theology.* 2 Vols. Edinburgh and London: Oliver and Boyd LTD, English edition published 1962.

53. Raven, John Howard. *Old Testament Introduction.* New York: Fleming H. Revell Company, 1906, revised 1910.

54. Rowley, H.H. *The Growth of the Old Testament.* London: Hutchinson's University Library, Hutchinson House. 1950.

55. Albright, Wm. F. "The Old Testament and the Archaeology of Palestine," *Old Testament and Modern Study.* Edited by H.H. Rowley. Oxford: Clarendon Press, 1st edition 1951.

56. Rowley, H.H. *Worship in Ancient Israel.* London: S.P.C.K., 1967.

57. Segal, M.H. *Grammar of Mishnaic Hebrew.* Oxford: Clarendon Press, 1927.

58. Segal, M.H. *The Pentateuch—Its Composition and Its Authorship.* Jerusalem: Magnes Press, Hebrew University, 1967.

59. Selleck, W.S. *The New Appreciation of the Bible.* Chicago: University of Chicago Press, 1906.

60. Torrey, R.A. *The Higher Criticism and the New Theology.* Montrose: Montrose Christian Literature Society. 1911.

61. Unger, Merrill F. *Introductory Guide to the Old Testament.* Grand Rapids: Zondervan Publishing House, 1956.

62. Vos, Howard F., ed. *Can I Trust the Bible?* Chicago: Moody Press, ©1963, Moody Press, Moody Bible Institute of Chicago. Used by permission.

63. Wellhausen, Julius. *Prolegomena to the History of Israel.* Translated by Black and Menzies. Edinburgh: Adam and Charles Black, 1885. (Originally published in 1878 under the title *History of Israel.*)

64. Whitelaw, Thomas. *Old Testament Critics.* London: Kegan, Paul, Trench, Trubner & Co., LTD., 1903.

65. Wilson, R.D. *A Scientific Investigation of the Old Testament.* London: Marshall Brothers Limited, 1926.

66. Wilson, R.D. *Studies in the Book of Daniel* (Series II). New York: Fleming H. Revell Company, 1938.

67. Wouk, Herman. *This Is My God.* New York: Doubleday and Co., 1959.

68. Mendenhall, George E. "Biblical History in Transition," *The Bible and the Ancient Near East.* Edited by G.E. Wright. New York: Doubleday and Company, 1961.

69. Wright, G.E. *God Who Acts.* London: SCM Press, LTD., 1958.

70. Yamauchi, Edwin M. "Stones, Scripts, and Scholars," *Christianity Today.* February 14, 1969. Vol. 13, No. 10, pp. 8-13.

71. Young, E.J. *An Introduction to the Old Testament.* Grand Rapids: Eerdmans Publishing Co., 1949.

72. Kitchen, K.A. "Some Egyptian Background to the Old Testament," *The Tyndale House Bulletin.* Nos. 5 and 6, 1960.

73. Sanders, C. *Introduction to Research in English Literary History.* New York: MacMillan, 1952.

74. *Strong's Exhaustive Concordance of the Bible.* New York: Abingdon-Cokesbury Press, 1944.

75. Encyclopaedia Britannica. Vol. 2. New York: University Press, 1969.

76. Reisner, G.A., and W.S. Smith. *A History of the Giza Necropolis,* Vol. 2. Cambridge: Harvard University Press, 1955.

77. North, C.R. "Pentateuchal Criticism," *The Old Testament and Modern Study.* Edited by H.H. Rowley. Oxford: Clarendon Press, 1951.

78. *The Geography of Strabo,* Vol. 8. English translation by Horace Leonard Jones. New York: Putnam's, 1932.

79. *Diodorus of Sicily,* Vol. 1. English translation by C.H. Oldlather. New York: Putnam's, 1933.

80. Driver, S.R. "Deuteronomy," *International Critical Commentary.* Edinburgh: T & T Clark, 1896.

81. Driver, S.R. "Book of Exodus," *Cambridge Bible for Schools and Colleges.* Cambridge: The University Press, 1911.

82. Pederson, Johannes, and Geoffrey Cumberlege. *Israel, Its Life and Culture.*

Vols. 1 and 2. Translated by Annie I. Fausboll. London: Oxford University Press, 1947.

83. Kline, Meredith. "Is the History of the Old Testament Accurate?" *Can I Trust My Bible?* Edited by Howard Vos. Chicago: Moody Press, ©1963. Moody Press, Moody Bible Institute of Chicago. Used by permission.

84. Ng, David, ed. *Sourcebook.* Philadelphia: Board of Christian Education—The United Presbyterian Church in the U.S.A., 1970.

85. Pfeiffer, Robert H. *Introduction to the Old Testament.* New York: Harper, 1941.

86. Wright, Ernest G. "Biblical Archaeology Today," *New Directions in Biblical Archaeology.* Edited by David N. Freedman and J.C. Greenfield. Garden City: Doubleday, 1969.

87. Manley, G.T. *The Book of the Law.* Grand Rapids: Wm. B. Eerdmans Publishing Co., 1957.

88. *The Interpreter's One-Volume Commentary on the Bible.* Edited by Charles M. Laymon. Nashville: Abingdon Press, 1971.

89. Albright, W.F. *History, Archaeology, and Christian Humanism.* New York: McGraw-Hill Book Company, 1964.

90. Allis, Oswald T. *The Old Testament, Its Claims and Its Critics.* Nutley, New Jersey: The Presbyterian and Reformed Publishing Company, 1972.

91. Anderson, G.W. *A Critical Introduction to the Old Testament.* London: Gerald Duckworth and Co., Ltd., 1959.

92. Barton, George A. *The Religion of Israel.* New York: MacMillan Co., 1918.

93. Barzun, J. and H. Graff. *The Modern Researcher.* New York: Harcourt, Brace and World, Inc., 1957.

94. Bewer, Julius A., Lewis Bayles Paton and George Dahl. "The Problem of Deuteronomy: A Symposium," *Journal of Biblical Literature.* 1929-30. Vol. 47, pp. 305-379.

95. Briggs, C.A. *The Higher Criticism of the Hexateuch.* New York: Charles Scribner's Sons, 1897.

96. Brightman, Edgar S. *The Sources of the Hexateuch.* New York: Abingdon Press, 1918.

97. Brown, Lewis, *This Believing World.* New York: MacMillan Company, 1961.

98. Cassuto, U. *Commentary on Genesis 1-11.* Jerusalem: Magnes Press, the Hebrew University, 1964.

99. Cheyne, T.K., *Founders of Old Testament Criticism.* London: Methuen & Co., 1893.

100. Cole, R. Alan. *Exodus.* Downers Grove, Ill.: Inter-Varsity Press, 1973.

101. Cornill, Carl. *Introduction to the Canonical Books of the Old Testament.* New York: G.P. Putnams Sons, 1907.

102. Davis, John J. *Conquest and Crisis.* Grand Rapids: Baker Book House, 1969.

103. Eerdmans, B.D. *The Religion of Israel.* Leiden: Universitaire Pers Leiden, 1947.

104. Engnell, Ivan. *A Rigid Scrutiny: Critical Essays on the Old Testament.* Translated and edited by John T. Willis. Nashville: Vanderbilt Press, 1969.

105. Flanders, Henry Jackson, Jr. and Robert Wilson Crapps and David Anthony Smith. *People of the Covenant.* New York: The Ronald Press Company, 1973.

106. Gordon, Cyrus. *Introduction to Old Testament Times.* Ventnor, N.J.: Ventnor Publishers, Inc., 1953.

107. Habel, Norman C. *Literary Criticism of the Old Testament.* Philadelphia: Fortress Press, 1971.

108. Harper, William R. and W. Henry Green. "The Pentateuchal Question." *Hebraica.* October, 1888. Vol. 5, No. 1, pp 18-73.

109. Harrison, R.K. "The Old Testament and its Critics," *Christianity Today,* May 25, 1959.

110. Kaiser, Walter C., Jr., "The Literary Form of Genesis 1-11," *New Perspectives on the Old Testament.* Edited by J. Barton Payne. Waco: Word Books, copyright 1970.

111. Kautzsch, E. *An Outline of the History of the Literature of the Old Testament.* Translated by John Taylor. Oxford: Williams and Norgate, 1898.

112. Kelso, James. *Archaeology and Our Old Testament Contemporaries.* Grand Rapids: Zondervan, 1966.

113. Kenyon, Sir Frederic. *Our Bible and the Ancient Manuscripts.* London: Eyre and Spottiswoode, 1939.

114. Kittel, R. *A History of the Hebrews.* Vol. 1. Translated by John Taylor. Edinburgh: Williams and Norgate, 1895.

115. Kittel, R. *The Scientific Study of the Old Testament.* Translated by J. Caleb Hughes. New York: G.P. Putnam's Sons, 1910.

116. Kuenen, A., *The Religion of Israel.* Translated by Alfred Heath May. Edinburgh: Williams and Norgate, 1874.

117. Kyle, Melvin G. *The Deciding Voice of the Monuments in Biblical Criticism.* Oberlin, Ohio: Bibliotheca Sacra Company, 1924.

118. Kyle, Melvin G. *The Problem of the Pentateuch.* Oberlin, Ohio: Bibliotheca Sacra Co., 1920.

119. Lewis, C.S. "Modern Theology and Biblical Criticism," *Christian Reflections.* Grand Rapids: Wm. B. Eerdmans Publishing Co., 1967.

120. Livingston, G. Herbert. *The Pentateuch in Its Cultural Environment.* Grand Rapids: Baker Book House, 1974.

121. Loetscher, Lefferts A., Editor-in-chief. "Pentateuch," *Twentieth Century Encyclopedia of Religious Knowledge.* Grand Rapids: Baker Book House, 1955.

122. MacDill, David, *The Mosaic Authorship of the Pentateuch.* Pittsburgh: United Presbyterian Board of Publication, 1896.

123. Manley, G.T. *The Book of the Law.* London: The Tyndale Press, 1957.

124. Meek, J.T. *Hebrew Origins.* Revised Edition. New York: Harper Brothers, 1950.

125. Moller, Wilhelm. *Are the Critics Right?* New York: Fleming H. Revell Co., 1899.

126. Montgomery, John Warwick. "Is Man His Own God?" *Christianity For the Tough Minded.* Edited by John Warwick Montgomery. Minneapolis: Bethany Fellowship, Inc., 1973.

127. Moore, James R. "Science and Christianity: Toward Peaceful Coexistence," *Christianity For the Tough Minded.* Edited by John Warwick Montgomery. Minneapolis: Bethany Fellowship, Inc., 1973.

128. Motyer, J.A. *The Revelation of the Divine Name.* London: The Tyndale Press, 1959.

129. Nielsen, Eduard. *Oral Tradition.* London: SCM Press, 1954.

130. North, C.R. "Pentateuchal Criticism," *The Old Testament and Modern Study.* Edited by H.H. Rowley. Oxford: Oxford University Press, 1967.

131. Payne, J.B. *An Outline of Hebrew History.* Grand Rapids: Baker Book House, 1954.

132. Pfeiffer, R.H. *Introduction to the Old Testament.* New York: Harper and Brothers Publishers, 1948.

133. Rast, Walter E. *Tradition, History and the Old Testament.* Philadelphia: Fortress Press, 1972.

134. Richardson, Alan. *The Bible in the Age of Science.* Philadelphia: The Westminster Press, 1961.

135. Sayce, A.H. *Fresh Light From the Ancient Monuments.* London: The Religious Tract Society, 1895.

136. Sayce, A.H. *The "Higher Criticism" and the Verdict of the Monuments.* London: Society for Promoting Christian Knowledge, 1895.

137. Sayce, A.H. *Monument Facts and Higher Critical Fancies.* London: The Religious Tract Society, 1904.

138. Schultz, Hermann. *Old Testament Theology.* Translated from the fourth edition by H.A. Patterson. Edinburgh: T & T Clark, 1898.

139. Segal, M.H. *The Pentateuch, Its Composition and Other Biblical Studies.* Jerusalem: Magnes Press, the Hebrew University, 1967.

140. Simpson, C.A. *The Early Tradition of Israel.* Oxford: Basil Blackwell, 1948.

141. Skinner, John. *A Critical and Exegetical Commentary on Genesis.* Edinburgh: T & T Clark, 1930.

142. Smith, W. Robertson. *Lectures on the Religion of the Semites.* London: Adam and Charles Black, 1907.

143. Tucker, Gene M. *Form Criticism and the Old Testament.* Philadelphia: Fortress Press, 1971.

144. Von Rad, Gerhard. *The Problem of the Hexateuch and Other Essays.* London: Oliver and Boyd, 1966.

145. Vos, Geerhardus. *The Mosaic Origin of the Pentateuchal Codes.* London: Hodder and Stoughton, 1886.

146. Wellhausen, J. *Sketch of the History of Israel and Judah.* London and Edinburgh: Adam and Charles Black, 1891.

147. Woudstra, Marten H. "The Tabernacle in Biblical-Theological Perspective," *New Perspectives on the Old Testament.* Edited by J. Barton Payne. Waco, Texas: Word Books, copyright 1970.

148. Wright, G.E. *The Old Testament Against Its Environment.* Chicago: Henry Regnery Co., 1950.

149. Albright, William F. "Arahaeological Discoveries and the Scriptures," *Christianity Today.* June 21, 1968. Vol. 12, pp. 3-5.

150. Albright, William F. "The Bible After Twenty Years of Archaeology," *Religion in Life.* 1952. Vol. 21, pp. 537-550.

151. Albright, W.F. "A Brief History of Judah from the Days of Josiah to Alexander the Great," *Biblical Archaeologist.* February, 1946. Vol. 9, pp. 1-16.

152. Albright, W.F. "King Jehoiachin in Exile," *Biblical Archaeologist.* December, 1942. Vol. 5, No. 4, pp. 49-55.

153. Albright, W.F. "The Oldest Hebrew Letters: Lachish Ostraca," *Bulletin of the American Schools of Oriental Research.* April, 1938. No. 70. pp. 11-16.

154. Albright, W.F. "Recent Progress in North-Canaanite Research," *Bulletin of the American Schools of Oriental Research.* April, 1938. No. 70, pp. 18-24.

155. Battenfield, James Richard. *Historicity of Genesis Fourteen.* Unpublished

Bachelor of Divinity Thesis submitted to Talbot Theological Seminary.

156. Burrows, Millar. *What Mean These Stones?* New York: Meridian Books, 1957.

157. Caiger, S.L. *Bible and Spade.* London: Oxford University Press, 1936.

158. Elder, John. *Prophets, Idols, and Diggers.* New York: Bobbs-Merrill Co., ©1960. Reprinted by permission of the publisher.

159. Feinberg, Charles L. "The Relation of Archaeology to Biblical Criticism," *bibliotheca Sacra.* June, 1947. Vol. 104, No. 414, pp. 170-181.

160. Finegan, Jack. *Light from the Ancient Past,* London: Oxford Press, distr. in the U.S. by Princeton University Press, 1946.

161. Frank, Henry Thomas. *Bible, Archaeology and Faith.* Nashville, Tenn.: Abingdon Press, 1971.

162. Free, Joseph P. *Archaeology and Bible History.* Wheaton, Ill.: Scripture Press, 1969.

163. Free, Joseph P. "Archaeology and the Bible," *His Magazine.* May, 1949. Vol. 9, pp. 17-20. reprinted by permission form *His,* student magazine of Inter-Varsity Christian Fellowship, ©1949.

164. Free, Joseph P. "Archaeology and Higher Criticism," *Bibliotheca Sacra.* January, 1957. Vol. 114, pp. 23-39.

165. Free, Joseph P. "Archaeology and the Historical Accuracy of Scripture," *Bibliotheca Sacra.* July, 1956. Vol. 113, pp. 214-226.

166. Free, Joseph P. "Archaeology and Liberalism," *Bibliotheca Sacra.* July, 1956. Vol. 113, pp. 322-338.

167. Free, Joseph P. "Archaeology and Neo-Orthodoxy," *Bibliotheca Sacra.* January, 1957. Vol. 114, pp. 123-132.

168. Garstang, John, *The Foundations of Bible History; Joshua, Judges.* New York: R.R. Smith, Inc., 1931.

169. Glueck, Nelson. *Rivers In the Desert.* New York: Farrar, Straus, and Cadahy, 1959.

170. Glueck, Nelson. "The Second Campaign at Tell el-Kheleifeh," *Bulletin of the American Schools of Oriental Research.* October, 1939. No. 75, pp. 8-22.

171. Glueck, Nelson. "The Third Season at Tell el-Kheleifeh," *Bulletin of the American Schools of Oriental Research.* October, 1940. No. 79, pp. 2-18.

172. Gordon, C.H. "Biblical Customs and the Nuzu Tablets," *T he Biblical Archaeologist.* February, 1940. Vol. 3, pp. 1-12.

173. Gordon, Cyrus. "The Patriarchal Age," *Journal of Bible and Religion.* October, 1955. Vol. 21, No. 4.

174. Hamilton, Floyd. *Basis of the Christian Faith.* New York: Harper, 1933.

175. Hauper, R.S. "Lachish—Frontier Fortress of Judah," *Biblical Archaeologist.* December, 1938. Vol. I, pp. 30-32.

176. Heidel, Alexander. *The Babylonian Genesis.* Chicago: University of Chicago Press, 1963.

177. Horn, S.H. "Recent Illumination of the Old Testament," *Christianity Today.* June 21, 1968. Vol. 12, pp. 925-929.

178. Irwin, W.A. "The Modern Approach to the Old Testament," *Journal of Bible and Religion.* 1953. Vol. 21, pp. 9-20.

179. Kenyon, Kathleen. *Beginning in Archaeology.* New York: Praeger, 1962.

180. Kline, Meredith G. "Is History of the Old Testament Accurate? *Can I Trust the Bible?* Edited by Howard Vos. Chicago: Moody, ©1963. Moody Press, Moody Bible Institute of Chicago. Used by permission.

181. Lapp, Paul W. *Biblical Archaeology and History*. New York: World Publishing, 1969.

182. Leemans, W.F. "Foreign Trade in the Old Babylonian Period as Revealed by Texts from Southern Mesopotamia," *Studia et Documenta ad iura Orientis Antiqui Pertinentia*. 1960. Vol. 6.

183. Little, Paul, *Know Why You Believe*. Wheaton, Ill.: Scripture Press, 1967.

184. Oesterley, W.O.E. and Theodore H. Robinson, *Hebrew Religion: Its Origin and Developments*. London: Society for Promoting Christian Knowledge, 1935.

185. Oman, Sir Charles. *On the Writing of History*. New York: Barnes and Noble. 1939.

186. Palmer, Humphrey. *Logic of Gospel Criticism*. London, Melbourne: MacMillan; New York: St. Martin's Press, 1968.

187. Peet, T. Eric. *Egypt and the Old Testament*. Liverpool: Univ. Press of Liverpool, 1942.

188. Price, Ira Maurice, *The Monuments and the Old Testament*. 17th edition. Philadelphia: The Judson Press, 1925.

189. Robertson, A.T. *A New Short Grammar of the Greek Testament*. Part I. New York: Richard R. Smith, Inc. 1931.

190. Stearns, M.B. "Biblical Archaeology and the Higher Critics," *Bibliotheca Sacra*. July-September, 1939. Vol. 96, No. 483, pp. 307-318.

191. Steele, Francis. "Lipit-Ishtar Law Code," *American Journal of Archaeology*. April-June, 1947. Vol. 51, No. 2, pp. 158-164.

192. Thiele, E.R. "The Chronology of the Kings of Judah and Israel," *Journal of Near Eastern Studies*. July, 1944. Vol. 3, pp. 137-186.

193. Unger, Merrill F. *Archaeology and the Old Testament*. Grand Rapids: Zondervan, 1954.

194. Unger, Merrill F. "Archaeological Discoveries," *Bibliotheca Sacra*. January, 1955. Vol. 112, Part 1; p. 55. Part II, p. 137.

195. Von Rad, Gerhard. *Genesis*. Translated by John H. Marks (in *The Old Testament Library*. G. Ernest Wright, *et. al.* eds. Philadelphia: The Westminster Press, 1961).

196. Külling, Samuel R. "The Dating of the So-Called 'P-Sections' in Genesis," *Journal of the Evangelical Theological Society*. Spring, 1972. Vol. 15.

197. Vos, Howard F. *Genesis and Archaeology*. Chicago: Moody Press, ©1963. Moody Press, Moody Bible Institute of Chicago. Used by permission.

198. Wight, Fred H. *Highlights of Archaeology in Bible Lands*. Chicago: Moody Press, ©1955. Moody Press, Moody Bible Institute of Chicago. Used by permission.

199. Wright, G. Ernest. "Archaeology and Old Testament Studies," *Journal of Biblical Literature*. December, 1958. Vol. 77, pp. 39-51.

200. Wright, G. Ernest. "The Present State of Biblical Archaeology," *The Study of the Bible Today and Tomorrow*. Edited by Harold R. Willoughby. Chicago: University of Chicago Press, 1947.

201. Wright, G. Ernest. "The Terminology of Old Testament Religion and Its Significance," *Journal of Near Eastern Studies*. October, 1942. Vol. I, No. 4, pp. 404-414.

202. Wright, G.E. "Two Misunderstood Items in the Exodus Conquest Cycle," *Bulletin of the American Schools of Oriental Research*. April, 1942. No. 86, pp. 33-34.

203. Albright, William F. "Historical and Mythical Elements in the Story of Joseph," *Journal of Biblical Literature*. 1918. Vol. 37, pp. 111-143.

204. Albright, William F. "The Old Testament and Archaeology," *Old Testament Commentary*. Edited by Herbert L. Alleman and Elmer E. Flack. Philadelphia: Muhlenberg Press, 1948.

205. Barton, G.A. "Archaeology and the Bible." Philadelphia: American Sunday School Union, 1937.

206. Unger, Merrill F. "Archaeological Discoveries and Their Bearing on Old Testament," *Bibliotheca Sacra*. April, 1955. Vol. 112, pp. 137-142.

207. Wellhausen, Julius. *Die Composition des Hexateuchs*. Third Edition, Berlin, 1899.

208. Smith, R.W. *The Prophets of Israel*. 1895.

209. Albright, William F. *Archaeology of Palestine and the Bible*. New York: Revell, 1933.

210. Sarna, Nahum. *Understanding Genesis*. New York: McGraw-Hill Book Co., 1966.

211. Anderson, Bernard W. "Changing Emphasis in Biblical Scholarship, *Journal of Bible and Religion*. April, 1955. Vol. 23, pp. 81-88.

212. Dahse, Johannes. "Texkritische Bedenken gegen den Ausgangspunkt der Pentateuchkritik" ("Textual-Critical Doubts About the Initial Premise of Pentateuchal Criticism"), *Archiven fur Religionswissenschaft*. 1903.

213. Orlinsky, Harry. *Ancient Israel*. Ithaca: Cornell University Press, 1954.

214. Gunkel, Hermann. *The Legends of Genesis*. Translated by W.H. Carruth. Chicago: The Open Court Publishing Co., 1901.

215. Hillers, Delbert. *Treaty-Curse and the Old Testament Prophets*. Rome: Pontifical Biblical Institute, 1964.

216. Huffmon, Herbert B. "The Exodus, Sinai, and the Credo," *Catholic Biblical Quarterly*. 1965. Vol. 27, pp. 101-113.

217. Kitchen, K.A. "Ancient Orient, 'Deuteronism' and the Old Testament," *New Perspectives on the Old Testament*. Edited by J. Barton Payne, Waco, Texas: Word, 1970.

218. Kline, Meredith. "The Concepts of Canon and Covenant," *New Perspectives on the Old Testament*. Edited by J. Barton Payne. Waco, Texas: Word, 1970.

219. McCarthy, Dennis J. "Covenant in the Old Testament," *Catholic Biblical Quarterly*. 1954. Vol. 27, pp. 217-40.

220. McCarthy, Dennis J. *Treaty and Covenant* Rome: Pontifical Biblical Institute, 1963.

221. Weinfeld, Moshe. *Deuteronomy and The Deuteronomic School*. Oxford: Oxford University Press, 1972.

222. Banks, Edgar J. *The Bible and the Spade*. New York: Association Press, 1913.

223. Gerhardsson, Birger. *Tradition and Transmission in Early Christianity*. Translated by Eric. J. Sharpe. Copenhagen: Ejnar Munksgaard, 1964.

224. Yaron, Reunen. *The Laws of Eshnunna*. Jerusalem: Magnes Press, 1969.

225. Youngblood, Ronald. *The Heart of the Old Testament*. Grand Rapids: Baker Book House, 1971.

226. Hasel, Gerhard F. "The Polemic Nature of the Genesis Cosmology." *The Evangelical Quarterly*. April-June, 1974. Vol. 46, No. 2, pp. 81, 91.

section III

form
criticism

The basic tenets of Form Criticism are examined. Practical answers are given to the basic assumptions and conclusions.

SECTION OUTLINE

chapter 16

introduction
to
new testament
form
criticism

Source criticism can only take one back to the written sources for the life of Christ, which appeared no earlier than 25 years after the events they recorded. The material was passed by word of mouth until it was written down in the form of the Gospels. Form Criticism tries to fill in this gap of oral transmission.

The form critics assume that the Gospels are composed of small independent units or episodes. These small single units (pericopes) were circulated independently. The critics teach that the units gradually took on the form of various types of folk literature, such as legends, tales, myths and parables.

According to Form Criticism, the formation and preservation of the units were basically determined by the needs of the Christian community *(Sitz im Leben)*. In other words, when the community had a problem, they either created or preserved a saying or episode of Jesus to meet the needs of that particular problem. Therefore, these units are not basically witnesses to the life of Christ but rather are considered to be the beliefs and practices of the early Church.

This criticism proposes that the evangelists were not so much the writers as the editors of the four Gospels. They took the small units and put them in an artificial framework to aid in preaching and teaching. Phrases such as "again," "immediately," "after a few days," "while on the way" and "after this" are not historical. Instead they provide a fictitious framework for gluing together the separate units or episodes. These chronological phrases serve as connectives for the various literary units.

The task of Form Criticism was to discover the "laws of tradition" which governed the collection, development and writing down of the isolated units. Then with the removal of the artificial (editorial) framework of chronology provided by the evangelists, Form Criticism attempts to recover the original form of the units (pericopes) and determine for what practical purpose (Sitz im Leben) the early Christians preserved them.

By this method it was thought that one could "pierce back beyond written sources into the period of oral transmission and account for the rise of the different types of episodes which eventually became a part of the Gospels." 48/445

Form Criticism eventually became more than a literary analysis. It developed into a historical analysis and began to pass judgment on the historicity of various passages or units.

1A. DEFINITIONS

1B. Form Criticism is basically the translation of the German word *Formgeschichte*. Its literal translation is "history of form."

Form Criticism is the study of forms of literature and "documents that preserve earlier tradition. Its basic assumption is that the earlier, oral use of the tradition shaped the material and resulted in the variety of literary forms found in the final written record. Study of these forms, therefore, throws light on the life and thinking of the people who thus preserved tradition." 46/436

2B. Robert Spivey and D. Moody Smith, in *The Anatomy of the New Testament*, further define the method of Form Criticism as "the classification of the 'forms' in which the tradition, especially the Gospel tradition, circulated before being written down and the attempt to determine the 'setting of life' of the church which they reflect." 113/463

3B. As E.B. Redlich, a form critic, observes:

"Form Criticism is a method of study and investigation which deals with the pre-literary stage of the Gospel tradition, when the material was handed down orally. It seeks to discover the origins and history of the material, that is to say, of the narratives and sayings which make up the Gospels, and to explain how the original narratives and sayings assumed their present form in the Gospels. It is concerned with the processes that led to the formation of the Gospels." 101/9

4B. G.E. Ladd defines Form Criticism by concluding that "the designation 'form criticism' refers to the various literary forms which the oral tradition assumed as it was passed from mouth to mouth. Back of this study was the assumption that certain laws of oral tradition when applied to the Gospels will lead to the recovery of the earliest form of the tradition. A close study of these forms led to the critical conclusion that in its earliest stages, the material in the Gospels was passed on orally as a series of disconnected units, anecdotes, stories, sayings, teachings, parables, and so on. Each unit of tradition had its own history in the church. The historical outline of Jesus' career as it is found in Mark and largely embodied in Matthew and Luke is no part of this tradition, but is the creation of the author of the Second Gospel, who collected many of these units of tradition, created a historical outline for Jesus' career, and used this outline as a narrative thread upon which to string the disconnected beads of independent traditions. This means that the indications in the Gospels of sequence, time, place, and the like are quite unhistorical and untrustworthy and must therefore be ignored by serious Gospel criticism. As a result, we have no 'life' or 'biography' of Jesus, but only a series of detached anecdotes and teachings artificially and unhistorically strung together." 74/144, 145

5B. Rudolf Bultmann, a radical form critic, explains the form critical approach by saying:

"For over forty years now, students of the New Testament have been aware of the existence of a school of gospel research known as Form Criticism—or, more accurately, *Formgeschichte*, Form History. Its attention has been devoted to the component units into which the tradition underlying the Synoptic Gospels may be analyzed. It endeavors to study the oral tradition at a stage prior to its crystallization in gospels, or even in sources underlying the gospels, whether written documents or cycles of fixed tradition—such as Q, the pre-Marcan outline of Jesus' ministry, the sequences in the narratives and discourse material, the Passion Narrative, and so on." 19/vii

He continues his explanation:

"Form Criticism begins with the realization that the tradition contained in the Synoptic Gospels originally consisted of separate units, which were joined together editorially by the evangelists. Form Criticism is therefore concerned to distinguish these units of tradition, and to discover their earliest form and origin in the life of the early Christian community. It views the gospels as essentially compilations of this older material. But it also studies them as finished works, in order to evaluate the literary activity of the evangelists, and to discover the theological motives that guided them." 19/3,4

6B. McGinley lists five basic principles of Form Criticism:

1). "The synoptic Gospels are popular, sub-literary compositions.
2). "They depict the faith of the primitive Christians who created them, not the historical Jesus.
3). "They are artificial collections of isolated units of tradition.
4). "These units originally had a definite literary form which can still be detected.
5). "This form was created by a definite social situation." 82/4

2A. PURPOSES OF FORM CRITICISM

R.H. Lightfoot summarizes the precepts of Form Criticism:

"They remind us that the early church is by no means likely to have expressed itself at once in a literary way, and they believe, first, that in the earliest years memories and traditions of the words and deeds of Jesus were only handed on from mouth to mouth, and secondly, that they were valued, not so much (as we might have expected) in and for themselves, as for their importance in solving problems connected with the life and needs of the young churches. These needs, they think, would be chiefly concerned with mission preaching, catechetical teaching, demonstration of the content and meaning of the Christian life, refutation of Jewish and other objections, and, perhaps above all, worship. They believe, further, that these memories and traditions would circulate at first chiefly in two forms: on the one hand, that of little, separate stories, and, on the other that of sayings of the Lord, whether in isolation or in small collections. Both would gradually assume a more or less fixed shape, through constant repetition in the churches; and, whatever may be true about the sayings, the stories would tend to form themselves upon the model of similar stories about teachers and leaders in the Jewish or the Hellenistic world. And, finally, they suggest that many of these pre-literary traditions are still discernible in our written gospels, especially St. Mark, and that to some extent they can be classified according to their type or form; whence the name of the new study." 76/30,31

Martin Dibelius provides an explanation:

"It tries to bridge the gap in the New Testament by setting forth the common basis upon which both the doctrine of Jesus Christ and the narrative of Jesus of Nazareth rests." 37/18

He continues by citing one of the objectives of the form critical method:

"In the first place, by reconstruction and analysis, it seeks to explain the origin of the tradition about Jesus, and thus to penetrate into a period previous to that in which our Gospels and their written sources were recorded." 36/Preface

Dibelius adds that "it seeks to make clear the intention and real interest of the earliest tradition. We must show with what objective the first churches recounted stories about Jesus, passed them from mouth to mouth as independent narratives, or copied them from papyrus to papyrus. In the same manner we must examine the sayings of Jesus and ask with what intention these churches collected them, learnt them by heart, and wrote them down." 36/Preface

Rudolf Bultmann has asserted, "The central principle of Form Criticism has been fully established, viz. that the earliest gospel traditions circulated orally within the church, whose religious needs they served, and were only gradually gathered together into groups, blocks, or sequences and finally gospels." 19/ix

He explains that Form Criticism has developed into "an attempt to apply to them [the Gospels] the *methods of form-criticism* which H. Gunkel and his disciples had already applied to the Old Testament. This involved discovering what the original units of the synoptics were, both sayings and stories, to try to establish what their historical setting was, whether they belonged to a primary or secondary tradition or whether they were the product of editorial activity." 21/2,3

3A. METHODOLOGY

Vincent Taylor notes the steps taken in Form Criticism:

(1) Classification of material by form.
(2) Recovering of original form.
(3) Search for *Sitz im Leben* (life-situation). 114/22

Robert Mounce, in an informal interview, has summarized the form critical procedure in the following manner:

"The form critic first lists the various types of forms into which the Bible narratives may be divided. Then he tries to determine the *Sitz im Leben*, the situation in life, of the early church that accounts for the development of each of the pericopes which are placed in the categories. Was it fear of persecution? Was it the movement of the Gentile church out of the Jewish setting? Was it heresy? Etc.

"After determination of the *Sitz im Leben*, one can account for the changes that have taken place and peel off the layers that have been added to the sayings of Jesus. The result is the return of the Gospel sayings, to their original or pure state." 144

4A. BACKGROUND AND HISTORY

1B. Background

Form Criticism originated in Germany in the years after the close of the War of 1914-1918. 101/16

Floyd V. Filson explains the early history of Form Criticism of the Synoptic Gospels:

"It appeared as a clear-cut method in works by K.L. Schmidt (1919), M. Dibelius (1919, and R. Bultmann (1921), the three scholars whose work still dominates this field of study. It built upon many forerunners: Olrick's studies of folktales; Gunkel's identification of oral traditions embedded in the Old

Testament; Wellhausen's critical attention to the individual items of the gospel tradition and to the early stages of that tradition; Norden's study of prose style and mission discourses; etc. It built upon the concept that identification of written sources could not fully bridge the gap between Jesus and the written Gospels. A period of oral tradition had intervened and called for study." 46/436

The outstanding scholars of the immediate pre-war age in Germany include Bernard Weiss, Holtzmann, Wrede, Johannes Weiss, Wellhausen, Gunkel and Wendland. 101/16

In the field of Form Criticism, Easton parallels some main authors and their works:

"Their authors are respectively, [Martin Albertz], [Rudolf Bultmann], [Martin Dibelius] and [Karl Ludwig Schmidt]. While their results are very diverse, all have in common the essential quality of endeavoring to define sharply the nature of the first Gospel tradition, and to determine something of the laws that governed its formation and transmission." 43/28,29

Among other notable form critics are D.E. Nineham and R.H. Lightfoot.

Some of the less radical form critics include Frederick Grant, C.H. Dodd, B.S. Easton, Vincent Taylor. They have been influenced by Bultmann and his followers, as evidenced in their writings and their use of the same or similar terminology. 57/2

Rudolf Pesch continues to trace the early development of Form Criticism as he relates that "at the beginning of the present century J. Weiss declared explicitly that the investigation of the literary forms of the gospels and of the individual groupings of material in them was one of the 'tasks for contemporary scientific research into the N.T.' (*Aufgaben der neutestamentlichen Wissenschaft in der Gegenwart* [1908], p. 35). But his predecessor, J.G. Herder, had already 'recognized for the first time the problems involved in form-critical research into the gospels' (W.G. Kümmel, p.98). Another predecessor towards the end of the previous century was F. Overbeck, who had called for 'a history of the forms' of 'the primitive literature of Christianity' (*Historische Zeitschrift* 48 [1882], p. 423). Before the First World War two classical scholars, P. Wendland (*Die urchristlichen Literaturformen* [1912]) and E. Norden (*Agnosthos Theos. Untersuchungen zur Formengeschichte religiöser Rede* [1913]), set in motion form-critical researches into the N.T. in certain important directions. After the War, the period of the form-critical approach really began." 97/337,338

C.F.D. Moule remarks that "the new impetus seems to have come at first from work on folklore, especially in the Old Testament, by scholars in Scandinavia and Germany, who claimed attention for the investigation of the laws of oral transmission. What actually happens, they asked, to stories when they are passed from mouth to mouth in an unliterary community? Gradually, at least two important principles formulated themselves in reply. First, that, by examining a sufficiently wide range of examples, one might become familiar enough with the standard 'shapes' or 'forms' assumed by stories in successive stages of transmission to be able, with some degree of accuracy, to strip the latest form of a given story down, by a kind of onion-peeling process, to its most primitive, original shape. And secondly, that it is a mistake to treat the sort of written documents which are now under discussion as though they were 'literary,' since the collective influence of communities was generally more important than any one individual in shaping a story, and even in moulding a whole document." 88/87

E.V. McKnight, in his short but thorough study of Form Criticism, *What Is Form Criticism?*, provides further background information concerning the positions arrived at through source criticism:

"By the early part of the twentieth century the critical study of the Synoptic Gospels had arrived at the following positions: (1) The 'two document' hypothesis was accepted. Mark and Q served as sources for Matthew and Luke. (2) Both Mark and Q, as well as Matthew and Luke, were influenced by the theological views of the early church. (3) Mark and Q contained not only early authentic materials but also materials of a later date." 83/9,10

2B. History

Bob E. Patterson, in an article entitled "The Influence of Form Criticism on Christology," has set forth a complete history of Form Criticism. (See appendix, p.345.)

Donald Guthrie has observed that there has been a noticeable rise in the acceptance of Form Criticism. He notes that many influences have helped to produce and maintain this movement. Among these influences are:

(1) Weak points in the theory of source criticism. Being a literary criticism, source criticism limited itself to the available documents. And, when studying Matthew and Luke, the source critic failed to deal with the 20 to 30 year span which came between the death of Jesus and the point in time when the written sources appeared. The form critics attempt to account for this time span.

(2) A general questioning of the historical accuracy of Mark. Wilhelm Wrede started this trend with his "Messianic Secret" theory (See page 277), which stated that Mark wrote his Gospel with the purpose of conveying the unfolding revelation of Jesus' Messiahship (or the conveyance of the "Messianic Secret").

Later, Julius Wellhausen put forth the idea that the original or first tradition in Mark was interlaced with added material from the Gospel writers and heavily dependent on the Christian thinking of that day.

(3) The desire to update the Gospels. Because the first century view of the world is no longer relevant, according to form critics, an avid wish arose among these theologians to bring the Gospels into the world of the 20th century.

(4) The attempt to position the literary materials in their original situation, life setting or *Sitz im Leben*. This thrust was readily observed in the form critics' appeal to the Gospel backgrounds. 131/188, 195

5A. MAJOR PROPONENTS OF FORM CRITICISM

1B. Martin Dibelius

Martin Dibelius, author of *From Tradition to Gospel, A Fresh Approach to the New Testament and Early Christian Literature, Gospel Criticism and Christology, Jesus* and other major works, was one of the first renowned form critics. A summary presentation of his approach to Form Criticism follows.

Initially, he comments that "in prosecuting a research in the history of the Form of the Gospels, we must concern ourselves first of all and most of all with only one section of primitive Christian literature, namely the synoptic Gospels." 36/2

He continues:

"The literary understanding of the synoptics begins with the recognition that they are collections of material. The composers are only to the smallest extent authors. They are principally collectors, vehicles of tradition, editors. Before all else their labour consists in handing down, grouping, and working over the material which has come to them." 36/3

Dibelius announces his personal goal in Form Criticism:

"We hoped to be able to test the trustworthiness of the tradition of the life of Jesus by the employment of new and less subjective criteria, to escape in this way from the arbitrary judgments of the psychological treatment of the life of Jesus, and finally in some measure to establish more firmly the knowledge of the words and deeds of Jesus." 155/42

He interprets that "the first understanding afforded by the standpoint of *Formgeschichte* is that there never was a 'purely' historical witness to Jesus. Whatever was told of Jesus' words and deeds was always a testimony of faith as formulated for preaching and exhortation in order to convert unbelievers and confirm the faithful. What founded Christianity was not knowledge about a historical process, but the confidence that the content of the story was salvation: the decisive beginning of the End." 36/295

Another theological goal of *Formgeschichte*, as Dibelius puts it, is to undertake to depict a comprehension of the story of Jesus, by which the frameworks of the material are dominated. 36/295

Dibelius alleges that the Gospels did not intend to portray the person of Jesus Christ. With this being the case, we should not question the tradition preserved in the Gospels. But, if we did search them for information concerning the character or qualities of Christ, none would be found. By using secular interrogation and finding no answers we must conclude that the tradition was not literary. 36/300

The fortune of primitive Christianity is reflected in the various forms of Gospel tradition. The form was "determined by ecclesiastical requirements arising in the course of missionary labour and of preaching." 36/287

The early church was a missionary church, and the "missionary purpose was the cause and preaching was the means of spreading abroad that which the disciples of Jesus possessed as recollections." 36/13

What drove the early Christians to such a propagation of the tradition "was the work of proselytizing to which they felt themselves bound, i.e. the missionary purpose." 36/13

When Dibelius speaks of preaching "all possible forms of Christian propaganda are included: mission preaching, preaching during worship, and catechumen instruction. The mission of Christendom in the world was the originative cause of all these different activities." 36/15

There was only one complete connected narrative about a portion of the life of Christ and that is the "Passion story." 36/23, 178 The main purpose of the "Passion story," according to Dibelius, was not to confirm the story but "to make clear what in the Passion took place by God's will." 36/186

All the other traditional units existed without any connection to other units.

In conclusion, Dibelius speaks of the formation of the Gospel tradition:

"When, however, we trace the tradition back to its initial stage we find no description of the life of Jesus, but short paragraphs or pericopae. This is the fundamental hypothesis of the method of Form Criticism (*formgeschichtliche Methode*) as a representative of which I am speaking here." 37/27

2B. Rudolf Bultmann

Rudolf Bultmann, a former professor of New Testament studies at Breslau, Giessen and Marburg, retired from his professorship in 1951. But he has continued to have a worldwide impact due to his outstanding contribution to contemporary New Testament critical scholarship. Bultmann has authored many books expressing the form critical viewpoint. Some of these are *The*

History of the Synoptic Tradition, Jesus and the Word, Theology of the New Testament and *Jesus Christ and Mythology.*

1C. The following represents a collection of statements about and by Bultmann:

Klaas Runia comments on the impact that Bultmann has made on the world:

"Bultmann's program has had a tremendous influence upon postwar theology. Nearly all leading theologians in Germany today are former students of his or at least have been strongly influenced, by his way of thinking. In the United States, similar but even more radical ideas have been advocated by Paul Tillich, and again we must say that many of the leading theologians belong to this school. Some go even so far as to say that the traditional idea of God, based on the Bible, is dead." 107/13

Rudolf Pesch continues:

"R. Bultmann, whose approach is more strongly influenced by comparative religion and historical criticism, formulated the truth 'that the literature in which the life of a given community, even the primitive Christian community, is reflected, springs out of quite definite social conditions and needs, which produce a quite definite style and quite specific forms and categories.'" 97/338

H.N. Ridderbos observes that Bultmann's approach to the New Testament is to compare it to non-Christian religions and their development. This approach is called the method of the history of religion (*Religiongeschichte*). 102/12

Bultmann has been noted for his skeptical approach to the Gospels. It is his conclusion that "one can only emphasize the uncertainty of our knowledge of the person and work of the historical Jesus and likewise of the origin of Christianity." 19/20

Bultmann describes the development of Form Criticism by stating that "the forms of the literary tradition must be used to establish the influences operating in the life of the community, and the life of the community must be used to render the forms themselves intelligible." 21/5

Bultmann discusses his method:

"The first step is to distinguish between the tradition material which the evangelists used and their editorial additions." 19/25

2C. A FEW COMMENTS AND CRITICISMS

G.E. Ladd points out that one of Bultmann's fundamental methods for reconstructing the early history of Christian thought and establishing the historicity of Jesus is the "comparative religious method."

"This is a method developed in German scholarship which assumes that any given religious phenomenon must be understood in terms of its religious environment." 74/8

Schubert Ogden, in his book *Christ Without Myth*, has observed:

"The first step in an imminent criticism of Bultmann's proposal is to show that its entire meaning may be reduced to two fundamental propositions: (1) Christian faith is to be interpreted exhaustively and without remainder as man's original possibility of authentic historical (*geschichtlich*) existence as this is more or less adequately clarified and conceptualized by an appropriate philosophical analysis. (2) Christian faith is actually realizable, or is a 'possibility in fact,' only because of the particular historical (*historisch*) event Jesus of Nazareth, which is the originative event of the church and its distinctive word and sacraments. The second step in the criticism is to demonstrate that, as Barth and Buri and many others have held, these two propositions are mutually incompatible." 91/111,112

Edward Ellwein interprets Bultmann's view of what we can know of Jesus in this way:

"Who is the man Jesus? He is a man like ourselves, not a mythical figure; he is without messianic radiance, a real man — but merely a man, a teacher and a prophet, who worked for a brief time, who prophesied the imminent end of the world and the breaking in of the rule of God, who renewed and radicalized the protest of the great Old Testament prophets against legalism and cultic worship of God, and who was delivered up by the Jews to the Romans and was crucified. Everything else is uncertain and legendary." 175/34

Donald Guthrie, in his *New Testament Introduction*, identifies the underlying cause of Bultmann's theology:

"Bultmann's disillusionment led him to seek an approach to the Gospels which would emancipate him from the need for historical demonstration. Only so could the simplest, in his opinion, ever come to faith. He was further prompted to this non-historical approach by his commitment to existential philosophy. Deeply influenced by Heidegger, Bultmann maintained that the most important element in Christian faith was an existential encounter with Christ." 131/93, 94

In conclusion Martin E. Marty from the University of Chicago states the different reactions toward Bultmann:

"Rudolf Bultmann has been the greatest New Testament scholar of the twentieth century. So say many of his colleagues and rivals. No, Bultmann has muddied theological waters by tying himself to the tortured philosophy of his fellow Marburger, Martin Heidegger. So say most anti-Heideggerians, and their number is legion. Another voice, from a large Lutheran party in Germany, about their fellow Lutheran: Rudolf Bultmann is the arch-heretic of the century." 179/10

3B. Vincent Taylor

Vincent Taylor, one of the major form critics, has actually been quite critical of the study which he supports. Taylor's primary work dealing with the area of Form Criticism has been *The Formation of the Gospel Tradition* which was first copyrighted in 1935. In this work he comments on what he concludes to be the major strengths and weaknesses of Form Criticism. Taylor does not possess the historical skepticism of Bultmann.

Initially, Taylor concurs with the form critics concerning their basic assumption:

"It remains for us to consider the fundamental assumption of Form-Criticism, that, in the main, the earliest tradition consisted of small isolated units without local or temporal connexions; and further, since the two questions are inseparable, to ask what place is to be given to the recollections of eyewitnesses. With the Gospel of Mark before us it is impossible to deny that the earliest tradition was largely a mass of fragments." 114/38,39

Concerning the oral tradition as presented by Dibelius and Bultmann, Taylor tends to agree with both:

"Form Criticism operates on the principle that the materials of the written Gospels can be divided into groups on the basis of differences in structure and form, and that these differences give us clues to the ways in which they developed in the pre-literary period. The differences grew out of the ways in which the elements of the Gospels were used in the day to day life of the Church, as material for preaching, for teaching, and for missionary propaganda." 119/470, 71

In reference to the crucial issue of community creativity and biographical interest, Taylor makes this assumption:

"Several reasons can be suggested for the want of a biographical interest. First, the early Christians were men of humble origin and attainments; they were not a literary people, and so did not face the problems which confront the chronicler. Further, their eyes were on the New Heaven and the New Earth which they believed Christ would soon bring. They did not know that nineteen centuries later we should still lack the consummation: nothing would have astonished them more. Their hopes were on the future; what need was there to record the past? Again, the formation of Jesus-tradition was largely a communal process. Stories had survival-value, not so much because they had interest for the individual, but because they ministered to the needs of Christians who met together in religious fellowship. Had the first Christians a biographical interest?

"So far as the Evangelists are concerned, somewhat different answers must be given. None of them aims at producing a biography in the modern sense of the term, although all wish to tell the Story of Jesus. In the Fourth Gospel the dominant aims are religious and doctrinal, but the material is presented in a historical framework. In Mark there is present a desire to sketch in outline the course of the Ministry of Jesus, and the same outline is followed in Matthew, although here it is subordinated to didactic and ecclesiastical interests. In Luke the sixfold date of iii. 1f., and the terms of the Preface (i. 1-4) indicate an intention to tell the Story in orderly succession, although we cannot assume that chronological succession is meant, or still less is achieved." 114/143,144

4B. Summary

To summarize these major proponents of Form Criticism it is necessary to consider some of the similarities and differences found among them.

1C. SIMILARITIES BETWEEN DIBELIUS AND BULTMANN

Although Bultmann and Dibelius classify the traditional material differently, that is, they see different forms with different life situations, they are in basic agreement as to their fundamental assumption. That assumption is twofold. They agree that the traditional material first existed as brief, rounded units, having the early community as their *Sitz im Leben* and that all historical contexts in the Gospels (with the exception of the Passion Story) are to be regarded as the editorial work of the evangelists. 57/24,25

E.V. McKnight continues to note the similarities between Dibelius and Bultmann: They "assume that the materials can be classified as to form and that the form enables the students to reconstruct the history of the tradition." 88/20

L.J. McGinley approaches Dibelius and Bultmann in a slightly different manner. He points out that they have agreed on style, disagreed on terminology, agreed on material, disagreed on the growth of the tradition, disagreed on the *Sitz im Leben* and finally agreed with a complete denial of the historical value of their categories. 82/45,46

McGinley continues:

"Bultmann and Dibelius agree that the description and classification of forms is but one part of the task undertaken by form-criticism. They maintain that since there exists a relationship between the different literary species produced in a community and the various functions of the community life, this relationship can be detected and the historico-social situation which created a definite form to satisfy a definite need can be determined." 82/18,19

McGinley observes that "in seeking parallels for the Gospel stories, Dibelius frequently refers to the rabbinic writings. Despite the relatively late redaction of this literature, he believes that the anecdotes themselves are of comparatively early origin and satisfactorily illustrate the synoptic narratives." 82/96

McGinley adds that "Bultmann also makes abundant use of illustrations and analogies from the rabbinic tradition. He believes, however, that the process that led to its fixation was more complicated than that which occurred with regard to the synoptic tradition. In the Gospels the forms were preserved more purely than in the rabbinic literature, where the formation was more conscious and where the motifs were artistically varied and individual units reshaped." 82/97

2C. SOME BASIC CRITICISM

One of the most basic differences between Bultmann and Dibelius is their concept of the "controlling motive" in the formation of the units.

1). Bultmann: The alleged debates between the early community and Judaism was the motive. 146/39-44; 149/350, 351

2). Dibelius: "Missionary goal" was the actual motive and "preaching" was the means of propagation. 36/13

Vincent Taylor provides a criticism of Bultmann when he claims that "Bultmann's tests of genuineness are much too subjective. Can we get very far by selecting a few characteristic features in the sayings of Jesus, and by making these a touchstone by which we decide the genuineness of the tradition as a whole? To decide what is characteristic is not easy, and, even if we can do this, the test must often fail because even the greatest of teachers often say familiar things. Great teachers refuse to be true to type, even their own type." 114/107, 108

Bultmann who follows Martin Dibelius in the chronological development of Form Criticism states that:

"In distinction from Dibelius I am indeed convinced that form-criticism, just because literary forms are related to the life and history of the primitive Church not only presupposes judgements of facts alongside judgements of literary criticism, but must also lead to judgements about facts (the genuineness of a saying, the historicity of a report and the like)." 21/5

Alfred Wikenhauser presents a serious criticism against the major form-critics:

"The ascription to the primitive Christian community of a really creative power is a serious defect in Form Criticism as it is applied by many of its exponents—notably by Bultmann and Bertram, and, less radically, by Dibelius; they maintain that certain parts of the synoptic Gospels were free creations of the community, or that motifs for their forming—especially for miracle stores or *Novellen*, and legends—were borrowed from Judaism and more particularly from Hellenism." 126/276

One of the major accusations against the form critics has been in the area of subjectivity. Robert Mounce, in a recent interview, has commented on this particular problem as he says:

"Form Criticism sounds like a scientific method. If it were, you would find consistency of interpretation. But the interpretations of a single saying vary widely. Not only are interpretations widespread but form critics often can't agree whether a pericopae is a miracle story or a pronouncement story—the two can be woven together. One would expect consistency in historical reconstruction if Form Criticism were a true science." 144

I.J. Peritz, also commenting on the area of subjectivity of the form critics, has concluded:

"Form Criticism thus brings face to face with the obligation either to acquiesce in its faulty method and conclusions or to combat them. What is involved, however, is not the alternative between an uncritical attitude and criticism, but between criticism and hypercriticism. A critical view of the Gospels does not claim strict objectivity. It is hard to tell sometimes where poetry ends and history begins. It is highly probable that there is no underlying strictly chronological or topographical scheme; and that they are not biography in 'our sense.' But this is far from admitting that we have no reliable testimony from eyewitnesses; that the Church from its Christ of faith created the Jesus of history, instead of from the Jesus of history its Christ of faith." 95/205

He adds:

"The great fault of Form Criticism is its imaginative subjectivity in evaluating tradition." 95/205

In a recent periodical Peritz sums up the views of form critics by stating that "it is only in one thing they all agree, namely, that the earliest disciples of Jesus were too ignorant in literary method or too indifferent to biography or history to make an effort to perpetuate the memory of their Master." 95/202

6A. IN SUMMARY

1B. Form Criticism seeks to discover the original literary forms in which the traditions of Jesus were written down.

2B. The form critics hope by discovering the original forms to be able to identify the needs of the early Church which prompted their creation.

3B. The form critical method involves dividing the Gospels as to literary form, then seeking the life situation which brought them into being. They seek to reduce the Gospels to their original pure state.

4B. Form Criticism was born in Germany following World War I.

5B. Among its major proponents are Martin Dibelius, Rudolf Bultmann and Vincent Taylor.

chapter 17

definition
of
terms

1A. A BASIC GLOSSARY

R.A. Spivey and D.M. Smith, in their *Anatomy of the New Testament,* provide the following glossary as an aid to the study of Form Criticism.

1B. "**Eschatology:** discourse about the last things or the end of the age (Greek *eschatos* meaning 'last'). Traditionally the term is used of Christian thought concerning all the events and actions associated with both the end of history and the end of human life.

2B. "**Gnosticism:** a religious movement or attitude widespread about the time of the emergence of the Christian faith. Believers possessed a secret knowledge (*gnosis*) and sought to escape the ephemeral earthly world for the eternal heavenly world.

3B. "**Hellenization:** the process or result of the spread of Greek language and culture in the Mediterranean world after Alexander the Great (died 323 B.C.).

4B. "**Kerygma** (literally 'proclamation'): the early Christian preaching about Jesus as the Christ intended to elicit the decision of faith.

5B. "**Myth:** the result of man's effort to communicate his faith in transcendent reality by means of story and symbol. This technical use of the term should be distinguished from the popular meaning of a fantastic or untrue story.

6B. "**Oral Tradition:** any teaching or similar material transmitted from person to person or generation to generation by word of mouth rather than by use of writing; also the process of such transmission.

7B. "**Parable:** a brief story that makes its point by the unusual development or imagery of the narrative. The various details do not function as allegory but are significant for the story itself. Although the parable was already known to the Jewish religious tradition, Jesus made especial use of it.

8B. "**Pericope:** a 'cutting around' or section. The term is used of the individual, complete units of tradition about Jesus that circulated separately in the early church and were ultimately joined together to form the Gospels.

9B. "**Redactor:** one who edits, revises, or shapes the literary sources that he has at hand. The separation of tradition and redaction is the primary task of form criticism.

10B. "**Source Criticism:** the work of identifying the written sources that were used in the composition of any given document, such as one of the Gospels.

11B. "**Synoptic Problem:** the problem of understanding the relationship between the Synoptic Gospels (Matthew, Mark, and Luke), taking account of their great similarities as well as their distinct differences. The generally accepted solution is that both Matthew and Luke used Mark, the Q source consisting largely of Jesus' sayings, and distinct material to which each had access separately." 113/463-466

2A. REDAKTION CRITICISM

Redaktion Criticism is defined by Norman Perrin, a prominent representative of this school:

"It is concerned with studying the theological motivation of the author as this is revealed in the collection, arrangement, editing, and modification of traditional material, and in the composition of new material or the creation of new forms within the traditions of early Christianity." 184/1

3A. RELIGIONSGESCHICHTLICHE METHODE

It is called the *religionsgeschichtliche Methode,* or the study of the Hebrew-Christian religion in terms of the history of religions in general. This method represents the most thorough-going application of a naturalistic historicism to the study of the Bible. It assumes "that biblical religion, in both the Old and New Testaments, passed through stages of growth and evolution like all ancient religions, and in this evolution was heavily influenced through interaction with its religious environment. This method involves the consistent application of the principle of analogy to biblical religion: the history and development of other ancient religions. This method is not at all interested in the truth of the Bible or in revelation. Hebrew religion is studied simply as one of many ancient Near Eastern religions, and the religion of the early church is seen as a syncretistic movement which had its ultimate origin with the teachings of Jesus of Nazareth and which borrowed and blended important elements from the first-century Jewish and Graeco-Roman religions." 74/195, 196

4A. GOSPEL TRADITION

Vincent Taylor interprets this term in the following way:

"[by] 'Gospel tradition' I mean that which we have received from the first Christians concerning the words and deeds of Jesus; and by its 'formation' I understand both the external characteristics of the tradition and the process by which it came into being." 114/1

5A. COMMUNITY

The form critics seek to define with this term the contemporary Christian church of the day when the Synoptic Gospels were written. Rudolf Bultmann often uses this term synonymously with the phrase "the primitive Christian church." 57/13

6A. CREATIVE COMMUNITY

Inherent in the fundamental assumptions of Form Criticism lies the concept of a creative community. Stanley Gundry explains this concept:

"The early Christian community is said to have been creative. By this is meant that anonymous forces in the community, operating according to fixed laws, either created tradition about Jesus or changed and molded existent tradition about Him." 57/13

7A. SITZ IM LEBEN

A translation of this German phrase could be "the life situation."

It refers to the characteristic mode or setting of life in the early Church. Form critics believe that every part or unit of the tradition of Jesus has been in some way influenced by the community, whether it was manufactured by the community or refined by the community. Therefore, the units are an adequate source for Sitz im Leben information or details. 57/13, 14

8A. UNITS OR PERICOPES

These are the individual, and at one time scattered, bits of tradition which, although complete in themselves, were gathered together by the Synoptic writers to form the Gospels. Examples of a pericope would be a short saying, a parable, an account of a healing or any similar bit of tradition from the life of Jesus which was complete by itself. 57/12, 13

9A. ARTIFICIAL CONTEXT

As stated above, the units (or pericopes) are to have been first connected with other units in the framework of Mark. The framework of Mark is the artificial context in which the units are supposedly imbedded. The artificial context is said to have been a result of the editorial work of the evangelist. Gundry adds that "this artificial context is also called the 'historical framework.'" 57/13

10A. DEMYTHOLOGIZATION

To have a proper understanding of Form Criticism and especially of Rudolf Bultmann's work, it is necessary to understand what the radical critics mean to convey by this term.

Donald Guthrie has defined this term by saying that "'demythologization,' is the attempt to interpret the Gospels stripped of all elements which form analysis have shown to belong to the first-century environment of the early Church." 131/190

G.E. Ladd adds that demythologizing "means the interpretation of mythological language in terms of the concept of human existence it embodies. It sees through the objectifying form of mythological language to the concept of human existence contained in it." 75/26,27

11A. HISTORY

J.P. Martin has distinguished between two different concepts of history. As he explains it, there is "Historie (mere history as an object of scientific study) and Geschichte (the event and its effects on present and future)." 79/21

Norman Perrin has made a similar distinction:

"In the first place we have history in the sense of 'what actually happened,' in the sense of historical factuality. For this kind of history Bultmann would use the word Historie.

"This kind of history is subject to investigation by the historical sciences." 96/37,38

Perrin adds that "the second of the conceptions linked to the word 'history is that of history in the sense of an event from the past living on in influence upon and significance for the future. The second of these two German words for history is 'Geschichte.'" 96/40

chapter 18

oral
tradition

Form Criticism assumes that before the Gospels were written there was a period of oral tradition.

1A. INTRODUCTION AND EXPLANATION

K. Groebel has enunciated the form critics' need for oral tradition. He shows that the "unit types grow out of the everyday life of their particular community: funerals, weddings, victories, defeats, worship and its liturgical acts, instruction, missionary propaganda, etc. These and the like are the 'seat in life' of each kind of tradition unit. Tradition is never preserved for its own sake with conscious antiquarian intent, but only because some need or interest of the community presses it into service. In such service it stays alive as oral tradition as long as that practical interest remains alive." 54/320

Floyd V. Filson notes that the form critics were the first to make an intensive study of oral tradition. Filson notes the effect of this study on the Gospel tradition (note the discounting of eyewitnesses):

"Moreover, not only is the function of the final editor of the material minimized, but the former tendency, still widely dominant, to bridge the decades between Jesus and the actual writing of the Gospels by some one eyewitness for each Gospel, is seriously discounted. Instead, for example, of seeing Peter as the sufficient guarantor of what Mk. contains, there is a tendency to see in Mk. the deposit of a collection of units of continually repeated oral tradition." 47/93

Ernst Käsemann, a post-Bultmannian form critic, but a disciple of Bultmann, has set forth the following proposition:

"The Synoptic Gospels as we have them today are the product of a tradition which was at least forty years in process of formation and the material of which is composed of very small units. At first it was individual sayings and isolated stories which were handed on; later, these were collected together probably for preaching purposes; this made it possible for the Evangelists, in a third and final stage, to set the appearance of Jesus on earth within a framework of space and time." 68/59

Vincent Taylor has provided the following summary of the radical critics' concept of oral tradition:

"During this period the tradition circulated mainly in separate oral units which can be classified according to their form. It is believed, further, that much may be inferred regarding the origin of these units, the causes which gave rise to them, and the changes they underwent until in the course of time they were given a written form." 114/10

G.E. Ladd has offered his support to the concept of an oral tradition:

"We may conclude, therefore, that the contention of form criticism that the Gospel tradition was preserved in oral form for a generation by the church is not only a fact which is attested strongly by the New Testament, but is also a fact of great theological importance. Not only was the Holy Spirit active in the writing of the books of the New Testament; he was also active in the history of the Gospel tradition before it assumed written form. This theological fact is seldom recognized by form critics, for they usually work as historians, not as theologians." 74/153

One of the main interests of the radical critics has been the division of the period of oral tradition into sections. Vincent Taylor has postulated that the first period of the tradition would extend from A.D. 30 to A.D. 50. He continues that "throughout the whole of this first period, no sign of a demand meets us for a connected record, apart from the Passion Story, and no interest is visible in the life of Jesus earlier than His Ministry." 114/174, 175

Taylor further remarks that "the second period extends approximately from about 50 to 65 A.D., though some of the processes now to be described may have begun in the earlier period." 114/175, 176

Taylor continues that "the characteristic mark of this second stage is the attempt to gather the scattered elements of the tradition into groups." 114/175, 176

The third period of the tradition extends from A.D. 65 to the initial writing of the Gospels. Concerning this period, Taylor remarks that "a special impulse to the task of Gospel compilation was given by the rapid expansion of the Gentile Mission, the lapse of time, and the increased need for Christian instruction and defence." 114/185

In conclusion, Taylor reflects on the development of oral tradition:

"The time is one in which precious fragments are treasured for their immediate interest and value; Christian hands are full of jewels, but there is no desire to weave a crown." 114/174, 175

2A. MAJOR PROPONENTS

1B. Martin Dibelius' Concept of Oral Tradition

"Before the Gospels were written, the source of preaching, teaching, and edification in the Church was the tradition about Jesus preserved either orally, or else in small collections capable of expansion. When the Gospels became current, the Church no longer held to the fluid tradition but to the writings in book form in which the old material had been recorded." 35/56

In trying to understand oral tradition, it is necessary to know what led to the handing down of tradition. Dibelius observes that "more than anything else, [that] led to the handing down of the tradition, viz. missionary purpose was the cause and preaching was the means of spreading abroad that which the disciples of Jesus possessed as recollections." 36/13

Dibelius goes on to clarify his understanding:

"If I speak of preaching in this connection, all possible forms of Christian propaganda are included: mission preaching, preaching during worship, and catechumen instruction. The mission of Christendom in the world was the originative cause of all these different activities." 36/15

Concerning the sayings of Jesus, Dibelius contends that they were regarded by the Christian churches to be "rules for right living" and were used to serve the purposes of the church. As he says:

"When the words of Jesus were assembled as ordinances for the churches it was easy to suit them to more advanced church-relationships by particularizing what was general, explaining what was misunderstood, and moderating prophetic severity." 35/33, 34

He adds that "these Christians believed themselves to be more faithful to their Master when they explained His sayings by expanding them and then followed them with understanding, than if they had abhorred any addition and passed on the original form of His words."

But he quickly qualifies this:

"Moreover those changes of form did not alter the essence of the gospel: the message of Jesus has been preserved for us in the first 3 Gospels self-consistently and unspoiled." 35/34, 35

In addition, Dibelius notes that the assembling together of Jesus' short and pithy "sayings" depended upon an oral tradition. He continues:

"We shall understand how these short and very pregnant utterances were treasured up and passed on by the hearers if we bear clearly in mind the strength of the memory of ancient people living in relatively simple social circumstances, and not driven to and fro by the modern desire for movement." 35/28

Dibelius attributes the collection of sayings to a group of unnamed and unknown people whose sole purpose was not to write books but rather to pass on tradition. He follows this thought by saying that "even the earliest Evangelists really intended nothing else." 35/52, 53

Dibelius notes that these sayings of Jesus were handed down with context. He says that "this fact is proved by the way in which the sayings have been assembled into the 'speeches' or 'sermons' of Jesus." 35/32

Another area of concern to which Dibelius addresses himself is the authenticity of the sayings of Jesus:

"Of course this stringing together of genuine sayings of Jesus with other Christian words of exhortation could become a source of error. In certain circumstances at a later date, other words standing in the neighbourhood of the authentic sayings could be held equally authentic and so increase the number of genuine words of Jesus by a few spurious ones. But that could only happen on the assumption that authentic words of Jesus were as a matter of fact to be found among the pieces of advice in the exhortations." 36/241

Concerning stories about Jesus, Dibelius states that "a glance shows that the narrative sections of the Gospels are not at all concerned with giving a chronicle of events, with biography, or with making a connected historical record. What is set down is essentially stories in narrative form, complete in themselves. In form at least they are similar to our anecdotes, and they deal with separate incidents in the life of Jesus. They would not have come down to us rounded off and complete in themselves, at any rate in Mark's Gospel, if they had not been current separately in the first instance, passed on from mouth to mouth independently of each other." 35/35

2B. Rudolf Bultmann's Concept of the Oral Tradition

Bultmann begins by stating that "the passing on of words of the Lord was motivated not by historical-biographical interest but by the practical concern to regulate the way of life of believers and to keep their hope alive. The one whom they heard speaking in the words was not the historical Jesus, but the Church's heavenly Lord." 25/124

Bultmann continues by referring to the problem of obscurance of the transmission of the tradition:

"As such narratives pass from mouth to mouth, or when one writer takes them over from another, their fundamental character remains the same, but the details are subject to the control of fancy and are usually made more explicit and definite." 19/32

Probably the best summary of Bultmann's concept of the oral tradition can be seen in his list of four laws which govern narrative and tradition:

(1)   The first law is that narrators do not give long, unified accounts, but rather, small, single pictures of utmost simplicity.

(2)   Secondly, as narratives pass from mouth to mouth, their fundamental character remains the same, but the details are subject to the control of fancy and are usually more explicit and definite.

(3)   In the third place, Bultmann thinks that he has discovered that indirect discourse tends to become direct discourse in the process of transmission.

(4)   Finally, he claims that there was an inclination to impose a schematic idea of the course of Jesus' activity on the tradition. With these principles as a basis, Bultmann analyzes the various types of traditional material. 146/32-34

3B. Vincent Taylor's Concept of Oral Tradition

Taylor, speaking as a representative of Form Criticism, acknowledges: "We gladly recognize the divine element in the Gospels, but we see that they came into existence in human ways, that in His wisdom God did not think it necessary to safeguard them by protective measures. but left them free to win their own way and to make their own conquests. We believe also that, while the results of this method are often perplexing to us, God's way has proved to be to His greater praise and glory. But if this is so it is all the more necessary to understand the process by which the tradition has been formed and transmitted." 114/2

Taylor cites B.S. Easton concerning the oral tradition:

"We have every reason to believe that the first tradition of the sayings-groups and the parables arose in Jesus' lifetime and under His personal direction; the earliest content of the tradition He Himself required His disciples to commit to memory." 43/41

Taylor remarks that "during the years which immediately followed the Resurrection, the first Christians preserved cycles of connected reminiscences associated with the various centres of the Ministry of Jesus." 114/69

Taylor continually alludes to a process of dissolution in transmission. He observes that "the stories have been shortened and rounded in the course of oral transmission; they have passed from hand to hand, and have been made the subject of comment and reflection, with the result that many a vivid detail has fallen by the way while the historical core remains." 114/158

He further explains that "the most important exception to the dissolving process continued to be the Passion Story which existed in the form of short accounts of the Arrest, Trial, and Crucifixion of Jesus current at different centres of primitive Christianity." 114/169, 170

Taylor introduces a new element into the concept of oral tradition. E.L. Abel comments on this by referring to Taylor:

"Those Christians who had lived to see both Jesus and the Gospels written would have been able to prevent imagination from spreading into the Gospels. Taylor proclaims that '...the presence of eyewitnesses, for at least a generation, would serve as a check on corruptions innocently due to imagination....' The late T.W. Manson held firmly to the view that a great deal of information in the Gospel of Mark comes directly from Peter the apostle. This supposition is based on statements similar to the following made by Papias (ca.A.D. 140): 'Mark was the interpreter of Peter and wrote down accurately, though not in order, that which he remembered of what was said or done by the Lord. He had, of course, neither heard the Lord nor did he follow Him, but later, as I said, Peter. The latter adapted his teaching to the needs of the moment, but not as if he wanted to make a collection of the Lord's sayings, so that Mark made no mistake when he wrote down some things as he remembered them. He intended only one thing, to omit or falsify nothing which he had heard.'" 1/273

One of the precepts of the form critics has been that as time passed, the oral tradition suffered in transmission. Vincent Taylor, a critic himself, attempts to answer to what degree this tradition has suffered and what has caused this suffering. But in so doing, he considers the greater importance to be in examining the causes that are responsible for the obscuring of the original tradition. The causes he notes are:

(1) "In the first place, most of the sayings must have been spoken in Aramaic, whereas we have them now in Greek; and translation, however faithful, must always mean some loss of accuracy and the possibility of error.

(2) "Again, there are cases where a saying is modified by the context in which it appears....

(3) "Further, a saying may be modified by religious interests. The phrase 'Son of man,' for example, may be introduced into a context to which it does not belong. We can see that this has happened when we compare an earlier and a later Gospel: in Mk. viii. 27 Jesus asks: 'Who do men say that I am?'; but in Mt. xvi. 13 the question appears in the form: 'Who do men say that the Son of man is?'

(4) "More debatable are the cases in which sayings have been modified by later dogmatic beliefs, by controversies, or by existing practices." 114/110-113

However, Taylor adds that personally "I have no hesitation in claiming that the tradition of the words of Jesus is far better preserved than we have any right to expect, and with much greater accuracy than is to be found in the record of the words of any great teacher of the past." 114/110-113

4B. Summary

James Martin, in *The Reliability of the Gospels*, has provided an excellent summation of the concepts of the oral tradition:

"The first might be termed the sphere of worship, where stories of Jesus were told to believers for their edification. This sphere includes the Christian church services, the catechumenical classes, the Christian family gatherings and, indeed, every situation where the stories of Jesus might be recounted to those who owned allegiance to Him for their instruction, their guidance, their encouragement, their comfort and, in general, their strengthening in the Christian way. The other might be termed the sphere of evangelism, where the stories of Jesus were told to unbelievers for their conviction and conversion. This sphere includes the preaching on the mission-field, the arguments employed in public debate and, indeed, every situation where Christians might be concerned to vindicate their faith in the eyes of those who did not share it." 80/52

Martin adds that perhaps the strongest and largest area of oral tradition was that of the early Christian worship service, which in form, was borrowed from the synagogue service, but whose flavor was distinctly Christian. "One of its distinctive and prominent features was the place given to recounting something of the life of Jesus. At some stage in the service, someone of authority was called upon to speak to the congregation about Jesus, and related some incident of His life or some aspect of His teaching. In this way the perpetuation of the tradition had an appointed and regular place in the services of worship in the early Church." 80/56

3A. BASIC ANSWER AND ANALYSIS

Criticism of Form Criticism has not been wanting. Filson includes the following points:

"It does not do justice to the historical sense, intelligence and integrity of the early Christians; while it rightly recognizes the extensive topical grouping of material in the Gospels, it goes too far in discrediting their basic outline of Jesus' ministry; while it correctly sees the importance of the early oral period, it hardly gives adequate weight to the fact that within some twenty years the writing of written sources began, and so the process of oral tradition was not so long as in folk tales and in the earliest Old Testament stories; its tendency to assume radical distortion of the tradition in the Hellenistic church is refuted by the prevailing Semitic character of the common Synoptic tradition; and its results are warped by unexamined assumptions, such as that miracle stories are largely late creations and that explicit Christology arose first in the church rather than in the mind of Jesus." 46/436, 437

Speaking of the brevity of the time element involved in the writing of the New Testament, Kistemaker writes:

"Normally, the accumulation of folklore among people of primitive culture takes many generations: it is a gradual process spread over centuries of time. But in conformity with the thinking of the form critic, we must conclude that the Gospel stories were produced and collected within little more than one generation. In terms of the form-critical approach, the formation of the individual Gospel units must be understood as a telescoped project with accelerated course of action." 186/48, 49

A.M. Hunter continues:

(1)   "The critics assumed that all the early tradition about Jesus was quite unfixed and relatively unreliable, though the first Christians, who

were Jews, had a serious care for the faithful and controlled transmission of their Lord's words and deeds.

(2)   "They drew dubious parallels between oral tradition in other cultures, where the time of transmission runs into centuries, and oral tradition in the Gospels, where it is a matter of two or three decades.

"They were prone to assume that the form of a Gospel story or saying was a reliable criterion of its authenticity, which of course it is not." 63/34

The accuracy of oral tradition is an additional matter of concern. The form critics tend to be skeptical of the reliability of oral tradition.

To this James Martin has answered:

"The Oral Tradition was made public through the knowledge of the Christians in the Church, and because it was made public the accuracy of it is sound." 80/65

He continues that it is reliable to believe that the church services and their construction of transmission was very trustworthy. In the services the stories of Jesus were repeated so often that these stories had to be well known. In light of this the Church would be unlikely to permit any kind of change in form or content. 80/61

E.F. Scott concurs that "while it was still in the oral phase it came to be invested with forms, which were more or less conventional. These conclusions are reasonably certain, and it does not follow from any of them or from all of them together that the record is untrustworthy." 111/188, 189

A.H. McNeile challenges Form Criticism's concept of oral tradition. He points out that form critics do not deal with the tradition of Jesus' words as closely as they should. A careful look at I Corinthians 7:10, 12, 25 shows the careful preservation and the existence of a genuine tradition of recording these words. In the Jewish religion it was customary for a student to memorize a rabbi's teaching. Mishna, Aboth, ii, 8: "A good pupil was like a plastered cistern that loses not a drop." If we rely on C.F. Burney's theory (*The Poetry of Our Lord* [1925]), we can assume that much of the Lord's teaching is in Aramaic poetical form, making it easy to be memorized. 85/4

Another area of conflict in the treatment of Form Criticism and oral tradition has been its failure to acknowledge the role of the Holy Spirit. Robert Mounce has commented that "Form Criticism has little or no place for the doctrine of the Holy Spirit and His role in the origin and transmission of the teachings of Jesus." 144

Taking into account the chronological considerations, McGinley comments on the theories of Dibelius and Bultmann:

"First of all, eyewitnesses of the events in question were still alive when the tradition had been completely formed; and among those eyewitnesses were bitter enemies of the new religious movement. Yet the tradition claimed to narrate a series of well-known deeds and publicly taught doctrines at a time when false statements could, and would, be challenged.

"Secondly, even though Christianity had widespread growth, the traditions of the gospels were so well formed that 30 years after Jesus' death, the Gospel of Mark, influenced by Peter, was instantly accepted in Rome.

"Thirdly, the fact that the whole process took less than thirty years, and that its essential part was accomplished in a decade and a half, finds no parallel in any tradition to which the Synoptic Gospels have been compared." 82/25

This time element, a definite control in the test of Form Criticism, shows up a major defect in the theory and Dibelius has not fully answered the implications while Bultmann has entirely overlooked it.

One of the major criticisms against the form critics' idea of the oral tradition is that the period of oral tradition (as defined by the critics) is not long enough to have allowed the alterations in the tradition that the radical critics have alleged.

It is very important to the critics to find a period that is analogous to the oral tradition period of the Gospels. A.H. McNeile observes that "the period which divides Jesus' Resurrection form the date of Mark's composition is little more than one generation. Dibelius sought for an analogy and found it in the *Apophthegmata Patrum*, though the tradition about the desert Fathers took not thirty or forty years to form but about one hundred. It is not unusual for men even of slight intellectual ability to recall and relate clearly important events occurring thirty-five years previously." 85/54

E.B. Redlich, a form critic, adds that "if, as is possible, the written source common to Matthew and Luke, generally known as Q, could be dated about A.D. 50, and if the special source of Luke, designated L, was a document which could be dated about the same time, and if our Lord died about A.D. 30, the strictly oral period would be no more than twenty years. In point of fact, it is another weakness of Form Criticism that it sits too lightly on the results of literary criticism and assumes that the formative period lasted about two generations or forty years. Thus, in their investigations there is a tendency to overlook the presence and influence of those who were eye-witnesses and ear-witnesses of the events of the life, death, and resurrection of Jesus, and could therefore guarantee the historical value of the tradition." 101/15, 16

L.J. McGinley believes that the formation of the tradition began after the death of Jesus, i.e., not earlier than A.D. 29-30, and was completed before Mark, i.e. A.D. 55-62. However, before Paul's captivity in 58, he had written to the Romans and Corinthians, the Thessalonians and Galatians in a way that assumed they had a prior detailed knowledge of Jesus. Taking these facts into consideration, we can conclude that the formative period cannot be extended beyond the year A.D. 50. From the form-critical viewpoint, the beginnings must have been slow, because the lack of biographical interest and expectation of a soon-to-happen Second Coming had to be overcome by the rise of other motives. 82/24

James Martin in *The Reliability of the Gospels* has remarked that "as a matter of fact, there was no time for the Gospel story of Jesus to have been produced by legendary accretion. The growth of legend is always a slow and gradual thing. But in this instance the story of Jesus was being proclaimed, substantially as the Gospels now record it, simultaneously with the beginning of the Church." 80/103, 104

L.J. McGinley, author of *Form Criticism of the Synoptic Healing Narratives*, adds:

"In developing such an intricate theory as form-criticism from either the analytic or constructive viewpoint, one of the investigator's primary concerns should be to discover a suitable external 'control' by which he can test his conclusion. Such a 'control' is at hand for form-criticism of the Gospels. It consists in determining *the length of time* required for a tradition to evolve in the manner proposed. This is not extremely difficult. The natural impression that such an evolutionary process extends over a long span of years can be tested by a study of those 'general laws governing popular narrative and tradition, such as stories and anecdotes.' [Rudolf Bultmann. *Die Erforschung der synoptischen Evangelien* (2nd. ed.; Giessen, 1930), p. 15.] and particularly by considering the development of the rabbinic and Hellenic literatures so much employed in form-criticism for analogies of style. Yet form-critics have consistently neglected any precise statements on this point, and it is significant that Dibelius considers the formation of the *Apophthegmata Patrum* a good analogy precisely because it was accomplished in so short a time [Martin Dibelius. "Zur Formgeschichte der Evangelien," *Theol. Rund.*, N.F.I. (1929), p. 173]." 82/23

He concludes by citing Köhler: "...that no more than fifteen years can be assigned to the active evolution of the synoptic tradition as understood by form-criticism]*Das formgeschichtliche Problem des N.T.* (Tubingen, 1927), p. 25]." 82/24

Steven H. Travis notes in his article, "Form Criticism":

"The assumption that there was an oral period before any of the gospel material came to be written down has been questioned by H. Schurmann. He suggests that during Jesus' ministry his disciples may have written notes on main aspects of his teaching." 6/159

F.G. Kenyon, a proven scholar, who questions the time element required by the form critical hypothesis, says that "there is simply not time for the elaborate processes required for Dibelius' *Formgeschichte*, which has won rather surprising popularity, but which presupposes, first the dissemination of stories of the life and teachings of Jesus, then their collection and classification into groups according to their character, and then the formation of continuous narratives in which they were utilized." 149/52

J. Warwick Montgomery has analyzed Form Criticism and has concluded that it fails because "the time interval between the writing of the New Testament documents as we have them and the events of Jesus' life which they record is too brief to allow for communal redaction by the Church." 87/37

4A. CONCLUSION

Babcock questions the validity of the basis of Form Criticism when he observes:

"This process of gradual moulding, in the course of which the stories were so modified that considerable allowance must be made for additions and diminutions before we can arrive at the true account of the event, would seem to demand a considerable interval of time. But it is now established that the Crucifixion took place in A.D. 33 and that all the Gospels were composed and in circulation by the end of the first century; we cannot therefore allow for a period of more than sixty years for the composition of any of them, and further, the Gospels according to St. Mark and St. Luke may well be all written within a quarter of a century after the last event narrated, while Q, which has been embodied in St. Luke and St. Matthew, may be at least ten years earlier. To the argument that form criticism demands a prolonged period and therefore that the composition of the Gospels must be put late there is thus an obvious reply, that other considerations both allow and suggest that their composition may be put far earlier, and this casts doubts on the validity of the theory of form criticism." 3/16

Paul L. Maier writes that "arguments that Christianity hatched its Easter myth over a lengthy period of time or that the sources were written many years after the event are simply not factual.' 153/122

5A. IN SUMMARY

1B. The form critics hold that the Gospel traditions were passed on in oral form for at least one generation after the death of Christ.

2B. Form critics believe the oral traditions were used mainly in worship and evangelism.

3B. Other scholars contend that there was not enough time between the death of Christ and the writing of the Gospels for the traditions to develop in the way the form critics propose.

4B. Many think the form critics are overly skeptical about the reliability of oral traditon.

chapter 19

pericopes
or
self-contained
units

Form Criticism assumes that during the oral period the narratives and sayings, with the exception of the Passion narrative, circulated mainly as single, self-contained, detached units, complete in themselves. These units are usually referred to as pericopes.

1A. BASIC ASSUMPTION

Floyd V. Filson, in *Origins of the Gospels*, stated that "fundamental to the form critic's method is the idea that the gospel material first circulated in small, independent units." 47/93

Filson suggests that it was continued repetition which tended to encourage the extension or oral tradition and it was this same tradition which tended to fix the form.

"According to form critics, it was largely through constant repetition during those days of oral use that the tradition received the form which it now possesses. Studies of folklore and popular stories in various languages lead to the conclusion that continued repetition of such material tends to give it a rather fixed form, which is suited to the material and to the setting in which it is used. These results are regarded as good guides for gospel study. Through constant repetition the material was given much of its present form." 47/92, 93

Alfred Wikenhauser, in his *New Testament Introduction*, has concluded that this assumption is the basic proposition of Form Criticism. He observes:

"The Gospels are not literary works of a single mould which owe their existence to the personality of a writer; they consist of a considerable number of small units or single passages (single stories and single sayings) which redactors have forged into a unity with the minimum of change. The Evangelists did not give shape to unformed tradition; they brought together into a unity the Gospel material which had been handed down in fairly set forms. Only the framework into which they set the individual passages is their own work, and this framework is an artificial creation." 126/255, 256

Wellhausen, cited by Bultmann, adds that "the oldest tradition consisted almost entirely of small fragments (sayings or words of Jesus), and did not present a continuous story of the deeds of Jesus or any complete collection of sayings. When these fragments were collected, they were connected so as to form a continuous narrative." 135/340

2A. PROPONENTS

1B. Karl Ludwig Schmidt

K.L. Schmidt, author of *Der Rahmen der Geschichte Jesu,* and a German form critic, has observed:

"Only now and then, from considerations about the inner character of a story, can we fix these somewhat more precisely in respect to time and place. But as a whole there is no life of Jesus in the sense of an evolving biography, no chronological sketch of the story of Jesus, but only single stories, *pericopae,* which are put into a framework." 147/47

2B. Martin Dibelius

Dibelius, concerning this element of the transmission of isolated pericopes, states that "when . . . we trace the tradition back to its initial stage we find no descriptions of the life of Jesus, but short, separate paragraphs or pericopae. This is the fundamental hypothesis of the method of form-criticism (*formgeschichtliche Methode*), as a representative of which I am speaking here." 37/27

Dibelius continues by explaining:

"In the earliest period there was no connected narrative of the life, or at least of the work of Jesus, i.e. a narrative comparable to a literary biography or the legendary life of a saint. The stories contained in the synoptic Gospels, whose essential categories I have attempted to describe, were at first handed down in isolation as independent stories. Fold tradition as contained in the Gospels could pass on Paradigms, Tales, and Legends, but not a comprehensive description of Jesus' work." 36/178

Martin Dibelius claims that by careful reading of the Gospels we should find that it is true that "the evangelists took over material which already possessed a form of its own. They joined some paragraphs together which beforehand had possessed a certain independent completeness." 36/4

Dibelius carries this concept of pericopes a little further by referring to another law of oral tradition which deals not with pericopes that are closely connected but rather with isolated units:

"We must presuppose the operation of still another law for the handing down of the sayings of Jesus. Here we have to do not with the words of Jesus which constituted either the kernel or the goal of the story, for the tradition of these sayings is closely connected with the handing down of the narratives, but rather we are now dealing with another class, viz. isolated sayings, especially proverbs, metaphors and commandments." 36/26, 27

3B. Rudolf Bultmann

Bultmann concurs with Martin Dibelius when he alleges that "it may be seen quite clearly that the original tradition was made up almost entirely of brief single units (sayings or short narratives), and that almost all references to time and place which serve to connect up the single sections into a larger context are the editorial work of the evangelists." 19/25

According to Bultmann, as the critics distinguish the "different stages of the synoptic tradition from one another in order to identify the oldest, the very first task is to make a critical distinction between tradition and editorial redaction in the Synoptic Gospels." 181/342

"It becomes clear" writes Bultmann, "that the original tradition underlying Mark (with perhaps the exception of the story of the Passion) consisted almost entirely of small isolated fragments; and that virtually all the descriptions of place or time which connect the individual fragments into a larger whole are due to redaction." 181/342

Bultmann, who has carried Form Criticism to its ultimate conclusion, has concentrated his thoughts on the transmission of pericopes in their relation to the evangelist. He writes that their problem was "how to localize historically, and assign to a definite place in the life of Jesus, his sayings which had been collected without any reference to the place or time when they were spoken." 19/26, 27

4B. Vincent Taylor

Vincent Taylor, a contemporary British form critic, has stated that "from the beginning then isolated sayings must have been current in Christian tradition. What Jesus said was remembered; where it was said, and under what conditions, was less easily recalled in circumstances less dramatic than those associated with the Pronouncement-Stories." 114/88

Taylor observes that the material in the oral tradition "was not guided and sustained by a biographical interest, and accordingly it soon began to perish by an inevitable process of attrition. Practical interests were uppermost, and thus it was that within about a decade the Gospel traditon came to be mainly a collection of isolated stories, sayings, and sayings-groups." 114/169, 170

Taylor's survey on the stories of oral tradition states that "the survey has shown that for the most part the stories are self-contained. This, again, is a feature of oral tradition which as a rule, is content to record incidents rather than a sequence of events." 114/167

Vincent Taylor presents the form critical argument concerning the Passion narrative, the one narrative that did not circulate as separate entities but rather as complete in itself. Taylor explains this by saying that "the situation in which the primitive community found itself demanded a continuous Passion Story. Almost from the first the followers of Jesus found themselves faced by a serious difficulty; both for themselves and others it was necessary to be able to show how a Crucified Messiah could be the subject of a message of Salvation. The first Christians were not long in discovering that such a message was 'unto Jews a stumbling-block, and unto Gentiles foolishness' (I Cor. i. 23). Arguments from Old Testament prophecies were not enough to meet this difficulty; such arguments made it the more necessary to tell the Story of the Cross and to tell it as a whole.... It was necessary to tell the connected Story, and so much the more as only the account of the succession of Passion and Easter solves the paradox of the Cross, only the combination of the events satisfies the need for interpretation, only the connexion of the individual incidents can answer the question of guilt." 114/47

5B. Comments on the Passion Narrative

M. Dibelius speaking as a representative of Form Criticism on the issue of a complete Passion narrative says that "we must presuppose the early existence of a Passion narrative complete in itself since preaching, whether for the purpose of the mission or of worship, required some such a text." 36/23

Dibelius adds that this necessary presupposition of Form Criticism "is justified by a glance at the tradition which has come down to us. The relatively fixed character of the Passion narrative in the synoptics, and the quite unique agreement between John and the other evangelists in this part of the narrative, show that this material had duly and uniformly reached its definite form." 36/23

Dibelius continues by observing the processes by which each evangelist records the Passion narrative. Of Matthew he says:

"Matthew increased the Passion material by introducing details copied from the Old Testament, e.g. the thirty pieces of silver, the gall in the drink, the detailed formulation of the scoffs of the passers-by (Matthew xxvi, 15; xxvii, 34, 43). He increased the material also by taking up Legends or legendary extensions of the narrative, such as the description of the traitor and his death, Pilate washing his hands, and the sentries at the grave and their expressions (xxvi, 25; xxvii, 3-10, 24, 25, 62-6; xxviii, 11-15)." 36/196

Referring to Mark, Dibelius asserts:

"It is probable that scriptural proof was at first only a postulate, a postulate rooted in the Easter faith. But this faith guaranteed the assurance that the very Passion of Jesus was in accordance with God's will, and God's will was to be found in the scriptures. Thus the witness of the scriptures may have been spoken of before it could really be adduced. Then in certain Old Testament passages, e.g. Psalms xxii, xxxi, lxix; Isaiah liii, the Passion of Jesus was found depicted in advance. These passages were read again and again as the evangel of the Passion. From this there grew, of a certainty still before the use of Mark's gospel, a conception of the *via dolorosa* and of the hour of suffering." 36/184

Dibelius claims that "Luke presents the Passion as a martyrdom. There were Jewish martyrdoms, as is proved by the literary record of them in the Martyrdom of Isaiah, and in II and IV Maccabees. Since these were read among the Christians the evangelist could expect that if he presented Jesus as a martyr he would be understood by Christian readers." 36/201

Dibelius concludes by professing that "the whole Lucan record presents an attempt to give the words of institution the force of history by putting them in the framework of a Passover meal. This framework and what belongs to it, as well as the dividing of the eschatological words into two sayings, is naturally the work of an evangelist who was pondering such an historization." 36/210

3A. BASIC ANSWERS AND ANALYSIS

1B. Critical Analysis of Pericope Transmission

It has been set forth that a "fundamental principle of the method called Form Criticism is this: the synoptic Gospels are a collection of small, independent units artificially linked together by the evangelists." 82/9, 10

L.J. McGinley has reacted to this by claiming that "while admitting readily that the evangelists employed various, independent sources in composing their Gospels, that the transition from scene to scene is frequently stereotyped and sometimes awkward, that Matthew, e.g., preferred topical arrangement to detailed chronological sequence, that the composition of all is simple and akin neither to the romantic biography nor the scientific history, we must still reject this concept of patchwork Gospels in which the role of the evangelist is restricted to that of a compiler." 82/9, 10

Vincent Taylor once again observes that form critical assumptions, such as the assumption of the oral tradition, "are constantly made which, to say the least, demand scrutiny, such as the too confident belief that the primitive tradition consisted almost entirely of isolated units and was purely popular in origin." 114/20

C.H. Dodd has observed that "none of the gospels would ever have come into being, were it not for fact that the individual pieces of the oral tradition were proclaimed from the beginning as elements of a coherent story." 148/55

The work which Mark did in his Gospel was done "not arbitrarily or irresponsibly, adds Dodd, "but under such guidance as he could find in tradition. It is hazardous to argue from the precise sequence of the narrative in detail; yet there is good reason to believe that in broad lines the Marcan order does represent a genuine succession of events, within which movement and development can be traced." 183/400

W.E. Barnes has challenged this fundamental assumption of Dibelius and the form critics by commenting:

"In his hardy rejection of connecting links in the Gospel narrative Dibelius overlooks (or dismisses) the several indications of a trustworthy geographical tradition of our Lord's wandering ministry, which these links supply. Is it reasonable to suppose that a late and ignorant evangelist-editor invented these scattered links, which when gathered together yield us so probable a story of the movements of Jesus?" 6/52

R.O.P. Taylor believes that the origin of the Gospels is based on a pattern that originated in the worship of the early Church rather than isolated pieces of oral tradition. He contends that there was a coherent story of Jesus' ministry described by the apostles that was regularly recited in a fixed form in church worship. As a result, Mark wrote down this pattern and it was also used by the other evangelists. Thus these evangelists were not depending on the Gospel of Mark, but this Gospel pattern of worship. cited by 136/119

James Martin writes that "the employment of artificial forms can not be pressed to mean more than that the Church was accustomed to tell particular kinds of Jesus-stories in particular ways. Many analogies can be cited where factual accounts are cast into a prescribed mould of narration without prejudice either to their truth or to the world's recognition of their truth. The illustration readiest to mind is that of policemen's reports and their evidence in court." 80/76

L.J. McGinley climaxes the criticism against the form critics' position regarding the transmission of isolated units in the oral tradition by emphasizing that "were the Gospels mere compilations, their heterogeneous origin should be conspicuous in the tenor of their story. Yet it is a striking fact that in these three converging and diverging narratives there reigns a simple but unmistakable consistency; there is no contradiction in Jesus' doctrine nor in His deeds, no inconsistency of word with action; the story of His success and failure flows logically to its end; the description of the land in which He lived and the people whom He encountered—a land and people never seen by many of the early Christians—has never been convicted of inaccuracy. Such unanimity of presentation would be impossible in a collection of isolated units." 82/10

2B. Critical Analysis of the Fallacy of Inaccurate Transmission of Pericopes

To begin with, James Martin explains two factors of influence on the transmission of oral tradition:

"Underlying the whole business of the transmission of the oral tradition are two factors whose influence on the preservation of accuracy must have been considerable. To these we make passing reference as we close the chapter.

"There is, for one, the fact that the early Church was Jewish in background and in outlook. Every Jew had been trained to treat tradition with great respect and with the utmost care. Those Jews who became Christians inevitably attached their reverence for tradition to the new tradition which had to do with Jesus: and, as they had been careful to preserve the old traditions with accuracy, so were they careful with regard to the new.

"The other factor is the early Church's deep conviction regarding Jesus' authority, for He was Messiah and more than Messiah—as the events of history had shown. This was the fundamental reason that stories of Him were told and preserved; and this was sufficient reason to ensure that these stories would be perpetuated with the utmost accuracy." 80/67

Kistemaker, writing of the 120 at Pentecost who received the Holy Spirit, says that "these people did not vanish but were active in many communities throughout Palestine, preaching the word which they had received from Jesus. In the letters of Paul, the words 'receive' and 'deliver' are technical terms referring to the transmission of a sacred trust. Hence, when Paul instructs the Christians at Corinth in the proper celebration of the Lord's Supper, he says: 'For I *received* from the Lord what I also *delivered* to you, that the Lord Jesus on the night when he was betrayed took bread' (I Cor. 13:23). And in Chapter 15 of that same epistle, he uses these terms again: 'For I *delivered* to you as of first importance what I also *received*' (v.3). The form critic fails to take note of the faithful transmission of the very words of Jesus which the apostles delivered to the churches. In this chain of receiving and delivering, he does not want to see Jesus as the originator of the gospel tradition." 186/48, 49

Martin continues that "it is easily forgotten and yet of considerable significance that in the oral period the traditions of Jesus were being quoted in the hearing of unbelievers, many of whom were antagonistic, as well as of believers. This also must have helped in no small measure to ensure that they suffered no substantial change in the course of their repetition. For the uncommitted and the hostile, quick to seize on any feature of the Christians' story which did not tally with its previous telling, would have made the most of the discrepancy. As a result, both in their public preaching and in debate and discussion, it would be impossible for the Christians to vary their stories in any material aspect from one telling to the other." 80/67

A.M. Hunter adds:

"In the last six years or so, however, Scandinavian reaction to Teutonic scepticism has taken a new and hopeful line in the work of Harald Riesenfeld and Birger Gerhardsson [*Memory and Manuscript*, 1961]. Their argument—and there is a lot to be said for it, even if it does not take us all the way—may be summed up thus: (1) The Jewish community was accustomed to transmit its oral tradition from teacher to pupil in a relatively fixed and controlled way; (2) New Testament references to 'tradition' suggest that the early Christians, most of them Jews, showed a like concern for faithful transmission; (3) this process of transmission began with Jesus, Himself a Teacher who made His disciples repeat and memorize what He taught them (*e.g.*, the sayings, many in poetic form, in the Sermon on the Mount). *Ergo* we may have confidence in the historical worth of our Gospels." 64/15-20

In dealing with this important concern of memorization of transmitted material, James Martin notes:

"The Jews of that day had a power of memory far superior to ours and the accuracy of their verbal transmission was, by our standards, most remarkable. For many generations—books being then, let us remember, a rare commodity—they had been accustomed to learn and to teach by word of mouth. As a result, their memories had become superbly trained and regularly performed feats that would be astonishing in Western circles." 80/66, 67

B.S. Easton adds to this thought when he writes:

"Furthermore, Jesus was popularly known and addressed as Rabbi, so that his method of teaching had recognizable elements in common with that of other rabbis. Like them, in particular, he gathered around himself a small group of very intimate disciples, who were being trained to become teachers in their turn; such training among the Jews always included the verbatim memorization of the teacher's most important sayings." 43/40, 41

James Martin reiterates that a significant fact which warrants discussion is that the Jews regarded spoken words as superior to written. Since the early Christians were Jews, they shared this outlook. They preferred to have spoken words to relate to the authority, so they found it unnecessary to have tradition put down in documentary form. But because the eyewitnesses were dying off, a change became necessary. 80/50

W.S. Taylor has commented that remembering, especially rote memory emphasized by the rabbis, played an important part in teaching in Jesus' time. Jesus showed concern with memory work in His teaching methods. He surrounded Himself with a small group of intimate disciples, whom He taught so that they could in turn teach others. Verbatim memorization was always used by the Jews for learning a teacher's most important sayings. Some of Jesus' sayings illustrate, in form, the rabbi's use of memorization methods. 119/478, 479

Recognizing this fallacy of inaccurate transmission of isolated bits of tradition, T.W. Manson writes that "we need some explanation why it was possible for the details of the story to be remembered and the general outline forgotten." 154/213

In *History and Christianity* John Warwick Montgomery states:

"We know from the mishna that it was Jewish custom to memorize a Rabbi's teaching, for a good pupil was like a 'plastered cistern that loses not a drop' [Mishna Aboth, II.8]. And we can be sure that the early Church, impressed as it was by Jesus, governed itself by this ideal. Moreover, none of the form-critical researches has ever been successful in yielding a non-supernatural picture of Jesus, for 'all parts of the Gospel record are shown by these various groupings to be pervaded by a consistent picture of Jesus as the Messiah, the Son of God' [16/33]." 87/37, 38

Taylor makes reference to B.S. Easton as he offers evidence on the Jewish Rabbis:

"He [Easton] reminds us that Jewish Rabbis used to instruct small groups of intimate disciples, requiring them to memorise their own most important sayings; and he argues that, since Jesus was frequently addressed as 'Rabbi,' and had to prepare His disciples within a brief space of time for popular preaching, it is probable that He used similar methods." 114/94

4A. IN SUMMARY

1B. Form critics contend that during the oral period the literary units (pericopes), which were complete in themselves, circulated separately.

2B. According to the form critics, the Passion story was the only extensive narrative which was in circulation during this period.

3B. Critics of Form Criticism feel that stories about Jesus would have been passed down accurately. They point to the Jewish tradition of accurate oral transmission and the fact that many who knew Jesus were still alive in this period.

chapter 20

classification according to the form

1A. BASIC ASSUMPTION

Material in the Gospels can be classified according to form.

1B. A good summary of the form classification held to by the form critics is provided by Everett F. Harrison:

"(1) **Pronouncement stories.** (Vincent Taylor's term) or *apophthegmata* (Bultmann) or Paradigms (Dibelius, in recognition of their use in Christian preaching). These involve incidents, quite brief as a rule, ending in an aphorism or famous saying that drives home the lesson. An example is the passage regarding the tribute money, ending in Jesus' notable pronouncement about rendering to Caesar and to God (Mark 12:17).

"(2) **Miracle stories.** Bultmann finds the same stylistic characteristics for the general run of Jesus' miracles as are common to those reported in the Hellenistic world: a statement of the malady, with special stress on its dire character so as to magnify the cure; the account of the healing; a statement of the effect on those who are present. Due to the correspondences, Bultmann concludes that these belong to the Hellenistic phase of the expanding church rather than to its Palestinian phase. Dibelius distinguishes miracles that are closely connected with the proclamation of the kingdom, which he therefore subsumes under Paradigms, and others that are stories complete in themselves and abounding in detail. These he calls 'tales,' and thinks that in them Jesus is simply pictured as a wonder-worker having exceptional potency.

"(3) Stories about Jesus. These have considerable variety and therefore are not easy to classify. It is readily admitted by the form critics that there are mythological elements in the portrayal of Jesus, for example, in the transfiguration. The tendency is regarded as full-blown in the Fourth Gospel. The category of myth is applied to those elements of the Gospel exposition of Jesus that present him in a guise transcending the human and the natural.

"(4) Sayings of Jesus. These are of several types. One is *wisdom words*. Since Judaism was rich in gnomic literature, this element in Jesus' teaching is to be expected. Yet there must be a suspicion, according to Bultmann, that at least some of the sayings of this type attributed to Jesus have been put in his mouth by the Evangelists. A second type may be called *prophetic sayings*. These include the Beatitudes and the utterances of a more apocalyptic nature, such as the prediction of the destruction of the temple. Again, there are statements that may be called *legislative*, in which Jesus gives teachings about prayer, fasting, divorce, forgiveness, and a variety of other topics. Sometimes these are classified as church words. Then there are certain 'I' sayings in which the person of Jesus is made prominent in some way. Finally, there is a well defined group of sayings known as *parables*, Jesus' favorite device for expounding the kingdom of God.

"(5) The Passion story. While complete agreement is lacking among the form critics, some seeing it as a sustained, well-knit narrative, in contrast to the fragmentary nature of the other Gospel materials, others seeing it as a piecing together of short fragments later embellished, it is nevertheless regarded as one of the forms." 58/148, 149

2B. A Further Breakdown of the Classifications Used by Martin Dibelius, Rudolf Bultmann and Vincent Taylor

  1C. CLASSIFICATIONS ACCORDING TO DIBELIUS:

     1) Paradigms - short incidents which climax in a teaching utterance of Jesus.
     2) Tales - stories told for their own sakes, miracle stories.
     3) Legends - stories about saintly people.
     4) Exhortations.
     5) Myths - stories of Jesus regarded as divine.
     6) Passion Story.

     The most historical of these are, according to Dibelius, paradigms, exhortations and elements of the Passion Story.

  2C. CLASSIFICATIONS ACCORDING TO BULTMANN:

     1) Apothegm - essentially coincidental with paradigms.
     2) Sayings - a) logia or wisdom utterances.
                b) prophetic and apocalyptic sayings.
                c) legal and ecclesiastical pronouncements.
                d) "I" use.
                e) parables.
     3) Miracle stories.
     4) Historical narratives and legends—grouping based on content more than form—Practically all of this material is a product of the Church.

  3C. CLASSIFICATIONS ACCORDING TO TAYLOR

     1) Passion narratives - definite and ordered form.
     2) Pronouncement Stories - equivalent to Dibelius' paradigms.
     3) Sayings and Parables.
     4) Miracle Stories.
     5) Stories about Jesus.

3B. The Forms of Martin Dibelius

The theory of form development is hypothesized by Dibelius:

"The fortune of primitive Christianity is reflected in the history of the Gospel-Form. The first beginnings of its shaping hardly deserve to be called literary. What Form was present was determined by ecclesiastical requirements arising in the course of missionary labour and of preaching. The Passion story, the most significant piece of tradition for Christian faith, was told relatively early as a connected story. Moreover isolated events from the life of Jesus, suitable for sermons, were told in short stories, and sayings and parables were used especially for a practical purpose. But pleasure in the narrative for its own sake arose and seized upon literary devices. The technique of the Tale developed, and lent meanwhile a fully secular character to the miracle stories. In addition, legendary narratives full of personal interest in the persons of the sacred story joined themselves to the periphery of the tradition. One told of these persons in the same way as similar narratives from the surrounding world spoke of other holy men. Already between the lines of the Gospel-Form one can see that the faith of Christendom moved from its fundamental strangeness in the world and its self-limitation to the religious interests of the Church, to an accommodation to the world and to harmony with its relationships." 36/287

1C. PARADIGMS

Dibelius recognizes five essential characteristics of the paradigms:

1) Brief and simple for possible sermon use.

2) Style that causes the words of Jesus to stand out clearly.

3) Independence from literary context.

4) Ending in a thought useful for preaching.

5) Religious emphasis rather than artistic.
   cited by 83/22

Some of the characteristics of this form include:

1) External rounding-off at beginning and end.

2) Brevity and simplicity - (lack portraiture).

3) Coloring of narrative in a totally religious and realistically unworldly manner.

4) Reaches climax and concludes with a word of Jesus.
   36/44-69

The purpose of the paradigm is preaching. Dibelius emphasizes that "the concentrated brevity of Paradigms rests upon a concern which makes the material subject to the purpose of the preacher, hinders wandering, and silences the unessential. Even what is only vivid or only arresting cannot be regarded as essential from the standpoint of a sermon." 36/53

McKnight, quoting Dibelius, says that sermons weren't just the bare Gospel message "but rather the message as explained, illustrated and supported with references and otherwise developed." 83/21

Dibelius further develops this preaching concept:

"Everywhere it is evident that what Jesus said possesses somehow a *general significance*, and, as a regulation for faith or life, gives the whole story an immediate relation with the hearer. It is no wonder then that we find this true of many Paradigms if by means of such sayings the story could be woven into the preaching." 36/56

He states why the sermon form is such a durable literary type:

"The nearer a narrative stands to the sermon the less is it questionable, or likely to have been changed by romantic, legendary, or literary influences." 36/61

He enumerates the positive points of the paradigm:

"The self-limitation of the Paradigm on stylistic grounds must be understood in the case of healings in the same manner as in those which we have already analysed. No question is raised about the technique of the miracle, and none about the technical skill of the miracle-worker. The only important points are that Jesus healed, and in what way He revealed the meaning and purpose of His work in a brief word to the man who had been healed and to the witnesses. Those are motives which have immediate significance for preaching, and thereby we pass over from the negative to the positive characteristics of a paradigmatic style." 36/55, 56

A list of eight paradigms of Dibelius are:

The Healing of the Paralytic .... Mark ii, 1 ff.
The Question of Fasting. .... Mark ii, 18f.
The Rubbing of the Ears of Corn .... Mark ii, 23 ff.
The Healing of the Withered Hand. .... Mark iii, 1 ff.
The Relatives of Jesus. .... Mark iii, 20 f., 30 ff.
Blessing the Children. .... Mark x, 13 ff.
The Tribute Money .... Mark xii, 13 ff.
The Anointing in Bethany. .... Mark xiv, 3 ff.
.36/42, 43

"In addition to these eight typical stories another ten of a less pure type can be regarded as illustrations—and will be so employed in the following research."

The Healing in the Synagogue .... Mark i, 23 ff.
The Call of Levi .... Mark ii, 13 ff.
Jesus in Nazareth .... Mark vi, 1 ff.
The Rich Young Man .... Mark x, 17 ff.
The Sons of Zebedee .... Mark x, 35 ff.
The Blind Man of Jericho. .... Mark x, 46 ff.
Cleansing the Temple. .... Mark xi, 15 ff.
The Question of the Sadducees. .... Mark xii, 18 ff.
The Inhospitable Samaritans. .... Luke ix, 51 ff.
The Man with the Dropsy .... Luke xiv, 1 ff.
36/42, 43

"The paradigms existed in isolation," states Dibelius. The repercussions of this, according to Dibelius are:

1) independent life must be noticeable in them today.

2) evidence of an external rounding off. 36/44

Dibelius is not concerned by the alleged unhistorical character of the paradigm:

"Therefore it should cause no surprise if in the Paradigms we were to come across sentences or at least words of Jesus of whose historical reliability there is doubt. They are not proved to be genuine by the fact of relatively primitive tradition, and on the other hand the paradigmatic nature of the matter is not spoiled by such unhistoric traits." 36/96

When talking of paradigms, Dibelius notes that a paradigm tends to be an example, a narrative with all interest centered upon the actual words of Jesus. 36/42

And concerning the originality of the paradigms Dibelius says:

"This manner of abbreviating the circumstances and giving the concluding saying as strikingly as possible is, therefore, apart from a few exceptions, not that of the original tradition, but is indicative of the secular style into which the gospel tradition was entering. The relative originality of the primitive Christian Paradigm in Greek literature comes out here once more." 36/163

2C. TALES OR *NOVELLEN*

Basil Redlich interprets Dibelius' definition of tales: "Stories about Jesus which set Him forth as a wonder-worker. These were formed not for edification, not to show Christ's power over the human soul, but to display the power of Jesus over nature and sickness. They were valued for themselves, and not for any saying in them, and might serve as examples to Christian healers and exorcists. They were the creation of a body of storytellers." 101/28

Dibelius' classification of tales is complete in itself. Its major difference from the seemingly similar paradigm is its broadness of description which tends to illustrate the same artistic element as exhibited in the Old Testament. All in all, it can be asserted that the tales provide far more detail than the paradigms. 36/76, 77

Dibelius remarks: "The paradigms aim at proselytising...the folk-tales aim at amusing and even perhaps impressing with a certain popular sagacity." 36/288

Another form critic, R.H. Lightfoot, defines this term:

"This word implies a prose narrative comparatively short in length, which presents something new in the sense of something striking, concentrates its attention on one point only, and is distinguished by a strict attention to form. It must possess a turning-point, after which it generally passes rapidly to its *denouement*." 76/45

Dibelius further clarifies that "it is not Jesus as the herald of the Kingdom of God with His signs, demands, threats and promises, who stands in the centre of these stories, but Jesus the miracle-worker. *The Tales deal with Jesus the thaumaturge*." 36/80

We can note six characteristics of these tales as we study Dibelius:

1) They are individual stories complete in themselves.

2) They tend to be detailed with secular motivation.

3) They have a lack of devotional motives and slackening of words of Jesus of general value.

4) They deal with Jesus as a miracle-worker.

5) They involve history of the illness.

6) They show success of the miracle. 36/72-103

Tales, a form classification, says McKnight, inaugurated by Dibelius, are said to originate in one of three ways: (1) by paradigmatic extension, (2) by the introduction of a foreign motif, or (3) by the borrowing of alien material. 83/23

Dibelius cites nine tales from the Gospel of Mark:

"Especially in Mark a number of narratives show the unmistakable signs of this category, so that we may recognize the following nine as Tales.

The Leper: Mark i, 40-5.
The Storm: Mark iv, 35-41.

The Demons and the Swine: Mark v, 1-20.
The Daughter of Jairus and the Woman with the Issue: Mark v, 21-43.
The Feeding of the Five Thousand: Mark vi, 35-44.
The Walking on the Sea: Mark vi, 45-52.
The Man, Deaf and Dumb: Mark vii, 32-37.
The Blind Man of Bethsaida: Mark viii, 22-6.
The Epileptic Boy: Mark ix, 14-29." 36/71, 72

He comments on the alleged relationship between Christian tales and other literary types:

"We can see the significance of primitive Christian Tales if we notice two processes within Hellenistic religious history: *(a)* the incidental *replacement of Myths by stories of miracles,* and *(b) the disappearance of the boundaries between God and the God-sent man.*" 36/96

Dibelius begins to question the historical reliability of the lives of tale authors: "It is true that we know nothing of those who put together these Christian tales, but we can describe the characteristics of their creations." 36/70, 71

He then goes on to question the historicity of the tales:

"The historical reliability of the Tales is in no way guaranteed by these demonstrations, rather analysis has already shown that the Tales are only to be used with great caution as historical sources. They lack the protection which preaching furnished to the Paradigms, and they were open to the invasion of foreign motives, since the shaping of their form was not influenced by missionary requirements, but by the pleasure of narrating the Tale." 36/292

Dibelius observes that "this type, as a whole, is less historical than the Paradigm." 36/102

"The category which it is meant to describe is more 'worldly' and has more of its literary forms than the Paradigm." 36/70, 71

"Indeed, *'literary style in reporting miracles,* a feature which we missed on the whole from Paradigms,...appears in the Tales with a certain regularity.'" 36/82

Dibelius summarizes:

"The Tales are meant to show Jesus as the Lord of divine powers, and they effect this object by a narrative style which does not despise colourful, or even 'secular,' means." 36/96

3C. LEGENDS

Dibelius notes another form which is used only occasionally in the New Testament, the legend. He defines it:

"By this term is meant a narrative written in an edifying style and telling of extraordinary things about a holy man or a holy place. Interest in the virtue and religiousness of the saint is in the foreground." 35/43

Another thought about Dibelius' "Legend":

"The term 'Legend' does not exclude historical traits, but only says that the main interest of the narrator lies elsewhere than in the historicity. It is directed to the religiousness and sanctity of the hero." 35/43

This form is a "legendary biography." Dibelius assumes that "simple events are surrounded with a heavenly light, or elements from other Legends are transferred to the hero in order to show the connection of his life with the divine world. But above all, his life is decorated with characters and scenes which correspond to the very nature of legendary biography." 36/108

Along with the biographical interest, an interest in man's fate is also discovered. Dibelius holds that "Legends are religious narratives of a saintly man in whose works and fate interest is taken. An aetiological interest is to be found alongside of the biographical; the endeavour is to give grounds for the significance of the saint's day by such narratives." 36/104

Concerning the purpose of legends, Dibelius states:

"Hence the Legends found among the Gospel narratives were intended to satisfy a double need: (1) the wish to know something of the holy men and women in Jesus' surroundings, their virtues and also their lot; (2) the desire which gradually came in, to know Jesus Himself in this way." 36/115

Finally, the central point of the legend is enunciated by Dibelius:

"The deeds and experiences of a man, who for his piety and sanctity is honoured by God with a special fate, stand as the middle point of a typical personal legend. He works miracles, reconciles enemies, tames animals; distress and danger lead him to salvation, and even as a martyr he is surrounded by signs of divine grace." 36/105

In a footnote from his book, *From Tradition to Gospel*, Dibelius notes three legends: Luke 4:29, 30; Mark 11:14, 21; Matthew 17:27. Of these three, only Matthew 17:27 is an independent legend. 36/106

Concerning legends and Christ's infancy, Dibelius remarks:

"Thus the infancy story shows itself to be a collection of legends of varied content, and also to be at different levels of historical significance." 35/51

A result of legends is commented on by Dibelius:

"Legends put halos round men, and set in a transfiguring light the very things with which religious men deal. Hence everything belonging to the very fact of holy men may become significant in a Legend." 36/132

And he further notes:

"A legendary form as such is in any case no decisive objection against the historicity of the hero, or even of an event, although again it is no guarantee for the faithfulness of the record to the truth. Rather the contrary, for it offers an argument for historical criticism of details." 36/109

4C. REMAINING FORMS OF DIBELIUS

Redlich seeks to establish the myth classification of Dibelius. He remarks that Dibelius uses "myths" to describe "many-sided interactions" or events which take place between mythological but not human persons. There are three: the Baptism, the Temptation and the Transfiguration. 101/30

Dibelius remarks about the sayings:

"Their Form is due to another standpoint; by placing together materially related words of Jesus the intention was to convey to Christendom a 'teaching' of Jesus on important questions of church life. Thus it is not to be wondered at that once and again actual problems of the church crop up, whether they do or do not suit the biographical occasion which the evangelist has given the whole." 36/222

Concerning the sayings of Jesus, Dibelius rather dogmatically states:

"The Gospels of Matthew and Luke frequently contain identical passages, which are lacking in Mark. These consist of sayings so closely related in form and style that the similarity cannot be due to accident nor to the parallelisms of oral tradition. Moreover, as far as we are able to judge, sometimes Matthew and sometimes Luke offers the more original formulation, a fact that excludes the presupposition that one had been used by the other. We must, therefore, presuppose that both made use of a common source, a collection of sayings of Jesus, which has been lost, and which has been called the Sayings Source, or, in accordance with the need for brevity in scientific terminology, simply Q." 36/52, 53

Dibelius notes that Jesus used such forms as:

Epic Repetition - Luke 15:18,21.
Antithesis of types - Luke 18:9-14; Luke 16:19-31.
Law of three-fold repetition - Matthew 25:14-39.
Parables - Matthew 7:24-27.
Proverbs - Matthew 7:3-5, 6.
Hebrew sense-parallelism - Matthew 10:26, 27.
Old Testament passages - Matthew 5:21-24.
Commandments - Matthew 6:17; Luke 14:26.
Prophecy - Matthew 24:4-14. 35/30-33

According to Dibelius, the type form chosen depended largely on the use intended:

"Thus the things which were remembered automatically took on a definite form, for it is only when such matters have received a form that they are able to bring about repentance and gain converts." 36/13, 14

Finally we may infer what the author (Dibelius) considers Jesus' role to be in the history of these forms. Dibelius states that Jesus, John the Baptist and Peter were "prophetic persons of the Orient." Like the other two, Jesus wrote nothing. Jesus' teachings were passed on orally in the definite forms necessary for preservation—forms like proverbs, parabolic narratives, riddles and fairy-tales. It is even asserted that Jesus not only used definite forms but also made use of stories that were already current. All He did was alter them to suit his purposes. 35/27, 31

4B. The Forms of Rudolf Bultmann

Bultmann, a modern proponent of the form critical method, asserts that "we must remind ourselves that certain forms were found close at hand in the environment of the early Christian community, and offered themselves for purposes of tradition. Similar sayings and brief narratives were handed down in Jewish literature, and their forms show remarkable similarity to those of the evangelical material." 19/30

Fredrich Muller adds three Bultmann principles for analysis of form and content in the Gospels:

"There is also the interpretation of its literary form, and here Bultmann has shown that this form can be understood only on the basis of three suppositions: (1) that the Evangelist himself depended on written Gnostic sources; (2) that an editor of the original text of the Gospel made additions to it; and (3) that in the copying of this Gospel later, a certain disarrangement of its content occurred." 176/207

1C. APOTHEGM OR APOPHTHEGM

Bultmann writes that he "should reckon as part of the tradition of the sayings a species of traditional material which might well be reckoned as stories—viz. such units as consist of sayings of Jesus set in a brief context. I use a term to describe them which comes from Greek literature, and is least question-begging—'apophthegms'." 21/11

Redlich summarizes some characteristics of Bultmann's apophthegms:

(1) "The interest of the story centers on a saying of Jesus.
(2) "The narrative is simple and brief, just long enough to make the story

intelligible.

(3) "The biographical interest, lacking in many of the narratives, forms an ingredient of the stories. Generally the parties concerned are vaguely described.

(4) "The narrative ends in the saying or an act of Jesus." 101/90

Bultmann defines the apophthegm:

"The distinguishing character of an apophthegma is the fact that it portrays a minor scene that furnishes the framework for an important utterance of a hero, a philosopher, a religious preacher, or some other such person. The important thing is the utterance itself; the narrative framework serves only to portray a situation giving occasion to the utterance."

About biographical apophthegmata he says:

"These are pictorial creations of the Christian community in which is brought to clear expression what the community held to be the character of their Master, what they experienced in relation to him, or how he fared in popular estimation." 18/46, 47

McGinley says that apophthegms, as defined by Bultmann, are comprised of controversies, instructions or biographical information. 82/37

And McKnight adds that Bultmann notes three different apophthegmatic types which arise due to various settings and causes. These are (a) controversy dialogues occasioned by conflict, (b) scholastic dialogues arising from opponents' questions and (c) biographical apophthegms which are in the form of a historical report. 83/26, 27

McKnight further notes that to Bultmann, any of the three apophthegmatic types can be considered an "ideal" Church construction. Bultmann concedes that the background for the form may be true but the apophthegm is not an historical report; it is a Church construction. 83/26, 27

Vincent Taylor lists one group of apophthegms:

"Bultmann's first group consists of twenty-four stories, sixteen of which appear also in the lists of Dibelius or Albertz. Of the sixteen stories, one, the Dropsical Man, is recorded by Luke alone (xiv. 1-6), and a second, the Baptist's Question (Lk. vii. 19ff. = Mt. xi. 2ff.), comes from Q. The remaining fourteen stories are Markan: the Paralytic (ii. 3ff.), Eating with Publicans and Sinners (ii. 15ff.), Fasting (ii. 18ff.), Cornfields on the Sabbath Day (ii. 23ff.), the Man with the Withered Hand (iii. 1ff.), the Beelzebub Controversy (iii. 22ff.), Clean and Unclean (vii. 5ff.), Divorce (x. 2ff.), the Rich Man (x. 17ff.), the Sons of Zebedee (x. 35ff.), Authority (xi. 27ff.), Tribute-money (xii. 13ff.), the Resurrection (xii. 18ff.) and the Great Commandment (xii. 28ff.). All these stories reward study, but it is not possible now to examine more than one or two." 114/63, 64

A second group is enumerated by Taylor:

"The story of the Centurion's Servant (Lk. vii. 2-10 = Mt. viii. 5-13), is from Q. Four are from Mark: the Calling of the First Disciples (i. 16-20; ii. 14), the Rejection at Nazareth (vi. 1-6), the Syro-Phoenician Woman (vii. 24-30), and the Cleansing (xi. 15-7); and the remaining five are found in Luke alone: Martha and Mary (x. 38-42), Jesus and Herod (xiii. 31-3), Zacchaeus (xix. 1-10), the Rejoicing of the Disciples (xix. 39f.), and the Weeping over Jerusalem (xix. 41-4). In these stories the interest appears to lie in the incidents themselves rather than in the words of Jesus." 114/75, 76

After citing two of Bultmann's apophthegms, Basil Redlich expresses his viewpoint about their validity. Of the genuine apophthegms, two are the Tribute-Money [Mark 12:13-17] and the Anointing [Mark 14:3-9]. In the same context:

"In short, the Apothegm-Stories are a reflection of the actual conditions of the days Jesus preached in Palestine. We must remember that Bultmann does not deny that Jesus ever lived. He forgets that Jesus did not live in isolation and that, as One who uttered historical *apothegmata*, He was attended by eye-witnesses anxious to hear and learn the words of wisdom which fell from the Rabbi's lips. To expect our Lord's hearers to forget every occasion but two, and when and in what circumstances every pronouncement was made is to expect the incredible." 101/113, 114

McGinley lists the "healing" apophthegms.

In the first such subdivision, the following healing stories are classed as apophthegms:

1) The man with the withered hand, Mark 3:1-6.
2) The man with dropsy, Luke 14: 1-6.
3) The woman with a spirit of infirmity, Luke 13: 10-14.
4) The blind and dumb possessed man, Mark 3:22-26; Matthew 12:22-28; Luke 11:14-20
5) The paralytic, Mark 2:1-12. 82/37

2C. SAYINGS

Bultmann comments that "not only have many of the older sayings of Jesus been modified in the course of tradition, but not seldom words have been placed in Jesus' mouth which in reality were either spoken by other Jewish teachers or first arose in the Christian community." 19/52

He points out the historicity of sayings:

"Even though we must give up the historicity of many of these narratives, still it remains possible, and even probable, that in many cases the saying of Jesus which they contain is thoroughly historical." 19/46

1D. Logia or Wisdom Sayings

Bultmann postulates that the birth of wisdom sayings is in community needs:

"Since the context or connection was really created by the later tradition (chiefly by the evangelists themselves), one must consider the question whether such Wisdom-sayings were not first admitted to the collection of Jesus' sayings at the time when, under the stress of the community's own needs, connected discourses of Jesus were first produced." 19/55

Or maybe they were derived from the treasure of Jewish thought. Bultmann professes:

"Now it is naturally possible that Jesus himself originated some of the Wisdom-sayings which the gospels record as spoken by him. It is equally possible that he made use now and then of proverbs which were current in his time. But it is quite clear that we must reckon with the possibility that the primitive community placed in his mouth many a beautiful saying that was really derived from the treasure of Jewish proverbial lore." 19/55

McKnight refers to three possibilities that authenticate "proverb," or wisdom saying, origin:

(1) Jesus was the actual originator.
(2) Jesus made use of proverbs that were popular in his time.
(3) The early Church put sayings in Jesus' mouth, sayings that were

taken from Jewish proverbial lore.

Bultmann's proverb illustrates Jesus as a wisdom teacher similar to other wisdom teachers in Israel, Judaism and the Orient. 83/28

2D. Prophetic Sayings

These sayings are described by Bultmann as those which "proclaimed the arrival of the Reign of God and preached the call to repentance, promising salvation for those who were prepared and threatening woes upon the unrepentant." 19/56, 57

Community creation is again noted with the wisdom saying by Bultmann:

"One may with perfect right recognize among them authentic words of Jesus; and though the Christian community itself produced many a prophetic saying, as may be clearly shown, it must nevertheless be recognized that, according to the testimony of the earliest Christians themselves, they owed their eschatological enthusiasm to the prophetic appearance of Jesus." 19/56, 57

3D. Legal Sayings

"Finally, a third group" writes Bultmann, "is formed by Jesus' words regarding the Law, to which have been attached many sayings setting forth the regulations of the community.... Though the formulation of one or another of them may be due to the church, as a whole these words of conflict with legalism, and expressing a spiritual obedience to the will of God, go back to the prophetic personality to whom the church owed its existence, that is to the personality of Jesus. Even though many of the sayings may have originated in the community, the spirit that lives in them goes back to the work of Jesus." 19/58

4D. "I" Sayings

One of Bultmann's form classifications is the "I" sayings, which consist of all the sayings that are attributed to Jesus where He speaks of His work or His destiny or Himself. Bultmann alleges that Jesus did not speak of Himself in first person but he admits that it is impossible to prove this.

Bultmann adds to the skepticism of historical accuracy when he says:

"Since such serious considerations arise against so many of these sayings, one can have but little confidence even in regard to those which do not come under positive suspicion, such as Lk. 12:49; Mk. 2:17b; Matt 15:24. We must now add that all these sayings which speak of the $\dot{\epsilon}\lambda\theta\epsilon\hat{\imath}\nu$ (or $\dot{a}\pi o\sigma\tau a\lambda\hat{\eta}\nu a\iota$ cp esp. Lk. 4:13 with Mk. 1:38) of Jesus, are also under suspicion of being Church products because this terminology seems to be the means of its looking back to the historical appearance of Jesus as a whole." 21/155

5D. Parables

McKnight defines a parable as a "concise and simple story which is much like a popular story in its concrete language, its use of dialectical language and soliloquy, and its repetition. It is a story told to call forth judgment on the part of the hearer; a judgment is made regarding the story of everyday human affairs and relations, then the judgment is applied in the realm of the spiritual life." 83/30, 31

Redlich distinguishes between the sayings and parables of the Gospels when he confines the term parables to the "longer" sayings where a comparison is made. 101/135

Bultmann provides some criteria by which we can judge the authenticity of a parabolic saying:

"We can only count on possessing a genuine similitude of Jesus where, on the one hand, expression is given to the contrast between Jewish morality and piety and the distinctive eschatological temper which characterized the preaching of Jesus; and where on the other hand we find no specifically Christian features." 21/205

Alfred Wikenhauser alludes to the creativity of the community concerning "I" sayings:

"Similarly most of the 'I sayings' are creations of the community expressing their faith in Jesus, his work, and his fate. In most cases the parables must be regarded as genuine traditional material, but in the course of transmission many of them were amplified with allegorical elements, or were interpreted and explained as allegories (Mk. 4, 14-20; Mt. 13, 36-43); indeed some of them must be regarded as creations of the community (e.g., Mk. 12, 1-12; Mt. 25, 1-13). It is also highly probable that there are parables from Jewish tradition, which were ascribed to Jesus by the Christian community (thus Lk. 16, 19-31; 14, 7-11, 12-14)." 126/268, 269

Criteria for authenticity of Jesus' sayings using the Form-Critical Method are:

By Bultmann:

    (1) It doesn't reflect early Church faith.
    (2) It doesn't arise out of Judaism.

By Jeremias:

    (3) It does have Aramaic traits.
    (4) It is consistent with other sayings of Jesus which are deemed authentic. 83/65-68

3C. MIRACLE STORIES

Schubert Ogden translates Bultmann's definition of miracle stories to be the following:

"Characteristic miracle stories are those in which the miracle constitutes the main theme and is described with considerable detail, such as the healing of the Gerasene demoniac, the cure of the woman with the issue of blood, the raising of the daughter of Jairus from death, the stories of the stilling of the storm, of walking on the sea, and others:

"Accounts of the miraculous healings run as follows: First, the condition of the sick person is depicted in such fashion as to enhance the magnitude of the miracle. After this introductory description of the illness comes the account of the healing itself. The close of the miracle story depicts the consequence of the miracle, frequently describing the astonishment or the terror or the approval of those who witnessed the miraculous event. In other cases, the close of the narrative shows the one who is healed demonstrating by some appropriate action that he is entirely cured." 18/43, 44

One of the two main groups of the narrative material as classified by Bultmann is the miracle stories. These are essentially the same as Dibelius' tales, characterized as stories consisting of miracles and healings with the miracle constituting the main theme. Miracles are also recorded in the apophthegms, but the miracle is secondary to the rest of the apophthegm. 83/31, 32

R. Fuller, author of *Interpreting the Miracles,* concludes that there is a strong tradition of Jesus as an exorcist and healer:

'But we can never be certain of the authenticity of any actual miracle story in the gospels. While a few of them may rest upon specific memory, most of them have probably been shaped out of generalized memories." 158/39

4C HISTORICAL NARRATIVES AND LEGENDS

McKnight relates that Bultmann defines a legend as a narrative which is both religious and edifying. It is not a miracle story or a history as such, but it may contain elements of both. Historical stories and legends are treated together by Bultmann, due to an inability to separate the two. 83/32

Taylor quotes Bultmann's definition (*Die Geschichte der Synoptischen Tradition*, 1921, p. 260):

"'As legends,' he says, 'I designate the narrative pieces of the tradition which are not properly speaking miracle-stories, but which nevertheless have no historical but a religious and edifying character.'" 114/31, 32

5C. MYTHS

Bultmann sets forth his understanding of myths:

"Myths speak about gods and demons as powers on which man knows himself to be dependent, powers whose favor he needs, powers whose wrath he fears. Myths express the knowledge that man is not master of the world and of his life, that the world within which he lives is full of riddles and mysteries and that human life is also full of riddles and mysteries." 22/19

"The whole conception of the world," continues Bultmann, "which is presupposed in the preaching of Jesus as in the New Testament generally is mythological; i.e., the conception of the world as being structured in three stories, heaven, earth and hell; the conception of the intervention of supernatural powers in the course of events; and the conception of miracles, especially the conception of the intervention of supernatural powers in the inner life of the soul, the conception that men can be tempted and corrupted by the devil and possessed by evil spirits. This conception of the world we call mythological because it is different from the conception of the world which has been formed and developed by science since its inception in ancient Greece and which has been accepted by all modern men." 22/15

Ogden stresses Professor Bultmann's restrictions about the classification:

"It does not include *all* discourse about the divine, but solely that type of such discourse in which God is spoken of in the categories of science, and the propositions of which, therefore, are open to verification or falsification by their coherence or incoherence with the propositions of genuine scientific thinking." 177/112

Ogden clarifies Bultmann's position on the "myth" classification when he states:

"Myth is that way of speaking in which the realm of the divine is conceptualized as though it were the object of the kind of thinking appropriate to science. To use one of his own favorite examples, myth speaks of God's transcendence over the world as if it were a matter of spatial distance and thus pictures him as located in a heaven situated somewhere above the world of mundane occurrences. The result of such speaking is that myth sooner or later comes into conflict with the thinking of science and, being no match for its adversary, inevitably gives way before it. Because it has the logical and grammatical form of objective scientific discourse, and yet intends to speak of a reality of which science in principle cannot speak, it can only be regarded by the scientist as a kind of primitive thinking that no longer has any reason for being." 177/112

5B. The Forms of Vincent Taylor

1C. PRONOUNCEMENT-STORIES

Vincent Taylor has used the term pronouncement-stories to classify a form of Gospel narrative:

"Their chief characteristic, it will be remembered, is that they culminate in a saying of Jesus which expresses some ethical or religious precept; the saying may be evoked by a question friendly or otherwise, or may be associated with an incident which is indicated in very few words." 114/63

Taylor disagrees with Bultmann and Dibelius on the terms paradigm and apophthegmata. He asserts that "*Paradigmen* ('models') is too general and is too exclusively associated with the theory that the stories were formed under the influence of preaching. On the other hand, *Apophthegmata* is literary rather than popular and, by concentrating attention too much on the final word of Jesus, it almost invites a deprecatory attitude to the narrative element. For these reasons I should like to suggest a name which has not yet been used. Why not call these narratives *Pronouncement-Stories?*" 114/30

He further emphasizes: "I suggest that neither of the names by which Dibelius and Bultmann designate the stories is satisfactory." 114/63

Taylor gives an illustration of this form:

"The Tribute-money (Mk. xii. 13ff.) illustrates the Pronouncement-Story at its best.

"'And they send unto him certain of the Pharisees and of the Herodians, that they might catch him in talk, And when they were come, they say unto him, "Master, we know that thou art true, and carest not for any one: for thou regardest not the person of men, but of a truth teachest the way of God: Is it lawful to give tribute unto Caesar, or not? Shall we give, or shall we not give?" But he, knowing their hypocrisy, said unto them, "Why tempt ye me? Bring me a penny, that I may see it." And they brought it. And he saith unto them, "Whose is this image and superscription?" And they said unto him, "Caesar's." And Jesus said unto them, "Render unto Caesar the things that are Caesar's, and unto God the things that are God's." And they marvelled greatly at him.'

"This section, which is longer than many Pronouncement-Stories, is a perfect unity. It is the one story in this group where Bultmann sees no reason to think of a community-formation.... There is not the slightest interest in individuals, or in questions of time or place. Everything leads up to the final word of Jesus, which for the early Christians must have had the force of a pronouncement. So Jesus had spoken, and there was no more to be said!" 114/64, 65

He professes that "the narrative element is not much more than a frame for the saying of Jesus." 114/71

Many of the pronouncement-stories have been lost. Taylor comments:

"The thirty or forty Pronouncement-Stories in the Gospels can be only a fraction of those which existed in the oral period. Many must have perished through the weakness of human memory; but the saying, the most virile element in the oral unit, would often survive, separated from the question which prompted it and the account of the events out of which it sprang." 114/81

2C. SAYINGS AND PARABLES

The concept of parables is highlighted by Taylor:

"In respect of form, the parables are more elaborate developments of the figures, comparisons, and metaphors which are so frequent in the sayings of Jesus." 114/100

Vincent Taylor alleges that the parables of Jesus circulated alone or in pairs and were collected at different centers. The parable introductions have been added by the evangelists with a comment on the parables themselves. So, inevitably there is a tendency to add sayings in the introduction which are similar to the parable itself. As Rudolf Bultmann has pointed out, the effect of this has been to introduce an element of uncertainty into the interpretation of parables. 114/102

Taylor concludes that the sayings-tradition is historically accurate. He writes:

"There is in the great majority of the sayings attributed to Jesus a self-authenticating note which stamps them as His, and not the formations of the community. This is an aesthetic judgment, and its limits cannot be precisely fixed, but it ought not to be neglected by any one who seeks to give a comprehensive opinion on the historical value of the sayings. Taken along with the more objective arguments, it confirms our conclusion that substantially the sayings-tradition is historically trustworthy." 114,10

3C. MIRACLE STORIES

Taylor alludes to a list of miracles:

"The Miracle-Stories proper include thirteen healing-miracles and five nature-miracles. The former include: the Demoniac in the Synagogue, Peter's Wife's Mother, the Leper, the Paralytic, the Gerasene Demoniac, the Daughter of Jaïrus, the Woman with the Issue, the Deaf Mute, the Blind Man near Bethsaida, the Epileptic Lad, Blind Bartimaeus, the Dumb Demoniac (Lk. xi. 14; Mt. xii. 22-4; cf. ix. 32-4), and the Young Man at Nain (Lk. vii. 11-7). The nature-miracles are the Stilling of the Storm, the Feeding of the Five Thousand, the Walking on the Water, the Cursing of the Fig Tree, and the Draught of Fishes." 114/120

6B. Other Authors

In concluding we include a few remarks about the various forms by different authors:

McGinley summarizes the method and assumptions of the form critical method by noting first that primitive literary expression has made use of fixed forms. This form is recognized in word choice, sentence construction and manner of literary presentation. The form is produced according to the needs of the community, and it evolves subject to certain transmission laws. 82/11

McKnight talks about paradigms and legends:

"The tales and legends are less historical than paradigms because of their very nature. Tales, however, are not all on the same level historically. They arose in three different ways: by extending paradigms, by introducing foreign motifs, and by borrowing foreign material; and the historical judgment upon a tale is related to its origin. A historical basis is to be presupposed when the tale developed from a paradigm. Only when a non-Christian story is the probable origin of a Christian tale is the historical reliability of the narrative really brought into question. Even legends must *not* be ruled out as possible vehicles of history, for legends too may contain some historical content." 83/34

Käsemann postulates the manner in which forms were created:

"First, there is secular material, previously circulating in the manner of proverbs, but now transferred to Jesus. Then the community, appealing in its internal disagreement to the Master or seeking to make his individuality more vivid, created in the so-called conflict discourses or apophthegms ideal scenes for his words and deeds." 68/60

Easton relates his view of form classifications and their importance when he states:

"The disputations show us Jesus as the Rabbi, the sayings as the Teacher, the miracles as the Wonder-worker. These literary types, poor in historic detail, little interested in the private life of their Hero, show Jesus purely objectively in his calling, which includes his criticism of the Law, preaching the Gospel, and healing the sick." 44/60

2A. BASIC ANSWER TO THE ASSUMPTION OF FORM CLASSIFICATIONS

1B. Criticism Posed by the Form Critics Themselves

The untrustworthiness of the forms is commented on by Dibelius. He not only writes that "Paradigms" are words relatively trustworthy (36/62) but also concludes that one cannot guarantee the historical reliability of "Tales."

Dealing with the questions of eyewitnesses, Dibelius concedes:

"Because the eye witnesses could control and correct, a relative trustworthiness of the Paradigms is guaranteed." 36/62

One wonders why he does not conclude that eyewitnesses actually wrote narrative stories, rather than form classified pieces of literature.

Vincent Taylor comments about the limits of Form Criticism:

"For the sayings of Jesus Bultmann's five-fold classification is useful, but here we discover the limitations of Form-Criticism; for the terms do little more than describe stylistic features; they do not denote popular forms into which an individual or a community unconsciously throws sayings.... We may certainly to advantage study the formal aspects of sayings, but when we try to classify them according to popular forms, the attempt breaks down. Morever, the method is almost bound to result in scepticism." 114/31

Taylor questions pronouncement-stories as products of imagination:

"The distribution of the Pronouncement-Stories has some bearing on the question of their early currency and genuineness. There are at least twenty in Mark, seven or nine in Luke's special source, four or five in Q, one in Matthew, and none in John. If the stories are products of Christian imagination, why do they not increase in number as time passes, and as new problems confront the growing Church? Why is there no Pronouncement-Story about the necessity of the Cross, or the Gentile Mission, or the foundation and organization of the Church? The absence of these topics in the stories which have come down to us gives us reasons to pause before views which credit the first Christians with a facility for invention and imagination always at command. If Bultmann is right, Christian imagination was potent where it was least needed, feeble or wanting where silence called for its exercise; it left undone the things which it ought to have done, and did the things it had no need to do." 114/86, 87

Taylor disagrees with Bultmann by alleging:

"Bultmann thinks that many of the *Apophthegmata* have been spun out of sayings of Jesus by the imagination of the community, and that even where a story is a 'uniform conception' it is often 'ideal' in character. I cannot think that this opinion is supported by a study of the stories themselves." 114/85

MORE EVIDENCE THAT DEMANDS A VERDICT

About myths and legends, Taylor frankly observes:

"'Myths' and 'Legends' are terms which do not define any particular structural forms." 114/31, 32

Taylor and Bultmann disagree over form classification. Taylor remarks about the second list (see page 225) of Bultmann's apophthegms:

"The remaining ten stories in Bultmann's second list seem to me to be Stories about Jesus rather than Pronouncement-Stories." 114/75, 76

Alfred Wikenhauser challenges the judgments of historicity of a passage on the basis of form:

"Many of its exponents use Form Criticism as a means of historical criticism; against them it must be strongly emphasized that the form of a traditional passage provides no foundation for a judgment concerning its historicity . The study of content must supplement the study of form; Form Criticism must be complemented by the study of facts." 126/275, 276

Redlich establishes an internal weakness of form classification concerning myths. It confuses subjective historical judgment with objective historical study. For instance, the title "myth" is an initial judgment of a narrative's historical value. Also, and this is admitted by even the form critics, "myth" stories have no literary form and are classifiable only according to their contents. "Form-less" stories are beyond the confines of "Form" Criticism. 101/15

Relating to the categorical form "miracles," Redlich exposes a major difference between Christian and non-Christian literature:

"Hence we may conclude that Jesus required this personal faith in Him and that it is a genuine part of the tradition. Now, in non-Christian tales such a demand is unknown: in them the cures are magical. There exists therefore a vital difference between the Christian and non-Christian parallel Miracle-Stories. An element is to be found in the Christian stories, which is unique. Parallelism fails in the most important element. 101/131

The inherent problem with classification of the Gospel material into created forms is pointed out by J.M. Robinson:

"The form critic conjectured that one way to identify the *Sitz im Leben* of the gospel tradition would be to classify the material on purely formal grounds, and then to identify the function in the Church's life responsible for the rise of each identified form. This procedure is methodologically sound, but did not in practice arrive at ultimately conclusive results. This was due to the indistinctness of the formal structure of much of the material, and the difficulty of making a clear correlation between formal tendencies and their setting in the Church's life. Consequently when the form critics came to discuss the historicity of the gospel tradition, a question for which their method was at best only indirectly relevant, they tended to arrive at the conclusion which their general orientation suggested, rather than a conclusion which form criticism as such required." 104/36, 37

A noted form critic comments on the myriad of forms which have been invented by form critics to suit the needs of their theory. Easton professes that:

"Paradigms, stories, legends, cult-legends, epiphanies, apothegms, miracles, parables, folk-tales, controversies, dialogues, parenesis, logia, prophetic and apocalyptic utterances, church rules, sayings in the first person, allegories, poem stanzas—the research of the past decade has exhibited no poverty of terminology! But how profitable is it all? Can we really analyze forms with such precision as to make form-criticism a true discipline?" 44/61

2B. Highly Subjective

The following criticism of one critic, Dibelius, is applicable to all of the critics.

McGinley alleges that Dibelius' method suffers due to his transition from a constructive methodology to an analytical one. He asserts that some stories have been subjectively chosen as typical paradigms without proof being presented that they were used in preaching or that they belong to a specific paradigmatic type. The arbitrary norms established, analysis begins by analytic exclusion and pruning leaving less than half of the eighteen chosen paradigms being of pure type. Thus, the exception becomes the rule! 82/35

W.E. Barnes claims faulty judgment is apparent in Dibelius's classifications:

"Why, for instance, is the healing of the leper [Mark 1:40-44] to be reckoned as a 'Tale,' and not as a 'Paradigm'? It stands first in Dibelius's list of Tales, but it has most of the characteristics of a Paradigm. It is brief: it can be easily isolated from the context: it is 'religious' in that it enjoins obedience to the Mosaic Law: it reaches its highest point in a saying of Jesus: it gives a direction which is strictly applicable to the place and to our Lord's attitude to the Law. The Twelve and other disciples needed to be taught that the Law of Moses was still valid for certain crises in their daily life [*From Tradition to Gospel*, p. 71, 72]. Dibelius's judgment becomes warped when he has to do with a 'miraculous' account [Matthew 5:17]." 6/58

1C. CRITICISM OF APOPHTHEGM AND PARADIGM

There are many divergences between these "parallel" forms. In comparing the apophthegm and paradigm we find that each author, Dibelius and Bultmann, is analyzing the same material. Bultmann's apophthegm includes 44 examples of other divergencies. For example, the terminology—Bultmann all but two are included in Bultmann's list. This obvious divergency is just an example of other divergencies. For example, the terminology—Bultmann alleges that the saying goes back to Jesus and the framework was created, while Dibelius holds that the saying results from the preacher and the story goes back to Jesus. 82/45

W.E. Barnes comments on the paradigm as defined by Dibelius:

"A Paradigm, as defined by Dibelius, must have none of the vivid touches in the narrative which suggest to most readers the eye-witness as the source of the story: 'Every expression of individual sensibility is absent [except that] which is in a high degree concerned with the matter itself [36/37] *i.e.* with the word or deed of Jesus himself. Dibelius postulates a severe and restrained type of oratory for the earliest missionaries, and ascribes to their sermons only the 'least adorned' of the Gospel narratives. How very *un*human these early missionaries must have been, and yet they won their fellow-men over to the Gospel." 6/50

He further challenges the paradigm:

"A second mark of a Paradigm is the brevity and simplicity of the narrative. In a Paradigm we learn of the actual circumstances only as much as we must know in order to understand the intervention of Jesus. Attractive details are left out. Only short passages could be introduced into a sermon. The Tribute Money is a case in point.

"These are rash assertions. Was all early Christian preaching, including that of the fiery St. Peter, limited thus? Dibelius is relying no doubt on the reports of Christian sermons which are found in the Acts of the Apostles. But does he suppose that these reports are complete, or even that they are sufficiently full to give us more than a taste of these sermons? His argument requires that we should be able to learn from these summaries not only the contents but also the method and style of the Christian preachers. But the reports are too brief." 6/52, 53

Laurence J. McGinley makes the following observation:

"As for the ending of the story with a thought useful for preaching, is it not at least possible that the actual incident originally so ended? Jesus might well point His deeds by a saying of universal significance, and there is no more natural reaction to a miraculous cure than a spontaneous exclamation of wonder from those present. Any one of these eighteen paradigms, and many other stories not listed here, might well have illustrated missionary sermons. But Dibelius has failed to prove that they were so used and by such use were molded to their present form." 82/36

Are the stories which don't fit the strict paradigm form closer to the authentic version? F.J. Babcock explains:

"In cases in which a story does not agree strictly with its type-pattern they would assert that these eccentricities, if we may so call them, were later additions and should be pruned away; though of course the very opposite may be the truer account, that while the mass have had their angles and edges worn off, these, by their very nonconformity to type, are shown to be closer to the original." 3/16

When Bultmann, says McGinley, begins to attempt to determine the apophthegmatic type, subjectivism enters the picture. He conjectures that acts have been thought up to provide occasion for dispute; he sets aside some verses because, to him, they weaken Jesus' sayings as intelligible apart from their context. He continually speaks of the procreativity of the apophthegm but he neglects the questions of how the category arose in the first place, if, as he asserts, the incidents never occurred. 82/43

McGinley continues that ultimately Bultmann "rejects as secondary corruptions of the primitive type almost all details of time and place, all initiative by Jesus, all definite names and characterization, the constant opposition of the Scribes and Pharisees. In so doing, he constructs a typical apothegm but destroys its reason for existence. Jesus lives at no time and in no place; He does nothing of His own account; He moves in a world of impersonal shadows; there is no reason for His rejection, trial, execution. While being molded to fit the theory, the facts have disappeared." 82/43

McGinley summarizes his argument by stating his analysis of the apophthegm:

"It is such a mixture of arbitrary statements and detailed analysis, of capricious bias and clever dissection that it leaves the reader overwhelmed and confused." 82/43

2C. CRITICISM OF NOVELLEN (TALES) AND PARABLES

Noting the arbitrariness of the distinctions between the novellen and the paradigm, L.J. McGinley writes that the key distinction between Dibelius's novelle (tale) and the paradigm rests in the extent of description. Granted some of the novellen are much more extensive and detailed than any paradigm (Mark 5:1), but by comparing healing narratives in each category, we find that four of five paradigms and four of seven novellen are of the same length, six verses. In addition, as regards detail, some novellen are told every bit as vividly as some paradigm; for example compare the novelle in Mark 10:46 to the paradigm in Mark 1:40. 82/57, 58

He goes on to comment about the lack of well-defined categories:

"The stylistic traits of this category, therefore, are conditioned by the content of the narratives rather than by their external form. Since there is no essential difference between the categories in breadth of style or religious tone, and since miracle-stories are also included among the paradigms—with gestures, proof of the cure, and choral-ending—we may reasonably conclude that the sharp distinction Dibelius has drawn between these categories is an exaggeration." 82/58

The origin and date of the *novellen* is vague. McGinley argues that "regarding the historical value of the novellen Dibelius maintains that some of these stories were developed by expansion of the paradigms. But this presupposes that the novellen are of later date, and for this no proof is given. Nor was it possible in the first two decades of Christianity, as it actually existed, for extraneous motifs and foreign material to penetrate the tradition in the manner Dibelius suggests." 82/59

3C. CRITICISM OF LEGENDS AND PARABLES

W.E. Barnes makes this observation about legends:

"To a third class of narrative Dibelius gives the name of 'Legends.' In surveying these, he starts with a general statement, a questionable assertion, which seems intended to prohibit any examination of his view. 'The oldest tradition,' he tells us, 'has no answer to give to questions about persons belonging to the most intimate circles of Jesus' [36/71]. In support of his statement, he gravely points out that in the account of the relatives 'seeking' Jesus, no names are given: they are described merely as 'his mother and his brethren' [36/49]. With equal gravity he points out in the story of Jesus' rejection in His own country that His neighbours, while mentioning His mother's name and the names of His four brethren and mentioning His sisters' existence, fail to give His sisters' names. His strange inference from this is that when names and details are given in other cases they do *not* come from the oldest tradition. His view is that Christian curiosity was aroused only at a later period concerning persons who came in contact with our Lord: and legends were invented to satisfy this curiosity." 6/71, 72

Commenting about the lack of structural form, Harold H. Hutson writes about myths and legends:

"The stories about Jesus present a more doubtful classification. This material has no definite structural form and shows form criticism at its weakest points. 'Myths' and 'legends' do not define particular structural forms, but depend largely upon historical references for decision between factual information and the accretion of details." 66/132

C.S. Lewis, former professor of Medieval and Renaissance Literature at Cambridge University states regarding legends:

"If he tells me that something in a Gospel is legend or romance, I want to know how many legends and romances he has read, how well his palate is trained in detecting them by the flavour; not how many years he has spent on that Gospel." 10/154

He then adds, referring to the Gospels:

"I have been reading poems, romances, vision-literature, legends, myths all my life. I know what they are like. I know that not one of them is like this." 10/155

4C. CRITICISM OF MIRACLES

L.J. McGinley, after analyzing Bultmann's concept of miracle stories, concludes that many of Bultmann's allegations concerning the form rest upon the simplicity of the synoptic style. He continues:

"These books are not modern psychological biographies; they imply, rather than depict, motives and inner dispositions. They are apologetic in aim and so interest centers on Jesus. They are concisely written and follow no complicated pattern in their narrative portions, However, they are not accounts composed along rigidly formalistic lines, comparable, for example, to the classical sonnet. Hence Bultmann errs in identifying as a 'subsequent development' any deviation from a theoretically pure type. It is not possible to establish the type with such detailed accuracy." 82/63

McGinley further relates a "common sense" reason for the form of healing miracles:

"Granted that two stories relate a cure, it is inevitable that there should be common traits: history of the illness, request for a cure, healing, verification of the healing, reactions [139/142]. In these general features, the Gospel miracle-narratives differ but little from the latest reports of the medical examiners at Lourdes; and yet—this is the important point- such common traits obviously do not prove a similarity of atmosphere, a parallel community creation of cult-legends, the influence of primitive literary laws, or a similar *Sitz im Leben* in the Palestine of long ago and the southern France of today. Details relatively unimportant regarding the cure itself will, therefore, be of prime importance as indications of the milieu in which the story arose." 82/76

F.F. Bruce questions the conclusions reached by form critical analysis:

"Again, the miracle-stories of the Gospels can be studied in terms of Form Criticism; they can be compared with stories of similar wonders in literature or folklore, and various interesting inferences can be drawn from a comparative examination of this kind. But this approach will not lead us to firm conclusions about the historical character of the Gospel miracles, nor will it explain the significance which these miracles have in the context of the life and activity of Jesus." 16/63

5C.   FINAL CRITICISMS

Observing historical studies, G.E. Wright proclaims:

"It is significant that most of the important new results in historical studies have little to do literary analysis." 128/50

John Warwick Montgomery cites H.J. Rose who comments on form analysis by saying:

"'The chief weapon of the separatists has always been literary criticism, and of this it is not too much to say that such niggling word-baiting, such microscopic hunting of minute inconsistencies and flaws in logic, has hardly been seen, outside of the Homeric field, since Rymar and John Dennis died' [H.J. Rose, *Handbook of Greek Literature from Homer to the Age of Lucian*. London: Methuen, 1934, pp. 42,43.]." 87/36

Neill rightly concludes:

"No one is likely to deny that there is value in the classification of material. The question at once arises, however, whether the classification really arises out of the material itself or whether it has been imposed upon it. The fact that various scholars analyse the words of Jesus in different ways suggests that not all is perfectly clear, and that the categories of which use has been made are not so much inherent in the New Testament itself as arrived at by other methods and imposed upon the material from without." 187/246

A.H. McNeile quotes M. Goguel about the form critics and their classifications:

"As M. Goguel [139/114-160] has said, 'It does not appear in the name of what principle it can be maintained that such a section as could be used for preaching is not to be used at the same time for instruction, for controversy, for mission work, and perhaps also quite simply to satisfy pious imagination and curiosity.'" 85/52

A correlation of the Gospels with a history of the early Christian life may be enlightening, but it does not reveal more than general patterns. McGinley continues with the deficiencies:

"It cannot tell us, at this late date, why many of the forms were chosen nor whether there ever was a definite relation between them and the life of the community. To postulate such a definite relationship and then employ it as a measure of the historicity of individual passages— as Bultmann and Dibelius have done—has been severely and justly criticized as a serious defect in the method." 82/20, 21

Although some of the Gospel stories and narratives fall into conventional forms and similar patterns, F.F. Bruce makes the following observation:

"There are occasions on which a stereotyped style is insisted upon even in modern life. When, for example, a police officer gives evidence in court, he does not adorn his narrative with the graces of oratory, but adheres as closely as he can to a prescribed and stereotyped 'form.' The object of this is that the evidence he gives may conform as closely as possible to the actual course of events which he describes. What his narrative lacks in artistic finish, it gains in accuracy. The stereotyped style of many of the Gospel narratives and discourses serves the same end; it is a guarantee of their substantial accuracy. It frequently happens that, because of this preservation of a definite 'form,' the reports of similar incidents or similar sayings will be given in much the same languages and constructed on much the same framework. but we must not infer from this similarity of language and framework that two similar narratives are duplicate accounts of one and the same event, or that two similar parables (e.g. the wedding feast of Matthew xxii. 2ff. and the great supper of Luke xiv. 16ff.) are necessarily variant versions of one and the same parable, any more than we should conclude that, because a police officer describes two street accidents in almost identical language, he is really giving variant accounts of one and the same street accident." 16/32, 33

Stan Gundry concludes "that material in stereotyped-forms is neither more nor less historical because of its form, which supposedly relates it to a *Sitz im Leben* in the church." 57/62

He goes on to say:

"Forms do not give the related material a relative historical value. Form is in no way related to truth or falsity. Nothing can be inferred from stereotyped forms other than that the church was accustomed to tell stories about Jesus in a certain way." 57/60

L.J. McGinley reiterates: "The serious defects in the general theory of Form Criticism will, naturally, vitiate its conclusions when it is applied to definite form-categories of the Gospels." 82/28

A.M. Hunter says that one "must never forget that the *form* in which a story is told can never tell us whether the substance of the story is true or false. The whole method is too subjective and speculative to afford us much sure guidance." 174/40

T.W. Manson acutely observes that "a paragraph of Mark is not a penny the better or the worse for being labelled 'Apothegm' or 'Pronouncement Story' or 'Paradigm.' In fact if Form-criticism had stuck to its proper business, it would not have made any real stir. We should have taken it as

we take the forms of Hebrew poetry or the forms of musical composition."
133/4

3A. IN SUMMARY

1B. Although there are similarities, each form critic has his own categories of forms which he finds in the Gospels.

2B. Often the form critics find fault with the forms of their colleagues.

3B. Other scholars find many of the form divisions to be unreliable.

4B. The form critics go astray when they use the form of a passage to prove its historical value.

The historicity of a saying is not determined by its form. By way of illustration, let's assume that I like antiques. As I am looking through the classified ads, I come across an advertisement (form) about an antique auction. The ad says there will be plenty of early American antiques. I attend the auction and find out there is only one antique up for auction. Everything else is mere used furniture.

Now, if the form (in this case the classified ad) determined the accuracy of the content, then I would automatically reject all classified ads about antique auctions. In reality, the form does not determine the reliability of its content. One must examine further than form to determine the dependability of content.

chapter 21

the
creative
community

Form Criticism assumes that vital factors which gave rise to and preserved forms are to be found in the practical interests of the Christian community.

1A. A CREATIVE COMMUNITY

1B. Basic Assumption

Spivey and Smith convey a common theory about the handing down of the traditions of Jesus, citing mainly the faith and circumstances of the early Church. In early Christianity, they believe, the Lord's authority did not stop with His life and death; He was a living Lord and the tradition was living and developing." The pressing needs of the community and church stimulated the writing down and hence partially fixing of this tradition.

"One obvious reason for writing Gospels was the death of the apostles, those who had been with Jesus. The church could not afford to lose the tradition of Jesus. Mark probably originated in the mid-sixties when, according to tradition, Paul and Peter, the two great apostles, were martyred.

"Other motives were also at work in the writing down of the Gospels. A church facing persecution needed to know the way in which Jesus himself had faced persecution. The early church, furthermore, had to struggle to understand itself apart from the law, organization, rites, and customs of Judaism. The early church also had to face the problem posed by the delay of the expected parousia (second coming of Jesus) and the end of the world. As the Christian mission expanded into the Gentile world, a further crisis was posed by the problem of how a religion basically Jewish in origin could appeal to the Hellenistic world without losing its identity and distinctiveness." 113/64, 65

In his book, *Origins of the Gospels,* Filson identifies these needs of the early church:

(1) Need for an outline to serve as a guide in matters of belief and conduct.

(2) Need for a guide to the meaning of their faith and understanding of their Savior.

(3) Need to express their faith in worship and need for the materials to express that faith.

(4) Need for material when in contact with problem of heresy or persecution. 47/95-97

Alluding to the "life situation" or *Sitz im Leben* of the early community, Barker, Lane and Michaels indicate:

"According to form critical reconstructions, as it expanded the church was confronted with a diversity of needs and interests. These concerns were *missionary* (presenting Jesus' life in such a way as to win new converts), *catechetical* (instructing the converts in their new faith), *apologetic* (answering the Jewish and pagan detractors of the faith), and *disciplinary* (protecting the church's life and belief against dangers from within). Such interests varied as the church moved into new environments. The materials required to instruct Christians in Palestine could be quite different from those necessary for the same purpose in Antioch, Ephesus, Corinth, or Rome. Cultural differences required adaptation. Diversity of need influenced not only what was remembered (and therefore taught), but also how it was remembered. Thus the form as well as the content of the gospel materials in the Hellenistic churches could differ considerably from what was adopted in the church at Jerusalem. Each church faced the problem of how to translate the gospel message into language that would be understood in a particular cultural environment, without distortion of the essential truth received from Jesus and the apostles." 5/68

1C. DIBELIUS' VIEW OF THE CREATIVE COMMUNITY

Dibelius points out the conflict between the authenticity of Jesus' words and the creation by the community:

"But we do not reach final certainty about Jesus' words, because we must reckon with the fact that, from the beginning, the development of the tradition took place amongst what were really the interests of the cultus." 36/209

Concerning development of tradition, Dibelius concludes about the community:

"In this way a large and fertile development took place in primitive Christian literature. The first traditions arose from the immediate requirements of the churches, without literary intention, without regard to the world or to the following ages." 35/271

He has also concluded that the *Sitz im Leben* of the oral tradition rests in the preaching of the early Church. He remarks:

"We may suppose that the manner in which the doings of Jesus was narrated was determined by the requirements of the sermon; in this way an illustrative style fitted for missionary work and for worship could arise." 36/26, 27

2C. BULTMANN'S VIEW OF THE CREATIVE COMMUNITY

Bultmann contends that "it is through the medium of the community, accordingly, that the figure of the historical Jesus appears." 10/60

It was the needs of Christian faith and life that provided the cause for Gospel tradition. Bultmann continues:

"It is perfectly clear that it was not the historical interest that dominated, but the needs of Chirstian faith and life. One may designate the final motive by which the gospels were produced as the *cultic* (that is, the needs of common worship), if one considers that the high point of Christian life was the gathering of the community for worship, when the figure of Jesus, his teaching as well as his life, was set forth before the eyes of the faithful, and when accordingly the gospels served for public reading." 19/64

Bultmann says that we "conclude that the whole framework of the history of Jesus must be viewed as an editorial construction, and that therewith a whole series of typical scenes, which because of their ecclesiastical use and their poetic and artistic associations we had looked upon as scenes in the life of Jesus, must be viewed as creations of the evangelists." 19/28

In the area of the authenticity of Jesus' sayings, Bultmann observes that "it is therefore possible that the picture which the Synoptists give us of the person and the message of Jesus has obliterated many an older trait, and that many a word is attributed to him which he did not utter." 19/20

Bultmann alleges:

"Not only have many of the older sayings of Jesus been modified in the course of tradition, but not seldom words have been placed in Jesus' mouth which in reality were either spoken by other Jewish teachers or first arose in the Christian community." 19/42

He goes on to say:

"The tradition gathered dominical sayings, gave them a new form, enlarged them by additions and developed them further: it collected other (Jewish) sayings, and fitted them by adaptation for reception into the treasury of Christian instruction, and produced new sayings from its consciousness of a new possession, sayings which they ingenuously put into the mouth of Jesus."

In summary of his challenge to the authenticity of the sayings of Jesus, Bultmann establishes that "in the synoptic tradition a series of sayings shows that Jesus' work was conceived as decisive happening, especially such as speak of him as having come or having been sent. They are scarcely (at least in the majority of cases) original words of Jesus, but mostly products of the Church. And so far as they had already arisen in the earliest (i.e. the Palestinian) Church (which cannot in every case be clearly made out) they testify that this Church in retrospect conceived the phenomenon of Jesus together with its meaning as a unity." 25/44

Bultmann would further establish the creative power of the community when he decides that Jesus had no desire to be the Father of a Church. The Church accepted Him:

"Still he did not found an order or a sect, far less a 'Church,' nor did he expect that everyone should or could forsake house and family.

"The saying about the building of the 'Church' (ἐκκλησία) Mt. 16:18 is, like the whole of Mt. 16:17-19, a later product of the Church." 24/10

In reference to the effect of the *Sitz im Leben* on community creation, Bultmann declares:

"The proper understanding of form-criticism rests upon the judgement that the literature in which the life of a given community, even the primitive Christian community, has taken shape, springs out of quite definite conditions and wants of life from which grows up a quite definite style and quite specific forms and categories. Thus every literary category has its 'life situation' (*Sitz im Leben:* Gunkel), whether it be worship in its different forms, or work, or hunting, or war. The *Sitz im Leben* is not, however, an individual historical event, but a typical situation or occupation in the life of a community." 21/4

Bultmann further asserts:

"Apparently the situation is to be understood only as follows: these traditions first arose in the Christian community and are to be explained by its situation. The 'disciples,' i.e. the primitive Christian church, have broken with the old customs in this matter, and they are defending themselves against criticism by means of the stories, through which they make their appeal to a saying of Jesus." 19/44, 45

Selecting one of the Gospels as an example of creative community, Bultmann interprets that "Mark is the work of an author who is steeped in the theology of the early Church, and who ordered and arranged the traditional material that he received in the light of the faith of the early Church—that was the result; and the task which follows for historical research is this: to separate the various strata in Mark and to determine which belonged to the original historical tradition and which derived from the work of the author." 21/1

Bultmann adds:

"What we find in Mark is for the most part a reflection of the later faith of the Church, 'a productive formation of the Church,' or the work of creative imagination. This not only accounts for the framework of the life of Jesus, but also to a large extent for the picture of Jesus within this framework. The historical reality of Jesus is very much covered over by myth and legend. The schema of the Christ myth has distorted the actual historical tradition." 175/30

Bultmann attributes the use of Old Testament Scripture to the community's debate concerning Jesus:

"It is certainly possible that the saying of Jesus enshrined in such a setting is old and authentic, as, for example, probably Mark ii, 19. In the other cases it is less probable, since here argumentative use is made of sentences from the Old Testament, and since most of the words of Jesus which cite the Old Testament are suspected of originating in the theological debates of the primitive community. Just as in this primitive community the faith in Jesus as the Messiah was defended by an appeal to Old Testament passages, so likewise an effort was made to found Christian practice upon a similar appeal." 19/44, 45

We must, therefore, according to Bultmann, conclude the following:

"As a result of this investigation it appears that the outline of the life of Jesus, as it is given by Mark and taken over by Matthew and Luke, is an editorial creation, and that as a consequence our actual knowledge of the course of Jesus' life is restricted to what little can be discovered in the individual scenes constituting the older tradition." 135/343

3C. TAYLOR'S VIEW OF THE CREATIVE COMMUNITY

The Gospel traditions have been molded by the influence of all aspects of early Christian life.

Taylor states that "every consideration bearing on the life of the first Christians must be taken into account—the practical demands arising from daily life, the need to explain the new faith to themselves and to others, the necessities of defence against objections and slanders from unfriendly and hostile neighbours. These and other considerations have determined the form which the tradition now has, and the changes it has undergone, and by taking them into account it is often possible to explain why this or that element in the tradition has survived and why much we should greatly desire to know has not been handed down to us." 114/36

Taylor asks:

"Have we not in all this a glimpse, not only of the Evangelist at work, but of the conditions of the primitive period in a typical community? All is determined by the needs, practical, religious, and apologetic of the first Christians, and the tradition is continuous or fragmentary as the needs dictate." 113/61

He agrees with the community or "social transmission of the Gospel:

"All the Form Critics rightly emphasize the social aspects of the formative process."

Taylor believes in the influence of the creative community:

"The narratives are mainly legends and ideal constructions, and most of the sayings, while Palestinian in origin, are products of primitive Christianity which puts back its own ideas and beliefs into the lips of Jesus. Fascher sums up the tendencies of the book well when he writes: 'The late and creative community is at work; it transforms everything into myth' [see 140/144]." 114/14

2B. Basic Answer to the Assumption that the Practical Interest of the Christian Community Gave Birth to the Gospels

Confronted by the problem of the Christian community's transmission of the traditions of their leader, W.D. Davies claims:

"Consider the alternatives placed before a student of the tradition about Jesus. The first alternative is to believe that for some time after his death and resurrection what Jesus did and said was neglected and so forgotten. But, as the Church developed, it became necessary for her to find rules for conduct, teaching for catechumens, material for 'sermons.' To meet this need, the Christian communities created their own sayings or borrowed materials from Jewish and Hellenistic sources and ascribed them to Jesus. The other alternative is to recognize that what Jesus actually taught was remembered by his followers and adapted by the Churches as the need arose." 333/115

Martin continues this line of reasoning:

"There was never any time when the Church lacked the historical tradition of Jesus. This indisputable fact has been blithely overlooked by those who wish to treat the Jesus-tradition of the Gospels as something that was either created or transformed by the Church. Either the Church had no authentic tradition of Jesus at all and fashioned a tradition for itself in conformity with its beliefs; or there were just a handful of vague recollections of Jesus in existence and the Church took these and developed the Gospels out of them. Such ideas could be written off as too absurd to merit any attention, were it not that in some quarters they appear to be seriously entertained." 80/62, 63

The description of a creative community in the New Testament is virtually nonexistent according to Redlich:

"Form Criticism in stressing the influence of the primitive community is blind to the influence of Jesus as a rabbi and a prophet. It makes the community a

creative body, of which there is little or no trace in the New Testament."
101/78

Easton continues:

"If we are to follow Wellhausen and Bultmann, we must hold that Jesus gave
no systematic teaching but was able, none the less, to inspire his followers with
the utmost moral and literary discrimination; so much so that when they
came to draw up rules for themselves they adopted only the basic content of
the Synoptists. That is, Wellhausen and Bultmann canonize the entire
Palestinian Church." 44/108

The receptive rather than the creative nature of any community, whether it
be in the New Testament or in today's society, is emphasized by Otto Piper:

"The documents of the N.T. confirm the findings of sociology and anthropology according to which collectives are receptive rather than creative
entities." 136/123

C.F.D. Moule, in an article which honors T.W. Manson, writes that the four
Gospels are "first and foremost addressed 'from faith,' indeed, but not 'to
faith' so much as to unbelief." 84/167

Moule argues that "all four Gospels alike are to be interpreted as more than
anything else evangelistic and apologetic in purpose...the Synoptic Gospels
represent primarily the recognition that a vital element in evangelism is the
plain story of what happened in the ministry of Jesus." 84/175, 176

Concerning the historical account of Jesus as an "ingredient in worship,"
Moule writes that "its very nature demands that, so far as possible, it be kept
in this distinguishable condition and not overlaid by interpretation. . . . Still
more, it was to equip Christians with a knowledge of their origins, for use in
evangelism and apologetic."

"The Christian communities," adds Moule, "were vividly aware of the
necessity of trying to avoid romancing, and of not confusing post-resurrection
experiences of incorporation in the Body of Christ with the pre-resurrection
process of discipleship—of following, learning, imitating...they have
generally resisted so phenomenally well the temptation to read back into the
narrative the contemporary interpretation of Christ; and was not this due to a
conscious resistance to the non-'historical' in the sense just indicated?" 84/175

"Christians knew well that if they lost sight of the story behind that experience
their worship could be like a house built on sand; and that if they preached
salvation without the story of how it came they could be powerless as
evangelists; and that if they could not explain how they came to stand where
they did, they would be failing to give a reason for their hope.

"Therefore, they cherished the narrative as something precious. . . . The point
is that the Christians knew the difference between the two—between the pre-
resurrection situation and the post-resurrection situation—and that their aim
was to tell faithfully the story of how the former led to the latter. And in
actual fact, they succeeded better than is often allowed." 84/173

1C.   DO COMMUNITIES PRODUCE MATCHLESS SAYINGS LIKE THOSE
      OF JESUS?

Easton comments that "it is easy enough to speak of the creation of sayings
by a community, but the phrase is really meaningless. Communities do not
create sayings; such creation comes from individuals and from individuals
only. Communities may adopt and transmit sayings, and may modify and
standardize them in transmission, but the sayings themselves must first
exist." 44/116

Vincent Taylor, a form critic, goes on to point out that it is doubtful that these communities could have formed so many of these sayings; this does not coincide with actual conditions of the time they were written. He points out that the first Christians were acutely aware of what Jesus said and what He didn't say, more so than Bultmann. As an example, in I Corinthians 7, Paul points out the difference between Christ's commands and his own; and he speaks of matters from which he acknowledges that he has no specific command from the Lord (vv. 25, 40). 114/107-109

Also, the time element necessary for community creation is lacking. Floyd Filson states:

"Any tendency to derive the bulk of the perennially vital Gospel tradition from the masses of believers instead of from Jesus must inevitably be suspected. If we do not place the beginning of written records of Jesus' words and deeds later than 50 A.D., we can hardly find room for such remarkable creative activity as would ascribe to the earliest Christians the elaboration of any large part of the tradition." 47/110

Robert Mounce summarizes a noted form critic's method of extracting the "actual" saying of Jesus from the Gospel narratives:

"After peeling off the layers of tradition, there are only a few of the sayings of Jesus that one can accept as authentic, according to Norman Perrin. He uses the 'criterion of dissimilarity' in a two-fold way.

(1)"If Jesus says anything which sounds like the early Church, then this can't be an authentic utterance.
[Mounce points out that Perrin ignores the possibility that the early Church took up and developed a saying of Jesus.]

(2)"If it sounds like ancient Judaism, then you can't trust it either, as being originally from Jesus.
[The Gospel, however, got underway in a Jewish setting. How else could Jesus talk but like a Jew?]"
[Norman Perrin, *Rediscovering the Teaching of Jesus*, p. 39] 144

Regarding the above observations, Barker, Lane and Michael list six detractions from the theory in the area of community's creation of Jesus' sayings:

(1)"The Gospel arose in a Jewish milieu where tradition was sacred and established procedures existed by which it was maintained.
(2)"From the beginning the apostles had a proprietary interest in this tradition and a zealous concern to preserve and protect it.
(3)"There had never been a concept of the church without ministry. Through the original apostles, as well as the prophets and teachers who followed, this ministry was a ministry of the word. The word of God therefore, in the form of gospel tradition, was never subservient to the community. It existed distinct from the church and had authority over it.
(4)"Even before Paul's labors, the tradition had come to possess a certain fixity.
(5)"The Gospel materials were reduced to writing within the lifetime of first-generation believers.
(6)"Rather extensive communication among individual churches throughout the Empire, including even Jerusalem, was a distinguishing feature of primitive Christianity."

2C. DID THE *SITZ IM LEBEN* INFLUENCE THE CREATION OF THE SAYINGS OF JESUS?

G.E. Ladd observes that while "we readily admit that each Gospel must be studied in terms of its supposed *Sitz im Leben*, it does not follow that this

Sitz im Leben, exercised a significant creative factor in the formation of the content of the Gospel tradition." 74/162

A factor guarding the evolutionary molding of Jesus' sayings if referred to by Martin:

"The fact that the history of Jesus was integral to the Christian proclamation from the beginning allows no scope for an evolutionary development of any extent. The interest and concern of the whole Christian community were too much focused on the facts of its origin for that." 80/112

Regarding the lifesetting, Guthrie inquires:

"But what Bultmann and his followers cannot explain is how the original Jesus became so 'coloured' or adapted to their own point of view by the later Christian community. Is it not much more credible to believe that the Christian community was 'coloured' by the authentic teaching of Jesus?" 131/201,202

Davies adds:

"The tradition about Jesus has its source in His activity: it is not the creation of the community, however much colored by its needs." 34/92, 93

Would not Jesus teach in the established norm of his day?

Ladd writes:

"Would we not expect that there would be parallels between Jesus' teaching and His Jewish environment? After all, He was a first-century Jew. Would we not expect His teachings to be useful in the church? This critical norm has, as a recent reviewer well pointed out, decided in advance that the result will be: 'a Jesus who was unorthodox, since anything that savours of orthodoxy, Jewish or Christian, has been excluded *a priori* [A.T. Hanson, "Essays on New Testament Themes," *Scottish Journal of Theology.* 18 (1965), p. 107],'" 74/164

McNeile observes that if there was any truth to the position of the Form Critics, then the problems in the early Church would have been evident in the Gospels or the practices of the Church would have been discussed or answered by Jesus. 85/55

Easton points out that there is no evidence of this sort in the Gospels—they are incredibly free from these problems. If anything, the treatment of Christ's words during the period of oral transmission is considered conservative. 44/108-115

The radical critics maintain that settings for the Gospel tradition originated in the early Church. But it seems much more realistic to ascribe the settings to the life and times of Jesus, rather than the life and times of the Church. It is here that Charles W.F. Smith claims that Form Criticism becomes very endangered. The form critics tend to use the Gospels as evidence for the life of the early Church and then they use that same evidence to criticize the Gospels. 112/273

3C. DID THE CREATIVE COMMUNITY LACK EYEWITNESS EVIDENCE?

Gundry writes:

"In the next place, it was demonstrated that the idea of a creative community is an impossible entity. Besides the fact that communities do not have this power, it would have been impossible for the community to function in this manner because of the presence of eyewitnesses. The community could only have passed on a tradition grounded in the facts." 57/64, 65

Questioning the ability of a community without eyewitnesses, Gundry reasons:

"Is it conceivable that in its own discussions and disputes the early church would not have examined doubtful statements concerning Jesus' ministry? If they, in fact, did not examine such statements with careful scrutiny, why is there such uniform agreement as to the nature and details of that ministry? A community that was purely creative and lacking in the powers of discrimination would have found it impossible to form a uniform and consistent tradition. The traditon must have been under the control of eyewitnesses within the church." 55/35, 36

Redlich comments that "some form critics in tracing the influence of the community mean to imply that much of the material, both narratives and sayings, were created by and in the communities. They were then attributed to Jesus. That is to say, the communities were bereft of apostles and eyewitnesses whose presence would check any unhistorical tendency. They only created myths. The early primitive Church consisted of men and women who were under the influence of fantasy." 101/60, 61

Guthrie challenges the principle of a "created" faith by stating:

"The uniqueness of the material is because of the uniqueness of the Person in whom it is centered and for whom the early Christians were prepared to suffer even death. Any Form Criticism which loses sight of this becomes at once divorced from reality. The Christians would not have been prepared to die in order to defend the products of their own imaginations." 131/211

4C. DID THE NEW TESTAMENT WRITERS PASS ON ACCURATE TRADITION?

Guthrie remarks about the Christian community's belief in the authenticity of the traditions of Christ:

"It seems most natural to assume that the Christian traditions were transmitted because they were believed to be authentic and were most probably regarded as authentic in the form in which they were transmitted. This means that the 'forms' were essential parts of the tradition and were not, as some form critics have maintained, the productions of the community." 131/231

Referring to the New Testament's accuracy, Manson proposes:

"There is a simple test that can be applied to theories that suggest the tradition about Jesus is in any considerable degree the creation of the Christian community. We possess a fair selection of the written works of one of the most influential figures in the Church during the period in which the Gopsel tradition took shape. St. Paul's letters were all written before the earliest Gospel. The Roman community—the traditional home of St. Mark's Gospel—possessed the Epistle to the Romans before it possessed the Roman Gospel of Mark. The Pauline letters abound in utterances which could easily be transferred to Jesus and presented to the world as oracles of the Lord. How many are? None. It seems a little odd that, if the story of Jesus was the creation of the Christian community, no use should have been made of the admirable materials offered by one of the most able, active, and influential members of the community." 133/

The form critics have a real hang-up in dealing with the different emphases in the Gospels, especially between Mark and Matthew. G.E. Ladd asserts that this is no problem; it makes historical sense to conclude that Mark was written to meet the needs of a Gentile audience and Matthew was written to a Jewish Christian community. Obviously the sketch that each author would present should vary so as to more adequately meet the needs of the audience. 74/161

Gundry questions the circumstances and qualities of a "creative community" and brings the accuracy dispute to light:

"From the book of Acts it is evident that the early Christians were men of varied races and cultures. Yet their faith demanded complete submission to the moral precepts of and worship of an obscure Jew, crucified by a Roman governor. It required complete severance from Judaism and heathenism. But this was accomplished in such far distant places as Rome in the short time between Jesus' death and Paul's letter to Rome. Can it seriously be supposed that this is the result of a creative community?" 56/142

5C. DOES THE EMPHASIS ON COMMUNITY CREATIVITY DIMINISH THE CHARACTER OF JESUS?

A.M. Hunter notes that "far too much is ascribed to the creation of the Early Church; far too little to the creative genius of the Church's Founder." 65/14

Bruch holds that "while the form in which much of the Gospel material has been preserved may be explained in terms of a life-setting in the primitive Church, the material itself demands a life-setting in the Palestinian ministry of Jesus." 15/12

Or, put more simply, Bruch says:

"A 'life-setting' in the early Church does not preclude a prior 'life-setting' in the life of Jesus Himself." 16/73

Davies comments on the teaching ability of Jesus:

"Much Form Criticism has been unnecessarily sceptical about the amount of teaching which can be traced back to Jesus himself. If the coming of the Christ in the flesh interested Christians, they must have been concerned with the details of his life in the flesh. Another way of asserting the same thing is to recognize that Form Criticism has ascribed to the Christian communities a role, in the creation of the tradition preserved in the Gospels, which is exaggerated. The New Testament witnesses to virile, expanding Christian communities, it is true, but also to confused and immature ones. It is more likely that the trust, the creativity, the originality which lies behind the Gospel tradition of the works and words of Jesus should be credited to him rather than to the body of Christians. The kind of penetrating insight preserved in the Gospels points not to communities—mixed and often muddled in their thinking—but to a supreme source in a single person, Jesus, Rabbi and prophet." 33/115

Filson continues the remarks about the distinctive teaching style:

"Finally, all attempts to make the apostolic age responsible for the creation of any considerable amount of the Gospel material shatter upon the evidence of the parables. This is the characteristic teaching form in the Synoptic Gospels. *It is noticeably absent from the rest of the New Testament and from other early Christian literature.* If the apostolic age had created these masterly mediums of teaching, other writings of that time would naturally have reflected the same method. But they do not. The primitive Church preserved a sense of the difference between Jesus' teaching method and their own ideas and methods.

"If the Gospels had been written in a Church lacking historical perspective, they would surely reveal the same traits found in the other literature written in that period. On the contrary, they prove to be sources for the life of Jesus which are not largely affected by the mood and movements of the apostolic age." 47/109

Guthrie further cites Jesus' teaching qualities:

(1) "Because Christ as a Teacher was greater than the community He founded, the form as well as the content of the oral tradition was characteristic of His teaching and personality, and not that of the community.

(2) "Variations of His teachings may not be considered unhistorical on this account, since Jesus may have repeated certain teachings at different times and in different forms." 131/211

The creative character of Jesus is referred to by Wikenhauser:

"It is false to ascribe the making of tradition to anonymous forces, to say that it was the community and the faith of the community which formed and handed on the tradition about Jesus. Creative power belongs not to a mass but only to individuals who tower over the mass." 126/277

Jesus' unique personality is again emphasized, this time by Peritz:

"It is the Jesus of history that is the only efficient genesis of the gospel tradition. If it had not been for His potent personality there would have been no gospel tradition. No explanation of the written Gospels is worthy of notice that minimizes the living and historic reality of the personality of Jesus. Form Criticism at this point is but one step removed from the myth theory. For whereas the myth theory resolved Jesus into an astral deity without historic existence, Form Criticism makes Him the product of the early Church. Against both errors we posit as the first stage in the gospel tradition the historic Jesus." 95/199

2A. AN ILLITERATE COMMUNITY

1B. Basic Assumption Pertaining to the Backgrounds of Early Christians

Grant theorizes that "the earliest Christians were into a literary, not even, for the most part, and educated group—as we should define 'educated.' 'Not many wise after the flesh, not many mighty, not many noble, are called; but God chose the foolish things of the world, that he might put to shame them that are wise....' (I Cor. i. 26ff.). They were the humble, the simple, and many of them were no doubt illiterate. God chose to reveal himself to 'babes'—'little ones' is an interchangeable synonym for disciples in one important section of the Palestinian or Syrian Gospel of Matthew (x. 42, xi. 25, etc.)." 53/40

Dibelius refers to this unusual paradox in the community:

"The paradox has become probable to us that unliterary men created a definite style." 36/37

He goes on to describe this illiterate people and their purpose:

"The company of unlettered people which expected the end of the world any day had neither the capacity nor the inclination for the production of books, and we must not predicate a true literary activity in the Christian Church of the first two or three decades. The materials which have been handed down to us in the Gospels lived in these decades an unliterary life or had indeed as yet no life at all." 36/9

Therefore Dibelius states how we can intrepret the production of the Gospel forms:

"To understand the categories of popular writings as they developed in the sphere of unliterary people we must enquire into their life and, in our special case, which deals with religious texts, into the customs of their worship." 36/8

2B. Basic Answer to an Illiterate Community Assumption

In consideration of the critics' assumption of an illiterate community, one must wonder how these men regard the scholarship of early Christian leaders such as Luke, James and, most notably, Paul. Filson clarifies the position on illiteracy of the community:

"It has already been pointed out that form criticism has erred and given a one-sided picture by depicting the transmission of the tradition as being exclusively in the hands of simple fold untrained in literary matters. Men of education and discernment were present and influential in the Church at all times. There were teachers whose special responsibility required their constant attention to the tradition. What form criticism learns about the perpetuation of folklore among simple, backward people is not a real parallel to the process in the primitive Church." 47/107

Filson specifically points out:

"However, a picture of primitive Christianity as composed solely of illiterate folk of the lowest class is not what any of our records suggest. There were 'teachers' who had both the ability and the zeal to give intelligent attention to the tradition. Moreover, there were educated people, among whom we may name Stephen, Philip, Barnabas, Mark, and Paul as examples, who are not to be ignored in any estimate of the intellectual and social level of the primitive Church." 47/104, 105

Peritz asserts that "the illiteracy and lack of literary and historical interest of the disciple circle, which form critics stress so extravagantly, are exaggerations and woefully needed *ex hypothesi.*" 95/199

3A. A PAROUSIA CONSCIOUS AND SALVATION-MINDED COMMUNITY

1B. Basic Assumption

Bultmann refers to the expectancy of the parousia as he notes that "in early Christianity history is swallowed up in eschatology. The early Christian community understands itself not as a historical but as an eschatological phenomenon. It is conscious that it belongs no longer to the present world but to the new Aeon which is at the door. The question then is how long this consciousness can remain vivid, how long the expectation of the imminent end of the world can remain unshaken." 20/51

He expounds further on the anticipation of the Second Coming:

"How did the developing Church endure and overcome its disappointment that the parousia of Christ failed to materialize? The first answer is that the disappointment did not take place suddenly, not everywhere at the same time. The 'time-between' was never reckoned by fixed months or years, as it once was in the Jewish apocalyptic and often later in the history of the Church; the parousia of Christ was never expected on a fixed day; it was believed that God had fixed the day and that no man knew it. By this faith the disappointment and the doubts which awoke here and there could be stilled, and it is a fact that the Christians gradually became accustomed to waiting. Certainly, in times of oppression or persecution the expectation of the near end of the world and the hope of it flamed up passionately. But, on the other hand, the Pastoral Epistles show that the Christians gradually slid into a manner of life which was both Christian and civic at the same time, and various admonitions here and there to be patient, waiting, and vigilant indicate the same." 20/51

Dibelius directs us toward the community's concentration on salvation:

"The oldest traditions of Jesus came into existence because the community was in need of them—a community which had no thought of biography or of world-history but of salvation—a community which had a desire to write books but only to preserve all that was necessary for preaching. That must be made absolutely clear unless we are to approach the Christian tradition with the wrong questions." 37/30

Thus he concludes about the information concerning Jesus that was preserved by the community:

"If they (the community) were eager to know about that past or describe it, they had only to think of the salvation which it had guaranteed to them." 37/28, 29

2B. Basic Answer

Redlich reveals Form Criticism's oversight of the faith of the early Church:

"Form Criticism by too great an emphasis on the expected Parousia has lost sight of the normal life which men lived though the Parousia was held to be imminent." 101/79

Then he challenges the form critics' belief in a "Parousia conscious" community:

"The Acts, Q, and the Epistles bear witness to the multiplicity of interests which affected the life of the Chruch. However much the expected Parousia controlled the life and conduct of the early Christians, we find them living a normal life, interested for example in supplying the needs of the poor (Acts 4:34, 6:1-6). Paul was insistent that the Corinthian Church should abound in the work of the Lord (I Cor. 15:58). The stories would therefore illustrate and encourage Christians as well as would be converts in giving teaching on all the practical interests of daily life." 101/59, 60

Martin points to the balanced faith of the Christians:

"The categories of the Synoptics do not easily fit the frame of existential historicity. Nor does the kerygma of Jesus about the kingdom of God fit the frame of individualistic pietism. Rather the Kerygma of Jesus with his awareness of an interval between Passion and Parousia points to a larger concept of the history of salvation in keeping with the Old Testament background." 79/23

4A. CONCLUSION

Piper professes that "the universal adherence to the gospel pattern proves that for the primitive church the gospel story had supernatural kerygmatic authority. That would hardly be the case if the gospel material had been invented to satisfy the desires and wishes of the congregation." 136/124

The division of forms and the appeal to the "Primitive Community " for their source does not belong in the realm of objective literary criticism.

Pierre Benoit concludes:

"It is plain that this method which at first sight seemed original and full of promise is revealed to be artificial and subjective as soon as it is rigidly applied. Admittedly there are certain distinct and recognisable forms in the Gospel. But it is impossible to refer them back to specific functions of the primitive community without artificiality; they include only part, and that a small one, of the gospel tradition; and lastly they are incapable, by themselves, of guaranteeing any judgement of the historical value of their content." 58/26

Benoit adds to the above that "in order to pass any judgement of this kind, it is necessary to pass from the study of the form to the study of the substance, from literary criticism to the analysis of reality; and, as we shall soon see, this leads to a return to a kind of criticism which has nothing new about it, but is only too well known." 58/26

Hunter underlines an interesting point about the creative Christian community. He points out that "the form critics make much of the creative part played by the early community in the formation of the Gospel tradition. The implication is that the Christian church manufactured much of the Gospel material in order to explain her faith. And we cannot help asking: if early Christian faith created the Gospel record, what created Christian faith?" 174/40

Guthrie reiterates the weakness of the "creative community" theory by concluding:

"Whatever part the community played in the process of transmission, it is inconceivable that the community created either the sayings of Jesus or the narratives about Him. The Christian communities were groups of people who had 'received' Christian traditions, and had believed them to be true and on the basis of them had made personal committal of themselves to Christ. No other explanation can make early Christian development intelligible. The future of form criticism will largely depend on the degree to which this fact is recognized." 131/231

Philospher, economist and noted historian, John Stuart Mill, proclaims:

"It is of no use to say that Christ as exhibited in the Gospels is not historical, and that we do not know how much of what is admirable has been super-added by the tradition of His followers. Who among His disciples, or among their proselytes, was capable of inventing the sayings ascribed to Jesus, or of imagining the life and character revealed in the Gospels?" cited by 138/154

Neill concludes that only Jesus had the capacity to create such a high caliber of spiritual truth:

"To sum up so much spiritual truth so simply, so briefly, and in such unforgettable images demands creative genius of the highest possible calibre. Who in the early Christian groups had such genius? Paul, on occasion, is capable of flights of lyric splendour; but he has not a plastic, visual imagination of the kind that expresses itself in such forms as the story of the temptation. In the first century we know of one man, and one only, who had that kind of imagination, and that kind of power over words. His name was Jesus of Nazareth." 187/251

Vincent Taylor, himself a form critic, makes known the results of overemphasizing the influence of the Christian community:

"Form-Criticism is justified in calling attention to the influence of the Christian community, but it has been carried beyond the bounds of probability. It has fostered a doubtful equanimity in the attitude of many scholars to the alleged activity of the Church in transforming the original tradition, and has encouraged a readiness to embark on the waters of an adventurous typology which travels far beyond its limited developments in the New Testament." 117/357

George Eldon Ladd believes that anyone who holds the view "that the Gospels do not preserve authentic traditions but embody to a considerable degree material created by the communities overlooks four important facts: (1) the brief period of time which elapsed between the events and the record of the events, (2) the role of eyewitnesses in preserving the tradition, (3) the role of the authoritative apostolic witness, and (4) the role of the Holy Spirit." 74/163

5A. IN SUMMARY

1B. Form Criticism assumes the Gospels were written because of the early Christian community's need to preserve and explain their faith and that the Gospels are not historic or authentic. A creative community, not the Holy Spirit, is the author of these four accounts.

2B. The answer to this assumption is that the early Christian community was too focused on the facts to "create" Jesus' sayings.

3B. Form Criticism assumes the early Christians were illiterate.

4B. The answer—evidence reveals that educated men (Paul) were very much a part of the primitive Church.

5B. Form Criticism assumes that the early Church was too Second Coming conscious and hope oriented to be rational and historical.

6B. The answer—Acts, Q and the Epistles reveal that the early Christians led normal, practical lives. They were admonished to abound in the work of the Lord, not as if they expected to be "taken up" at any moment.

7B. The caliber of the Gospel message is too high to have originated with a creative community.

chapter 22

no biographical interest

1A. BASIC ASSUMPTION

Form Criticism assumes that the early Christian community had no biographical interest, so the Gospels have no biographical, chronological or geographical value.

Gundry begins:

"This assumption postulates a creative community that is lacking in biographical interest and yet creates a tradition to meet its own needs. What these needs were can be discovered by the form of each unit. Thus, the Gospels are primarily sources of information about the life of the early church, not the life of Christ. The units were then strung together in an artificial context by the evangelists, whose primary task was redaction. Such is the assumption with its implications." 57/42

The original purpose of the Gospels is set forth by McKnight:

"The Gospels are not biographies of Jesus written for historical purposes by the original disciples of Jesus; rather, they are religious writings produced a generation after the earthly Jesus to serve the life and faith of the early church." 83/2

And what was eventually included in the Gospels is deduced by Filson:

"It was not mere historical or biographical interest that governed the choice of what survived. The choice, according to the form critic, was governed by the usage and needs of the Church." 47/95

Wikenhauser confirms:

"The Gospels are not biographies, but testimonials to faith. They do not describe the life of Jesus in the sense of following the exterior and interior development of his life and work, depicting his personality and demonstrating his significance in history. They are connected with the primitive Christian proclamation of faith, and in so far as they are a record of Jesus' words and deeds they tell of the works, teaching, and Passion of the God-sent Saviour of men; they thereby make his work as Saviour live before the eyes of the Christian community. But they lack almost entirely what is indispensable to a biography: the origin and youth of the hero, his spiritual development, the depiction of his character, a theme, and a chronology." 126/255, 256

Smith states the position of most radical critics:

"To say that the Gospels do not yield material for a biography of Jesus is by now a cliché. The attempt to recover history from the Gospels is beset by such grave difficulties that only those who have studied the attempt can gage the dimensions of the problem. It is popularly supposed that form-criticism has necessitated this conclusion." 112/266

1B. The Position of Dibelius

Dibelius proclaims:

"All these considerations confirm this judgment: the oldest traditions of Jesus came into existence because the community was in need of them—a community which had no thought of biography or of world-history but of salvation—a community which had no desire to write books but only to preserve all that was necessary for preaching." 37/30

The concern for the tradition which culminated in the Gospels arose around the interest of the churches in preaching, worship and teaching. As Dibelius writes:

"Concern for the tradition arose from this necessity, and not from literary or biographical requirements." 36/30

Dibelius notes that with the growth and spread of public worship people desired to see an overall picture of Jesus in the story of salvation. He continues:

"That could be accomplished if traits proper to worship were introduced, e.g. into individual miracle stories." 35/47

Dibelius would have us "cast our vote" for Jesus, a "political candidate with no qualifications" when he writes:

"The fact that Jesus was a man is decisive for faith; how this earthly life was lived seems to be of no importance." 37/12

2B. The Position of Bultmann

Bultmann's position is summarized by McGinley who relates his position on Jesus:

"We know nothing of Jesus' life, only His message. We possess this message only as it was presented by the community. The Gospel of John is not a source of this presentation. In the synoptic Gospels everything of Hellenistic origin is to be set aside. Of the remainder, all that betrays community interests or advanced development is to be excluded. The resultant oldest stratum was possibly the product of a complicated process no longer discernible. It is questionable how far the picture of Jesus presented by the community in this oldest stratum is a true one. The thought-content of the stratum is probably Jesus', but it makes no difference if it is not." 82/27

In one of his most famous books, *Jesus and the Word*, Bultmann declares:

"I do indeed think that we can now know almost nothing concerning the life and personality of Jesus, since the early Christian sources show no interest in either, are moreover fragmentary and often legendary; and other sources about Jesus do not exist." 23/8

Bultmann doesn't agree with those that say the early Christians had a biographical interest, but he circularly argues:

"Those apothegms which are of a biographical character are likewise for the most part creations of the community, since they give expression to what Christians had experienced of their Master or what he had experienced at the hands of his people." 19/45

3B. The Position of Taylor

Taylor asserts the complete lack of a biographical interest in the community:

"The Evangelists could not succeed because for a generation at least a Christianity had existed which was destitute of the biographical interest: no one thought of recording the life of Christ." 114/143, 144

He then clarifies the biographical interest question:

"If by a 'biographical interest' we mean a wish to tell stories from the life of Jesus, the first Christians had such an interest; but if we mean the desire to trace the course of a man's life, to show how one thing led to another, to depict the development of his personality, to make him real to the imagination and the understanding, the first Christians had no such interest." 114/144

Finalizing his argument, he asserts:

"Nothing is so revealing as a biography—about the author! But we can dispense with fuller knowledge about the Evangelists because we have been spared the veil which well-intentioned biographers would have cast over the face of Jesus. Because the Gospels are not biographies, we know Him better." 114/145

2A. BASIC ANSWER

1B. Description of a Biography

Davies defines the three forms of biographies:

"Of late it has been frequently asserted that the Gospels are not biographies. But this admission must not be too exclusively interpreted. As a genre of literature, biography, in its mature form, has only emerged in the last three centuries and it has assumed three forms: (1) That in which the biographical data are fused, the biographer himself being present in the work as omniscient narrator (we think of Morley's *Life of Gladstone* as one example of this). Obviously the Gospels are not biographies in this sense. (2) That in which there is a free creation, in the biographer's own words, the result being something akin to the painter's portrait—an impression, which may, in fact, be more 'true' than the first type of biography mentioned. But, again, the Gospels are not such individualistic, impressionistic creations; the role of the community in the formation of the tradition rules out such extreme personalism. (3) That in which the biographer arranges traditional documentary and other material to produce an integrated work. With this last type the Gospels can broadly be compared, i.e., they manipulate traditional material with seriousness." 34/94

Filson extends the modern definition further:

"Let a number of modern biographies be examined. They will follow a rough chronological framework, but within those limits the various interests of the person depicted will become centers around which material is gathered. Each chapter will trace one line of interest." 47/103

2B. Biographical Interest of Gospels Established

Barnes brings to light the biographical interest:

"When critics deny the preservation of an 'historical' (or, better, a 'biographical') tradition of the ministry of Jesus, they forget that Jesus had a mother who survived Him, and also devoted followers both women and men. Are we to believe that these stored up no memories of the words (and acts also) of the Master? And the Twelve—though they often misunderstood Him, would they not preserve among themselves either by happy recollection or by eager discussion many of His startling sayings and of His unexpected deeds? And was not the eager expectation itself of the second coming based on a lively memory of the blessings of the first coming manifested in the Galilean ministry? Such, surely, are the probabilities, and the probabilities receive confirmation from vivid touches which are seen constantly in Mark, which is confessedly the earliest of our Gospels." 6/15, 16

Davies explains that the interest of the Church in the life of Jesus accounts for the emergence of the Gospels by concluding that "it is difficult to understand—if the early churches were uninterested in the life of Jesus to any considerable degree—why Gospels should have emerged at all. On the other hand, if the early Churches were concerned to witness to the 'story' of Jesus, the emergence of the Gospel form becomes easily intelligible, and the preservation of geographic and chronological data in the Gospels natural." 33/117

Peritz reasons why the critics are against biographical interest:

"Discarding the testimony of Papias and Luke that these sources are based on the reports of eye witnesses and contain biographical and historical data, Form Critics substitute for an alleged internal evidence to the effect that these sources contain no historical or biographical data for the construction of a life of Jesus." 95/200, 201

Martin declares that:

"It was not a little only of Jesus that was remembered but a great deal (cf. John 21:25). What took place in the first decades of the Christian Church was not the adaptation and elaboration of a few reminiscences to increase their usefulness but the selection from a host of reminiscences of those that appeared most valuable." 80/112

An important point is established by Gundry concerning community biographical interest in Jesus:

"The centrality of Jesus to the Christian message indicates that the early church had a very intense desire to know more about Jesus, and that they would have been very discriminating in their acceptance of accounts of His life." 55/39

3B. Evidence of Biographical Interest in the Gospels

Concerning biographical, historical, and geographical evidence in Mark, Barnes writes:

"From the fact of the preservation of these geographical details, as well as of the names of persons by the Second Evangelist, we have good reason to draw the conclusion that the vivid touches also, which illuminate many of the episodes related by St. Mark, are due not to the literary art of the Evangelist but to the fact that he drew from a living tradition." 6/11, 12

Barnes cites a specific example in Mark:

"But St. Mark's treatment of Pilate and of the condemnation of Jesus warns us that the Christian tradition was biographical rather than 'historical.' This

Evangelist does not tell us even that Pilate was governor ('Procurator') of Judaea: he was not interested in Pilate, but only in Pilate's belief in the innocence of Jesus. But the Christian tradition which St. Mark followed had a vivid biographical memory. It told that Simon of Cyrene, the father of Alexander and Rufus, had borne the cross of Jesus, and it recorded the names of three of the women who saw Jesus die— Mary Magdalene, Mary the mother of James the less, and Salome [Mark 15]." 6/11, 12

Manson strengthens the biographical evidences in Mark with a pointed query:

"But if the outline had then to be created *ad hoc*, it can only be that for the thirty years between the end of the Ministry and the production of *Mark*, Christians in general were not interested in the story of the Ministry and allowed it to be forgotten. One would like to know why the first generation were not interested while the second generation demanded a continuous narrative. More than that, we need some explanation why it was possible for the details of the story to be remembered and the general outline forgotten. It is not the normal way of remembering important periods in our experience." 133/5

Burkitt strongly asserts a biographical interest in Mark:

"In reviewing Sundwall's *Die Zusammensetzung des Markus-evangeliums* in the *Journal of Theological Studies* (April, 1935, pp.186-8) Burkitt wrote: 'In opposition to the opinion of many scholars I feel that Mark *is* a Biography, if by Biography we mean the chief outlines of a career, rather than a static characterization. In Mark there is movement and progression.... It does not sound to me like *Gemeindetheologie*, the unconscious secretion of a community of believers. Nothing but a strong element of personal reminiscence could have produced it. And therefore I still hold to the belief that it embodies the private reminiscences of Peter, supplemented for the last week by the reminiscences of the young Mark himself.'" cited by 114/ix

Vincent Taylor adds to Burkitt's observation:

"In no way, it seems to me, does Form-Criticism weaken this judgment." 114/ix

Ladd observes the biographical methodology in Matthew:

"In other words, Matthew deliberately rearranges Mark's order of events, not because he thought they were historically wrong and he wishes to correct Mark's errors, but because a topical rearrangement better suited Matthew's purpose. A failure to recognize fully that the Evangelists obviously had no biographical concerns will result in attributing to them alleged historical errors that are in reality no part of their purpose and should not therefore be seen as errors at all." 74/167

G.N. Stanton in his chapter, "Ancient Biographical Writing," in *Jesus of Nazareth in New Testament Preaching*, referring to the view that Gospel accounts offer no comparison to Hellenistic biography, states:

"This view, which seeks to establish the perspective of the Gospels partly from a comparison with ancient biographical writing, has been extremely influential, but it is based on a quite surprisingly inaccurate assessment of ancient biographical writing." 11/118

Stanton continues by demonstrating that the Gospels are not so different from ancient biography so as to preclude any similarity. The evidence is quite substantial for the Gospels to be placed in that literary and historical milieu. 11/117-136

Moreland concludes his excellent section on "The Gospels and Ancient Biographies" with:

"An important conclusion has been reached. The Gospels do have enough in common with ancient biographies to be called biographical. And one purpose of biography was to give a prose narrative presenting supposedly historical facts which were to reveal the character of the figure, often with a view toward affecting the reader's behavior. More specifically, the Gospels at least partially served the purpose of distortions. But a question arises at this point." 9/87

Concerning the biographical interest of the early Church, Gundry observes the words of Paul and Luke:

(1)   "If there were no biographical interest in the early church, why did Paul distinguish between his words and the Lord's words (I Cor. 7:10, 12, 25)?

(2)   "If the early church had no biographical interest, why had many taken in hand to draw up narratives of the events of Jesus' life,

(3)   "and why had they used the material of eyewitnesses (Luke 1:1-2)? If such were the case, why did Luke add to this collection an accurate account of the Lord's ministry after having done his own careful research (Luke 1:3-4)?

(4)   "If these early Christians had no biographical interest, why did they bother to appeal constantly to the fact that they were eyewitnesses of the events concerning which they spoke?

(5)   "The Form Critics must discredit the book of Acts and Luke's prologue if they are to claim seriously that the early church had no biographical interest." 55/38

4B. Conclusion

Bultmann writes, in his *History of the Synoptic Tradition*, that tradition is not the product of Jesus' life, but that Jesus' life is the product of tradition. When tradition is removed, very little of Jesus is left.

G.E. Ladd articulates his criticism of the form critics' stand on the biographical interest of the community:

"We must insist that it is poor criticism to demand biographical precision of the Evangelists when they themselves obviously did not intend it. This does not mean that we can go all the way with the form critics. Their conclusion that we have no trustworthy historical outline for the life of Jesus does not follow." 75/168

Manson asserts that "it is at least conceivable that one of the chief motives for preserving the stories at all, and for selecting those that were embodied in the Gospels, was just plain admiration and love for their hero. It is conceivable that he was at least as interesting, for his own sake, to people in the first century as he is to historians in the twentieth." 133/6

Harrison affirms that "the very idea that there was no biographical interest on the part of the early church in Jesus of Nazareth is incredible." 58/150

3A. IN SUMMARY

1B.   The form critic assumes the early Christian community had no biographical, chronological or geographical interest.

2B.   The answer—Why did Mark state geographical and biographical details if he had no interest in preserving interest? Why did the disciples stress the fact they were eyewitnesses? Why did the disciples remember and write down the events of Jesus' life if they had no biographical interest?

chapter 23

laws
of
tradition

Form Criticism assumes that the original form of tradition can be recovered and its history before being written down can be traced by discovering the laws of tradition.

1A. BASIC ASSUMPTION

Form critics believe that by comparing the pre-literary forms of oral tradition in other societies with those of the gospel that we can come to some conclusions concerning "the laws which operate as formative factors in popular tradition, [M. Dibelius, *From Tradition to Gospel*, Ivor, Nicholson, and Watson, 1934, p.7] certain definite principles of transformation [143/20]." 119/471

These laws are:

"(1) As time goes on, the oral tradition becomes embellished by the elaboration of simple themes and by the addition of new detail. It becomes both longer and more complex. Consequently, it can be taken as virtually axiomatic that 'the simpler version represents the original' [143/23]. (2) As time goes on, there is a tendency for the particular to become general, and for a statement with local significance to become a statement with universal significance. In the situation faced by the expanding Church, this tendency was accentuated. (3) As time goes on, the material often changes in form, becoming more dramatic by the addition of vivid detail, by the transformation of indirect into direct narration, etc. (4) And, as time goes on, concepts are added which would have been unfamiliar and unnatural in the original situation." 119/471

L.J. McGinley has analyzed the approach that the radical critics have taken concerning the authentication of the Synoptic material. He has concluded:

"While reconstructing the transmission of the synoptic material, form-critics have attempted to estimate whether it could have been transmitted with historical truthfulness. Their conclusions have been negative." 82/12

Filson notes what the critics concluded:

"The Gospels become an important source of information about the life, interests, problems, and development of the apostolic age. In fact, that is precisely what the form critic claims. This position may be most sharply and drastically formulated in the statement that the Gospels are a primary source for the study of the apostolic age, but only secondarily of value for study of the life of Jesus." 47/99

A.H. McNeile has observed that "a rule about such traditions appears to be that a cycle of legends is less primitive than the separate story, which serves as the basic unit. Each unit has its particular colouring so that if two stories are combined the colours are blurred. In a primitive unit the actors are few and the action is short, vivid, and direct. The unit is apt to end with an oral generalization or to include a striking saying which would be easily remembered and for which the framework of the story may serve simply as the scaffolding." 85/48

1B. Martin Dibelius

Dibelius approaches this particular issue in the following manner:

"In each case we must inquire (1) as to *the motive* which caused the spreading of the reminiscences, although the feelings and desires of the people were directed towards the future, and (2) as to *the law* which governed their spreading and which helped to form and to preserve what had been said. If there is no such law, then the writing of the Gospels implies not an organic development of the process by means of collecting, trimming, and binding together, but the beginning of a new and purely literary development. If there was no such motive, then it is quite impossible to understand how men who made no pretentions to literature could create a tradition which constituted the first steps of the literary production which was even then coming into being." 36/11

Dibelius continues by alleging that "the first Christians had no interest in reporting the life and passion of Jesus objectively to mankind, *sine ira et studio*. They wanted nothing else than to win as many as possible to salvation in the last hour just before the end of the world, which they believed to be at hand. Those early Christians were not interested in history." 37/16

Dibelius concludes by remarking that "a further limitation of the historicity of the tradition is entailed by this concentration of interest on its missionary application. The stories are couched in a certain style, that is to say, they are told in a way calculated to edify believers and to win over unbelievers. They are not objective accounts of events." 37/76

2B. Rudolf Bultmann

Rudolf Bultmann concurs with Dibelius' skeptical approach to the study of the tradition:

"The doubt as to whether Jesus really existed is unfounded and not worth refutation. No sane person can doubt that Jesus stands as founder behind the historical movement whose first distinct stage is represented by the oldest Palestinian community. But how far that community preserved an objectively true picture of him and his message is another question." 23/13

Much of what Bultmann claims is based upon the position held by Julius

Wellhausen, another noted biblical scholar. Here Bultmann refers to his predecessor:

"Wellhausen said the Spirit of Jesus undoubtedly breathes in the utterances derived from the community at Jerusalem; but we do not derive a historical picture of Jesus himself from the conception of Jesus which prevailed in the community." 135/341

3B. Vincent Taylor

Taylor does not concur with Bultmann and Dibelius. He maintains that "Bultmann takes no account of the existence of eyewitnesses. The orphaned Christian community has no leaders to whom it can appeal for an account of what Jesus said: it might have been marooned on an island in the Greek Archipelago! This attitude is due to Bultmann's preoccupation with forms, but it vitiates a study of the question of genuineness from the beginning." 114/107

Taylor tends to accept the historic authenticity of the tradition, for as he states:

"The presence of eyewitnesses, for at least a generation, would serve as a check on corruptions innocently due to the imagination." 114/207

4B. Summary

The radical critics have alleged that the tradition is historically unsound. Their basic criterion has been the laws of tradition and their ramifications.

Ernst Käsemann helps to approach this problem as he explains:

"To state the paradox as sharply as possible: the community takes so much trouble to maintain historical continuity with him who once trod this earth that it allows the historical events of this earthly life to pass for the most part into oblivion and replaces them by its own message." 68/20

R.H. Lightfoot adds:

"It seems, then, that the form of the earthly no less than of the heavenly Christ is for the most part hidden from us. For all the inestimable value of the gospels, they yield us little more than a whisper of his voice; we trace in them but the outskirts of his ways." 76/225

Eyewitness testimony is noticeably absent from the considerations of the Form Critics. Bultmann explains this by noting:

"Is it enough to say that faith grows out of the encounter with the Holy Scriptures as the Word of God, that faith is nothing but simple hearing? The answer is yes. But this answer is valid only if the Scriptures are understood neither as a manual of doctrine nor as a record of witnesses to a faith which I interpret by sympathy and empathy." 22/71

H.N. Ridderbos goes one step further:

"What can we do with the mythological story of the resurrection? We can no longer accept it as a miraculous event which supplies us with the objective proof of Christ's significance. It is true that it is so thought of repeatedly in the New Testament (Acts 17:31). and Paul also tries to establish with certainty the resurrection as a historical event by enumerating the eye witnesses (I Corinthians 15:3-8). But this argumentation is fatal. The return of the dead to life is a mythical event; the resurrection cannot be established by witnesses as an objective fact, a guarantee of faith; the resurrection itself is an object of faith." 102/24, 25

2A. BASIC ANSWER

1B. The basic criterion of the historical authenticity judgment was the laws of tradition. But note:

"Even a quick comparison will show how striking are the differences between most of the principles of remembering as Bartlett [Bartlett, F.C. *Remembering*. (Cambridge: Cambridge University Press, 1932)] demonstrates them, and the principles of the transmission of narrative material which govern the conclusions of form criticism. According to the principles of form criticism, 'the simpler version represents the original'; according to the principles of remembering, the simpler form represents the end of a process of change. According to the former, unfamiliar material is added in the process of transmission; according to the latter, unfamiliar material is reduced in the process of remembering. According to the former, particular statements tend, with the passage of time, to become general, and local references to become universal; according to the latter, general statements almost invariably tend to become particular. Thus, if a general statement is found in a remembered narrative, it is likely to belong to an early stage in the process of remembering." 119/474, 475

W.S. Taylor continues, again referring to Bartlett's work titled *Remembering*:

"The process of remembering, he [Bartlett] says, always tends to produce a shortened and simplified version of the original. 'With frequent reproduction, omission of detail, simplification of events and structure...may go on almost indefinitely.' 'When a readily recognizable form is presented, this tends to undergo simplification into a genuinely conventionalized representation.' When the material presented is not originally in a readily recognizable form, then once memory has reduced it to 'some readily recognizable form...simplification sets in.'" 119/473

Vincent Taylor has conducted a study of oral tradition, and his conclusion is that orally transmitted material tends to be shortened or abbreviated. In spite of material being added to the tradition, Taylor finds it remarkable that the accounts almost always shorten. Things such as names of persons or places usually begin to be omitted the longer something is orally transmitted. And a general rounding of material with the subsequent omission of details is the normal end product of such a process. 114/124

E.L. Abel has observed:

"Contrary to the conclusions derived from Form Criticism, studies of rumor transmission indicate that *as information is transmitted, the general form or outline of a story remains intact, but fewer words and fewer original details are preserved*." 1/375, 376

As a result of his personal experiments, Vincent Taylor postulates:

"The experiments show that the tendency of oral transmission is definitely in the direction of *abbreviation*. Additions are certainly made in all good faith through misunderstandings and efforts to picture the course of events, but almost always the stories become shorter and more conventional.

"Such experiments suggest that longer Miracle-Stories, which are not products of literary art, stand near the records of eyewitnesses, and that the shorter and more conventional stories have passed through many hands before they were committed to writing." 114/124, 125

C.H. Dodd cites the emphasis the Gospel writers placed on facts, about Jesus as well as the teaching of Jesus:

"So far, the tradition behind the Gospels is strictly comparable with the contemporary oral traditions of Judaism. But in one point the Christian tradition departs from the Jewish model. The disciples of Jesus not only handed down what he taught. They laid at least equal stress upon certain facts about him. When Gospels came to be written, these facts bulked largely." 39/17

2B. The Effect of Eyewitnesses

As to the beginnings of the writings of the gospels, W.E. Barnes observes that "because of the wide-spread growth of the stories of Jesus and lack of Ministers, who were also eyewitnesses, it became very evident for the Word to be put full account in writing. St. Luke [Luke 1:2-4] acknowledged the need for writings. The converts too felt the need for written material to remind them of what they had heard." 6/2

James Martin concurs by adding that the disciples and followers of Jesus did not forget Him or His teachings due to constant repetition among themselves and occasional debate with their opponents. For the most part, this maintenance was oral but there was some early writing down of the tradition. As time passed and eyewitnesses died, the tradition began to be written into an official form, thus, our four Gospels. 80/24, 25

In conclusion, Harrison cites E. Fascher, author of *Die Formgeschichtliche Methode* (140), and his objection to form study:

"Because the materials of the Gospels are vastly different from the substance of folk literature, the literary laws governing popular tradition are not applicable. The subject matter of the Gospels is far more important than any literary form." 58/150

In reference to the lack of mention of the eyewitnesses' influence on the oral tradition, James Martin establishes that "it is easily forgotten and yet of considerable significance that in the oral period the traditions of Jesus were being quoted in the hearing of unbelievers, many of whom were antagonistic, as well as of believers. This also must have helped in no small measure to ensure that they suffered no substantial change in the course of their repetition. For the uncommitted and the hostile, quick to seize on any feature of the Christians' story which did not tally with its previous telling, would have made the most of the discrepancy. As a result, both in their public preaching and in debate and discussion, it would be impossible for the Christians to vary their stories in any material aspect from one telling to the other." 80/67, 68

Floyd Filson calls this lack of reference to eyewitnesses "the most flagrant" error of the form critics. He points out that "the most flagrant errors of form critics calls for mention. Folk tales do not reckon with eyewitnesses. Form critics also tend to forget them. Vincent Taylor reproaches extreme critics by saying that they act as though all eyewitnesses had been caught up to heaven immediately after Jesus' death. In contrast to this serious fault of much form criticism, we must hold that the eyewitnesses mentioned in Lk. 1:2 exercised a great control over the tradition in its early and crucial stage." 47/107, 108

Gundry adds:

"The failure of form criticism to account adequately for the role of eyewitnesses in the early church is sufficient to discredit its basic assumption with its implications. If there were eyewitnesses, there could have been no creative community that formed and transformed tradition to suit its own needs without regard to the truth. But the form critic ignores the possibility of eyewitnesses, for he is totally occupied with forms and the smooth working of a theory. He has not taken the time to examine the historical evidence." 55/34, 35

Vincent Taylor, who finds himself diametrically opposed to the form critics in this particular area, charges:

"It is on this question of eyewitnesses that Form-Criticism presents a very vulnerable front. If the Form-Critics are right, the disciples must have been translated to heaven immediately after the Resurrection. As Bultmann sees it, the primitive community exists *in vacuo*, cut off from its founders by the walls of an inexplicable ignorance." 114/41

He adds:

"All this is absurd; but there is a reason for this unwillingness to take into account the existence of leaders and eyewitnesses. Indeed, there are two reasons. By the very nature of his studies the Form-Critic is not predisposed in favour of eyewitnesses; he deals with oral forms shaped by nameless individuals, and the recognition of persons who enrich the tradition by their actual recollections comes as a disturbing element to the smooth working of the theory." 114/41

Taylor concludes by reiterating:

"However disturbing to the smooth working of theories the influence of eyewitnesses on the formation of the tradition cannot possibly be ignored. The one hundred and twenty at Pentecost did not go into permanent retreat; for at least a generation they moved among the young Palestinian communities, and through preaching and fellowship their recollections were at the disposal of those who sought information. . . . But when all qualifications have been made, the presence of personal testimony is an element in the formative process which it is folly to ignore. By its neglect of this factor Form-Criticism gains in internal coherence, but it loses its power to accomplish its main task which is to describe the *Sitz im Leben* of the tradition." 114/42, 43

Alfred Wikenhauser suggests:

"Against this it must be emphasized vigorously that we may not exclude from the formation of tradition the eyewitnesses of the life and work, passion and death of Jesus. Luke says explicitly that the accounts of his predecessors, which he knows and uses, were guaranteed by those 'who from the beginning were eye-witnesses and ministers of the word' (that is, of the proclamation of the Gospel), and he intends his own work to be a proof of all that his readers had learned (1, 1-4). Enough firsthand witnesses were still alive in the few decades during which tradition got its final shaping; we have only to think of Peter, James, and John, the pillars 'of the Church of Jerusalem (Gal. 2, 9) at the time of the Council of Jerusalem (cf. also 1 Cor. 15, 6).'" 126/276, 277

E.B. Redlich agrees:

"It will not follow that every detail of every narrative of our Lord's life can be guaranteed to be historically true because eye witnesses were alive when the first records were made. We must allow for personal errors, want of powers of scientific observation, the Eastern outlook and Modes of thought, misunderstandings and such like. Our claim is that there is prima-facie ground for assuming the substantial accuracy of the Gospel narrative." 101/36

A.M. Hunter comments on the form critics' view of the eyewitnesses at the time tradition was taking place:

"Reading the Form Critics, we get the impression that when the Gospel tradition was taking shape, all the eye-witnesses of our Lord's ministry were either dead or in hiding." 65/14

Robert Mounce concurs with the conclusion of Hunter when he states that apparently the eyewitnesses of the event were either dead or sleeping! There was not that long a period of time between the teachings of Jesus and the development of the Gospels. Eyewitnesses to the events still had to be on the scene. 144

On this volatile issue, E.B. Redlich upholds the questionable character of eyewitness testimony:

"In the earliest days there was no clamant need for an ordered Resurrection narrative. Eye-witnesses could testify to having seen Jesus after His Resurrection, and there were hundreds of them (1 Corinthians 15:6). The fact of the tremendous happening on Easter Day was assured by first-hand evidence of an indisputable character." 101/178, 179

Stanley Gundry summarizes by saying that "it cannot be successfully argued that the eyewitnesses had died before the oral tradition had reached a fixed form and then was finally put down into written form. F.F. Bruce, who accepts the priority of Mark, argues for written sources of the Synoptic Gospels not later than about A.D. 60.

"Even assuming that Source Criticism is valid, one must still allow for a crystallization of the tradition that is complete some years before it is written down. However, according to Galatians 2:9, James, Peter, and John were still alive." 57/47

Gundry adds that "the earliest that the event there recorded can be dated is A.D. 48. The earliest that I Corinthians can be dated is A.D. 55; but according to I Corinthians 15:6, a good number of eyewitnesses were still alive. In other words, it is not at all unlikely that by the time the gospel tradition was crystallized in its oral form according to the Form Critic and that by the time it was recorded in documents according to the Source Critic, there were still eyewitnesses alive that could either affirm or deny the authenticity of the material. It is not only unlikely that these eyewitnesses all would have died, it is almost impossible." 57/47

Even Dibelius himself admits the terrific impact that eyewitnesses must have played on the oral tradition:

"At the period when eye-witnesses of Jesus were still alive, it was not possible to mar the picture of Jesus in the tradition. Chronology furnished criterion for judging the evangelical tradition." 36/293

Allan Barr has concluded:

"If the Christians had a real interest in the accuracy of their traditions, they must have tested them by their own standards of evidence. Now it need hardly be said that we cannot expect these to be the standards of the modern historian. The impartial criticism of sources, the weighing of probabilities, the sifting and appraising of indirect evidence, were beyond the range of the early Christians and their contemporaries. Where, then, could men of the time and cultural level of the early Christians find standards to verify the facts reported to them, if so they wished to do? The answer is simply this—in the principle of corroboration by eye-witnesses." 8/401

Another possibility that the form critics failed to deal with is the influence that hostile eyewitnesses might have played on the oral tradition. With reference to these hostile eyewitnesses, Gundry remarks that "there were individuals antagonistic to Christianity outside the church who had been eyewitnesses of Jesus' ministry. Again, is it possible that they would have allowed false statements to pass as facts concerning His life which they also knew so well? Christianity would have opened itself to ridicule if it had created such stories to perpetuate itself." 55/36

James Martin adds:

"There can be little doubt that, if the Christians had been guilty of inconsistency in the repetition of their tradition, their enemies would have been able to rout them ignominiously from the field, making them a public laughing-stock and effectively ensuring that their preaching would have no impact on the minds of any who heard it." 80/68

The apostles, who surely desired to honor the Lord, would not have been a party to the habit of ascribing to Him facts that did not originate with Him. Further, hundreds of people in the early Church must have been a powerful restraining factor in keeping the tradition true to fact. 50/150

L.J. McGinley also recognizes the impact of the hostile witnesses:

"First of all eyewitnesses of the events in question were still alive when the tradition had been completely formed; and among these eyewitnesses were bitter enemies of the new religious movement. Yet the tradition claimed to narrate a series of well-known deeds and publicly taught doctrines at a time when false statements could, and would, be challenged." 82/25

3B. The Value of Hostile Witnesses

In *The New Testament Documents: Are They Reliable?* F.F. Bruce emphasizes the value of hostile witnesses:

"And it was not only friendly eyewitnesses that the early preachers had to reckon with; there were others less well disposed who were also conversant with the main facts of the ministry and death of Jesus. The disciples could not afford to risk inaccuracies (not to speak of wilful manipulation of the facts), which would at once be exposed by those who would be only too glad to do so. On the contrary, one of the strong points in the original apostolic preaching is the confident appeal to the knowledge of the hearers; they not only said, 'We are witnesses of these things,' but also, 'As you yourselves also know' (Acts ii. 22). Had there been any tendency to depart from the facts in any material respect, the possible presence of hostile witnesses in the audience would have served as a further corrective." 16/45, 46

He adds:

"We are, in fact, practically all the way through in touch with the evidence of eyewitnesses. The earliest preachers of the gospel knew the value of this first-hand testimony, and appealed to it time and again. 'We are witnesses of these things,' was their constant and confident assertion. And it can have been by no means so easy as some writers seem to think to invent words and deeds of Jesus in those early years, when so many of His disciples were about, who could remember what had and had not happened. Indeed, the evidence is that the early Christians were careful to distinguish between sayings of Jesus and their own inferences or judgments. Paul, for example, when discussing the vexed questions of marriage and divorce in I Corinthians vii, is careful to make this distinction between his own advice on the subject and the Lord's decisive ruling: 'I, not the Lord,' and again, 'Not I, but the Lord.'" 16/45, 46

In conclusion, Stan Gundry reiterates:

"An equally important factor is that there were individuals antagonistic to Christianity outside the church who had been eyewitnesses of Jesus' ministry. Again, is it possible that they would have allowed false statements to pass as facts concerning His life which they also knew so well? Christianity would have opened itself to ridicule if it had created such stories to perpetuate itself." 57/45

3A. CONCLUSION

L.J. McGinley has decided that using the methodology assumed by the form critics "leaves a mangled text, of interest neither to the primitive Christian nor the modern exegete." 82/70

P.G. Duncker refers to P. Benoit who asks if anything of historical worth can remain after the form critics have eliminated from the tradition most of the gospel material as unhistorical. He answers:

"Very little; a quite inoffensive residue: Jesus of Galilee, who thought himself to be a prophet, who must have spoken and acted accordingly, without our being able to say exactly what he spoke and how he acted, who eventually died in a lamentable way. All the rest: his divine origin, his mission of salvation, the proof he gave for these by his words and miracles, finally the resurrection which set a seal on his work, all this is pure fiction, proceeding from faith and cult, and clothed with a legendary tradition, which was formed in the course of the preachings and the disputes of the primitive community [Benoit, Pierre. *Exégèse et Théologie*. Vol. I, p. 46. Paris: Éditions du Cerf. 1961]." 42/28

J. Martin observes that the Gospels cannot be ignored as historical documents and that the evangelists wrote them to be considered as such. Martin believes that too often the Gospels are classified as legends without considering their historical claims. He points out that at the time these were written there was no historical method to use as a standard, but rather, the evangelists accepted their material and recorded it without question. The writer concludes that the question of the historicity of the Gospels should not be sloughed off so easily but that the facts show they are historically accurate and they read like historical writings. Martin points out that it is obvious that they were intended to be historical. 80/101

E.F. Scott claims that in examining the Gospels we usually take two approaches, looking at them for their religious message and as historical fact. As works of history, Scott says, we should subject them to all the normal tests of truth that any document of history is put through. However, Scott argues that while evaluating the Gospels one should not be influenced by their religious value apart from their historical value. This, because Christians believe that God entered history at a point in time and brought salvation through a human life lived in historical time, and the foundations of the Christian faith depend on the facts recorded in the gospels. 111/196

3A. IN SUMMARY

1B. The form critic assumes that tradition is historically unsound by nature. Therefore the early Christian tradition is historically unsound.

2B. The answer—Studies on oral transmission show that although original material is often shortened, the story's outline remains intact. The presence of antagonistic eyewitnesses would not allow false statements to be recorded.

chapter 24

the historical
skepticism

1A. BASIC ASSUMPTION

The New Testament writings do not portray a historical picture of Jesus.

Rudolf Bultmann quotes Julius Wellhausen as saying:

"The spirit of Jesus undoubtedly breathes in the utterances derived from the community at Jeruslaem; but we do not derive a historical picture of Jesus himself from the conception of Jesus which prevailed in the community." 135/341

In order to establish a principle for historical research of Jesus, Wellhausen goes on to say:

"We must recognize that a literary work or a fragment of tradition is a primary source for the historical situation out of which it arose, and is only a secondary source for the historical details concerning which it gives information." 135/341

This assertion leads us to view the Gospels as a secondary source for the facts concerning Jesus. J. Martin concurs:

"Gospels must be taken as reliable renderings of *what the Church believed at the time of writing* concerning the facts on which its faith was founded." 80/44

Therefore, R. H. Lightfoot, a noted critic, infers:

"It seems, then, that the form of the earthly no less than of the heavenly Christ is for the most part hidden from us. For all the inestimable value of the gospels, they yield us little more than a whisper of his voice; we trace in them but the outskirts of his ways." 76/225

1B. The Opinion of Albert Schweitzer

The search for a historical Jesus, a Jesus whose existence could be concretely proven (outside the Bible and Christian experience), was led by critic Albert Schweitzer. He writes:

"The Jesus of Nazareth who came forward as the Messiah, who preached the ethic of the Kingdom of God, who founded the Kingdom of Heaven upon earth, and died to give His work its final consecration, never had any existence. He is a figure designed by rationalism, endowed with life by liberalism, and clothed by modern theology in an historical garb." 109/396

Schweitzer continues with an observation about the problem of our study of a historical Jesus, which itself, he claims, has had erratic background:

"The study of the Life of Jesus has had a curious history. It set out in quest of the historical Jesus, believing that when it had found Him it could bring Him straight into our time as a Teacher and Savior. It loosed the bands by which He had been riveted for centuries to the stony rocks of ecclesiastical doctrine, and rejoiced to see life and movement coming into the figure once more, and the historical Jesus advancing, as it seemed, to meet it. But He does not stay; He passes by our time and returns to His own." 109/397

2B. The opinion of Martin Dibelius

Martin Dibelius doubts any historical interest in Jesus:

"The first Christians had no interest in reporting the life and passion of Jesus objectively to mankind, *sine ira et studio*. They wanted nothing else than to win as many as possible to salvation in the last hour just before the end of the world, which they believed to be at hand. Those early Christians were not interested in history." 37/16

Attacking the objectivity of biblical events, Dibelius elaborates on the aspect of Christian "propaganda" clouding the true historical picture:

"A further limitation of the historicity of the tradition is entailed by this concentration of interest on its missionary application. The stories are couched in a certain style, that is to say, they are told in a way calculated to edify believers and to win over unbelievers. They are not objective accounts of events." 37/76

3B. The Opinion of Rudolf Bultmann

The skepticism of the historical truth of Jesus' life often surfaces in Bultmann's theology:

"I do indeed think that we can now know almost nothing concerning the life and personality of Jesus, since the early Christian sources show no interest in either, are moreover fragmentary and legendary; and other sources about Jesus do not exist." 23/8

He proclaims "the *character* of Jesus, the vivid picture of his personality and his life, cannot now be clearly made out." 19/61

Bultmann comments on a historical method of searching the Scriptures, and his view of how an event, such as a miracle, should be interpreted (actually ruled out):

"The historical method includes the presupposition that history is a unity in the sense of a closed continuum of effects in which individual events are connected by the succession of cause and effect. This does not mean that the process of history is determined by the causal law and that there are no free decisions of men whose actions determine the course of historical happenings.

But even a free decision does not happen without cause, without a motive; and the task of the historian is to come to know the motives of actions. All decisions and all deeds have their causes and consequences; and the historical method presupposes that it is possible in principle to exhibit these and their connection and thus to understand the whole historical process as a closed unity.

"This closedness means that the continuum of historical happenings cannot be rent by the interference of supernatural, transcendent powers and that therefore there is no 'miracle' in this sense of the word. Such a miracle would be an event whose cause did not lie within history....It is in accordance with such a method as this that the science of history goes to work on all historical documents. And there cannot be any exceptions in the case of biblical texts if the latter are at all to be understood [as] historical." 18/291,292

He adds:

"All this goes to show that the interest of the gospels is absolutely different from that of the modern historian. The historian can make progress toward the recovery of the life of Jesus only through the process of critical analysis. The gospels, on the other hand, proclaim Jesus Christ, and were meant to be read as proclamations." 19/70

It is not the existence of Jesus that Bultmann questions; rather, he questions how objective the Gospel writers were.

Bultmann concludes that "the doubt as to whether Jesus really existed is unfounded and not worth refutation. No sane person can doubt that Jesus stands as founder behind the historical movement whose first distinct stage is represented by the oldest Palestinian community. But how far that community preserved an objectively true picture of him and his message is another question." 23/13

Fuller sums up Bultmann's view:

"All we know, he says, is that Jesus was executed by the Romans as a political criminal. But what we can reconstruct does not take us very far." 51/14

The extreme skepticism of Bultmann is not adhered to by Dibelius. He admits that some of the earliest pieces of tradition possess "authentic memories" conveyed by eyewitnesses.

4B. The Opinion of Ernst Käsemann

A former student of Rudolf Bultmann, Ernst Käsemann holds that "it was not historical but kerygmatic interest which handed them [the individual units of Gospel tradition] on. From this standpoint it becomes comprehensible that this tradition, or at least the overwhelming mass of it, cannot be called authentic. Only a few words of the Sermon on the Mount and of the conflict with the Pharisees, a number of parables and some scattered material of various kinds go back with any degree of probability to the Jesus of history himself. Of his deeds, we know only that he had the reputation of being a miracle-worker, that he himself referred to his power of exorcism and that he was finally crucified under Pontius Pilate. The preaching about him has almost entirely supplanted his own preaching, as can be seen most clearly of all in the completely unhistorical Gospel of John." 68/59, 60

In approaching the problem of historical revision of the Gospel material by the community, Ernst Käsemann maintains:

"To state the paradox as sharply as possible: the community takes so much trouble to maintain historical continuity with him who once trod this earth that it allows the historical events of this earthly life to pass for the most part into oblivion and replaces them by its own message." 68/20

His fixation on one's existential identification with the cross, instead of a historically based faith, leads him to conclude that "for this reason the historical element in the story of Jesus has, in these other writings, shrunk almost to vanishing point." 68/21

2A. Rebuttal

The consequence of employing the historical skepticism of the form critics is exposed by Ladd:

"The Son of God incarnate in Jesus of Nazareth becomes a product rather than the creator of Christian faith. He is no longer seen as the Saviour of the Christian community." 74/147

1B. The Result of Following Bultmann

What remains after Bultmann and his followers have eliminated from tradition most of the Gospel material as historically inaccurate and as creations of the community?

Peter G. Duncker cites P. Benoit concerning what would be left:

"Very little; a quite inoffensive residue: Jesus of Galilee, who thought himself to be a prophet, who must have spoken and acted accordingly, without our being able to say exactly what he spoke and how he acted, who eventually died in a lamentable way. All the rest: his divine origin, his mission of salvation, the proof he gave for these by his words and miracles, finally the resurrection which set a seal on his work, all this is pure fiction, proceeding from faith and cult, and clothed with a legendary tradition, which was formed in the course of the preachings and the disputes of the primitive community [Benoit, Pierre. *Exégèse of Théologie*. (p. 46, Vol. I) Paris: Editions du Cerf. 1961]." 42/28

One author, David Cairns, has made this conclusion about Bultmann's form of theology, which runs away from the historical towards the existential:

"Our provisional conclusion in this chapter must be that none of the justifications urged by Bultmann in support of his flight from history carries conviction. The whole enterprise resembles too much the remedy of decapitation as a cure for a headache." 30/149

A frightening aspect of Bultmann's approach to the New Testament is observed by Ellwein when he notes Bultmann's existential basis:

"Is it not a disturbing feature of Bultmann's interpretation of the New Testament message when the historical reality of the historical Jesus of Nazareth becomes a 'relative X'? This means that the occurrence of God's revelation which has assumed bodily and historical form in Jesus evaporates and is, so to speak, placed within parentheses." 175/42

Ellwein continues:

"All that remains is the punctual event of preaching, a kind of 'mathematical point' which lacks any extension just because this very extension would illicitly render the 'other-worldly' into something 'this-worldly.'" 175/42

Bultmann's desire to exclude historical framework and analysis "leaves a mangled text, of interest neither to the primitive Christian nor the modern exegete." 82/70

2B. The Historical Accounts of the Disciples

Peritz cites the purpose of the disciples to be the recording of the Gospels. He claims:

"To declare, as Form Critics do, that the early disciples of Jesus expected the end of the age and had no interest in history, may be true of a small group; but it was not true of all. If it were true of all, we should have no gospel records whatever; and Luke's 'many' who had attempted gospel accounts could not have existed." 95/205

A. N. Sherwin-White makes a comparison between the methods of writing history used by the Roman writers and the Gospel writer. He concludes that "it can be maintained that those who had a passionate interest in the story of Christ, even if their interest in events was parabolical and didactic rather than historical, would not be led by that very fact to pervert and utterly destroy the historical kernel of their material." 182/191

F. F. Bruce comments on the historical accuracy of Luke:

"A man whose accuracy can be demonstrated in matters where we are able to test it is likely to be accurate even where the means for testing him are not available. Accuracy is a habit of mind, and we know from happy (or unhappy) experience that some people are habitually accurate just as others can be depended upon to be inaccurate. Luke's record entitles him to be regarded as a writer of habitual accuracy." 16/90

Blackman notes the dependability of the Gospel writers as he indicates that "Luke's awareness that the salvation-history concerning Jesus of Nazareth is a part of history as a whole. In this Luke is not to be completely differentiated from his fellow evangelists. All of them are conscious of being reporters of real events played out by a real historical person. For all their effort to create a conviction about that person, and to testify to the divine power that operated through him, they are essentially reporters, not free to invent or falsify the data which the tradition of their churches presented as having happened in Galilee and Judaea a generation earlier." 11/27

3B. The Unique Character of Jesus as the Foundation of the Authenticity of the New Testament

E. F. Scott makes the following observation about the attack of the critics:

"...(their) evidence would hardly be challenged if they were concerned with some other hero of antiquity, and it is only because they recount the life of Jesus that they are viewed suspiciously." 111/1

If one is to judge the historicity of Jesus, then He ought to be judged as impartially as any other figure in history. F. F. Bruce testifies that "the historicity of Christ is as axiomatic for an unbiased historian as the historicity of Julius Caesar. It is not historians who propagate the 'Christ-myth' theories.

"The earliest propagators of Christianity welcomed the fullest examination of the credentials of their message. The events which they proclaimed were, as Paul said to King Agrippa, not done in a corner, and were well able to bear all the light that could be thrown on them. The spirit of these early Christians ought to animate their modern descendants. For by an acquaintance with the relevant evidence they will not only be able to give to everyone who asks them a reason for the hope that is in them, but they themselves, like Theophilus, will thus know more accurately how secure is the basis of the faith which they have been taught." 16/119, 120

The claims by the New Testament writers about the character of the historical Jesus are not seen to be a problem by Montgomery:

"However, the inability to distinguish Jesus' claims for himself from the New Testament writers' claims for him should cause no dismay, since (1) the situation exactly parallels that for all historical personages who have not themselves chosen to write (e.g., Alexander the Great, Augustus Caesar, Charlemagne). We would hardly claim that in these cases we can achieve no adequate historical portraits. Also, (2) the New Testament writers, as we saw in the previous chapter, record eyewitness testimony concerning Jesus and can therefore be trusted to convey an accurate historical picture of him.." 87/48

4B. Ancient Historiography

J. P. Moreland presents the main issue:

"Were ancient historians able to distinguish fact from fiction? Is there any evidence that they desired to do so? The works of Greek, Roman and Jewish historians all probably influenced the New Testament writers." 9/87

Thus, a major objection often penned against the Gospels as ancient documents is that their authors (as well as authors of other ancient documents) lived in a different historical arena where factual accuracy was not important.

Moreland continues by discussing some of the evidence:

"Among Greek writers, many discussed the importance of giving an accurate account of what happened. Herodotus emphasizes the role of eyewitnesses in historical reporting. The historian must, however, evaluate and verify their reports using common sense. Reports of superhuman and miraculous occurrence should be regarded with suspicion. Thucydides also attempted to evaluate the accuracy of reports that came to him. In *History of the Peloponnesian War*, 1.22.1, he does admit that on occasion he did invent speeches. But in those cases he attempted to be consistent with what was known of the speaker. In any case, he did not feel free to invent narrative. Polybsius held very exacting standards. He advocated examination of sources, objectivity, and castigated superstition and a 'womanish love of the miraculous.' He also advocated the questioning of reliable eyewitnesses." 9/88

A. W. Mosley concludes his article, "Historical Reporting in the Ancient World," with the following summation:

"The survey shows clearly, then, that the question, 'Did it happen in this way?' was a question which made sense to the people living at that time, and was a question which was often asked. People living then knew that there was a difference between fact and fiction.

Mosely further states:

"Generally it was easier to be inaccurate when a writer was dealing with events that had happened a long time before. Writers who were dealing with events of the recent past — eyewitnesses being still alive — seem generally to have tried to be as accurate as possible and to get the information from the eyewitnesses. They knew they could not get away with inventing freely stories of events and personalities of the recent past. We note that Josephus accused Justus of holding back publication of his history until eyewitnesses were no longer available and this is strongly condemned.

"We have seen that these historians (e.g., Lucian, Dionysius, Polybius, Ephorus, Cicero, Josephus and Tacitus) were quick to criticize their fellow writers if they gave inaccurate accounts. A person who gave an inaccurate account of something that had happened was regarded as having — in some measure at least — failed. We would expect to find that such charges were brought against the New Testament writers if they had failed in this way.

"Our survey has not proved anything conclusive about the attitude of the New Testament writers to the historicity of the traditions they received and passed on about the historical Jesus, but it would suggest that we should not assume from the start that they could not have been interested in the question of authenticity. It is quite possible that people were concerned to distinguish which reports were factually true, and that this influenced the development of the Christian tradition, both in the period where reports were passed on orally, and later when the tradition came to be written down." 12/26

5B. The View of the Critics — Is It Truly Impartial?

Objecting to form critics' personal opinions, Redlich writes:

"Historical Criticism must not be identified, as Form Critics often do, with the critic's own personal opinion of the historical truth of a narrative or saying. This latter is a historical value-judgment. It has no connection with laws of the tradition or with formal characteristics." 101/11

McNeile believes that the form critics have gone too far in passing judgment on the contents of the Gospels, for their method is a literary one — not historical. 85/54

G. E. Ladd reasons: "It must be recognized that modern biblical criticism was not the product of a believing scholarship concerned with a better understanding of the Bible as the Word of God in its historical setting, but of scholarship which rejected the Bible's claim to be the supernaturally inspired Word of God." 74/38

6B. Conclusion

"The Christians," concludes Pierre Benoit, "may not have been interested in 'history'; but they were certainly interested in the 'historical'. The preachers of the new faith may not have wanted to narrate *everything* about Jesus, but they certainly did not want to relate anything that was not real." 58/32

Benoit poses the following question:

"Is it credible that the converts accepted so novel a faith, which demanded so much of them, on the strength of mere gossip-sessions, at which Dibelius and Bultmann's preachers invented sayings and actions which Jesus never uttered and never performed merely to suit themselves?" 58/32

Filson notes the ultimate result of extending the form critic's historical skepticism:

"As may readily be seen, if the Gospels thus reflect the life and thought of the primitive Church, the problem of the reliability of the material for the study of Jesus' life arises. This is frankly recognized by the form critic, and when an element of the tradition shows a developed church interest, or a Hellenistic character, it is rejected from the fund of usable data for the life of Jesus. Since all the material preserved was used by the Church, this skepticism may go so far as practically to deny that we have any dependable data left with which to picture the historical Jesus." 47/99

Stressing the need for external evidence, Albright holds that "the ultimate historicity of a given datum is never conclusively established nor disproved by the literary framework in which it is imbedded; there must always be external evidence." 129/12

Albright adds: "From the standpoint of the objective historian data cannot be disproved by criticism of the accidental literary framework in which they occur, unless there are solid independent reasons for rejecting the historicity of an appreciable number of other data found in the same framework." 156/293, 294

Finally, the testimony of contemporary historians of Jesus' day should be acknowledged. Laurence J. McGinley confirms:

"In any study of the Synoptic Gospels whether it's Dibelius' concentration on transmission and composition or Bultmann's historical portrayal of the synoptic tradition from origin to crystallization, something should be said for historical testimony. But, it's not! [H. Dieckmann, *"Die Formgeschichtliche Methode und ihre Anwendung auf die Auferstehungs Berichte,"* Scholastik, I, 1926, p. 389] External testimony such as Irenaeus Tertullian, and Origen is noticeably not referred to. Justin's observation that the Gospels are merely apostolic memoirs [*Apologia*, I, 66] is mentioned only to be rejected as misleading [Bultmann, *Die Erforschung der Synoptischen Evangelien, The New Approach*, p. 397]. Papias' testimony [Eusebius, *Ecclesiastical History*, III, 39 (MP6, xx, 296-300) pp. 22, 23] of Matthew and Mark fares no better. Bultmann refers to Papias' reference to Mark as the interpreter of Peter — as an error; Dibelius refers to Papias' testimony on the authorship of Matthew and Mark but concludes that he has been mislead by thinking that the evangelists were really authors [Bultmann, *Zur Formgeschichte der Evangelien*, Theol. Rund. N.F.I. 1929, p. 10]. This neglect of historical testimony seems to show a lack of completeness and perspective.

"As De Grandmaison remarks, 'it is the wisest method in these matters to prefer an ounce of ancient information which is authentic to a bookful of learned conjectures' [De Grandmaison, *Jesus Christ*, I, 1935, p. 115]." 82/22, 23

Norman Pittenger declares:

"Let us take it for granted that all attempts to deny the historicity of Jesus have failed." 100/89, 90

3A. IN SUMMARY

1B. Form Criticism assumes the New Testament portrays what the Church *believed* to be true of Jesus, rather than what *was* true.

2B. The answer—Bultmann's conclusions concerning the historical inaccuracy of the Gospels are unsound, for not even the Christian would be interested in the end product of a Gospel taken out of its historical framework.

1C. Luke proved himself to be habitually accurate.

2C. No other historical figure is attacked as Jesus is. Critics' views are not impartial.

3C. Attempts to deny the historicity of Jesus have failed.

chapter 25

the
messianic
secret theory

Reginald Fuller poses the problem that is dealt with in this section:

"But what of the Messianic problem? Did Jesus claim to be Messiah? Did He possess a 'Messianic consciousness'? Form criticism had eliminated the Messianic categories from the sayings of the historical Jesus on the ground that these categories reflect the faith of the post-Easter church." 51/37

1A. THE MESSIANIC CONCEPT OF WREDE

Basil Redlich outlines Wrede's theory of the Messianic Secret:

"The diciples were not gradually educated to believe who Jesus was, and the confession of Jesus as Messiah did not begin until after the Resurrection. This belief in the Messiahship was the outcome of the experiences of that event, which convinced the disciples that He was risen. The Messiahship was therefore not revealed to anyone during the ministry and the idea of it was not revealed to anyone before the Resurrection. Even Jesus did not believe He was the Messiah. What we find in Mark is a theory imposed by Mark on the narrative." 101/20

A further development of this idea is commented on by Edgar McKnight. He says that Wrede came up with the Messianic Secret concept. He states that before the Resurrection no one supposed that Jesus was the Messiah, but afterwards He was interpreted in this way. Mark in his effort to overcome the non-Messianic tradition attempted to harmonize the historical and dogmatic elements by using the idea of an intentional secrecy of Jesus' Messiahship." 83/8

G. E. Ladd sheds more light on the subject when he says that Wrede's renowned Messianic Secret theory holds that Jesus did not claim to be Messiah nor was His mission Messianic. The Resurrection alone brought about belief in Jesus' Messiahship, especially after the Resurrection when the Church read Messiahship back into His life. The Church possessed a non-Messianic tradition, which was embarrassing because it did hold a Messianic faith—hence, in order to alleviate the embarrassment of this contradiction, the Messianic Secret was created—that Jesus knew He was the Messiah, but kept this knowledge from His disciples. 74/157

A modern day interpretation of the Messianic Secret is detailed by Martin Stallman in his essay entitled, "Contemporary Interpretation of the Gospels as a Challenge to Preaching and Religious Education":

"As is well known, the confidence with which earlier investigators had hoped to lay bare behind the Marcan Gospel a substratum of reliable historical information about Jesus was first shaken by W. Wrede's book, *The Messianic Secret of the Gospels* (1901). He was the first to focus attention upon the procedures of the second Evangelist, because he sought to explain the curious way in which the latter incorporates the 'injunctions to silence' into his narrative. No one whose attention has once been called to it can fail to be impressed by what Wrede observed and then traced to the theory of the 'Messianic secret.' On the one hand, the Evangelist unmistakably treats the career of Jesus as the arena in which the final conflict between God and the demonic powers takes place. He tells of exorcisms and healings in which this struggle is victoriously carried through; even the so-called 'conflict narratives' (Mark 3:1-6, 22-30; 2:1-12), which are connected with healing miracles and which culminate in a saying of Jesus, portray the same drama. On the other hand, wherever Jesus' authority comes clearly into view, it is suppressed with a command to silence. Jesus does not wish recognition as Messiah; he encounters profound misunderstanding not only from the people but from his very disciples (4:40 f.; 6:52; 8:16 ff.; 9:10, 32). Even his parables are intentionally enigmatic; they are aimed at rendering their hearers obdurate, and they are explained only for the benefit of the disciples (4:10 ff.). This combination of the theme of the manifestation of Jesus' Messianic authority with the motif of the Messianic secret imparts to the Evangelist's presentation a uniquely contradictory flavor. The aptness of M. Dibelius' characterization of the Gospel of Mark as 'a book of secret epiphanies' is widely recognized.

"To explain these features Wrede drew upon pragmatic historical considerations. He held that Mark needed to explain to his readers why Jesus was believed to be the Messiah only after Easter; to meet this need, Mark put forth the theory that Jesus himself did not wish to be recognized as Messiah and for that reason had in fact not been. In actual fact, Jesus' earthly career had possessed no observable Messianic traits. It was in the gospel account that his activity on earth was first represented as that of the Son of God. In producing this representation, however, Mark was not able without resulting contradiction to combine the historical actualities of Jesus' career—and what was remembered of them—with the conceptions of Jesus' Messianic authority which had in the meantime become current in the Christian community." 178/238

2A. WREDE'S CONCEPT AS ELABORATED BY BULTMANN

Bultmann wonders about the consistency of the Messianic Secret:

"It was soon no longer conceivable that Jesus' life was unmessianic—at least in the circles of Hellenistic Christianity in which the synoptics took form. That Jesus Christ, the Son of God, should have legitimated himself as such even in his earthly activity seemed self-evident, and so the gospel account of his ministry was cast in the light of messianic faith. The contradiction between this point of view and the traditional material finds expression in the theory of the Messiah-secret, which gives the Gospel of Mark its peculiar character: Jesus functioned as the Messiah, but his messiah-ship was to remain hidden until the resurrection (Mk. 9:9). The demons, who recognize him, are commanded to be quiet; silence is also commanded after Peter's Confession (8:30), after the Transfiguration (9:9), and after some of the miracles. The motif of the disciples' incomprehension likewise serves the secrecy-theory: Though the disciples receive secret revelation, they fail to understand it. Of course, this secrecy-theory, whose existence and importance W. Wrede pointed out, was incapable of being consistently carried through; hence the Gospel of Mark has been rightly characterized by the paradoxical term, book of 'secret epiphanies' (Dibelius)." 24/32

To Bultmann there was a notable distinction to be made between Jesus' teaching and the early Church's teaching:

"Jesus viewed himself only as the herald of the imminent end of the world, announcing the coming of the heavenly Son of Man. The early church believed that Jesus had been exalted to heaven and would himself be the Messianic Son of Man in the coming kingdom." 75/13

Bultmann summarizes any Messianic purpose that Jesus might have had:

"He does not proclaim himself as the Messiah, i.e. the king of the time of salvation, but he points ahead to the Son of Man as another than himself. *He in his own person signifies the demand for decision*, insofar as his cry, as God's last word before the End, calls men to decision." 24/9

The result of Bultmann's view is commented on by Herman Ridderbos. When asked what remains of the Christ of the Apostles' Creed, Ridderbos quotes a critic of Bultmann as concluding that Jesus Christ "was not conceived by the Holy Ghost, not born of the Virgin Mary. He did suffer under Pontius Pilate, he was crucified, he did not descend into hell and did not rise again on the third day from the dead; he did not ascend into heaven and does not sit on the right hand of God the Father, and will not come to judge the living and the dead." 102/27

3A. BASIC ANSWER

Concerning the tradition of the non-Messianic Jesus, Ladd says:

"The fact is that *we do not have a non-messianic tradition*. Such a 'neutral' tradition is a purely hypothetical critical reconstruction, which rests on rather flimsy evidence." 74/158

T. W. Manson, a recent British critic, ads to the above: "The farther we travel along the Wredestrasse, Wrede Avenue, the clearer it becomes that it is the road to nowhere." 154/216

Filson concurs with Ladd about the tradition, when he adds a comment about the impossibility of the apostles creating the title of Messiah for Jesus:

"A second example of the respect paid the tradition is found in the way that the title 'Son of man' is frequently used in all the Gospels, and always by Jesus alone, while in the rest of the New Testament the title is used but once of him outside of the Gospels (Acts 7:56). This is so clear and unanimous a testimony that all attempts to say the apostolic age first brought this title into use are futile and unreasonable. They did not originate it; it was not their spontaneous way of referring to him; they did know that it was a favorite expression of Jesus himself." 47/108, 109

Montgomery follows the same line of thought with this conclusion:

"Moreover, were these early followers of Jesus psychologically or temperamentally capable of carrying out such a deification process? Certainly they, no less than Jesus himself, were then charlatans or psychotics. Yet the picture of them in the documents is one of practical, ordinary people, down-to earth fishermen, hardheaded tax gatherers, etc., and people with perhaps more than the usual dose of skepticism. Think of Peter returning to his old way of life after Jesus' death; think of 'doubting' Thomas. Hardly the kind of men to be swept off their feet into mass hallucination of technicolor proportions." 87/71, 72

4A. IN SUMMARY

  1B. The form critic says the Messianic Concept was created by Jesus' followers. Not even Jesus believed He was the Messiah. Bultmann says Jesus "points ahead to the Son of Man as another than Himself." (24/9)

  2B. The answer—

  1C. Jesus, Not His disciples, uses the title "Son of Man" in the Gospels.

  2C. The disciples lives show they were practical, ordinary men, not charlatans or psychotics.

chapter 26

gnosticism

1A. BULTMAN'S DEFINITION

G. E. Ladd interprets Bultmann as saying that Gnosticism gave rise to the concept of the existence of a "redeemer of man." The concept of a heavenly redeemer who comes from the realm of light to the fallen world to release man and restore him to light does not factually reflect the Gospels nor is it distinctly and uniquely Christian. It is a Gnostic myth which developed in oriental dualism before Jesus ever lived. 75/17

Bultmann gives his own description of a Gnostic redeemer:

"Redemption comes from the heavenly world. Once more a light-person sent by the highest god, indeed the son and 'image' of the most high, comes down from the light-world bringing *Gnosis.* He 'wakes' the sparks of light who have sunk into sleep or drunkenness and 'reminds' them of their heavenly home. He teaches them concerning their superiority to the world and concerning the attitude they are to adopt toward the world. He dispenses the sacraments by which they are to purify themselves and fan back to life their quenched light-power or at least strengthen its weakened state—by which, in other words, they are 'reborn.' He teaches them about the heavenly journey they will start at death and communicates to them the stations of this journey—past the demonic watchmen of the starry spheres. And going ahead he prepares the way for them, the way which he, the redeemer himself, must also take to be redeemed. For here on earth he does not appear in divine form, but appears disguised in the garment of earthly beings so as not to be recognized by the demons. In so ap-

pearing, he takes upon himself the toil and misery of earthly existence and has to endure contempt and persecution until he takes his leave and is elevated to the world of light." 24/167

Ladd explains Bultmann's attempt to relate Gnostic and New Testament thought patterns:

"At this point Bultmann makes his biggest leap. He postulates a conflation of the mystery redemption myth and the Gnostic myth as background for New Testament thought. The idea of a dying and rising cult deity (mystery religions) was conflated with the idea of a heavenly redeemer who comes to earth to save fallen man (Gnostic religion). These two were in turn added to the Jewish myth of a heavenly Son of Man. Out of this threefold conflation of Jewish apocalyptic, mystery, and Gnostic myths emerged the syncretistic figure of a heavenly being who comes from the realm of light to bring men the knowledge of God (Gnostic), who dies and rises again (mystery), who ascends to heaven and will come again as the Son of Man to break off history and inaugurate the Kingdom of God (Jewish apocalyptic)." 74/205

The following is a list of discoveries of Gnostic sources compiled by W. F. Albright:

"Our last category of outstanding discoveries carries down into the Christian era and may seem too late to be of significance for biblical studies. First comes the discovery in 1930 of seven Manichean codices composed in part by Mani, founder of this Gnostic sect, in the third century A.D., translated into Coptic soon afterwards and copied for us by fourth-century scribes. The publication, chiefly due to the talent of H. J. Polotsky, began in 1934 and was interrupted in 1940 by the war. Before this our only firsthand knowledge of Manichean literature came from fragments translated into Central Asiatic languages and discovered in Turkestan by German explorers before the First World War. Now we have a mass of original material, which among other things, establishes the secondary character of Mandeanism in relation to Manicheism; the former has been regarded by many scholars as in part older than the Gospel of John.

"In 1947 a second, even more remarkable, discovery of Gnostic books was made in Egypt, this time a lot of some forty treatises bound together in codices, at Chenoboscium (Chenoboskion) in Upper Egypt. These books are also in Coptic; the extant copies date from the third and fourth centuries and the original Greek works from which they were translated must go back to the second and third centuries. We have here for the first time the original writings of the strange early Gnostic groups called the Barbelo Gnostics, the Ophites, Sethians, and others, as well as several Hermetic treatises. At last we can control and expand the information given us by Hippolytus, Irenaeus, and Epiphanius about these early Gnostics and their beliefs. The new documents will have extraordinary significance in connection with the debate about the alleged Gnostic affinities of the Gospel of John. Fortunately all (or nearly all) of these codices have been acquired by the Egyptian government, and it is to be hoped that they will be published before long. Meanwhile we have very reliable information from the first student of these texts, Jean Doresse." 157/540, 541

2A. ORIGINS OF CHRISTIANITY RELATING TO GNOSTIC, JUDAISTIC, AND "EARLY CIVILIZATION" THOUGHT PATTERNS

1B. According to Martin Dibelius

Dibelius compares the style of the Gospels' rendition of Christ's healing power to secular renditions. He compares the Gospels' inclusion of the severity of the illness and the technique of the miracle that Christ used to such secular renditions of other thaumaturges in the Talmud or antiquities. 36/82, 83

Dibelius notes use of Judaism's traditions in the origins of Christianity:

1.) Halakha—"the tradition of rules concerning life and worship"
2.) Haggada—"the tradition of historical and theological material" 36/28

2B. According to Rudolf Bultmann

Gnosticism came from the Orient, and then developed side-by-side with the Christian religion, influencing it in many ways. Or so theorizes Bultmann:

"Gnosticism is not a phenomenon that first appeared within the Christian Church. It cannot be described as a speculative Christian theology under the influence of Greek philosophical tradition. It is not properly regarded as the 'acute Hellenization' of Christianity, as Harnack in his time supposed. It has its roots in a dualistic redemption-religion which invaded Hellenism from the orient. Seen as a whole, it is a phenomenon parallel or competitive to the Christian religion. Each of these movements, the Gnostic and the Christian, influenced the other in many ways, but of that we shall have to speak later on. At any rate, there was very soon a Christian Gnosticism which, in its radical form, completely rejected the Old Testament, thus constituting the most extreme of the possibilities to be surveyed; that is why it is here named first." 24/109, 110

He goes on to say:

"But sometimes Christianity and Gnosticism combined. On the whole, one could be tempted to term Hellenistic Christianity a syncretistic structure. The only reason one may not do so is that it is not just a conglomerate of heterogeneous materials; in spite of all its syncretism in detail it retains from its origin an inherent drive toward an independent understanding, all its own, of God, world, and man. But the question is: Will this drive triumph and achieve clear form in a genuinely Christian theology?" 24/164, 165

Professor Bultmann stresses the relationship of Gnosticism to Christianity:

"Now it must be carefully noted that in all this Gnosticism is combatted not as if it were a foreign, heathen religion into which Christians are in danger of apostatizing. Rather, it is only dealt with so far as it is a *phenomenon within Christianity.* And it is also clear that the Gnostics here opposed by no means regard the Christian congregations as a mission field which they want to convert from Christianity to Gnosticism. Rather, they consider themselves Christians teaching a Christian wisdom—and that is the way they appear to the churches, too....

"At first, Gnosticism probably penetrated into the Christian congregations mostly through the medium of a Hellenistic Judaism that was itself in the grip of syncretism." 24/170, 171

Ridderbos comments on the Gnostic and Greek myths and their relation to Jesus as viewed by some critics:

"Here the Old Testament idea of a king or the Hellenistic conception of a divine essence was not developed as strongly as the mysterious, miraculous power over which Jesus had command, and which placed him upon the same niveau, in the consciousness of the Christian church, as the well-known Hellenistic miracle workers who also called themselves 'Sons of God,' and were thought of as intermediary beings, God-men, or heroes. These God-men were viewed as the product of a mixture of a divine and a human essence. They appear not only in the Greek tradition but also in the Babylonian, and especially in the Egyptian legends of the kings.

"Later on, however, this conception of Jesus as a divine man is entirely surpassed by the previously mentioned conception according to which Jesus was a self-sufficient or an independent divine being who descended from the heavens. This latter conception receives its particular form not from the old Greek religions but from the later pre-Christian gnosticism, according to which a pre-existent divine being came upon the earth in order to conduct the conflict or struggle against the powers of darkness." 102/13, 14

3A. THE EFFECTS OF GNOSTICISM ON CHRISTIAN THOUGHT

Bultmann distinguishes a so-called "apparent" Gnostic influence in the Gospels:

"It is Gnostic language when Satan is called 'the god of this world' ($a\grave{\iota}\tilde{\omega}\nu o s$) (II Cor. 4:4), the 'ruler of this world' (Jn. 12:31; 14:30; 16:11), 'the prince of the power of the air' (Eph. 2:2), or 'the ruler of this Aeon' (Ign. Eph. 19:1). Both in name and meaning 'the rulers of this age' who brought 'the Lord of glory' to the cross (I Cor. 2:6, 8) are figures of Gnostic mythology—viz. those demonic world-rulers who are also meant by the terms 'angels,' 'principalities,' 'authorities,' 'powers' (Rom. 8:38f.; I Cor. 15:24, 26; Col. 1:16; 2:10, 15; Eph. 1:21; 3:10; 6:12; I Pet. 3:22) and are at least included in the 'many gods and many lords' of I Cor. 8:4. As in Gnosticism, they are conceived to be in essence star-spirits; as such they are called 'elemental spirits of the universe' (Gal. 4:3, 9; cf. Col. 2:8, 20) who govern the elapse and division of time (Gal. 4:10). Also Gnostic are the 'world rulers of this present darkness' and the 'spiritual hosts of wickedness in the heavenly places' (i.e. in the region of air, the lower sphere of the firmament, Eph. 6:12).

"Aside from the terms for mythological figures, the *terminology* in which dualism is expressed shows extensive Gnostic influence. This is most apparent in John, whose language is governed by the antithesis 'light—darkness.'" 24/173

Bultmann professes a decided existential influence upon man as a result of Gnosticism:

"For Christian missions, *the Gnostic movement* was a competitor of the most serious and dangerous sort because of the far-reaching relatedness between them. For the essence of Gnosticism does not lie in its syncretistic mythology but rather in a new understanding—new in the ancient world—of man and the world; its mythology is only the expression of this understanding. Whereas to ancient man the world had been home—in the Old Testament as God's creation, to classic Greece as the cosmos pervaded by the deity—the *utter difference of human existence from all worldly existence* was recognized for the first time in Gnosticism and Christianity, and thus the world became foreign soil to the human self; in fact, in Gnosticism, his prison." 24/165

Bultmann presents another reference to Gnostic thought and its effect on the Christian community's idea of salvation:

"While in the presentation of Luke-Acts this paradox was resolved in favor of a theology of history which knows only a history of salvation unrolling as world history...it was also resolved in another direction by sacrificing from the kerygma its reference to the historical occurrence. This happened in Gnosticism. In it the occurrence of salvation is understood with a consistent one-sidedness as transcendental, and, in consequence of divorcing it from history, the occurrence of salvation becomes mythical. Unlike heathen Gnosticism, Christian Gnosticism naturally could not give up all connection with the historical person Jesus and thus transplant the occurrence of salvation into a mythical past. But it did surrender the historical reality of the Redeemer when it denied the identity of the Son of God with the historical Jesus by teaching either that the Son of God only temporarily—from the baptism of Jesus, say—united with the human Jesus and then left him before the passion, or that the Redeemer's human form was only seemingly a body (docetism)." 25/126, 127

Bultmann claims that the "powers beyond" come to the present as a result of gnosticism:

"In the sacramental Church eschatology is not abandoned, but it is neutralized in so far as the powers of the beyond are already working in the present. The interest in eschatology diminishes. And for this there is the further peculiar reason that the cosmic drama, which was expected in the future, was thought of as having in a certain sense already happened. The influence of the gnostic mythology was effective here. The Gnostics believed that, although there is to be an end of the world, the decisive event has already happened in that the heavenly Saviour came into this world and then left it and so prepared a way to the heavenly world of light for his adherents. His descent and ascent are combat with and victory over the hostile cosmic powers, which have incarcerated the heavenly sparks of light in human souls and then obstruct their way back into the heavenly home." 20/54

Bultmann further elaborates:

"Insofar as Christian preaching remained true to the tradition of the Old Testament and Judaism and of the earliest Church, *definitive contrasts between it and Gnosticism* are straightway apparent. In harmony with that tradition the Christian message did by and large hold to the idea that *the world is the creation of the one true God,* and hence that the creator-God and the redeemer-God are one. That immediately results in a contrast in *anthropology.* For in the genuinely Christian view, man is, body and soul, the creature of God, and no pre-existent spark of heavenly light—as if that were his real being—is to be distinguished from his psychosomatic existence. Hence, that division between those who bear the spark of light within, the 'spiritual ones' (who, Gnostically speaking, are *fvaei awyouevoi:* 'by nature saved') and the mere 'men of soul' or 'men of flesh' who lack the heavenly self, was not considered *a priori* to run through all mankind, though this Gnostic differentiation was taken over in another way. Correspondingly, a contrast in *eschatology* persists almost consistently, insofar as the Christian proclamation does not know the idea of the heavenly journey of the self made possible by Gnosis and sacraments, but does teach the resurrection of the dead and the last judgment." 24/168

Dibelius puts forth a form critical view of how the tradition of Jesus developed eventually to its end stage of *gnosis:*

"And further, right at the beginning of the history of primitive Christian literature, there stood a tradition of an unliterary nature, consisting of short narratives and striking sayings, which were repeated for practical purposes. Those who gather them gradually try not only to give their context, but also to interpret them and indeed, to make their point of view explicit. Thus it comes about at length that the mythological element takes charge of the entire material of evangelical history. But this also corresponds to the general development of primitive Christianity which passes from a historical person to his formal worship and finally to the cosmic mythological Christ of Gnosis, and to ecclesiastical Christology." 36/287, 288

4A. BASIC ANSWER

1B. The Evidence Against a Gnostic Influence

W. F. Albright questions the veracity of Gnostic influence on Christianity:

"The New Testament, according to many scholars, exhibits pronounced gnostic features, and in fact is unintelligible, historically speaking, unless understood against a gnostic background. Gnostics believed that salvation came through esoteric mysteries, 'gnosis,' a mysterious, superhuman, enigmatic knowledge, which was hidden from ordinary men. Now these scholars claimed that there was a pre-Christian gnosticism, and that this is best illustrated by the books of the Mandaeans, the so-called Christians of John the Baptist, who still survive in Iraq on the lower Tigris. This is rather a surprising claim, since, although John the Baptist is their great hero, the Mandaeans consider Jesus as their great demon or devil, and are bitterly hostile to both Christianity and Judaism." 2/40

Albright continues his attack:

"In fact, two discoveries have now proved this theory to be entirely wrong. The first is the Dead Sea Scrolls. The second is the Chenoboskion papyri." 2/41

He notes:

"Before this discovery, nothing was known about the early gnostics except what was preserved in the writings of the specialists in heresies, the so-called heresiographers, notably Irenaeus of Lyons (late second century), Hippolytus (early third century), and Epiphanius in the fourth century." 2/41

Finally he tells of the archaeological finds confirming the reliability of the Church fathers as opposed to the gnostics:

"The gnostics were believed by many scholars to be fairly orthodox Christians—the church fathers were said to have exaggerated their divergences. We now know that the church fathers were very reliable. They did not tell us everything by any means, but what they did tell us has been confirmed in large part by these new finds, and nothing of what they said has been shown to be wrong. This is just what we should expect, since they would have played directly into the hands of the gnostics, if they had misrepresented them. On the other side, there is no evidence today for pre-Christian gnosticism." 2/42

2B. The Inconsistencies of Dibelius and Bultmann

Dibelius notes that there is infrequent use of "Legend" in the Canonical Gospels even though its use is prevalent in the apocryphal Gospels. What little "Legend" is used is a result of accession from outside the Christian world and sparse use seems to indicate that as Dibelius puts it:

"That is a sign that the tradition of Jesus was at first closed to accessions from the 'world' and was only open to them when Christianity itself entered further into that 'world.'" 35/45

Dibelius' question is, if the tradition of Jesus was at first closed to accessions from the outside world, how could pagan mysteries and miracles and Gnostic heresies have had such a dominant effect on the Gospel as is noted by both Dibelius and Bultmann? 35/45, 46

In reference to Bultmann's pre-Christian era hypothesis of a Gnostic personal redeemer Ladd says that "there is no clear evidence that the concept of a Gnostic heavenly redeemer ever existed in the pre-Christian era; and the hypothesis of a conflation of the Gnostic and the mystery religion myths is equally tenuous." 75/48

Finally, Ladd questions Bultmann concerning another problem:

"The *religionsgeschichtliche* reconstruction will show the need of thorough historical scholarship. Bultmann holds that Jesus was finally interpreted in the Gentile world in terms of the Gnostic mythology of a pre-existent heavenly redeemer who descends to earth to deliver men imprisoned in the realm of fallen matter and to lead them back to the realm of light where they belong. It is, however, a fact that none of the ancient sources knows of such a heavenly redeemer in pre-Christian times [R. McL. Wilson, *The Gnostic Problem.* (London: Mowbray, 1958), p. 217]. Such an alleged figure is a critical hypothesis derived from post-Christian sources which were influenced by Christian faith. The historical fact is that 'there is no hint of the figure of the redeemer in any non-Christian Gnostic source' [Hugh Anderson, *Jesus and Christian Origins.* (New York: Oxford, 1964), p. 52]. One of the main foundations of Bultmann's historical reconstruction is without firm historical support." 74/210

One of the best books on Gnosticism is *The Gnostic Problem* by Robert M. Wilson.

Wilson writes that "to the Christian...the primary ideas are the forgiveness of sins, reconciliation with God [by the 'redeemer'], and eternal life, the first two of which are not known to the Gnostic." 185/217 To this Wilson adds that "there are similarities and differences, but in the end Gnosticism is fundamentally un-Christian and un-Jewish." 185/218

A book that should be consulted for further research on Gnosticism is *Pre-Christian Gnosticism* by Edwin M. Yamauchi. This work is a survey of the proposed evidence for pre-Christian Gnosticism.

5A. IN SUMMARY

1B. Form Criticism says the heavenly redeemer concept originated with the Gnostics, not the Christians. Gnosticism influenced much of the Christian theology and terminology.

2B. The answer—

1C. The Dead Sea Scrolls and the Chenoboskion papyri show that Christianity could not possibly be a product of Gnostic thought.

2C. The liberal argument is inconsistent—it says early tradition was "closed to accessions from the outside world" (35/45, 46), but then says the early tradition was open to Gnostic influence.

3C. Gnosticism is fundamentally un-Christian and un-Jewish. How could it then be incorporated into Christianity?

chapter 27

conclusion
to form
criticism

Every critical method or study has its pros and cons, its contributions and short-comings.

This section gives some of the contributions and limitiations of the "Form Critical" approach.

1A. CONTRIBUTION OF FORM CRITICISM

B. S. Easton highlights a contribution made through the form critical study when he concludes:

"Form-study brings us into contact with the earliest Christian pedagogy, and so should prove a fruitful field of study, particularly in the light it will throw on the early Palestinian Christian interests. This is reason enough to give the new discipline our full attention." 44/77

Barker, Lane, and Michaels establish the following contributions of Form Criticism:

1) "It helps immeasurably in the appreciation of the distinctive style and structure of synoptic tradition. The form of the written Gospels essentially mirrors that of the oral tradition which preceded them.

2) "It is neither possible nor necessary to demand a complete har-monization of the chronologies of the different Gospels. Con-sequently the Gospel narratives are grouped according to a variety of patterns.

3)   "Form criticism helps explain some otherwise perplexing variations in parallel accounts of the same incident. A detail omitted by one evangelist may be included by another because it carries for him a certain relevance with respect to the situation out of which he writes." 5/70

Some other results are noted by Floyd Filson:

"It is true that the gospel tradition was orally preserved for a time. It is also true that this early period was of the greatest importance for the dependability of all later forms of the tradition, and therefore merits our closest scrutiny.

"It is true that small units of tradition, whether teaching tradition or narrative material, were known and utilized for practical purposes as occasion demanded. It may also be accepted as reasonable that typical incidents or utterances were preserved, and in some cases these units may have been composite.

"Beyond question it is true that the surviving gospel material is but a very small portion of the total amount that might have been preserved. It is likewise true that the selection of what was to survive was governed largely by practical interests connected with the faith and life of the Church. Just as a preacher in our day will remember particularly those features of an address or book which affect his own life, thinking, and preaching, so the memory of those early Christians was much governed by their needs and interests.

"It is also true that the needs of guidance, instruction, worship, and controversy were prominent influences in this whole process, and that the attitude of those who transmitted the tradition was not that of the research fellow or detached biographer. And this means that to some extent even a careful and cautious critical study of the Gospels will see reflected in them the life of the primitive Church, for the interests and problems of the early Christians can be inferred from them." 47/103-105

Another important aspect, as New Testament scholar Harold W. Hochner has pointed out, is that form criticism has focused our attention on the oral period. 7/NP

Steven Travis agrees:

"Form criticism has helped us, however tentatively, to penetrate into the "tunnel period" between A.D. 30 and 50, before any of our New Testament documents were written down. For instance, it has given us clues about methods of preaching and teaching among the early Christians, and about their debates with Jewish opponents. 6/161

One important conclusion of form critical study is contributed by Mounce:

"Form Criticism is a good reminder of the nature of Jesus' teaching: its conciseness and its wide applicability. What we have in the Gospels is a select body of teaching capable of universal application." 144

Two important conclusions of Form Criticism are revealed by Redlich:

(1)   "Form Criticism by admitting that collections of saying were made early has pointed to the possibility that the ipsissima verba ['exact words'] of our Lord were treasured as oracles to guide and control the destinies of individuals and of the Church.

(2)   "Form Criticism has stimulated the study of Gospel origins, and its method of research and investigation may lead to a wider scientific study in the future." 101/79

2A. LIMITATIONS OF FORM CRITICISM

Basil Redlich summarizes the limitations of the Form Critical technique:

1)   "Classification should be according to form and nothing else, as in

Apothegm-Stories, Miracle-Stories and Parables. Where forms do not exist, classification according to contents is not Form Criticism.

2) "Form-less groups should not be given historical value-judgments before investigation. Also where a type or form does not exist, no historical valuation can be justified. Form Criticism should investigate the forms of the tradition, explain the forms, and attempts to trace the development of forms and of forms only.

3) "Form Criticism has not made adequate use of the results of Literary Criticism of the Gospels, e.g., the dating of the documentary sources of the synoptic gospels, and the connexion of these sources with the great centres of Christendom.

4) "Form Criticism in stressing the influence of the primitive community is blind to the influence of Jesus as a Rabbi and a prophet. On the one hand, it makes the community a creative body, of which there is little or no trace in the New Testament. The primitive Christians were not all Rabbis nor all Solomons. On the other hand, it is not recognized that Jesus was not a teacher who perpetually repeated the same maxims or memorized addresses which He delivered without variation. He is likely to have repeated the same saying in different form and constantly varied His discourses. Also variations in the Gospels may have been due to fuller information. Matthew and Luke and John, who composed their Gospels after Mark, would have been able to revise the narrative from further knowledge.

5) "Form Criticism neglects far too much the presence of eyewitnesses in the formative period and their ability to check the tradition and to safeguard it.

6) "Form Criticism neglects the evidence of second-century and later writers.

7) "Form Criticism has not clearly defined the extent of the formative period.

8) "Form Criticism has unjustifiably assumed that the contexts and settings and chronological details are of no historical or biographical value.

9) "Form Criticism is not justified in assuming that analogy is a guide to the historical truth of their legends and myths.

10) "Form Criticism in evaluating the vital factors does not take account of all the varied interests of the early Church.

11) "Form Criticism gives a wide scope for subjective treatment and to this its supporters are partial.

12) "Form Criticism overlooks the undoubted fact that the primitive Church was willing to suffer and die for its belief in Jesus and the power of His name. Jesus was a real Jesus and their Christ, Who had proved Himself by His deeds and His teaching.

13) "Form Criticism by too great an emphasis on the expected Parousia has lost sight of the normal life which men lived though the Parousia was held to be imminent." 101/77, 78

McGinley comments on the defects in Form Criticism developed by Bultmann and Dibelius, as he states:

"It has failed to work out a position in independence of the Two-Source theory [140/51]. It has neglected the essential differences between the Gospels and *Kleinliteratur*. It has accepted the discredited theory of collective creation and applied it to a community in which it did not and could not exist. It has mistaken simplicity of style for patchwork compilation. Forms have been too sharply defined and at the price of much excision of the text. A *Sitz im Leben* has been sought in every phase of primitive Christian life except the most important one: the Christian's desire to know the life of Jesus. Throughout, no place is given to historical testimony; substance is neglected in preoccupation with form; the controlling factor of time is disregarded; there is prejudice against the historical value of the whole Gospel story." 82/154

One of the peripheral goals of radical form critics has been to establish a historical Jesus authenticated through for analysis.

Form Criticism has contributed to the modern evangelical understanding of the Gospels in a negative sense by failing in this quest. As G. E. Ladd summarizes:

"Form criticism has failed to discover a purely historical Jesus." 74/157

F. J. Babcock concludes:

"But when by using this evidence we have been enabled to penetrate some little way into the mind of the early converts and their teachers, we find that whole basis of the form criticism theory has been dissolved and has vanished. It is ingenious, it is to some extent plausible, there are suggestions that it might contain fragments of truth. So it was with the Tübingen theory, and there is no reason to doubt that in a short time the theory of form criticism will share the same fate." 3/20

Rogers states:

"The method assumes solutions to questions that are still open, such as the source and synoptic questions. It assumes the validity of the two documentary theory of Mark and Q as the basis for Matthew and Luke. The priority of Mark is also assumed." 209/NP

A general impression by McGinley of Form Criticism:

"At best, much of what is true in form criticism is not new and much of what is new is not true, still, at the worst, there is wheat in the chaff for the winnowing." 82/154

McGinley states his opinion of Bultmann's work:

"If, as Bultmann contends, Schmidt has destroyed the framework of the Gospel story, then his successor has mutilated the picture itself beyond recognition, and analysis has become annihilation." 82/68

In concluding, F. F. Bruce has a suggestion for the form critic:

"When this painstaking work has been accomplished and the core of the tradition authenticated as securely as possible, he will do well to stand back among the rank and file of Gospel readers and, listening with them to the witness of the Evangelists, join in acknowledging that this witness has the 'ring of truth' [J. B. Phillips, *Ring of Truth: A Translator's Testimony* (London, 1967)]." 17/57

chapter 28

an assessment
of the
historical
critical
method

The documentary hypothesis and form criticism are facets of what is more broadly known in theology as the historical-critical method. This method, which essentially saw its birth as a child of the enlightenment, has attracted a strong following in theological circles. It is the leading method by which liberal scholars (radical or higher critics) study the Scripture in Europe and has taken an increasing toll on American biblical scholarship as well.

Some evangelical leaders are quick to point out that this method has its strengths, especially with regard to the importance of understanding the historical milieu in which the document was written, as well as appraising the evidence critically; i.e., with scrutiny. This is certainly true and to be commended. Scripture must be examined historically; i.e., in its historical background.

Scripture also must be examined critically. By this we mean, scrutinizing the text, we must ascertain such things as its authorship, date of writing and the reliability and accuracy of the text. For if the Scriptures are true, they will certainly stand the scrutiny of scholarship.

However, the radical presuppositions of the historical-critical method are so tightly bound up with this method, it is impossible to separate the form of the method (its use) from its negative presuppositions or axioms. All methods have presuppositions, yet as pointed out earlier in this work, the negative presuppositions of this method, such as anti-supernaturalisms, *ipso-facto* preclude an entire arena in testimony and evidence (especially from the biblical text itself). So by "critically" the radical critic who uses this method, not only means looking at the text with close scrutiny, but also looking at it with a number of ill-founded presuppositions.

This method, when applied to the Scriptures has seen an ever widening gap between those who expound it from the pulpit and the scholar's chair to those who attempt to understand it and apply it in their lives, as students and laymen. This is for a number of reasons.

One is due to its faulty presuppositions. If the supernatural is divorced from reality, why listen to the Bible? It is just another natural book. Theology becomes no more than religious humanism. Second, in recent years the historical-critical method has become so complex in its method and scope that it can be used competently and understood only by a limited number of educated specialists.

As a simplified example, the person who is hurting in his marriage may turn to the Bible for help in rough times. As the couple contemplates divorce, they look over the Scriptural injunctions and make some positive applications to help them weather the storm as they rely on the bedrock of Scripture, only then to find out from their pastor the next day: (1) it was not a miracle of a supernatural God to bring man and woman together as the story recounts in Genesis, and (2) all the New Testament teaching on divorce really did not come from Christ anyway. Some zealous Gospel writer just penned his thoughts as they meshed with the community around him, and put them in Jesus' mouth to lend authority to what is being said. After all, Jesus might have said it anyway! No one would want to rely on that type of authority for his marriage.

Robin Scroggs, himself a liberal critic, in the *Chicago Theological Seminary Register* in his article, "Beyond Criticism to Encounter: The Bible in the Post-Critical Age," makes this present observation with regard to the success and usefulness of the historical-critical method.

"By placing the texts in their historical, political, sociological and economical contexts, people quickly get a glimpse of a human reality with which they can more easily identify." 221/5

James A. Sanders, also a liberal critic, makes this evaluation of biblical criticisms:

"But as with most other such movements, this one, too, has created some problems: there apparently came a point when its work seemed to produce more negative than positive results for the ongoing believing communities. The charge that biblical scholarship has locked the Bible into the past and rendered it irrelevant has been made with increasing volume since the demise of neo-orthodox theology."

Walter Wink, another liberal critic, in his book *The Bible in Human Transformation*, categorically asserts, "The historical-critical method has reduced the Bible to a dead letter." 223/4

O. C. Edwards summarizes Wink's analysis of the historical-critical method and states:

"It produces a trained incapacity to deal with the real problems of actural living persons in their daily lives." 224/116

It must be noted, although it cannot be elaborated on here, that not all of those who believe the historical-critical method is presently a liability believe it should be scrapped altogether. Many call for a major overhaul. However, no overhaul will be of benefit until their presuppositions are altered.

chapter 29

redaction criticism

Within the last 50 years a new discipline has developed known as Redaction Criticism. This new approach finds its roots in the form critical method, and depends to some extent on its methodology. As with New Testament form criticism, Redaction Criticism up to this point has had its primary focus on the synoptic Gospels rather than on Pauline or Johannine writings. However, unlike form criticism which focuses on the period of oral transmission, the redaction critical method centers on the Gospels themselves.

This method adds a new dimension to New Testament criticism, that of the *sitz-em-leben* of the author. The writers of the Gospels are not seen simply as compilers of different forms, but rather as authors in their own right. They are as men who carefully orchestrated a literary symphony using the Gospel "form" pioneered by the evangelist Mark. The Gospel writers are seen as both theological composers and redactors putting together primarily a literary and theological work, not a historical one.

Redaction criticism seeks to determine the theological viewpoint of the evangelist who wrote the Gospel. The critics attempt to ascertain what sources or accounts did the Gospel writers choose and why, and where these are fitted together in his particular account (known as "seams"). The critics want to find the specific theological "glue" the authors used to build their Gospels.

But as the redaction critic attempts to determine why each author chose to develop his Gospel as he did, he completely ignores the author's own claims and reasons for writing. The critics also do not view the Gospels as historical accounts in any accepted sense of the idea. The critics pass judgment on the documents before they are allowed to speak for themselves.

A short presentation of the tenets of redaction criticism follows:

1A. DEFINITIONS

1B. The authors are seen as active rather than passive instruments in the development of the Gospels. Gunther Bornkamm comments:

"The Synoptic writers show—all three and each in his own special way—by their editing and construction, by their selection, inclusion and omission, and not least by what at first sight appears an insignificant, but on closer examination is seen to be a characteristic treatment of the traditional material, that they are by no means mere collectors and handers-on of the tradition, but are also interpreters of it." 189/11

2B. Norman Perrin defines redaction criticism this way:

"It is concerned with studying the theological motivation of an author as this is revealed in the collection, arrangement, editing, and modification of traditional material, and in the composition of new material or the creation of new forms within the traditions of early Christianity." 191/1

He then adds:

"The prime requisite for redaction criticism is the ability to trace the form and content of material used by the author concerned or in some way to determine the nature and extent of his activity in collecting and creating, as well as in arranging, editing and composing." 191/2

3B. Stephen Smalley, in his essay, "Redaction Criticism," from *New Testament Interpretation: Essays on Principles and Methods*, explains Redaction Criticism this way:

"The term 'redaction' in Gospel criticism describes the editorial work carried out by the evangelists on their sources when they composed the Gospels. It has been suggested by Ernst Haenchen that 'composition criticism' would better describe the study of this process."

Smalley further describes the difference between "redaction criticism" and "composition criticism":

"Although they are close together, they are strictly speaking different disciplines. One (redaction criticism) is the study of the observable changes introduced by the Gospel writers into the traditional material they received and used. The other (composition criticism) examines the *arrangement* of this material, an arrangement which is motived by the theological understanding and intention of the evangelists. And some scholars expand the term 'composition' in this context to include the construction of wholly new sayings by the Gospel writers, which are then (so it is claimed) attributed by them to Jesus.

"It is possible that in the future composition criticism will need to be distinguished from redaction criticism, just as redaction criticism is currently distinguished from form criticism. But meanwhile, and for convenience, the term 'redaction criticism' can be understood as the detection of the evangelists' creative contribution in all its aspects to the Christian tradition which they transmit." 194/181

2A. PURPOSE

Integrally related to the purpose of redaction criticism is its relation to form criticism

1B. Purpose

As with form criticism, redaction criticism seeks to uncover the traditions regarding Jesus Christ. Yet according to the redaction critics, the discipline of form criticism had overlooked an important point. Robert Stein comments:

"As a result the form critics forgot that the individual Gospels are also units which demand consideration and must be investigated as individual entities. This error was due in part to the fact that the form critics looked upon the Gospel writers as merely collectors or *Sammler*. They were only 'scissors and paste men' who assembled together the various pericopes. As a result the first three books of the NT were viewed not as 'gospels' but as 'pericope collections.' Form critics therefore felt justified in treating each pericope as an individual gem. Each bit of tradition was treated as a separate pearl and carefully analyzed. But what of the setting into which these gems were placed? The form critics overlooked the fact that the setting provided by the evangelists gave a distinct appearance to these gems. They overlooked the fact that these pearls of tradition were strung together in a particular manner and revealed a particular design. 193/45-46

Ralph Martin amplifies the above:

"Put simply, the aim and intention of a *redaktionsgeschtlich* treatment of the gospels is concerned to upturn by reversal of Harvyns and Davey that 'the evangelist write as historians and not as theologians.' The evidence adduced in support of this reversal which turns the gospel writers into theologians lies in the *Tendenz* of the gospel material, that is, in the reason why certain incidents are included in just the ways they are and couched in the particular language used." 192/46-47

Joachim Rohde in *Rediscovering the Teaching of the Evangelists* comments:

"The most important discovery of redaction criticism which goes beyond form criticism is that it is not the gospels as a whole which must be claimed as composite material but only their content, whilst the redaction of it, that is to say, its grouping, its composition and arrangement into a definite geographical and chronological framework with quite definite theological viewpoints, must be regarded as the work of the evangelist. This investigation of redaction criticism into the gospel as a whole led to the realization that the evangelists' choice of material, the order in which they placed what they had collected, especially the arrangement of their compositions, and the alterations they made in the traditional matter, are all determined by their theology; in other words, the evangelists did their work as theologians and from theological viewpoints." 195/14-15

Thus the major purpose of redaction criticism is to determine what theological viewpoints shaped the Gospel writers' thinking and how did their doctrine guide them in writing, collecting and arranging their Gospel. All this is undertaken to ascertain what the Gospel writers have to say to us today.

2B. Relationship to Form Criticism

Redaction criticism those arose out of the need to fill a void left by form criticism. Yet the two disciplines, although different, are distinctly related. Smalley elucidated:

"Why is it necessary at all in the study of the Gospels to move beyond form criticism into redaction criticism? Since both disciplines are concerned with the editing and shaping of the tradition about Jesus, although at different stages, need they be separated? The answer to these questions is straightforward. There is an important difference between the approaches of form criticism and redaction criticism in the method used and the conclusions reached, as well as in the fact that they are concerned with different stages in the history of the Christian tradition.

"Form criticism (especially in its older versions) tends to view the Gospels as collections of material which originated as independent units (an assumption that itself needs qualification), and the evangelists as little more than 'scissors and paste men' who gathered these units together with a special interpretative slant in mind. Redaction criticism, on the other hand, looks at the Gospels as complete documents, and sees the evangelists as individual theologians (even 'authors') in their own right. Form criticism deals with the origins of the Gospel tradition, redaction criticism with its later stages.

"Redaction criticism thus builds on redaction criticism, in the sense that form-critical method enables us to detect the work of the evangelists themselves more clearly. The newer discipline of redaction criticism moves away from form criticism, however, in that it sets out to discover the theological uniqueness of the evangelists *in relation to their sources*. To this extent redaction criticism is not a real part of form criticism. But once the two have been separated, it is important to notice that redaction criticism does not then become simply a study of 'the theology' of the evangelists. It is rather a consideration of the creative way in which these writers have handled their sources at the final stages of composition." 194/182

3A. BACKGROUND AND HISTORY

1B. Background

In the nineteenth century the old quest for the historical Jesus was taking place. The movement was initiated by the works of H. S. Reimanus published posthumously by G. Lessing. Reimanus believed the Gospel accounts were colored by the news of the disciples. He held to a rationalistic base and believed that the resurrection accounts were contradictory and not part of Christ's teaching.

Later, D. F. Strauss, with the publication of his *Life of Jesus, Critically Examined*, touched off a strong debate as he contended that the truth of the historical Jesus was shrouded in myth. The quest for the historical Jesus continued, however, as the critics attempted to reconstruct the liberal lives of Christ. Many of these men held to a rationalistic, objective view of history, that Jesus was no more than an ordinary man, and historical (non-supernatural) evidence could be found to reconstruct his life. These men also held the historicity of the Markan account in fairly high esteem (seen through their rational presuppositions), believing the Gospels presented basically an historical picture, especially Mark, the first Gospel written.

The factors which contributed to the demise of the old quest also served as a foundation for the eventual rise of redaction criticism. One such factor was William Wrede's *The Messianic Secret*. Wrede's book served to shatter the idea that Mark was historically accurate in his approach (see page 277). Wrede believed Mark wrote from a personal rather than historical viewpoint. Perrin comments on Wrede's contribution:

"So far as the development of redaction criticism is concerned, Wrede's thesis opened the way for the study of the dogmatic ideas and theological conceptions that were at work in the tradition. The study of these ideas and conceptions is the task of redaction criticism, and Wrede's work on the Messianic Secret is in many ways the first product of this discipline." 191/12

As mentioned earlier, form criticism served as the historical base for redaction criticism. As the Gospels were studied using the form critical approach, the need to consider the Gospel writers as authors rather than simply collectors became a major concern. Another important work anticipating this viewpoint was R. H. Lightfoot's *History and Interpretation in the Gospels*. In this work, which is actually a series of lectures given at the University of Oxford in 1934, Lightfoot discusses the Gospels from a *formgeschichte* approach, paying special attention to the previous work on the subject. In his third lecture, Lightfoot argues that Mark sets forth his purpose for writing his Gospel, and that it is theological in nature. Lightfoot believes Mark's theological viewpoint affected his historical reporting and was colored by it. He states:

"In St. Mark's gospel the case seems very different. Here our first impression may well be that we are dealing with a plain historical record, to which we must assign our own interpretation; and the attempt to do so has been constantly made in the last two generations. But it is becoming probable that in this gospel also the significance which the evangelist believes to belong to and inhere in the history is constantly suggested in the form of fact, and that St. Mark's gospel is built upon the basis of a definite doctrine, although the latter is much less obtrusively and pervadingly present than in the gospel of St. John. 196/58-59

With these slowly emerging emphases redaction criticism came to the fore. One other factor contributed to the rise of the discipline and that was the oversight of form criticism to see the writers of the Gospels as more than mere editors. (See "Purpose" on page 306 for a discussion of this factor.)

2B. History

Redaction criticism is relatively a new discipline with the majority of the scholarship taking place in the last 30 years, after World War II. The scholarly lull in Germany during the war years served to focus attention on the apparent weaknesses in the form critical method. This focus, together with works such as Lightfoot's, saw three different works appear, on each of the three synoptic Gospels, all written independently of each other in the late forties to mid-fifties.

The works were: (1) On Matthew: "End-Expectation and Church in Matthew" (1954, in a brief in a German publication; 1956, a more expanded form), and "The Stilling of the Storm in Matthew" (1948, original German publication) by Gunther Bornkamm. They are now found in English in *Tradition and Interpretation in Matthew*, 1963. (2) On Luke: *The Theology of St. Luke* (1953, original German edition; 1960, for the English translation. (3) On Mark: *Mark the Evangelist* (1956, original German publication; 1969 for the English translation).

These three books are the seminal works which helped usher in the redaction criticism approach.

Perrin comments on this origin of the discipline:

"Redaction criticism burst into full flower immediately after the Second World War in Germany. Just as three scholars emerged with independent works marking the beginning of form criticism proper after the hiatus caused by the First World War, so three scholars came forward with independent works denoting the beginning of redaction criticism proper after the hiatus caused by the Second World War. After the First World War it was Karl Ludwig Schmidt, Martin Dibelius, and Rudolf Bultmann, as we have already noted; after the Second World War it was Gunther Bornkamm, Hans Conzelmann, and Willi Marzsen. Though working independently of one another—Bornkamm on Matthew, Conzelmann on Luke, and Marxsen on Mark—they moved in the same general direction. One of them, Willi Marxsen, gave the new movement its German name, *Redaktionsgeschichte*." 191/25

4A. MAJOR PROPONENTS

1B. Gunther Bornkamm

Bornkamm, a pupil of Bultmann, is considered the first of the true redaction critics." 191/26

Bornkamm believes Matthew's theological emphasis is ecclesiological in nature. The Church's relationship to the imminent return of Christ is examined in Bornkamm's "End-Expectation and Church in Matthew." In the short essay, "The Stilling of the Storm," he illustrates how Matthew used the Markan accounts of the narrative and then structured his own in such a way as to bring across his specific emphasis.

Focusing on the individual contributions of the Gospel writers, Bornkamm states:

"The evangelists do not hark back to some kind of church archives when they pass on the words and deeds of Jesus, but they draw them from the kerygma of the Church and serve this kerygma. Because Jesus is not a figure of the past and thus is no museum piece, there can be no 'archives' for the primitive Christian tradition about him, in which he is kept. This insight into the nature of the tradition about Jesus is confirmed in detail again and again. The pericope which is here to serve as an example for making clear the evangelist's method of working is the story of the stilling of the storm. 189/52-53

Referring to Bornkamm's contribution to redaction criticism, Smalley states:

"Gunther Bornkamm's work on the Gospel of Matthew marks the rise of redaction criticism. As a pupil of Rudolf Bultmann, he proceeded from form-critical assumptions to the further stage of analyzing Matthew's own theological outlook and intention as this is to be discerned in his handling of traditional material. In two articles which were later included in the volume now translated as *Tradition and Interpretation in Matthew*, Bornkamm set out his conclusions about the first evangelist and his work. The earlier essay is a study of the episode of the stilling of the storm in Matthew 8: 23-27, and attempts to show how Matthew treated the source from which he derived this pericope (Mk. 4:35-41). The new context and presentation given to the incident, Bornkamm claims, reveal the independent meaning it has for the evangelist. The miracle thus becomes to him 'a kerygmatic paradigm of the danger and glory of discipleship.' The other essay of Bornkamm deals with the construction of the discourses of Jesus in Matthew, and discusses the extent to which these are controlled by the evangelist's own understanding of the church, the end, the law, Christ himself, and the interrelation of all four. Together, these two studies reflect Bornkamm's dominant conviction that Matthew is a distinctive redactor; an 'interpreter of the tradition which he collected and arranged.'" 194/183

Rohde comments on his use of form criticism and how it relates to the redaction method in Bornkamm's interpretation of the Matthenian accounts. Rohde points to Bornkamm's shift in emphasis to the authors themselves:

"We must begin with Bornkamm's first article. His introductory remarks make it evident how far he is building on the form-critical method. He attributes to form criticism the methodical elaboration of the insight that the gospels must be understood as *kerygma*, and not as biographies of Jesus of Nazareth; and that they cannot be fitted into any of the literary categories of antiquity, but that they are stamped and determined in every respect by faith in Jesus Christ, the Crucified and Risen One, both in their content and their form, as a whole and in detail." 195/11

He further adds:

"In conclusion, Bornkamm declares that in this interpretation of the stilling of the storm he does not intend to attack the principles of form criticism, according to which the single pericopes are regarded as the primary data of the tradition. In the future, however, even greater care must be taken to enquire about the motives for the composition by the *individual* evangelists. It is true that they had worked to a large extent as collectors; yet it is important to ascertain the definite theological intentions revealed by the composition. By its connection with the sayings about discipleship, the stilling of the storm has become *kerygma* and a paradigm of the danger and glory of discipleship." 195/13

2B. Hans Conzelmann

Of Conzelmann, Perrin states:

"If Gunther Bornkamm is the first of the true redaction critics, Hans Conzelmann is certainly the most important. His *Theology of St. Luke*, first published in German in 1954, is the one work above all others which focused attention upon this new discipline and convinced a whole world of New Testament scholarship that here, indeed, was a major new departure in New Testament Studies. His book ranks with Bultmann's *History of the Synoptic Tradition* or Jeremias's *The Parables of Jesus* as one of the few truly seminal works of our time in the field of New Testament research; neither the discipline of New Testament theology as a whole nor the understanding of Luke in particular will ever be the same again." 191/28-29

Conzelmann comments on the need to see Luke primarily as a theologian rather than a historian. This is a major directive in Conzelmann's approach:

"In what sense then can Luke be described as a 'historian'? Modern research concerns itself essentially with the reliability of his reporting, but if we are interested in the first place not in what is reported, but in the report as such, the problem takes a different form: what is Luke's conception of the meaning of his account? We must start from a methodical comparison with his sources, in so far as these are directly available or can be reconstructed. What is Luke's attitude to his forerunners and how does he conceive his task in the context of the contemporary Church's understanding of doctrine and history? Our aim is not to investigate the models and sources as such, nor is it to reconstruct the historical events. This is of course an indispensable task, but first of all the meaning of the text before must be investigated regardless of our idea of the probable course of historical events, regardless, that is, of the picture which Luke gives of the latter.

"We must of course define Luke's own historical position in the context of the development of the Church. Only in this way can we understand how on the one hand he looks back to the 'arche' of the Church as something unique and unrepeatable, which presupposes a certain distance in time, and how on the other hand he looks forward to the eschatological events. What distinguishes him is not that he thinks in the categories of promise and fulfillment, for this he has in common with others, but the way in which he builds up from these categories a picture of the course of saving history, and the way in which he employs the traditional material for this purpose." 197/12-13

Of Conzelmann's contribution Smalley remarks:

"Hans Conzelmann's work as a redaction critic has been concerned mainly with Luke-Acts. His book *Die Mitte der Zeit*, first published in 1954, and translated into English as *The Theology of St. Luke,* marks a watershed in Gospel studies and an important advance in the method of redaction criticism itself; for it is an analysis of Luke's unique role as a theologian." 194/183

3B. Willi Marxsen

Marxsen's redaction critical study of Mark is a highlight in its field. In his work *Mark the Evangelist, Marxsen first used the term redaktionsgeschichte.* He also proposed a three-fold *sitz-em-leben*, rather than two-fold as advocated by the form critics. His three *sitz-em-leben* are (1) of Jesus, (2) of the church, and (3) (the new contribution) of the author. This new emphasis set the standard for future work in redaction criticism.

Some have disagreed with Marxsen over the use of three *sitz-em-leben* (some seeing two and three as one unit) but the disagreement is mainly one of semantics. 193/49ff

Marxsen desires to make a clear distinction between form and redaction criticism. 190/215

Perrin comments on Marxsen's distinctions between form and redaction criticism:

"First, he stresses the difference between the understanding of the evangelists in the one discipline and the other. Form criticism regarded the evangelists primarily as collectors of tradition, whereas redaction criticism regards them as authors in their own right. Secondly, form criticism was mostly concerned with breaking down the tradition into small units and particularly with the way in which these small units came into being in the first place.

"Redaction criticism, however, concerns itself with the larger units down to and including the particular form of Gospel and asks questions about the purpose of the formation of these larger units of tradition. Thirdly, form criticism with its concern for the individual units of tradition and its understanding of the evangelists as collectors of tradition could never do justice to that bold new step taken by the evangelist Mark, who gathers together individual units and larger collections of tradition and out of them fashions something wholly new—a 'Gospel.'

"Both Matthew and Luke inherit this form, 'Gospel,' from Mark and make further use of it themselves; in no small measure it is the purpose of redaction criticism to do justice to both the Marcan theology lying behind the creation of the form 'Gospel,' and to those aspects of the Lucan and Matthean theology which become evident as we consider the way in which they use the form as well as the tradition which they inherit from Mark. Fourthly in keeping with his understanding of the totality of the transmission of tradition from its creation in the early church to its reformulation by the synoptic evangelists, Marxsen claims that one should be prepared to consider three separate 'settings-in-life' for synoptic tradition. 191/33-34

Smalley discusses Marxsen's contribution to the field:

"Marxsen accepts the method and conclusions of form criticism as a basis for his work. But once more, like them, he goes beyond this to emphasize the important contribution made by Mark himself when he collected together the independent units of the evangelic tradition and wrote them up into a Gospel as such, characterized by his own theological outlook.

"That outlook is seen particularly, Marxsen claims, in Mark's treatment of such features as the tradition about John the Baptist and the geographical references in his narratives. (Galilee, for example, is 'obviously the evangelist's own creation.') Throughout, Marxsen sees the second evangelist as a theologically motivated redactor, whose doctrinal interpretations become clearer when the use by Matthew and Luke of the Marcan tradition and its interpretations is considered.

"One of Marxsen's more important contributions to the whole discussion of redaction criticism is his clarification of the threefold setting of all Gospel material (in the teaching of Jesus, in the life of the early church and in the writing and intention of the evangelists), of which mention has already been made. In this as in many other ways, Marxsen laid down methodological precedents which other redaction critics have followed." 194/184

5A. METHODOLOGY

1B. Presuppostions

The major presuppositions of the redaction critical approach are the following.

1C. TWO SOURCE HYPOTHESIS

Redaction criticism depends heavily on Markan priority, along with the necessity of the Q source. Should Markan priority be seriously questioned with evidence to doubt its veracity, most of redaction criticism in its present form would crumble.

All three major proponents depend on Mark as the primary source for their work, each one trying to understand how the different evangelists made use of Mark. For Marxsen it is a comparison to determine how Mark was used by both Matthew and Luke.

Rohde comments:

"Most of the scholars who use the redaction-critical method start with the two-source theory and try to grasp the specific theology of the individual evangelist by comparing the synoptists." 195/19

Perrin also comments:

"The prime requisite for redaction criticism is the ability to trace the form and content of material used by the author concerned or in some way to determine the nature and extent of his activity in collecting and creating, as well as in arranging, editing and composing. The most successful redaction-critical work has been done on the Gospels of Matthew and Luke, since in these we have one major source which each evangelist used, the Gospel of Mark, and can reconstruct a good deal of another, the sayings source 'Q.'

"But similar work can be done wherever the use of traditional material can be determined or the particular activity of the author detected, and it is interesting to note that redaction criticism really began with work on the Gospel of Mark." 191/2

2C. FORM CRITICISM

As previously mentioned and emphasized, the discipline of form criticism is a primary requisite to redaction studies (see purpose). Not all proponents would put the same stress on its usefulness or advantages, but it nevertheless is needed.

Perrin comments:

"In the field of New Testament criticism, the discipline of redaction criticism is the latest of the three major developments which are the subjects of the volumes in this series: literary criticism, form criticism, and redaction criticism. Though the distinctions between the three disciplines are somewhat artificial, they do call attention to the fact that the critical work has proceeded by stages and that one type of work builds upon the results of another. Form criticism and redaction criticism in particular are very closely related to one another. They are in fact the first and second stages of a unified discipline, but their divergence in emphasis is sufficient to justify their being treated separately." 191/2

3C. THEOLOGIANS VS. HISTORIANS

The redaction critics presuppose that the theological viewpoint of the author was the dominant factor which shaped the composition of his Gospel. Historical accuracy and objectivity were secondary to the need to present a specific picture of Christ as seen by the community and the author.

Perrin comments on this attitude:

"In our view Mark is a significant and creative literary figure and deserves to be read in the form in which he chose to write rather than in summary. Mark has the right to be read on his own terms, and after several generations of being read mistakenly, as a historian, he has earned the right to be read as a theologian." 191/53

Soulen puts it this way:

"It is important to note that RC (redaction criticism) as applied to the synoptic Gospels is based on the Two Source Hypothesis which names Mark and Q as sources in the writing of Matthew and Luke. Should the priority of Matthew be established, as some suggest, the redaction-critical analysis of the synoptics would have to begin all over again." 199/143-44

4C. BASIC ASSUMPTIONS

As with other liberal critics, the redaction critics hold to a rationalistic foundation.

In the main, they hold to a rigid scientific world view where the supernatural is ruled out on *a priori* grounds.

This procrustean bed also shapes their historiography. Their view rules out any real possibility of objective history.

These presuppositions shape all their thinking.

2B. Procedure

The methodology of the redaction critics involves the need to ascertain what sources or accounts the Gospel writers chose and why, as well as where these accounts are fitted together in his particular account (known as seams). This is undertaken by determining the various *sitz-em-lebens* from which the material arose, including the authors'.

The general goals of the procedure are listed by Martin:

"Attention is shifted from the small, independent units into which form-criticism had separated the gospel materials, and interest is turned to the gospels as literary wholes.

"An important corollary of this change of perspective is that the evangelists emerge from the role of simple collectors and *Tradents* (i.e. handers-on) of the material they assemble and are reinstated in their own right as authors why by their selecting and editing the material impose on that material a distinctive theological stamp. In a phrase used by J. Rohde (*op. cit.*, p. 12; cf. p. 20), they do not simply hand on the story, but by placing it in a particular context and editing its details they become the earliest exegetes of it.

"This means that we are invited to penetrate beneath the layers of the gospel data which can be identified as traditional and seek to locate the elements of the evangelist's editorializing work. We are encouraged to enter and explore the world of the evangelist himself—or more plausibly the community of which he was a member and seek to understand what the gospel sections *and the completed whole of the gospels* would have meant in those situations.

"So we are bidden, at the behest of redaction criticism, the 'third life-setting' of the gospels, i.e., the setting which provides explanatory contexts for the evangelist's own work. For W. Marxsen who pioneered the redactional study of Mark's gospel this entailed a study of the historical and theological background which provoked the evangelist to publish his literary work under the novel caption of 'gospel.' Marxsen needed to find an 'occasion,' called by him a catalyst which is required to cause the author to assemble, edit and then make public in written form what we know as a gospel book.

"Assuming that Mark had before him a collection of loosely connected sections of narrative and teaching, what impulse moved him to set them into a coherent pattern which conveyed a unified message? It cannot have been by accident that his gospel was born, for 'it is not at all obvious that this totally disparate material should finally find its way into the unity of a Gospel." 192/47-8

Stein in his article, "What Is Redaktionsgeschichte?" delineates this further as he discusses the concerns in the redaction critical procedure:

"Rather we are concerned with ascertaining the unique contribution to and understanding of the sources by the evangelists. This will be found in their seams, interpretative comments, summaries, modification of material, selection of material, omission of material, arrangement, introductions, conclusions, vocabulary, christological titles, etc. In the redaktionsgeschichte investigation of the gospels we do not seek primarily the theology of the evangelist's sources as form criticism does, but having ascertained the evangelist's redaction, we seek to find:

"*What unique theological views does the evangelist present which are foreign to his sources?* Redaktionsgeschichte is not primarily concerned with any unique literary style or arrangement that an evangelist may have used. It seeks rather the unique theological views of the evangelist. An example of this is the twofold division of Galilee-Jerusalem found in Mark. If this is due to literary and stylistic motives, redaktionsgeschichte is not involved, but, if this scheme is due to a theological motive, then redaktiongeschichte is very much involved.

"*What unusual theological emphasis or emphases does the evangelist place upon the sources he received?* An evangelist may give to his sources an emphasis which is not necessarily a *de novo* creation. The evangelist reveals his redaktionsgeschichte in this instance by the unusual stress he places upon a certain theme found in the tradition. An example of this is the 'messianic secret' found in Mark.

"*What theological purpose or purposes does the evangelist have in writing his gospel?*

"*What is the* Sitz im Leben *out of which the evangelist writes his gospel?* It is hoped that the results of (1) and (2) can be systematized so that the purpose and *Sitz im Leben* of the evangelist can be ascertained. This will not always be so. Some of the evangelists' redaktionsgeschichte will concern peripheral matters, for not every change or stress will involve a major problem, concern, or purpose of the evangelists. As a result some of the results of (1) and (2) may at times not be of great importance or relevance for (3) and (4)." 193/53-54

For a more detailed look at procedure see Robert H. Stein's "The Redaktionsgeschcichtlich Investigation of a Markan Seam (MC/21ff)." 200/70-94

Also for a treatment on specifics N. Perrin's chapter, "Redaction Criticism at Work: A Sample" in *What Is Redaction Criticism?* is helpful. 191/40-63

Dan O. Via, Jr. summarizes:

"Redaction criticism is the most recent of the three disciplines to have become a self-conscious method of inquiry. It grew out of form criticism, and it presupposes and continues the procedures of the earlier discipline while extending and intensifying certain of them. The redaction critic investigates how smaller units—both simple and composite—from the oral tradition or from written sources were put together to form larger complexes, and he is especially interested in the formation of the Gospels as finished products. Redaction criticism is concerned with the interaction between an inherited tradition and a later interpretive point of view. Its goals are to understand why the items from the tradition were modified and connected as they were, to identify the theological motifs that were at work in composing a finished Gospel, and to elucidate the theological point of view which is expressed in and through the composition. Although redaction criticism has been most closely associated with the Gospels, there is no reason why it could not be used—and actually it is being used—to illuminate the relationship between tradition and interpretation in other New Testament books." 191/vi-vii

6A. BASIC CRITICISMS

1B. Many of the criticisms which apply to form criticism will also clearly apply here since redaction criticism builds on this discipline.

2B. The two-source theory of the Gospels and Markan priority has never been established and is in dispute today.

3B. Professor Harold W. Hehner, Ph.D. in New Testament at Cambridge, makes the following summary assessments:

    1C. The sitz-em-leben position is not historically substantiated. The evidence points to the fact that the Gospels created the Christian community rather than the fact that the communities created the Gospel.

    2C. The role of eyewitnesses is forgotten. Their testimony is clear in the Gospels, and if one of them was wrong they could have corrected him. The critics believe that theologians would distort history to fit their theology. This is not necessarily the case. The critics attempt to reconstruct the Gospel accounts totally apart from the eyewitnesses, who were there.

    3C. The uniqueness of Jesus is minimized. The critics assume that the Gospel writers made the brilliant statements in the Gospels rather than Jesus.

    4C. Christian ethics are minimized. Christ emphasized the truth, yet the Gospel writers fabricated a story. They told us that the story of Christ happened a certain way, yet in reality it did not. It was a community creation. A small lie may have small consequences, yet here their lie is believed by thousands and thousands thus have even died for a lie.

    5C. There is no room for the Holy Spirit. Their naturalistic theology almost excludes the work of God in the believer's life.

    6C. Simply because the authors have a theological purpose in writing does not negate authenticity or historical accuracy.

7A. IN SUMMARY

1B. Redaction criticism seeks to discover the theological viewpoint of the Gospel writer, both how he arrived at it and how it influenced the shaping of his work.

2B. Redaction criticism came into existence in Germany following World War II.

3B. Its major proponents are Gunther Bornkamm, Willi Marxsen and Hans Conzelmann.

4B. The redaction critics seek to understand three major sitz-em-lebens, that of Jesus' day, of the church, and of the author.

5B. The redaction critics have little, if any, historical substantiation or evidence for their view and operation of their method.

BIBLIOGRAPHY

1. Abel, E.L. "Psychology of Memory and Rumor Transmission and Their Bearing on Theories of Oral Transmission in Early Christianity," *Journal of Religion.* October, 1971. Vol. 51, pp. 270-281.

2. Albright, W.F. *New Horizons in Biblical Research.* New York: Oxford University Press, 1966.

3. Babcock, F.J. "Form Criticism," *The Expository Times.* October, 1941. Vol. 53, No. 1, pp. 16-20.

4. Baker, Dom Aelred. "Form and the Gospels," *Downside Review.* January, 1970. Vol. 88, pp. 14-26.

5. Barker, Glenn W., William L. Lane, J. Ramsey Michaels. *The New Testament Speaks.* New York: Harper & Row Publishers, 1969.

6. Barnes, W.E. *Gospel Criticism and Form Criticism.* Edinburgh: T. & T. Clark, 1936.

7. Barr, Allan. "Bultmann's Estimate of Jesus," *Scottish Journal of Theology.* December, 1954. Vol. 7, pp. 337-352.

8. Barr, Allan. "The Factor of Testimony in the Gospels," *Expository Times.* June, 1938. Vol. 49, No. 9, pp. 401-408.

9. Barrett, C.K. "Myth and the New Testament, *Expository Times.* September, 1957. Vol. 68, No. 12, pp. 359-362.

10. Bartsch, Hans-Werner, ed. *Kerygma and Myth.* Translated by Reginald H. Fuller. London: S P C K, 1962.

11. Blackman, E.C. "Jesus Christ Yesterday: The Historical Basis of the Christian Faith," *Canadian Journal of Theology.* April, 1961. Vol. 7, No. 2, pp. 118-127.

12. Bowman, John Wick. "From Schweitzer to Bultmann," *Theology Today.* July, 1954. Vol. 11, pp. 160-178.

13. Braaten, Carl E. and Roy A. Harrisville, editors and translators. *The Historical Jesus and the Kerygmatic Christ.* Nashville, Tenn.: Abingdon Press, 1964.

14. Braaten, Carl E. and Roy A. Harrisville, selectors, editors, and translators. *Kerygma and History.* New York: Abingdon Press, 1962.

15. Bruce, F.F. "Criticism and Faith," *Christianity Today.* November 21, 1960. Vol. 5, No. 4, pp. 9-12.

16. Bruce, F.F. *The New Testament Documents: Are They Reliable?* Fifth edition. Downers Grove, Illinois: Inter-Varsity Press, 1960.

17. Bruce, F.F. *Tradition Old and New.* Grand Rapids: Zondervan Publishing House, 1970.

18. Bultmann, Rudolf. *Existence and Faith.* Shorter writings of R. Bultmann selected, translated and introduced by Schubert M. Ogden. Cleveland and New York: Meridian Books—The World Publishing Co., 1960.

19. Bultmann, Rudolf and Karl Kundsin. *Form Criticism.* Translated by F. C. Grant. Original Publisher—Willett, Clark, and Co., 1934. Harper and Brothers—Torchbook Edition, 1962.

20. Bultmann, Rudolf. *History and Eschatology.* Edinburgh: The Edinburgh University Press, 1957.

21. Bultmann, Rudolf. *The History of the Synoptic Tradition.* Translated by John Marsh. New York: Harper and Row, 1963.

22. Bultmann, Rudolf. *Jesus Christ and Mythology.* New York: Charles Scribner's Sons, 1958.

23. Bultmann, Rudolf. *Jesus and the Word.* Translated by Louise Pettibone Smith and Erminie Huntress Lantero. New York: Charles Scribner's Sons, 1958.

24. Bultmann, Rudolf. *Theology of the New Testament.* Vol. 1. Translated by Kendrick Grobel. New York: Charles Scribner's Sons, 1951.

25. Bultmann, R. *Theology of the New Testament.* Vol. 2. Translated by Kendrick Grobel. New York: Charles Scribner's Sons, 1955.

26. Burkitt, F. Crawford. *The Gospel History and Its Transmission.* Edinburgh: T. & T. Clark, 1925.

27. Burkitt, F.C. *Jesus Christ.* London and Glasgow: Blackie and Sons, Ltd., 1932.

28. Cadbury, Henry J. "Some Foibles of N.T. Scholarship," *Journal of Bible and Religion.* July, 1958. Vol. 26, pp. 213-216.

29. Cadoux, Arthur Temple. *The Sources of the Second Gospel.* London: James Clarke and Co. Ltd., n.d.

30. Cairns, David, *A Gospel Without Myth?* London: SCM Press Ltd., 1960.

31. Campbell, Richard. "History and Bultmann's Structural Inconsistency," *Religious Studies.* March, 1973. Vol. 9, pp. 63-79.

32. Culpepper, Robert H. "The Problem of Miracles," *Review and Expositor.* April, 1956. Vol. 53, pp. 211-224.

33. Davies, W.D. *Invitation to the New Testament.* New York: Doubleday and Co., Inc., 1966.

34. Davies, W.D. "Quest to Be Resumed in New Testament Studies," *Union Seminary Quarterly.* January, 1960. Vol. 15, pp. 83-98.

35. Dibelius, Martin. *A Fresh Approach to the New Testament and Early Christian Literature.* New York: Charles Scribner's Sons, 1936.

36. Dibelius, Martin. *From Tradition to Gospel.* Translated by Bertram Lee Woolf. New York: Charles Scribner's Sons, 1935.

37. Dibelius, Martin. *Gospel Criticism and Christology.* London: Ivor Nicholson and Watson, Ltd., 1935.

38. Dibelius, Martin. *Jesus.* Translated by Charles B. Hedrick and Frederick C. Grant. Philadelphia: The Wesminster Press, 1949.

39. Dodd, C.H. *About the Gospels, The Coming of Christ.* Cambridge: at the University Press, 1958.

40. Dodd, C.H. *History and the Gospel.* New York: Charles Scribner's Sons, 1938.

41. Dodd, C.H. *The Parables of the Kingdom.* London: Nisbet and Co., Ltd., 1935.

42. Duncker, Peter G. "Biblical Criticism," *The Catholic Biblical Quarterly.* January, 1963. Vol. 25, No. 1, pp. 22-33.

43. Easton, Burton Scott. *Christ in the Gospels.* New York: Charles Scribner's Sons, 1930.

44. Easton, Burton Scott. *The Gospel Before the Gospels.* New York: Charles Scribner's Sons, 1928.

45. Ferré, Nels F. S. "Contemporary Theology in the Light of 100 Years," *Theology Tday.* October, 1958. Vol. 15, pp. 366-76.

46. Filson, Floyd V. "Form Criticism," *Twentieth Century Encyclopedia of Religious Knowledge.* Vol. 1. Edited by Lefferts A. Loetscher. Grand Rapids: Baker Book House, 1955.

47. Filson, Floyd V. *Origins of the Gospels.* New York: Abingdon Press, 1938.

48. Fitzmyer, Joseph A. "Memory and Manuscript: The Origins and Transmission

of the Gospel Tradition," *Theological Studies.* September, 1962. Vol. 23, pp. 442-457.

49. Fuller, Reginald Horace. "Rudolf Bultmann," *Encyclopedia Britannica.* Vol. 4. Chicago: William Benton, 1962.

50. Fuller, Reginald H. *The Mission and Achievement of Jesus.* London: SCM Press Ltd., 1967.

51. Fuller, Reginald H. *The New Testament in Current Study.* New York: Charles Scribner's Sons, 1962.

52. Grant, F. C. "Biblical Studies; Views and Reviews," *Theology Today.* April, 1957. Vol. 14, pp. 48-60.

53. Grant, Frederick C. *The Growth of the Gospels.* New York: The Abingdon Press, 1933.

54. Groebel, K. "Form Criticism," *The Interpreter's Dictionary of the Bible.* Edited by Emory Stevens Bucke. New York: Abingdon Press, 1962. Vol. 2, pp. 320, 321.

55. Gundry, Stanley N. "A Critique of the Fundamental Assumption of Form Criticism, Part I," *Bibliotheca Sacra.* April, 1966. No. 489, pp. 32-39.

56. Gundry, Stanley N. "A Critique of the Fundamental Assumption of Form Criticism, Part II," *Bibliotheca Sacra.* June, 1966. No. 490, pp. 140-149.

57. Gundry, Stan. *An Investigation of the Fundamental Assumption of Form Criticism.* A thesis presented to the Department of New Testament Language and Literature at Talbot Theological Seminary, June, 1963.

58. Benoit, Pierre. *Jesus and the Gospels.* Vol. 1. Translated by Benet Weatherhead. New York: Herder and Herder, 1973.

59. Henderson, Ian. *Rudolf Bultmann.* Richmond: John Knox Press, 1965.

60. Henry, C.F. H. "The Theological Crisis in Europe: Decline of the Bultmann Era?" *Christianity Today.* September 25, 1964. Vol. 8, pp. 12-14.

61. Hodges, Zane C. "Form-Criticism and the Resurrection Accounts," *Bibliotheca Sacra.* October-December, 1967. Vol. 124, No., 496, pp. 339-348.

62. Hoskyns, Sir Edwyn and Noel Davey *The Riddle of the New Testament.* London: Faber and Faber Ltd., 1947.

63. Hunter, Archibald M. *Introducing the New Testament.* Philadelphia: Westminster Press, Third Revised Edition, 1972.

64. Hunter, A.M. "New Testament Survey," *The Expository Times.* October, 1964. Vol. 76, No. 1, pp. 15-20.

65. Hunter, A.M. *The Work and Words of Jesus.* Philadelphia: The Westminster Press, 1950.

66. Hutson, Harold H. "Form Criticism of the New Testament," *Journal of Bible and Religion.* July, 1951. Vol. 19, pp. 130-133.

67. Johnson, Sherman E. "Bultmann and the Mythology of the New Testament," *Anglican Theological Review.* January, 1954. Vol. 36, pp. 29-47.

68. Käsemann, Ernst. *Essays on New Testament Themes.* Naperville, Ill.: Alec R. Allenson, Inc.; London: SCM Press Ltd., 1964.

69. Käsemann, Ernst. *New Testament Questions of Today.* Philadelphia: Fortress Press, 1969.

70. Kee, H.C. "Aretalogy and Gospel," *Journal of Biblical Literature.* September, 1973. Vol. 92, pp. 402-422.

71. Kegley, Charles W., ed. *The Theology of Rudolf Bultmann.* New York: Harper and Row Publishers, 1966.

72. Kenyon, Sir Frederic. *The Story of the Bible.* London: John Murray, 1936.
73. Kunneth, Walter. "Dare We Follow Bultmann?" *Christianity Today.* October 13, 1961. Vol. 6, No. 1, pp. 25-28.
74. Ladd, G.E. *The New Testament and Criticism.* Grand Rapids: Wm. B. Eerdmans Publishing Co., 1967.
75. Ladd, George Eldon. *Rudolf Bultmann.* Chicago: Inter-Varsity Press, 1964.
76. Lightfoot, Robert Henry. *History and Interpretation in the Gospels.* New York: Harper and Brothers Publishers, 1934.
77. Malevez, L. *The Christian Message and Myth.* London: SCM Press, Ltd., 1958.
78. Manson, T.W. *The Sayings of Jesus.* London: SCM Press Ltd., 1949.
79. Martin, J.P. "Beyond Bultmann, What?" *Christianity Today.* November 24, 1961. Vol. 6, No. 4, pp. 20-23.
80. Martin, James. *The Reliability of the Gospels.* London: Hodder and Stoughton, 1959.
81. McClymont, J.A. *New Testament Criticism.* New York: Hodder and Stoughton, 1913.
82. McGinley, Laurence J. *Form Criticism of the Synoptic Healing Narratives.* Woodstock, Maryland: Woodstock College Press, 1944.
83. McKnight, Edgar V. *What Is Form Criticism?* Philadelphia: Fortress Press, 1969.
84. Moule, C.F.D. "The Intentions of the Evangelists," *New Testament Essays.* Edited by A.J.B. Higgins. Manchester: at the University Press, 1959.
85. McNeile, A.H. *An Introduction to the Study of the New Testament.* London: Oxford University Press, 1953.
86. Miegge, Giovanni. *Gospel and Myth in the Thought of Rudolf Bultmann.* Translated by Bishop Stephen Neill. Richmond, Virginia: John Knox Press, 1960.
87. Montgomery, John Warwick. *History and Christianity.* Downers Grove, Illinois: Inter-Varsity Press, copyright 1964.
88. Moule, C.F.D. "Form Criticism and Philological Studies," *London Quarterly and Holborn Review.* April, 1958. Vol. 183, pp. 87-92.
89. Mounce, Robert H. "Is the New Testament Historically Accurate?" *Can I Trust My Bible?* Edited by Howard Vos. Chicago: Moody Press, 1963.
90. Nineham, D.E. "Eyewitness Testimony and the Gospel Tradition," *The Journal of Theological Studies.* October, 1960. Vol. 11, pp. 255-264.
91. Ogden, Schubert M. *Christ Without Myth.* New York: Harper and Row Publishers, 1961.
92. Ogden, S. "Debate on Demythologizing," *Journal of Bible and Religion.* January, 1959. Vol. 27, pp. 17-27.
93. Parkin, Vincent. "Bultmann and Demythologizing," *The London Quarterly and Holborn Review.* October, 1962. Vol. 187. Sixth series, Vol. 31, pp. 258-263.
94. Patterson, Bob E. "The Influence of Form-Criticism on Christology," *Encounter.* Winter, 1970. Vol. 31, pp. 5-24.
95. Peritz, Ismar J. "Form Criticism as an Experiment," *Religion in Life.* Spring, 1941. Vol. 10, No. 2, pp. 196-211.
96. Perrin, Norman. *The Promise of Bultmann.* In a series—the Promise of Theology, edited by Martin E. Marty. New York: J.P. Lippincott Co., 1969.

97. Pesch, Rudolf. "Form Criticism," *Sacramentum Mundi*. Edited by Karl Rahner. New York: Herder and Herder, 1968. Vol. 2, pp. 334-337.

98. Pinnock, Clark H. "The Case Against Form-Criticism," *Christianity Today*. July 16, 1965. Vol. 9, pp. 1064-1065.

99. Piper, Otto A. "Myth in the New Testament," *Twentieth Century Encyclopedia of Religious Knowledge*. Vol. 2. Edited by Lefferts A. Loetscher. Grand Rapids: Baker Book House, 1955.

100. Pittenger, W. Norman. "The Problem of the Historical Jesus," *Anglican Theological Review*. April, 1954. Vol. 36, pp. 89-93.

101. Redlich, E. Basil. *Form Criticism*. Edinburgh: Thomas Nelson and Sons, Ltd., 1939.

102. Ridderbos, Herman N. *Bultmann*. Translated by David H. Freeman. Grand Rapids: Baker Book House, 1960.

103. Riddle, Donald Wayne. *Early Christian Life as Reflected in Its Literature*. New York: Willett, Clark and Company, 1936.

104. Robinson, James M. *A New Quest of the Historical Jesus*. Naperville, Illinois: Alec R. Allenson, Inc., 1959.

105. Robinson, James M. "The Recent Debate on the New Quest," *Journal of Bible and Religion*. July, 1962. Vol. 30, No. 3, pp. 198-206.

106. Rosche, Theodore R. "The Words of Jesus and the Future of the 'Q' Hypothesis, Part III," *Journal of Biblical Review*. September, 1960. Vol. 79, pp. 210-220.

107. Runia, Klaas. "The Modern Debate Around the Bible," *Christianity Today*. July 5, 1968. Vol. 12, No. 20, pp. 12-15.

108. Schweitzer, Albert. *Out of My Life and Thought*. Translated by C.T. Campton. New York: Henry Holt and Company, 1949.

109. Schweitzer, Albert. *The Psychiatric Study of Jesus*. Translated by Charles R. Joy. Boston: The Beacon Press, 1948.

110. Scott, Ernest Findlay. *The New Testament Today*. New York: Macmillan Company, 1927.

111. Scott, Ernest Findlay. *The Validity of the Gospel Record*. New York: Charles Scribner's Sons, 1938.

112. Smith, Charles W.F. "Is Jesus Dispensable?" *Anglican Theological Review*. July, 1962. Vol. 44, No. 3, pp. 263-280.

113. Spivey, Robert A. and D. Moody Smith, Jr. *Anatomy of the New Testament*. London: The Macmillan Company—Collier Macmillan Limited, 1969.

114. Taylor, Vincent. *The Formation of the Gospel Tradition*. London: Macmillan and Co. Limited, Second edition, 1935.

115. Taylor, Vincent. *The Gospels, A Short Introduction*. Fifth Edition. London: The Epworth Press, 1945.

116. Taylor, Vincent. "Modern Issues in Biblical Studies," *The Expository Times*. December, 1959. Vol. 71, pp. 68-72.

117. Taylor, Vincent. "Second Thoughts—Formgeschichte." *The Expository Times*. September, 1964. Vol. 75, No. 12, pp. 356-358.

118. Taylor, Vincent. "State of New Testament Studies Today," *London Quarterly and Holborn Review*. April, 1958. Vol. 183, pp. 81-86.

119. Taylor, W.S. "Memory and Gospel Tradition," *Theology Today*. January, 1959. Vol. 15, pp. 470-479. Used by permission of *Theology Today*.

120. Throckmorton, Burton H. Jr. *The New Testament and Mythology*. Philadelphia: The Westminster Press, 1949.

121. Vardaman, E. Jerry. "The Gospel of Mark and 'The Scrolls.'" *Christianity Today.* September 28, 1973. Vol. 17, pp. 4-7.

122. Vokes, F.E. "The Context of Life—*Sitz im Leben*," *Church Quarterly Review.* July 5, 1952. Vol. 153, pp. 350-354.

123. Wallace, H.C. "Miracle as a Literary Device," *The Modern Churchman.* April 27, 1961. Vol. 4, No. 3, pp. 168-171.

124. Wedel, T.O. "Bultmann and Next Sunday's Sermon," *Anglican Theological Review.* January, 1957. Vol. 39, pp. 1-8.

125. Weiss, Johannes. *Earliest Christianity.* Translated by Frederick C. Grant. New York: Harper and Brothers, 1959.

126. Wikenhauser, Alfred. *New Testament Introduction.* Translated by Joseph Cunningham. Freiburg, West Germany: Herder and Herder, 1958.

127. Wrede, W. *Paul.* Translated by Edward Lummis. London: Elsom and Co., 1907.

128. Wright, G.E. *The Bible and the Ancient Near East* New York: Doubleday & Co., 1961.

129. Albright, W.F. "The Israelite Conquest of Canaan in the Light of Archaeology," *Bulletin of the American Schools of Oriental Research.* April, 1939. Vol. 74, pp. 11-23.

130. Thomas, W.H. Griffith. *Christianity's Christ.* Grand Rapids: Zondervan, n.d.

131. Guthrie, Donald. *New Testament Introduction.* Downer's Grove, Ill: Inter-Varsity Press, Third edition, 1970.

132. Palmer, Humphrey. *The Logic of Gospel Criticism.* London and Melbourne: Macmillan; New York: St. Martin's Press, 1968.

133. Manson, T.W. "The Quest of the Historical Jesus—Continues." *Studies in the Gospels and Epistles.* Edited by Matthew Black. Manchester: Manchester University Press, 1962.

134. Dodd, C.H. *New Testament Studies.* Manchester: Manchester University Press, 1954.

135. Bultmann, Rudolf. "A New Approach to the Synoptic Problem." *Journal of Religion.* July, 1926. Vol. 6, pp. 337-362.

136. Piper, Otto. "The Origin of the Gospel Pattern," *Journal of Biblical Literature.* June, 1959. Vol. 78. pp. 115-124.

137. Stonehouse, Ned B. *Origins of the Synoptic Gospels.* Grand Rapids: Wm. B. Eerdmans Publishing Co., 1963.

138. Schaff, Philip. *The Person of Jesus.* New York: American Tract Society, n.d.

139. Gouguel, M. "Une nouvelle école de critique évangélique: la form-und traditiongeschichliche Schule," *Revue de l'histoire des relilgions.* Paris: E. Leroux, 1926. t. XCIV, pp. 115-160.

140. Fascher, E. *Die Formgeschichtliche Methode.* Giessen: Töpelmann, 1924.

141. Schweitzer, Albert. *Quest of the Historical Jesus.* Translated by W. Montgomery. New York: The Macmillan Company, 1906.

142. Riesenfeld, Harald, *The Gospel Tradition and its Beginnings: A Study in the Limits of 'Formegeschichte.'* London: A.R. Mowbray & Co. Limited, 1957.

143. Jeremias, Joachim. *The Parables of Jesus.* Translated by S.H. Hooke. London: SCM Press Ltd., Sixth edition, 1963.

144. Mounce, Robert. Interview. July 2, 1974.

145. Thiessen, Henry Clarence. *Introduction to the New Testament.* Grand Rapids: Wm. B. Eerdmans Publishing Co., 1943.

146. Bultmann, R. "The Study of the Synoptic Gospels," *Form Criticism.* Edited by Frederick C. Grant. Chicago: Willett, Clark & Co., 1934.

147. Schmidt, K.L. *Der Rahman der Geschichte Jesus.* Berlin: Trowitzsch & Sohn, 1919.

148. Dodd, C.H. *The Apostolic Preaching.* London: Hodder and Stoughton Limited, 1936.

149. Kenyon, Frederic. *The Bible and Modern Scholarship.* London: J. Murray, 1948.

150. Manson, T.W. "Is It Possible to Write a Life of Christ?" *The Expository Times.* May, 1942. Vol. 53, pp. 248-251.

151. Manson, T.W. *Jesus the Messiah.* Philadelphia: Westminister Press, 1946.

152. Harrison, Everett F. "Are the Gospels Reliable?" *Moody Monthly.* February, 1966.

153. Maier, Paul L. *First Easter: The True and Unfamiliar Story.* New York: Harper and Row, 1973.

154. Manson, T.W. "Present Day Research in the Life of Jesus," *The Background of the New Testament and Its Eschatology.* Edited by W.D. Davies and D. Daube. Cambridge: at the University Press, 1956.

155. Dibelius, Martin. "The Contribution of Germany to New Testament Science," *The Expository Times.* October, 1930. Vol. 42, pp. 39-43.

156. Albright, Wm. F. *From Stone Age to Christianity.* Baltimore: Johns Hopkins Press, 1940.

157. Albright, Wm. F. "The Bible After Twenty Years of Archaeology," *Religion in Life.* Autumn, 1952. Vol. 21, pp. 537-550.

158. Fuller, R. *Interpreting the Miracles.* Philadelphia: Westminster Press, 1963.

159. Enslin, Morton Scott. *Christian Beginnings.* New York: Harper and Brothers Publishers, 1938.

160. Eusebius. *The Ecclesiastical History.* Vol. 1 Translated by Kirsopp Lake. London: William Heinemann Ltd., 1926.

161. Harrison, Everett F. *Introduction to the New Testament.* Grand Rapids: Wm. B. Eerdmans Publishing Company, 1971.

162. Hayes, D.A. *The Synoptic Gospels and the Book of Acts.* New York: The Methodist Book Concern, 1919.

163. *The International Standard Bible Encyclopedia.* Edited by James Orr. Chicago: Howard-Severance Co., 1915.

164. Redlich, E. Basil. *The Student's Introduction to the Synoptic Gospels.* London: Longmans, Green and Co., 1936.

165. Ropes, James Hardy. *The Synoptic Gospels.* Cambridge: Harvard University Press, 1934.

166. Sanday, William, ed. *Oxford Studies in the Synoptic Problem* Oxford: at the Clarendon Press, 1911.

167. Schaff, Philip. *History of the Christian Church.* Vol. 1. New York: Charles Scribner's Sons, 1882.

168. Scott, Ernest Finlay. *The Literature of the New Testament.* Morningside Heights, New York: Columbia University Press, 1936.

169. Stanton, Vincent Henry. *The Gospels as Historical Documents.* Vol. 2. Cambridge: at the University Press, 1909.

170. Streeter, Brunett Hillman. *The Four Gospels.* London: Macmillan and Co., Fifth Impression, 1936.

171. Tenney, Merrill C. *The Genius of the Gospels*. Grand Rapids: Wm. B. Eerdmans Publishing Co., 1951.

172. Tenney, Merrill C. "Reversals of New Testament Criticism," *Revelation and the Bible*. Edited by Carl F. H. Henry. Grand Rapids: Baker Book House, 1969.

173. Westcott, Brooke Foss. *Introduction to the Study of the Gospels*. London: Macmillan and Co., 1888.

174. Hunter, A.M. *Interpreting the New Testament: 1900-1950*. London: SCM Press Ltd., 1951.

175. Ellwein, Eduard. "Rudolf Bultmann's Interpretation of the Kerygma," *Kerygma and History*. Edited by Carl E. Braaten and Roy A. Harrisville. New York: Abingdon Press, 1962.

176. Muller, Fredrich. "Bultmann's Relationship to Classical Philology," *The Theology of Rudolf Bultmann*. Edited by Charles W. Kegley. London: SCM Press, 1966.

177. Ogden, Schubert M. "The Significance of Rudolf Bultmann for Contemporary Theology," *The Theology of Rudolf Bultmann*. Edited by Charles Kegley. London: SCM Press, 1966.

178. Stallman, Martin. "Contemporary Interpretation of the Gospels as a Challenge to Preaching and Religious Education." *The Theology of Rudolf Bultmann*. Edited by Charles Kegley. London: SCM Press, 1966.

179. Marty, Martin E. "Foreword" to *The Promise of Bultmann* by Norman Perrin. New York: J.B. Lippincott Company, 1969.

180. Taylor, R.O.P. *The Ground Work of the Gospels*. Oxford: B. Blackwall, 1946.

181. Bultmann, R. "The New Approach to the Synoptic Problem," *The Journal of Religion*. July, 1926. Vol. 6, pp. 337-362.

182. Sherwin-White, A.N. *Roman Society and Roman Law in the New Testament*. Oxford: at the Clarendon Press, 1963.

183. Dodd, C.H. "The Framework of the Gospel Narrative," *The Expository Times*. June, 1932. Vol. 43, pp. 396-400.

184. Perrin, Norman. *What is Redaction Criticism?* Philadelphia: Fortress Press, 1969.

185. Wilson, Robert M. *The Gnostic Problem*. London: A.R. Mowbray & Co. Limited, 1958.

186. Kistemaker, Simon. *The Gospels in Current Study*. Grand Rapids: Baker Book House, 1972.

187. Neill, Stephen. *The Interpretation of the New Testament*. London: Oxford University Press, 1964.

188. Yamauchi, Edwin. *Pre-Christian Gnosticism*. Grand Rapids: Wm. B. Eerdman's Publishing Co., 1973.

189. Bornkamm, Günther. *Tradition and Interpretation in Matthew*, Philadelphia: The Westminster Press, 1963.

190. Guthrie, Donald. *New Testament Introduction*, Downers Grove: Inter-Varsity Press, 1970.

191. Perrin, Norman. *What Is Redaction Criticism?* Philadelphia: Fortress Press, 1969.

192. Martin, Ralph, *Mark, Evangelist and Theologian*, Grand Rapids: Zondervan Publishing House, 1973.

193. Stein, Robert M. "What is Redaktiongeschichte?" *Journal of Biblical Literature*, Vol. 88, 1969, pp. 45-56.

194. Smalley, Stephen S. "Redaction Criticism," in *New Testament Interpretation.* Grand Rapids: Eerdmans, 1977, pp. 181-198.

195. Rohde, Joachim. *Rediscovering the Teaching of the Evangelists,* Philadelphia: The Westminster Press, 1968.

196. Lightfoot, Robert Henry. *History and Interpretation in the Gospels,* London: Hodder and Stoughton, 1935.

197. Conzelmann, Hans. *The Theology of St. Luke,* Translated by Geoffrey Boswell. New York: Harper and Row, Publishers, 1961.

198. Marxsen, Willi. *Mark the Evangelist,* Translated by Roy A. Harrisville. New York: Abingdon Press, 1969.

199. Soulen, Richard N. *Handbook of Biblical Criticism,* Atlanta: John Knox Press, 1976.

200. Stein, Robert H. "The Redaktionsgeschichtliche Investigation of a Markan Seam," *Zeitschrift für die Neutestamentliche Wissenschaft* 61 (1970): 70-94.

201. Hoehner, Harold W. "Jesus the Source or Product of Christianity," Lecture taped at the University of California at San Diego, La Jolla, California, January 22, 1976.

202. Nash, Ronald H., ed. *Philosophy of Gordon Clark.* Philadelphia: The Presbyterian and Reformed Publishing Company, 1968.

203. Glueck, Nelson. "The Bible as a Divining Rod," *Horizon* 2:2, November, 1959.

204. Erlandsson, Seth. Tr. by Harold O.J. Brown, "Is Biblical Scholarship Possible Without Presuppositions?" *Trinity Journal* Vol. VII, No. 1, Spring 1978.

205. Albright, W.F. *The American Scholar,* 1941.

206. Waltke, Bruce K. "A Critical Reappraisal of the Literary Analytical Approach," Unpublished Paper. Dallas Theological Seminary, 1975.

207. Marshall, I. Howard, ed. *New Testament Interpretation, Essays on Principles and Methods,* Grand Rapids: William B. Eerdmans Publishing Co., 1977.

208. Hoehner, Harold W. "Unpublished Lecture Notes in Biblical Introduction 902," Dallas Theological Seminary, Spring, 1975.

209. Rogers, Cleon. "Unpublished Lecture Notes from Contemporary New Testament Issues in European Theology 232." Dallas Theological Seminary, Spring, 1979.

210. Moreland, J.P. *An Apologetic Critique of the Major Presuppositions of the New Quest of the Historical Jesus,* Th.M. Thesis, Dallas Theological Seminary, 1979.

211. Lewis, C.S. *Christian Reflections.* Edited by Walter Hooper. Grand Rapids: Eerdmans, 1967.

212. Stanton, G.N. *Jesus of Nazareth in New Testament Preaching.* London: Cambridge University Press, 1974.

213. Mosely, A.W. "Historical Reporting in the Ancient World," *New Testament Studies* 12 (1965-66): 10-26.

214. Campbell, E.F., Jr. "The Amarna Letters and the Amarna Period," *The Biblical Archaeologist,* Vol. 23, Feb., 1960.

215. Kitchen, K.A. "The Old Testament in the Context: 1 from the Origins to the Eve of the Exodus," *TSF Bulletin,* Vol. 59, Spring, 1971.

216. Wright, G. Ernest, *Biblical Archaeology,* Westminster Press, Philadelphia, 1962.

217. Albright, W.F. *The Archaeology of Palestine and the Bible,* Fleming H. Revell Co., New York, 1932.

218. Kitchen, K.A. *The Bible in Its World,* Downers Grove, Ill.: Inter-varsity Press, 1978.

219. Pettinato, Giovanni, "The Royal Archives of Tell-Mardikh-Ebla," *The Biblical Archaeologist,* Vol 39, No. 2, pp. 44-52. May, 1976.

220. Freedman, David Noel. "The Real Story of the Ebla Tablets; Ebla, and the Cities of the Plain," *Biblical Archaeologist,* Vol. 4, No. 4, pp. 143-164. December, 1978.

221. Scroggs, Robin. "Beyond Criticism to Encounter: The Bible in the Post-Critical Age." *Chicago Theological Seminary Register* 68 (Fall 1978):1-11.

222. Sanders, James A. "Biblical Criticism and the Bible as Canon," *Union Seminary Quarterly Review* 32 (Spring and Summer 1977): 157-165.

223. Wink, Walter. *The Bible in Human Transformation.* Philadelphia: Fortress Press, 1973.

224. Edwards, O.C. Jr. "Historical-Critical Method's Failure of Nerve and a Prescription for a Tonic: A Review of Some Recent Literature," *Anglican Theological Review* 59 (April 1977): 115-134.

225. Smedley, C. Donald. "The Theological Shift of Method and Perspective in Contemporary Biblical Criticism," Th.M. Research Project, Dallas Theological Seminary, 1980.

226. Maier, Gerhard. *The End of the Historical-Critical Method.* Translated by E.W. Leverenz and R.F. Norden. St. Louis: Concordia Publishing House, 1974.

section IV

appendices

THE STONES CRY OUT
(archaeological examples)

1A. THE STORIES OF ISAAC, JACOB AND JOSEPH

This section deals with what archaeology has to say about the setting in which Isaac, Jacob and Joseph lived. It deals with certain of the episodes that have long perplexed biblical commentators and critics.

1B. Isaac: The Oral Blessing Episode (Genesis 27)

It would seem, indicates Joseph Free, a most unusual event that Isaac did not take his oral blessing back when he discovered Jacob's deception. However, the Nuzi Tablets tell us that such an oral declaration was perfectly legal and binding. Thus he could not retract the oral blessing. One tablet records a law suit involving a woman who was to wed a man, but his jealous brothers contested it. The man won the suit because his father had orally promised the woman to him. Oral statements carried a very different weight then than they do today. The Nuzi texts came from a similar culture to that in Genesis. 21/322, 323

G. Ernest Wright explains this serious action:

"Oral blessings or death-bed wills were recognized as valid at Nuzi as well as in Patriarchal society. Such blessings were serious matters and were irrevocable. We recall that Isaac was prepared to keep his word even though his blessing had been extorted by Jacob under false pretenses. 'And Isaac trembled with a very great trembling and said: "Whoever it was that hunted game and brought it to me and I ate...even he shall be blessed."' (27:33)." 44/43

In commenting further on the above Nuzi record, Cyrus Gordon draws three points:

"This text conforms with Biblical blessings like those of the Patriarchs in that it is (a) an oral will, (b) with legal validity, (c) made to a son by a dying father." 25/8

Thus a clearer light is thrown on a culture which we know inadequately at best.

2B. Jacob

1C. THE PURCHASE OF ESAU'S BIRTHRIGHT

Gordon provides information on this episode in Genesis 25:

"Few incidents in family life seem more peculiar to us than Esau's sale of his birthright to his twin brother, Jacob. It has been pointed out that one of the [Nuzi] tablets...portrays a similar event." 25/3,5

The tablet which Gordon refers to is explained by Wright:

"Esau's sale of his birthright to Jacob is also paralleled in the Nuzi tablets where one brother sells a grove, which he has inherited, for three sheep! This would seem to have been quite as uneven a bargain as that of Esau: 'Esau said to Jacob: "Give me, I pray, some of that red pottage to eat..." And Jacob said: "Sell me first thy birthright." And Esau said: "Behold I am about to die (of hunger); what is a birthright to me?" And Jacob said: "Swear to me first." And he swore to him and sold his birthright to Jacob. Then Jacob gave Esau bread and a mess of lentils and he ate and drank' (25:30-4)." 44/43

Free explains further.

"In one Nuzi tablet, there is a record of a man named Tupkitilla, who transferred his inheritance rights concerning a grove to his brother, Kurpazah, in exchange for three sheep. Esau used a similar technique in exchanging his inheritance rights to obtain the desired pottage." 18/68, 69

S.H. Horn, in "Recent Illumination of the Old Testament" (*Christianity Today*), draws a colorful conclusion:

"Esau sold his rights for food in the pot, while Tupkitilla sold his for food still on the hoof." 28/14, 15

2C. THE JACOB AND LABAN EPISODE (Genesis 29)

Cyrus Gordon claims that we can understand even Genesis 29 by episodes in the Nuzi Tablets:

"Laban agrees to give a daughter in marriage to Jacob when he makes him a member of the household; 'It is better that I give her to thee than that I give her to another man. Dwell with me!' (Genesis 29:9). Our thesis that Jacob's joining Laban's household approximates Wullu's [person mentioned in the Tablets] adoption is borne out by other remarkable resemblances with the Nuzu document." 25/6

3C. THE STOLEN IMAGES EPISODE (Genesis 31)

This has been explained by other Nuzi discoveries. The following, from J.P. Free's "Archaeology and the Bible" (*His Magazine*), gives a good explanation of not only the episode, but also the background on the Nuzi Tablets themselves:

"Over 1000 clay tablets were found in 1925 in the excavation of a Mesopotamian site know today as Yorgan Tepe. Subsequent work brought forth another 3000 tablets and revealed the ancient site as 'Nuzi.' the tablets, written about 1500 B.C., illuminate the background of the Biblical patriarchs, Abraham, Isaac, and Jacob. One instance will be cited: When Jacob and Rachel left the home of Laban, Rachel stole Laban's family images or 'teraphim.' When Laban discovered the theft, he pursued his daughter and son-in-law, and after a long journey overtook them (Genesis 31:19-23). Commentators have long wondered why he would go to such pains to recover images he could have replaced easily in the local shops. The Nuzi tablets record one instance of a son-in-law who possessed the family images having the right to lay legal claim to his father-in-law's property, a fact which explains Laban's anxiety. This and other evidence from the Nuzi tablets fits the background of the Patriarchal accounts into the early period when the partriarchs lived, and does not support the critical view—which holds that the accounts were written 1000 years after their time." 19/20

Thanks to archaeology, we are beginning to understand the actual setting of much of the Bible.

3B. Joseph

1C. SELLING INTO SLAVERY

K.A. Kitchen brings out in his book, *Ancient Orient and Old Testament,* that Genesis 37:28 gives the correct price for a slave in the 18th century B.C.:

"Finally, the price of twenty shekels of silver paid for Joseph in Genesis 37:28 is the correct average price for a slave in about the eighteenth century B.C.: earlier than this, slaves were cheaper (average, ten to fifteen shekels), and later they became steadily dearer. this is one more little detail true to its period in cultural history. 30/52, 53

2C. THE VISIT TO EGYPT

The possibility of Joseph's visit to Egypt has been questioned by some. Millar Burrows *(What Mean These Stones?)* points out:

"Accounts of going down to Egypt in times of famine (12:10; 42:1, 2) bring to mind Egyptian references to Asiatics who came to Egypt for this purpose. A picture of visiting Semites may be seen on the wall of a tomb at Beni Hasan which comes from a time not far from that of Abraham." 13/266, 267

Howard Vos *(Genesis and Archaeology)* also points out the presence of the Hyksos in Egypt.

"But we have much more than the pictorial representation from Knumhotep's tomb to support the early entrance of foreigners into Egypt. There are many indications that the Hyksos began to infiltrate the Nile Valley around 1900 B.C. Other contigents came about 1730 and overwhelmed the native Egyptian rulers. So if we take an early date for the entrance of the Hebrews into Egypt, they would have come in during the period of Hyksos infiltration—when many foreigners were apparently entering. If we accept a date of about 1700 or 1650 B.C. for the entrance of the Hebrews, the Hyksos would have been ruling Egypt and likely would have received other foreigners." 42/102

Vos goes on to draw four connections between the Hyksos tribes and the Bible. One, the Egyptians considered the Hyksos and the Hebrews as different. Two, it is a possibility that the rising Egyptian king who was antagonistic toward Joseph's people (Exodus 1:8) was the nationalistic

Egyptian king. Naturally such a fever of nationalism would not be healthy for any foreigners. Three, Genesis 47:17 is the first time horses are mentioned in the Bible. The Hyksos introduced horses to Egypt. Four, after the Hyksos expulsion, much land was concentrated in the hands of the monarchs; this fits with the events of the famine which Joseph predicted and through which he strengthened the crown. 42/104

3C. JOSEPH'S PROMOTIONS

The following is a summary of Howard Vos's discussion of the question of Joseph's admittedly unique rise, found in his *Genesis and Archaeology*:

Joseph's being lifted from slavery to prime minister of Egypt has caused some critical eyebrows to rise, but we have some archaeological accounts of similar things happening in the Land of the Nile.

"A Canaanite Meri-Ra, became armor-bearer to Pharaoh; another Canaanite, Ben-Mat-Ana, was appointed to the high position of interpreter; and a Semite, Yanhamu or Jauhamu, became deputy to Amenhotep III, with charge over the granaries of the delta, a responsibility similar to that of Joseph before and during the famine."

When Pharaoh appointed Joseph prime minister, he was given a ring and a gold chain or a collar which is normal procedure for Egyptian office promotions [cf. 35/161, 162]. 42/106.

G.E. Campbell, commenting on the Amorna period, further discusses this parallel of Joseph's rise to power:

"One figure in the Rib-Adda correspondence constitutes an interesting link both with the princes of the cities in Palestine to the south and with the Bible. He is Yanhamu, whom Rib-Adda at one point describes as the *musallil* of the king. The term means, in all likelihood, the fanbearer of the king, an honorary title referring to one who is very close to the king, presumably sharing in counsels on affairs of state. Yanhamu held, then, a very prominent position in Egyptian affairs. His name appears in correspondence from princes up and down Palestine-Syria. At the beginning of the Rib-Adda period, Yanhamu seems to have been in charge of the issuing of supplies from the Egyptian bread-basket called Yarimuta, and we have already seen that Rib-Adda was apparently constantly in need of his services.

"Yanhamu has a Semitic name. This, of course, suggests further parallel to the Joseph narrative in Genesis, beyond the fact that both are related to the supplies of food for foreigners. Yanhamu offers an excellent confirmation of the genuinely Egyptian background of the Joseph narrative, but this does not mean, of course, that these men are identical, or that they functioned at the same time. Indeed Joseph may better fit into the preceding period for a number of reasons, although the evidence as yet precludes anything approaching certainty. It is clear that Semites could rise to positions of great authority in Egypt: they may even have been preferred at a time when indigenous leadership got too powerful or too inbred." 13/16, 17

With regard to Semites rising to power in Egyptian government, Kitchen— with reference to previously recovered stelae and the Brooklyn and Illahun papyri, comments:

"We know that Semites in the Egypt of the XIIth-XIIIth Dynasties (c. 1991-1633 B.C.) got into Egyptian administrative documents and were mentioned on private family monuments. On the eve of the Hyksos regime and during its course we find Semites as princelings and officials having their names written in hieroglyphics on scarab-seals and the like. In this context, a Joseph could have done likewise.

Though slaves today are not normally promoted instantly to prime minister without at least a minimal breaking-in position to get their feet wet in the responsibility of office, this was not necessarily the case in ancient Egypt.

4C. JOSEPH'S TOMB

John Elder in his *Prophets, Idols, and Diggers* made an interesting comment:

"In the last verses of Genesis it is told how Joseph adjured his relatives to take his bones back to Canaan whenever God should restore them to their original home, and in Joshua 24:32 it is told how his body was indeed brought to Palestine and buried at Shechem. For centuries there was a tomb at Shechem reverenced as the tomb of Joseph. A few years ago the tomb was opened. It was found to contain a body mummified according to the Egyptian custom, and in the tomb, among other things, was a sword of the kind worn by Egyptian officials." 15/54

4B. Conclusion

Needless to say, the Nuzi discoveries have played a central role in illuminating the different portions of this section; in fact, they have been of singular importance. S.H. Horn lists six areas of influence which the texts have exercised.

"Other [Nuzi] texts show that a bride was ordinarily chosen for a son by his father, as the patriarchs did; that a man had to pay a dowry to his father-in-law, or to work for his father-in-law if he could not afford the dowry, as poor Jacob had to do; that the orally expressed will of a father could not be changed after it had been pronounced, as in Isaac's refusal to change the blessings pronounced over Jacob even though they had been obtained by deception; that a bride ordinarily received from her father a slave girl as a personal maid, as Leah and Rachel did when they were married to Jacob; that the theft of cult objects or of a god was punishable by death, which was why Jacob consented to the death of the one with whom the stolen gods of his father-in-law were found; that the strange relationship between Judah and his daughter-in-law Tamar is vividly illustrated by the laws of the ancient Assyrians and Hittites." 28/14

Archaeology has indeed had an impact on our knowledge of Bible backgrounds.

2A. THE PENTATEUCH: Other Archaeological Examples

1B. Genesis

The first book of Moses, especially chapters 1-11, have been viewed as saga or legend, stories in a mythological rather than an historical setting. Recent archaeological finds do not favor the mythological stance. Here is a sampling of some of the evidence.

1C. TABLE OF NATIONS

The Table of Nations in Genesis appears accurate and unique in ancient history, commenting on its accuracy, Albright says:

"In view of the inextricable confusion of racial and national strains in the ancient near East it would be quite impossible to draw up a simple scheme which would satisfy all scholars; no one system could satisfy all the claims made on the basis of ethnic predominance, ethnographic diffusion, language, physical type, culture, historical tradition. The Table of Nations remains an astonishingly accurate document.

"(It) shows such a remarkably 'modern' understanding of the ethnic and linguistic situation in the ancient world, in spite of all its complexity, that scholars never fail to be impressed with the author's knowledge of the subject. ("The Old Testament and Archaeology, in *Old Testament Commentary*, Philadelphia, 1948, p. 138). 40/77

Concerning its uniqueness in historical literature, Albright states:

"It stands absolutely alone in ancient literature, without a remote parallel even among the Greeks, where we find the closest approach to a distribution of peoples in genealogical framework. But among the Greeks the framework is mythological and the people are all Greeks or Aegean tribes." (Young's Analytical Concordance to the Bible, p. 25)

2C. DATE OF PATRIARCHS

Rather than an early first millennium date, the evidence points strongly to late third millennium or early second millennium date for the partiarchs. Albright explains:

"In this connection it must again be stressed that a date for Abraham in the fifteenth or fourteenth century B.C. is unacceptable for the following basic reasons.

"1. The names of early Hebrew individuals and tribal groupings belong to the first half of the second millenium, and few of them survive as names in actual usage into the Late Bronze Age, to which the names of the Mosaid Age clearly belong. . .

"2. The Hebrew genealogies include only the Patriarchs and the heads of clans belonging to them. There is then a jump to the fathers of the leading figures of the Exodus. This is parallel to the situation found in Africa (especially Sudan and Rhodesia). Arabia and the Pacific Islands, where excavation and radiocarbon datings have forced the chronology based on Polynesian generations back centuries. . .

3C. USE OF CAMELS

Kenneth Kitchen remarks:

"It is often asserted that the mention of camels and of their use is an anachronism in Genesis. This charge is simply not true, as there is both philological and archaeological evidence for knowledge and use of this animal in the early second millenium B.C. and even earlier." 30/79

He further explains:

"While a possible reference to camels in a fodder-list from Alalakh (c. eighteenth century B.C.) has been disputed, the great Mesopotamian lexical lists that originated in the Old Babylonian period show a knowledge of the camel c. 2000/1700 B.C. including its domestication. Furthermore, a Sumerian text from Nippur from the same early period gives clear evidence of domestication of the camel by then, by its allusions to camel's milk. Camel bones were found in house-ruins at Mari of the pre-Sargonic age (twenty-fifth to twenty-fourth centuries B.C.), and also in various Palestinian sites from 2000 to 1200 B.C. From Byblos comes an incomplete camel figurine of the nineteenth/eighteenth centuries B.C. This and a variety of other evidence cannot be lightly disregarded. For the early and middle second millenium B.C., only limited use is presupposed by either the biblical or external evidences until the twelfth century B.C." 30/79-80

2B. Exodus - Leviticus

The following examples provide additional confirmation for the historicity of the Pentateuchal accounts.

1C. THE TEN COMMANDMENTS

The antiquity of the first and second commandments of the Decalogue has found support in archæology. G. Ernest Wright states:

"Equally surprising is the prohibition against images. 'Thou shalt not make unto thee a graven image' or any 'molten gods' (Exodus 20:4; 34:17). This is a significant commandment since there was nothing like it in the world about. Archaeology offers support for the antiquity of this commandment in Israel in that a figure of Yahweh has yet to be found in debris of an Israelite town. The interesting fact is that Canaanite cities possess quite a series of copper and bronze figurines of male deities, most of which are identified with Baal. But when we come to Israelite towns, the series gives out. Yet Israelites were familiar with such images, as we know from the denunciations in Deuteronomy, Jeremiah, Habbakuk, and Isaiah. In the city of Megiddo, for example, a tremendous amount of debris was moved from the first five town-levels (all Israelite), and not a single example has been discovered. 15/116-117

"At the same time, however, large numbers of figurines representing the mother-goddess are found in every excavation into Israelite houses, indicating that many homes had one or more of them. To be sure, they are no longer as sensuous as the Canaanite examples (cf. Fig. 72), but they are nevertheless indisputable evidence of the widespread syncretism, verging on polytheism, among the common people. They probably owned them, however, not so much for theological as for magical reasons, using them as 'good luck' charms. It would not be surprising to find an occasional image of Yahweh among such unenlightened and tolerant circles in Israel, but the fact remains that the people seemed to understand that God was simply not honored in that way. The antiquity of the Second Commandment thus receives support, and by implication also the First Commandment; and these two prohibitions are certainly among the distinguishing features of Israelite belief. 15/117-118

2C. THE TABERNACLE

W.F. Albright, writing in *The Archaeology of Palestine and the Bible*, finds a number of archaeological discoveries which support the historicity of the Tabernacle:

"On the other hand, recent archaeologcal discoveries have warned us against undue skepticism with regard to the age of the material preserved by P. It has quite generally been assumed, for example, that the Priestly Source gives a fanciful account of the Tabernacle, its installation and cult, which at best only reflects priestly ideals of the Exilic Age. Against this attitude the writer wishes to protest most vigorously." 2/159

Albright discusses the geographic background:

"Many indications point to a desert background of the Tent of Meeting (*ohel moed*, the term used by P most frequently). Whereas cedar and olive-wood were employed in building the Temple of Solomon, acacia alone is mentioned in the account of the construction of the Tabernacle. The predominant use of goats' hair tent-cloth and of ram-skins and lamb-skins (*orot elim, orot tehaskim*, Ex. 25:5, etc.) surely rests on authentic tradition. Quite aside from all other considerations, the wholesale deviation from the plans of the Temple of Solomon and of the ideal Temple of Ezekiel remains inexplicable if we must suppose that the Tabernacle is a fanciful construction of Exilic priests, nor can we explain the admittedly composite structure of the description unless we suppose that it had some tangible background in tradition.." 2/161

Concerning the altar of incense, which was connected with the Tabernacle, Albright states:

"While we cannot go into detail, for lack of space, with regard to the apparatus of the Mosaic cult, as described by P., we may refer again to the discussion of the altar of incense in chapter II. in connection with our discovery of the top of such an altar in the level of the tenth or eleventh centuries B.C. at Tell Beit Mirsim. The description of the altar of incense used in the Tabernacle (Ex. 30:1-3) agrees with that of the *hammanim* discovered here and in other sites, though it was considerably larger. Now the Priestly Code would never have introduced such a hamman into its Tabernacle unless there had been a warrant for it in old tradition. During the Prophetic Age the use of *hammanim* had been denounced and incense eliminated from official Mosaic ritual."

Finally, he comments on the seven-branched candlestick, which was used inside the Tabernacle:

"It is a common view among biblical scholars today that the seven branched candlestick of the Tabernacle (Ex. 25:31ff., 37:17ff.) reflects the Babylonian or even the Persian period. Unhappily for this *a priori* conception, however, it is precisely in the Early Iron I—never afterwards—that we find pottery lamps with seven places for wicks, the rim of the lamp being pinched together seven times. Such lamps are found in Tell Beit Mirsim B, as well as in contemporary deposits elsewhere in Palestine." 2/161-162

3C. FORM OF THE COVENANT

Most liberal scholars claim the Pentateuch was not written by Moses but was the product of a much later age. However, as K.A. Kitchen (among others) points out, the particular form of the covenant found in the Pentateuch has its historical parallel *only* in the age of Moses:

"The central feature of the book of Exodus is the giving of the covenant-commandments, the law and the cult at Sinai. Exodus from chapter 19 onwards, and all of Leviticus, both center upon Sinai, the founding-point of the Israelite nation in all later biblical tradition. After the time in the wilderness and Israel's arrival (as a new generation) in Moab before crossing the Jordan, there was a renewal of the covenant and its laws—enshrined in Deuteronomy. The *form* of covenant found in Exodus-Leviticus and in Deuteronomy (plus Joshua 24) is neither arbitrary nor accidental. It is a form proper to the general period of the exodus, current in the 14th/13th centuries B.C. and *neither earlier nor later* on the total available evidence." 17/79

3A. THE CONQUEST OF CANAAN

1B. The Basic Assumption

Some critics reject the biblical picture of the conquest of Canaan in Joshua, replacing it with another picture of the culture and setting at that time. Paul Lapp in *Biblical Archaeology and History* has claimed that this "perspective has led some scholars to take the view that there was virtually no conquest by Joshua at all. Instead, there was a gradual and peaceful infiltration of the sparsely settled central hill country of Palestine by the Joshua tribes. The actual destructive conquest of Joshua is also dismissed by another hypothesis which considers the arrival of the Joshua tribes a trigger that touched off popular revolts overthrowing the leaders of the Palestinian city-states." 31/108

Lapp gives a good background to the question:

"The [Canaan] conquest provides another example of the search for connections between biblical and historical-archaeological material. This concerns an event for which there is a considerable amount of archaeological evidence, a great amount of detailed description in the biblical sources, and volumes of diverse opinions and hypotheses produced by modern scholars." 31/107

Indeed this has been a popular battlefield.

2B. Basic Answer

G. Ernest Wright in "The Present State of Biblical Archeology" gives an excellent evaluation of the trend. Wright points out that archaeology is causing breakthroughs in the understanding of the Bible, a case in point being the concept of Israelite conquest of Canaan. The original concept deleted actual combat and considered it a gradual one of "osmosis," the two cultures being "progressively amalgamated." The excavation of Bethel, Lachish and Debir overthrows such a view, since these sites were destroyed furiously at about 1200 B.C. Apparently the farthest thing from the mind of the conquerers was a synthesis of culture. Joshua 10 and 11 was said to be in conflict with Judges 1, but this has been overstated. It is incorrect to assume that assimilation, though widely practiced, was the rule. Israel was much too nationalistic for such cultural indecisiveness. 44/1-15

Lapp continues:

"The archaeological evidence supports the view that the biblical traditions developed from an actual historical conquest under Joshua in the late thirteenth century B.C." 31/111

1C. AMARNA TABLETS

Archer explains how this discovery has helped clarify the historical picture. The Tell el-Amarna Tablets, Archer says, came to light from the Egyptian site of el-Amarna (1887), ancient capital of Egypt (called Akhetaten then). They are from officials of Palestine and Syria who were upset about attacking Habiru (or 'Apiru). They describe a disorganized turmoil among the states there, speak of how many are deserting their allegiance to Egypt and ask for military aid to stop the onslaught. One letter from Megiddo lists some of the fallen cities, all of which are in the south (region of Arad). This conforms with the Israel conquest pattern. Cities like Gezer, Ashkelon and Lachish are reported as fallen.

In Joshua these were recorded as among the first taken. Jericho, Beersheba, Bethel and Gibeon are not even heard from once. These were the first to fall to Joshua. We may conclude, therefore, that these tablets record the Hebrew conquest of Canaan in 1400-1380 from the standpoint of the Canaanites themselves." 12/164

J.P. Free evaluates their significance:

"The tablets illuminate and confirm the picture which the Bible gives of Palestine at that time. Canaan in the period of conquest was subject to many local kings, who ruled over individual cities with perhaps their surrounding territory." 18/136

Unger quotes one of the tablets:

"Abdi-Hiba, governor of Jerusalem wrote numerous letters to the Pharaoh Akhnaton (1387-1366 B.C.) beseeching Egyptian aid against the encroaching Habiru, if the country were to be saved for Egypt:

'The Habiru plunder all lands of the king.
If archers are here
this year, then the lands of the king,
the Lord, will remain; but if the archers are not here,
then the lands of the king, my lord, are lost.'

[Taken from Samuel Mercer, *The Tell el-Amarna Tablets* (Toronto 1939), Vol. II, no. 287, lines 56-60.]" 40/146

A big question arises as to whether "Habiru" means "Hebrew." Henry Thomas Frank asserts that this cannot be:

"Some time ago it was fashionable to equate these people with the biblical Hebrews and to see in the Amarna Letters evidence of the Hebrew invasion of Canaan. This equation is no longer possible. First, other archaeological evidence shows it is still at least a century too early for the Hebrew incursion. Second, while the question of the Hapiru is still complex, archaeologically recovered documents now indicate that they were an ethnically mixed group, speaking several different languages, but bound together by their occupation: brigandage. While there may have been Hebrews among them, they were not *the* Hebrews nor were they even nomads. Their name *Hapiru* may originally have meant 'tramp,' 'dusty one,' or perhaps 'wanderer,' but it came to designate a 'robber,' a 'bandit.' These were stateless persons, a fourth class in a highly stratified society. They lived by stealing, smuggling, and increasingly by raiding and destroying settled areas. Eventually they became a threat even to the cities. Over and over again in the Amarna Letters princes accuse one another of being allied with these outlaws. Indeed, in some cases the very word Hapiru seems used as a term of abuse." 17/69

W.F. Albright, however, does feel the two are related:

"During the past fifteen years (1947-1962) it has become possible to pinpoint the background of the stories of Abraham (Gen. 12-24) with a precision wholly undreamed of when the first edition of this survey was written. The meaning of the term *'Apiru-'Abiru*, later 'Ibri, 'Hebrew,' has now been established; it meant something like 'donkey-man, donkey driver, huckster, caravaneer.' Originally it may have meant 'dusty,' with obvious reference to the dust raised by donkeys on a much-travelled road." 4/5

Unger also maintains a connection:

"In the light of the interesting fact that Abraham is the first person in the Bible to bear the name Hebrew, *'Ibri*, (Gen. 14:13), the occurrence of the term 'Habiru' in the Mari letters (eighteenth century B.C.) and earlier in the Cappadocian texts (nineteenth century B.C.) as well as in the later Nuzian, Hittite, Amarna and Ugaritic texts (fifteenth-fourteenth centuries B.C.) is significant, since the philological equation Hebrew-Habiru seems assured." 40/124, 125

The Amarna Tablets seem to aid greatly in a better knowledge of the conquest of Canaan. J.P. Free adds:

"For their betrayal of the Canaanite-Amorite cause, the Hivite group was attacked by a coalition of five Amorite kings (Josh. 10:5). The Amarna Tablets confirm this picture of Canaan, for they were actually written by such kinglets who ruled over various cities. Seven of the letters were written by the king of Jerusalem, and others were from the kings of such places as Tyre and Sidon. They reflect the same general lack of unity among the city-states of Canaan as indicated in the Biblical record." 18/136

2C. THE SETTING

Lapp sets forth an interesting case:

"This evidence, coupled with the obvious differences in character of occupation and quality of pottery, makes it very difficult to refute a postulation favorable to a substantial conquest by Joshua. Intercity struggles would scarcely have produced a new culture, and popular revolutions would hardly have led to major destructions of larger towns. If the conquest merely amounted to peaceful infiltration, to whom are the destructions and occupations between the end of the Late Bronze age and the arrival of the Sea Peoples to be attributed? The destruction of large and heavily fortified towns like Lachish and Hazor can best be explained by a concerted effort on the part of a sizable body of troops under Joshua. It is possible to attribute these destructions to Egyptian campaigns, Sea Peoples without their characteristic pottery, or internecine struggles, but why promote such postulations in the face of clear statements in the biblical sources that these two sites were destroyed by Joshua?" 31/110

The 1200 plus B.C. burning levels violate the explicit statement of the narratives that Joshua burned *none* of the cities in their falls except Jericho, Ai and Hazor (c.f. Joshua 11:13). So those burning levels may indeed be due to the sea peoples' invasion or Egyptian campaigns.

Free further shows how archaeology can be used to double check ancient works.

"Several of the cities indicated as taken by the Israelites have been excavated, including Jericho, Lachish, Debir, and Hazor; and evidence has been found at each one indicating destruction about 1400 B.C. or a little later. On the other hand, certain cities are indicated as not having been taken, such as Bethshan, Taanach, and Megiddo (Josh. 17:11), and excavation at these sites has shown that they were not taken at this time." 18/237

G.E. Wright evaluates the evidence in "The Present State of Biblical Archaeology":

"The violent destruction which occurred at such sites as Bethel, Lachish, and Debir during the thirteenth century indicates that we must take seriously the biblical claims for a storming of at least central and southern Palestine with such violence and such contempt for the inhabitants that there was small opportunity or desire for amalgamation on a large scale." 44/83

Further, in "The Terminology of Old Testament Religion," Wright speaks of the cultural difference:

"Likewise unique in Israel, as compared with Canaan, are the moral tone of the religion with its apodictic legal tradition, the conception of covenant relation between God and people, and the cosmological conceptions." 45/413

Albright, in *From the Stone Age to Christianity*, points out the character of the Israelites:

"Archaeological excavation and exploration are throwing increasing light on the character of the earliest Israelite occupation, about 1200 B.C. [The author would place this occupation at 1400 B.C.—middle of Late Bronze age.] First it is important to note that the new inhabitants settled in towns like Bethel and Tell Beir Mir-sim almost immediately after their destruction. The Israelites were thus far from being characteristic nomads or even seminomads, but were ready to settle down at once and live the life of peasants, tilling the soil and dwelling in stone houses. A second main point is that the new Israelite occupation was incomparably more intensive than was the preceding Canaanite one." 6/212

3B. Conclusion

Gleason Archer notes Albright's conclusions:

"It is because of the cumulative impact of all these findings that archaeologists like W.F. Albright have felt constrained to concede the essential accuracy of the Pentateuch." 12/165

W.F. Albright:

"M. Noth and K. Möhlenbrink have recently made a vigorous attack on the historical reliability of the stories of the Conquest in Joshua, on various literary and aetiological grounds, but they have been opposed with equal vigor by the writer (1939); archaeological discoveries of the past few years have proved that their attack far overshoots the mark." 6/209

Anderson of Drew Theological Seminary comments on behalf of biblical criticism:

"In these days we speak less dogmatically of the 'assured gains' of Biblical criticism, for someone is just apt to pull the rug out from under our feet. For instance, if one has said with great assurance that scholars are agreed that the conquest of Canaan was a slow gradual process and that the book of Joshua is a falsification of the actual state of affairs, it is very disconcerting to hear scholars like Albright, Wright, Bright, and Orlinsky say that archaeological research in central Palestine indicates a decisive phase of conquest." 11/81

Free concludes:

"In summary, we find that efforts to set aside the historicity of the Conquest are not supported by archeological evidence." 22/221, 222

4A. THE HITTITES

1B. Introduction

The Bible mentions the Hittites many times. But until recently scholars had found no other ancient writings which referred to them. Therefore the very existence of this civilization was often doubted. John Elder (*Prophets, Idols, and Diggers*) explains that "one of the striking confirmations of Bible history to come from the science of archeology is the 'recovery' of the Hittite peoples and their empires. Here is a people whose name appears again and again in the Old Testament, but who in secular history had been completely forgotten and whose very existence was considered to be extremely doubtful." 15/75

Elder goes on to mention some of the popular biblical references.

"In Genesis 23:10, it is told that Abraham bought a parcel of land for a burying place from Ephron the Hittite. In Genesis 26:34, Esau takes a Hittite girl for wife, to the great grief of his mother. In the Book of Exodus, the Hittites are frequently mentioned in the lists of people whose land the Hebrews set out to conquer. In Joshua 11:1-9, the Hittites join in the confederation of nations that try to resist Joshua's advance, only to be defeated by the waters of Merom. In Judges, intermarriage occurs between the Hebrews and the Hittites. In I Samuel 26, Hittites enroll in David's army, and during the reign of Solomon he makes slaves of the Hittite element in his kingdom and allows his people to take Hittite wives. But until the investigations of modern archeologists, the Hittites remained a shadowy and undefined people." 15/75

Finally, he gives us a brief summary of the archaeological finds in this area:

"Clay tablets found in Assyria and Egypt give us our first picture of the Hittites and their way of life. Egyptian artists depicted them as having features we identify as Armenian, and it seems more than likely that the Hittites were the ancestors of the Armenian race. An Egyptian tablet records a fierce battle between Ramses II and the Hittites at Kadesh on the Orontes River in 1287 B.C." 15/75

2B. Brief History

M.B. Stearns, in his *Bibliotheca Sacra* article, "Biblical Archaeology and the Higher Critics," mentions the coming of the Hittites into the limelight:

"It is interesting to know that Sir Leonard Woolley, whose name has become a household word because of his remarkable discoveries at Abraham's city of Ur, is at present engaged in the excavation of a great Hittite palace near Antioch in Syria, built about 1600 B.C. Of this discovery he himself has written to the London Times, 'The frequent references in the Old Testament to Hittites living in Syria and Palestine in the Patriarchal age, which have often been rejected as anachronisms, may yet prove sound history.' For if the Hittites were established in Antioch as early as 1600 B.C., there may well have been some members of their race farther South." 37/317

Merrill Unger, in an article for *Bibliotheca Sacra,* gives an excellent description of the history of these people:

"Like the Horites, the Biblical references to the Hittites used to be regarded in critical circles as historically worthless." 39/139

He also says:

"Less than a century ago the Hittite meant little more to the reader of the Bible than the Hivite or the Perizzite." 39/140

The Hittites were in contact with Bible characters as early as Abraham and as late as David and Solomon. Though the Old Testament claims the significance of the Hittite might, broad acceptance was not enjoyed until archaeology began to point out how significant the Hittite Empire really was, rivaling at times Egyptian dynasties and Mesopotamian kingdoms.

Hittite artifacts and monuments began to surface about 1871, first around Carchemish. In 1884, William Wright published a history, *The Empire of the Hittites* and A.H. Sayce published *The Hittites—The Story of a Forgotten Empire.* A breakthrough came in 1906-07 with the discovery of 10,000 clay tablets in many languages at Boghazkoi. These revolutionized knowledge of the Hittites.

These pointed out two periods of great Hittite power, the first around 1800 B.C., the second of about 1400 to 1200 B.C. In the second, we see a definite empire tendency, and the Hittites seemed to be the nation to look out for during Subbiluliuma's reign (1300's B.C.). Contact was strong with Egypt at this time.

But the wole thing came to a halt about 1200 B.C.; Boghazkoi stumbled, though Hittite influence would remain through other cities that had not fallen, such as Carchemish, Hamath and North Syria.

"The Assyrian emperor Tiglathphileser I, around 1100 B.C., fought with the Hittites and other peoples of western Asia. Ashurnaisirpal (885-860 B.C.) put Sangara, king of Carchemish, under tribute. In 717 B.C. Carchemish finally fell into the hands of Sargon II, and the Hittites were absorbed by the great Assyrian empire. But meanwhile they had become the cultural tie between the Tigris-Euphrates valley and Europe." 39/141

These discoveries have increased greatly our knowledge of the ancient Near East and the Old Testament is much more clear as a result.

"The manner in which archeology has brought to light the ancient Horites and Hittites furnishes a good example of the way this important science is expanding Biblical horizons." 39/140, 141

3B. The Story of Their Discovery

1C. SAYCE'S WORK

Acceptance of the above history did not come easily. Fred Wight in his *Highlights of Archaeology in Bible Lands* gives a brief picture of what had to endure:

"A.H. Sayce, of Oxford, was the first scholar to identify the Hittite people from the monuments. In 1876 he read a paper to the Society of Biblical Archaeology wherein he attributed certain inscriptions found in Hamath and at Aleppo to the Hittites. In 1879 he visited the Near East and in 1880 he read another paper to the archaeologists, asserting that the Hittites had lived in the mountainous country north of Mesopotamia and also in all of Asia Minor." 43/92, 93

J.P. Free continues:

"Then A.H. Sayce, a British assyriologist, identified the Hittites of the Bible with the mysterious Hatti of the monuments, and published his 'Story of a Forgotten Empire' (1892), but E.A.W. Budge of the British Museum as late as 1902 rejected this identification 'on insufficient grounds.' But when in 1906, Hugo Winckler of Berlin went to the site of Boghaz-koi in central Turkey and examined the remains of what proved to be the Hittite capital, there could be no more doubt. Winckler found an archive of clay tablets, which contained among other documents a military treaty between the Hittites and the Egyptians nearly 1300 years before Christ." 19/19

Albright in *Recent Discoveries in Bible Lands* gives this evaluation:

"In 1871 some inscriptions in a previously unknown type of hieroglyphic script were discovered at Hamath in Syria, and eight years later A.H. Sayce identified the script with that of inscriptions already known from Asia Minor. Applying the term 'Hittite' to all of the Bible was doubted by many, but it has proved to be correct." 9/53

2C. HOFNER

One of the leading experts on the Hittites is Harry A. Hofner, formerly of the faculty of Yale University, now with the Oriental Institute at the University of Chicago.

Hofner warns about the pitfalls posed by the term 'Hittites." He writes that "it is possible to identify at least four distinct ethnic groups in antiquity to whom the name 'Hittite' (Nesite LÚ^{uru}*HATTI*, Egyptian *ht*, Ugaritic *hty*, Hebrew *hittī* = LXX *khettaios*, Akkadian *hattu*) has at some time been applied." 47/198

The first group, according to Hofner, is the Hattians who inhabited the central plateau of Asia Minor about 2,000 B.C. The second group was the Indo-Europeans who also settled in Asia Minor and ruled over the urban centers about 1,700 B.C. They were identified with the phrase "men of Hatti." A third group were the "Neo-Hittites" who ruled Syria the first half of the first millennium B.C. The fourth group is almost entirely identified by the Old Testament.

"It is my opinion," asserts Hofner, "that we never encounter Hittites of my first two categories (i.e. Hattians or Nesites) in the Old Testament. The 'kings of the Hittites' spoken of during the time of Solomon (2 Chr. 1:17) and Jehoram son of Ahab (2 Kings 7:6) were Syrians ('Hittites' of category three). But apart from the expression 'the land of Hittites,' which sometimes denotes Syria, all other references to 'Hittites' in the Old Testament are to a small group living in the hills during the era of the Patriarchs and the later descendants of that group." 42/214

Hofner continues that the "real-estate transaction between Abraham and 'Ephron, the Hittite' in Genesis 23 does not presuppose 'intimate knowledge of intricate subtleties of Hittites laws and customs,' as has been claimed. These 'Hittites' would seem to be natives in every sense of the word. 42/214

4B. Evaluation

Fred Wight:

"Now the Bible picture of this people fits in perfectly with what we know of the Hittite nation from the monuments. As an empire they never conquered the land of Canaan itself, although Hittite local tribes did settle there at an early date. Nothing discovered by the excavators has in any way discredited the Biblical account. Scripture accuracy has once more been proved by the archaeologists." 43/94, 95

5A. THE LACHISH LETTERS

1B. Introduction

1C. OLD TESTAMENT BACKGROUND

Jeremiah 34:6, 7 read as follows:

"Then Jeremiah the prophet spoke all these words to Zedekiah king of Judah in Jerusalem when the army of the king of Babylon was fighting against Jerusalem and against all the remaining cities of Judah, that is, Lachish and Azekah, for they alone remained as fortified cities among the cities of Judah."

Israel had been in a futile rebellioin against Nebuchadnezzar. Judah was not united in this revolt. Jeremiah preached submission, while the Jewish leaders could only speak of resistance, and resist they did, though they were soundly defeated by the powers of Nebuchadnezzar. In the final days of the rebellion, the last vestiges of Hebrew independence were embodied in a pair of outposts, Lachish and Azekah, 35 miles southwest of Jerusalem. From Lachish came a series of letters giving a graphic picture of what it was like to be in such a situation. These add greatly to our knowledge of Old Testament background. This discovery is known as the Lachish Letters (or Ostraca).

2C. BACKGROUND TO FIND

William F. Albright, in his *Religion in Life* article, "The Bible After Twenty Years of Archaeology," introduces us to this find:

". . . we mention the new documents from the sixth and fifth centuries B.C. which have come to light since 1935. In 1935 the late J.L. Starkey discovered the Ostraca of Lachish, consisting chiefly of letters written in ink on potsherds. Together with several additional ostraca found in 1938, they form a unique body of Hebrew prose from the time of Jeremiah. Further light on the time of the Exile comes from the ration lists of Nebuchadnezzar, found by the Germans at Babylon and partly published by E.F. Weidner in 1939. Other new evidence will be discussed below. Somewhat later but of decisive value for our understanding of the history and literature of the Jews in the time of Ezra and Nehemiah are the continuing finds and publications of Aramaic papyri and ostraca from Egypt. Four large groups of this material are being published, and their complete publication will more than double the total bulk of such documents available twenty years ago." 3/539

R.S. Haupert wrote a survey article on these finds, "Lachish—Frontier Fortress of Judah." He goes into the authorship and background of the letters:

"Most of the best preserved are letters written by a certain Hoshaiah (a good Biblical name: Neh. 12:32, Jer. 42:1;43:2), apparently a subordinate military officer stationed at an outpost or observation point not far from Lachish, to Yaosh, the commanding officer of Lachish. That the letters were all written within a period of a few days or weeks is indicated by the fact that the pieces of pottery on which they were wrtten were from jars of similar shape and date, and five of the pieces actually fit together as fragments of the same original vessel. The fact that all but two of the letters were found on the floor of the guardroom naturally suggest that they were deposited there by Yaosh himself upon receiving them from Hoshaiah." 27/30, 31

2B. Dating and Historical Setting

Albright wrote a special article on this find, "The Oldest Hebrew Letters: Lachish Ostraca," in the *Bulletin of the American Schools of Oriental*

Research, and he deals with the setting of the Letters:

"In the course of this sketch it will have become increasingly evident to the attentive reader that the language of the Lachish documents is perfect classical Hebrew. The divergences from biblical usage are much fewer and less significant than supposed by Torczner. In these letters we find ourselves in exactly the age of Jeremiah, with social and political conditions agreeing perfectly with the picture drawn in the book that bears his name. The Lachish Letters take their place worthily between the Ostraca of Samaria and the Elephantine Papyri as epigraphic monuments of Biblical Hebrew history." 8/17

G.E. Wright, in "The Present State of Biblical Archaeology," dates the letters by internal evidence:

"On Letter XX are the words 'the ninth year,' that is, of King Zedekiah. That is the same year in which Nebuchadnezzar arrived to begin the reduction of Judah: 'in the ninth year . . ., in the tenth month' (II Kings 25:1; this would be about January 588 B.C., the siege of Jerusalem continuing to July 587 B.C.— II Kings 25:2-3)." 44/179

Millar Burrows (*What Mean These Stones?*) agrees with Wright:

"At Lachish evidence of two destructions not far apart has been found; undoubtedly they are to be attributed to Nebuchadnezzar's invasions of 597 and 587 B.C. The now famous Lachish letters were found in the debris from the second of these destructions." 13/107

Albright sums up the question of the dating of the finds:

"Starkey has contributed a useful sketch of the discovery, explaining the archaeological situation in which the ostraca were found and fixing their date just before the final destruction of Lachish at the end of Zedekiah's reign. The facts are so clear that Torczner has surrendered his objections to this date, which is now acccepted by all students." 8/11, 12

3B. The Letters

For sake of convenience, each of the letters was labeled with a number. Haupert gives an overview of Letters II through VI:

"Throughout this group of letters [Letters II-Vi] Hoshaiah is continually defending himself to his superior, although the charges against him are not always clear. It is tempting to think that he is in sympathy with the Jeremiah faction which wanted to submit to the Babylonians instead of rebelling; but, of course, we cannot be sure." 27/31

He then touched on several of them.

1C. LETTER I

"Letter I . . . though only a list of names, is of striking significance since three of the nine names which occur—Gemariah, Jaazaniah, and Neriah—appear in the Old Testament only in the time of Jeremiah. A fourth name is Jeremiah, which, however, is not limited in the Old Testament to the prophet Jeremiah, and need not refer to him. A fifth name, likewise not limited to this period, is Mattaniah, which Biblical students will recognize as the pre-throne name of King Zedekiah." 27/31

2C. LETTER III

Haupert continues:

"In Letter III Hoshaiah reports to Yaosh that a royal mission is on the way to Egypt, and that a company of this group has been sent to his outpost (or to Lachish) for provisions, an allusion which points directly to the intrigues of the pro-Egyptian party under Zedekiah. Of unusual interest is the reference in the same letter to 'the prophet.' Some writers have confidently identified this prophet with Jeremiah. This is entirely possible, but we cannot be certain and should be careful about pushing the evidence too far." 27/32

3C. LETTER IV

J.P. Free *(Archaeology and Bible History)* speaks of Letter IV, an often-mentioned one:

"In the days of Jeremiah when the Babylonian army was taking one town after another in Judah (about 589-586 B.C.), we are told in the Bible that, as yet, the two cities of Lachish and Azekah had not fallen (Jer. 34:7). Striking confirmation of the fact that these two cities were among those still holding out is furnished by the Lachish letters. Letter No. 4, written by the army officer at a military outpost to his superior officer at Lachish, says 'We are watching for the signals of Lachish according to all indications which my Lord hath given, for we cannot see Azekah.' This letter not only shows us how Nebuchadnezzar's army was tightening its net around the land of Judah, but also evidences the close relationship between Lachish and Azekah which are similarly linked in the book of Jeremiah." 18/223

Haupert sees it at another angle:

"The final statement of Letter IV affords an intimate glimpse into the declining days of the Kingdom of Judah. Hoshaiah concludes: 'Investigate, and (my lord) will know that for the fire-signals of Lachish we are watching, according to all the signs which my lord has given, for we cannot see Azekah.' This statement calls to mind immediately the passage in Jer. 34:7." 27/32

Wright adds his view of the reference to not seeing Azekah:

"When Hoshaiah says that he 'cannot see Azekah,' he may mean that the latter city has already fallen and is no longer sending signals. At any rate, we here learn that Judah had a signal system, presumably by fire or smoke, and the atmosphere of the letters reflects the worry and disorder of a besieged country. A date in the autumn of 589 (or 588) B.C. has been suggested for the bulk of the letters." 44/179

4C. LETTER VI

Joseph Free points out the close relationship between Letter VI and Jeremiah's writings:

"J.L. Starkey found (1935) a group of eighteen potsherds bearing on their surface several military messages written by an army officer to his superior officer stationed at Lachish. W.F. Albright has pointed out ["A Brief History of Judah from the Days of Josiah to Alexander the Great," *Biblical Archaeologist*, Vol. 9, No. 1, February, 1946, p. 4.] that in one of these letters (No. 6) the army officer complains that the royal officials (sarim) had sent out circular letters which 'weaken the hands' of the people. The army officer who wrote this Lachish letter used the expression, 'weaken the hands,' to describe the effect of the over-optimism of the royal officials, whereas the officials, referred to in the book of Jeremiah (38:4), in turn had used the same expression in describing the effect of Jeremiah's realistic prophecy concerning the approaching fall of Jerusalem. The royal officials were deemed guilty of the very action which they sought to ascribe to Jeremiah." 18/222

4B. Significance

1C. GEDALIAH SEAL

John Elder points out yet another find in addition to the Ostraca, which adds even more weight to the biblical story of Lachish:

"The nearby city fortress of Lachish provides clear proof that it had been twice burned over a short period of time, coinciding with the two captures of Jerusalem. In Lachish the imprint of a clay seal was found, its back still shows the fibers of the papyrus to which it had been attached. It reads: 'The property of Gedaliah who is over the house.' We meet this distinguished individual in II Kings 25:22, where we are told: 'And as for the people that remained in the land of Judah, whom Nebuchadnezzar king of Babylon had left, even over them he made Gedaliah... ruler.'" 15/108, 109

2C.   THE LACHISH FINDINGS

Haupert concludes:

"The real significance of the Lachish Letters can hardly be exaggerated. No archaeological discovery to date has had a more direct bearing upon the Old Testament. The scribes who wrote the letters (for there was more than one) wrote with genuine artistry in classical Hebrew, and we have virtually a new section of Old Testament literature: a supplement to Jeremiah." 27/32

6A.   THE EXILE

1B.   Introduction

It woulld be a pleasant state if one were able to say that controversies over the Old Testament taper off after the patriarchs, but this is simply not the case. In fact, some scholars take issue with even the very basic events in the Old Testament which occur long after the early days of Genesis.

This section deals with a very interesting, though less broadly known, part of Israelite history, that of the Exile, or "Babylonian Captivity," the history of which is recorded in II Kings 17ff, II Chronicles 36ff, Ezra and Nehemjah. William F. Albright, in *From the Stone Age to Christianity*, gives a good thesis statement for this section:

"The post-exilic matter in Chronicles and Ezra-Nehemiah has been regarded by a number of scholars (notably by C.C. Torrey) as largely apocryphal, but recent discoveries and investigations have strikingly discredited this extreme position." 6/208

If the allegations against the traditional interpretation become established, then it will strategically damage the integrity of the Old Testament with the inevitable result of confusion as to which statements are "accurate" and which are to be rejected. Archaeology requires no such drastic modification, and in the following pages we will examine what can be said about this period.

2B.   Characters

For clarity, since the history of the Exile is not so popular as that of Moses, a brief introduction to the four main characters of this study follows.

1C.   JEHOIACHIN (JOICHIN)

The *International Standard Bible Encyclopaedia* gives us some of the facts: Jehoiachin reigned three months (597 B.C.) in Judah before being taken to Babylon to spend 37 years in prison. This marked the first deportation into Babylon after the very small group to leave under his father. 29/1577

Jehoiachin should not be confused with his father, Jehoiakim, who was an unfortunately poor ruler for eleven years starting in 608 B.C. 29/1579

Jack Finegan goes on to explain his plight in Babylon. He claims that from the excavations at Babylon it is known that, though he was given no ruling power, Jehoiachin was considered the legal king of Judah. He had a certain degree of freedom of movement and after his 37-year captivity was given even better treatment (II Kings 25:27-30). 16/188, 189

Albright, in "King Jehoiachin in Exile" *(Biblical Archaeology)*, explained the scene in Judah.

He commented that those who stayed behind liked Jehoiachin as ruler more than his successors; they called them "bad figs" in Jeremiah 24.

Nebuchadnezzar's son was benevolent with the displaced king, though Jehoiachin never was allowed to return and died in Babylon. 7/50

2C. CYRUS

Joseph P. Free *(Archaeology and Bible History)* mentions Cyrus. He explains that the empire of Nebuchadnezzar centered in Babylon fell to Cyrus the Great of Persia in 539 B.C. He was the king that allowed the Jews of Babylon to return to their home (note II Chronicles 36:22, 23 and Ezra 1:1-4). He reversed what the Assyrians and Nebuchadnezzar did in the deportations. 18/236, 237

Ira Price, in *The Monuments and the Old Testament*, picks up the evaluation of Cyrus, praising him as "a shrewd politician, and a kind-hearted ruler." He made the place of the conquered people as comfortable as possible, allowing cultural autonomy within the empire. He had reasons for returning the Jews. First, it was a normal procedure to allow many captive people to return to wherever they had been taken from, not just Jews. Second, Cyrus might have been shown Isaiah 44:28 or heard the essence of the prophecy that he, Cyrus, would allow the Jews to rebuild the temple and city. Third, he may have wanted a buffer state between Egypt and himself and Israel would fit in quite well. 35/382, 383

3C. EZRA

R. Dick Wilson's article, "Ezra," in *The International Standard Bible Encyclopaedia*, gives a brief summary of Ezra. He was born a priest in Babylon, though his profession as he grew up was a scribe. In about the year 459-458 B.C., he presented the King of Persia, Artaxerxes I, with a request to return to Judah and re-establish the law of Jehovah in Jerusalem. The king consented in an astonishingly positive way. At Jerusalem, Ezra saw a number of repentances of the people and also set to work rebuilding the temple. This Jewish scribe was a major leader of Judah during the rebuilding of Jerusalem after the Exile. 29/1082, 1083

4C. NEHEMIAH

In the same encyclopedia, under "Nehemiah," Wilson goes into his story. He was appointed at an early age to be the cupbearer to the King of Persia, Artaxerxes, who ruled in 464-424 B.C. This was an extremely strategic office, in which Nehemiah came in very close contact with one of the most influential men in the world. Small wonder that he was later put into the position of governor of Judea (444 B.C.). With the influence and power he had, he was able to have the walls of Jerusalem built, as well as gates, in addition to bringing about numerous social reforms. Ezra helped in all these projects. 29/2131

3B. Archaeological Finds

Before getting into what archaeological finds we have, a brief foreshadowing of the actual controversies will help us to see the impact that these finds have made. Albright, in "The Bible After Twenty Years of Archaeology" *Religion in Life)*, summarized the critics' viewpoint:

"Then in 1895 and 1896 W.H. Kosters and C.C. Torrey began their onslaughts on post-exilic history, followed by S.A. Cook and others. Torrey started by denying the authenticity of the Ezra Memoirs and went on to reject that of the Book of Ezekiel and finally that of the Book of Jeremiah. Continuing with remorseless logic (given his totally unacceptable premises), he denied that there had been a thoroughgoing devastation of Judah and Jerusalem by the Chaldeans in the time of Nebuchadnezzar, that there had been any real Exile or Restoration, and that there was an Ezra. The figure of Nehemiah he regarded as obscure and unimportant." 3/545

This is a picture of what the critics attack when considering the Exile.

1C. POTTERY

Albright, in *Archaeology of Palestine and the Bible,* made a point about pottery, which is a valuable archaeological consideration:

"There is fortunately a marked difference between the pottery of the pre-exilic and of the post-exilic periods, so that confusion is impossible. Practically all the ancient Judaean sites of the southern Shephelah and the adjacent Negeb, and many in the southern hill-country to the east show no occupation after the Exile (unless in the Roman or Byzantine periods.)" 2/171

2C. CYRUS CYLINDER

This is a record of goings on during the time of Cyrus the Great, as Free affirms:

"Archaeological evidence that Cyrus pursued a liberal and tolerant policy toward deported peoples, such as the Jews whom he found in Babylonia, was discovered during the nineteenth century by Rassam, who found the Cyrus Cylinder. This cylinder states concerning such groups, 'All of their peoples I assembled and restored to their own dwelling-places.' A picture of one of Cyrus' cylinders appears in several handbooks on archaeology. It tells of his taking the city of Babylon without violence, and, later, of returning people to their former dwellings." 18/237

Fred Wight adds:

"On a broken cylinder discovered at Ur, Cyrus is recorded as having said: 'Sin (the moon-god), the illuminator of heaven and earth, with his favorable sign delivered into my hands the four quarters of the world, and I returned the gods to their shrines.' This recalls to mind the proclamations of II Chronicles 36:22, 23 and Ezra 1:2, 3." 43/68

Finegan draws a conclusion from this:

"The spirit of Cyrus's decree of release which is quoted in the Old Testament (II Chronicles 36:23; Ezra 1:2-4) is confirmed by the Cyrus cylinder, where the king relates that he allowed the captives to return to their various countries and rebuild their temples." 16/191

The significance of this cylinder will become obvious as the section continues.

3C. ELEPHANTINE TABLETS

W.F. Albright, in "The Bible After Twenty Years of Archaeology," explained that these papyrus documents are of fifth century vintage and were found in an Upper Egyptian Jewish colony. They were published between 1904 and 1911. They have seriously jolted critical positions. 3/546

Jack Finegan commented on the contents:

"The contents of the Elephantine papyri are varied, ranging from the copy of the Behistun inscription of Darius mentioned above... to such a document as a Jewish marriage contract. In one letter, dated about 419 B.C., the Jews of Elephantine are instructed by the authority of the Persian government to celebrate the Passover according to the official practice of the Jerusalem temple as embodied in the priestly code (Exodus 12:1-20)." 16/201

4C. BABYLONIAN RATION LISTS AND JAR HANDLES

Finegan mentioned the Ishtar Gate of Babylon:

"In the ruins of the vaulted building near the Ishtar Gate which was mentioned above... some 300 cuneiform tablets were unearthed. Upon study these have been found to date from between 595 and 570 B.C., and to contain lists of rations such as barley and oil paid to craftsmen and captives who lived in and near Babylon at that time.... But the name of most significance to us is none other than that of Yaukin, king of Judah, with whom also five royal princes are listed." 16/188

Yaukin is the same as Jehoiachin. Albright has more to say:

"In recently published tablets from a royal archive of Nebuchadnezzar, dating in and about the year 592 B.C., Jehoiachin and five of his sons, as well as at least five other Jews, are mentioned among recipients of rations from the royal court. It is significant that Jehoiachin was still called 'king of Judah' in official Babylonian documents." 4/85

This is what G. Ernest Wright said concerning the Babylonian jar handles recently unearthed. He begins:

"Further confirmation of the status of Jehoiachin in Babylon comes from the discovery in Palestine of three stamped jar-handles which bore the words, 'Belonging to Eliakim, steward of Yaukin.'" 44/178

These jar handles are not significant in themselves, but the seals impressed upon them make them very valuable; they can be dated about 598-587 B.C. Eliakim was a caretaker of the royal possessions of Yaukin. There were seals saying other things as well. One bearing a rooster's image was discovered eight miles north of Jerusalem. Wright explains this one and another:

"It belonged 'To Jaazaniah, servant of the king,' a Judean royal official mentioned in II Kings 25:23 and Jer. 40:8 (cf. also Jer. 42:1 and 'Azariah' in 43:2, all of whom may be the same person). The other was a seal impression found in the ruins of Lachish.... It bears the inscription, 'To Gedaliah who is over the house.' This is undoubtedly the same man as the governor whom Nebuchadnezzar appointed 'over the people who remained in the land of Judah' after the fall of Jerusalem and who was soon murdered (II Kings 25:22-26; Jer. 40-1)." 44/178

4B. Controversies

With this background knowledge of the main characters of this period, as well as the illumination which archaeology can provide, we are now able to examine the controversial issues at hand. Joseph Free ("Archaeology and the Historical Accuracy of Scriptures" in *Bibliotheca Sacra*) summarized Torrey's basic allegations thus:

"Torrey denied, among other things, the following:

(1) The authenticity of the record in Ezra;

(2) the fact of any real devastation as recorded in the Biblical account of the destruction and devastation of Judah at the beginning of the Exile;

(3) the fact of any real Exile or Restoration;

(4) even the implications of the details of the Exile, e.g., II Kings 25:11-12 indicates that virtually all the skilled workers were taken away in the Exile, and the poor of the land had to replace the vinedressers and gardeners (husbandmen) so taken away. Torrey's denial of the details of the Exile went so far that he asserted that no Jewish gardeners could possibly have been taken as captives to Babylon." 22/223, 224

1C. C.C. TORREY

Torrey wrote *The Composition and Historical Value of Ezra-Nehemiah*, a short booklet which dealt mainly with the composition of Ezra and Nehemiah. Toward the latter part, he investigated the historical value of the Old Testament accounts of this period. What follows are short excerpts from the pamphlet:

"The results reached in the preceding investigation will, if accepted, necessitate a decided change in our estimate of the value of Ezra-Nehemiah as a source for the post-exilic history of the Jews." 38/51

"No fact of O.T. criticism is more firmly established than this; that the Chronicler, as a historian, is thoroughly untrustworthy. He distorts facts deliberately and habitually; invents chapter after chapter with the greatest freedom; and, what is most dangerous of all, his history is not written for its own sake, but in the interest of an extremely one-sided theory." 38/52

"As for the story of the Return under Zerubbabel, told in Ezra 1.2, each one of its several features has been repeatedly shown to be unworthy of credence. The Cyrus edict cannot possibly be regarded as genuine." 38/52

Torrey was careful, however, to give praise honestly.

"The story of Ezra is the Chronicler's masterpiece. It is the best exemplification of the traits that appear so prominently in the long passages in the book of Chronicles, his own qualities as a writer of fiction and his idea of the history of Israel." 38/57

He cannot be accused of ambiguity. He concluded the book with the following paragraph:

"The result of the investigation as to the historical content of Ezra-Neh. has thus been to show, that aside from the greater part of Neh. 1-6 the book has no value whatever, as history. It may have served a useful purpose in its own day. The Chr. [Chronicler] was not trying to write history for us, but for what he supposed to be the benefit of his people. He had his own motive, which we shall do well not to judge harshly. But his work, whatever else may be said of it, certainly throws no light on the history of the Jews in the Persian period." 38/65

It might be argued that Torrey was at a disadvantage by not having the modern finds of archaeology available. However, it would be difficult to show how Torrey was expecting any finds to cause him to modify his opinions. It would seem probable that if any significant archaeological discoveries were to be coming, he would expect them to validate not refute, his skepticism. In light of what we know today, the scarce archaeological facts of his day seem to merely bring out more clearly the hypothetical, not factual, learning of the early critics.

With a quote from Albright, we will begin our brief review of the individual questions:

"The views of these scholars have been categorically disproved by the archaeological discoveries of the past twenty years." 3/546

2C. NO REAL EXILE OR RESTORATION

Ezra purposed to restore Jewish laws. Did he succeed? *The Archaeology of Palestine and the Bible* by W.F. Albright gives a decided yes:

"The famous Passover letter proved that normative Judaism was imposed upon the colonies of the Diaspora by the aid of the Persian Government, in corroboration of the statements in Ezra." 2/170

Does archaeology say the children of Israel went to Babylon? Jack Finegan concludes that they did:

"Amidst the splendors of Babylon, however, our greatest interest lies in the inquiry as to whether any traces of the Jewish exiles remain. A discovery of much importance to the biblical archaeologist now makes it possible to give an affirmative answer to this question (Ernst F. Weidner in *Mélanges Syriens offerts a Monsieur René Dussaud* II (1939), pp. 923-927; W.F. Albright in BA v. 4 (Dec. 1942), pp. 49-55.)." 16/188

3C. DETAILS OF THE EXILE

One interesting question is how many details are confirmed by archaeology? To begin with, we can look to the Babylonian Lists and W.F. Albright ("King Jehoiachin in Exile," *Biblical Archaeologist*):

"The contents of the tablets, in Dr. Weidner's [the discoverer] resume, prove to be extraordinarily interesting, since they list payments of rations in oil and barley, etc., to captives and skilled workmen from many nations, all living in and around Babylon, between the years 595 and 570 B.C. Among them are Yaukin, king of Judah, and five royal princes, as well as numerous other men of Judah; the songs of Aga, king of Ascalon in the land of the Philistines, together with mariners and musicians from that seaport; mariners and craftsmen from Tyre, Byblus and Arvad in Phoenicia; Elamites, Medes and Persians; many Egyptians, who were mariners, ship-builders, horse-trainers and monkey-trainers." 7/51

He goes on to explain that "Father L.H. Vincent, identified the name 'Yaukin' as an abbreviated form of 'Joiachin,' just as the name 'Yauqim' of contemporary documents is an abbreviation of 'Joiakim.' 7/50

In II Kings 24:14, we read of the king of Babylon taking the Jews into exile, not only the Judean King, but also the "craftsman and smiths." Albright takes Torrey to issue on this point:

"Incidentally, Torrey asserted that no Jewish *gardeners* can possibly have been taken as captives to Babylon—but we have in these same ration lists, among other captive Jews, a Jewish *gardener*! The attempt by Torrey and Irwin to show that there was no Jewish dispersion in Babylonia to which Ezekiel can have preached—assuming that he existed at all—has collapsed entirely. That neither language nor content of the Book of Ezekiel fits any period or place outside of the early sixth century B.C. and Babylonia, has been proved in detail by C.G. Howie (1950)." 3/546

Free comments on the presence of King Jehoiachin in Babylon:

"It is thrilling to be able to find even the 'ration receipts' of King Jehoiachin from twenty-five hundred years ago." 18/221

4C. QUESTION OF EZRA-NEHEMIAH

One big reason for the late dating of Ezra, and thus an allowance for less respect due its historical value, is the so-called late words found therein. This is one reason Torrey felt so much at liberty to abuse the integrity of the book. Albright again, however, raises a difficulty with such a view.

"For example, Torrey insisted that certain words, among them *pithgama*, 'matter, affair,' were of Greek origin and could not, therefore, have been taken into biblical Aramaic before 330 B.C. In the last twenty years these very same words have turned up in Egyptian Aramaic and Babylonian cuneiform documents from the late fifth century, that is, from the very time of Ezra! The forced Greek etymologies which he proposed are now mere curiosities." 3/546, 547

In "Archaeology and Higher Criticism," J.P. Free notes that the "rationalistic critical view" maintains a single authorship of Ezra, Nehemiah and Chronicles (20/36). R.H. Pfeiffer (*Introduction to the Old Testament*) can be cited:

"The book of Ezra-Nehemiah is the sequel of Chronicles and was written by the Chronicler (II Chron. 36:22f. is repeated verbatim in Ezra 1:1-3a). It relates the history of the Jews during the century which elapsed from the edict of Cyrus allowing the Exiles to return (538 B.C.) to Nehemiah's second visit to Jerusalem (432 B.C.; Neh. 13:6f.; cf. 5:14)." 34/813

Free then returns to the words used in the book of Ezra:

"The late dating of these books by the liberal was based, among other things, on the assumption that the Aramaic letters in Ezra were written in a late type of Aramaic. The discovery of the Elephantine Letters on an island in the Nile River showed that the Aramaic of Ezra may easily date back to the fourth century, if not to the end of the fifth." 20/36

In dealing with Nehemiah, he says,

"The reference in Nehemiah to the drachma, a Greek coin, was also held to be evidence of the late date of that book. But the discovery of six drachmas in the Persian level in the excavation of Beth-zur, south of Bethlehem, showed that Nehemiah would not have been ahead of himself in mentioning the drachma about 450 B.C." 20/36, 37

Free goes on to cite Albright accusing Pfeiffer of being "far behind the van of Old Testament scholarship" (2/253) in his maintaining of a third century (B.C.) date of Ezra-Nehemiah-Chronicles. Then, he concludes:

"Thus, at point after point the reasons for late dating of many of the books of the Old Testament is shown by archaeological discovery not to be supported." 20/37

Before closing the case on Ezra-Nehemiah, we have an interesting story of one man who stood up strongly against this popular late-date theory, even though he did not have the benefits of modern archaeology. The man is Eduard Meyer.

Albright, in *From the Stone Age to Christianity*, introduces him to us:

"E. Meyer's brilliant defense of its authenticity in 1897 was not only fully justified as far as it went but was not even sufficiently comprehensive." 6/208

In another book, he adds:

"The language alone undoubtedly forms a powerful argument in favour of the essential authenticity of the Aramaic letters in Ezra, which has been denied by most modern scholars, with the brilliant exception of Eduard Meyer." 2/170

In an article he goes further:

"The great ancient historian, Eduard Meyer, fifty-five years ago insisted on the substantial authenticity of the Persian decrees and official letters preserved in Ezra; during the past twenty years strong additional evidence for them has been published by H.H. Schaeder and Elias Bickerman. If it were practicable to quote from still unpublished Aramaic documents from fifth-century Egypt, the weight of factual evidence would crush all opposition." 3/547

To Albright, the case is closed:

"Again Torrey and others have insisted that the language of the book is late, dating from the third century B.C., after Alexander the Great. The publication of the fifth-century Elephantine Papyri (1904-1911) from a Jewish colony near Assuan in upper Egypt had already made Torrey's position difficult, but subsequent discoveries by Mittwoch, Eilers, and others have dealt it the *coup de grâce*." 3/546

5C. NO DESTRUCTION OF JUDAH

This final category will not take long, but it is included because at one time it actually was believed that there was no real destruction of Judah when Nebuchadnezzar marched through.

Free says:

19 yrs

"The invasions of Nebuchadnezzar in 605, 597, and 587-586 B.C. caused much damage and destruction in Judah. Archaeological evidence shows that many of the cities of Judah were destroyed and not rebuilt, a fact particularly evidenced in the excavations at Azekah, Bethshemesh, and Kirjathsepher, and also by surface examination elsewhere." 18/227

What have the excavations shown? Albright gives a clue:

"The views of these scholars have been categorically disproved by the archaeological discoveries of the past twenty years. Excavation and surface exploration in Judah have proved that the towns of Judah were not only completely destroyed by the Chaldeans in their two invasions, but were not reoccupied for generations—often never again in history. This is solidly demonstrated by the evidence of pottery (which serves the archaeologist as fossils serve the geologist in dating periods), confirmed by a steadily increasing number of inscriptions from the last years of the Kingdom of Judah. Vivid light is shed on these events by the Lachish Ostraca and other recently discovered documents." 3/546

And in conclusion, he is most clear:

✗ ✗ ✗ "Archaeological data have thus demonstrated the substantial originality of the Books of Jeremiah and Ezekiel, Ezra and Nehemiah, beyond doubt."

7A. TELL MARDIKH: The Discovery of Ebla

One of the greatest archaeological finds in this century has only recently come to light. In 1964 Professor Paolo Matthiae, archaeologist from the University of Rome, began a systematic excavation of a then unknown city. Due to the determination and foresight of Matthiae, in 1974-75 a great royal palace was uncovered which eventually yielded over 15,000 tablets and fragments. Giovanni, Pettinato, epigrapher, had worked closely with Matthiae in helping to determine some of the paleographic significance of the find. At present, only a fraction of the tablets have been translated. It is now certain that upon this ancient site the once prestigious city of Ebla ruled the Near East as the seat of a great empire. Ebla is located near the modern-day city of Aleppo in North Syria.

Location of EBLA

The zenith of Ebla was principally in the third millennium B.C. (co-terminous with the time of the patriarchs). Although the Ebla texts, at present, do not specifically mention biblical people or events (although there is much debate over this issue) they do provide an abundance of background material and biblical place names for evaluating the biblical narratives. The importance of Ebla for Syrian history is most impressive. The significance of Ebla for biblical studies is phenomenal. So far only the tip of the iceberg has been seen. Although the evidence has taken time to surface, listed here is some of the support for the biblical narratives.

1B. Biblical Towns

In reference to the identification of biblical towns in the Ebla archives, Kitchen notes:

"Not a few towns of biblical interest appear in the Ebla tablets, which preserve (in most cases) the earliest-known mention of these in written records.

"More useful, potentially, are the Eblaite mentions of familiar Palestinian place-names such as Hazor, Megiddo, Jerusalem, Lachish, Dor, Gaza,

3,000 BC

Ashtarot (-Qarnaim), etc. Several of these places are known archaeologically to have been inhabited towns in the third millennium B.C. (Early Bronze Age III-IV), and these tablets confirm their early importance, possibly as local city-states. Finally, Canaan itself now appears as a geographical entity from the later third millennium B.C., long before any other dated external mention so far known to us—it will be interesting to learn what extent is accorded to Canaan in the Ebla texts." 218/53-54

2B. Biblical Names

"Not a few of the proper names of inhabitants of Ebla have struck Pettinato and others by their obvious resemblances to a wide range of personal names of individuals in the Bible." 218/52

"The most important contributions of the Ebla occurrences of these and other such names are (i) to emphasize once more that these are names used by *real* human individuals (never by gods, or exclusively [if ever] by tribes, or by fairytale figures), and (ii) to indicate the immense antiquity of names of this type, and of these names in particular." 218/53

Dr. Pettinato gives clear Eblaite variations on such Hebrew names as Israel, Ishmael and Micaiah. 219/50

3B. Ancient Near Eastern Tribute

Some consider the tribute received by Solomon at the height of his empire as fanciful exaggeration. But the find at Ebla offers another interpretation of the accounts.

Gold

"Imperial Ebla at the height of its power must have had a vast income. From one defeated king of Mari alone, a tribute of 11,000 pounds of silver and 880 pounds of gold was exacted on one occasion. This *ten tons* of silver and over *one third of a ton* of gold was no mean haul in itself. Yet it was simply one 'delectable extra' so far as the treasury-accounts of Ebla were concerned. In such an economic context, the 666 talents (about twenty tons) of gold as Solomon's basic income from his entire 'empire' some 15 centuries later (I Kings 10:14; II Chronicles 9:13) loses its air of exaggeration and begins to look quite prosaic as just part of a wider picture of the considerable (if transient) wealth of major kingdoms of the ancient biblical world.

"The comparisons just given do *not* prove that Solomon actually did receive 666 talents of gold, or that his kingdom was organized just as Kings describes. But they do indicate clearly (i) that the Old Testament data must be studied in the context of their world and *not* in isolation, and (ii) that the *scale* of activity portrayed in the Old Testament writings is neither impossible nor even improbable when measured by the relevant external standards." 218/51-52

4B. Religious Practices

Temples

The Ebla texts reveal that many of the Old Testament religious practices are not as "late" as some critical scholars have espoused.

"In matters like priests, cult and offerings the records from Ebla so far merely reinforce for Syria-Palestine what we already know for Egypt, Mesopotamia and Anatolia in the third, second and first millennia B.C., and from the records of North-Syrian Qatna and Ugarit for the second millennium B.C. Namely, that well-organized temple cults, sacrifices, full rituals, etc., were a *constant* feature of ancient Near-Eastern religious life at *all* periods from prehistory down to Graeco-Roman times. They have nothing to do with baseless theories of the nineteenth century A.D., whereby such features of religious life can only be a mark of 'late sophistication,' virtually forbidden to the Hebrews until after the Babylonian exile—alone of *all* the peoples of the ancient East. There is simply no rational basis for the quaint idea that the simple rites of Moses' tabernacle (cf. Leviticus) or of Solomon's temple, both well over 1000 years later than the rituals practiced in half-a-dozen Eblaite temples, must be the idle invention of idealizing writers as late as the fifth century B.C." 218/54

G. Pettinato comments on the source of the specifics referred to by Kitchen:

"Passing on to the divine cult, we note the existence of the temples of Dagan, Astar, Kamos, Rasap, all attested in the texts from Ebla. Among the offerings are listed bread, drinks, or even animals. Two tablets in particular, TM, 75, G, 1974 and TM, 75, G, 2238, stand out because they record the offerings of various animals to different gods made by all the members of the royal family during a single month. For example, '11 sheep for the god Adad from the en as an offering,' '12 sheep for the god Dagan from the en as an offering,' '10 sheep for the god Rasap of the city Edani from the en as an offering.'

"Among the more interesting aspects of the divine cult at Ebla is the presence of diverse categories of priests and priestesses, including two classes of prophets, the *mahhu* and the *nabiutum*, the second of which finds a natural counterpart in the Old Testament. To explain the biblical phenomenon scholars have hitherto looked to Mari for background, but in the future Ebla will also claim their attention." 219/49

5B.   Hebrew Words

K.A. Kitchen speaks of the critical view of Scripture held by many liberal scholars:

"Seventy or a hundred years ago, no such vast depth of perspective was possible; and to suit the purely theoretical reconstructions of Old Testament books and history by German Old Testament scholars in particular, many words in Hebrew were labelled 'late'—600 B.C. and later, in effect. By this simple means, mere philosophical prejudices could be given the outward appearance of a 'scientific' reconstruction down to the present day." 218/50

As a reply, he continues:

"However, the immense growth in our knowledge of the earlier history of words found in Old Testament Hebrew tends now to alter all this. If a given word is used in Ebla in 2300 B.C., and in Ugarit in 1300 B.C., then it *cannot* by any stretch of the imagination be a 'late word' (600 B.C.!), or an 'Aramaism' at periods when standard Aramaic had not yet evolved. It becomes instead an *early* word, a part of the ancestral inheritance of biblical Hebrew. More positively, the increased number of contexts that one gains for rarer words can provide useful confirmation—or correction—of our understanding of their meaning." 218/50

Referring to specific words, Kitchen states:

"Thus, to go back to the survey of city-officials at Ebla, the term used for those scores of 'leaders' was *nase*, the same word as *nasi*, a term in biblical Hebrew used for leaders of the tribes of Israel (e.g., Numbers 1:16, 44, etc.), and applied to other purely human rulers such as Solomon (I Kings 11:34). Old-fashioned biblical criticism declared the word to be 'late,' a mark of the hypothetical 'priestly code' for example.

"The word *ketem*, 'gold,' is in Hebrew a rare and poetic synonym for *zahab*, and is commonly dismissed as 'late.' Unfortunately for this mis-dating, the word was borrowed into Egyptian from Canaanite back in the twelfth century B.C., and now—over 1000 years earlier still—recurs as *kutim* in the Paleo-Canaanite of Ebla, 2300 B.C." 218/50

He continues:

"As remarked in Chapter 2, the Hebrew word *tehom*, 'deep,' was not borrowed from Babylonian, seeing that it is attested not only in Ugaritic as *thmt* (thirteenth century B.C.) but also Ebla a thousand years earlier (*ti'amatum*). The term is Common Semitic.

"As an example of a rare word confirmed in both existence and meaning, one may cite Hebrew *'ereshet*, 'desire,' which occurs just once in the Bible, in Psalm 21:2 (Heb. 21:3). Besides being found in Ugaritic in the thirteenth century B.C., this word now appears a millennium earlier at Ebla as *irisatum* (Eblaite or Old-Akkadian) in the Sumerian/Eblaite vocabulary tablets.

"Finally, the supposed 'late' verb *hadash/hiddesh*, 'be new'/'to renew' goes back—again—via Ugaritic (*hadath*) to Eblaite (*h)edash(u)*. And so on, for many more besides." 218/50-51

Kitchen concludes:

"The lessons here are—or should be—clear. Set against 2½ thousand years of history and development of the West Semitic dialects, the whole position of the dating of the vocabulary and usages in biblical Hebrew will need to be completely reexamined. The truth appears to be that early West Semitic in the third and second millennia B.C. had in common a vast and rich vocabulary, to which the later dialects such as Canaanite, Hebrew, Phoenician, Aramaic, etc., fell heirs—but in uneven measure. Words that remained in everyday prosaic use in one of these languages lingered on only in high-flown poetry or in traditional expressions in another of the group. Thus, not a few supposed 'late words' or 'Aramaisms' in Hebrew (especially in poetry) are nothing more than early West-Semitic words that have found less use in Hebrew but have stayed more alive in Aramaic." 218/51

6B. Future Value

More evidence from Ebla will soon be forthcoming and will shed more light on the biblical account.

Temporarily, some of the potentially very significant finds concerning biblical historicity have been clouded with uncertain reports. One of these finds centers on the five cities of the plain mentioned in Genesis 14. The historicity of these cities and their kings has long been questioned by critical scholars. But evidence came to light in the early stages of the Ebla excavation that shed important new background on the historicity of these cities. 220/143-164

However, new excavations of the data have called some of these findings into question. 220/143

Hopefully these issues will be resolved soon for the benefit of all.

8A. CONCLUSION

Archaeology does not prove the Bible. It does not prove beyond a shadow of a doubt all aspects of the history of the Exile. It does, however, put the one who wishes to maintain the traditional view on at least an equal footing with the skeptics. A person must no longer feel required to believe scholarship like that of Torrey. Free put a simple closing to his study of the subject thus:

"In summary, archaeological discoveries show at point after point that the Biblical record is confirmed and commended as trustworthy. This confirmation is not confined to a few general instances." 22/225

NOTE: For further study of this area, see either Free, or better, Albright. These two have done extensive work in this area, as this section indicates: Free, Joseph P.— *Archaeology and Bible History* and an article series in *Bibliotheca Sacra* in 1956-57; Albright, William Foxwell—*Archaeology of Palestine and the Bible*, "King Jehoiachin in Exile" in *Biblical Archaeologist* and "The Bible After Twenty Years of Archaeology" in *Religion in Life*.

APPENDIX BIBLIOGRAPHY

1. Albright, William F. *The Archaeology of Palestine.* Baltimore: Penguin Books, 1960.

2. Albright, William F. *Archaeology of Palestine and the Bible.* New York: Revell, 1932.

3. Albright, William F. "The Bible After Twenty Years of Archaeology," *Religion in Life.* Autumn, 1952. Vol. 21, pp. 537-550.

4. Albright, William F. *The Biblical Period from Abraham to Ezra.* New York: Harper, 1960.

5. Albright, William F. "A Brief History of Judah from the Days of Josiah to Alexander the Great." *Biblical Archaeologist.* February, 1946. Vol. 9, No. 1, pp. 1-16.

6. Albright, William F. *From the Stone Age to Christianity.* Baltimore: John Hopkins Press, 1940.

7. Albright, William F. "King Jehoiachin in Exile," *Biblical Archaeologist.* December, 1942. Vol. 5, No. 4, pp. 49-55.

8. Albright, William F. "The Oldest Hebrew Letters: Lachish Ostraca," *Bulletin of the American Schools of Oriental Research.* April, 1938. No. 70, pp. 11-16.

9. Albright, William F. *Recent Discoveries in Bible Lands.* New York: Funk and Wagnall, 1955.

10. Albright, William F. "Recent Progress in North-Canaanite Research," *Bulletin of the American Schools of Oriental Research.* April, 1938. No. 70, pp. 18-24.

11. Anderson, Bernhard W. "Changing Emphasis in Biblical Scholarship," *Journal of Bible and Religion.* April, 1955. Vol. 23, pp. 81-88.

12. Archer, Gleason L. *A Survey of Old Testament Introduction.* Chicago: Moody,© 1964, 1974. Moody Press, Moody Bible Institute of Chicago. Used by permission.

13. Burrows, Millar. *What Mean These Stones?* New York: Meridian Books, 1957.

14. Caiger, S.L. *Bible and Spade.* London: Oxford University Press, 1936.

15. Elder, John. *Prophets, Idols, and Diggers.* New York: Bobbs-Merrill Co., 1960.

16. Finegan, Jack. *Light from the Ancient Past.* London: Oxford Press, distributed in the U.S. by Princeton University Press, 1946.

17. Frank, Henry Thomas. *Bible, Archaeology and Faith.* Nashville: Abingdon Press, 1971.

18. Free, Joseph P. *Archaeology and Bible History.* Wheaton, Ill.: Scripture Press, 1969.

19. Free, Joseph P. "Archaeology and the Bible," *HIS Magazine.* May, 1949. Vol. 9, pp. 17-20. Reprinted by permission from *HIS*, student magazine of Inter-Varsity Christian Fellowship, ©1949.

20. Free, Joseph P. "Archaeology and Higher Criticism," *Bibliotheca Sacra.* January, 1957. Vol 114, pp. 23-29.

21. Free, Joseph P. "Archaeology and Liberalism," *Bibliotheca Sacra.* October, 1956. Vol. 113, 322-338.

22. Free, Joseph P. "Archaeology and the Historical Accuracy of Scripture," *Bibliotheca Sacra.* July, 1956. Vol. 113, pp. 214-226.

23. Glueck, Nelson. "The Second Campaign at Tell el-Kheleifeh," *Bulletin of the American Schools of Oriental Research.* October, 1939. Vol. 75, pp. 8-22.

24. Glueck, Nelson. "The Third Season at Tell el-Kheleifeh," *Bulletin of the American Schools of Oriental Research.* October, 1940. Vol. 79, pp. 2-18.

25. Gordon, C.H. "Biblical Customs and the Nuzu Tablets," *The Biblical Archaeologist.* February, 1940. Vol. 3, No. 1, pp. 1-12.

26. Hamilton, Floyd. *Basis of the Christian Faith.* New York: Harper, 1933.

27. Haupert, R.S. "Lachish—Frontier Fortress of Judah," *Biblical Archaeologist.* December, 1938. Vol. 1, No. 4, pp. 30-32.

28. Horn, Siegfried H. "Recent Illumination of the Old Testament," *Christianity Today.* June 21, 1968. Vol. 12, No. 19, pp. 13-17.

29. *International Standard Bible Encyclopaedia.* 5 vols. Edited by James Orr, John L. Nielsen, and James Donaldson. Grand Rapids: Wm B. Eerdmans Publishing Co., 1939.

30. Kitchen, K.A. *The Ancient Orient and the Old Testament.* Chicago: Inter-Varsity Press. 1966.

31. Lapp, Paul W. *Biblical Archaeology and History.* New York: World Publishing, 1969.

32. Little, Paul. *Know Why You Believe.* Wheaton, Ill.: Scripture Press, 1967.

33. Peet, T. Eric. *Egypt and the Old Testament.* Liverpool: University Press of Liverpool, 1942.

34. Pfeiffer, Robert H. *Introduction to the Old Testament.* New York: Harper, 1948.

35. Price, Ira M. *The Monuments and the Old Testament.* 17th edition. Philadelphia: The Judson Press, 1925.

36. Sayce, A.H. *Monument Facts and Higher Critical Fancies.* London: The Religious Tract Society. 1910.

37. Stearns, M.B. "Biblical Archaeology and the Higher Critics," *Bibliotheca Sacra.* July, 1939. Vol. 96, No. 383, pp. 307-318.

38. Torrey, Charles C. *The Composition and Historical Value of Ezra-Nehemiah.* Giessen, Germany: J. Ricker'sche Buchhandlung, 1896.

39. Unger, Merrill F. "Archaeological Discoveries and Their Bearing on Old Testament," *Bibliotheca Sacra.* April, 1955. Vol. 112, pp. 137-142.

40. Unger, Merrill R. *Archaeology and the Old Testament.* Grand Rapids: Zondervan, 1954.

41. Vos, Howard, ed. *An Introduction to Bible Archaeology.* Chicago: Moody, ©1959. Moody Press, Moody Bible Institute of Chicago. Used by permission.

42. Vos, Howard. *Genesis and Archaeology.* Chicago: Moody Press, ©1963.

43. Wight, Fred H. *Highlights of Archaeology in Bible Lands.* Chicago: Moody, ©1955. Moody Press, Moody Bible Institute of Chicago. Used by Permission.

44. Wright, G.E. "The Present State of Biblical Archaeology," *The Study of the Bible Today and Tomorrow.* Edited by Harold R. Willoughby. Chicago: University of Chicago Press, 1947.

45. Wright, G.E. "The Terminology of the Old Testament Religion and Its Significance," *Journal of Near East Studies.* October, 1942. Vol. 1, No. 4, pp. 404-414.

46. Oesterley, W.O.E. and Theodore H. Robinson. *Hebrew Religion: Its Origin and Developments.* London: Society for Promoting Christian Knowledge, 1935.

47. Hofner, Harry A. "The Hittites and the Hurrians," *Peoples of the Old Testament.* Edited by D.J. Wiseman. London: Oxford Press, 1973.

RECENT ILLUMINATION OF THE OLD TESTAMENT

SIGFRIED H. HORN

We Christians have a particular interest in the past of the Near East, because our religious and cultural roots lie there. Our beliefs are guided by an ancient book, the Bible, that was produced in its entirety in lands strange to us by people who did not speak our tongue and whose customs were not ours. If the message contained in that ancient book is to have maning for us moderns of the Western world, we must understand it and have confidence in its authenticity, its veracity, its timelessness, and its eternal values.

During the last two centuries, the Old Testament more than the New has been subjected to much critical investigation. We know it was written in Hebrew by Jews 2,500 years ago and more. It contains accounts of miracles that cannot be verified, events that seem unreal or fantastic, and prophecies in a symbolism that requires special study to be understood. Little wonder that many thinking people have questioned the value of the Old Testament for this modern age and have subjected it to a scrutiny that no other book, ancient or modern, has ever experienced.

Many fields have undergone revolutions during the last few centuries. In the space of 150 yearss, traveling has been accelerated from 4 to 17,000 miles an hour. Electronic computers now make calculations with breath-taking speed. Electric and atomic power has been harnessed and can be released at will. The worlds of the Arctic and the Antarctic, of the deep sea, of the air that surrounds us and of the empty space beyond our atmosphere—all these have been explored. No wonder the inquisitive mind of modern man began also to question traditional religious beliefs, when he saw that values changed in many areas and that the views of his forbears in many fields of knowledge proved false. It is only natural, then, that the basis of our Christian faith, the Bible, has been subjected to careful scrutiny.

For some results of this investigation seemed to threaten doom for the Bible, particularly the Old Testament. The culmination was reached at the time of World War I. Scholars did not yet know that a Hebrew alphabetic script existed before the eighth or ninth century B.C.; therefore they thought that the Pentateuch could not have been produced any earlier than the period of the Hebrew kings. Since ancient parallels for the strange customs described in the patriarchal stories had not been discovered, practically all scholars of standing in Europe and America considered these stories ficticious. Furthermore, the earliest known Hebrew Old Testament manuscripts came from the tenth century A.D. and thus were less than a thousand years old. This strengthened the suspicion that the Bible text had undergone substantial changes during its transmission from one generation to another over a period of many centuries from which no witnesses seemed to have survived.

Not surprisingly, many scholars therefore abandoned belief in traditional views about the Old Testament. Friedrich Delitzsch, a great German Assyriologist and Old Testament scholar, wrote in 1921 that "the books of Moses, Joshua and Judges suffer under the fault that history is indiscriminately mixed with legends and fairy tales, as is also the case in the Book of Kings" (*Die gross Täuschung*, I, 10). He also asserted that "the Old Testament works, the alleged Word of God, has been transmitted in a much more faulty and careless way than we can comprehend" (II, 5). Julius Wellhausen, the famous higher Bible critic, proclaimed unchallenged his idea that the conditions of the later Jewish monarchy were retrojected into the hoary past, and that the patriarchal stories were no more than a transfigured mirage of unreality. He was so fully convinced of the unreliability of the biblical narratives that he exclaimed: "If it [the Israelite tradition] were only possible, it would be folly to prefer any other possibility" (*Komposition des Hexateuch*, p. 346).

But thanks to archaeological discoveries made during the last forty years, this situation has changed completely. In 1917 Alan Gardiner, noted British Egyptologist, made the first decipherment of the Proto-Semitic inscriptions found at Mt. Sinai by Flinders Petrie more than ten years earlier. These inscriptions, written in a pictorial script by Canaanites before the middle of the second millennium B.C., prove that alphabetic writing existed before the time of Moses. Numerous other inscriptions in the same script have since that time come to light in Palestine and near Mt. Sinai, showing that the art of writing in an alphabetic script was already widespread in the patriarchal age.

The discovery of a whole archive of legal and social texts at Nuzi, a small place in northeastern Iraq, has revealed that the social and legal background of the patriarchal age is reflected accurately and in great detail in the Old Testament patriarchal narratives. Nothing has done more in recent years to restore confidence in the reliability of these narratives than the humble Nuzi texts. Scholar after scholar has testified that "there is today no reason to doubt the authenticity of the general background of the patriarchal narratives" (E.A. Speiser, *Annual of the American Schools of Oriental Research*, XIII, 43). To the discoveries at Nuzi must be added the finding of several law codes from the early second millennium B.C. that have revealed the legal background for many strange customs encountered in the patriarchal period.

Since 1929, annual excavations carried out at Ras Shamra in northern Syria have given us a large mass of Canaanite literature, written in an alphabetic cuneiform script that was deciphered in an incredibly short time, chiefly through the ingenuity of two scholars, one German and one French. These texts have illuminated the religion as well as the moral and social conditions of the ancient Canaanites and have provided much linguistic help for a better understanding of the poetical sections of the Old Testament.

Excavations of numerous sites in Palestine, Syria, and other Bible lands have brought to light many bits of evidence that have made major or minor contributions to a better understanding or verification of the Bible Stories. Professor W.F. Albright, the greatest living Orientalist made the following significant remarks in 1958 when he reviewed the archaeological accomplishment of the recent past:

> Thanks to modern research we now recognize its [the Bible's] substantial historicity. The narratives of the patriarchs, of Moses and the exodus, of the conquest of Canaan, of the judges, the monarchy, exile and restoration, have all been confirmed and illustrated to an extent that I should have thought impossible forty years ago [*The Christian Century*, November 19, 1958, p. 1329].

Then came the culmination of all discoveries in the field of biblical archaeology: the finding of Hebrew scrolls in the vicinity of the Dead Sea, scrolls that have given us samples, dating from the period from the third century B.C. to the second century A.D., of all Old Testament books save one. The few well-preserved documents as well as the tens of thousands of fragments of worm-eaten and rotten Bible scrolls, which patient scholars have deciphered and published, have already done much to restore confidence in the reliability of the Hebrew text. One can find scores of published testimonials by reputable scholars who as the result of their studies of the Dead Sea scrolls have declared their surprise that the changes the Masoretic Hebrew text experienced in the course of transmission were so few and so insignificant. Professor Albright said in this respect that the Dead Sea scrolls prove "conclusively that we must treat the consonantal text of the Hebrew Bible with the utmost respect and that the free emending of difficult passages in which modern critical scholars have indulged cannot be tolerated any longer" (*Recent Discoveries in Bible Lands*, 1955, p 128).

Having taken this general look at the phenomenal changes in the evaluation of the reliability of the Old Testament, let us turn to some concrete examples of illumination and verification of the Old Testament by archaeological discoveries. First, in the patriarchal stories we find several strange accounts of a barren wife who asked her husband to produce a child for her by her maid servant. Sarah did this, and later also Jacob's two wives, Rachel and Leah. Today we know that this practice was not unusual during the patriarchal age. The laws of that period as well as ancient marriage contracts mention it. For example, in a marriage contract from Nuzi, the bride Kelim-ninu promises in written form to procure for her husband Shennima a slave girl as second wife, if she fails to bear him children. She also promises that she will not drive out the offspring of such a union. In no other period besides the patriarchal age do we find this strange custom.

Another example is the sale of Esau's birthright to Jacob for a dish of lentils. It is hard to believe that that status of an older brother or sister could ever have been attained by purchase. Nowever, a Nuzi text deals with this very custom. In a written contract between Tupkitilla and Kurpazah, two brothers, Tupkitilla sells his inheritance rights to his younger brother for three sheep. Esau sold his rights for food in the pot, while Tupkitilla sold his for food still on the hoof.

Other texts show that a bride was ordinarily chosen for a son by his father, as the patriarchs did; that a man had to pay a dowry to his father-in-law, or to work for his father-in-law if he could not afford the dowry, as poor Jacob had to do; that the orally expressed will of a father could not be changed after it had been pronounced, as in Isaac's refusal to change the blessings pronounced over Jacob even though they had been obtained by deception; that a bride ordinarily received from her father a slave girl as personal maid, as Leah and Rachel did when they were married to Jacob; that the theft of cult objects of a god was punishable by death, which was why Jacob consented to the death of the one with whom the stolen gods of his father-in-law were found; that the strange relationship between Judah and his daughter-in-law Tamar is vividly illustrated by the laws of the ancient Assyrians and Hittites. These are only some of the many parallels to customs reflected in the patriarchal stories that archaeologists have discovered. Such evidence shows clearly that these narratives were written soon after the events described had occurred, when these strange customs either still existed or had not yet been forgotten.

Leaving the patriarchal period, let us see how archaeological material can illuminate biblical records without providing a scrap of written material. The excavations at Shiloh by Danish scholars provide an example. The early chapters of the first book of Samuel describe the story of Eli and Samuel at the tabernacle located at Shiloh. This city was at that time the seat of the desert sanctuary originally constructed under Moses' direction at Mt. Sinai. Its greatest treasure was the Ark of the Covenant. Then we read that the Ark was captured by the Philistines in the battle of Aphek and held by them for some time. Finally it was returned to Israel, but not to the city of Shiloh. For many years it remained at Kirjath-jearim, until David transferred it to Jerusalem, his capital. Moreover, when we read again of the family of Eli, the Ark resides not at Shiloh but at Nob; nothing is said about the fate of Shiloh and its sanctuary.

What happened to it? In the book of Jeremiah, references are made to some great disaster that befell Shiloh at some unspecified period of Israel's history. Nothing in Jeremiah's references suggests that this disaster had occurred in the distant past. However, scholars have long supposed that the Philistines destroyed Shiloh and its tent sanctuary after they defeated the Israelites and took the Ark at the battle of Aphek. When the Danes excavated Shiloh, they found evidence that satisfactorily answers the question. The broken pieces of pottery discovered there provide a means for reconstructing the ancient history of Shiloh. This pottery evidence shows that there was a break in the city's history from the eleventh century B.C. until the sixth century. From biblical evidence we know that the early eleventh century B.C. is precisely the period of the Philistine defeat of Israel and the capture of the Ark; hence we have proof that at that time the city of Shiloh and the Tabernacle must have been destroyed.

I want to inject a personal note about the discoveries at Shechem, for I have participated in its excavation. Our 1960 work at Shechem revealed that the city and its great temple of Baal were destroyed in the twelfth century B.C. That is exactly the time indicated in the Bible for the destruction of Shechem by Abimelech, the bastard son of the judge Gideon. The archaeological evidence—broken pieces of pottery—sets that date at about 1150 B.C. The agreement between the two dates, one obtained from biblical evidence and the other from archaeological data, could hardly have been closer. This is certainly a source of great satisfaction for us biblical archaeologists.

For another illustration of the value of archaeological evidence for a better understanding of the Old Testament, let us go to Jerusalem. Archaeological explorations have shed some interesting light on the capture of Jerusalem by David. The biblical accounts of that capture (II Sam. 5:6-8 and I Chron. 11:6) are rather obscure without the help obtained from archaeological evidence. Take for example II Samuel 5:8, which in the King James Version reads: "And David said on that day, Whosoever getteth up to the gutter, and smiteth the Jebusites, and the lame and the blind, that are hated of David's soul, he shall be chief and captain." Add to this statement I Chronicles 11:6—"So Joab the son of Zeruiah went first up and was chief."

Some years ago I saw a painting of the conquest of Jerusalem in which the artist showed a man climbing up a metal downspout, running on the outside face of the city wall. This picture was absurd, because ancient city walls had neither gutters nor downspouts, although they had weeping holes in the walls to drain water off. The Revised Standard Version, produced after the situation had become clear through archaeological discoveries made on the spot, translates the pertinent passages: "And David said on that day, 'Whoever would smite the Jebusites, let him get up on the water shaft to attack the lame and the blind, who are hated by David's soul,'" "And Joab the son of Zeruiah went up first, so he became chief." What was this water shaft that Joab climbed?

Jerusalem in those days was a small city lying on a single spur of the hills on which the large city eventually stood. Its position was one of great natural strength, because it was surrounded on three sides by deep valleys. This was why the Jebusites boastfully declared that even blind and lame could hold their city against a powerful attacking army. But the water supply of the city was poor; the population was entirely dependent on a spring that lay outside the city on the eastern slope of the hill.

So that they could obtain water without having to go down to where the spring was located, the Jebusites had constructed an elaborate system of tunnels through the rock. First they had dug a horizontal tunnel, beginning at the spring and proceeding toward the center of the city. After digging for ninety feet they hit a natural cave. From the cave they dug a vertical shaft forty-five feet high, and from the end of the shaft a sloping tunnel 135 feet long and a stair case that ended at the surface of their city, 110 feet above the water level of the spring. The spring was then concealed from the outside so that no enemy could detect it. To get water the Jebusite women went down through the upper tunnel and let their water skins down the shaft to draw water from the cave, to which it was brought by natural flow through the horizontal tunnel that connected the cave with the spring.

However, one question remained unanswered. The excavations of R.A.S. Macalister and J.G. Duncan some forty years ago had uncovered a wall and a tower that were thought to be of Jebusite and Davidic origin respectively. This tract of wall ran along the rim of the hill of Ophel, west of the tunnel entrance. Thus the entrance was left outside the protective city wall, exposed to the attacks and interference of enemies. Why hadn't the tunnel been built to end inside the city? This puzzle has now been solved by the recent excavations of Kathleen Kenyon on ophel. She found that Macalister and Duncan had given the wall and tower they discovered wrong dates: these things actually originated in the Hellenistic period. She uncovered the real Jebusite wall a little farther down the slope of the hill, east of the tunnel entrance, which now puts the entrance safely in the old city area.

David, a native of Bethlehem, four miles south of Jerusalem, may have found out about the spring and its tunnel system in the days when as a youth he roamed through the countryside. Later, as king he based his surprise attack on this knowledge, and made the promise that the first man who entered the city through the water shaft would be his commander-in-chief. Joab, who was already general of the army, did not want to lose that position and therefore led the attack himself. The Israelites apparently went through the tunnel, climbed up the shaft, and were in the city before any of the besieged citizens had any idea that so bold a plan had been conceived.

This water system, constructed more than three thousand years ago, is still in existence and can be examined by any tourist. Some good climbers have even climbed the shaft in modern times, though it is not easy to do so because the rock walls are smooth and slick and give little hold for hand or foot. The shaft is also a little too wide for a comfortable climb, as I learned in my unsuccessful attempt to climb it.

Among many other illustrations of how archaeology clears up disputed points of biblical history, I want to mention one more, involving the conquests of Jerusalem by Nebuchadnezzar II. Various biblical records mention three conquests of Judah's capital by the Babylonian king, first in 605 B.C., in the third year of King Jehoiakim, then in 597 after a three-month reign of Jehoiachin, and finally in 586 in the eleventh year of King Zedekiah. For a long time scholars did not doubt that Nebuchadnezzar had taken Jerusalem, for the biblical statements seemed quite clear on this point. However, many scholars became somewhat suspicious when a hundred years of excavations in Babylonia failed to turn up one single text of Nebuchadnezzar referring to any one of these conquests of Jerusalem, though numerous texts written by this monarch had come to light during these hundred years. Also, the city of Babylon, which the Germans excavated during a long campaign of eighteen years, failed to provide a single document to show that Nebuchadnezzar had ever been at war with the kingdom of Judah or had ever taken their capital, Jerusalem. A number of well-known scholars began to doubt that Nebuchadnezzar had ever taken Jerusalem during his reign. But today these doubts are groundless; at least one of Nebuchadnezzar's three conquests of Jerusalem is well attested by several pieces of archaeological evidence, of which I shall mention two recent ones.

Shortly before the last war, Professor Ernst Weidner worked in the Berlin Museum on unimposing tablets that had been found in some storerooms of Nebuchadnezzar's palace in Babylon many years ago. These tablets contained day-by-day records of the issuance of grain and oil to dependents of the royal palace, such as workmen engaged in royal building operations, musicians employed as entertainers, and hostages from foreign countries. As Weidner studied these somewhat dry records, he suddenly came upon the name of King Jehoiachin of Judah as recipient of royal rations of grain and oil. The tablets mentioning the king were written in 592 B.C., five years after he had been taken captive, and his five sons and their tutor are mentioned also. Jehoiachin received twenty times as much foodstuff as any other person listed, an indication that he was still considered an honorable personage and may have been allowed to keep servants for his use. His imprisonment, to which the Bible also refers, seems to have begun at a later time, probably when efforts were made during a rebellion (described by Jeremiah) to put him back on the throne of Judah.

The second interesting discovery bearing on this subject was made in 1955 by Donald Wiseman of the British Museum. Among tablets that had been in that museum for many decades Wiseman discovered one that chronicled several years of Nebuchadnezzar's reign. This tablet describes briefly the military campaign of Nebuchadnezzar against Judah in 597 B.C. and the capture of Jerusalem on March 16 of that year — the first exact date of a biblical event obtained from a factual non-biblical record. The tablet also states that Nebuchadnezzar deposed King Jehoiachin and replaced him by Zedekiah.

These two discoveries teach us a valuable lesson. That some excavations from which we expect some information seem to shed no light on biblical events should not be taken as evidence that the biblical records are at fault. We should never forget that all our evidence is fragmentary and incomplete, spotty in some parts and more full in others. Conclusions based on incomplete or negative evidence can be entirely misleading, as this illustration clearly shows. Time after time, after a long period of patient waiting, solutions ot our problems have been found. There are still many points awaiting clarification, which may come as more archaeological evidence comes to light.

Many more examples could be given of how archaeological evidence has shed light on interesting details of biblical history. The unpretentious castle at Gibeah, King Saul's residence, has been excavated, and Solomon's copper and iron mines in Edom have been rediscovered and in part are being exploited again by modern Israelis. The Assyrian cuneiform documents mention nine of the thirty-six Hebrew kings that reigned during the period of Assyria's existence and give us much valuable information about the history of the divided kingdom. Egypt has produced welcome historical evidence, both in documents and in other material. There are records of King Shishak's invasion of Judah and Israel after Solomon's death, recorded in two Old Testament books. A large existing archive consists of scores of papyrus documents written by Jews of the post-exilic period; these have illustrated many obscure points of that interesting time we glimpse in the books of Ezra and Nehemiah.

The archaeologist's pick and hoe have produced for the biblical scholar an abundance of auxiliary material that enables him to understand and defend the historical narratives much better than before. And we can assume that there is more to come.

Reprinted from *Christianity Today.*
June 21, 1968. Vol. 12, No. 19, pp. 13-17.
Used by permission

HIGHER CRITICS AND FORBIDDEN FRUIT

CYRUS H. GORDON

Though Bible scholars live in an age of unprecedented discovery, they stand in the shadow of nineteenth-century higher criticism. There was a time when the label "conservative" meant the rejection of that higher criticism, but now the conservative mind often latches onto higher criticism even though archaeology has rendered it untenable. My conservative critics, some of whom are on the faculties of Protestant, Catholic, and Jewish seminaries, find fault not because my writings run counter to any particular religious tenet, but because I am not devoted to JEDP: the badge of inter-confessional academic respectability.

INTELLECTUAL COMMITMENT

All of my Bible professors were conservative higher critics with a positive appreciation—and in some instances, with a profound knowledge—of the archaeological discoveries bearing on the Bible. I was trained simultaneously in higher criticism and biblical archaeology without at first realizing that the two points of view were mutually exclusive. By this I mean that a commitment to any hypothetical source-structure like JEDP is out of keeping with what I consider the only tenable position for a critical scholar: to go wherever the evidence leads him.

When I speak of a "commitment" to JEDP, I mean it in the deepest sense of the word. I have heard professors of Old Testament refer to the integrity of JEDP as their "conviction." They are willing to countenance modifications in detail. They permit you to subdivide (D_1, D_2, D_3, and so forth) or combine (JE) or add a new document designated by another capital letter; but they will not tolerate any questioning of the basic JEDP structure. I am at a loss to explain this kind of "conviction" on any grounds other than intellectual laziness or inability to reappraise.

The turning point in my own thinking came after (and in large measure because of) a four-year hiatus in my academic career during World War II. Coming out of the army and back into teaching, I offered a course on the Gilgamesh Epic. In the eleventh tablet I could not help noting that the Babylonian account of the construction of the Ark contains the specifications in detail much like the Hebrew account of Noah's Ark. At the same time, I recalled that the Genesis description is ascribed to P of Second Temple date, because facts and figures such as those pertaining to the Ark are characteristic of the hypothetical Priestly author. What occurred to me was that if the Genesis account of the Ark belonged to P on such grounds, the Gilgamesh Epic account of the Ark belonged to P on the same grounds—which is absurd. The pre-Abrahamic Genesis traditions (such as the Deluge) are not late P products; they are essentially pre-Mosaic and it is not easy to single out even details that are late. This has been indicated by Sumero-Akkadian tablets for a long time; it is now crystal-clear from the Ugaritic texts, where whole literary themes as well as specific phrases are now in our possession on pre-Mosaic tablets, as well as in our canonical Bible. Ezekiel (14:13-19) thus refers to an ancient Daniel: a model of virtue who emerged together with his progeny from a major disaster. We now have the Ugaritic Epic of this Daniel on tablets copied in the fourteenth century B.C., when the story was already old. Like many another psalm ascribed to David, psalm 68, far from being late, is full of pre-Davidic expressions some of which were not even understood before the discovery of the Ugaritic poems. In verse 7, for example, kosharot means "songstresses" as in Ugaritic so that we are to translate "He brings out prisoners with the songstresses," meaning that when God rescues us from trouble, he brings us joy as well as relief. He frees the prisoner not into a cold world but into one of joyous song. The Kosharot were just as much a part of the classical Canaanite heritage of the Hebrews as the Muses are a part of our classical Greek heritage.

The question the biblical scholar now asks is not "How much post-Mosaic (or post-Exilic) is this or that?" but rather "How much pre-Mosaic (or pre-Abrahamic)?"

The urge to chop the Bible (and other ancient writings) up into sources is often due to the false assumption that a different style must mean a different author.

AUTHORSHIP AND STYLE

When the subject matter is the same, different styles do ordinarily indicate different authorship. But any one author will employ different styles for different types of subject matter. A lawyer uses different styles depending on whether he is preparing a brief, or writing a letter to his mother. A clergyman does not use the same style in making a benediction and in talking to his children at the breakfast table. No physician writes in prescription style except on prescription blanks. Accordingly the technical style of Genesis in describing the Ark is no more an indication of different authorship from the surrounding narrative than a naval architect's style in describing the specifications of a ship makes him a different author from the same architect writing a love letter to his fiancée.

Minds that are incapable of grasping whole entities are tempted to fractionalize the whole into smaller units. The Book of Job, for all its difficulties, is infinitely greater than the sum of its parts after the critics have hacked it to bits. Ancient Near East literature makes it abundantly clear that Job as it stands is a consciously constructed *single* composition. The kind of criticism that detaches the prose prologue and epilogue from the poetic dialogues on stylistic grounds (that is, that "prose and poetry don't mix") runs counter to ancient Near Eastern rules of composition. From many available illustrations, let us single out Hammurapi's Code in which the prose laws are framed within a poetic prologue and epilogue, giving the composition what may be called the ABA form. This means that the main body of the composition is enclosed within language of a contrasting style. The structure of Job ("prose-*poetry*-prose") exemplifies this ABA scheme. Moreover, the structure of Daniel ("Hebrew-*Aramaic*-Hebrew") also reflects the ABA pattern, and the book should be understood as a whole, consciously composed unit.

No one in his right mind would want to outlaw the study of the component parts of biblical (or any other) books, but a sane approach to scriptural (or and [sic] other) literature requires that we take it on its own terms, and not force it into an alien system.

One of the commonest grounds for positing differences of authorship are the repetitions, with variants, in the Bible. But such repetitions are typical of ancient Near East literature: Babylonian, Ugaritic, and even Greek. Moreover, the tastes of the Bible World called for duplication. Joseph and later Pharaoh, each had prophetic dreams in duplicate. In Jonah 4, the Prophet's chagrin is described at two stages, each accompanied by God's asking "Are you good and angry?" (vv. 4, 9). Would anyone insist that such duplicates stem from different pens?

One particular type of duplicate is especially interesting because of the extrabiblical collateral material at our disposal. Judges 4 gives the prose and Judges 5 the poetic account of Deborah's victory. The two accounts confront us with variants. The usual critical position is that the poetic version is old; the prose version later. The assumption of disparity in age or provenance between the two accounts on stylistic grounds is specious. Historic events were sometimes recorded in Egypt simultaneously in prose and poetic versions, with the major differences appropriate to the two literary media. (Sometimes the Egyptians added a third version—in pictures.) In approaching matters such as the date and authorship of Judges 4 and 5, it is more germane to bear in mind the usages of the Bible World than it is to follow in the footsteps of modern analytic scholars who build logical but unrealistic systems.

A FRAGILE CORNERSTONE

One of the fragile cornerstones of the JEDP hypothesis is the notion that the mention of "Jehovah" (actually "Yahweh") typifies a J document, while "Elohim" typifies an E document. A conflation of J and E sources into JE is supposed to account for the compound name Yahweh-Elohim. All this is admirably logical and for years I never questioned it. But my Ugaritic studies destroyed this kind of logic with relevant facts. At Ugarit, deities often have compound names. One deity is called Qadish-Amrar; another, Ibb-Nikkal. Usually "and" is put between the two parts (Qadish-and-Amrar, Nikkal-and-Ibb, Koshar-and-Hasis, and so forth), but the conjunction can be omitted. Not only biblical but also classical scholars will have to recognize this phenomenon. In Prometheus Bound, *Kratos Bia-te* "Force-and-Violence" is such a combination. If any further proof were necessary, Herodotus provides it in his history (8:111), where he relates that Themistocles tried to extort money from the Andreans by telling them that he came with two great gods "Persuasion-and-Necessity." The Andrians refused to pay, and their way of telling him "you can't squeeze blood from a turnip" was that their gods were unfortunately "Poverty-and-Impotence." Thus it was a widespread usage to fuse two names into one for designating a god. The most famous is perhaps Amon-Re who became the great universal deity as a result of Egyptian conquest under the eighteenth dynasty. Amon was the ram-headed god of the capital city, Thebes. Re was the old universal Sun god. The fusion of Re's religious universalism with the political leadership in Amon's Thebes underlies the double name "Amon-Re." But Amon-Re is one entity. Scholars can do much to explain the combination of elements in Yahweh-Elohim. Yahweh was a specific divine name, whereas Elohim designated "Deity" in a more general, universal way. The combination Yahweh-Elohim is probably to be explained as "Yahweh = Elohim," which we may paraphrase as "Yahweh is God." But when we are told that "Yahweh-Elohim is the result of documentary conflation, we cannot accept it any more than we can understand Amon-Re to be the result of combining an "A" document with an "R" document.

THE GENUINE SOURCES

Older documents do underlie much of the Old Testament. Our Book of Proverbs is compiled from collections indicated as "The proverbs of Solomon, son of David" (1:1), "The proverbs of Solomon" (10:1), "These also are saying of the wise" (24:23), "These also are proverbs of Solomon which the men of Hezekiah king of Judah copied" (25:1), "The words of Agur" (30:1), and "The words of Lemuel, king of Massa, which his mother taught him" (31:1). The individual psalms must have existed before our canonical book of 150 Psalms was compiled. Many of the psalms bear titles ascribing them to specific authors. But other biblical books do not have titles heading the text. The scroll of Ruth begins "Now it came to pass in the days when the judges ruled"; Leviticus opens "And Jehovah called unto Moses"; and so on. Since some biblical books are compilations (like Proverbs and Psalms) and since titles were often omitted (as in Ruth or Leviticus), it follows that certain biblical books can be compilations of earlier sources unidentified by titles.

If JEDP are artificial sources of the Pentateuch, are there any real ones? Yes, and one of them happens to be the book of Wars of Jehovah cited in Numbers 21:14. Another ancient source used by the authors of both Joshua and Samuel is the book of Jashar, excerpted in Joshua 10:13 and II Samuel 1:18 ff. The second of these excerpts is the beautiful dirge of David for Saul and Jonathan, which was used for teaching the troops of Judah heroism and skill in the art of war (note, for teaching the sons of Judah bowmanship—in v. 18). There can be little doubt that the book of Jashar was a national epic, commemorating the heroic course of Hebrew history from at least the conquest under Joshua to the foundation of the Davidic dynasty. Like other national epics, including the Iliad and Shah-nameh, the book of Jashar was used for inspiring warriors to live, and if necessary to die, like their illustrious forerunners. If the entire book of Jashar was characterized by the high quality reflected in David's dirge, we can only hope that future discoveries will restore it to us. It might successfully compete with the Homeric epic as a masterpiece of world literature.

The books of Kings draw on earlier documents, such as, "the book of the acts of Solomon" (I Kings 11:41); and "the chronicles of the kings of Judah" and "the chronicles of the kings of Israel." The canonical books of Chronicles cite a host of sources by name. The time is ripe for a fresh investigation of such genuine sources of Scripture, particularly against the background of the Dead Sea Scrolls.

THE MODERN IDOLS

No two higher critics seem to agree on where J, E, D or P begins or ends. The attempt to state such matters precisely in the Polychrome Bible discredited the use of colors but not the continuance of less precise verbal formulations. The "history" of Israel is still being written on the premise that we can only do so scientifically according to hypothetical documents to which exact dates are blandly assigned. While most critics place P last chronologically, some of the most erudite now insist that P is early, antedating D in any case. Any system (whether P is earlier or later than D in such a system makes no difference) that prevents us from going where the facts may lead is not for me. I prefer to deal with the large array of authentic materials from the Bible World and to be unimpeded by any hypothetical system.

There may well be quite a few sources designated but not generally recognized as such in the Bible. Just as an older Deluge story is incorporated in the Gilgamesh Epic, another older variant Flood account has been, I think, excerpted in Genesis. The Hebrew word *toledot* (literally "generations") can designate a "narrative" or "story." In Genesis 6:9 "This is the Narrative of Noah" (literally, "generations of Noah") may well have conveyed to an ancient Hebrew what a title does to us. The account of nature in Genesis 2:4 ff. is introduced by "This is the Account of the Cosmos" (literally, "the generations of the heavens and the earth") and might possibly have been intended as a title indicating a biblical source.

Let us keep our eyes open and our minds sharp. Let us make observations and check them against the available facts. But let us not erect vast edifices on shifting sands.

The excavations at Ugarit have revealed a high material and literary culture in Canaan prior to the emergence of the Hebrews. Prose and poetry were already fully developed. The educational system was so advanced that dictionaries in four languages were compiled for the use of scribes, and the individual words were listed in the Ugaritic, Babylonian, Sumerian, and Hurrian equivalents. The beginnings of Israel are rooted in a highly cultural Canaan where the contribution of several talented peoples (including the Mesopotamians, Egyptians, and branches of the Indo-Europeans) had converged and blended. The notion that early Israelite religion and society were primitive is completely false. Canaan in the days of the Patriarchs was the hub of a great international culture. The Bible, hailing from such a time and place, cannot be devoid of sources. But let us study them by taking the Bible on its own terms and against its own authentic background.

If there is any expression in the Hebrew language that is charged with meaning for the intellectual person devoted to his biblical heritage, it is *simhat torah* "the delight in studying Scripture." I am familiar with this delight and I like to see others have the opportunity of experiencing it. I am distressed to meet ever so many intelligent and serious university students who tell me that their teachers of Bible have killed the subject by harping on the notion that biblical study consists of analyzing the text into JEDP. The unedifying conclusion of all such study is that nothing is authentic. That this type of teaching should go on in our age of discovery when biblical scholarship is so exciting is, so to speak, a perverse miracle.

A professor of Bible in a leading university once asked me to give him the facts on JEDP. I told him essentially what I have written above. He replied: "I am convinced by what you say but I shall go on teaching the old system." When I asked him why, he answered: "Because what you have told me means I should have to unlearn as well as study afresh and rethink. It is easier to go on with the accepted system of higher criticism for which we have standard textbooks." What a happy professor! He refuses to forfeit his place in Eden by tasting the fruit of the tree of knowledge.

Reprinted from *Christianity Today*.
November 23, 1959. Vol. 4, pp. 131-134.
Used by permission.

A COMPARISON OF
FORM CRITICISM AND CLASSICAL CRITICISM
OF THE GOSPELS

BY GORDON R. LEWIS

By way of introduction to this brief paper I should like to state two hypotheses and focus upon the precise nature of this issue regarding them.

THE HYPOTHESIS OF CLASSICAL CRITICISM

Criticism of the Gospels is not new. Attempts to discover the way in which such remarkably similar and yet different accounts of Jesus' life were composed and have been made since the early days of church history. Among the scholars who treated the problems of harmonizing the Gospels were: Tatian (died A.D. 172), Ammonius of Alexandria (220), Eusebius of Caesarea (died 340), Augustine (400); in the sixteenth century: Osiander, Jansen, Robert Stephens, John Calvin, Du Molin, Chemnitz; in the 17th and 18th centuries: Lightfoot, Bengal, Newcome; in the 19th century: Wieseler, Tischendorf, Greswell, William Thomson, Rushbrooke, Edward Robinson, S.J. Andrews, and Frederik Gardner.[1] The work of these men varied in linguistic and historical skill, and in many detailed conclusions. But for the present purposes they are classified together because as they faced the charges of unreliability against the Gospels and examined the complex data, they did not find irreconcilable contradictions in the Gospel records nor insuperable discrepancies with fact. Classical critics concluded that the Gospels portrayed Jesus as He was and that Christian faith confessed that Jesus was both Lord and Christ.

THE HYPOTHESIS OF FORM CRITICISM

Another trend in investigation of the Gospels has found irreconcilable contradictions and insuperable discrepancies with fact. Consequently, form critics concluded that little could be known about Jesus as He was, but that this did not disturb their faith in the Christ. While there were many forerunners, major recent proponents of form criticism have been Martin Dibelius, Rudolf Bultmann, Gunther Bornkamm and Joachim Jeremias.[2] Again there are varieties of emphasis, but for shorthand purposes we shall refer to the general conclusions of these men as Form Criticism.

THE ISSUE

A responsible student will recognize that he cannot be completely objective in his evaluation of the evidence or the assessment of these two perspectives. None of the scholars mentioned on either side has been perfectly objective, no one ever is. At the same time, responsible scholarship is cognizant of its biases, examines other alternatives than its own and tests the possibilities in terms of as objective an analysis of the relevant data as possible.

A responsible student of the Gospels will examine both form criticism and classical criticism as possible hypotheses. He will identify and assess the similarities and the differences between them. Where they differ, he will accept the hypothesis which consistently accounts for the greatest number of facts with the fewest difficulties. As Alan Richardson explained,

> The way to approach the New Testament is by framing of an hypothesis (whether consciously or unconsciously) and then testing it by continual checking with the New Testament documents and other relevant evidence from the period. This is in fact the way in which historical critical interpretation is done nowadays in every field of historical reconstruction. It necessarily involves a personal or subjective element, but this is now seen to be unavoidable, as the illusion of scientific or presuppositionless history recedes. It does not, however, involve an absolute subjectivism or historical relativism for the pursuit of history as a humane science involves the conviction that one historical interpretation can be rationally shown to be better than another.[3]

It is not necessary to choose between form criticism and classical criticism at every point, however, because in a number of significant points their outlook is similar.

AGREEMENTS

1. Both classical criticism and form criticism seek to obtain the meaning of the Bible through grammatical, historical exegesis.

2. Both insist that dogmatic theology must not be allowed to determine the interpretation of biblical texts.

3. Both hold that the Gospel tradition was preserved in largely oral form for a generation by the church.

4. The Gospels did not arise in a neutral vacuum, but in the life of an active, witnessing church. The life setting of the church explains why many sayings and incidents in the Gospels were put on record.

5. The forms in which the preaching and teaching were cast became stereotyped.

6. There is interpretive value in determining the literary form of the passages under investigation.

7. A literary document is to be interpreted in terms of the author's purpose.

Undoubtedly other convictions are also shared, but these are sufficient to indicate a significant amount of common ground.

DIFFERENCES

Differences will be pointed out in relation to the points of agreement as numbered.

1. Classical criticism divorces the grammatical, historical *method* of interpretation from a naturalistic *world-view*, seeking to interpret the literature in terms of its inherent supernatural presuppositions. Form criticism assumes the truth of positivistic world-view from the 19th and early 20th century and imposes this upon the Gospels.

2. If classical criticism occasionally yields to the dictates of orthodox theology, does not form criticism continuously yield to the dictates of Bultmann's 19th century "scientific" view of the cosmos as a closed system of natural causes, and to Heidegger's demand for a Jesus as an authentic *repeatable* human possibility?

3. While form criticism assumes that an oral tradition of twenty to thirty years allows for the growth of folk tales and considerable distortion of the truth concerning Jesus, classical criticism regards a generation insufficient for the production of folklore. T.W. Manson explained,

> In the first decades of the life of the original Palestinian community, the tradition concerning the teaching of Jesus rested on a broader base than we commonly imagine. We tend to think of it as being in the hands of a few distinguished persons who were leaders in the Church, and to forget the common people who heard Jesus gladly, and who also had memories. When this is realized we can see that the Church's task in meeting the problems which arose in its own life and in its relations with the Jewish authorities was not that of creating words of Jesus applicable to these situations, but rather that of selecting what was relevant from the available mass of reminiscences.[4]

Put more popularly still, "Legends, like mushrooms grow best in the dark out of stuff that has time to decay. Not so for the Gospels, there was not enough time and there was too much light!"

4. Form criticism assumes a complete difference between life situations in the experience of Jesus and that of the early church. Classical criticism sees the possibility of considerable similarity. For example, when questions arose in the church about divorce or paying a temple tax, it was natural to recall what Jesus had said on the subject.[5] Similarly, form criticism assumes a radical distortion of the tradition in the Hellenistic church. Classical criticism denies that distortion on

the basis of the prevailingly Semitic character of the common Synoptic tradition.[6] As William Barclay concludes his ironic assessment of form criticism,

The Form Critics have done an immeasurable service in enabling us to understand the formation, the genesis and the aim of the gospels, but. . . their one mistake is their failure to see that the gospel writers sought to awaken faith in Jesus as He was. This is not to say that they have the standards and the methods of accuracy of a modern scientific historian, but it is to say that their aim was to show Jesus as He was in the days of His flesh in order that men might by faith find the risen Lord.[7]

5. Form criticism assumes that the form of statement somehow determines the truth or falsity of its content. Classical criticism questions the wisdom of testing truth-claims by their linguistic form. Healing stories from all over the world follow a recurrent form stressing the intractability of the disease, the completeness of the cure, and the effect on the spectators. But the fact that a story follows this stereotype tells us nothing about its historicity. The classification of sayings of Jesus according to their form tells us little about their authenticity.[8]

6. Form criticism makes little of the difference between the tradition of the scribes and the Gospel tradition. Classical criticism sees a marked difference between the preservation of the traditions of men who frustrated the Word of God (Matt. 15:6) and preservation of the Gospel tradition which was the Word of God. Early Christians, in fact, made a clear distinction between their own judgments and Christ's pronouncements (I Cor. 7:10, 12, 25).

7. Assuming that history must be totally objective and give a complete, connected development of a person's life from beginning to end, form critics have concluded that a life of Jesus is no longer possible.[9] Classical criticism, recognizing that all history is interpretive and that no history is complete, maintain that the writers of the Gospel disclose informed selection and interpretation in terms of their discernible purposes. Obviously they did not attempt a complete, chronological account of Jesus' life and times. The important thing to them was who Jesus was in order that men might believe on Him. Since their concerns were topical rather than chronological, "errors" may be attributed to them that are no errors at all. They can only be errors if the critic forces upon the material standards which were no part of the Evangelists' purpose.[10]

One other difference is particularly significant. Form critics do not regard the Holy Spirit's superintendence of all the written and oral processes of composition of the Gospels a necessary hypothesis, possibly because they try to work as historians rather than as theologians.[11] Classical criticism questions the possibility of divorcing the sciences completely, and affirms that the Holy Spirit's activity not only guided the writing of the Gospels, but also the preservation of authentic written and oral sources for the writers.

WHICH VIEW BEST FITS THE FACTS?

Form criticism has developed on the basis that the classical view could not consistently account for the phenomena of the Gospels. If there are logical contradictions between the accounts and discrepancies with known facts, of course, it is impossible to defend a careful preservation of the testimony of eyewitnesses under the inspiration of the Holy Spirit.

Classical criticism, on the other hand, finds that a careful use of logic and assessment of relevant data does not come up with actual contradictions or discrepancies. "Variations in different reports of the same event are to be expected because of the complexity of antecedents to the event, the varied facets of it, and the multiple perspectives possible for different purposes. In order to show distortion of the facts concerning the historical Jesus, form critics must produce more than mere differences in accounts, they must produce actual contradictions. Two different assertions are only contradictory when they affirm and deny the same thing at the same time and in the same respect. Many alleged contradictions are not contradictions at all, but in logical terminology sub contraries.

For example, form critics observe that in John Jesus' ministry is primarily in Jerusalem; in the Synoptics in Galilee. Since Jesus admittedly ministered in both areas, and it was no part of the purpose of either John or the Synoptics to give a complete travelogue, this difference is not of the kind to support invention by the church, or any hypothesis of historical inaccuracy.

Form critics see difficulty in the fact that Matthew and Luke give two reasons for Jesus' having been born in Bethlehem though he was a citizen of Nazareth. If the reason in Matthew is Micah's prophecy (5:2), that in no way conflicts with Luke's reference to instrumental reason—the census which took Mary and Joseph to Bethlehem, the original home of David's family.

Is Luke's census at A.D. 6 not impossible to reconcile with the statement that Herod was alive at the time, since he died in 4 B.C.? Here is a genuine difficulty. But a monument inscription indicates that Quirinius was twice Governor of Syria and that the first governorship was from 7 or 8 B.C. to A.D. 1. The preceding census was probably ordered in Rome in 7 B.C. and delays in its implementation bring it to 4 or 5 B.C.[12]

In the Synoptics, form critics point out, Jesus refuses to give signs while in John the signs are listed. Signs are also given by Jesus to John the Baptist in the Synoptics (Matt. 11:4). On one occasion when the Pharisees were particularly obtuse and would not have been disturbed by any facts (Mark 8:12), Jesus refused to perform any further signs, other than his resurrection from the dead. It is unhistorical criticism to take a statement from a limited context and give it a universal and necessary reference to manufacture difficulties.

Form critics find a problem in that John has a realized eschatology in which the kingdom is not coming as in the Synoptics, but has arrived in the eternal Christ. However, John also has futuristic elements (5:28 and 11:25, resurrection from the dead). It is important to know that there are several uses of the word "kingdom" and there is no contradiction if a different sense is involved in these different contexts. The kingdom may refer to God's providential rule over all, to Christ's present spiritual rule in the hearts of believers, and to a future social and political kingdom. It is quite possible that the gospels teach all three without contradiction.

Numerous problems are raised in connection with the resurrection accounts. Mark has the women fearful upon their discovery of the empty tomb and telling no one. Matthew has them run at once to tell the disciples. John, Matthew and Mark disagree about how many women came to the tomb. Luke and Acts disagree about how long the appearances continued. Mark has Jesus instruct the disciples about the resurrection, yet they are surprised when the news reaches them.

In response let me quote John (*Honest to God*) Robinson in his unusually good article on the resurrection in *The Interpreter's Dictionary of the Bible:*

"When we turn to the gospels, their evidence on the empty tomb is in substance unanimous. There are, indeed, differences of detail which at times have been given an exaggerated prominence... None of these, however, is the kind of difference that impugns the authenticity of the narrative. Indeed they are all precisely what one would look for in genuine accounts of so confused and confusing a scene... [The recent mythological view fails to do justice to the scriptural evidence.] *Many in fact will continue to find it easier to believe that the empty tomb produced the disciples' faith than that the disciples' faith produced the empty tomb.*"

Robinson concludes, "All the appearances, in fact, depict the same phenomenon, of a body identical, yet changed, transcending the limitations of the flesh yet capable of manifesting itself within the order of flesh." Again, "According to all our accounts it was the appearances, not the tomb, that were decisive for the disciples' faith."

The calendar, the Lord's day, the Christian Church, and the New Testament all stand today as witnesses of a world-shaking, history-making event that took place in the first century. If not the resurrection, then what? Although critics have tried every conceivable way to explain away the evidence, one after another the theories collapsed. *The Interpreter's Dictionary of the Bible* reports, "Recent scholars have, therefore, tended to abandon the attempt to give rationalistic explanations of the narrative as it stands."

CONCLUSIONS

This brief study has not been able to make anything like a thorough investigation of the problem, but it has attempted to indicate the lines such an investigation would take. Each hypothesis must be evaluated by the evidence available. As Alan Richardson says,

> Thus, for example, R. Bultmann's hypothesis that the theology of the New Testament is a mythological conglomeration of Jewish apocalyptic and Hellenistic gnostic ideas which have somehow coagulated round the name of Jesus of Nazareth, about whom little certain historical knowledge can be attained, must be studied to see whether it gives a rational and coherent explanation of the New Testament evidence. In this respect it should be compared with the other hypotheses, such as that Jesus himself is the prime author of the striking reinterpretation of the Old Testament theology which is found in his own reported teachings and in the New Testament as a whole (the new covenant, the new Israel, the reinterpreted Messiahship, the reign of God, and so on).

The Phenomenon of the New Testament C.F.D. Moule adds the phenomena of the Christian community which possessed nothing distinctive except the conviction that Jesus had been raised from the dead—that the one who Jesus was had been raised to life absolute. The origin and rise of other movements may be explained by factors anyone can recognize as valid even if their peculiarities are discounted as invalid. But if the basic Christian conviction is discounted, it is difficult to know where to look for an explosion powerful enough to launch the missile.[13]

In addition to the phenomenon of the church, are the astounding phenomena of the change of the day of worship from Saturday to Sunday, the production of the New Testament itself and the personal experience of disciples such as Saul who became Paul. These and other phenomena can be accounted for by the classical view that we can know who Jesus was and that he in fact rose from the dead. If not the Jesus of Nazareth as portrayed in the Gospels, then what? Form criticism has not only failed to establish logical contradictions and actual discrepancies but also has failed to provide an adequate hypothesis to account for these astounding events of the years immediately following Jesus' life.

It is not enough for Jeremias to take misleading narratives as a "call" to faith in another "Christ."[14] To what Christ shall we respond? If we cannot believe the church's witness to the historical Jesus, why should we accept its human, fallible witness to an unknown Christ? As Jesus said, "If I have told you earthly things, and ye believe me not, how shall you believe if I tell you heavenly things?" (John 3:12).

A call went out from Norad to the radio and TV networks of America on Saturday, February 20, 1971. It proclaimed a national emergency and told all stations to go off the air and await instructions from the government. If such untrustworthy "calls" became habitual we could hardly be expected to prepare ourselves for a real emergency upon hearing another. If the Gospels habitually distort the message about Jesus, can we trust them concerning the Christ?

Brought up on form criticism, William Hamilton through a false biblical record sought revelatory encounters with the true God. But he lost all confidence in misguiding pointers to a transcendent realm and pronounced a Lord of history dead.

Uncertain biblical sounds provided no check upon J.J. Altizer's claim to have experienced not merely the absence of God, but the death of God. Such contradictory claims for personal experience must be tested by evidence and truth (I John 4:1-3). The early Christians knew what we need to know, that if Jesus the Christ were not raised from the dead faith is futile (I Cor. 15:17).

But now is Christ risen from the dead! (I Cor. 15:20). The Lord of history reversed the irreversible forces of nature, transformed history's greatest moral tragedy into a triumph of holy love, and laid the foundation of a community of forgiveness.

Used by permission of:

Dr. Gordon Lewis
Professor of Systematic Theology
  and Christian Philosophy
Conservative Baptist Theological Seminary
Denver, Colorado

REFERENCES

[1]For a survey of these productions see R.M. Riddle, "Introductory Essay" to Augustine's *Harmony of the Gospels*, ed. Philip Schaff in *A Select Library of the Nicene and Post-Nicene Fathers of the Christian Church*, Vol. VI (Grand Rapids: Wm. B. Eerdmans Publishing Company, 1956), pp. 67-70.

[2]For a survey of the history of form criticism see E. Basil Redlich, *Form Criticism* (London: Duckworth, 1948), pp. 9-33.

[3]Alan Richardson, "New Testament Theology" ed. by Alan Richardson, *A Dictionary of Christian Theology* (London: SCM Press, Ltd., 1969), p. 229.

[4]Cited by R.W. Catterall, "Modern Reason and the Gospels" ed. by John J. Heaney, *Faith, Reason and the Gospels* (Westminster: The Newman Press, 1964), p.167.

[5]F.F. Bruce, "Form Criticism," ed. Everett F. Harrison, *Baker's Dictionary of Theology* (Grand Rapids: Baker Book House, 1960), pp. 227-28.

[6]Floyd V. Filson, "Form Criticism," *Twentieth Century Encyclopedia of Religious Knowledge*, I (Grand Rapids: Baker Book House, 1955), p. 437.

[7]William Barclay, *The First Three Gospels* (Philadelphia: The Westminister Press, 1966), p. 115.

[8]F.F. Bruce, *op. cit.*

[9]K. Grobel, "Form Criticism," *The Interpreter's Dictionary of the Bible*, II (New York: Abingdon Press, 1962).

[10]George Ladd, *The New Testament and Criticism* (Grand Rapids: Wm. B. Eerdmans Publishing Company, 1967), p.167.

[11]*Ibid.*

[12]W.M. Ramsay, *Was Christ Born at Bethlehem?* (New York: G.P. Putnam's Sons, 1898), pp. 227-244.

[13]C.F.D. Moule, *The Phenomenon of the New Testament* (Naperville, Ill.: Alec R. Allenson, 1967), p. 21.

[14]Joachim Jeremias, *The Problem of the Historical Jesus* (Philadelphia: Fortress Press, 1964), pp. 23-24.

MODERN THEOLOGY
AND BIBLICAL CRITICISM

BY C.S. LEWIS

The undermining of the old orthodoxy has been mainly the work of divines engaged in New Testament criticism. The authority of experts in that discipline is the authority in deference to whom we are asked to give up a huge mass of beliefs shared in common by the early Church, the Fathers, the Middle Ages, the Reformers, and even the nineteenth century. I want to explain what it is that makes me skeptical about this authority. Ignorantly skeptical, as you will all too easily see. But the skepticism is the father of the ignorance. It is hard to persevere in a close study when you can work up no *prima facie* confidence in your teachers.

First then, whatever these men may be as Biblical critics, I distrust them as critics. They seem to me to lack literary judgement, to be imperceptive about the very quality of the texts they are reading. It sounds a strange charge to bring against men who have been steeped in those books all their lives. But that might be just the trouble. A man who has spent his youth and manhood in the minute study of New Testament texts and of other people's studies of them, whose literary experiences of those texts lacks any standard of comparison such as can only grow from a wide and deep and genial experience of literature in general, is, I should think, very likely to miss the obvious things about them. If he tells me that something in a Gospel is legend or romance, I want to know how many legends and romances he has read, how well his palate is trained in detecting them by the flavour; not how many years he has spent on that Gospel. But I had better turn to examples.

In what is already a very old commentary I read that the Fourth Gospel is regarded by one school as a 'spiritual romance', 'a poem not a history', to be judged by the same canons as Nathan's parable, the Book of Jonah, *Paradise Lost* 'or, more exactly, *Pilgrim's Progress'.* After a man has said that, why need one attend to anything else he says about any book in the world? Note that he regards *Pilgrim's Progress*, a story which professes to be a dream and flaunts its allegorical nature by every single proper name it uses, as the closest parallel. Note that the whole epic panoply of Milton goes for nothing. But even if we leave out the grosser absurdities and keep to *Jonah*, the insensitiveness is crass—*Jonah*, a tale with as few even pretended historical attachments as *Job*, grotesque in incident and surely not without a distinct, though of course edifying, vein of typically Jewish humour. Then turn to John. Read the dialogues: that with the Samaritan woman at the well, or that which follows the healing of the man born blind. Look at its pictures: Jesus (if I may use the word) doodling with his finger in the dust; the unforgettable ἦν δὲ νύξ (xiii, 30). I have been reading poems, romances, vision-literature, legends, myths all my life. I know what they are like. I know that not one of them is like this. Of this text there are only two possible views. Either this is reportage—though it may no doubt contain errors—pretty close up to the facts; nearly as close as Boswell. Or else, some unknown writer in the second century, without known predecessors or successors, suddenly anticipated the whole technique of modern, novelistic, realistic narrative. If it is untrue, it must be narrative of that kind. The reader who doesn't see this has simply not learned to read.

Here, from Bultmann's *Theology of the New Testament* (p. 30) is another: 'Observe in what unassimilated fashion the prediction of the parousia (Mk. viii, 38) follows upon the prediction of the passion (viii, 31).' What can he mean? Unassimilated? Bultmann believes that predictions of the parousia are older than those of the passion. He therefore wants to believe—and no doubt does believe—that when they occur in the same passage some discrepancy or 'unassimilation' must be perceptible between them. But surely he foists this on the text with shocking lack of perception. Peter has confessed Jesus to be the Anointed One. That flash of glory is hardly over before the dark prophecy begins—that the Son of Man must suffer and die. Then this contrast is repeated. Peter, raised for a moment by his confession, makes his false step; the crushing rebuff 'Get thee behind me' follows. Then, across that momentary ruin which Peter (as so often) becomes, the voice of the Master, turning to the crowd, generalizes the moral. All His followers must take up the cross. This avoidance of suffering, this self-preservation, is not what life is really about. Then, more definitely still, the summons to martyrdom. You must stand to your tackling. If you disown Christ here and now, He will disown you later. Logically, emotionally, imaginatively, the sequence is perfect. Only a Bultmann could think otherwise.

Finally, from the same Bultmann; 'The personality of Jesus has no importance for the kerygma either of Paul or of John... Indeed the tradition of the earliest Church did not even unconsciously preserve a picture of his personality. Every attempt to reconstruct one remains a play of subjective imagination.'

So there is no personality of Our Lord presented in the New Testament. Through what strange process has this learned German gone in order to make himself blind to what all men except him see? What evidence have we that he would recognize a personality if it were there? For it is Bultmann *contra mundum*. If anything whatever is common to all believers, and even to many unbelievers, it is the sense that in the Gospels they have met a personality. There are characters whom we know to be historical but of whom we do not feel that we have any personal knowledge—knowledge by acquaintance; such are Alexander, Attila, or William of Orange. There are others who make no claim to historical reality but whom, none the less, we know as we know real people: Falstaff, Uncle Toby, Mr. Pickwick. But there are only three characters who, claiming the first sort of reality, also actually have the second. And surely everyone knows who they are: Plato's Socrates, the Jesus of the Gospels, and Boswell's Johnson. Our acquaintance with them shows itself in a dozen ways. When we look into the Aprocryphal gospels, we find ourselves constantly saying of this or that *logion*, 'No. It's a fine saying, but not His. That wasn't how He talked.'—just as we do with all pseudo-Johnsoniana.

So strong is the flavour of the personality that, even while He says things which, on any other assumption than that of Divine Incarnation in the fullest sense, would be appallingly arrogant, yet we—and many unbelievers too—accept Him at His own valuation when He says 'I am meek and lowly of heart.' Even those passages in the New Testament which superficially, and in intention, are most concerned with the Divine, and least with the Human Nature, bring us face to face with the personality. I am not sure that they don't do this more than any others. 'We beheld His glory, the glory as of the only begotten of the Father, full of graciousness and reality... which we have looked upon and our hands have handled.' What is gained by trying to evade or dissipate this shattering immediacy of personal contact by talk about 'that significance which the early church found that it was impelled to attribute to the Master'? This hits us in the face. Not what they were impelled to do but what I should call impersonality: what you'd get in a D.N.B article or an obituary or a Victorian *Life and Letters of Yeshua Bar-Yosef* in three volumes with photographs.

That then is my first bleat. These men ask me to believe they can read between the lines of the old texts; the evidence is their obvious inability to read (in any sense worth discussing) the lines themselves. They claim to see fern-seed and can't see an elephant ten yards away in broad daylight.

Now for my second bleat. All theology of the liberal type involves at some point—and often involves throughout—the claim that the real behaviour and purpose and teaching of Christ came very rapidly to be misunderstood and misrepresented by His followers, and has been recovered or exhumed only by modern scholars. Now long before I became interested in theology I had met this kind of theory elsewhere. The tradition of Jowett still dominated the study of ancient philosophy when I was reading Greats. One was brought up to believe that the real meaning of Plato had been misunderstood by Aristotle and wildly travestied by the new-Platonists, only to be recovered by the moderns. When recovered, it turned out (most fortunately) that Plato had really all along been an English Hegelian, rather like T.H. Green. I have met it a third time in my own professional studies; every week a clever undergraduate, every quarter a dull American don, discovers for the first time what some Shakesperian play really meant. But in this third instance I am a privileged person. The revolution in thought and sentiment which has occurred in my own lifetime is so great that I belong, mentally, to Shakespeare's world far more than to that of these recent interpreters. I see—I feel it in my bones—I know beyond argument—that most of their interpretations are merely impossible; they involve a way of looking at things which was not known in 1914, much less in the Jacobean period. This daily confirms my suspicion of the same approach to Plato or the New Testament. The idea that any man or writer should be opaque to those who lived in the same culture, spoke the same language, shared the same habitual imagery and unconscious assumptions, and yet be transparent to those who have none of these advantages, is in my opinion preposterous. There is an *a priori* improbability in it which almost no argument and no evidence could counterbalance.

Thirdly, I find in these theologians a constant use of the principle that the miraculous does not occur. Thus any statement put into Our Lord's mouth by the old texts, which, if He had really made it, would constitute a prediction of the future, is taken to have been put in after the occurrence which it seemed to predict. This is very sensible if we start by knowing that inspired prediction can never occur. Similarly in general, the rejection as unhistorical of all passages which narrate miracles is sensible if we start by knowing that the miraculous in general never occurs. Now I do not here want to discuss whether the miraculous is possible. I only want to point out that this is a purely philosophical question. Scholars, as scholars, speak on it with no more authority than anyone else. The canon 'If miraculous, unhistorical' is one they bring to their study of the texts, not one they have learned from it. If one is speaking of authority, the united authority of all the Biblical critics in the world counts here for nothing. On this they speak simply as men; men obviously influenced by, and perhaps insufficiently critical of, the spirit of the age they grew up in.

But my fourth bleat—which is also my loudest and longest—is still to come.

All this sort of criticism attempts to reconstruct the genesis of the texts it studies; what vanished documents each author used, when and where he wrote, with what purposes, under what influences—the whole *Sitz im Leben* of the text. This is done with immense erudition and great ingenuity. And at first sight it is very convincing. I think I should be convinced by it myself, but that I carry about with me a charm—the herb *moly*—against it. You must excuse me if I now speak for a while of myself. The value of what I say depends on its being first-hand evidence.

What forearms me against all these Reconstructions is the fact that I have seen it all from the other end of the stick. I have watched reviewers reconstructing the genesis of my own books in just this way.

Until you come to be reviewed yourself you would never believe how little of an ordinary review is taken up by criticism in the strict sense: by evaluation, praise, or censure, of the book actually written. Most of it is taken up with imaginary histories of the process by which you wrote it. The very terms which the reviewers use in praising or dis-praising often imply such a history. They praise a passage as 'spontaneous' and censure another as 'laboured'; that is, they think they know that you wrote the one *currente calamo* and the other *invita Minerva*.

What the value of such reconstructions is I learned very early in my career. I had published a book of essays; and the one into which I had put most of my heart, the one I really cared about and in which I discharged a keen enthusiasm, was on William Morris. And in almost the first review I was told that this was obviously the only one in the book in which I had felt no interest. Now don't mistake. The critic was, I now believe, quite right in thinking it the worst essay in the book; at least everyone agreed with him. Where he was totally wrong was in his imaginary history of the causes which produced its dullness.

Well, this made me prick up my ears. Since then I have watched with some care similar imaginary histories both of my own books and of books by friends whose real history I knew. Reviewers, both friendly and hostile, will dash you off such histories with great confidence; will tell you what public events had directed the author's mind to this or that, what other authors had influenced him, what his over-all intention was, what sort of audience he principally addressed, why—and when—he did everything.

Now I must first record my impression; then, distinct from it, what I can say with certainty. My impression is that in the whole of my experience not one of these guesses has on any one point been right; that the method shows a record of 100 per cent failure. You would expect that by mere chance they would hit as often as they miss. But it is my impression that they do no such thing. I can't remember a single hit. But as I have not kept a careful record my mere impression may be mistaken. What I think I can say with certainty is that they are usually wrong....

Now this surely ought to give us pause. The reconstruction of the history of a text, when the text is ancient, sounds very convincing. But one is after all sailing by dead reckoning; the results cannot be checked by fact. In order to decide how reliable the method is, what more could you ask for than to be shown an instance where the same method is at work and we have facts to check it by? Well, that is what I have done. And we find, that when this check is available, the results are either always, or else nearly always, wrong. The 'assured results of modern scholarship', as to the way in which an old book was written, are 'assured', we may conclude, only because the men who knew the facts are dead and can't blow the gaff. The huge essays in my own field which reconstruct the history of *Piers Plowman* or *The Faerie Queene* are most unlikely to be anything but sheer illusions.

Am I then venturing to compare every whipster who writes a review in a modern weekly with these great scholars who have devoted their whole lives to the detailed study of the New Testament? If the former are always wrong, does it follow that the latter must fare no better?

There are two answers to this. First, while I respect the learning of the great biblical critics, I am not yet persuaded that their judgement is equally to be respected. But, secondly, consider with what overwhelming advantages the mere reviewers start. They reconstruct the history of a book written by someone whose mother-tongue is the same as theirs; a contemporary, educated like themselves, living in something like the same mental and spiritual climate. They have everything to help them. The superiority in judgement and diligence which you are going to attribute to the biblical critics will have to be almost superhuman if it is to offset the fact that they are everywhere faced with customs, language, race-characteristics, a religious background, habits of composition, and basic assumptions, which no scholarship will ever enable any man now alive to know as surely and intimately and instinctively as the reviewer can know mine. And for the very same reason, remember, the biblical critics, whatever reconstructions they devise, can never be crudely proved wrong. St. Mark is dead. When they meet St. Peter there will be more pressing matters to discuss.

You may say, of course, that such reviewers are foolish in so far as they guess how a sort of book they never wrote themselves was written by another. They assume that you wrote a story as they would try to write a story; the fact that they would so try, explains why they have not produced any stories. But are the biblical critics in this way much better off? Dr. Bultmann never wrote a gospel. Has the experience of his learned, specialized, and no doubt meritorious, life really given him any power of seeing into the minds of those long dead men who were caught up into what, on any view, must be regarded as the central religious experience of the whole human race? It is no incivility to say—he himself would admit—that he must in every way be divided from the evangelists by far more formidable barriers—spiritual as well as intellectual— than any that could exist between my reviewers and me.

This essay is from a published collection of Lewis' lectures and articles, "Christian Reflections," edited by Walter Hooper. It is used by permission of the publisher, William B. Eerdmans Publishing Company.

THE INFLUENCE OF FORM
CRITICISM ON CHRISTOLOGY

BY BOB PATTERSON

New Testament form criticism did not appear suddenly around 1919. Two movements in biblical studies led to its birth. Hermann Gunkel, building on the work of the Wellhausen school, pioneered from [sic] criticism in the Old Testament at the turn of the century. Gunkel started with the principle that the authors of Old Testament were compilers of the tradition rather than professional writers. Assuming that the collected traditions contained a great variety of literary types and forms, Gunkel proposed to sift out each separate type and study it according to its form, content, style, and structure. "Thereafter each type had to be traced back to its 'Sitz im Leben,' its life-situation in the daily environment and activity of the Hebrew people, at which stage the tradition was spoken, not written." The original types during the oral period consisted of songs celebrating victory in war, funeral laments, prophetic sermons, and cult liturgies, among others. In his commentary on Genesis in 1901 he demonstrated the wide-ranging possibilities of form criticism for biblical studies.

At the same time distinguished German scholars in the field of literary criticism were also paving the way for New Testament form criticism. David F. Strauss (1835) had set the stage by denying the historical value of the Gospels, claiming that they were legends formed years after their supposed occurrence. In 1901 Bernard Weiss (and Holtzmann) countered this skepticism by affirming that the Gospel of Mark, the primary Gospel, and a secondary source designated as Q (the "two document hypothesis" of literary criticism), were historically trustworthy. In the same year, however, a new and different attack on the historical reliability of Mark was made by Wilhelm Wrede.

Wrede said that (1) Mark artificially [sic] constructed the framework of his narratives, (2) that he included later and less reliable as well as earlier traditions, and (3) that he imposed a doctrinal theory on his Gospel. Wrede held that Mark must have imposed on his narrative the idea that the disciples were trained by Jesus during his ministry to believe that Jesus was the Messiah (the "Messianic Secret"), because every evidence indicated that it was not revealed to anyone until after the resurrection. Even Jesus himself did not know He was the Messiah. Wrede concluded that the "Messianic Secret" was "a device invented by Mark in order to reconcile the non-Messianic materials of his source with his own christological beliefs." Wrede said that the Jesus of Mark was unhistorical, and that the supernatural divine Christ in Mark reflects the faith of the church a generation after Easter. By 1914 this debate centering about Mark had reached a general consensus.

> The Two-document hypothesis was accepted, but the historical value of Mark and the trustworthiness of Q were being questioned. Secondly, it was being argued that Mark and Q were influenced by the theological views of the early Church. Thirdly, it was being asserted that Mark was a collection not only of traditional narratives and sayings of Jesus, but of material of a later date [101/24].

In the fourth place, it was being said that there were legendary elements in Mark.

From these studies scholars began to recognize that there were "forms" of oral tradition in Mark, but they could not get at them with the tools of literary criticism. Out of the inability of literary criticism to answer many of the questions about the pre-literary stage of Mark and the other Gospels, New Testament form criticism, "the child of disappointment" was born. Three scholars, Martin Dibelius, Rudolf Bultmann, and K.L. Schmidt working simultaneously but independently on the primitive Christian tradition and the laws of their formation and transmission, founded New Testament form criticism ("formgeschichte," form history).

They took up the principles enunciated by Gunkel for Old Testament studies and applied them to the New Testament. These pioneers accepted the main results of literary criticism, then moved on to investigate the traditions (pre-literary oral traditions) and the way they were moulded before they received literary shape.

According to the Form Critics, the evangelists were not authors, but collectors and editors. Their work consisted in collecting, choosing, grouping, re-shaping, and handing down the traditions. They had nothing to do with the original moulding, for they took over material which had a "form" and which existed in independent self-contained units.

They assumed that the original oral tradition behind the Gospels took shape as they did in any folklore traditions (China, India, Persia, Greece) which were moulded by constant repetition. The first aim of the form critics, then, was to discover the laws of oral tradition in the "twilight period," when the tradition was still circulating "orally as a series of disconnected units, anecdotes, stories, saying, teaching, parables, and so on."

The second aim of the form critics was to arrive at the actual happenings and sayings of Jesus and thus resolve any doubts about the trustworthiness of the knowledge concerning the historical Jesus. Back of this aim stood the skepticism of Wrede and his principle of the "messianic Secret." The form critics assumed that the traditions about Jesus had been transformed by the collective consciousness of the primitive Christian community, that the Gospels are expressions of the community's faith. But by following the form critical method they felt that they would know the Jesus of history as he was before the Gospels were written. K.L. Schmidt, in examining the framework in which the Markan materials were set, distinguished between the "tradition" (the isolated units of material) and the "redactions" (the connecting links between the units, the contributions of the evangelist). He concluded that the Markan geography and chronology were unreliable and that the "redactions" provided clues to Mark's own distinctive theology. Schmidt set the task for form criticism, i.e., to discover the previous history of the units of material.

As Bultmann and Dibelius applied the form critical method to the Gospels the process comprised three operations. First, the oral units were classified according to a form. Second, the forms were assigned to a life setting in the community or group which created them ("Sitz im Leben," life situation, creative milieu). Third, the historical value of each unit was assessed. Dibelius felt that the oral traditions [sic] were first shaped by the preaching needs of the church. He lists the forms as follows: 1. *Paradigms* (sermon illustrations); 2. Miracle stories about Jesus (tales or *Novellen*); 3. Catechetical teaching (sayings); 4. Edifying narratives (legends); 5. Supernatural stories (*mythen*); 6. Passion narratives. Bultmann's grouping of the material is as follows: 1. *Apothegms* (may be controversial or biographical, practically the group called *paradigms* by Dibelius); 2. Sayings, which he divides into five groups (wisdom words, "I" words, prophetic and apocalyptic words, law words and community rules, and parables); 3. Miracle stories; 4. Legends.

Dibelius, a conservative form critic, was quite cautious in his assessment of the trustworthiness of the historical records.

He found that the forms of the units of the tradition had been determined largely by the kind of people to whom they could be traced back: Preachers, teachers or missionaries. Yet while Dibelius clearly saw that the tradition had undergone considerable change in the preaching, teaching, and missionary interest of the primitive Church, he did not deny the possibility of its historicity as going back in the first instance to Jesus himself.

To Bultmann, however, the Gospels lose much of their trustworthiness as historical records and the Jesus of history is lost. In his hands form criticism took a skeptical direction. He accounts as historically trustworthy only about forty of the group that he lists as Sayings, none of the Miracle Stories, and none of the Legends. He rejected the idea that the Gospel traditionists "had any kind of historical intention, and characterized the materials of the tradition about Jesus as the legendary or mythological fabrications of the primitive Christian community, which gave objective expression to its faith in concrete stories regarding Jesus."

Not all form critics think that the early church completely transformed the original tradition about Jesus. Vincent Taylor, author of one of the best books in English on form criticism, says that form criticism "seems to me to furnish constructive suggestions which in many ways confirm the historical trustworthiness of the Gospel tradition." Taylor further remarks that if the skeptical form critics such as Bultmann are right "the disciples must have been translated to heaven immediately after the Resurrection." The skeptical form critic, by the very nature of his assumptions, is not predisposed in favour of any original eyewitnesses. Form criticism is limited in that the form does not always give clues to the life setting of the narrative and by the face [sic] that the form does not always serve as the best way for ascertaining the legitimacy of historical authenticity.

During the '20's two other movements were arraigning the liberal attempts to reconstruct the life of Jesus—form criticism and Karl Barth's Dialectical Theology. Both movements emphasized that the New Testament must be understood from the point of view of the post-Easter church. These "kerygma theologians" made two devastating criticisms against the "life of Jesus" enterprise. First, they demonstrated that the New Testament documents are primarily kerygmatic proclamations in which Jesus is pointed to as God's saving act on man's behalf, and not historical sources for the life of Christ. To suppress the kerygmatic element is to miss the faith element of the post-Easter community. Second, they questioned the ability of the historical method to grasp the nature of God's revelation of Himself in Christ." God's presence for man's salvation is not an objective phenomenon within the grasp of men, not even of learned historians who are able to work their way back to supposedly certain facts about Jesus." The only way to perceive God's revelation is through learning the kerygma and responding in faith and obedience. By these assertions the historical-critical method and form criticism in particular entered into an alliance with classical christology to preserve the mystery of Jesus.

In 1953 Ernst Käsemann started what is known as the "post-Bultmann" phase of New Testament study by returning to the problem of the historical Jesus. To rid the New Testament of the docetism implicit in Bultmann's program of demythologizing (the "myths" of the kerygma are interpretative rather than objective statements) is the primary motive behind the new quest. Käsemann and others [sic] want to show that there is at least a consistent frame of reference between Jesus and the church's kerygma. These scholars, regarding the resurrection as a matter that can be known only by faith, try to find elements in the tradition that have not been fully assimilated by the post-Easter faith.

> To the extent that they are not assimilated by faith, they point to Jesus as he really was. But these elements must not be irrelevant or contrary to Easter faith, for the whole purpose of the new quest, in distinction from the old, is to demonstrate a parallel between the Jesus of history and Easter faith, so that it cannot be said that faith must be a myth [Reginald H. Fuller, Easter Faith and History, p. 112].

Reprinted from Encounter.
Winter, 1970. Vol. 31, No. 1, pp. 5-24.
Used by permission.

AUTHOR INDEX

SUBJECT INDEX

Let's Stay In Touch!

If you have grown personally as a result of this material, we should stay in touch. You will want to continue in your Christian growth, and to help your faith become even stronger, our team is constantly developing new materials.

We publish a monthly newsletter called **5 Minutes with Josh** which will:

1) tell you about those new materials as they become available,
2) answer your tough questions,
3) give creative tips on being an effective parent,
4) let you know our ministry needs, and
5) keep you up-to-date on my speaking schedule (so you can pray).

If you would like to receive this publication, simply fill out the coupon below and send it in. By special arrangement **5 Minutes with Josh** will come to you regularly — <u>no charge</u>.

Let's keep in touch!

Josh

Yes! I want to receive the free subscription to **5 Minutes with JOSH**

Name_____

Address_____

City_____State_____Zip_____

Mail to: Josh McDowell Ministry, **5 Minutes with Josh**,
Box 1000, Dallas, TX 75221